INSIDE MACINTOSH

Networking

Addison-Wesley Publishing Company

Reading, Massachusetts   Menlo Park, California   New York
Don Mills, Ontario   Wokingham, England   Amsterdam   Bonn
Sydney   Singapore   Tokyo   Madrid   San Juan
Paris   Seoul   Milan   Mexico City   Taipei

Apple Computer, Inc.
20525 Mariani Avenue
Cupertino, CA 95014
408-996-1010

Apple, the Apple logo, APDA, AppleLink, AppleShare, AppleTalk, EtherTalk, ImageWriter, LaserWriter, LocalTalk, Macintosh, MPW, ProDOS, and TokenTalk are trademarks of Apple Computer, Inc., registered in the United States and other countries.

System 7 is a trademark of Apple Computer, Inc.

Adobe Illustrator, Photoshop, and PostScript are trademarks of Adobe Systems Incorporated, which may be registered in certain jurisdictions.

America Online is a service mark of Quantum Computer Services, Inc.

CompuServe is a registered service mark of CompuServe, Inc.

FrameMaker is a registered trademark of Frame Technology Corporation.

Helvetica and Palatino are registered trademarks of Linotype Company.

Internet is a trademark of Digital Equipment Corporation.

ITC Zapf Dingbats is a registered trademark of International Typeface Corporation.

NuBus is a registered trademark of Texas Instruments, Inc.

Optrotech is a trademark of Orbotech Corporation.

Simultaneously published in the United States and Canada.

ISBN 0-201-62269-6

2 3 4 5 6 7-CRW-97969594
Second printing, May 1994

The paper used in this book meets the EPA standards for recycled fiber.

Library of Congress Cataloging-in-Publication Data

Inside Macintosh.   Networking   /   by Apple Computer, Inc.
        p.   cm.
      Includes index.
      ISBN 0-201-62269-6
      1. Macintosh (Computer)   2. AppleTalk.   3. Computer networks.
I. Apple Computer, Inc.
QA76.8.M3152   1994
004.6'8—dc20   93-46639
                                                                      CIP

Contents

Chapter 2	AppleTalk Utilities 2-1

Chapter 3 Name-Binding Protocol (NBP) 3-1

Chapter 6   **AppleTalk Transaction Protocol (ATP)**   6-1

Chapter 7	Datagram Delivery Protocol (DDP) 7-1

Chapter 11

Ethernet, Token Ring, and Fiber Distributed Data Interface   11-1

Glossary

Index

Figures, Tables, and Listings

Multinode Architecture   12-1

About This Book

This book, *Inside Macintosh: Networking,* describes the AppleTalk protocols and the application programming interfaces to them. AppleTalk is a network system including hardware and software that supports communication over a variety of data-link types. Using AppleTalk, applications and processes can transfer and exchange data and share resources. The central part of the AppleTalk software consists of a number of protocols arranged in layers, with each protocol offering different services.

To familiarize you with the functions that each of these protocols provide so that you can determine which protocols to use for your application, this book includes an overview of the AppleTalk protocols. This book describes how to write a networked application that uses the AppleTalk application programming interfaces to send and receive data. It describes how to use different methods to send data, such as establishing a sustained connection across which you can transfer streams of data or transferring data in small, discrete units called packets.

To gain an understanding of AppleTalk as a whole and a perspective of the types of services that each AppleTalk protocol provides, see the chapter "Introduction to AppleTalk." This chapter explains some basic networking concepts and how they apply to AppleTalk. It describes how addressing is implemented in AppleTalk networks and how this affects your application. It also explains how you can use each of the AppleTalk protocols for specific application requirements, and finally, it discusses a feature that is common to all routines across AppleTalk protocol interfaces: how to use either of two methods, synchronous or asynchronous, to specify when control is returned to your program after you call a routine.

To learn how to obtain information about the AppleTalk drivers and the networking environment and how to send packets to other applications and processes on your own node, see the chapter "AppleTalk Utilities."

To determine how to register your application with AppleTalk so that it is visible on the network and available for other applications and processes to contact and also how to obtain the addresses of other applications and processes so that you can contact them, see the chapter "Name-Binding Protocol (NBP)."

To obtain zone location information for the node that is running your application or other applications on an AppleTalk network, see the chapter "Zone Information Protocol (ZIP)."

To provide support for a networked application that establishes and maintains a peer-oriented session connection between your application and its partner on the network and that allows the applications to send streams of data to each other, see the chapter "AppleTalk Data Stream Protocol (ADSP)." This chapter also discusses how you can establish a secure connection that provides for user authentication and data encryption.

To provide support for a transaction-based session application in which one end of the connection controls the session and issues a transaction request that the other end carries out, see the chapter "AppleTalk Transaction Protocol (ATP)."

To gain access to the underlying AppleTalk transport protocol that allows you send discrete packets of data across the network without imposing on your application the additional overhead required to set up and maintain a session, see the chapter "Datagram Delivery Protocol (DDP)." To use DDP, you must provide socket-listener code that you must write in assembly language.

To provide complete coverage of the AppleTalk protocols, this book includes in the chapters "AppleTalk Session Protocol (ASP)" and "AppleTalk Filing Protocol (AFP)" a discussion of two higher-level protocols that are not commonly used by application program developers: AppleTalk Session Protocol (ASP) and AppleTalk Filing Protocol (AFP). ASP allows you to establish an asymmetrical session between an ASP workstation application and an ASP server application. The primary use of ASP is to provide services for the AppleTalk Filing Protocol (AFP) that, in turn, provides all of the services necessary to access an AppleTalk AppleShare server. AFP allows a workstation on an AppleTalk network to access and manipulate files on an AFP file server, such as an AppleShare server. Because you can use the native file system to access an AFP server from a workstation, in most cases you should not need to use AFP directly.

To register your application with the LAP Manager so that you will be notified when an AppleTalk transition event occurs that can affect your application, and to define a transition event that your application causes to occur that can affect other applications, see the chapter "Link-Access Protocol (LAP) Manager." This chapter also describes how to install a protocol handler as a client of the LAP Manager if your application processes 802.2 Type 1 packets.

To learn how to write data directly to an Ethernet, token ring, or Fiber Distributed Data Interface (FDDI) driver instead of using the AppleTalk protocol stack, see the chapter "Ethernet, Token Ring, and Fiber Distributed Data Interface." This chapter also describes how to read data directly from an Ethernet driver.

To implement a special-purpose application that receives and processes AppleTalk packets in a custom manner instead of passing them directly on to a higher-level AppleTalk protocol for processing, see the chapter "Multinode Architecture."

Because the AppleTalk network system includes both hardware and software—and because the software includes not only the AppleTalk protocol stack and the programming interfaces to it, but also file servers, print servers, internet routers, drivers for circuit card or network interface controllers, and so forth—the information in this book constitutes only a small part of the body of literature documenting AppleTalk.

For a detailed description of the AppleTalk protocol specifications, see *Inside AppleTalk,* second edition. For a complete description of the LAP Manager, EtherTalk, and other AppleTalk connections, see the *Macintosh AppleTalk Connections Programmer's Guide.* To learn how to install and operate an AppleTalk internet, see the *AppleTalk Internet Router Administrator's Guide* and the *AppleTalk Phase 2 Introduction and Upgrade Guide.* For an introduction to the hardware and software of an entire AppleTalk network, see *Understanding Computer Networks* and the *AppleTalk Network System Overview.* For information on designing circuit cards and device drivers for Macintosh computers, see *Designing Cards and Drivers for the Macintosh Family,* second edition.

What to Read

If you are new to AppleTalk, you should begin with the chapter "Introduction to AppleTalk." This chapter describes some basic networking concepts that pertain to AppleTalk, and it summarizes each of the AppleTalk protocols and features, suggesting possible uses for them.

The chapter also includes a section that provides an overview of the two execution modes that you can use to execute routines that belong to the AppleTalk protocol programming interfaces. Even if you are already familiar with AppleTalk, you should read this section.

Each of the remaining chapters is devoted to a separate AppleTalk protocol or feature. Most of the chapters are self-contained; unless otherwise stated, there are no dependencies on preceding or following chapters. However, in some cases you may find it helpful to familiarize yourself with the information in other chapters that address related protocols. In most cases, your application will use more than one protocol.

The higher-level protocols are described first, followed by the lower-level protocols and the interfaces to the hardware device drivers, and ending with the chapter that describes multinode architecture.

Chapter Organization

Most chapters in this book follow a standard general structure. For example, the chapter "Name-Binding Protocol (NBP)" contains these major sections:

■ "About NBP." This section provides an overview of the Name-Binding Protocol and its features.

■ "Using NBP." This section describes how to use the most common NBP functions, gives related user interface information, provides code samples, and supplies additional information. For example, the section describes how to register your application with NBP so that users and other applications can locate and contact your application. It also describes how to look up another application's address based on its name and how to cancel a pending NBP request that you have made.

■ "NBP Reference." This section provides a complete reference to NBP by describing the constants, data structures, and routines that you use to gain access to the NBP services. Each routine description follows a standard format that gives the routine declaration; a description of every parameter; the routine result, if any; and a list of errors, warnings, and notices. Most routine descriptions give additional information about using the routine and include cross-references to related information elsewhere. Many of the AppleTalk programming interface routines use parameter blocks to pass information to and receive it from the software driver that implements the protocol. The parameter block data type is described in the data structures section, and any parameter block fields that are common to all the routines that use the parameter block are defined in that section. Fields particular to a routine, but not common to all routines, are described along with the routine to which they pertain.

■ "Summary of NBP." This section shows the Pascal, C, and assembly-language interfaces for the constants, data types, and routines associated with NBP. It also lists the result codes.

Conventions Used in This Book

This book uses various conventions to present certain types of information. For example, parameter blocks are presented in a certain format so that you can scan them quickly.

Special Fonts

All code listings, reserved words, and the names of data structures, constants, fields, parameters, and functions are shown in Courier (`this is Courier`).

When new terms are introduced, they are in **boldface.** These terms are also defined in the glossary.

Types of Notes

There are several types of notes used in this book.

Note

A note formatted like this contains information that is interesting but possibly not essential to an understanding of the main text. The wording in the tag may say something more descriptive, such as "Calling `ReadPacket` and `ReadRest` when LocalTalk is the data link." (This example appears on page 7-19.) Notes with descriptive titles contain useful information about a particular aspect of the feature being described. ◆

IMPORTANT

A note like this contains information that is especially important. (An example appears on page 7-10.) ▲

▲ **WARNING**

Warnings like this indicate potential problems that you should be aware of as you design your application. Failure to heed these warnings could result in system crashes or loss of data. (An example appears on page 7-18.) ▲

Assembly-Language Information

Inside Macintosh provides information about the registers for specific routines like this:

Registers on entry

A0   Contents of register A0 on entry

Registers on exit

D0   Contents of register D0 on exit

In addition, *Inside Macintosh* presents information about the fields of a parameter block in this format:

Parameter block

→	input1	Ptr	Input parameter.
←	output1	Ptr	Output parameter.
↔	inAndOut	Integer	Input/output parameter.

Numerical Formats

Hexadecimal numbers are preceded by a dollar sign ($).

The numerical values of constants are shown in decimal, unless the constants are flag or mask elements that can be summed, in which case they are shown in hexadecimal.

Development Environment

The system software routines described in this book are available using Pascal, C, or assembly-language interfaces. How you access these routines depends on the development environment you are using. This book shows system software routines in their Pascal interface using the Macintosh Programmer's Workshop (MPW).

All code listings in this book are shown in Pascal. They suggest methods of using various routines and illustrate techniques for accomplishing particular tasks. However, Apple Computer, Inc., does not intend for you to use these code samples in your applications.

Developer Products and Support

APDA is Apple's worldwide source for over three hundred development tools, technical resources, training products, and information for anyone interested in developing applications on Apple platforms. Customers receive the quarterly *APDA Tools Catalog* featuring all current versions of Apple development tools and the most popular third-party development tools. Ordering is easy; there are no membership fees, and application forms are not required for most of our products. APDA offers convenient payment and shipping options, including site licensing.

To order products or to request a complimentary copy of the *APDA Tools Catalog*, contact

APDA
Apple Computer, Inc.
P.O. Box 319
Buffalo, NY 14207-0319

Telephone	800-282-2732 (United States)
	800-637-0029 (Canada)
	716-871-6555 (International)
Fax	716-871-6511
AppleLink	APDA
America Online	APDA
CompuServe	76666,2405
Internet	APDA@applelink.apple.com

If you provide commercial products and services, call 408-974-4897 for information on the developer support programs available from Apple.

Introduction to AppleTalk

Contents

This chapter provides an overview of the AppleTalk networking system and the AppleTalk Manager. AppleTalk is a communications network system interconnecting personal computer workstations, computers acting as file servers and print servers, printers, and shared modems allowing them to exchange information through a variety of types of communications hardware and software. The AppleTalk Manager consists of a set of programming interfaces to the various components of AppleTalk for applications and processes running on Macintosh computers.

This chapter introduces some of the AppleTalk terminology that is used throughout the rest of this book. Read this chapter if you want to gain an overview of the AppleTalk networking system and its component protocols. You should also read this chapter for suggestions on which AppleTalk protocols to use for various application requirements.

- This first section of this chapter, "About Networking on the Macintosh," provides an introduction to AppleTalk networking concepts and terminology, and then it discusses
    - □ the AppleTalk protocols and their functions
    - □ the AppleTalk Manager
    - □ the layers of the Open Systems Interconnection (OSI) model and how the AppleTalk protocol stack relates to this model
- The second section of this chapter, "Deciding Which Protocol to Use," discusses how you can use each of the AppleTalk protocols that has an application programming interface.
- The third section of this chapter, "The AppleTalk Pascal Interface," describes the two modes in which you can execute the routines that make up the interfaces to the AppleTalk protocols. This information applies to each of the protocols covered individually throughout the chapters of this book. You should read this section before you use any of the programming interfaces to the AppleTalk protocols.

The chapters that make up the rest of this book describe how to use the AppleTalk Manager and the hardware device drivers. Because the AppleTalk network system includes both hardware and software—and because the software includes not only the AppleTalk Manager but also file servers, print servers, internet routers, drivers for circuit cards, and so forth—the information in this book constitutes only a small part of the body of literature documenting AppleTalk.

About Networking on the Macintosh

Networking on the Macintosh is implemented through AppleTalk. Applications and processes can communicate across a single AppleTalk network or an AppleTalk internet, which is a number of interconnected AppleTalk networks. Using AppleTalk, applications and processes can transfer and exchange data and share resources.

The AppleTalk networking system includes a number of protocols arranged in layers, which are collectively referred to as the **AppleTalk protocol stack.** Each of these protocols provides a set of functions and services that a protocol above it can use and build upon. A higher-level protocol is considered a **client** of the protocol that is below it in the AppleTalk protocol stack. (For information on how these protocols are implemented, see "The AppleTalk Protocol Stack" beginning on page 1-11.)

Many of the AppleTalk protocols provide application programming interfaces that you can use to access the services of the protocol. The programming interfaces to these protocols are collectively referred to as the **AppleTalk Manager.**

This section provides

- an introduction to some AppleTalk networking fundamentals, including a discussion of addressing in AppleTalk

- an overview of the AppleTalk protocol stack, with a brief discussion of each protocol

- an overview of the AppleTalk Manager, which includes the LAP Manager programming interface

AppleTalk Networking

This section introduces some networking concepts and terms that pertain to AppleTalk and that are used throughout the chapters of this book. It discusses

- fundamental networking concepts and AppleTalk

- addressing in AppleTalk

- AppleTalk connectivity

Basic AppleTalk Networking Concepts

A networking system, such as AppleTalk, consists of hardware and software. Hardware on an AppleTalk network includes physical devices such as Macintosh personal computer workstations, printers, and Macintosh computers acting as file servers, print servers, and routers; these devices are all referred to as **nodes** on the network.

AppleTalk interconnects these nodes through transmission paths that include both software and hardware components. The software that governs the transfer of data across a computer network is commonly designed using a layered architecture or model. (For more information on networking models and AppleTalk, see "AppleTalk and the OSI Model" beginning on page 1-19.)

For each layer of a model, protocols exist that specify how the networking software is to implement the functions which that layer provides and interact with the layer above and below it. A **protocol** is a formalized set of procedural rules for the exchange of information and the interactions between the network's interconnected nodes. A network software developer implements these rules in programs that carry out the functions specified by the protocol. AppleTalk consists of a number of protocols, many of which are implemented in software programs called *drivers*.

Note

This book uses the abbreviated term *protocol* to refer to the implementation of those rules in software drivers, instead of always using the complete term *protocol implementation*. ◆

There are many ways to characterize networks. One characteristic of a network is whether it is connection-oriented or connectionless. (A protocol can also be considered connectionless or connection-oriented.) A connection-oriented network is one in which two nodes on the network, such as computers, that want to communicate must go through a connection-establishment process, which is called a *handshake.* This involves the exchange of predetermined signals between the nodes in which each end identifies itself to the other. Once a connection is established, the communicating applications or processes on the nodes at either end can send and receive streams of data.

A **connectionless network** is one in which two nodes that want to communicate do so by going directly into a data-transfer state without first setting up a connection. A connectionless network is also called a **datagram** or **packet-oriented network** because data is sent as discrete packets; a **packet** is a small unit of data that is sent across a network. This means that each packet must carry the full addressing information required to deliver the data from its source node to its destination node. A packet includes a **header** portion that holds the addressing information along with some other information, such as a checksum value that can be used to verify the integrity of the data delivered, and a data portion that holds the message text. The terms *packet* and *datagram* are synonymous.

A connection-oriented network is analogous to a telephone system. The party who initiates the call knows whether or not the connection is made because someone at the other end of the line either answers or not. A connectionless network is analogous to electronic mail. A person sends a mail message expecting it will be delivered to its destination. Although the mail usually arrives safely, the sender doesn't know this unless the recipient initiates a response affirming it.

There are trade-offs between the two types of networks: a connection-oriented network provides more function, but at a cost. A connectionless network is less costly in terms of overhead, but it offers limited support.

A connection-oriented network ensures **reliable delivery of data,** which includes error checking and recovery from error or packet loss. Connection-oriented networks provide support for sessions. In AppleTalk networking, a **session** is a logical (as opposed to physical) connection between two entities on an internet. The two communicating parties can send streams of data across a session, rather than being limited to sending the data as individual packets. When data is sent as a stream, the networking system provides flow control to manage the data that makes up the stream. A session must be set up at the beginning and broken down at the end. All of these services entail overhead.

There is no connection setup or breakdown required for a connectionless network, and no session is established. A connectionless network offers best-effort delivery only. **Best-effort delivery** means that the network attempts to deliver any packets that meet certain requirements, such as containing a valid destination address, but the network does not inform the sender when it is unable to deliver the packet, nor does it attempt to recover from error conditions and packet loss. A connectionless network involves less overhead because it does not provide network-wide acknowledgments, flow control, or error recovery.

The terms *connectionless* and *connection-oriented* can also be applied to individual protocols that make up the networking software, as well as to the entire network system itself. AppleTalk includes protocols that provide connection-oriented services, although, as a whole, AppleTalk is considered a connectionless network because data is delivered across an AppleTalk network or internet as discrete packets. One of the AppleTalk protocols, the Datagram Delivery Protocol (DDP), implements packet delivery. However, the AppleTalk Data Stream Protocol (ADSP) and the AppleTalk Transaction Protocol (ATP) provide connection-oriented services, such as session establishment and reliable delivery of data. The AppleTalk protocols that provide connection-oriented services are built on top of the datagram services that DDP provides.

In developing AppleTalk applications, you must decide whether to use a connection-oriented or connectionless AppleTalk protocol. How to choose a protocol to use is described in "Deciding Which AppleTalk Protocol to Use" beginning on page 1-22.

The connection-oriented AppleTalk protocols support the following two kinds of sessions:

■ **symmetrical.** This session is also referred to as a *peer-to-peer session.* It is one in which both ends have equal control over the communication. Both ends can send and receive data at the same time and initiate or terminate the session. This type of session offers more capability and is more commonly used than an asymmetrical session.

■ **asymmetrical.** In this type of session, only one end of the connection can control the communication. One end of the connection makes a request to which the other end can only respond. This type of session is best suited to a transaction in which a small amount of data is transferred from one side to the other.

When both ends can send and receive data, the process is called a **full-duplex dialog.** When both sides must alternate between sending and receiving data, the process is called a **half-duplex dialog.**

Addressing and Data Delivery on AppleTalk Networks

This section discusses some of the aspects of AppleTalk networking that are part of its addressing and data-delivery scheme. Many components contribute to the addressing information that is used to identify the location of an application or a process on an AppleTalk internet. This section defines these names and numbers, and Table 1-1 highlights them.

Table 1-1   AppleTalk addressing numbers and names

Addressing information	Description
Network number	A unique 16-bit number that identifies the network to which a node is connected. A single AppleTalk network can be either extended or nonextended. An extended network is defined by a range of network numbers.
Node ID	A unique 8-bit number that identifies a node on an AppleTalk network.
Socket number	A unique 8-bit number that identifies a socket. A maximum of 254 different socket numbers can be assigned in a node.
Zone name	A name assigned to an arbitrary subset of nodes within an AppleTalk internet.

A single AppleTalk network can be interconnected with other AppleTalk networks through **routers** to create a large, dispersed AppleTalk internet. A router in an internet can select the most efficient path to the data's intended destination, while allowing connected networks to remain fully independent and to retain separate addresses.

Each network is assigned a **network number** so that packets destined for a particular network on an AppleTalk internet can be routed to the correct network. A router consults the packet's destination network number and forwards the packet throughout the internet from one router to another until the packet arrives at its destination network. AppleTalk supports a number of types of networks including LocalTalk, TokenTalk, EtherTalk, and FDDITalk networks.

AppleTalk assigns a **node ID** to a node when it connects to the network. Every node on an AppleTalk network is identified by its unique 8-bit node ID. (Extended networks include the 16-bit network number.) Once a packet arrives at its destination network, the packet is delivered to its destination node within that network, based on the node ID.

More than one application or process that uses AppleTalk may be running on a single node at the same time. Because of this, AppleTalk must have a way to determine for which application or process a packet that is delivered to the node is intended. AppleTalk uses sockets to satisfy this requirement. A **socket** is a piece of software that serves as an addressable entity on a node. Each process or application that runs on an AppleTalk network "plugs into" a socket that is identified by a unique number. Applications or processes exchange data with each other across an internet through sockets. Because each application or process has its own socket address, a node can have two or more concurrent open connections, for example, one to a file server and one to a printer.

The **socket number** identifies the process to which the Datagram Delivery Protocol (DDP) is to deliver a packet. The combination of the socket number, the node ID, and the network number creates the **internet socket address** of an application or process. An internet socket address provides a unique identifier for any socket in the AppleTalk internet. When an application or process is associated with a socket, it is referred to as a **socket client.**

An application or process becomes accessible from any point in the AppleTalk internet through its association with an internet socket address and a special name that is associated with the internet socket address through the AppleTalk Name-Binding Protocol (NBP). An NBP name contains three parts: object, type, and zone. The zone field of the name is the zone in which the node resides.

A **zone** is a logical grouping of nodes in an AppleTalk internet. The use of zones allows a network administrator to set up departmental or other logical groupings of nodes on an internet. A single extended network can contain nodes belonging to any number of zones; an individual node on an extended network can belong to only one zone. Each zone is identified by a zone name.

An **AppleTalk internet** always consists of more than one AppleTalk network. It can be made up of a mix of LocalTalk networks, TokenTalk networks, EtherTalk networks, and FDDITalk networks. It can also consist of more than one network of a single type, such as several LocalTalk networks. A single AppleTalk network can be either a nonextended network or an extended network. An AppleTalk internet can include both nonextended and extended networks.

Note

The term *internet* is used throughout this book to refer to an AppleTalk internet exclusively. It is not within the scope of this book to discuss other types of internets, such as Arpanet. ◆

An AppleTalk **nonextended network** is one in which

- the network has one network number assigned to it

- the network supports only one zone

- all nodes on the network share the same network number and zone name

- each node on the network has a unique node ID

LocalTalk is an example of a nonextended network. Each node on a nonextended network, such as LocalTalk, has a unique 8-bit node ID. Because there are 256 combinations of 8 bits, and two combinations are not available (ID 255 is reserved for broadcast messages and the ID 0 is not allowed), a nonextended network supports up to only 254 active nodes at a time.

An AppleTalk **extended network** is one in which

- the network has a range of network numbers assigned to it

- the network supports multiple zones

- each node on the network has a unique node ID (Nodes can also have different network numbers that fall within the network number range and different zone names.)

A network number range defines the extended network. An extended network uses what is referred to as **extended addressing:** in principle, a range of network numbers allows each extended network to have over 16 million (2^{24}) nodes. In any specific implementation, the hardware or software might limit the network to fewer nodes.

You can think of an extended network as a number of nonextended networks forming a single network, each providing up to 254 possible node IDs.

Whether the network is extended or nonextended, data is always delivered in DDP packets that include the DDP header that contains addressing information followed by the data itself. As the DDP packet is passed down the protocol stack to the layer below, the packet is extended to include additional information.

At the data-link layer, additional addressing information is prepended to the DDP header, and the packet is now called a *frame*. At the physical layer, a frame preamble is prepended to the frame header and a frame trailer is appended to the end of the data portion of the DDP packet. (You don't need to be concerned with the frame preamble and frame trailer; they are mentioned here and shown in Figure 1-1 for completeness.) The frame is then transmitted across the network or internet to its destination node.

At the destination node, the frame is received, and as it is passed up through the protocol stack the additional information that was added to the DDP packet at each layer on the sending node is used and removed at the corresponding layer on the destination node. The frame preamble and frame trailer are removed at the physical layer. The frame header is removed at the data-link layer. You can think of the data that your application sends as being enclosed successively at each of these layers in envelopes that contain addressing information necessary to deliver the data; at the corresponding layer on the destination node, the envelope is removed. Figure 1-1 illustrates this concept.

Figure 1-1   Data delivery on AppleTalk networks

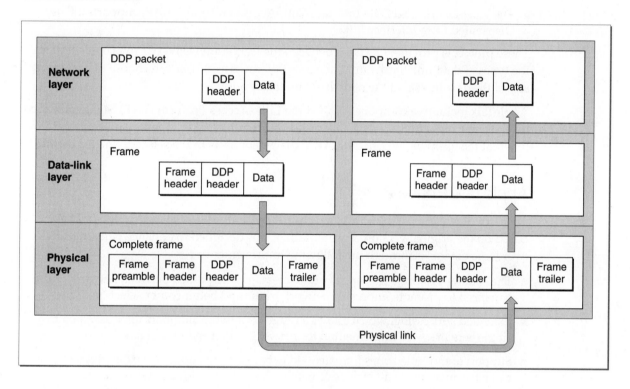

AppleTalk Connectivity

A fundamental part of a network system is its **connectivity** infrastructure, which includes the communication hardware and the protocols for controlling the hardware. The communication hardware can consist of various media including wire cabling, fiber optics cabling, and a network interface controller (NIC), if one is used. This hardware and software constitute the data transmission medium, which is called a data link. A data link provides nodes with access to the network.

Nodes on a network share and compete for access to the link. The link-access protocol implemented in the software controls the access of a node to the network hardware and makes it possible for many nodes to share the same communications hardware. It also handles the delivery of packets from one node to another over a network. When a packet is delivered to the link-access protocol for transmission across the network, additional addressing and control information is added to the packet, and the packet is called a **frame.**

AppleTalk connectivity is designed to be **link independent,** which means that it allows for the use of various types of data links accessed through the various link-access protocols, which it supports. AppleTalk provides the following data-link support:

■ The LocalTalk Link-Access Protocol (LLAP) supports a LocalTalk link.

■ The EtherTalk Link-Access Protocol (ELAP) supports an Ethernet link.

■ The TokenTalk Link-Access Protocol (TLAP) supports a token ring link.

■ The Fiber Distributed Data Interface Link-Access Protocol (FLAP) supports a Fiber Distributed Data Interface link.

These protocols provide interfaces between the Datagram Delivery Protocol (DDP) and the types of data-link hardware that AppleTalk can use. A user can choose to connect to any of the data links that the node is set up to support.

AppleTalk includes a component called the **Link-Access Protocol (LAP) Manager,** which insulates the higher-level AppleTalk protocols from having to identify and connect to the link that the user has chosen; the LAP Manager connects to the selected link for them.

AppleTalk Phase 2

The current version of AppleTalk, which was introduced in 1989, is AppleTalk Phase 2. Based on the original version of AppleTalk, it was designed to enhance performance over large networks through the following improvements:

■ The routing protocols that specify how messages are passed between networks were enhanced to promote improved network traffic and better router selection.

■ Extended addressing, which allows a range of network numbers to be assigned to a single network, was implemented for networks other than LocalTalk.

■ Support of multiple zones for extended networks was added. An extended network can have an associated list of zone names. A single extended network can be associated with more than one zone name, or a single zone name can be associated with more than one extended network. Two nodes on the same extended network can belong to different zones.

Note
The Phase 2 versions of the AppleTalk drivers are included as part of system software version 7.0 and later. They can be installed on any Macintosh computer other than the Macintosh 128K, Macintosh 512K, Macintosh 512K enhanced, and Macintosh XL computers. If you want to provide AppleTalk Phase 2 drivers with your product, you must obtain a license from Apple Software Licensing. ◆

Historical note

AppleTalk Phase 1, the original AppleTalk protocol architecture, was designed to support small local workgroups. AppleTalk Phase 1 supported the LocalTalk Link-Access Protocol (LLAP), which was originally called the *AppleTalk Link-Access Protocol (ALAP)*. With the addition of the EtherTalk Link-Access Protocol (ELAP) and other link-access protocols, ALAP was renamed to indicate the specific data link that it supports. ◆

The AppleTalk Protocol Stack

This section explains what an AppleTalk protocol is, then it provides a brief discussion of each component of the AppleTalk protocol stack, followed by a discussion of how the AppleTalk protocols are implemented in software drivers.

This section also introduces the LAP Manager, multivendor support, and multinode architecture, which are components of AppleTalk, although strictly considered, they are not protocols.

To develop applications that use AppleTalk networking services, you don't need to understand how AppleTalk implements the protocols it supports. However, understanding the functions that each protocol provides will help you determine which application programming interfaces to use for your application.

The AppleTalk system architecture consists of a number of protocols arranged in layers. The various AppleTalk protocols are sets of rules, not computer programs, and so can be implemented in many different ways on many different systems. All of the AppleTalk protocol functions that you can address or control from a Macintosh application are implemented as Macintosh device drivers or managers. Many other features of these protocols are implemented in software located only on internet routers that are not used to run general applications. Some parts of protocols are implemented by server software such as file servers or print servers.

When this book refers to a protocol as *doing* or *controlling* something, you should understand the statement to mean that some program that implements the protocol actually carries out the operation. Each protocol in a specific layer provides services to one or more protocols in a higher-level layer, which is then the client of the lower-level protocol. The higher-level protocol builds on the services provided by the lower-level one. Figure 1-2 on page 1-12 shows the AppleTalk protocols and how they relate to one another in layers. The following sections describe each protocol in turn, beginning with AFP, and progressing through the protocols as they appear in the figure.

Figure 1-2   AppleTalk protocol stack

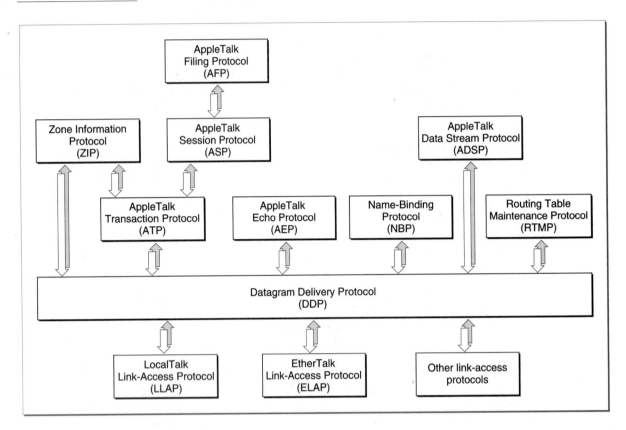

AppleTalk Filing Protocol (AFP)

The **AppleTalk Filing Protocol (AFP)** allows a workstation on an AppleTalk network to access files on AppleShare file servers. When the user opens a session with an AppleShare file server over an internet, it appears to any application running on the workstation that uses File Manager routines as if the files on the file server were located on a disk drive connected to the workstation. The AFP protocol is not commonly used because the native file system commands allow users to access an AFP server, such as AppleShare, from a workstation. There is no server-based interface.

The chapter "AppleTalk Filing Protocol (AFP)" in this book describes the application programming interface to the workstation implementation of AFP. For additional information about AFP, see "Accessing AppleShare and Other File Servers" on page 1-27.

Zone Information Protocol (ZIP)

The **Zone Information Protocol (ZIP)** provides applications and processes with access to zone names. Each node on a network belongs to a zone. Zone names are typically used to identify groups of nodes belonging to a particular department or area. ZIP allows applications and processes to gain access to

■ their own node's zone name

■ the names of all the zones on their local network

■ the names of all the zones throughout the internet

The chapter "Zone Information Protocol (ZIP)" in this book describes the ZIP application programming interface. For additional information about ZIP, see "Identifying Zones" on page 1-23.

AppleTalk Session Protocol (ASP)

The **AppleTalk Session Protocol (ASP)** sets up and maintains sessions between a workstation and a server. ASP is an asymmetrical protocol in which one side of the dialog, the workstation client of ASP, initiates the session and sends commands to the other side of the dialog. A higher-level protocol that is built on top of the ASP server interprets and executes the command, and the ASP server returns a reply. ASP also provides a means by which the server can send a message to the workstation; for example, a file server can use this messaging system to notify all of the workstations that are using the file server that it is shutting down. ASP is used by the AppleTalk Filing Protocol to allow a user to manipulate files on a file server. Because ADSP provides socket clients at both ends of the connection with equal control, ADSP is more commonly used than ASP when a session protocol is required.

The chapter "AppleTalk Session Protocol (ASP)" in this book describes the ASP application programming interface. For additional information about ASP, see "AppleTalk Session Protocol" on page 1-25.

AppleTalk Data Stream Protocol (ADSP)

The **AppleTalk Data Stream Protocol (ADSP)** is a connection-oriented protocol that supports sessions over which applications and processes that are socket clients can exchange full-duplex streams of data across an AppleTalk internet. ADSP is a symmetrical protocol; the socket clients at either end of the connection have equal control over the ADSP session and the data exchange. Through attention messages, ADSP also provides for out-of-band signaling, a process of sending data outside the normal session dialog so as not to interrupt the data flow.

The chapter "AppleTalk Data Stream Protocol (ADSP)" in this book describes the ADSP application programming interface. For additional information about ADSP, see "AppleTalk Data Stream Protocol" on page 1-24.

AppleTalk Transaction Protocol (ATP)

The **AppleTalk Transaction Protocol (ATP)** is a transaction protocol that allows one socket client to transmit a request that some action be performed to another socket client that carries out the action and transmits a response reporting the outcome. ATP provides reliable delivery of data by retransmitting any data packets that are lost and ensuring that the data packets are delivered in the correct sequence.

The chapter "AppleTalk Transaction Protocol (ATP)" in this book describes the ATP application programming interface. For additional information about ATP, see "Performing a Transaction" on page 1-25.

AppleTalk Echo Protocol (AEP)

The **AppleTalk Echo Protocol (AEP)** exists on every node as a DDP client process called the **AEP Echoer.** The AEP Echoer uses a special socket to *listen* for packets sent to it from socket clients on other nodes. When it receives such a packet, the AEP Echoer returns it directly to the sender. A socket client can send a packet to the AEP Echoer on another node to determine if that node can be accessed over the internet and to determine how long it takes a packet to reach that node. There is no application programming interface to AEP. A socket client can send packets to an AEP Echoer socket on another node from a DDP socket, but it cannot access the AEP implementation directly.

The chapter "Datagram Delivery Protocol (DDP)" in this book describes how to send packets to the AEP socket. For additional information about AEP, see "Measuring Packet-Delivery Performance" on page 1-26.

Name-Binding Protocol (NBP)

The **Name-Binding Protocol (NBP)** provides your application or process with a way to map names that are useful to people using your program to numbers or addresses that are useful to computers. NBP associates a user-friendly three-part name that can be displayed to end users with the internet socket address of the application or process. When a user launches it, your application can register itself with NBP. When a user quits the application or when you no longer wish to advertise your application, your application can delete its entry from the NBP names table. Once your application registers itself with NBP, other applications can locate it.

All applications and processes that use AppleTalk use NBP to make their services known and available throughout an AppleTalk internet and to locate other applications and processes in the internet. An application or process can use NBP to

- register itself with NBP. Registering an application or process with NBP makes that process a network-visible entity. (NBP lets your application or process bind a three-part name to its internet socket address.)

- look up or confirm the address of another application or process that is registered with NBP.

- remove its entry from the NBP names table when it no longer wants to advertise its services.

The chapter "Name-Binding Protocol (NBP)" in this book describes the NBP application programming interface. For additional information about NBP, see "Making Your Application Available Throughout the Internet" on page 1-22.

Routing Table Maintenance Protocol (RTMP)

The **Routing Table Maintenance Protocol (RTMP)** provides AppleTalk internet routers with a means of managing routing tables used to determine how to forward a datagram from one socket to another across an internet based on the datagram's destination network number. The RTMP implementation on a router maintains a table called a routing table that specifies the shortest path to each possible destination network number. The AppleTalk protocol software in a workstation (that is, a node other than a router) contains only a small part of RTMP, called the RTMP stub, that DDP uses to determine the network number (or range of network numbers) of the network cable to which the node is connected and to determine the network number and node ID of one router on that network cable. There is no application programming interface to the RTMP stub; therefore, RTMP is not discussed in this book.

Datagram Delivery Protocol (DDP)

The **Datagram Delivery Protocol (DDP)** is a connectionless protocol that transfers data between sockets as discrete packets, or datagrams, with each packet carrying its destination internet socket address. DDP provides best-effort delivery. It does not include support to ensure that all packets sent are received at the destination or that those packets that are received are in the correct order. Higher-level protocols that use the services of DDP provide for reliable delivery of data. DDP uses whichever link-access protocol the user selects; that is, DDP can send its datagrams through any type of data link and transport media.

The chapter "Datagram Delivery Protocol (DDP)" in this book describes the DDP application programming interface. For additional information about DDP, see "Sending and Receiving Data as Discrete Packets" on page 1-26.

Link-Access Protocols

AppleTalk supports various network (or link) types and allows the user to select and switch among the types of networks to be used based on how the user's machine is configured; that is, if the machine has the proper hardware and software installed for a link type, the user can select that link. AppleTalk includes the link-access protocols for LocalTalk, EtherTalk, TokenTalk, and FDDITalk (Fiber Distributed Data Interface). AppleTalk uses connection files of type `'adev'` that contain software that supports a particular type of data link.

To achieve link independence, AppleTalk relies on the **Link-Access Protocol (LAP) Manager,** which is a set of operating-system utilities, not an AppleTalk protocol. The main function of the LAP Manager is to act as a switching mechanism that connects the AppleTalk link-access protocol for the link type that the user selects to both the higher-level AppleTalk protocols and the lower-level hardware device driver for that data link. From the Network control panel, a user can select which network is to be used for the node's AppleTalk connection.

The AppleTalk connection files of type 'adev' and the LAP Manager work together with the Network control panel file of type 'cdev'. When the user selects a network type from the Network control panel, the LAP Manager routes AppleTalk communications through the link-access protocol for the selected network.

The LAP Manager also provides an application with access to the AppleTalk Transition Queue. You can place an entry for your application in the AppleTalk Transition Queue so that the LAP Manager will notify you when an AppleTalk transition occurs or is about to occur. An AppleTalk transition is an event, such as an AppleTalk driver being opened or closed, that can affect your AppleTalk application.

The chapter "Link-Access Protocol (LAP) Manager" in this book describes the LAP Manager and the AppleTalk Transition Queue. For additional information about the LAP Manager, see the *Macintosh AppleTalk Connections Programmer's Guide*.

Multivendor Architecture

In addition to supporting various types of networks, Apple also provides what is known as *multivendor support*. The **multivendor architecture** allows for multiple brands of Ethernet, token ring, and FDDI NuBus™ network interface controllers (NICs) to be installed on a single node at the same time. In addition to selecting the type of network connection, the user can now select a particular device to be used for the network connection. The chapter "Ethernet, Token Ring, and Fiber Distributed Data Interface" in this book describes multivendor architecture.

Multinode Architecture

Multinode architecture is an AppleTalk feature that allows an application to acquire node IDs in addition to the standard node ID that is assigned to the system when the node joins an AppleTalk network. Multinode architecture is provided to meet the needs of special-purpose applications that receive and process AppleTalk packets in a custom manner instead of passing them directly on to a higher-level AppleTalk protocol for processing. A multinode ID allows the system that is running your application to appear as multiple nodes on the network. The prime example of a multinode application is Apple Remote Access (ARA). The chapter "Multinode Architecture" in this book describes this feature.

How the AppleTalk Protocols Are Implemented

Above the data-link level, all of the AppleTalk protocols that you can address or control from a Macintosh application through a programming interface as well as multinode architecture are implemented as Macintosh device drivers. Table 1-2 identifies the AppleTalk drivers and the protocols they implement.

Table 1-2   AppleTalk drivers and the protocols they implement

AppleTalk driver	Protocols it implements
.MPP	DDP, NBP, AEP, RTMP stub, multinode
.ATP	ATP
.XPP	ASP, workstation portions of ZIP and AFP
.DSP	ADSP

Figure 1-3 shows the AppleTalk protocols with the name of the driver that implements the protocol and the connection files of type `'adev'` that AppleTalk provides for various types of links. Notice how the LAP Manager acts as a switching mechanism between the higher-level protocols and the link-access protocols. Many other features of these protocols are implemented in software located only on internet routers that are not used to run general applications. Some parts of protocols are implemented by server software such as file servers and print servers.

Figure 1-3   Device drivers and connections files that implement AppleTalk protocols

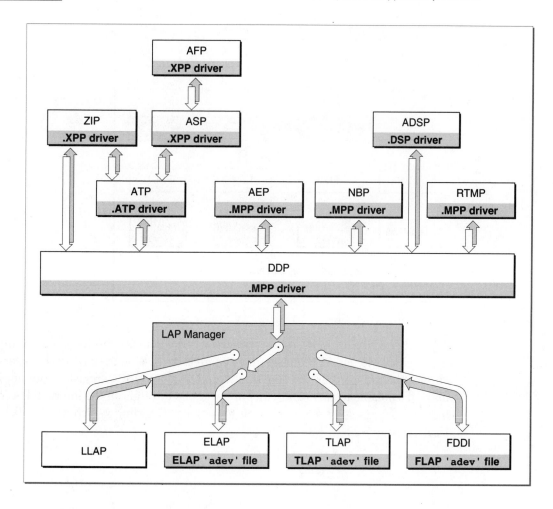

The AppleTalk Manager

Your application accesses the services of the AppleTalk protocols through the AppleTalk Manager, which is a collection of the application programming interfaces to the AppleTalk protocols. The AppleTalk Manager includes the LAP Manager, which collects together the interfaces to the supported AppleTalk data links. Note that not all AppleTalk protocols have programming interfaces.

Figure 1-4 shows the AppleTalk protocols; those protocols that have programming interfaces are shaded.

Figure 1-4   AppleTalk protocols with programming interfaces

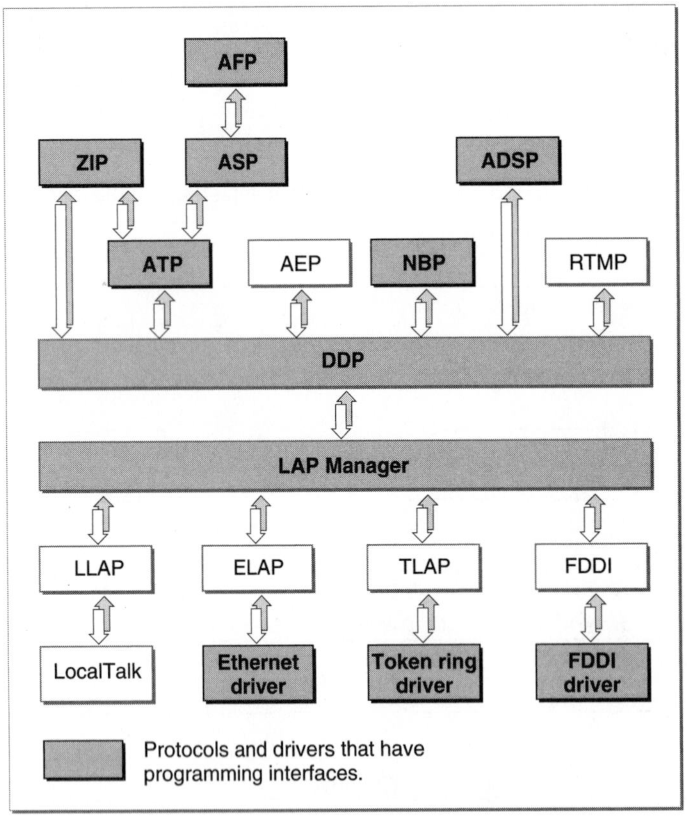

Typically, an application uses the services of more than one protocol. For example, you might choose to use ADSP to set up a symmetrical session over which the users of your application can transfer data, but you would also use NBP to register your application to make it available to users and other applications throughout the internet. For information on how to select which protocols to use, see "Deciding Which AppleTalk Protocol to Use" on page 1-22.

AppleTalk and the OSI Model

This section provides general information about the relationship between AppleTalk and an industry-standard networking model. You do not need to read this section to understand the AppleTalk protocols or to use the AppleTalk Manager.

Most networking systems are designed as layered architectures that relate to what are called *reference models.* These matrices offer a structure that network designers can refer to in developing a network architecture; they are guidelines and not rules. Each layer of a model collects together those functions that are similar or highly interrelated and provides services to the layer above it. Network designers develop protocols that encompass the functions of each layer. Often more than one protocol is defined and implemented to handle the requirements of a layer in different ways. Some protocols include functions that span more than one layer specified by a model. For example, in favor of efficiency, a network protocol developer may elect to define a single protocol that spans two or more layers of a reference model.

Various layered models have been developed that provide standards for the design and development of networking software. One of these models is the Open Systems Interconnection (OSI) model, which is a seven-layered standard that was published by the International Standards Organization (ISO) in the 1970s. This is the model with which the AppleTalk network system architecture is most closely aligned.

Note

Although this section discusses AppleTalk in relation to the OSI model, it does not claim a protocol compatibility of AppleTalk with the OSI protocols currently in various stages of definition, approval, and deployment. ◆

Figure 1-5 on page 1-20 shows the relationships among the AppleTalk protocols and how they map to the OSI model. The shaded area of the graphic shows the name of the OSI layer. A connection between one protocol and another above or below it in the figure indicates that the upper protocol is a client of the lower protocol, that is, the upper protocol uses services provided by the lower protocol in order to carry out some functions.

Application Layer

The highest layer of the OSI model is the application layer. This layer allows for the development of application software. Software written at this layer benefits from the services of all the underlying layers. There is no AppleTalk protocol that maps directly to this layer, although some of the functions of the AppleTalk Filing Protocol (AFP) fulfill this layer.

Figure 1-5   AppleTalk protocol stack and the OSI model

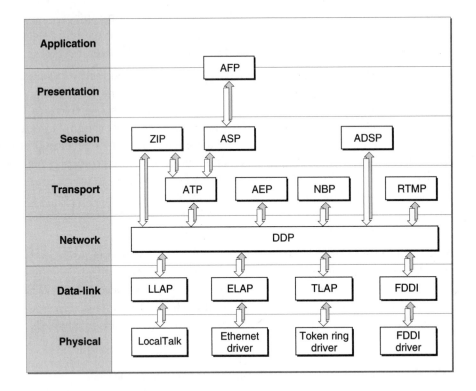

Presentation Layer

The presentation layer assumes that an end-to-end path or connection already exists across the network between the two communicating parties, and it is concerned with the representation of data values for transfer, or the *transfer syntax*. In the OSI model, the AppleTalk Filing Protocol (AFP) spans the presentation and application layers. AFP provides an interface between an application and a file server. It uses the services of ASP, which, in turn, is a client of ATP.

AFP allows a workstation on an AppleTalk network to access files on an AFP file server, such as an AppleShare file server. When the user opens a session with an AppleShare file server over an internet, it appears to any application running on the workstation that uses File Manager routines as if the files on the file server were located on a disk drive connected to the workstation.

Session Layer

The session layer serves as an interface into the transport layer, which is below it. The session layer allows for **session establishment,** which is the process of setting up a connection over which a dialog between two applications or processes can occur. Some of the functions that the session layer provides for are flow control, establishment of synchronization points for checks and recovery for file transfer, full-duplex and half-duplex dialogs between processes, and aborts and restarts.

The AppleTalk protocols implemented at the session layer are

■ the AppleTalk Data Stream Protocol (ADSP), which provides its own stream-based transport layer services that allow for full-duplex dialogs

■ the AppleTalk Session Protocol (ASP), which uses the transaction-based services of ATP to transport workstation commands to servers

■ the Zone Information Protocol (ZIP), which provides applications and processes with access to zone names. Each node on a network belongs to a zone.

Transport Layer

The transport layer isolates some of the physical and functional aspects of a packet network from the upper three layers. It provides for end-to-end accountability, ensuring that all packets of data sent across the network are received and in the correct order. This is the process that is referred to as *reliable delivery of data,* and it involves providing a means of identifying packet loss and supplying a retransmission mechanism. The transport layer also provides connection and session management services.

The following AppleTalk protocols are implemented at the transport layer:

■ Name-Binding Protocol (NBP)

■ AppleTalk Transaction Protocol (ATP)

■ AppleTalk Echo Protocol (AEP)

■ Routing Table Maintenance Protocol (RTMP)

In addition to these transport layer protocols, the AppleTalk Data Stream Protocol (ADSP) includes functions that span both the transport and the session layers. ADSP provides for reliable delivery of data, and in that capacity it covers the transport layer requirements.

Network Layer

The network layer specifies the network routing of data packets between nodes and the communications between networks, which is referred to as *internetworking.* The Datagram Delivery Protocol (DDP) is the AppleTalk protocol implemented at the network layer. DDP is a connectionless datagram protocol providing best-effort delivery. This means that DDP transfers data as discrete packets and that DDP does not include support to ensure that all packets sent are received at the destination or that those packets that are received are in the correct order. Higher-level protocols that use the services of DDP provide for this kind of reliability.

Data-Link and Physical Layers

The data-link layer and the physical layer provide for connectivity. The communication between networked systems can be via a physical cable made of wire or fiber optic, or it can be via infrared or microwave transmission. In addition to these, the hardware can include a network interface controller (NIC), if one is used. The hardware or transport media and the device drivers for the hardware comprise the physical layer. LocalTalk, token ring, Ethernet, and Fiber Distributed Data Interface (FDDI) are examples of types of networking hardware that AppleTalk supports.

The physical hardware provides nodes on a network with a shared data transmission medium called a *link*. The data-link layer includes a protocol that specifies the physical aspects of the data link and the link-access protocol, which handles the logistics of sending the data packet over the transport medium. AppleTalk is designed to be data-link independent, allowing for the use of various types of hardware and their link-access protocols.

Deciding Which AppleTalk Protocol to Use

The AppleTalk Manager consists of a collection of application programming interfaces to the AppleTalk protocols and the LAP Manager. Each of the AppleTalk protocols implements a different set of functions and services, and the programming interface for a specific protocol includes a set of routines that give your application access to the protocol's functions and services.

AppleTalk offers programming interfaces to a variety of communications protocols at different levels. Your choice of protocol or protocols to use depends primarily on your application's needs.

This section provides a brief discussion of how your application can use each protocol. The AppleTalk protocols are layered in a stack with each protocol benefiting from the services of the protocols in layers below it. Looked at from a top-down approach, the high-level protocols provide an accretion of all the services of the underlying protocols.

A developer who uses the higher-level protocols that provide for reliable delivery of data and error recovery does not have to implement these services as part of an application. An application developer who wants to write a program for end users that runs on an AppleTalk network would typically use the interfaces to one or more higher-level protocols. For example, you might use NBP to register the program with the network so that it is visible to users and other applications, and, perhaps, ADSP to transfer data.

A network software developer who wants to implement a custom session-oriented protocol, instead of using ADSP or ASP, would typically use the interface to a protocol such as DDP or any of the protocols below it. A network software developer who wants to implement a custom protocol stack instead of using AppleTalk can use a low-level protocol interface to attach a protocol handler that receives data from the network.

Making Your Application Available Throughout the Internet

This section discusses the Name-Binding Protocol (NBP) that you can use to make your application or process visible to users and other applications and processes throughout an AppleTalk internet.

NBP binds the internet socket address assigned to a process or application to a special human-readable name that contains three parts: the object, type, and zone fields. The NBP name is different from the name of the application. The object and type are assigned by the process itself and can be anything the user or application developer selects; the zone is the one in which the node resides.

NBP maintains a table on each node that contains the name-and-address pair for each application or process on that node that is registered with NBP. Once an application or process is registered with NBP, it becomes visible to users and other applications and processes throughout the internet. When a process or application is registered with NBP, it is referred to as a **network-visible entity.**

Users can select an application by its NBP name. Based on the name or a part of the name, applications and processes can request NBP to look up the internet socket address for the entity.

When you use other AppleTalk protocols that send and receive data, your application or process becomes associated with an internet socket address. Although applications and processes need the internet socket addresses of other applications and processes that they want to connect with, a name identifying the type of application and its location is more meaningful to an end user. Your application or process can use NBP to find all other applications or processes of the same type and get their internet socket addresses. Your application could then display the NBP names of other applications to an end user so that the user can select an application to connect to. Your application could then use another AppleTalk protocol, such as ADSP, to connect to the partner application.

An application, such as a network management tool, could use NBP to collect information so that it can provide an inventory of all nodes belonging to a zone and list the applications running on each of those nodes. It could sort the applications by type. For example, it could provide a list of all file servers on an AppleTalk internet.

Identifying Zones

The Zone Information Protocol (ZIP) maintains a zone information table in each internet router that lists the relationships between zone names and network numbers. You can use the part of ZIP that is implemented on a nonrouter node to get the name of the zone to which the node that is running the application belongs. Your application can also call ZIP to get a list of all the zones in the internet.

An application running on a node that belongs to an extended network can call ZIP to get a list of all the zone names associated with that network. For example, an application that supports network administration might use these service to provide a network administrator with a list of the zones for a particular network so that the administrator can select the correct zone for a node when adding nodes to a network.

An application could collect other kinds of information, such as what services are running on nodes, and then sort the information by zone.

Using a Session Protocol to Send and Receive Data

AppleTalk includes two session protocols that you can use to send and receive data:

- ADSP provides a symmetrical session.
- ASP provides an asymmetrical session.

Most applications use ADSP, which was made available after ASP.

AppleTalk Data Stream Protocol

Your application can use ADSP to set up and maintain a connection with another application over an internet. Through this connection, both applications can send and receive streams of data at any time. Because ADSP allows for the continuous exchange of data, any application that needs to support the exchange of more than a small amount of data should use ADSP. In addition to providing for a duplex data stream, ADSP also provides an application with a means of sending attention messages to pass control information between the two communicating applications without disrupting the main flow of data.

In most cases, ADSP is the protocol that Apple recommends applications use for sending and receiving data. In addition to ensuring reliable delivery of data, ADSP provides a peer-to-peer connection, that is, both ends of the connection can exert equal control over the exchange of data.

Note
Because ADSP is connection-oriented, it entails additional processing and memory usage in setting up and maintaining the connection between the two applications. Therefore, if your application needs to send a small amount of data, such as a request that the other end perform a task and report the result in response, and you don't want to incur the overhead involved in establishing, maintaining, and breaking a connection, you should consider using ATP rather than ADSP for data transfer. ◆

ADSP appears to its clients to maintain an open pipeline between the two entities at either end. Either entity can write a stream of bytes to the pipeline or read data bytes from the pipeline. However, because ADSP, like all other higher-level AppleTalk protocols, is a client of DDP, the data is actually sent as datagrams. This allows ADSP to correct transmission errors in a way that would not be possible for a true data stream connection. Thus, ADSP retains many of the advantages of a connectionless protocol while providing to its clients a connection-oriented full-duplex data stream.

An application that uses ADSP can treat the data to be transferred as continuous streams of data, or it can treat it as discrete messages to be interpreted individually. Applications that might use ADSP include server software applications such as mail servers, terminal emulation programs, or any application that requires two-way communication between computers. ADSP also includes features that let you authenticate the identity of the party at the other end of the connection and send encrypted data across the session, which is then decrypted at the other end. The authentication and encryption features of ADSP are referred to as *AppleTalk Secure Data Stream Protocol (ASDSP)*.

AppleTalk Session Protocol

You can use the AppleTalk Session Protocol (ASP) to implement workstation applications that require an asymmetrical dialog with a server in which the workstation application initiates and controls the dialog. The workstation application tells the server application what to do and the server responds. ASP provides for the setting up, maintaining, and closing down of a session between a workstation and a server.

A workstation application that requires a state-dependent service should use ASP instead of ATP. **State dependence** means that the response to a request is dependent on a previous request. Consider the example of a workstation application connecting to a file server to read a file: before the application can read the file, it must have first issued a request to open the file. (For example, the AppleTalk Filing Protocol [AFP] uses ASP. However, only the client side of ASP is implemented on the Macintosh.) When a dialog is state dependent, all requests must be delivered in order and duplicate packets must not be sent: ASP provides for this.

An ATP transaction-based request, such as a workstation application requesting a server to return the time of day, is independent of other requests and not state dependent.

ASP assigns each session a unique identifier called a **session reference number** that allows more than one workstation to establish a session with the same server at the same time. For example, a server might use session reference numbers to distinguish between commands received from various clients of sessions.

ASP ensures that commands from a workstation are delivered without duplication and in the same order in which they were sent. ASP conveys the results of these commands back to the workstation. As long as the session is open, the workstation can request directory information, change filenames, and so forth. The file server must respond to the workstation's commands and cannot initiate any actions on its own.

Performing a Transaction

If you want to write an application that performs a transaction, you can use the AppleTalk Transaction Protocol (ATP). A transaction is an interaction between two applications that are clients of ATP in which one application, known as the *requester*, sends a request to the other application, known as the *responder*, to perform a task and return a response that reports the outcome of the task. The transaction request must fit in a single packet; however, the response can contain up to eight packets. ATP transactions are an efficient means of transporting small amounts of data across the network. ATP provides a reliable loss-free transport service. ATP's means of ensuring reliable delivery of data is based on the request-response paradigm as opposed to the data stream model that ADSP uses for reliable delivery of data.

You should use ATP

- if you want to send a small amount of data
- if your application requires delivery of all packets
- if your application can tolerate a minor degree of performance degradation
- if you do not want to incur the overhead and more extensive performance degradation involved in maintaining a session

ATP is useful for collecting status information; for example, a network management application might include a responder program on each node to which the central application sends out ATP requests asking for version information, such as the version of AppleTalk that the node is running. The responder program could check the version and send the information back to the main application in response to the request. Games that are based on request-and-response types of dialogs can make efficient use of ATP.

Sending and Receiving Data as Discrete Packets

Your application can use the Datagram Delivery Protocol (DDP) to transmit data in the form of packets across an AppleTalk internet. Because DDP provides best-effort delivery of datagrams with no recovery when packets are lost or discarded because of errors, it involves less overhead and provides for faster performance than do the higher-level protocols that add reliable delivery.

For applications, such as some games that don't require reliable delivery of data and can tolerate possible packet loss or diagnostic tools that retransmit at regular intervals to estimate averages, DDP suffices, and it offers the value of good performance. In fact, if you develop a game application that limits players to nodes on a single network, DDP will use short addressing headers on packets, requiring 8 fewer bytes per packet, which are faster to send.

If you are a network software developer who wants to develop a session-oriented protocol, a client-server protocol, or a transaction-based protocol that offers services different from those provided by ADSP, ASP, or ATP, you can design and implement your protocol as a client of DDP. However, this can entail providing your own server implementation in some cases. For a detailed description of DDP and the other AppleTalk protocols, see *Inside AppleTalk,* second edition.

If you use the DDP interface, you must provide a process called a *socket listener* to receive datagrams addressed to the socket. The chapter "Datagram Delivery Protocol (DDP)" in this book describes how to write a socket listener.

Measuring Packet-Delivery Performance

You can use the AppleTalk Echo Protocol (AEP) to measure the timing of send-receive cycles and to determine if another node is online. There is no application programming interface to AEP. However, to measure the round-trip packet delivery time from your node to another node, your application or process can send a packet that is addressed to the AEP socket, referred to as the *AEP Echoer,* on the destination node, and AEP will return a copy of that packet directly to you.

You can use this echo test as part of a diagnostic tool application, for example. A diagnostic tool could troubleshoot a suspect node and report how long it took the packet to travel to and from the node. Your application could use repeated transmissions to determine if a packet takes longer than the typical amount of time to reach the node, if it contains corrupted data, or if it doesn't make it back at all.

To determine if another node is on the network, you can send a packet to that node's AEP socket. For a conclusive test, you should send more than one packet, in case the first packet is lost or discarded by DDP.

Accessing AppleShare and Other File Servers

The AppleTalk Filing Protocol (AFP) provides an interface between an application and an AFP file server. For example, it allows workstations on an AppleTalk network to access files on AppleShare file servers. AFP uses the services of ASP.

Only the workstation side of AFP is implemented on the Macintosh. Few application developers use AFP because the existing File Manager commands perform most functions needed to access and manipulate files on an AppleShare server.

If you choose to use AFP, your application can provide support that allows a workstation user to use the workstation's own local or native file system commands to manipulate files on a remote node. The chapter "AppleTalk Filing Protocol (AFP)" in this book describes how to use AFP.

Receiving Packets Using a Virtual Node and Processing Them in a Custom Manner

Your application can use the AppleTalk multinode architecture to acquire node IDs that are in addition to the standard user node ID assigned to the system. You can use these virtual node IDs, called *multinodes*, to receive all broadcast packets and all AppleTalk packets addressed to the multinode. You can then process the packets in a custom manner. A multinode ID is not connected to the AppleTalk protocol stack above the data-link layer; this means that an application that uses a multinode is not connected to the AppleTalk protocol above the data-link level, and it cannot use their services. For example, Apple Remote Access (ARA) uses this multinode capability to implement remote access. The chapter "Multinode Architecture" describes how to acquire a multinode ID and send and receive packets using the multinodes.

The LAP Manager

The LAP Manager acts as an interface between the link types and the higher-level AppleTalk protocols. The LAP Manager contains a protocol handler that it attaches directly to the hardware device driver to receive 802.2 Type 1 packets for Ethernet, token ring, and FDDI. If your application handles 802.2 Type 1 packets, you must provide a protocol handler to read the packets and install your protocol handler as a client of the LAP Manager. A **protocol handler** is a piece of assembly-language code that controls the reception of a packet of a particular protocol type. When an 802.2 packet for your application arrives, the LAP Manager will call your protocol handler to read the packet.

The LAP Manager also provides and maintains a service called the **AppleTalk Transition Queue (ATQ)** that you can use to ensure that your application is not adversely affected when an AppleTalk transition occurs.

An example of an AppleTalk transition is an AppleTalk driver being closed or opened by another routine or the operating system. At any given time, there might be two or more applications running that use AppleTalk. If one of these applications closes the AppleTalk drivers, all AppleTalk applications are affected.

Your application can register itself with the AppleTalk Transition Queue by placing an entry in the queue. The LAP Manager sends a message to each entry in the AppleTalk Transition Queue when a transition occurs. Your application or other routines can also define their own AppleTalk events and call the AppleTalk Transition Queue to inform it that such an event occurred.

The AppleTalk Transition Queue also allows an application that uses the **Flagship Naming Service** to place an entry in the queue that enables it to stay informed as to changes to the flagship name. A **flagship name** is a personalized name that users can enter to identify their nodes when they are connected to an AppleTalk network. The flagship name is different from the Chooser name that a node uses for server-connection identification. The LAP Manager uses the transition queue message system to communicate name changes between applications and processes whenever the user resets the flagship name.

The chapter "Link-Access Protocol (LAP) Manager" in this book describes the LAP Manager services and interface. For more information about the LAP Manager, see the *Macintosh AppleTalk Connection Programmer's Guide*.

Using AppleTalk's link independence to write portable applications

If you write an application that uses one of the high-level AppleTalk protocols, such as ADSP or ATP, your program will run over any link type. A user running your application can switch between link types, for example, move from one type of network, such as token ring, to another, such as Ethernet, without affecting your program. The LAP Manager handles the interface and connection to the correct link-access protocol based on the link type the user selects. ◆

Directly Accessing a Driver for a Network Type

The .ENET, the .TOKN, or the .FDDI driver is normally called by the AppleTalk Manager through the AppleTalk connection file for the link type (EtherTalk, TokenTalk, or FDDITalk) when the user has selected one of these network types from the Network control panel. You can write your own protocol stack or application that uses one of these drivers directly rather than through AppleTalk.

The interface at this level allows you to open the driver and send data to it directly for transmission over the network. However, to receive data from the network, you need to provide a protocol handler written in assembly language.

For Phase 1 Ethernet packets, that is, the original version of Ethernet packets, you can read data directly from an Ethernet driver using the default protocol handler that Apple provides or your own protocol handler.

For IEEE 802.2 packets, you must use the interface to the Link-Access Protocol (LAP) Manager to attach your protocol handler to read data from an Ethernet, token ring, or FDDI driver. Token ring and FDDI support only 802.2 packets.

The chapter "Ethernet, Token Ring, and Fiber Distributed Data Interface" in this book describes how to use the interface for Phase 1 Ethernet packets. The chapter "Link-Access Protocol (LAP) Manager" in this book describes how to use the interface for IEEE 802.2 packets.

The AppleTalk Pascal Interface

This section provides an overview of the two execution modes that you can use to execute routines that belong to the AppleTalk protocol interfaces.

When your application calls an AppleTalk routine, you set a Boolean value as a parameter to the routine that directs the system software to execute the routine synchronously or asynchronously:

- If you set the routine to run synchronously, your application program cannot continue executing until the operation completes.

- If you set the routine to execute asynchronously, the system software returns control to your application program immediately and one of two methods is used to signal your program later when the operation completes; these methods are the use of a completion routine or a polling strategy.

The first version of the AppleTalk Pascal interfaces is now referred to collectively as the **alternate interface.** Routines belonging to the alternate interface that were executed asynchronously signaled the application that the operation had completed through the use of a network event.

Note
The use of network events introduced problems that were remedied by the creation of a new interface whose routines relied on the use of a completion routine or a result-field polling strategy rather than a network event as a completion-signaling mechanism for asynchronous calls. ◆

The new interface was designed to be similar to that of the Device Manager and the File Manager. Its routines use parameter blocks to pass input and output values. The interface glue code converts the parameter block values into a Device Manager `PBControl` call to the appropriate AppleTalk device driver. Called the **preferred interface** in the past, this interface is now the standard AppleTalk interface.

When writing new applications that use AppleTalk, you should use the routines belonging to the interface described in this book. Use of the alternate interface calls could cause compatibility problems with current and future system software, although the alternate interface is still provided in the header files for backward compatibility.

Note

For functions that execute asynchronously, you must not move or
dispose of the parameter block before the function completes execution;
while the function is executing, AppleTalk owns the memory that you
allocated for the function's use. *After* the call returns, you need to
dispose of the memory allocated for the parameter block unless you
intend to reuse the parameter block, for example, for another function. ◆

Executing Routines Synchronously or Asynchronously

Your program can execute the routines that make up the interface to the AppleTalk
protocols either synchronously or asynchronously. **Synchronous execution** means that
your program is prevented from doing any other processing until the current operation
completes. **Asynchronous execution** means that the system returns control to your
program after your program calls the routine so that your program can continue with
other processing while the asynchronous operation completes.

If you execute a routine synchronously, the call does not return until the operation
completes; you do not have to use a completion routine that runs at interrupt level or
poll a result field to determine when the operation completes; on the other hand, your
program cannot continue running until the call returns, which causes the system to come
to a standstill. Synchronous calls are useful for operations that execute and return to the
calling program quickly, such as opening or closing sockets. On an AppleTalk internet,
data is transferred between sockets, which must be opened before they can be used and
closed when they are no longer needed.

Calling a routine asynchronously directs the system software to begin the operation
process now, return control to the calling program, then complete execution of the
routine as soon as possible. Asynchronous execution eliminates program execution delay
time, but it requires that your application provide a means of determining when the
operation has completed execution. There are two methods an application can use to
determine when an operation completes execution:

- An application can provide a completion routine to be called at interrupt level.

- An application can poll the routine's parameter block result field.

The parameter block that is used to contain input and output information for
a function includes a result field called `ioResult`. When your application calls a
function asynchronously,

- the driver executes the function, if possible.

- if the driver is busy, the driver queues the function and sets the `ioResult` field to 1.

When the function completes execution, the driver sets the result field to a value that
indicates either that no error occurred (`noErr`) or an error condition code value that
identifies the type of error.

Polling the Result Field

Your application can poll the result field to determine when the result value changes. Your application can use the polling process to inform the user that the system is still busy performing the operation that handles the request; for processes that may take a long time, your application can display a progress dialog box to the user.

Note
If you use polling, you must set the call's parameter block `ioCompletion` field to `NIL`. ◆

Using a Completion Routine

Instead of polling the result field, your application can supply a completion routine to be executed at interrupt level when the operation completes. You provide the address of the completion routine in the call's parameter block `ioCompletion` field. Because completion routines are executed at interrupt level, they cannot call any routines that move memory.

AppleTalk Utilities

Contents

This chapter describes the AppleTalk functions and services that do not belong to a specific AppleTalk protocol interface but that apply to AppleTalk as a whole.

The chapter describes how to

- obtain a wide variety of information about AppleTalk and the network environment of your node, including the maximum number of protocol handlers and concurrent NBP calls that the installed .MPP driver supports

- obtain the addresses of your node and its local internet router

- enable intranode delivery, which lets you send packets to your own application or other applications and processes running on the same node as yours

- determine if the AppleTalk Phase 2 drivers are installed on your system

- select a node ID in the server range

- open the .MPP and .XPP drivers

The .MPP driver opens the .ATP driver. The chapter "AppleTalk Data Stream Protocol (ADSP)" in this book describes how to open the .DSP driver. Although Apple Computer, Inc. recommends that you not close any of the AppleTalk drivers because other applications that are coresident may be using them, this chapter explains how to close the .MPP driver, if, for some reason, you must.

About the AppleTalk Utilities

The AppleTalk Utilities are a group of diverse functions, some of which allow you to obtain information about AppleTalk and the networking environment of your node and some of which allow you change values that affect AppleTalk features.

The `PGetAppleTalkInfo` function returns a wide range of information, including some information that other functions belonging to the AppleTalk Utilities also return. For example, both `PGetAppleTalkInfo` and `GetNodeAddress` return the node ID and network address of the user node that is running your application. The `PGetAppleTalkInfo` function returns the node ID and the network number of the last router from which the node that is running your application has heard; the `GetBridgeAddress` function also returns the node ID of the internet router on your node's local network.

Note

The `PGetAppleTalkInfo` function was developed and made available after the `GetNodeAddress` and `GetBridgeAddress` functions. Apple Computer, Inc. recommends that you use the `PGetAppleTalkInfo` function to obtain addressing information for a user node or router instead of using the `GetNodeAddress` and `GetBridgeAddress` functions. ◆

Although the AppleTalk interface does not include a function that you can use to direct AppleTalk to select a node ID from the server node range when you open AppleTalk, this chapter describes how you can do this. If your application or the application that

opened AppleTalk directed AppleTalk to assign a server node ID to the node, the
PGetAppleTalkInfo function will return a flag that tells you this request was made.

AppleTalk includes a feature called **intranode delivery** that allows two programs
running on the same node to communicate with each other through the AppleTalk
protocols. The AppleTalk Utilities include the PSetSelfSend function, which you can
use to enable or disable intranode delivery. The PGetAppleTalkInfo function will
tell you if intranode delivery is on or off.

Using the AppleTalk Utilities

This section describes how to use some of the functions and services that make up the
AppleTalk Utilities. It explains how to

- check the version of the AppleTalk drivers that are installed

- get information about the .MPP driver and the network environment

- get the address of your node and locate your local router

- enable intranode delivery

- request AppleTalk to assign to your node an ID that is in the range of numbers that
  are reserved for server nodes

Determining Whether AppleTalk Phase 2 Drivers Are Supported

Once the .MPP driver has been loaded into memory, you can use the Gestalt function
with the gestaltAppleTalkVersion selector to check the version of AppleTalk. The
Gestalt function returns the version of the .MPP driver. If the version is equal to or
greater than 53, then the .MPP driver supports AppleTalk Phase 2.

Alternatively, you can call the SysEnvirons function. If the atDrvrVersNum field of
the SysEnvRec data structure returned by this function is equal to or greater than 53,
then the .MPP driver supports AppleTalk Phase 2.

Getting Information About the .MPP Driver and the Network Environment

This section describes how you can use the PGetAppleTalkInfo function to obtain
information about the installed version of the .MPP driver, the network environment,
and the .MPP driver's maximum capacities, such as the number of sockets and the
number of NBP calls that the .MPP driver supports. The .MPP driver implements
these protocols:

- Datagram Delivery Protocol (DDP)

- Routing Table Maintenance Protocol (RTMP) stub

- Name-Binding Protocol (NBP)

- AppleTalk Echo Protocol (AEP)

Before you call the `PGetAppleTalkInfo` function, you must allocate memory for and define a parameter block of type `MPPParmType`. The section "MPP Parameter Block" beginning on page 2-9 shows this data structure. You must also allocate memory for and provide pointers to the data buffers into which the `PGetAppleTalkInfo` function returns the data-link address and zone name for extended networks.

The `PGetAppleTalkInfo` function's Boolean parameter allows you to specify whether the function is to be executed synchronously or asynchronously. This function is generally executed synchronously. (For information on these two modes, see the chapter "Introduction to AppleTalk" in this book.)

The `PGetAppleTalkInfo` function returns the following information:

- a pointer to the MPP global variables

- a pointer to the .MPP driver's device control entry (DCE) data structure

- configuration flags that indicate the status of certain conditions that are set at startup

- a value (the `selfSend` flag) that indicates whether the node can send packets to itself (See "Sending Packets to Applications and Processes on Your Own Node" on page 2-6 and "Enabling Intranode Delivery of DDP Packets" on page 2-15 for more information.)

- the range of network numbers for the network to which the node is attached

- the 8-bit node ID and 16-bit network number of the node

- the 8-bit node ID and 16-bit network number of the last router from which the node has heard

- the maximum capacities of the .MPP driver, such as the maximum number of protocol handlers and the maximum number of static sockets allowed by this driver

- a pointer to the registered names queue

- the address of the node on the underlying data link (for example, the Ethernet hardware address)

- the node's zone name

The data-link address and the zone name are returned only for extended networks—that is, network types that allow more than one network number per network. You use the `laLength` parameter to specify the length of the data-link address you want returned; the function returns the actual length of the data in the `laLength` parameter and returns the data in the buffer you provide.

The `ExtendedBit` flag returned by the `PGetAppleTalkInfo` function is `TRUE` if the node is connected to an extended AppleTalk network. (The `ExtendedBit` flag is bit 15 of the configuration parameter returned by this function.) Note that the presence of the AppleTalk Phase 2 drivers does not of itself indicate that the node is connected to an extended network. For more information, see "PGetAppleTalkInfo" beginning on page 2-11.

Note

Always use the PGetAppleTalkInfo function to obtain information about the .MPP driver. You cannot rely on the validity of the MPP global variables pointed to by the varsPtr parameter block field value for this information. ◆

Getting the Address of Your Node or Your Local Router

You can use the AppleTalk Utilities GetNodeAddress function to get the node ID of the node that is running your application and the number of the network to which that node is connected.

Note

If GetNodeAddress returns a network number of 0, this means that there is no internet router available. However, your application or process should call GetBridgeAddress to determine if there are router-like services, such as Apple Remote Access (ARA), available to that node. ◆

To locate your local router, you can first call GetNodeAddress for the router's network number; the network number that GetNodeAddress returns for a node is also valid for the internet router on that local network. To get the node ID part of a local router's address, you can call the GetBridgeAddress function. If there is not a router on the local network, GetBridgeAddress returns a function result of 0.

Note

You can also use GetZoneList to determine if there is a router on the local network. For information on GetZoneList, see the chapter "Zone Information Protocol (ZIP)" in this book. ◆

Sending Packets to Applications and Processes on Your Own Node

Because more than one application or process can be running on a single node at the same time, it is reasonable to assume that you may want to send packets from your application or process to other applications and processes running on the same node. To support this, AppleTalk includes a function that lets you turn on (or off) an intranode delivery feature.

When intranode delivery is on, two programs running on the same node can communicate with each other through the AppleTalk protocols. You can address and send a packet to another application or process that is an internet socket client running on your own node from any of the AppleTalk protocols that provide programming interfaces.

You use the PSetSelfSend function to enable or disable intranode delivery. The PSetSelfSend function returns the value of the previous setting, so that you can save it and reinstate the value later if it differs from the setting that you specify. For more information about enabling or disabling intranode delivery, see "PSetSelfSend" beginning on page 2-15.

Note

Intranode delivery applies to user node applications and processes. Sending packets between a multinode application and user node applications on the same machine is independent of the intranode delivery feature. A multinode is treated as a virtual node distinct from the user node; both the user node and the multinode have their own node IDs. ◆

Selecting a Node in the Server Range

AppleTalk node IDs are divided into two classes: **user node IDs** and **server node IDs.**

- User node IDs are in the range 1–127 ($01–$7F).

- Server node IDs are in the range 128–254 ($80–$FE).

AppleTalk's dynamic node assignment occurs through a process in which the node acquiring a node ID sends out enquiry packets to determine if the ID that the node suggests is available. Although unlikely, problems can occur if a node that owns the suggested ID fails to respond to the enquiry because it is busy.

User nodes are switched on and off more frequently than are server nodes. Separating user node ID assignment from server node ID assignment allows for different degrees of verification.

Within the user node ID range, verification is performed quickly with fewer retransmissions of the enquiry control packet than are sent for server node ID verification; this decreases the initialization time for user nodes. A more thorough node ID verification is performed for servers. This scheme increases the initialization time for server nodes but is not detrimental to the server's operation because server nodes are rarely switched on and off.

You can start up AppleTalk so that it will assign a node ID within the server range by making an extended Open call to the .MPP driver. To do this, you set the immediate bit in the _Open trap. To request a server node ID, set to 1 the high bit (bit 31) of the extension longword field ioMix in the extended call. Set to 0 the remaining bits in the ioMix field and the bits of all the other unused fields in the queue element. The code in Listing 2-1 sets the high bit in the ioMix field, then it calls an assembly-language routine that is not shown in this listing, PBOpenImmedSync, to make the extended open call. The code uses the following global constants:

```
SPConfig      = $01FB;
portBClearMask = $F0;
```

The code in Listing 2-1 assumes that the .MPP driver is not currently open. It is important to remember that you can only request a server node ID when you first open the .MPP driver.

Listing 2-1   Opening the .MPP driver and obtaining a node ID in the server range

```
FUNCTION PBOpenImmedSync(paramBlock: ParmBlkPtr): OSErr;
INLINE $205F,$A200,$3E80;
FUNCTION OpenNodeInServerRange: OSerr;
IMPLEMENTATION
FUNCTION OpenNodeInServerRange: OSerr;
VAR
    MPPPtr:         ParmBlkPtr;
    err:            OSerr;
    MPPName:        Str31;
    SpConfigPtr:    Ptr;
BEGIN
    IF IsMPPOpen THEN
        BEGIN
            OpenNodeInServerRange := openErr;
        END
    ELSE
        BEGIN
            SPConfigPtr  := Ptr(SPConfig);
            SPConfigPtr^ := BYTE(BAND(SPConfigPtr^, portBClearMask));
            SPConfigPtr^ := BYTE(BOR(SPConfigPtr^, UseATalk));
            MPPName := '.MPP';
            MPPPtr := ParmBlkPtr(NewPtrClear(sizeof(ParamBlockRec)));
            MPPPtr^.ioMix := Ptr($80000000);
            MPPPtr^.ioNamePtr := @MPPName;
            OpenNodeInServerRange := PBOpenImmedSync(MPPPtr);
        END
END;
```

AppleTalk Utilities Reference

This section describes the data structure and the routines that make up the AppleTalk Utilities. The "Data Structures" section shows the MPP parameter block required for the PSetSelfSend and the PGetAppleTalkInfo functions.

The "Routines" section describes the routines for

■ getting information about the installed .MPP driver and the current network environment

■ enabling intranode delivery

■ getting the addresses of your node and your local internet router

■ opening the .MPP and .XPP drivers (The .MPP driver opens the .ATP driver.)

Data Structures

This section describes the MPP parameter block that you use for the `PSetSelfSend` and `PGetAppleTalkInfo` functions.

MPP Parameter Block

The `PSetSelfSend` and `PGetAppleTalkInfo` functions require a pointer to the MPP parameter block. The `MPPParamBlock` data type defines the MPP parameter block.

■ The `PGetAppleTalkInfo` function uses the MPP parameter block with the `GetAppleTalkInfoParm` variant record to pass information to and receive it from the .MPP driver.

■ The `PSetSelfSend` function uses the MPP parameter block with the `SetSelfSendParm` variant record to pass information to and receive it from the .MPP driver. The `MPPParamBlock` data type defines the MPP parameter block.

This section defines the fields common to both of these functions. The fields for the variant records are defined in the function description that uses the record.

```
TYPE
    MPPParmType     =        (...SetSelfSendParm,
                             GetAppleTalkInfoParm...);
    MPPPBPtr        =        ^MPPParamBlock;
    MPPParamBlock   =
    PACKED RECORD
        qLink:               QElemPtr;        {reserved}
        qType:               Integer;         {reserved}
        ioTrap:              Integer;         {reserved}
        ioCmdAddr:           Ptr;             {reserved}
        ioCompletion:        ProcPtr;         {completion routine}
        ioResult:            OSErr;           {result code}
        ioNamePtr:           StringPtr;       {reserved}
        ioVRefNum:           Integer;         {reserved}
        ioRefNum:            Integer;         {driver reference }
                                              { number}
        csCode:              Integer;         {primary command code}
    CASE MPPParmType OF
        SetSelfSendParm:
            (newSelfFlag:    Byte;            {self-send toggle flag}
             oldSelfFlag:    Byte);           {previous self-send }
                                              { state}

        GetAppleTalkInfoParm:
            (version:        Integer;         {requested info version}
             varsPtr:        Ptr;             {pointer to MPP }
                                              { variables}
```

```
            DCEPtr:           Ptr;          {pointer to MPP DCE}
            portID:           Integer;      {port number [0..7]}
            configuration:    LongInt;      {32-bit configuration }
                                            { word}
            selfSend:         Integer;      {nonzero if self-send }
                                            { enabled}
            netLo:            Integer;      {low value of network }
                                            { range}
            netHi:            Integer;      {high value of network }
                                            { range}
            ourAddr:          LongInt;      {our 24-bit AppleTalk }
                                            { address}
            routerAddr:       LongInt;      {24-bit address of }
                                            { last router}
            numOfPHs:         Integer;      {max. number of }
                                            { protocol handlers}
            numOfSkts:        Integer;      {max. number of static }
                                            { sockets}
            numNBPEs:         Integer;      {max. concurrent NBP }
                                            { requests}
            ntQueue:          Ptr;          {pointer to registered }
                                            { name queue}
            LAlength:         Integer;      {length in bytes of }
                                            { data-link address}
            linkAddr:         Ptr;          {data-link address }
                                            { returned}
            zoneName:         Ptr);         {zone name returned}
END;
```

Field descriptions

ioCompletion   A pointer to a completion routine that you can provide. When you
               execute the PGetAppleTalkInfo function or the PSetSelfSend
               function asynchronously, the .MPP driver calls your completion
               routine when it completes execution of the function. Specify NIL for
               this field if you do not wish to provide a completion routine. If you
               execute the function synchronously, the .MPP driver ignores the
               ioCompletion field.

ioResult   The result of the function. When you execute the function asynchro-
               nously, the function sets this field to 1 and returns a function result
               of noErr as soon as the function begins execution. When the
               function completes execution, it sets the ioResult field to the
               actual result code.

ioRefNum   The .MPP driver reference number. The MPW interface fills in
               this field.

csCode   The routine selector command code of the .MPP command
                          to be executed. The MPW interface fills in this field. For
                          the `PGetAppleTalkInfo` function, `csCode` is always
                          `GetATalkInfo`. For the `PSetSelfSend` function, `csCode`
                          is always `setSelfSend`.

Routines

This section describes the routines that you use to obtain information about AppleTalk
and the network environment, enable intranode delivery of DDP packets, obtain your
node's address and your local network router's address, and open and close the .MPP,
.ATP, and .XPP drivers.

Obtaining Information About the .MPP Driver and the Current Network Environment

You can use the `PGetAppleTalkInfo` function to obtain a wide variety of information
about the .MPP driver that is installed on the node that is running your application
and the network environment of that node. Among the information that the
`PGetAppleTalkInfo` function returns are

■ the address and zone name of the node that is running your application

■ the number of concurrent NBP calls that the installed .MPP driver supports

■ the range of network numbers for the network, if it is an extended network

PGetAppleTalkInfo

The `PGetAppleTalkInfo` function returns information about the currently installed
version of the .MPP driver and the network environment.

```
FUNCTION PGetAppleTalkInfo (thePBptr: MPPPBPtr; async:
                              Boolean): OSErr;
```

thePBptr   A pointer to an MPP parameter block.

async   A Boolean that specifies whether the function should be executed
            asynchronously. Specify TRUE for asynchronous execution.

Parameter block

→	ioCompletion	ProcPtr	A pointer to a completion routine.
←	ioResult	OSerr	The result code.
→	ioRefNum	Integer	The .MPP driver reference number.
→	csCode	Integer	Always GetATalkInfo.
→	version	Integer	The version of the function.
←	varsPtr	Ptr	A pointer to the MPP globals.

continued

←	DCEPtr	Ptr	A pointer to DCE for the .MPP driver.
←	portID	Integer	The port number.
←	configuration	LongInt	The configuration flags.
←	selfSend	Integer	Nonzero if self-sending is enabled.
←	netLo	Integer	The low value of the network range.
←	netHi	Integer	The high value of the network range.
←	ourAddr	LongInt	The local 24-bit AppleTalk address.
←	routerAddr	LongInt	The 24-bit address of the router.
←	numOfPHs	Integer	The maximum number of protocol handlers.
←	numOfSkts	Integer	The maximum number of static sockets.
←	numNBPEs	Integer	The maximum concurrent NBP requests.
←	ntQueue	Ptr	A pointer to registered names table.
↔	LAlength	Integer	The length in bytes of data-link address (extended networks only).
→	linkAddr	Ptr	A pointer to data-link address buffer (extended networks only).
→	zoneName	Ptr	A pointer to zone name buffer.

Field descriptions

version
: The version number of the `PGetAppleTalkInfo` function you are calling. For version number 53 and greater of the .MPP driver, this number is always 1.

varsPtr
: A pointer to the MPP global variables. This parameter is reserved for the use of Apple Computer, Inc.; you cannot rely on the validity of the variables pointed to by this parameter.

DCEPtr
: A pointer to the device control entry (DCE) data structure for the .MPP driver. For information about the DCE, see the chapter "Device Manager" in *Inside Macintosh: Devices*.

portID
: The port number for the .MPP driver. The port number is always 0 unless you are requesting information for an .MPP driver being used by a router.

configuration
: A 32-bit longword of configuration flags. The following flags are currently defined:

Bit	Flag	Description
31	SrvAdrBit	TRUE (equal to 1) if the routine that opened the .MPP driver requested a server node number. For more information on server nodes, see "Selecting a Node in the Server Range" on page 2-7. This flag indicates only that the server node number was requested, not that it was returned. Some AppleTalk data links, such as EtherTalk, TokenTalk, and FDDITalk, do not honor a request for a server node number.

continued

Bit	Flag	Description
30	RouterBit	TRUE (equal to 1) if an AppleTalk internet router was loaded at system startup (that is, there's a router operating on the same node as your application). A router can be loaded and not active.
15	ExtendedBit	TRUE (equal to 1) if the node is on an extended network. Testing this bit is the only way to determine whether you are on an extended network.
7	BadZoneHintBit	TRUE (equal to 1) if the zone name of the node you are on was not the same as the zone name stored in parameter RAM (sometimes referred to as the *zone name hint*) when the .MPP driver was opened. If the zone name hint is invalid, then the AppleTalk Manager uses the default zone for the network. The default zone is defined by the network administrator.
6	OneZoneBit	TRUE (equal to 1) if only one zone is assigned to your extended network or if you are not on an extended network. Use the ExtendedBit flag to determine whether you are on an extended network.

selfSend
: The ability of a node to send packets to itself. This feature, called *intranode delivery*, is enabled when this parameter is nonzero. Use the PSetSelfSend function, which is described beginning on page 2-15, to enable or disable this feature.

netLo
: The low value of the range of network numbers on the local cable. Only extended networks can have a range of network numbers. For a nonextended network, this parameter returns the network number.

netHi
: The high value of the range of network numbers on the local cable. Only extended networks can have a range of network numbers. For a nonextended network, this parameter returns the network number.

ourAddr
: The 24-bit AppleTalk network address of the node you are on. The least significant byte of the longword is the node ID. The middle 16 bits are the network number. The most significant byte of the longword is reserved for use by Apple Computer, Inc.

routerAddr
: The 24-bit AppleTalk network address of the last router from which your node heard traffic. The least significant byte of the longword is the node ID. The middle 16 bits are the network number. The most significant byte of the longword is reserved for use by Apple Computer, Inc. You should always use this address when you want to communicate with a router.

numOfPHs	The maximum number of protocol handlers that this .MPP driver allows.
numOfSkts	The maximum number of statically assigned sockets that this .MPP driver allows. Statically assigned sockets are described in *Inside AppleTalk*, second edition. For more information about sockets, see the chapter "Datagram Delivery Protocol (DDP)" in this book.
numNBPEs	The maximum number of concurrent requests to NBP that this .MPP driver allows.
ntQueue	A pointer to the first entry in the names table for the local node. You can use NBP routines to look up and register names in the names table. The names table is described in the chapter "Name-Binding Protocol (NBP)" in this book.
LAlength	The number of bytes of the data-link address that the function should place in the buffer pointed to by the LinkAddr parameter. You use this parameter when you call the PGetAppleTalkInfo function on a node on an extended network. If you request more bytes than the total number of bytes in the address, then the function returns in the LAlength parameter the actual number of bytes it placed in the buffer. If the address is longer than the size of the buffer, then the PGetAppleTalkInfo function fills the buffer and returns in the LAlength parameter the actual length of the address, not the number of bytes returned. The function does *not* return an error when the buffer is too large or too small for the address. A value of 6 bytes for LAlength is sufficient for most purposes.
linkAddr	A pointer to a buffer for the data-link address returned for extended networks only. You use the LAlength parameter to specify the number of bytes of the address that you want placed in this buffer. You must allocate a buffer large enough to hold the number of bytes you specify. Specify NIL for this parameter if you do not want the function to provide a data-link address.
zoneName	A pointer to a buffer into which the PGetAppleTalkInfo function places the local node's zone name. You must allocate a buffer of at least 33 bytes to hold this data, or you must specify NIL for the zoneName parameter if you do not want to obtain the zone name. This field is returned only if the node is on an extended network.

DESCRIPTION

The PGetAppleTalkInfo function returns a variety of information about the current networking environment. For example, it returns information telling you whether or not applications running on the node can send packets to themselves or to other applications or processes on the same node. An application can call PGetAppleTalkInfo to determine if the node on which it is running has an ID that falls within the server node ID range. It can also obtain the address of the last router that the node communicated with and the node's own address.

You must allocate memory for and define a parameter block of type MPPParmType and pass that parameter block's pointer to PGetAppleTalkInfo when you call the function. You must also allocate memory for and provide pointers to the data buffers into which the `PGetAppleTalkInfo` function returns the data-link address and zone name. You pass a pointer to the buffer for the returned data-link address as the value of the `linkAddr` field. You pass a pointer to the buffer for the returned zone name as the value of the `zoneName` parameter block field.

SPECIAL CONSIDERATIONS

If the node on which your application is running happens also to be running AppleTalk internet router software in the background, more than one set of MPP global variables may be in RAM. To make sure you obtain information about the .MPP driver that handles application software, always use the `PGetAppleTalkInfo` function rather than the Device Manager's `PBControl` function. However, if you want to use the `PBControl` function, you must use a device driver reference number of –10 for the .MPP driver.

The memory that you allocated for the parameter block and data buffers belongs to the .MPP driver until the `PGetAppleTalkInfo` function completes execution. The memory must be nonrelocatable. After the `PGetAppleTalkInfo` function completes execution, you can reuse the memory or release it.

ASSEMBLY-LANGUAGE INFORMATION

If you use assembly language to call this function, you must use a device driver reference number of –10 for the .MPP driver.

RESULT CODES

noErr	0	No error
paramErr	–50	Version number is too high

Enabling Intranode Delivery of DDP Packets

This section describes how the `PSetSelfSend` function allows applications and processes running on the same node to send packets to one another.

PSetSelfSend

The `PSetSelfSend` function enables or disables the AppleTalk intranode delivery service.

```
FUNCTION PSetSelfSend (thePBptr: MPPPBPtr; async: Boolean): OSErr;
```

thePBptr   A pointer to an MPP parameter block.

async   A Boolean that specifies whether the function should be executed asynchronously. Specify TRUE for asynchronous execution.

AppleTalk Utilities

Parameter block

→	ioCompletion	ProcPtr	A pointer to a completion routine.
←	ioResult	OSErr	The function result.
→	ioRefNum	Integer	The .MPP driver reference number.
→	csCode	Integer	Always setSelfSend.
→	newSelfFlag	Byte	A flag that turns intranode delivery on or off.
←	oldSelfFlag	Byte	A flag that reports the previous state of intranode delivery, whether it was on or off.

Field descriptions

newSelfFlag   A flag that enables or disables the intranode delivery feature. Set this field to a nonzero number to enable the feature; set it to zero to turn off the feature.

oldSelfFlag   A flag indicating the previous state of the intranode delivery feature. The PSetSelfSend function returns this value. A nonzero value indicates that intranode delivery was enabled; a value of zero indicates it was disabled.

DESCRIPTION

The PSetSelfSend function turns on or off the intranode delivery feature that allows you to send a packet to another socket on the same node. You can use this feature, for example, to send data from an application to a print spooler that is running in the background on the same node.

When PSetSelfSend is enabled, you can send packets to socket clients on your node from all levels of the AppleTalk protocol stack for which there are programming interfaces. The PSetSelfSend function returns in the oldSelfFlag field the previous setting for the intranode delivery feature so that you can restore it later, if you want to. Because intranode delivery is enabled on most systems running AppleTalk, you should assume that it is turned on and take this into account when you write your code.

Note that intranode delivery applies to the user node applications. Sending packets between a multinode application and user node applications on the same machine is independent of the intranode delivery feature. A multinode is treated as a virtual node distinct from the user node; both the user node and the multinode have their own node IDs.

SPECIAL CONSIDERATIONS

Enabling or disabling the intranode delivery feature affects the entire node. For example, an application that uses NBP to look up names and then display them to a user might not expect to receive names of other network-visible entities within its own node; when intranode delivery is enabled, this will occur.

ASSEMBLY-LANGUAGE INFORMATION

To execute the PSetSelfSend function from assembly language, call the _Control trap macro with a value of setSelfSend in the csCode field of the parameter block.

RESULT CODES

noErr   0   No error

Getting the Addresses of Your Node and Local Internet Router

This section describes the GetNodeAddress and GetBridgeAddress functions, which you can use to get the address of the node that is running your application or process and to determine if the local network to which that node is connected includes a router. If there is a router on the local network, GetBridgeAddress will return the node ID of that router. The router's network number is the same as that of your local network.

GetNodeAddress

The GetNodeAddress function returns the current node ID and network number of the node on which the calling program is running.

```
FUNCTION GetNodeAddress (VAR myNode,myNet: Integer): OSErr;
```

myNode   The node ID of the node on which your application or process is running.

myNet   The network number of the network to which the node is attached that is running your application or process. If myNet returns 0, this means that there is no internet router available. However, your application or process should call GetBridgeAddress to determine if there are router-like services available to that node.

DESCRIPTION

The GetNodeAddress function returns the address of a node on a network. If the network is not an extended network, the network number that GetNodeAddress returns is 0. Note that even if GetNodeAddress returns a network number of 0, there may be a router service on the local network. For example, a node can be on a network whose network number is 0 and be connected to a remote network through Apple Remote Access (ARA).

If the .MPP driver is not installed, the GetNodeAddress function returns a function result of noMPPErr. To install the .MPP driver, open it using the Device Manager's OpenDriver function or the MPPOpen function.

ASSEMBLY-LANGUAGE INFORMATION

This function is implemented in the MPW glue code only. It is not accessible from assembly language.

RESULT CODES

noErr	0	No error
noMPPErr	–3102	The .MPP driver is not installed

GetBridgeAddress

The GetBridgeAddress function returns the node ID of the router on your local network.

```
FUNCTION GetBridgeAddress: Integer;
```

DESCRIPTION

The GetBridgeAddress function returns the current node ID of an internet router in the low-order byte of the function result. If the function result is 0, there is no router on the local network. The router's network number is that of the local network; you can use the GetNodeAddress function to get the network number.

ASSEMBLY-LANGUAGE INFORMATION

This function is implemented in the MPW glue code only. It is not accessible from assembly language.

SEE ALSO

To obtain the network number of the local network, use the GetNodeAddress function described on page 2-17.

Opening and Closing Drivers

This section describes the functions that you can use to open the .MPP and .XPP drivers, MPPOpen and OpenXPP. The .MPP driver opens the .ATP driver. This section also describes the function that closes the .MPP driver, MPPClose.

The MPPOpen and OpenXPP functions are included to provide a complete description of the AppleTalk programmatic interface. Apple Computer, Inc. recommends that you use the Device Manager's OpenDriver function to open the .MPP and .XPP drivers. In addition to opening a driver, the OpenDriver function returns the driver reference number. If the driver is already open, the OpenDriver function simply returns the driver reference number. For information on the OpenDriver function, see the chapter "Device Manager" in *Inside Macintosh: Devices*.

The .MPP, .ATP, and .XPP drivers must always be open before you can use the AppleTalk protocols that they implement. The .MPP driver must be open before you open the .XPP driver. How to open the .DSP driver is described in the chapter "AppleTalk Data Stream Protocol (ADSP)" in this book.

▲ **WARNING**
Because coresident programs might also be using AppleTalk,
you should not close the AppleTalk drivers. ▲

This section also includes the `IsMPPOpen` and `IsATPOpen` functions that determine if
the .MPP and the .ATP drivers are already open.

MPPOpen

If the .MPP driver has not already been opened, the `MPPOpen` function opens
the .MPP driver, initializes the driver's variables, and assigns a node ID to the
Macintosh computer.

```
FUNCTION MPPOpen: OSErr;
```

DESCRIPTION

The `MPPOpen` function first determines whether the .MPP driver has already been
opened. If it has, `MPPOpen` returns an error code. If the .MPP driver is not open,
`MPPOpen` loads the driver into the system heap and then initializes the driver's variables
before dynamically assigning a node ID to the system. It also loads the .ATP driver
and the NBP code into the system heap.

Apple Computer, Inc. recommends that you use the Device Manager's `OpenDriver`
function to open the .MPP driver instead of using the `MPPOpen` function.

SPECIAL CONSIDERATIONS

For versions of AppleTalk before AppleTalk version 56, if serial port B isn't configured
for AppleTalk or if it is already in use, the .MPP driver is not loaded and the `portInUse`
result code is returned.

RESULT CODES

noErr	0	No error
portInUse	–97	Driver open error code indicating that the port is in use
portNotCf	–98	Driver open error code indicating that the parameter RAM is not configured for this connection

SEE ALSO

The `MPPOpen` function does not return the .MPP driver reference number, as the
`OpenDriver` function does. For information on the `OpenDriver` function, see
the chapter "Device Manager" in *Inside Macintosh: Devices*.

MPPClose

The `MPPClose` function closes the .MPP driver and removes from memory any data structures associated with it.

```
FUNCTION MPPClose: OSErr;
```

DESCRIPTION

In addition to closing the .MPP driver, the `MPPClose` function also closes and removes from memory the .ATP driver and the NBP code if they are installed. Calling `MPPClose` completely disables AppleTalk.

▲ **WARNING**
Apple Computer, Inc. strongly recommends that you *not* use this call because other coresident applications could also be using AppleTalk. ▲

Calling `MPPClose` completely disables AppleTalk.

SPECIAL CONSIDERATIONS

If the current connection is LocalTalk, `MPPClose` also returns the use of port B to the serial driver.

RESULT CODES

noErr   0   No error

IsMPPOpen

The `IsMPPOpen` function determines and reports whether or not the .MPP driver is loaded and running.

```
FUNCTION IsMPPOpen: Boolean;
```

DESCRIPTION

If the .MPP driver is open, the `IsMPPOpen` function returns a value of **TRUE**; if the .MPP driver is not open, it returns **FALSE**. If you want to obtain a node ID in the server range, you can request the assignment only when you first open the .MPP driver. In this case, you can use the `IsMPPOpen` function to determine if the .MPP driver has already been opened.

RESULT CODES

noErr   0   No error

SEE ALSO

You can also use the Device Manager's OpenDriver function to ensure that the .MPP driver is open. If it is not, OpenDriver will open the .MPP driver and return the driver reference number. If the .MPP driver is already open, the OpenDriver function will return the reference number without performing additional processing, and therefore without incurring much additional overhead.

IsATPOpen

The IsATPOpen function determines and reports whether or not the .ATP driver is loaded and running.

FUNCTION IsATPOpen: Boolean;

DESCRIPTION

If the .ATP driver is open, the IsATPOpen function returns a value of TRUE; if the .ATP driver is not open, it returns FALSE. Because the .MPP driver opens the .ATP driver, this function is seldom used. It is included to provide a complete description of the AppleTalk programmatic interface.

RESULT CODES

noErr   0   No error

SEE ALSO

To open the .ATP driver, you open the .MPP driver. You can use the Device Manager's OpenDriver function to ensure that the .MPP driver is open. If the .MPP driver is open, then the .ATP driver is also open. If the .MPP and .ATP drivers are already open, the OpenDriver function will return the .MPP driver reference number without performing additional processing, and therefore without incurring much additional overhead.

For information on the OpenDriver function, see the chapter "Device Manager" in *Inside Macintosh: Devices.*

OpenXPP

The OpenXPP function opens the .XPP driver and returns the driver reference number.

```
FUNCTION OpenXPP (VAR xppRefnum: Integer): OSErr;
```

xppRefnum   The .XPP driver reference number, which the function returns.

DESCRIPTION

Before you can use the protocol interfaces (ZIP, ASP, and AFP) that are implemented by the .XPP driver, you must open the driver. You can use the OpenXPP function to open the .XPP driver, or you can call the Device Manager's OpenDriver function. In either case, before you open the .XPP driver, you must ensure that the .MPP driver and the .ATP driver are open.

Apple Computer, Inc. recommends that you use the Device Manager's OpenDriver function to open the .XPP driver instead of using the OpenXPP function. The OpenXPP function is included to provide a complete description of the AppleTalk programmatic interface.

SPECIAL CONSIDERATIONS

Under most circumstances, you should not close the .XPP driver because other applications and processes could be using it. However, if you must close the .XPP driver, you can use the Device Manager's CloseDriver function. The CloseDriver function should be used only by system-level applications.

RESULT CODES

noErr	0	No error
portInUse	–97	Either AppleTalk is not open or the AppleTalk port is in use by another driver

SEE ALSO

The OpenXPP function does not return the .MPP driver reference number, as does the OpenDriver function. For information on the OpenDriver and CloseDriver functions, see the chapter "Device Manager" in *Inside Macintosh: Devices*.

Summary of AppleTalk Utilities

Pascal Summary

Constants

```
CONST
   setSelfSend          =  256;        {allow intranode delivery, csCode}
   GetATalkInfo         =  258;        {get AppleTalk information, csCode}
```

Data Types

MPP Parameter Block for PSetSelfSend and PGetAppleTalkInfo

```
TYPE MPPParmType =    (...SetSelfSendParm,
                         GetAppleTalkInfoParm...);
TYPE MPPParamBlock =
   PACKED RECORD
      qLink:             QElemPtr;        {reserved}
      qType:             Integer;         {reserved}
      ioTrap:            Integer;         {reserved}
      ioCmdAddr:         Ptr;             {reserved}
      ioCompletion:      ProcPtr;         {completion routine}
      ioResult:          OSErr;           {result code}
      ioNamePtr:         StringPtr;       {reserved}
      ioVRefNum:         Integer;         {reserved}
      ioRefNum:          Integer;         {driver reference number}
      csCode:            Integer;         {primary command code}
   CASE MPPParmType OF
      SetSelfSendParm:
         (newSelfFlag:   Byte;            {self-send toggle flag}
          oldSelfFlag:   Byte);           {previous self-send state}
      GetAppleTalkInfoParm:
         (version:       Integer;         {requested info version}
          varsPtr:       Ptr;             {pointer to MPP variables}
          DCEPtr:        Ptr;             {pointer to MPP DCE}
          portID:        Integer;         {port number [0..7]}
```

```
      configuration:    LongInt;       {32-bit configuration word}
      selfSend:         Integer;       {nonzero if self-send enabled}
      netLo:            Integer;       {low value of network range}
      netHi:            Integer;       {high value of network range}
      ourAddr:          LongInt;       {our 24-bit AppleTalk address}
      routerAddr:       LongInt;       {24-bit address of last router}
      numOfPHs:         Integer;       {maximum number of protocol }
                                       { handlers}
      numOfSkts:        Integer;       {maximum number of static sockets}
      numNBPEs:         Integer;       {maximum concurrent NBP requests}
      ntQueue:          Ptr;           {pointer to registered name queue}
      LAlength:         Integer;       {length in bytes of data-link addr}
      linkAddr:         Ptr;           {data-link address returned}
      zoneName:         Ptr);          {zone name returned}
END;


MPPPBPtr =  ^MPPParamBlock;
```

Routines

Obtaining Information About the .MPP Driver and the Current Network Environment

```
FUNCTION PGetAppleTalkInfo  (thePBptr: MPPPBPtr; async: Boolean): OSErr;
```

Enabling Intranode Delivery of DDP Packets

```
FUNCTION PSetSelfSend       (thePBptr: MPPPBPtr; async: Boolean): OSErr;
```

Getting the Addresses of Your Node and Local Internet Router

```
FUNCTION GetNodeAddress     (VAR myNode: Integer; VAR myNet: Integer): OSErr;
FUNCTION GetBridgeAddress:  Integer;
```

Opening and Closing Drivers

```
FUNCTION MPPOpen:           OSErr;
FUNCTION MPPClose:          OSErr;
FUNCTION IsMPPOpen:         Boolean;
FUNCTION IsATPOpen:         Boolean;
FUNCTION OpenXPP            (VAR xppRefnum: Integer): OSErr;
```

C Summary

Constants

```
/*csCodes/
enum {
   setSelfSend      =     256,      /*intranode packet delivery*/
   GetATalkInfo     =     258      /*get AppleTalk information*/
};
```

Data Types

MPP Parameter Block for PSetSelfSend and PGetAppleTalkInfo

```
union ParamBlockRec {
   MPPparms          MPP;           /*general MPP parms*/
};

typedef MPPParamBlock *MPPPBPtr;

#define MPPATPHeader \
   QElem          *qLink;         /*reserved*/\
   short          qType;          /*reserved*/\
   short          ioTrap;         /*reserved*/\
   Ptr            ioCmdAddr;      /*reserved*/\
   ProcPtr        ioCompletion;   /*completion routine*/\
   OSErr          ioResult;       /*result code*/\
   long           userData;       /*reserved*/\
   short          reqTID;         /*reserved*/\
   short          ioRefNum;       /*driver reference number*/\
   short          csCode;         /*call command code*/

typedef struct {
   MPPATPHeader
   char     newSelfFlag;          /*self-send toggle flag*/
   char     oldSelfFlag;          /*previous self-send state*/
}SetSelfparms;

typedef struct {
   MPPATPHeader
   short    version;          /*requested info version*/
   Ptr      varsPtr;          /*pointer to well-known MPP vars*/
```

```
    Ptr        DCEPtr;              /*pointer to MPP DCE*/
    short      portID;              /*port number [0..7]*/
    long       configuration;       /*32-bit configuration word*/
    short      selfSend;            /*nonzero if self-send enabled*/
    short      netLo;               /*low value of network range*/
    short      netHi;               /*high value of network range*/
    long       ourAdd;              /*our 24-bit AppleTalk address*/
    long       routerAddr;          /*24-bit address of last router*/
    short      numOfPHs;            /*maximum number of protocol handlers*/
    short      numOfSkts;           /*maximum number of static sockets*/
    short      numNBPEs;            /*maximum number of concurrent NBP requests*/
    Ptr        nTQueue;             /*pointer to registered name queue*/
    short      LAlength;            /*length in bytes of data-link addr*/
    Ptr        linkAddr;            /*data-link address returned*/
    Ptr        zoneName;            /*zone name returned*/
}GetAppleTalkInfoParm;

typedef union {
    MPPparms                MPP;             /*general MPP parms*/
    SetSelfparms            SETSELF;
    GetAppleTalkInfoParm    GAIINFO;
}MPPParamBlock;

typedef MPPParamBlock *MPPPBPtr;
```

Routines

Obtaining Information About the .MPP Driver and the Current Network Environment

```
pascal OSErr PGetAppleTalkInfo
                    (MPPPBPtr thePBptr,Boolean async);
```

Enabling Intranode Delivery of DDP Packets

```
pascal OSErr PSetSelfSend    (MPPPBPtr thePBptr,Boolean async);
```

Getting the Addresses of Your Node and Local Internet Router

```
pascal OSErr GetNodeAddress
                    (short *myNode,short *myNet);
pascal short GetBridgeAddress
                    (void);
```

Opening and Closing Drivers

```
pascal OSErr MPPOpen          (void);
pascal OSErr MPPClose         (void);
pascal Boolean IsMPPOpen      (void);
pascal Boolean IsATPOpen      (void);
pascal OSErr OpenXPP          (short *xppRefnum);
```

Assembly-Language Summary

Constants

Unit Number for the .MPP driver

```
mppUnitNum      EQU      9          ;MPP unit number
mppRefNum       EQU      -10        ;MPP driver reference number
```

Command Codes

```
setSelfSend     EQU      256        ;set to allow writes to self, control call
GetATalkInfo    EQU      258        ;get AppleTalk information, control call
```

Zone and Router Bits

```
BadZoneHintBit EQU       7          ;1, if zone hint was found invalid when the
                                    ; .MPP driver was opened
RouterBit       EQU      30         ;1, if this is a router port
```

MPP Queue Element Standard Structure

```
;arguments passed in the CSParam area
newSelfFlag     EQU      $1C        ;offset, new value for self-send flag
oldSelfFlag     EQU      $1D        ;old value of self-send flag
```

GetAppleTalkInfo

```
GAIVersion      EQU      1          ;highest version for GAI params
```

Data Structures

MPP Parameter Block Common Fields for PGetAppleTalkInfo and PSetSelfSend

0	qLink	long	reserved
4	qType	word	reserved
6	ioTrap	word	reserved
8	ioCmdAddr	long	reserved
12	ioCompletion	long	address of completion routine
16	ioResult	word	result code
18	ioNamePtr	long	reserved
22	ioVRefNum	word	reserved
24	ioRefNum	word	driver reference number

GetAppleTalkInfo Parameter Variant

16	ioResult	word	result code
26	csCode	word	command code; always GetAppleTalkInfo
28	version	word	version of function
30	varsPtr	long	pointer to the .MPP driver variables
34	DCEPtr	long	pointer to DCE for the .MPP driver
38	portID	word	port number
40	configuration	long	configuration flags
44	selfSend	word	nonzero if self-send is enabled
46	netLo	word	low value of network range
48	netHi	word	high value of network range
50	ourAddr	long	local 24-bit AppleTalk address
54	routerAddr	long	24-bit address of router
58	numOfPHs	word	maximum number of protocol handlers
60	numOfSkts	word	maximum number of static sockets
62	numNBPEs	word	maximum number of concurrent NBP requests
64	ntQueue	long	pointer to registered names table
68	LAlength	word	length in bytes of data-link address (extended networks only)
70	linkAddr	long	pointer to data-link address buffer (extended networks only)
74	zoneName	long	pointer to zone name buffer

PSetSelfSend Parameter Variant

26	csCode	word	always setSelfSend
28	newSelfFlag	byte	flag that turns intranode delivery on or off
29	oldSelfFlag	byte	flag that reports the previous state of intranode delivery, whether it was on or off

Result Codes

noErr	0	No error
paramErr	−50	Version number is too high
portInUse	−97	Driver open error code indicating that the port is in use
portNotCf	−98	Driver open error code indicating that the parameter RAM is not configured for this connection
noMPPErr	−3102	The .MPP driver is not installed

Name-Binding Protocol (NBP)

Contents

Contents

This chapter describes the Name-Binding Protocol (NBP) that you can use to make your process or application available to other processes or applications across the network. This chapter also describes how you can use NBP to obtain the addresses of other processes and applications on the network.

This chapter uses the term *entity* to refer to processes and applications that run on an AppleTalk network. You use NBP in conjunction with another protocol that allows you to send and receive data. For example, you can register your entity with NBP and then use a transport protocol such as ADSP to communicate with other entities; ADSP opens a socket for your entity to use and assigns that socket number to the entity. Your entity registers an NBP name in conjunction with this socket number.

You should read this chapter if you want to

- register an entity with NBP to make it available for other network entities to contact

- obtain another entity's address so that you can contact it

- obtain the NBP names and internet socket addresses of all registered entities whose NBP names match your partial specified name

For an overview of the Name-Binding Protocol and how it fits within the AppleTalk protocol stack, read the chapter "Introduction to AppleTalk" in this book, which also introduces and defines some of the terminology used in this chapter. For a description of the Name-Binding Protocol specification, see *Inside AppleTalk,* second edition.

About NBP

NBP allows you to bind a name to the internal storage address for your entity and register this mapping so that other entities can look it up. Applications can display NBP names to users and use addresses internally to locate entities. When you register your entity's name and address pair, NBP validates its uniqueness.

An **entity name** consists of three fields: **object, type,** and **zone.** The value for each of these fields can be an alphanumeric string of up to 31 characters. The entity name is not case sensitive. You specify the value for the object and type fields.

The object field typically identifies the user of the system, or the system itself, in the case of a server. Applications commonly set this value to the owner name, which the user specifies through the Sharing Setup control panel.

The type field generally identifies the type of service that the entity provides, for example, "Mailbox" for an electronic mailbox on a server. Entities of the same type can find one another and identify potential partners by looking up addresses based on the type portion of the name alone.

The zone field identifies the zone to which the node belongs. You do not specify this value; when you register your process, you specify an asterisk (*) for this field. NBP interprets the asterisk to mean the current zone or no zone, in the case of a simple network configuration not divided into zones.

Name-Binding Protocol (NBP)

The mapping of names to addresses that NBP maintains is important for AppleTalk because the addressing numbers that AppleTalk uses are not fixed. AppleTalk assigns an address dynamically to a node when the node first joins the network and whenever the node is rebooted. Because of this, the address of a node on an AppleTalk network can change from time to time. Although a network number corresponds to a particular wire and the network number portion of an address is relatively stable, the socket number that is assigned to an entity is usually randomly generated. (For an overview of AppleTalk addresses and the addressing scheme, see the chapter "Introduction to AppleTalk" in this book.) Although NBP is not a transport protocol, that is, you do not use it to send and receive data, NBP is a client of DDP. Figure 3-1 shows NBP and its underlying protocols.

Figure 3-1   The Name-Binding Protocol and the underlying AppleTalk protocols

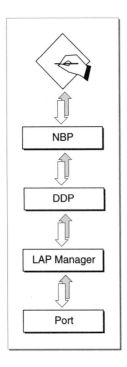

NBP provides network entities with access to current addresses of other entities. The name part of an NBP mapping is also important in identifying and locating an entity on the network. The NBP entity name is different from the application name. An application can display entity names to users and look up addresses based on names.

For example, an entity name can include a portion that identifies that entity type. An application can request NBP to return the names of all of the registered entities of a certain type, such as a particular type of game. The application can then display those entity names to a user to allow the user to select a partner. When the user selects an entity name, the application can request NBP to return the address that is mapped to the entity name.

When you register your entity with NBP, it is made visible to other entities throughout the network. A network entity that is registered with NBP is referred to as a **network-visible entity.** A mail server application is an example of a network-visible entity. When a mail server is registered with NBP, workstation clients with mailboxes can access the mail server program to send and receive mail.

A server application might call NBP to register itself at initialization time so that its clients can access the server when they come online. However, a game application might register itself when a user launches it so that partner applications of the same type can locate it, then remove its entry from the NBP names directory when the user quits the application.

You use the NBP routines to register your entity so that other entities can find it and to retrieve the addresses of other entities with which you want to communicate. You specify an entity name that adheres to a defined format and register that name with NBP in conjunction with the socket number that your entity uses. NBP then makes your entity's complete address available to other entities. To retrieve the address of another entity that is registered with NBP, you supply that entity's NBP name. You can retrieve the addresses of more than one entity by using wildcards instead of a fully qualified NBP name.

Although you register your entity's NBP name in association with the socket that it uses, NBP maintains an entry that contains your entity's complete internet socket address. The **internet socket address,** also called the *internet address*, includes the socket number, the node ID, and the network number. All network-visible entities on an internet are **socket clients,** which means that each one is associated with a socket. Each socket has a unique number, and every entity has a unique internet socket address that identifies it. The socket number part of the internet address ensures that data intended for an entity is delivered to that particular entity.

The link-access protocol dynamically assigns a unique node ID to each node when it joins the network. When the user reboots the system, sometimes the same node ID is available and sometimes a new node ID is assigned. The network number is the number of the network to which the node is directly connected, and it remains the same as long as the node is physically connected to that network. NBP fills in the node ID and the network number in a names table entry. You don't supply these parts of the internet address.

NBP maintains a **names table** in each node that contains the name and internet address of each registered entity in that node. Each name and address pair is called a **tuple.** When you register your process with NBP, you provide a names table entry. NBP builds its names table on a node from the entries that entities supply.

The NBP routines include a procedure, NPBSetNTE, that you can use to fill in a names table entry that is in the format that NBP expects. The NPBSetNTE procedure takes the name and the socket ID that you specify and builds a names table entry in the buffer that you provide. (For information on using NPBSetNTE, see "Registering Your Entity With NBP" beginning on page 3-7.)

To form a names table for a node, NBP connects together as a linked list the names table entries of all the registered entities on that node. The collection of names tables on all the nodes in an internet is known as the **NBP names directory.** Figure 3-2 shows a number of nodes on a network, each with its own names table; each names table contains an entry for each registered entity on its node.

Figure 3-2   The NBP names table on each node, collectively forming an NBP names directory

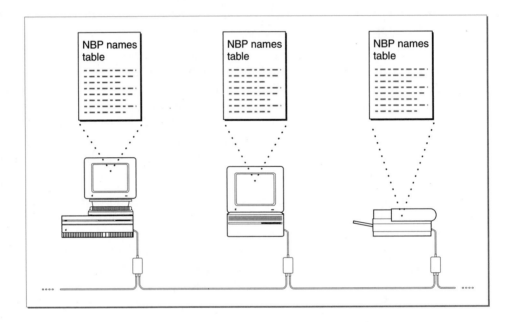

Whenever a node receives an NBP lookup request, NBP searches through its names table for a match and, if it finds a match, returns the information to the requester.

Using NBP

This section describes how you can use NBP to

■ set up a names table entry for your entity and register your entity's name and address pair with NBP for other entities to access

■ look up an address based on a name

■ confirm a name and address that you already have

■ remove your entity's name and address from the NBP names directory

■ cancel a pending NBP request

The .MPP driver implements the NBP protocol. Your application should check to ensure that the .MPP driver is already loaded on the system running your application before it attempts to call NBP. If the driver is not already open, your application should open it by calling the Device Manager's `OpenDriver` function. The following example shows how to open the .MPP driver.

```
BEGIN
    myErr := OpenDriver('.MPP', mppRefNum);    {open .MPP driver}
    IF myErr <> noErr THEN DoErr(myErr);       {check and handle }
                                               { error}
```

For more information on determining if the .MPP driver is open and opening the AppleTalk drivers, see the chapter "AppleTalk Utilities" in this book.

Your application can have multiple concurrent active NBP requests. For example, your application can perform a number of `PRegisterName`, `PLookupName` and `PConfirmName` requests concurrently. The maximum number of concurrent requests is machine dependent. You can use the `PGetAppleTalkInfo` function to determine the maximum number of concurrent NBP requests supported by the .MPP driver on the node running your application. For information about the `PGetAppleTalkInfo` function, see the chapter "AppleTalk Utilities" in this book.

All of the NBP functions use parameter blocks to hold input and output values. Whether you execute a function synchronously or asynchronously, you must not alter the contents of the parameter block until after the NBP function that uses it completes the operation. In effect, the parameter block belongs to the NBP function until the function completes execution. (For a discussion of synchronous and asynchronous execution, see the chapter "Introduction to AppleTalk" in this book.) When the operation completes, you can either reuse the memory allocated for the parameter block or release it.

In addition to the parameter block used for the function, the memory that you allocate for any records and buffers whose pointers you pass to NBP through a parameter block field must also be nonrelocatable until the function completes execution. When the operation completes, you can reuse these data structures or release the memory that you allocated for them.

To allocate nonrelocatable memory, you can use the Memory Manager's `NewPtr` or `NewPtrSys` function. If you use `NewHandle` instead, you need to lock the memory. For more information about these functions, see *Inside Macintosh: Memory*.

Registering Your Entity With NBP

You register your entity with NBP to make its services available to other entities throughout the network. Once the entity is registered, other entities can look up its name and address pair based on its name or a part of that name.

Your process can register itself with several names all associated with the same socket.

To register itself, your entity calls two NBP routines:

- the set names table entry (`NBPSetNTE`) procedure, which prepares the names table entry

- the register name (`PRegisterName`) function, which provides NBP with a pointer to the names table entry so that NBP can register the entry on the node

Setting Up a Names Table Entry

The `NBPSetNTE` procedure creates a names table entry in the format that Figure 3-4 on page 3-9 shows. You associate an NBP entity name with the socket number assigned to your entity.

When you create the names table entry, you provide NBP with the socket number that your entity uses. This is the socket ID that was assigned to your entity when it opened a socket.

Figure 3-3 shows a complete internet socket address belonging to an entity and the entity name that is associated with the address.

Figure 3-3   The internet socket address and entity name of an application

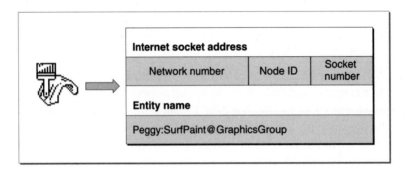

Along with the individual fields of the name and the socket number, you pass `NBPSetNTE` a pointer to a buffer that is 108 bytes long. You create a record of type `NamesTableEntry` as the buffer to be used for the names table entry. When you register your entity, NBP uses the buffer that you pass it as the actual names table entry for that entity; it does not make a copy of the buffer. NBP links the `NamesTableEntry` record that you provide to other names table entries on the node to create a names table for that node. For this reason, memory that you allocate for the buffer must be nonrelocatable.

Figure 3-4 shows the structure of the names table entry record.

Notice that the first field in the `NamesTableEntry` record is a pointer to the next entry in the linked list. NBP maintains the value of this field. You do not supply this value. However, you can get a pointer to the first entry in the names table on the node where the entity is running by calling the `PGetAppleTalkInfo` function. For information about the `PGetAppleTalkInfo` function, see the chapter "AppleTalk Utilities" in this book.

Figure 3-4   Names table entry record format

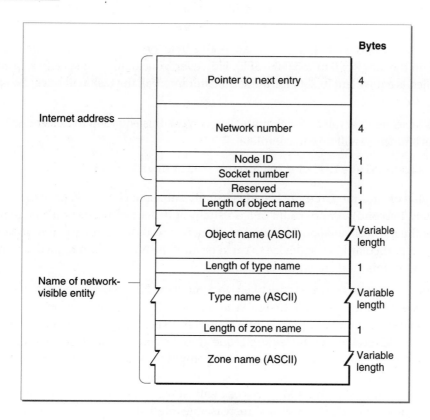

Registering a Names Table Entry

After you create the names table entry using NBPSetNTE, you register it by calling the PRegisterName function. When you call PRegisterName, NBP fills in the network number and node ID for the names table entry; because these values are the same for all entities on the node, you do not need to supply them.

Before you call the PRegisterName function, you must supply values for the function's parameter block input fields. These fields are interval, count, entityPtr, and verifyFlag. If you execute the function asynchronously, you must also supply a value for the ioCompletion field. After you call the PRegisterName function, you must not alter the contents of the parameter block until the function completes execution, and you must not modify or manipulate the names table entry until you remove it from the NBP name and address pair directory.

You set the parameter block's entityPtr field to the names table entry's pointer. For released software, you should always set the verifyFlag field to a nonzero number. This directs NBP to check throughout the network to determine that the name you want to register is unique. Ensuring that a name is unique avoids the occurrence of problems that can arise when two entities are registered with the same name. If the entity name is already registered for another entity, the PRegisterName function result indicates that the name is a duplicate by returning a function result of nbpDuplicate.

You can specify how many times NBP should attempt to verify the name's uniqueness by assigning a value to the count field. You can control how long NBP waits between each check by assigning a value to the interval field.

The interval and count parameters are both 1 byte long, which limits them to a value within the range of 0 to 255 ($00–$FF). However, you should not specify a value of 0 (which is equivalent to 256) for the retransmit interval; the task will never be executed if you do.

You measure intervals in 8-tick units. You can use this equation to determine how long in ticks a function will take to complete:

```
TimeToCompleteInTicks := count * interval * 8;
```

A value of 7 for the interval field is usually sufficient ($7 \times 8 = 56$ ticks equals approximately 1 second). A retry count of 5 is usually sufficient. However, on a large network, base the interval value on the speed of the network. Base the retry count on how likely it is for a particular kind of device to catch or miss the NBP lookup request and how many devices of this kind are on the network.

Some kinds of devices are more likely to receive the NBP lookup request than are others. For example, the AppleTalk ImageWriter has a dedicated processor on the LocalTalk option card to handle AppleTalk processing. A dedicated processor is likely to be available to receive an NBP lookup request, so the count for a device of this type can be relatively low. However, most Macintosh computers and LaserWriter printers depend on the system's shared processor to handle all processing, so the count for these kinds of devices should be higher. On a network with slow connections, for example, one that uses a modem bridge, you should increase the interval.

You can use different values for different types of devices. You can store these values in a preferences resource so that you can easily change them to correspond to changes in the network. For example, you could include values such as the following for these devices:

Device	Interval	Count
AppleShare	$07	$05
AppleTalk ImageWriter	$07	$02
LaserWriter	$0B	$05

You pass to the PRegisterName function a pointer to a parameter block and a Boolean value indicating if the function is to be executed asynchronously or synchronously. If you set the async Boolean parameter to TRUE, you must either provide a completion routine or set the ioCompletion field value to NIL, in which case, your process must poll the parameter block's ioResult field to determine when the function completes the operation. For a discussion of synchronous and asynchronous execution, see the chapter "Introduction to AppleTalk" in this book.

Listing 3-1 shows a segment of code that registers an application with NBP. First the code allocates nonrelocatable memory for the names table entry. Then the code calls NBPSetNTE to set up the names table entry in the format that the PRegisterName function expects.

Name-Binding Protocol (NBP)

Next, the code assigns values to the input fields of the parameter block to be used for the PRegisterName function. The code doesn't assign values to the ioRefNum and csCode fields because these field values are filled in by the PRegisterName function's glue code in the MPW interface.

Notice that the code assigns to the entityPtr field the ntePtr pointer to the buffer that the code passed to the NBPSetNTE function. After it sets up the parameter block, the code makes a synchronous call to the PRegisterName function to register the names table entry. If the PRegisterName function returns an error, the code releases the nonrelocatable memory that it allocated for the names table entry.

Listing 3-1   Registering an application with NBP

```
FUNCTION MyRegisterName (entityObject: Str32; entityType: Str32;
                          socket: Integer; VAR ntePtr: Ptr): OSErr;
VAR
   mppPB: MPPParamBlock;
   result: OSErr;
BEGIN
   ntePtr := NewPtrSys(sizeof(NamesTableEntry));
   IF ntePtr = NIL THEN
      BEGIN
         result := MemError;                    {return memory error}
         ntePtr := NIL;
      END
   ELSE
      BEGIN
         {Build the names table entity.}
         NBPSetNTE(ntePtr, entityObject, entityType, '*', socket);
         WITH mppPB DO
            BEGIN
               interval := $0F;                 {reasonable values for the }
               count := $03;                    { interval and retry count}
               entityPtr := ntePtr;             {pointer to NamesTableEntry}
               verifyFlag := Byte(TRUE);        {ensure that name is unique}
            END;
         result := PRegisterName(@mppPB, FALSE);{register the name}
         IF (result <> noErr) THEN
            BEGIN
               DisposPtr(ntePtr);               {if error, release memory}
               ntePtr := NIL;
            END;
      END;
   MyRegisterName := result;
END;
```

Using NBP   3-11

Handling Names Table Entry Requests

In addition to providing services that let you register an entity name and socket address for your process, NBP lets you look up addresses of other entities based on a name, confirm that a process whose entity name and address you already have is still registered with NBP and that the address is correct, remove your process's name and address from the names table when you no longer want to make the entity available, and cancel a pending request. You use

- the `NBPSetEntity` procedure to prepare an entity name in the format required by the NBP functions

- the `PLookupName` function to retrieve another entity's address based on the entity's complete NBP name, or to retrieve the addresses of multiple entities that match an NBP name that includes wildcards

- the `NBPExtract` function to read a retrieved address from the return buffer

- the `PConfirmName` function to verify a name and address

- the `PRemoveName` function to remove your process's name and address from the NBP names directory

- the `PKillNBP` function to cancel a request to register, confirm, or look up a names table entry if the function was called asynchronously and it has not already been executed

Preparing an Entity Name

To prepare an entity name using `NBPSetEntity`, you allocate a buffer that is at least 99 bytes long. You can allocate a record of type `EntityName` for this buffer. You pass `NBPSetEntity` a pointer to the buffer along with the three parts of the name (object, type, and zone), and `NBPSetEntity` writes the entity name to the buffer in the format that the `PLookupName`, `PConfirmName`, and `PRemoveName` functions require. Figure 3-5 shows the format of the entity name record.

Figure 3-5   Entity name record format

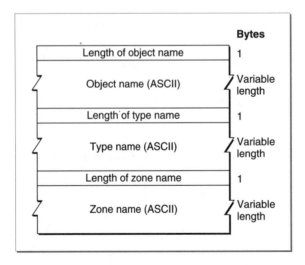

For the `PConfirmName` and `PRemoveName` functions, you must specify explicit values for the `nbpObject`, `nbpType`, and `nbpZone` parameters. However, you can specify wildcards for these parameters for `PLookupName`.

Looking Up a Name

You can use the `PLookupName` function to look up the address of a particular entity whose NBP name you know. You can also use the `PLookupName` function to find the addresses of more than one entity whose NBP names match a partial name that includes wildcards.

If you want to retrieve the address of a particular entity, you assign to the `entityPtr` field of the parameter block a pointer to a fully qualified entity name that you provided using `NBPSetEntity`. You create a buffer to hold the name and address that `PLookupName` returns and set the parameter block's return buffer pointer (`retBuffPtr`) field to this buffer's pointer. Because the data is packed and each tuple takes a maximum of 104 bytes, to look up a particular name you need to set the return buffer size (`retBuffSize`) field to the buffer size of 104 bytes. Figure 3-6 shows the format of the record for a tuple that `PLookupName` returns.

Figure 3-6   Tuple returned by the `PLookupName` function

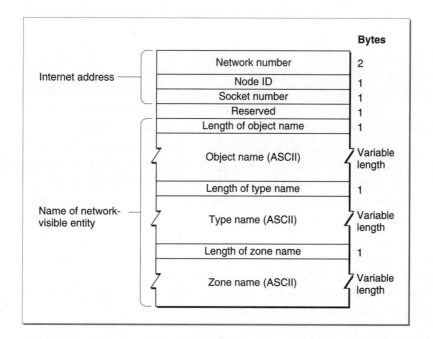

If you want only one name and address pair returned, you set the maximum number of matches (`maxToGet`) field to 1. When you call the function asynchronously, you must assign to the `ioCompletion` field a pointer to your completion routine or set this field to `NIL`. For more information about executing routines synchronously or asynchronously, see the chapter "Introduction to AppleTalk" in this book.

If you want to obtain the addresses of other instances of the same type of entity that are running on other nodes in the network, you can look up the addresses of these entities by specifying wildcards. In this case, you specify a type field value and wildcards for the object and zone fields.

Table 3-1 shows the wildcards that you can use to control the kind of matches that you want NBP to return.

Table 3-1   NBP wildcards

Character	Meaning
=	All possible values. You can use the equal sign (=) alone instead of specifying a name in the object or type field.
≈	Any or no characters in this position. You can use the double tilde (≈) to obtain matches for object or type fields. For example, *pa≈l* matches *pal*, *paul*, *paper ball*, and so forth. You can use only one double tilde in any string. Press Option-X to type the double tilde character on a Macintosh keyboard. If you use the double tilde alone, it has the same meaning as the equal sign (=). NOTE Any node not running AppleTalk Phase 2 drivers will not recognize this character.
*	This zone. You can use the asterisk (*) in place of the name of the zone to which this node belongs.

For example, if you want to retrieve the names and addresses of all the mailboxes in the same zone as one in which your process is running, you can set the entity name object field to the equal sign (=), the type field to `Mailbox`, and the zone field to the asterisk (*). The `PLookupName` function will return the entity names and internet addresses of all mailboxes in that zone excluding your own entity's name and address.

You can specify how thorough the lookup should be by defining the number of times that NBP should broadcast the lookup packets and the time interval between these retries. To do this, you assign values to the parameter block's `count` and `interval` fields. See the discussion on how to determine these values in the section "Registering a Names Table Entry" beginning on page 3-9.

You must also create a buffer large enough to hold all of the tuples for the matches that NBP returns. (See Listing 3-3 on page 3-17.) You assign the buffer's pointer to the parameter block's `retBuffPtr` field and the buffer's size in bytes to the `retBuffSize` field. Allow 104 bytes for each match. You set the maximum number of matches for NBP to return as the value of the `maxToGet` field.

The `PLookupName` function keeps track of the number of matches it writes to the return buffer each time it receives a returned packet containing one or more matches, and it updates the number of matches returned (`numGotten`) field after it returns each match. Because `PLookupName` maintains `numGotten`, you can start reading the names and addresses in the buffer and storing them or displaying them for the user before the function completes execution.

A single lookup request or retry can return more than one match in a reply packet. When this happens, the PLookupName function will return as many of the matches that the packet contains as will fit in the buffer. In cases such as this, you will find that the number of tuples that PLookupName writes to the return buffer may exceed the maximum number of matches to be returned as specified by maxToGet. When this occurs you can assume that there may be additional matches that did not fit in the buffer or additional reply packets containing matches that PLookupName did not process. To receive all the matches, you should increase the size of the buffer and the maxToGet number, and call the PLookupName function again.

If the buffer is too small to accommodate all of the returned matches in a packet, the PLookupName function returns a function result of nbpBuffOvr. In any case, the numGotten field always indicates the actual number of tuples returned in the buffer. (See also "PLookupName" beginning on page 3-30 for more information about this function.)

The code in Listing 3-2 assigns values to the fields of the parameter block to be used for the PLookupName function call. The value theEntity points to a packed entity-name record that you prepared using NBPSetEntity. This is the name that will be looked for. The value returnBufferPtr points to the buffer where PLookupName will return any matches that it finds. The buffer must be able to hold the number of matches specified by the input value of entityCount; each match is 104 bytes long. On return, entityCount contains the number of matches that the PLookupName function found and returned in the buffer pointed to by returnBufferPtr. The PLookupName function's glue code in the MPW interface fills in the values for the ioRefNum and csCode fields.

Listing 3-2 Calling PLookupName to find matches for an entity name

```
FUNCTION MyLookupName (theEntity: EntityName; VAR entityCount: Integer;
                       returnBufferPtr: Ptr): OSErr;
CONST
   kTupleSize = 104;          {sizeof(AddrBlock) + a one-byte enumerator + }
                              { sizeof(EntityName)}
VAR
   mppPB: MPPParamBlock;

BEGIN
   WITH mppPB DO
      BEGIN
         interval := $0F;              {reasonable values for the }
         count := $03;                 { interval and retry count}
         entityPtr := @theEntity;      {pointer to the entity name to }
                                       { look for}

         retBuffPtr := returnBufferPtr; {pointer to the buffer for the }
                                       { tuples}
```

```
      RetBuffSize := entityCount * kTupleSize;
                                        {return buffer size}
      maxToGet := entityCount;          {the number of entities that the }
                                        { return buffer can hold}
   END;
MyLookupName := PLookupName(@mppPB, FALSE);
                            {look up the entity name}
entityCount := mppPB.numGotten;
                            {return the number of matches found}
END;
```

The tuples in the buffer are in the format used in the NBP names table, as shown in Figure 3-6 on page 3-13. Because data is packed, the object, type, and zone names in this format are of arbitrary length; you cannot use Pascal to read these tuples. You can use the NBPExtract function to read tuples from the buffer.

Extracting a Name From a List of Returned Names

After NBP returns the matches to your buffer, you need to extract the match or matches that you want to use. You can use the NBPExtract function to read a name and address pair from the return buffer that you supplied to PLookupName. Before you call NBPExtract, you need to allocate memory for two buffers: one buffer that is at least 102 bytes long to hold the name part of the tuple and another buffer that is 4 bytes long to hold the address. You pass the NBPExtract function pointers to these buffers. The NBPExtract function unpacks the name and address data and writes it to the buffers that you supply.

You also pass NBPExtract a pointer to the buffer containing the returned tuples; this is the pointer that you assigned to the PLookupName function's retBuffPtr parameter block field. For the numInBuf parameter, you specify the number of tuples in the return buffer; this is the value that the PLookupName function returned in the numGotten parameter block field. Counting the first returned tuple as one and following in sequence to the value of numGotten, you identify which name and address pair you want to extract as the value of the whichOne parameter. You can use the NBPExtract function in a loop that varies the value of the whichOne parameter (entityCount in the following code example) from 1 to the total number of tuples in the list to extract all the names in the list.

Listing 3-3 shows an application-defined procedure, DoMyLookupName, that allocates a buffer to hold the matches that the PLookupName function returns; the MyLookupName function, shown in Listing 3-2 on page 3-15, calls the PLookupName function. The DoMyLookupName procedure calls the MyLookupName function.

If the MyLookupName function returns a result code of noErr, then the code calls the NBPExtract function to read the matches that are in the buffer and write them to the application's buffer with an application-defined routine, MyAddToMatchList; the listing does not show the MyAddToMatchList routine. After the matches are extracted, the code disposes of the return buffer.

Listing 3-3 Creating a buffer to hold name matches found, then using `NBPExtract` to read the matches

```
PROCEDURE DoMyLookupName;
    CONST
        kTupleSize = 104;          {sizeof(AddrBlock) + a one-byte enumerator + }
                                   { sizeof(EntityName)}
        kMaxMatches = 100;         {number of matches to get}
    VAR
        result:           OSErr;
        returnBufferPtr:  Ptr;
        theEntity:        EntityName;
        entityCount:      Integer;
        index:            Integer;
        entityAddress:    AddrBlock;
BEGIN
    returnBufferPtr := NewPtr(kMaxMatches * LongInt(kTupleSize));
    IF returnBufferPtr <> NIL THEN
        BEGIN
        {Create a packed entity name.}
            NBPSetEntity(@theEntity, '=', 'AFPServer', '*');
            entityCount := kMaxMatches;        {maximum number of matches we want}
            result := MyLookupName(theEntity, entityCount, returnBufferPtr);
            IF result = noErr THEN
            {Extract the matches and add them to the match list.}
                FOR index := 1 TO entityCount DO
                    IF NBPExtract(returnBufferPtr, entityCount, index, theEntity,
                                entityAddress) = noErr THEN
                        AddToMatchList(theEntity, entityAddress)
                DiposPtr(returnBufferPtr);     {release the memory}
    END;
END;
```

Confirming a Name

If you know the name and address of an entity, and you only want to confirm that the tuple is still registered with NBP and that the address hasn't been changed, you should call the `PConfirmName` function instead of calling `PLookupName`.

The `PConfirmName` function is faster than `PLookupName` because NBP can send a request packet directly to the node based on the address that you supply rather than having to broadcast lookup packets throughout the network to locate the names table entry based on the entity name alone.

The code in Listing 3-4 sets up the parameter block to be used for the `PConfirmName` function and calls `PConfirmName` to verify that the name and address still exist, and that the address is unchanged. If the application is using a different socket, PConfirmName returns a function result of nbpConfDiff and gives the new socket number in the parameter block's newSocket field.

Listing 3-4   Confirming an existing NBP name and address

```
FUNCTION MyConfirmName (theEntity: EntityName; entityAddress: AddrBlock;
                        VAR socket: Integer): OSErr;
VAR
   mppPB: MPPParamBlock;
BEGIN
   WITH mppPB DO
      BEGIN
         interval := $0F;              {reasonable values for the interval }
         count := $03;                 { and retry count}
         entityPtr := @theEntity;      {entity name to look for}
         confirmAddr := entityAddress; {entity's network address}
      END;
   MyConfirmName := PConfirmName(@mppPB, FALSE);
   socket := mppPB.newSocket;          {return the socket number, which is }
                                       { the new socket number if }
                                       { PConfirmName's result is }
                                       { nbpConfDiff}
END;
```

Removing an Entry From the Names Table

After you close the socket that your process uses or when you no longer want to make the process available throughout the network, you remove the names table entry from the node on which it resides using the PRemoveName function.

There are two ways to remove a names table entry:

- For the first method, you use the NBPSetEntity procedure to put the entity name of an existing registered entity into the structure that NBP requires. Then you specify the pointer to this record as the value of the entityPtr field of the parameter block.

- For the second method, you provide the PRemoveName function with a pointer to the names table entry record that you used to register the name.

The PRemoveName function removes the entry from the node's names table unless the name is no longer registered, in which case, PRemoveName returns a function result of nbpNotFound. An entity name may not be included in the node's names table if, for example, the request to register the name had been canceled by the PKillNBP function before the PRegisterName function used to register the name was executed.

The code in Listing 3-5 shows how to remove a names table entry using PRemoveName. The PRemoveName function's glue code fills in the ioRefNum and csCode values. The code in Listing 3-5 provides the pointer to the names table entry record that was used to register the name; it assigns this value to the `entityPtr` field of the parameter block used for the `PRemoveName` function call. (The code in Listing 3-1 on page 3-11 created the names table entry record.) If the application-defined `MyRemoveName` function returns a function result of `noErr`, the code disposes of the memory block pointed to by `ntePtr`.

Listing 3-5   Removing an NBP names table entry

```
FUNCTION MyRemoveName (ntePtr: Ptr): OSErr;
VAR
   mppPB: MPPParamBlock;
   result: OSErr;
BEGIN
   mppPB.entityPtr := Ptr(ORD4(ntePtr) + 9);
                     {the entity name is at offset 9 in the NTE}
   result := PRemoveName(@mppPB, FALSE);{remove the name}
   IF (result = noErr) THEN
      DisposPtr(ntePtr); {release the memory}
   MyRemoveName := result;
END;
```

Canceling a Request

You can use the `PKillNBP` function to cancel a request to register, look up, or confirm a names table entry if the function was called asynchronously and it has not already been executed.

When you call `PRegisterName`, `PLookupName`, or `PConfirmName`, NBP calls the Device Manager, which places your request in the .MPP driver queue with other requests waiting to be executed. To queue the request, the Device Manager places a pointer to the function's parameter block in the .MPP driver queue. You assign this pointer to the `PKillNPB` parameter block's queue element (`nKillQEl`) field.

If the function request that you want to cancel is not in the queue, `PKillNBP` returns a function result of `cbNotFound`. If `PKillNBP` cancels the function, it returns a function result of `noErr`, and the function that it canceled returns a function result of `reqAborted`.

The code in Listing 3-6 on page 3-20 shows how to cancel a `PRegisterName`, `PLookupName`, or `PConfirmName` function call. The application-defined `MyKillNBP` function takes as an input parameter a pointer to the parameter block that was used to make the `PLookupName`, `PRegisterName`, or `PConfirmName` function call to be canceled. The code assigns this pointer to the `nKillQEl` field of the parameter block to be passed to the `PKillNBP` function. The `ioRefNum` and `csCode` field values are filled in by the `PKillNBP` function's glue code in the MPW interface.

Listing 3-6   Canceling a request to look up a name

```
FUNCTION MyKillNBP (requestPBPtr: MPPPBptr): OSErr;
   VAR
   mppPB: MPPParamBlock;
BEGIN
   mppPB.nKillQEl := Ptr(requestPBPtr);
   MyKillNBP := PKillNBP(@mppPB, FALSE);
END;
```

NBP Reference

This section describes the data structures and routines that are specific to the Name-Binding Protocol (NBP). The "Data Structures" section shows the Pascal data structures for the records and the parameter block that the NBP functions use. The "Routines" section describes the NBP routines.

Data Structures

This section describes the data structures that you use to provide information to and receive it from NBP.

Address Block Record

The address block record is a data structure of type `AddrBlock` that defines a packed record that is used to contain an internet socket address. The names table entry record includes a field that takes a value of this record type.

```
AddrBlock = PACKED RECORD
   aNet:      Integer;
   aNode:     Byte;
   aSocket:   Byte;
END;
```

Field descriptions

aNet   The network number.
aNode   The node ID.
aSocket   The socket number.

Names Table Entry Record

The names table entry record is a data structure of type `NamesTableEntry` that is used to hold an NBP names table tuple, consisting of a name and address. Because the object, type, and zone names in a names table entry are packed data of arbitrary length, you cannot create this record in Pascal (which requires you to declare the length of character strings when you define the record). If you are using the NBP Pascal interface, you use the `NPBSetNTE` procedure to create a names table entry. For illustration of the names table record format, see Figure 3-4 on page 3-9.

```
TYPE
   NamesTableEntry =
   RECORD
      qLink:      QElemPtr;
      nteAddress: AddrBlock;
      nteData: PACKED ARRAY[1..100] OF Char;
   END;
```

Field descriptions

`qLink`	A pointer to the next names table entry in the names table linked list that NBP maintains on the node. (This field is used internally by NBP.)
`nteAddress`	The internet socket address.
`nteData`	The NBP name associated with the entity's address.

Entity Name Record

The entity name record is a data structure of type `EntityName` that is used to hold the NBP name for an entity that is associated with a socket address. Your application looks up or confirms an address or removes a names table entry based on an entity name.

Because the object, type, and zone names that constitute the entity name in this format are packed data and of arbitrary length, you cannot create this record in Pascal (which requires you to declare the length of character strings when you define the record). If you are using the NBP Pascal interface, you put an existing entity name into the structure that NBP requires using the `NBPSetEntity` procedure.

```
TYPE
   EntityName =
   RECORD
      objStr:  Str32;
      typeStr: Str32;
      zoneStr: Str32;
   END;
   EntityPtr = ^EntityName;
```

Field descriptions

objStr	The object part of an entity name. It consists of an alphanumeric string of up to 31 characters. The object part of the name can be any valid string; it is commonly used to identify the user of the system.
typeStr	The type part of an entity name. It consists of an alphanumeric string of up to 31 characters. The type part of the name can be any valid string, but it is commonly used to identify the type of service that the entity provides.
zoneStr	The zone part of an entity name. It consists of an alphanumeric string of up to 31 characters that identifies the zone to which the node belongs that is running the process.

The MPP Parameter Block for NBP

The NBP functions use the MPP parameter block defined by the `MPPParamBlock` data type to pass information to and receive it from the .MPP driver. You use these fields to specify input values to and receive output values from an NBP function. This section defines the fields common to all NBP functions, except those that are reserved for internal use by the .MPP driver or not used.

```
TYPE
   MPPParmType      =      (...RegisterNameParm, LookupNameParm,
                           ConfirmNameParm,RemoveNameParm, KillNBPParm...);
   MPPPBPtr         =      ^MPPParamBlock;
   MPPParamBlock    =
   PACKED RECORD
      qLink:               QElemPtr;       {reserved}
      qType:               Integer;        {reserved}
      ioTrap:              Integer;        {reserved}
      ioCmdAddr:           Ptr;            {reserved}
      ioCompletion:        ProcPtr;        {completion routine}
      ioResult:            OSErr;          {result code}
      ioNamePtr:           StringPtr;      {reserved}
      ioVRefNum:           Integer;        {reserved}
      ioRefNum:            Integer;        {driver reference number}
      csCode:              Integer;        {primary command code}
   CASE MPPParmType OF
      RegisterNameParm,
      LookupNameParm,
      ConfirmNameParm,
      RemoveNameParm:
         (interval:        Byte;           {retry interval}
          count:           Byte;           {retry count}
          entityPtr:       Ptr;            {pointer to entity name or }
                                           { names table element}
```

```
    CASE MPPParmType OF
      RegisterNameParm:
          (verifyFlag:      Byte;         {verify uniqueness of name or not}
           filler3:         Byte;)
      LookupNameParm:
          (retBuffPtr:      Ptr;          {pointer to return buffer}
           retBuffSize:     Integer;      {return buffer size}
           maxToGet:        Integer;      {matches to get}
           numGotten:       Integer;)     {matches gotten}
      ConfirmNameParm:
          (confirmAddr:     AddrBlock;    {pointer to entity name}
           newSocket:       Byte;         {socket number}
           filler4:         Byte);
      )
    KillNBPParm:
        (nKillQEl:          Ptr;)         {pointer to queue element to cancel}
END;
```

The fields for each variant record are defined in the function description that uses the record.

Routines

This section describes the NBP routines. The NBP routines allow you to

- create an NBP names table entry

- register an NBP names table entry with the NBP names directory

- put an existing NBP entity name into the structure that NBP requires for you to look up, confirm, or remove an existing registered entity name

- look up the address of a network entity based on its NBP name

- read a name and address from a list of pairs that NBP returns

- confirm that a name and address pair is registered with NBP

- remove a registered name from the NBP names directory

- cancel an NBP request

An arrow preceding a parameter indicates whether the parameter is an input parameter, an output parameter, or both:

Arrow	Meaning
→	Input
←	Output
↔	Both

You can use the PGetAppleTalkInfo function to determine the maximum number of concurrent NBP requests that the .MPP driver installed on the system that is running your process supports. See the chapter "AppleTalk Utilities" for information on the PGetAppleTalkInfo function.

Registering an Entity

This section describes the NBPSetNTE and the PRegisterName routines. You can use the NBPSetNTE procedure to create an NBP names table entry to be used to register the name and address of an entity with NBP so that the entity is made visible throughout the network. You use the PRegisterName function to register a names table entry that you created through the NBPSetNTE procedure.

NBPSetNTE

The NBPSetNTE procedure creates a new NBP names table entry to be added to the NBP names table through the PRegisterName function.

```
PROCEDURE NBPSetNTE (ntePtr: Ptr; nbpObject,nbpType,nbpZone: Str32;
                     socket: Integer);
```

ntePtr   A pointer to a buffer that you provide that is at least 108 bytes long. The NBPSetNTE procedure fills this buffer with a names table entry based on the remaining parameter values that you specify. This buffer should be a record of type NamesTableEntry.

nbpObject   The object part of the name for the names table entry. This value can be up to 31 characters long. You cannot use any wildcard characters in this name. (An object name typically identifies the node and is commonly set to the Chooser name that the user specified.)

nbpType   The type part of the name for the names table entry. This value can be up to 31 characters long. You cannot use any wildcard characters in this name. This part of an NBP name usually identifies the type of service to which the name is assigned.

nbpZone   The zone part of the name for the names table entry. You must use an asterisk (*) for this name, indicating the local zone.

socket   The number of the socket that was returned and assigned to your process when you opened a socket using one of the AppleTalk transport protocols. The NBP entity name is associated with the socket number that you specify.

DESCRIPTION

The NBPSetNTE procedure creates a names table entry that you can register with the NBP names directory using the PRegisterName function. When you call PRegisterName to register the name, you must provide a pointer to the NBP names table entry that you created previously.

Because the object, type, and zone names in a names table entry are packed data of arbitrary length, you cannot create this record in Pascal (which requires you to declare the length of character strings when you define the record). Use the NBPSetNTE procedure to create the names table entry.

SPECIAL CONSIDERATIONS

The names table entry that you provide remains the property of NBP once you register it using PRegisterName and until you remove it using the PRemoveName function. You can allocate a block of nonrelocatable memory for the names table entry buffer using the Memory Manager's NewPtr or NewPtrSys function.

If instead you use the NewHandle function to allocate the buffer memory, you must lock the memory before you call PRegisterName to register the name because NBP adds the actual names table entry to the NBP names table for that node, and the names table entry remains part of the table until you remove it.

ASSEMBLY-LANGUAGE INFORMATION

The NBPSetNTE procedure is implemented entirely in the MPW interface files. There is no assembly-language equivalent for this procedure.

SEE ALSO

For the names table entry record format, see Figure 3-4 on page 3-9.

For the NamesTableEntry data type declaration, see "Data Structures" on page 3-20.

For information on allocating memory, see *Inside Macintosh: Memory*.

The PRegisterName function is described next.

PRegisterName

The PRegisterName function adds a unique names table entry to the local node's NBP names table.

```
FUNCTION PRegisterName (thePBptr: MPPPBPtr; async: Boolean): OSErr;
```

thePBptr   A pointer to an MPP parameter block.

async   A Boolean that indicates whether the function should be executed asynchronously or synchronously. Specify TRUE for asynchronous execution.

Parameter block

→	ioCompletion	ProcPtr	A pointer to a completion routine.
←	ioResult	OSErr	The function result.
→	ioRefNum	Integer	The .MPP driver reference number.
→	csCode	Integer	Always registerName.
→	interval	Byte	The retry interval.
↔	count	Byte	The retry count.
→	entityPtr	Ptr	A pointer to a names table entry.
→	verifyFlag	Byte	A flag to indicate whether NBP is to verify NBP names as unique.

Field descriptions

ioCompletion   A pointer to a completion routine that you can provide. When you execute a function asynchronously, the .MPP driver calls your completion routine when it completes execution of the function if you specify a pointer to the routine as the value of this field. Specify NIL for this field if you do not wish to provide a completion routine. If you execute a function synchronously, the .MPP driver ignores the ioCompletion field. For information about completion routines, see the chapter "Introduction to AppleTalk" in this book.

ioResult   The result of the function. When you execute the function asynchronously, the function sets this field to 1 and returns a function result of noErr as soon as the function begins execution. When the function completes execution, it sets the ioResult field to the actual result code.

ioRefNum   The .MPP driver reference number. The MPW interface fills in this field.

csCode   The command code of the .MPP command to be executed. The MPW interface fills in this field.

interval   The retry interval to be used by NBP when it verifies the uniqueness of the name. The retry interval value specifies how long the function is to wait between retries in 8-tick units. A value of 7 for the interval field is usually sufficient ($7 \times 8 = 56$ ticks equals approximately 1 second).

count   On input, the retry count to be used by NBP when it verifies the uniqueness of the name. Its value tells the PRegisterName function how many times to retry. A retry count of 5 is usually sufficient. On return, the number of times that NBP actually attempted to verify the uniqueness of the name.

entityPtr   A pointer to a names table entry. You can use the NBPSetNTE procedure to create a names table entry. You cannot use wildcard characters in the object name and type name fields of the names table entry, but you must use an asterisk (*)—indicating the local zone—for the zone name field.

verifyFlag   A flag that determines whether NBP attempts to verify that the name you are adding to the names table is unique. Set this flag to a nonzero number to have NBP verify the name. You can set this flag to zero during program development, but to avoid confusion caused by duplicate names on a network, you should always set the verifyFlag parameter to a nonzero number in released software.

DESCRIPTION

Before another entity can send information to your entity over AppleTalk, it must have your entity's internet socket address. Also, for users to be able to select your application, the entity must be made visible throughout the network.

The `PRegisterName` function adds an entry for a network entity to the node's NBP names table, making it possible for a user or another process to locate that entity through its NBP name (consisting of object, type, and zone names). The process whose name is registered with NBP is referred to as a *network-visible entity*.

Because the object, type, and zone names in a names table entry are of arbitrary length, you cannot create this record in Pascal (which requires you to declare the length of character strings when you define the record). Use the `NBPSetNTE` procedure to create the names table entry. If you execute the function asynchronously and you do not specify a completion routine, your process can poll the `ioResult` field to determine when the function completes execution.

You can assign any number of names to a single socket. If you use a single socket for more than one process, you must provide a socket listener.

If you use the `PKillNPB` function to cancel the `PRegisterName` function and the cancel request is successful, `PRegisterName` returns a function result of `reqAborted`.

SPECIAL CONSIDERATIONS

The names table entry that you provide remains the property of NBP until you use the `PRemoveName` function to remove the entry from the names table. You must allocate a nonrelocatable block for the names table entry, or lock any relocatable block that you use for it until you are ready to remove the entry.

ASSEMBLY-LANGUAGE INFORMATION

To execute the `PRegisterName` function from assembly language, call the `_Control` trap macro with a value of `registerName` in the `csCode` field of the parameter block. To execute the `_Control` trap asynchronously, include the value `,ASYNC` in the operand field. To execute this function from assembly language, you must also specify the driver reference number.

RESULT CODES

noErr	0	No error
nbpDuplicate	–1027	Name already exists
tooManyReqs	–1097	Too many concurrent requests; wait a few minutes, then try the request again
reqAborted	–1105	Request canceled

To create a names table entry, use the NBPSetNTE procedure, described on page 3-24.

For the names table entry record format, see Figure 3-2 on page 3-6.

For the NamesTableEntry data type declaration, see "Names Table Entry Record" on page 3-21.

To cancel a name registration request, use the PKillNBP function, described on page 3-38.

For information about socket listeners, see the chapter "Datagram Delivery Protocol (DDP)" in this book.

Handling Name and Address Requests

This section describes

- the NBPSetEntity procedure, which you can use to put an existing NBP entity name into the structure that NBP requires for you to look up, confirm, or remove an existing registered entity name

- the PLookupName function, which you can use to look up the network address of an entity, based on the NBP registered name for that entity, or using wildcards

- the NBPExtract function, which you can use to read a name and address pair from the buffer containing the list of tuples that PLookupName returns

- the PConfirmName function, which you can use to confirm that a name whose address you know is still associated with that address, and that the pair is still registered with the NBP names directory

- the PRemoveName function, which you can use to remove a name and address pair from the NBP names directory when you no longer want to make the service associated with the tuple available throughout the network

- the PKillNBP function, which you can use to cancel requests to NBP

NBPSetEntity

The NBPSetEntity procedure puts an existing NBP name of a network-visible entity into the packed-record format that the PLookupName, PConfirmName, and PRemoveName functions require.

```
PROCEDURE NBPSetEntity (buffer: Ptr;
                        nbpObject,nbpType,nbpZone: Str32);
```

buffer   A pointer to a buffer that you provide that is at least 99 bytes long. The NBPSetEntity procedure fills this buffer with the entity name you specify in the other three parameters.

nbpObject   The object part of the registered NBP name. You can specify wildcard characters in this part of the name only for use with the PLookupName function.

nbpType   The type part of the registered NBP name. You can use wildcard characters in this part of the name only for use with the PLookupName function.

nbpZone   The zone part of the registered NBP name. You can use wildcard characters in this part of the name only for use with the PLookupName function.

Table 3-1 on page 3-14 describes the wildcard characters that you can specify for the nbpObject, nbpType, and nbpZone fields for use with the PLookupName function.

DESCRIPTION

When you call the PRemoveName function to remove the name of a network-visible entity from the NBP names table, or call the PLookupName or PConfirmName function to look up network-visible entities, you must specify an entity name in the format shown in Figure 3-5 on page 3-12. (For PRemoveName, instead of creating the entity-name record, you can provide a pointer to the names table entry record that you used to register the name.)

The object, type, and zone names that constitute the entity name in this format are packed data and of arbitrary length. Therefore, you cannot create this record in Pascal (which requires you to declare the length of character strings when you define the record). Use the NBPSetEntity procedure to provide the entity name in the format that NBP requires.

SPECIAL CONSIDERATIONS

The memory that you allocate for the entity name buffer belongs to NBP until the function completes execution. You can reuse it or dispose of it after the operation completes.

ASSEMBLY-LANGUAGE INFORMATION

The NBPSetEntity procedure is implemented entirely in the MPW interface files. There is no assembly-language equivalent for this procedure.

SEE ALSO

The PLookupName function is described next.

For a discussion of how to use NBPSetEntity, see "Preparing an Entity Name" beginning on page 3-12.

To confirm that an entity is still registered with NBP, use the PConfirmName function, described on page 3-34.

To remove a registered name from the NBP names table, use the PRemoveName function, described on page 3-36.

PLookupName

The PLookupName function returns the names and addresses of all the network-visible entities that match a name that you supply, which can include wildcard characters.

```
FUNCTION PLookupName (thePBptr: MPPPBPtr; async: Boolean): OSErr;
```

thePBptr   A pointer to an MPP parameter block.

async   A Boolean that specifies whether the function should be executed asynchronously or synchronously. Specify TRUE for asynchronous execution.

Parameter block

→	ioCompletion	ProcPtr	A pointer to a completion routine.
←	ioResult	OSErr	The function result.
→	ioRefNum	Integer	The .MPP driver reference number.
→	csCode	Integer	Always lookupName.
→	interval	Byte	The retry interval.
↔	count	Byte	The retry count.
→	entityPtr	Ptr	A pointer to an entity name.
→	retBuffPtr	Ptr	A pointer to the return data buffer.
→	retBuffSize	Integer	The return buffer size in bytes.
→	maxToGet	Integer	The maximum number of matches to get.
←	numGotten	Integer	The number of addresses found and returned.

Field descriptions

ioCompletion   A pointer to a completion routine that you can provide. When you execute a function asynchronously, the .MPP driver calls your completion routine when it completes execution of the function if you specify a pointer to the routine as the value of this field. Specify NIL for this field if you do not wish to provide a completion routine. If you execute a function synchronously, the .MPP driver ignores the ioCompletion field. For information about completion routines, see the chapter "Introduction to AppleTalk" in this book.

ioResult   The result of the function. When you execute the function asynchronously, the function sets this field to 1 and returns a function result of noErr as soon as the function begins execution. When the function completes execution, it sets the ioResult field to the actual result code.

ioRefNum   The .MPP driver reference number. The MPW interface fills in this field.

csCode   The command code of the .MPP command to be executed. The MPW interface fills in this field.

interval   The retry interval to be used by NBP when it looks on the internet for matching names. The retry interval value specifies how long the function is to wait between retries in 8-tick units. The retry interval equals the interval field value × 8 ticks. A value of 7 for the interval field is usually sufficient ($7 \times 8 = 56$ ticks equals approximately 1 second). However, on a large network, you should base the interval value on the speed of the network and how many devices of this type you expect to be on the network.

count
: The retry count to be used by NBP when it looks on the internet for matching names. Its value specifies the number of times PLookupName is to retry the operation. A retry count of 3 or 4 is usually sufficient. However, on a large network, you should base the value on how likely it is for the type of device to miss the NBP request. For example, the AppleTalk ImageWriter has a dedicated processor on the LocalTalk option card to handle AppleTalk processing, so the retry count for a device of this type can be low, whereas most Macintosh systems and LaserWriter printers depend on their shared processor to handle all system processing, so a retry count for a device of these types should be higher. The PLookupName function decrements this field each time it looks for names.

entityPtr
: A pointer to an entity name in the format shown in Figure 3-5 on page 3-12. You can use the NBPSetEntity procedure to prepare the entity name record.

retBuffPtr
: A pointer to a buffer you provide into which the PLookupName function puts the names and addresses that it finds. Each matching tuple takes a maximum of 104 bytes, and you use the maxToGet field to specify the maximum number of tuples to be returned.

retBuffSize
: The size of the buffer you are providing.

maxToGet
: The maximum number of matches to be returned.

numGotten
: The actual number of matches that PLookupName returned. The PLookupName function updates this field each time it receives an NBP returned packet and adds names to the return buffer. If there is space remaining in the buffer, NBP may return more matches than the number specified by maxToGet. If numGotten is greater than or equal to maxToGet, there may be additional matches. In this case, you should increase the size of the buffer pointed to by retBuffPtr and call the PLookupName function again.

DESCRIPTION

Before you can send data to another entity, you must have the network address of that entity. The PLookupName function returns the names and addresses of any network-visible entities whose names match the entity name you specify. The entity name can include any of the wildcard characters given in Table 3-1 on page 3-14.

The PLookupName function completes execution when the number of matches returned is equal to or greater than the number in the maxToGet field, the function exceeds the retry count, the buffer overflows, or the request is canceled through the PKillNBP function.

The number of matches returned can be greater than the number specified in the maxToGet field under the following circumstances: A single lookup request or retry can return more than one match in a reply packet. If there is space remaining in the buffer and NBP receives a packet containing multiple matches, PLookupName will return as many of the matches as fit in the buffer. If this occurs, you should increase the size of the buffer and call the PLookupName function again to ensure that you obtain all of the matches.

If all of the tuples returned in a reply packet do not fit in the buffer, then the function completes with as many tuples as can fit. Whether NBP returns more or fewer matches than you specify as the value of maxToGet, the value of numGotten reflects the actual number of tuples that PLookupName writes to the return buffer.

Because the function updates the numGotten field each time it receives a returned packet containing one or more matches and writes those name and address pairs to the return buffer, you can start reading the names in the buffer and displaying them for the user before the function completes execution.

The tuples in the buffer are in the format used in the NBP names table, as shown in Figure 3-6 on page 3-13. Because the object, type, and zone names in this format are of arbitrary length, you cannot use Pascal to read these tuples. Use the NBPExtract function to read tuples from the buffer.

SPECIAL CONSIDERATIONS

Memory used for the entity name record and the return buffer belongs to PLookupName until the function completes execution and must be nonrelocatable.

ASSEMBLY-LANGUAGE INFORMATION

To execute the PLookupName function from assembly language, call the _Control trap macro with a value of lookupName in the csCode field of the parameter block. To execute the _Control trap asynchronously, include the value ,ASYNC in the operand field. To execute this function from assembly language, you must also specify the driver reference number.

RESULT CODES

noErr	0	No error
tooManyReqs	–1097	Too many concurrent requests; wait a few minutes, then try the request again
reqAborted	–1105	Request canceled

SEE ALSO

To read tuples from the buffer, use the NBPExtract function, described next.

To create the entity name record, use the NBPSetEntity procedure, described on page 3-28.

To check that a network-visible entity whose name and address you already know is still available on the network, use the PConfirmName function, described on page 3-34.

To cancel a name lookup request, use the PKillNBP function, described on page 3-38.

NBPExtract

The `NBPExtract` function returns one tuple (entity name and internet address) from the list of tuples placed in a buffer by the `PLookupName` function.

```
FUNCTION NBPExtract (theBuffer: Ptr; numInBuf: Integer;
                     whichOne: Integer;
                     VAR abEntity: EntityName;
                     VAR address: AddrBlock): OSErr;
```

theBuffer   A pointer to the buffer containing the tuples returned by the `PLookupName` function.

numInBuf   The number of tuples returned by the `PLookupName` function in the `numGotten` parameter.

whichOne   The sequence number of the tuple that you want the function to return. This parameter can be any integer in the range 1 through `numInBuf`.

abEntity   A pointer to a buffer that you provide to hold the name returned by the function. This buffer must be at least 102 bytes long.

address   A pointer to a buffer that you provide to hold the address returned by the function. The buffer must be at least 4 bytes long.

DESCRIPTION

The `NBPExtract` function extracts a name and address pair from the list of tuples that the `PLookupName` function returns. The `PLookupName` function returns the names of network-visible entities in a packed format that you cannot read from Pascal. Use the `NBPExtract` function in a loop that varies the value of the `whichOne` parameter from 1 to the total number of tuples in the list to extract all the names in the list.

ASSEMBLY-LANGUAGE INFORMATION

The `NBPExtract` function is implemented entirely in the MPW interface files. There is no assembly-language equivalent to this procedure.

RESULT CODES

noErr	0	No error
extractErr	–3104	Can't find tuple in buffer

SEE ALSO

To look up the name and address of an entity registered with NBP, use the `PLookupName` function, described on page 3-30.

For a description of the `EntityName` data type, see "Entity Name Record" on page 3-21.

For a description of the `AddrBlock` data type, see "Address Block Record" on page 3-20.

PConfirmName

The PConfirmName function confirms that a network-visible entity whose name you know is still available on the network and that the address associated with the name has not been changed.

```
FUNCTION PConfirmName (thePBptr: MPPPBPtr; async: Boolean): OSErr;
```

thePBptr   A pointer to an MPP parameter block.

async   A Boolean that specifies whether the function should be executed asynchronously or synchronously. Specify TRUE for asynchronous execution.

Parameter block

→	ioCompletion	ProcPtr	A pointer to a completion routine.
←	ioResult	OSErr	The function result.
→	ioRefNum	Integer	The .MPP driver reference number.
→	csCode	Integer	Always confirmName.
→	interval	Byte	The retry interval.
↔	count	Byte	The retry count.
→	entityPtr	Ptr	A pointer to an entity name.
→	confirmAddr	AddrBlock	The entity address.
←	newSocket	Byte	The current socket number.

Field descriptions

ioCompletion   A pointer to a completion routine that you can provide. When you execute a function asynchronously, the .MPP driver calls your completion routine when it completes execution of the function if you specify a pointer to the routine as the value of this field. Specify NIL for this field if you do not wish to provide a completion routine. If you execute a function synchronously, the .MPP driver ignores the ioCompletion field. For information about completion routines, see the chapter "Introduction to AppleTalk" in this book.

ioResult   The result of the function. When you execute the function asynchronously, the function sets this field to 1 and returns a function result of noErr as soon as the function begins execution. When the function completes execution, it sets the ioResult field to the actual result code.

ioRefNum   The .MPP driver reference number. The MPW interface fills in this field.

csCode   The command code of the .MPP command to be executed. The MPW interface fills in this field.

interval   The retry interval to be used by NBP when it looks on the internet for the entity. The retry interval value specifies how long the function is to wait between retries in 8-tick units. A value of 7 for the interval field is usually sufficient ($7 \times 8 = 56$ ticks equals approximately 1 second).

count	The retry count to be used by NBP when it looks on the internet for the entity. The value of count specifies the number of times the PConfirmName function is to retry the operation. A retry count of 3 or 4 is usually sufficient. The PConfirmName function decrements this field each time it looks for names.
entityPtr	A pointer to an entity name that you want to confirm. The entity name must be in the format that Figure 3-5 on page 3-12 shows. You can use the NBPSetEntity procedure to create the entity name record.
confirmAddr	The last known address of the network-visible entity whose existence you wish to confirm.
newSocket	The current socket number of the entity. If the socket number of the entity has changed, the PConfirmName function returns the new socket number in this field and returns the nbpConfDiff result code.

DESCRIPTION

If you already know the name and address of a network-visible entity, but want to confirm that the name is still registered with NBP and that the address hasn't changed before you attempt to send data to it, you can use the PConfirmName function. If the address is no longer associated with the name, PConfirmName returns a result code of nbpNoConfirm, indicating that the name may have been removed from the socket. If the name is assigned to another socket, PConfirmName returns the current socket number in the parameter block's newSocket field and a result code of nbpConfDiff. This function generates less network traffic than the PLookupName function.

SPECIAL CONSIDERATIONS

Memory used for the buffer containing the entity name and the record containing the entity address belongs to PConfirmName until the function completes execution.

ASSEMBLY-LANGUAGE INFORMATION

To execute the PConfirmName function from assembly language, call the _Control trap macro with a value of confirmName in the csCode field of the parameter block. To execute the _Control trap asynchronously, include the value ,ASYNC in the operand field. To execute this function from assembly language, you must also specify the driver reference number.

RESULT CODES

noErr	0	No error
nbpNoConfirm	−1025	Name not confirmed
nbpConfDiff	−1026	Name confirmed for different socket
tooManyReqs	−1097	Too many concurrent requests; wait a few minutes, then try the request again
reqAborted	−1105	Request canceled

SEE ALSO

For a description of the AddrBlock data type, see "Address Block Record" on page 3-20.

To find the address of a network-visible entity whose name or address you do not already know, use the PLookupName function, described on page 3-30.

To cancel a name confirmation request, use the PKillNBP function, described on page 3-38.

PRemoveName

The PRemoveName function removes a previously registered name from the NBP names table.

```
FUNCTION PRemoveName (thePBptr: MPPPBPtr; async: Boolean): OSErr;
```

thePBptr   A pointer to an MPP parameter block.

async   A Boolean that specifies whether the function should be executed asynchronously or synchronously. Specify TRUE for asynchronous execution.

Parameter block

→	ioCompletion	ProcPtr	A pointer to a completion routine.
←	ioResult	OSErr	The function result.
→	ioRefNum	Integer	The .MPP driver reference number.
→	csCode	Integer	Always removeName.
→	entityPtr	Ptr	A pointer to an entity name.

Field descriptions

ioCompletion   A pointer to a completion routine that you can provide. When you execute a function asynchronously, the .MPP driver calls your completion routine when it completes execution of the function if you specify a pointer to the routine as the value of this field. Specify NIL for this field if you do not wish to provide a completion routine. If you execute a function synchronously, the .MPP driver ignores the ioCompletion field. For information about completion routines, see the chapter "Introduction to AppleTalk" in this book.

ioResult   The result of the function. When you execute the function asynchronously, the function sets this field to 1 and returns a function result of noErr as soon as the function begins execution. When the function completes execution, it sets the ioResult field to the actual result code.

ioRefNum   The .MPP driver reference number. The MPW interface fills in this field.

csCode   The command code of the .MPP command to be executed. The MPW interface fills in this field.

entityPtr   A pointer to the name of the network-visible entity that you wish
                   to remove from the names table. The name must be in the format
                   shown in Figure 3-5 on page 3-12. You cannot use any wildcard
                   characters in the name.

DESCRIPTION

When you close a socket or terminate an application or process that you registered in the
NBP names table as a network-visible entity, you must use the PRemoveName function
to remove the name from the names table.

To remove the names table entry, you assign to the entityPtr field of the parameter
block a pointer to a fully qualified entity name. The entity name is a packed array of
Pascal strings. Because the object, type, and zone names in this format are of arbitrary
length, you cannot create this record in Pascal (which requires you to declare the length
of character strings when you define the record). You can use the NBPSetEntity
procedure to create this record, or you can provide PRemoveName with a pointer to the
names table entry record that you used to register the name.

SPECIAL CONSIDERATIONS

Memory used for the buffer containing the entity name belongs to the PRemoveName
function until the function completes execution and must be nonrelocatable. After you
remove the names table entry, you can reuse the memory or release it.

ASSEMBLY-LANGUAGE INFORMATION

To execute the PRemoveName function from assembly language, call the _Control trap
macro with a value of removeName in the csCode field of the parameter block. To
execute the _Control trap asynchronously, include the value ,ASYNC in the operand
field. To execute this function from assembly language, you must also specify the driver
reference number.

RESULT CODES

noErr	0	No error
nbpNotFound	−1028	Name not found
reqAborted	−1105	Request canceled

SEE ALSO

To create an entity name record of the form required by the PRemoveName function, use
the NBPSetEntity procedure, described on page 3-28.

PKillNBP

The PKillNBP function cancels NBP function calls to the PLookupName, PRegisterName, or PConfirmName function.

```
FUNCTION PKillNBP (thePBptr: MPPPBPtr; async: Boolean): OSErr;
```

thePBptr   A pointer to an MPP parameter block.

async   A Boolean that specifies whether the function should be executed
            asynchronously or synchronously. Specify TRUE for asynchronous
            execution.

Parameter block

→	ioCompletion	ProcPtr	A pointer to a completion routine.
←	ioResult	OSErr	The function result.
→	ioRefNum	Integer	The .MPP driver reference number.
→	csCode	Integer	Always killNBP.
→	nKillQEl	Ptr	A pointer to a queue element.

Field descriptions

ioCompletion   A pointer to a completion routine that you can provide. When you
               execute a function asynchronously, the .MPP driver calls your
               completion routine when it completes execution of the function if
               you specify a pointer to the routine as the value of this field. Specify
               NIL for this field if you do not wish to provide a completion
               routine. If you execute a function synchronously, the .MPP driver
               ignores the ioCompletion field. For information about completion
               routines, see the chapter "Introduction to AppleTalk" in this book.

ioResult   The result of the function. When you execute the function asynchro-
               nously, the function sets this field to 1 and returns a function result
               of noErr as soon as the function begins execution. When the
               function completes execution, it sets the ioResult field to the
               actual result code.

ioRefNum   The .MPP driver reference number. The MPW interface fills in
               this field.

csCode   The command code of the .MPP command to be executed. The
               MPW interface fills in this field.

nKillQEl   A pointer to the MPP parameter block for the NBP request you
               want to cancel.

DESCRIPTION

When you call the PLookupName, PRegisterName, or PConfirmName function asynchronously, the Device Manager puts your request in the .MPP driver's queue with
other requests. If you want to cancel a pending NBP request, you pass a pointer to the
parameter block for that request to the PKillNBP function.

If the function's parameter block is in the .MPP driver's queue waiting for the function to be executed, the PKillNBP function deletes the entry from the queue and returns a function result of noErr. The function whose parameter block is deleted completes execution and returns a function result of reqAborted, indicating that the function was canceled.

If the function has already been executed, that is, it is no longer in the queue, PKillNBP returns a function result of cbNotFound, indicating that the parameter block for the function to be canceled was not in the .MPP driver's queue.

The function also calls the completion routine for the canceled request with the result code reqAborted (–1105) in the D0 register.

ASSEMBLY-LANGUAGE INFORMATION

To execute the PKillNBP function from assembly language, call the _Control trap macro with a value of killNBP in the csCode field of the parameter block. To execute the _Control trap asynchronously, include the value ,ASYNC in the operand field. To execute this function from assembly language, you must also specify the driver reference number.

RESULT CODES

| noErr | 0 | No error |
| cbNotFound | –1102 | NBP queue element not found |

Summary of NBP

Pascal Summary

Constants

```
CONST
   {.MPP driver unit and reference number}
   mppUnitNum    =    9;            {MPP driver unit number}
   mppRefNum     =   -10;           {MPP reference number}

   {csCodes for NBP}
   confirmName   =   250;           {confirm name}
   lookupName    =   251;           {lookup name}
   removeName    =   252;           {remove name from names table}
   registerName  =   253;           {register name in names table}
   killNBP       =   254;           {kill outstanding NBP request}
```

Data Types

Address Block Record

```
   AddrBlock =
   PACKED RECORD
      aNet:      Integer;           {network number}
      aNode:     Byte;              {node ID}
      aSocket:   Byte;              {socket number}
   END;
```

Names Table Entry Record

```
TYPE  NamesTableEntry =
   RECORD
      qLink:       QElemPtr;        {pointer to next NTE in names table}
      nteAddress:  AddrBlock;       {pointer to this names table entry}
      nteData: PACKED ARRAY[1..100] OF Char;
                                    {names table entry}
   END;
```

Entity Name Record

```
EntityName =
RECORD
    objStr:        Str32;        {object name}
    typeStr:       Str32;        {type name}
    zoneStr:       Str32;        {zone name}
END;
EntityPtr = ^EntityName;
```

MPP Parameter Block for NBP

```
MPPParmType    =      (...RegisterNameParm, LookupNameParm,
                         ConfirmNameParm,RemoveNameParm...);
TYPE MPPParamBlock =
    PACKED RECORD
        qLink:                 QElemPtr;       {reserved}
        qType:                 Integer;        {reserved}
        ioTrap:                Integer;        {reserved}
        ioCmdAddr:             Ptr;            {reserved}
        ioCompletion:          ProcPtr;        {completion routine}
        ioResult:              OSErr;          {result code}
        ioNamePtr:             StringPtr;      {reserved}
        ioVRefNum:             Integer;        {reserved}
        ioRefNum:              Integer;        {driver reference number}
        csCode:                Integer;        {primary command code}
    CASE MPPParmType OF
        RegisterNameParm,
        LookupNameParm,
        ConfirmNameParm,
        RemoveNameParm:
            (interval:        Byte;            {retry interval}
             count:           Byte;            {retry count}
             entityPtr:       Ptr;            {pointer to entity name or }
                                              { names table entry}
            CASE MPPParmType OF
                RegisterNameParm:
                    (verifyFlag:   Byte;      {verify uniqueness of name or not}
                     filler3:      Byte;)
                LookupNameParm:
                    (retBuffPtr:   Ptr;        {pointer to return buffer}
                     retBuffSize:  Integer;    {return buffer size}
                     maxToGet:     Integer;    {matches to get}
                     numGotten:    Integer;)   {matches gotten}
```

```
        ConfirmNameParm:
            (confirmAddr:   AddrBlock;    {pointer to entity name}
             newSocket:     Byte;         {socket number}
             filler4:       Byte);
        )
    KillNBPParm:
        (nKillQEl:        Ptr;)          {pointer to queue element to cancel}
    END;


MPPPBPtr    =       ^MPPParamBlock;
```

Routines

Registering an Entity

```
PROCEDURE NBPSetNTE         (ntePtr: Ptr; nbpObject,nbpType,nbpZone: Str32;
                             socket: Integer);
FUNCTION PRegisterName      (thePBptr: MPPPBPtr; async: Boolean): OSErr;
```

Handling Name and Address Requests

```
PROCEDURE NBPSetEntity      (buffer: Ptr; nbpObject,nbpType,nbpZone: Str32);
FUNCTION PLookupName        (thePBptr: MPPPBPtr; async: Boolean): OSErr;
FUNCTION NBPExtract         (theBuffer: Ptr; numInBuf: Integer; whichOne:
                             Integer; VAR abEntity: EntityName; VAR address:
                             AddrBlock): OSErr;
FUNCTION PConfirmName       (thePBptr: MPPPBPtr; async: Boolean): OSErr;
FUNCTION PRemoveName        (thePBptr: MPPPBPtr; async: Boolean): OSErr;
FUNCTION PKillNBP           (thePBptr: MPPPBPtr; async: Boolean): OSErr;
```

C Summary

Constants

```
/*NBP parameter constants*/
#define MPPioCompletion MPP.ioCompletion
#define MPPioResult MPP.ioResult
#define MPPioRefNum MPP.ioRefNum
#define MPPcsCode MPP.csCode
#define NBPinterval NBP.interval
#define NBPcount NBP.count
```

```
#define NBPntQElPtr NBP.NBPPtrs.ntQElPtr
#define NBPentityPtr NBP.NBPPtrs.entityPtr
#define NBPverifyFlag NBP.parm.verifyFlag
#define NBPretBuffPtr NBP.parm.Lookup.retBuffPtr
#define NBPretBuffSize NBP.parm.Lookup.retBuffSize
#define NBPmaxToGet NBP.parm.Lookup.maxToGet
#define NBPnumGotten NBP.parm.Lookup.numGotten
#define NBPconfirmAddr NBP.parm.Confirm.confirmAddr
#define NBPnKillQEl NBPKILL.nKillQEl
#define NBPnewSocket NBP.parm.Confirm.newSocket
```

```
enum {                              /*.MPP driver unit and reference */
                                    /* number*/
   mppUnitNum     =    9,           /*.MPP driver unit number*/
   mppRefNum      =    -10};        /*MPP reference number*/


enum {                              /*.MPP csCodes*/
   confirmName    =    250,         /*confirm name*/
   lookupName     =    251,         /*lookup name*/
   removeName     =    252,         /*remove name from names table*/
   registerName   =    253,         /*register name in names table*/
   killNBP        =    254};        /*kill outstanding NBP request*/
```

Data Types

Address Block Record

```
struct AddrBlock {
   short          aNet;      /*network name*/
   unsigned char  aNode;     /*node name*/
   unsigned char  aSocket;   /*socket number*/
};

typedef struct AddrBlock AddrBlock;
```

Names Table Entry Data Structure

```
struct {
   Ptr          qNext;             /*pointer to next names table element*/
   NTElement    nt;
}NamesTableEntry;
```

Entity Name Record

```
struct EntityName {
    Str32           objStr;         /*object name*/
    char            pad1;           /*Str32's aligned on even word boundaries*/
    Str32           typeStr;        /*type name*/
    char            pad2;
    Str32           zoneStr;        /*zone name*/
    char            pad3;
};


typedef struct EntityName EntityName;
typedef EntityName *EntityPtr;
```

MPP Parameter Block for NBP

```
#define MPPATPHeader \
    QElem           *qLink;         /*reserved*/\
    short           qType;          /*reserved*/\
    short           ioTrap;         /*reserved*/\
    Ptr             ioCmdAddr;      /*reserved*/\
    ProcPtr         ioCompletion;   /*completion routine*/\
    OSErr           ioResult;       /*result code*/\
    long            userData;       /*command result (ATP user bytes)*/\
    short           reqTID;         /*request transaction ID*/\
    short           ioRefNum;       /*driver reference number*/\
    short           csCode;         /*primary command code*/

typedef struct {
    MPPATPHeader
}MPPparms;

typedef struct {
    MPPATPHeader
    char            interval;       /*retry interval*/
    char            count;          /*retry count*/
    union {
        Ptr             ntQElPtr;   /*pointer to queue element to cancel*/
        Ptr             entityPtr;

                                    /*pointer to entity name or names */
                                    /* table entry*/

    } NBPPtrs;
```

```
    union {
        char            verifyFlag;     /*verify uniqueness of name or not*/
    struct {
        Ptr             retBuffPtr;     /*pointer to return buffer*/
        short           retBuffSize;    /*return buffer size*/
        short           maxToGet;       /*matches to get*/
        short           numGotten;      /*matches gotten*/
    } Lookup;
    struct {
            AddrBlock       confirmAddr; /*pointer to entity name*/
            char            newSocket;   /*socket number*/
        } Confirm;
    } parm;
}NBPparms;


struct {
    MPPATPHeader
    Ptr             nKillQEl;
                                        /*pointer to queue element to cancel*/
}NBPKillparms;

union ParamBlockRec {
    MPPparms        MPP;                /*general MPP parms*/
    NBPparms        NBP;                /*NBP calls*/
    NBPKillparms    NBPKILL;            /*cancel call to NBP*/
};
typedef MPPParamBlock *MPPPBPtr;
```

Routines

Registering an Entity

```
pascal void NBPSetNTE       (Ptr ntePtr, Ptr nbpObject, Ptr nbpType,
                             Ptr nbpZone, short socket);

pascal OSErr PRegisterName  (MPPPBPtr thePBpt, Boolean async);
```

Handling Name and Address Requests

```
pascal void NBPSetEntity    (Ptr buffer, Ptr nbpObject, Ptr nbpType,
                             Ptr nbpZone);

pascal OSErr PLookupName    (MPPPBPtr thePBptr, Boolean async);
```

```
pascal OSErr NBPExtract      (Ptr theBuffer, short numInBuf, short whichOne,
                              EntityName *abEntity, AddrBlock *address);
pascal OSErr PConfirmName    (MPPPBPtr thePBptr, Boolean async);
pascal OSErr PRemoveName     (MPPPBPtr thePBptr, Boolean async);
pascal OSErr PKillNBP        (MPPPBPtr thePBptr, Boolean async);
```

Assembly-Language Summary

Constants

Unit Number for the .MPP Driver

```
mppUnitNum        EQU   9              ;MPP unit number
```

NBP Symbolic Characters

```
equals            EQU   '='            ;wildcard symbol
NBPWildCard       EQU   '≈'            ;wildcard symbol
star              EQU   '*'            ;"This zone" symbol
```

NBP Command Codes

```
registerName      EQU   253            ;register name in names table
lookupReply       EQU   242            ;used internally
lookupName        EQU   251            ;look up an NBP name
confirmName       EQU   250            ;confirm name
removeName        EQU   252            ;remove name from names table
killNBP           EQU   254            ;kill outstanding NBP request
```

NBP Packet

```
nbp               EQU   $02            ;DDP protocol type code for NBP
nbpControl        EQU   0              ;control code
nbpTCount         EQU   0              ;tuple count
nbpID             EQU   1              ;NBP ID
nbpTuple          EQU   2              ;start of the first tuple
```

NBP Tuple Header Offsets

```
tupleNet          EQU   0              ;offset to network number (word)
tupleNode         EQU   2              ;offset to node ID (byte)
tupleSkt          EQU   3              ;offset to socket number (byte)
```

```
tupleEnum          EQU    4              ;offset to enumerator (byte)
tupleName          EQU    5              ;offset to name part of tuple (byte)
tupleAddrSz        EQU    5              ;tuple address field size
```

NBP Packet Types

```
brRq               EQU    1              ;broadcast request
lkUp               EQU    2              ;lookup request
lkUpReply          EQU    3              ;lookup reply
```

NBP Names Information Socket (NIS) Number

```
nis                EQU    2              ;NIS number
```

Maximum Number of Tuples in NBP Packet, Maximum Size of a Tuple Name

```
tupleMax           EQU    15             ;maximum number of tuples returned from
                                         ; a lookup request
NBPMaxTupleSize    EQU    32             ;maximum size of a tuple name
```

Data Structures

MPP Parameter Block Common Fields for NBP

0	qLink	long	reserved
4	qType	word	reserved
6	ioTrap	word	reserved
8	ioCmdAddr	long	reserved
12	ioCompletion	long	address of completion routine
16	ioResult	word	result code
18	ioNamePtr	long	reserved
22	ioVRefNum	word	reserved
24	ioRefNum	word	driver reference number

PRegisterName Parameter Variant

26	csCode	word	command code; always registerName
28	interval	byte	retry interval
29	count	byte	retry count
30	entityPtr (ntQElPtr)	long	names table queue element pointer
34	verifyFlag	byte	verify name flag
40	filler	byte	reserved

PLookupName Parameter Variant

26	csCode	word	command code; always lookupName
28	interval	byte	retry interval
29	count	byte	retry count
30	entityPtr	long	pointer to entity name
34	retBuffPtr	long	pointer to return data buffer
38	retBuffSize	word	size in bytes of return buffer
40	maxToGet	word	maximum number of matches to get
42	numGotten	word	number of matches returned

PConfirmName Parameter Variant

26	csCode	word	command code; always confirmName
28	interval	byte	retry interval
29	count	byte	retry count
30	entityPtr	long	pointer to entity name
34	confirmAddr	long	address of names table entry to confirm
38	newSocket	byte	socket number, if different from specified one
39	filler	byte	reserved

PRemoveName Parameter Variant

26	csCode	word	command code; always removeName
28	filler	word	reserved
30	entityPtr	long	pointer to entity name

PKillNBP Parameter Variant

26	csCode	word	command code; always killNBP
28	nKillQEl	long	pointer to queue element to remove

Result Codes

noErr	0	No error
nbpNoConfirm	−1025	Name not confirmed
nbpConfDiff	−1026	Name confirmed for different socket
nbpDuplicate	−1027	Name already exists
nbpNotFound	−1028	Name not found
tooManyReqs	−1097	Too many concurrent requests; wait a few minutes, then try the request again
cbNotFound	−1102	NBP queue element not found
reqAborted	−1105	Request canceled
extractErr	−3104	Can't find tuple in buffer

Zone Information Protocol (ZIP)

Contents

This chapter describes the Zone Information Protocol (ZIP) that maintains mappings of zone names to network numbers on internet routers. ZIP is primarily implemented by routers. A small portion of ZIP is implemented on nodes that are not routers to allow you to obtain zone information from a router node. This chapter describes only the portion of ZIP that is implemented on a node that is not a router.

You should read this chapter if you want to obtain

- the name of the zone to which the node belongs that is running your application

- the names of the zones for the local network to which your application's node is connected

- the names of all the zones that exist throughout the AppleTalk internet to which your local network belongs

The portion of ZIP that is implemented on nodes that are not routers uses the AppleTalk Transaction Protocol (ATP) to send requests for zone information to a router node. To better understand how ZIP handles your requests for information and returns to you responses to those requests, you should read the chapter "AppleTalk Transaction Protocol (ATP)" in this book.

For an overview of the Zone Information Protocol and how it fits within the AppleTalk protocol stack, read the chapter "Introduction to AppleTalk" in this book, which also introduces and defines some of the terminology used in this chapter. For a description of the Zone Information Protocol specification, see *Inside AppleTalk,* second edition.

About ZIP

The Zone Information Protocol (ZIP) provides applications and processes with access to zone names. A **zone** is a logical grouping of nodes in an AppleTalk internet, and each zone is identified by a name. A zone name is typically used to identify an affiliation between a group of nodes, such as a group of nodes belonging to a particular department within an organization.

ZIP maintains the mapping of networks and the zones they include for all networks belonging to an AppleTalk internet:

- Every node on a network belongs to a zone; a node can belong to only one zone at a time.

- A nonextended network contains only one zone, and all nodes in that network belong to the same zone.

- A single extended network can contain nodes that belong to up to 255 different zones. A single zone can include nodes that belong to different extended networks. Each AppleTalk extended network has associated with it a list of the zones to which its nodes can belong. A node joining the network can select its zone from this list.

On each router node in the internet, ZIP builds a zone information table that includes each network's number (extended networks have network number ranges) in association with the network's list of zones. Nodes that are not routers, such as end-user systems, do not contain a zone information table. However, a portion of ZIP is implemented on each nonrouter node so that applications and processes can gain access to their own node's zone name, names of all the zones on their local network, or names of all the zones throughout the internet. The .XPP driver implements the part of ZIP that is on nonrouter nodes, and it provides an interface that allows an application or process to request zone name information in a transaction-based dialog. ZIP uses the transaction-based services of ATP to transport requests from workstation nodes to router nodes. Figure 4-1 shows ZIP and its underlying protocols. The portion of ZIP that is implemented on nonrouter nodes, such as workstations, uses the services of ATP.

Figure 4-1   The Zone Information Protocol (ZIP) and the underlying AppleTalk protocols

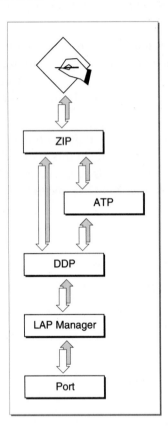

Using ZIP

The Zone Information Protocol provides three functions that you can use to obtain the names of registered zones. You can use these functions to obtain

■ the name of the zone to which your application and its node belong

■ the names of the zones in your local network or the names of all the zones that exist throughout the AppleTalk internet to which your local network belongs

Applications running on nodes connected to both extended and nonextended networks can use ZIP to get the name of their node's zone. An application running on a node that belongs to an extended network can call ZIP to get a list of all the zone names associated with that network. For example, a network administration application might use ZIP to provide an administrator with a list of the zones for a particular network so that the administrator can select the correct zone for a node when adding nodes to a network.

You can use ZIP in conjunction with NBP. For example, you can use ZIP to look up zones on the network, then use NBP to look up names in each zone.

ZIP sends the `GetMyZone`, `GetLocalZones`, and `GetZoneList` functions as AppleTalk Transaction Protocol (ATP) requests. These requests always ask for a single response. For example, when you call ZIP to request zone name information, the portion of ZIP implemented on the node running your application sends a request using the transaction-based services of ATP to the portion of ZIP implemented on a local router that contains the zone information table; using ATP, ZIP on the router node transmits a response to your request.

When you call `GetMyZone` to get the name of your node's zone, ZIP returns the complete zone name in a single ATP response and writes that zone name to the buffer you provide. However, when you want to retrieve a list of zone names belonging either to your local network or to all of the networks forming the internet, ZIP may not always be able to return the complete list of names in a single ATP response. In this case, you need to call the ZIP function repeatedly in a loop in order to retrieve all of the zone names.

The `GetMyZone`, `GetLocalZones`, and `GetZoneList` functions each use a parameter block of type `XPPParamBlock` to contain input and output values for the call. You use the `xCallParam` variant record to the XPP parameter block for the ZIP functions. This parameter block contains an `ioRefNum` field, which the MPW interface sets to the .XPP driver reference number.

The parameter block for each of the three ZIP functions includes a `csCode` field and an `xppSubCode` field. You do not need to set these field values before you call the function; the MPW interface fills in the value for each of these fields. The value for the `csCode` field is always `xCall`. The `xppSubCode` field value identifies the specific ZIP function, and it differs for each of the three functions.

For the three ZIP functions, you specify timeout and retry values that determine the behavior of the ATP transaction that the ZIP call relies on. You need to set values for these fields before you call the ZIP function. You use the parameter block's `xppTimeout` field to set the timeout value and the `xppRetry` field to set the retry value. The timeout tells ATP how long in seconds to wait between each attempt, and the retry value tells it how may retries it should attempt. For information on how ATP uses these values, see the chapter "AppleTalk Transaction Protocol (ATP)" in this book.

For each function, you supply a buffer to hold the returned zone name data and a buffer that ZIP requires for its own use. These two buffers and the `XPPParamBlock` parameter block that you allocate for the function belong to ZIP for the life of the call; you must not manipulate them or alter their contents during the operation. The memory for these buffers and the parameter block belongs to the function until the function completes execution.

If you set the function's `async` Boolean parameter to TRUE, either you must provide a completion routine or your application must poll the parameter block's `ioResult` field to determine when the function completes the operation. See the chapter "Introduction to AppleTalk" in this book for a discussion of synchronous and asynchronous execution as it applies to the Boolean parameter.

Getting the Name of Your Application's Zone

Your application can get the name of the zone for the node on which it is running by calling the `GetMyZone` function. The zone name is a data structure of type `Str32`, and the `GetMyZone` function writes the zone name to a buffer that you supply. You set the parameter block's `zipBuffPtr` field to a pointer for a buffer that must be at least 33 bytes in size.

You also supply a buffer that is 70 bytes in size as the value of the `zipInfoField`. You must set the first word of this buffer to 0 before you call the function. This buffer is for ZIP to use.

Listing 4-1 shows the application-defined `DoGetMyZone` function, which illustrates the use of the `GetMyZone` function. The `DoGetMyZone` function declares the parameter block and the return buffer. Then it assigns values to the some of parameter block fields and initializes to 0 the first word of the `zipInfoField` parameter before it calls `GetMyZone`. The MPW interface fills in the XPP parameter block `ioRefNum`, `csCode`, and `xppSubCode` fields, so the `DoGetMyZone` function doesn't need to assign these values.

Listing 4-1   Using the `GetMyZone` function

```
FUNCTION DoGetMyZone(VAR myZoneName: Str32): OSErr;
VAR
    xppPB: XPPParamBlock;
    myZoneName:     ARRAY[1..33] OF Char;
BEGIN
    WITH xppPB DO
        BEGIN
            xppTimeout := 3;              {timeout interval}
            xppRetry := 4;                {retry count for ZIP requests}
            zipBuffPtr := @myZoneName; {buffer for returned zone name}
            zipInfoField[1] := 0;         {initialize first word to 0}
            zipInfoField[2] := 0;
        END;
    DoGetMyZone := GetMyZone(@xppPB, FALSE);
END;
```

If there is no router present in the network, the function returns a function result of `noBridgeErr`. If the retry count is exceeded before the ATP transaction that ZIP relies on receives a valid response, the function returns a function result of `reqFailed`. The function returns a function result of `tooManyReq` when too many concurrent ATP requests have been made. If you receive a function result of `tooManyReq`, wait a minute or so, and then try again; some transactions can take up to 30 seconds to complete. For the complete list of function results, see the description of the function `GetMyZone` beginning on page 4-12.

Getting a List of Zone Names for Your Local Network or Its Internet

If your application is running on a node that belongs to an extended network, the application can use the `GetLocalZones` function to obtain a list of the names of the zones in its node's local network. An application running on a node that belongs to an extended network can also use the `GetZoneList` function to obtain a list of the names of the zones throughout the AppleTalk internet to which its node's local network belongs. These functions behave similarly.

ZIP returns a single ATP response per request. Because the complete list of zone names may not fit in a single ATP response, you need to make repeated calls to either `GetLocalZones` or `GetZoneList` until you receive all of the zone names. You must allocate a buffer to hold the zone names data that the ZIP function returns and point to that buffer from the function's `zipBuffPtr` parameter block field. This buffer must be 578 bytes in size, large enough to hold an entire ATP response. ZIP returns the zone names into this buffer as a packed array of packed Pascal strings.

The `zipNumZones` field returns the actual number of zone names that ZIP placed in the buffer. You must set the `zipLastFlag` field to 0 before you execute the `GetZoneList` or `GetLocalZones` function. If the `zipLastFlag` parameter is still 0 when the command has completed execution, then ZIP is waiting to return more zone names. In this case you must empty the buffer, or allocate a new one, and call the `GetZoneList` or `GetLocalZones` function again immediately. When there are no more zone names to return, ZIP sets the `zipLastFlag` field to a nonzero value. The `zipInfoField` field is a 70-byte data buffer that you must allocate for use by ZIP. The first time you call any of these functions, you must set the first word of this field to 0. You must not change any values in this field subsequently.

Listing 4-2 shows the application-defined `DoGetZoneList` function, which illustrates how to use the `GetZoneList` function. The `GetLocalZones` function operates in exactly the same fashion.

This `DoGetZoneList` function allocates a buffer for zone names and repeatedly calls the `GetZoneList` function to get a list of zone names. If `GetZoneList` returns a function result of `noErr`, then the `DoGetZoneList` code calls the application-defined `MyZIPExtract` function, shown in Listing 4-3, to remove a zone name from the `GetZoneList` buffer and place it in the application's buffer. The `DoGetZoneList` code in Listing 4-2 does not show the application-defined `MyAddToZoneList` that writes the zone name to the application's buffer.

Listing 4-2   Using `GetZoneList` to retrieve names of zones throughout the AppleTalk internet

```
FUNCTION DoGetZoneList: OSErr;
CONST
    kZoneBufferSize = 578;                  {required size of zone list buffer}
VAR
    xppPB: XPPParamBlock;
    result: OSErr;
    zoneBuffer: Ptr;
    index: Integer;
    zoneName: Str32;
BEGIN
    {Allocate buffer for returned zone names.}
    zoneBuffer := NewPtr(kZoneBufferSize);
    IF zoneBuffer = NIL THEN
        result := MemError
    ELSE
    BEGIN
        WITH xppPB DO
        BEGIN
            xppTimeout := 3;                {timeout interval}
            xppRetry := 4;                  {retry count}
            zipBuffPtr := zoneBuffer;       {zone names returned here}
            zipLastFlag := 0;               {set to 0 first time through}
            zipInfoField[1] := 0;           {first word of zipInfoField must be }
            zipInfoField[2] := 0;           { initialized to 0 the first time}
        END;

        {Loop to get all of the zone names.}
        REPEAT
            result := GetZoneList(@xppPB, FALSE);
            IF (result = noErr) THEN
                FOR index := 1 TO xppPB.zipNumZones DO
                    IF MyZIPExtract(zoneBuffer, xppPB.zipNumZones, index,
                                zoneName) = noErr THEN
                        MyAddToZoneList(zoneName);
        UNTIL (xppPB.zipLastFlag <> 0) OR (result <> noErr);
        DisposPtr(zoneBuffer);              {release memory}
    END;
    DoGetZoneList := result;
END;
```

When you call the `GetZoneList` function or the `GetLocalZones` function to obtain a list of zone names, ZIP returns the zone names as a packed array of packed Pascal strings. Your application must include a routine to extract the zone names that you want from the buffer.

Listing 4-3 shows an application-defined function called `MyZipExtract` that extracts a particular zone name from the buffer of packed zone names returned by either `GetZoneList` or `GetLocalZones`.

The `MyZipExtract` function takes a `numInBuf` input parameter that specifies the number of zone names in the buffer pointed to by the `theBuffer` parameter. For the `numInBuf` parameter, you specify the value that ZIP returned in the `zipNumZones` field of the XPP parameter block used for the `GetZoneList` or `GetLocalZones` function.

You use the `whichOne` input parameter to identify the zone name to extract. The `MyZIPExtract` function returns the zone name in the `zoneName` string parameter.

The `MyZIPExtract` function returns a result of `paramErr` if `whichOne` is 0 or `whichOne` is greater than the number of zones in the buffer. Otherwise, the function returns a function result of `noErr`.

Listing 4-3   Extracting a zone name from the list of zone names returned in the buffer

```
FUNCTION MyZIPExtract (theBuffer: Ptr; numInBuf: Integer; whichOne: Integer;
                  VAR zoneName: Str32): OSErr;
VAR
    result: OSErr;
    zonePtr: Ptr;
BEGIN
    {preflight the input parameters}
    IF (whichOne = 0) OR (whichOne > numInBuf) THEN
        result := paramErr
    ELSE
    BEGIN
        zonePtr := theBuffer;
        {Look for whichOne}
        REPEAT
            whichOne := whichOne - 1;
            IF whichOne <> 0 THEN
                {move pointer to next zone name}
                zonePtr := Ptr(ORD4(zonePtr) +
                    Length(StringPtr(zonePtr)^) + 1);
        UNTIL whichOne = 0;
                {return the zone name}
        BlockMove(zonePtr, @zoneName,
                Length(StringPtr(zonePtr)^) + 1);
        result := noErr;
    END;
    MyZIPExtract := result;
END;
```

ZIP Reference

This section describes the data structure and the functions that are specific to the Zone Information Protocol (ZIP). The "Data Structures" section shows the Pascal data structure for the XPP parameter block. The "Routines" section describes the ZIP functions.

Data Structures

This section describes the XPP parameter block that you use to provide information to and receive it from ZIP.

The XPP Parameter Block for ZIP

The Zone Information Protocol's `GetMyZone`, `GetLocalZones`, and `GetZoneList` functions implemented by the .XPP driver use the `xCallParam` variant record to the XPP parameter block defined by the `XPPParamBlock` data type. Your application uses this parameter block to specify input values to and receive output values from a ZIP function. This section defines the parameter block fields that are common to all of the ZIP functions and that are filled in by the MPW interface or returned by the function; your application does not need to fill in these fields. This section does not define reserved fields, which are used either internally by the .XPP driver or not at all. The fields for the `xCallParam` variant record are defined in the function descriptions.

```
TYPE XPPParamBlock =
    PACKED RECORD
        qLink:          QElemPtr;   {reserved}
        qType:          Integer;    {reserved}
        ioTrap:         Integer;    {reserved}
        ioCmdAddr:      Ptr;        {reserved}
        ioCompletion:   ProcPtr;    {completion routine}
        ioResult:       OSErr;      {result code}
        cmdResult:      LongInt;    {reserved}
        ioVRefNum:      Integer;    {reserved}
        ioRefNum:       Integer;    {driver reference number}
        csCode:         Integer;    {primary command code}
    CASE XPPPrmBlkType OF
        xCallParam
            xppSubCode: Integer;    {secondary command code}
            xppTimeout: Byte;       {.XPP timeout period}
            xppRetry:   Byte;       {retry count}
            filler1:    Integer;    {reserved}
```

```
             zipBuffPtr:     Ptr;          {returned zone names}
             zipNumZones:    Integer;      {number of zones returned}
             zipLastFlag:    Byte;         {nonzero when all zone names }
                                           { have been returned}
             filler2:        Byte;         {reserved}
             zipInfoField:   PACKED ARRAY[1..70] OF Byte;
                                           {reserved}
END;
XPPParmBlkPtr = ^XPPParamBlock;
```

Field descriptions

ioCompletion	A pointer to a completion routine that you can provide. When you execute a function asynchronously, the .XPP driver calls your completion routine when it completes execution of the function if you specify a pointer to the routine as the value of this field. Specify NIL for this field if you do not wish to provide a completion routine. If you execute a function synchronously, the .XPP driver ignores the ioCompletion field. For information about completion routines, see the chapter "Introduction to AppleTalk" in this book.
ioResult	The result of the function. When you execute the function asynchronously, the function sets this field to 1 and returns a function result of noErr as soon as the function begins execution. When the function completes execution, it sets the ioResult field to the actual result code.
ioRefNum	The .XPP driver reference number. The MPW interface fills in this field.
csCode	The command code of the XPP command to be executed. The MPW interface fills in this field.

Routines

This section describes the ZIP functions. The ZIP functions allow you to

■ obtain the name of the zone to which the node belongs that is running your application

■ obtain a list of all the zones for the local network of the node that is running your application

■ obtain a list of all the zones associated with the internet that the node running your application belongs to

An arrow preceding a parameter indicates whether the parameter is an input parameter, an output parameter, or both:

Arrow	Meaning
→	Input
←	Output
↔	Both

Obtaining Zone Information

This section describes the Zone Information Protocol (ZIP) functions: GetMyZone, GetLocalZones, and GetZoneList. The GetMyZone function returns the name of the zone that your application's node belongs to. The GetLocalZones function returns a list of zone names on the local network that your application's node belongs to. The GetZoneList function returns a complete list of zones on the internet that your application's node belongs to.

Assembly-language note

The .XPP driver functions all use the same value (xCall, which is equal to 246) for the csCode parameter to the XPP parameter block. The xCall routine uses the value of the xppSubCode parameter to distinguish between the functions, as follows:

Function	xppSubCode	Value
GetMyZone	zipGetMyZone	7
GetLocalZones	zipGetLocalZones	5
GetZoneList	zipGetZoneList	6 ◆

GetMyZone

The GetMyZone function returns the zone name of the node on which your application is running.

```
FUNCTION GetMyZone (thePBptr: XPPParmBlkPtr;
                    async: Boolean): OSErr;
```

thePBptr   A pointer to an XPP parameter block.

async   A Boolean that indicates whether the function should be executed asynchronously or synchronously. Specify TRUE for asynchronous execution.

Parameter block

→	ioCompletion	ProcPtr	A pointer to a completion routine.
←	ioResult	OSErr	The function result.
→	csCode	Integer	Always xCall for this function.
→	xppSubCode	Integer	Always zipGetMyZone for this function.
→	xppTimeout	Byte	The retry interval in seconds.
→	xppRetry	Byte	The retry count.
→	zipBuffPtr	Ptr	A pointer to data buffer.
→	zipInfoField	PACKED ARRAY	A data buffer for use by ZIP; first word set to 0.

Field descriptions

xppSubCode	A routine selector. This field is automatically set by the MPW interface to zipGetMyZone for this function.
xppTimeout	The amount of time, in seconds, that the .ATP driver should wait between attempts to obtain the data. A value of 3 or 4 seconds for the xppTimeout field is usually sufficient.
xppRetry	The number of times the .ATP driver should attempt to obtain the data before returning the request failed (reqFailed) result code. A value of 3 or 4 is usually sufficient.
zipBuffPtr	A pointer to a 33-byte data buffer that you must allocate. ZIP returns the zone name into this buffer as a Pascal string.
zipInfoField	A 70-byte data buffer that you must allocate and initialize for use by ZIP. You must set the first word of this buffer to 0 before you call the GetMyZone function.

DESCRIPTION

Before you call GetMyZone, you must allocate a buffer that is 33 bytes in size and set the zipBuffPtr parameter block field to point to this buffer. ZIP writes the zone name that it retrieves to this buffer that you supply. You must also supply a buffer that is 70 bytes in size as the value of the zipInfoField field. This buffer is for ZIP to use. An application running on a node on either an extended or a nonextended network can use this function to retrieve the node's zone name.

SPECIAL CONSIDERATIONS

The memory that you allocate for the parameter block and the two buffers required by the GetMyZone function belongs to the .XPP driver until the function completes execution. You can reuse the memory or dispose of it after the operation completes.

ASSEMBLY-LANGUAGE INFORMATION

To execute the GetMyZone function from assembly language, call the _Control trap macro with a value of xCall in the csCode field of the parameter block and a value of zipGetMyZone in the xppSubCode field of the parameter block. To execute this function from assembly language, you must also specify the .XPP driver reference number.

RESULT CODES

noErr	0	No error
noBridgeErr	–93	No router is available
reqFailed	–1096	Request to contact router failed; retry count exceeded
tooManyReqs	–1097	Too many concurrent requests
noDataArea	–1104	Too many outstanding ATP calls

SEE ALSO

For the XPPParamBlock data type, see "The XPP Parameter Block for ZIP" beginning on page 4-10.

To get the correct reference number for the .XPP driver, you can use the Device Manager's OpenDriver function, which returns the driver reference number. For information about the OpenDriver function, see the chapter "Device Manager" in *Inside Macintosh: Devices*.

GetLocalZones

The GetLocalZones function returns a list of all the zone names on the local network—that is, the network that includes the node on which your application is running.

```
FUNCTION GetLocalZones (thePBptr: XPPParmBlkPtr;
                        async: Boolean): OSErr;
```

thePBptr   A pointer to an XPP parameter block.

async   A Boolean that indicates whether the function should be executed
              asynchronously or synchronously. Specify TRUE for asynchronous
              execution.

Parameter block

→	ioCompletion	ProcPtr	A pointer to a completion routine.
←	ioResult	OSErr	The function result code.
→	csCode	Integer	Always xCall for this function.
→	xppSubCode	Integer	Always zipGetLocalZones.
→	xppTimeout	Byte	The retry interval in seconds.
→	xppRetry	Byte	The retry count.
→	zipBuffPtr	Ptr	A pointer to data buffer.
←	zipNumZones	Integer	The number of names returned.
←	zipLastFlag	Byte	A flag that is nonzero if there are no more names.
→	zipInfoField	PACKED ARRAY	A data buffer for use by ZIP; first word set to 0.

Field descriptions

xppSubCode   A routine selector. This field is automatically set by the MPW
               interface to zipGetLocalZones for this function.

xppTimeout   The amount of time, in seconds, that the .ATP driver should wait
               between attempts to obtain the data. A value of 3 or 4 seconds for
               the xppTimeout field is usually sufficient.

xppRetry   The number of times the .ATP driver should attempt to obtain the
               data before returning the request failed (reqFailed) result code. A
               value of 3 or 4 is usually sufficient.

`zipBuffPtr`	A pointer to a 578-byte data buffer that you must allocate. ZIP returns the zone names into this buffer as a packed array of Pascal strings.
`zipNumZones`	The number of zone names that ZIP placed in the data buffer.
`zipLastFlag`	A value that indicates if there are more zone names for your network beyond those that ZIP returned in the `zipBuffPtr` field. The .XPP driver sets this field to 1 if there are no more zone names for your network.
`zipInfoField`	A 70-byte data buffer that you must allocate for use by ZIP. You must set the first word of this buffer to 0 before you call the `GetLocalZones` function the first time through the loop, and you must not change the contents of this field thereafter.

DESCRIPTION

A single extended network can have more than one zone associated with it. Your application can use the `GetLocalZones` function to retrieve the list of zones for its node's local network. The `GetLocalZones` function uses ATP to retrieve the zone information. The buffer that you allocate to hold the returned zone names is the size of a single ATP response. You must call the `GetLocalZones` function repeatedly until all of the zones for the local network have been returned.

Your application must check the `zipLastFlag` field to determine if there are more zone names for your network. If the value of this field is 1, there are no more zone names for your local network. If the value of this field is still 0 when the `GetLocalZones` function completes execution, you must empty the data buffer pointed to by the `zipBuffPtr` parameter and immediately call the `GetLocalZones` function again without changing the value in the `zipInfoField` parameter.

If you receive a `GetLocalZones` function result of `tooManyReqs`, wait a minute or so, and then try again; some transactions can take up to 30 seconds to complete.

This function works for extended networks only. If the node that is running your application is on a nonextended network and you want the name of that node's zone, use the `GetMyZone` function.

SPECIAL CONSIDERATIONS

The memory that you allocate for the parameter block and the two buffers required by the `GetLocalZones` function belongs to the .XPP driver until the function completes execution. You can reuse the memory or dispose of it after the operation completes.

ASSEMBLY-LANGUAGE INFORMATION

To execute the `GetLocalZones` function from assembly language, call the `_Control` trap macro with a value of `xCall` in the `csCode` field of the parameter block and a value of `zipGetLocalZones` in the `xppSubCode` field of the parameter block. To execute this function from assembly language, you must also specify the .XPP driver reference number.

RESULT CODES

noErr	0	No error
noBridgeErr	–93	No router is available
reqFailed	–1096	Request to contact router failed; retry count exceeded
tooManyReqs	–1097	Too many concurrent requests
noDataArea	–1104	Too many outstanding ATP calls

SEE ALSO

For the XPPParamBlock data type, see "The XPP Parameter Block for ZIP" beginning on page 4-10.

To get the correct reference number for the .XPP driver, you can use the Device Manager's OpenDriver function, which returns the driver reference number. For information about the OpenDriver function, see the chapter "Device Manager" in *Inside Macintosh: Devices*.

GetZoneList

The GetZoneList function returns a complete list of all the zone names on the internet.

```
FUNCTION GetZoneList (thePBptr: XPPParmBlkPtr;
                      async: Boolean): OSErr;
```

thePBptr   A pointer to an XPP parameter block.

async   A Boolean that indicates whether the function should be executed asynchronously or synchronously. Specify TRUE for asynchronous execution.

Parameter block

→	ioCompletion	ProcPtr	A pointer to a completion routine.
←	ioResult	OSErr	The function result.
→	csCode	Integer	Always xCall for this function.
→	xppSubCode	Integer	Always zipGetZoneList for this function.
→	xppTimeout	Byte	The retry interval in seconds.
→	xppRetry	Byte	The retry count.
→	zipBuffPtr	Ptr	A pointer to data buffer.
←	zipNumZones	Integer	The number of names returned.
←	zipLastFlag	Byte	A flag that is nonzero if there are no more names.
→	zipInfoField	PACKED ARRAY	A data buffer for use by ZIP; first word set to 0.

Field descriptions

`xppSubCode`	A routine selector. This field is automatically set by the MPW interface to `zipGetZoneList` for this function.
`xppTimeout`	The amount of time, in seconds, that the .ATP driver should wait between attempts to obtain the data. A value of 3 or 4 seconds for the `xppTimeout` field generally gives good results.
`xppRetry`	The number of times the .ATP driver should attempt to obtain the data before returning the request failed (`reqFailed`) result code. A value of 3 or 4 is usually sufficient.
`zipBuffPtr`	A pointer to a 578-byte data buffer that you must allocate. ZIP returns the zone names into this buffer as a packed array of Pascal strings.
`zipNumZones`	The number of zone names that ZIP placed in the data buffer.
`zipLastFlag`	A value that indicates if there are more zone names for your network beyond those that ZIP returned in the `zipBuffPtr` field. The .XPP driver sets this field to 1 if there are no more zone names for your network.
`zipInfoField`	A 70-byte data buffer that you must allocate for use by ZIP. Typically, you call `GetZoneList` repeatedly from within a loop. You must set the first word of this buffer to 0 before you call the `GetZoneList` function the first time through the loop, and you must not change the contents of this field thereafter.

DESCRIPTION

The `GetZoneList` function returns a complete list of all the zone names on the internet to which the local network of the node running your application belongs. The `GetZoneList` function uses ATP to retrieve the zone information. The buffer that you allocate to hold the returned zone names is the size of a single ATP response. You must call the `GetZoneList` function repeatedly until all of the zones for the local network have been returned.

Your application must check the `zipLastFlag` field to determine if there are more zone names for your network. If the value of this field is 1, there are no more zone names for your local network. If the value of this field is still 0 when the `GetZoneList` function completes execution, you must empty the data buffer pointed to by the `zipBuffPtr` parameter and immediately call the `GetZoneList` function again without changing the value in the `zipInfoField` parameter.

If you receive a `GetZoneList` function result of `tooManyReqs`, wait a minute or so, and then try again; some transactions can take up to 30 seconds to complete.

To obtain a list of only the zone names on the local network, use the `GetLocalZones` function instead. If you use the `GetZoneList` function on a nonextended network, the function returns the `reqFailed` result code.

SPECIAL CONSIDERATIONS

The memory that you allocate for the parameter block and the two buffers required by the GetZoneList function belongs to the .XPP driver until the function completes execution. You can reuse the memory or dispose of it after the operation completes.

ASSEMBLY-LANGUAGE INFORMATION

To execute the GetZoneList function from assembly language, call the _Control trap macro with a value of xCall in the csCode field of the parameter block and a value of zipGetZoneList in the xppSubCode field of the parameter block. To execute this function from assembly language, you must also specify the .XPP driver reference number.

RESULT CODES

noErr	0	No error
noBridgeErr	–93	No router is available
reqFailed	–1096	Request to contact router failed; retry count exceeded
tooManyReqs	–1097	Too many concurrent requests
noDataArea	–1104	Too many outstanding ATP calls

SEE ALSO

For the XPPParamBlock data type, see "The XPP Parameter Block for ZIP" beginning on page 4-10.

To get the correct reference number for the .XPP driver, you can use the Device Manager's OpenDriver function, which returns the driver reference number. For information about the OpenDriver function, see the chapter "Device Manager" in *Inside Macintosh: Devices*.

Summary of ZIP

Pascal Summary

Constants

```
CONST
   {csCode for .XPP extended calls}
   xCall           =    246;

   {.XPP driver unit and reference number}
   xppUnitNum      =    40;
   xppRefNum       =    -41;

   {routine selectors}
   zipGetLocalZones =   5;      {routine selector for local zone names}
   zipGetZoneList   =   6;      {routine selector for internet zone list}
   zipGetMyZone     =   7;      {routine selector for node's zone name}
```

Data Types

The XPP Parameter Block for ZIP

```
TYPE XPPParamBlock =
     PACKED RECORD
         qLink:              QElemPtr;   {reserved}
         qType:              Integer;    {reserved}
         ioTrap:             Integer;    {reserved}
         ioCmdAddr:          Ptr;        {reserved}
         ioCompletion:       ProcPtr;    {completion routine}
         ioResult:           OSErr;      {result code}
         cmdResult:          LongInt;    {reserved}
         ioVRefNum:          Integer;    {reserved}
         ioRefNum:           Integer;    {driver reference number}
         csCode:             Integer;    {primary command code}
```

```
        CASE XPPPrmBlkType OF
          xCallParam
              xppSubCode:    Integer;    {secondary command code}
              xppTimeout:    Byte;       {timeout period for .XPP}
              xppRetry:      Byte;       {retry count}
              filler1:       Integer;    {reserved}
              zipBuffPtr:    Ptr;        {returned zone names}
              zipNumZones:   Integer;    {number of zones returned}
              zipLastFlag:   Byte;       {nonzero when all zone }
                                         { names have been returned}
              filler2:       Byte;       {reserved}
              zipInfoField:  PACKED ARRAY[1..70] OF Byte;
                                         {reserved for use by .XPP}
        END;
        XPPParmBlkPtr = ^XPPParamBlock;
```

Routines

Obtaining Zone Information

```
FUNCTION GetMyZone          (thePBptr: XPPParmBlkPtr; async: Boolean): OSErr;
FUNCTION GetLocalZones      (thePBptr: XPPParmBlkPtr; async: Boolean): OSErr;
FUNCTION GetZoneList        (thePBptr: XPPParmBlkPtr; async: Boolean): OSErr;
```

C Summary

Constants

```
/*MPP parameter constants*/
#define MPPioCompletion MPP.ioCompletion
#define MPPioResult MPP.ioResult
#define MPPioRefNum MPP.ioRefNum
#define MPPcsCode MPP.csCode

enum {                              /*.XPP csCode*/
   xCall          =    246};        /*csCode for .XPP extended calls*/

enum {                              /*.XPP driver unit and reference */
                                    /* numbers*/
   xppUnitNum     =    40,          /*XPP unit number */
   xppRefNum      =    -41};        /*XPP reference number */
```

```
enum {                              /*XPP routine selectors*/
    zipGetLocalZones    =   5,      /*routine selector for local zone names*/
    zipGetZoneList      =   6,      /*routine selector for internet zone list*/
    zipGetMyZone        =   7};     /*routine selector for node's zone name*/
```

Data Types

The XPP Parameter Block for ZIP

```
#define XPPPBHeader
    QElem           *qLink;                 /*reserved*/\
    short           qType;                  /*reserved*/\
    short           ioTrap;                 /*reserved */\
    Ptr             ioCmdAddr;              /*reserved*/\
    ProcPtr         ioCompletion;           /*completion routine*/\
    OSErr           ioResult;               /*result code*/\
    long            cmdResult;              /*reserved*/\
    short           ioVRefNum;              /*reserved*/\
    short           ioRefNum;               /*driver reference number*/
    short           csCode;                 /*primary command code*/

typedef struct {
    XPPPBHeader
        short       xppSubCode;             /*secondary command code*/
        char        xppTimeout;             /*retry interval in seconds*/
        char        xppRetry;               /*retry count*/
        short       filler1;
        Ptr         zipBuffPtr;             /*pointer to buffer of 578 bytes*/
        short       zipNumZones;            /*number of zone names in response*/
        char        zipLastFlag;            /*nonzero if no more zones*/
        char        filler2;                /*filler*/
        char        zipInfoField[70];       /*initial call, set first word to 0*/
}XCallParam;
```

Routines

Obtaining Zone Information

```
pascal OSErr GetMyZone       (XPPParmBlkPtr thePBptr, Boolean async);
pascal OSErr GetLocalZones   (XPPParmBlkPtr thePBptr, Boolean async);
pascal OSErr GetZoneList     (XPPParmBlkPtr thePBptr, Boolean async);
```

Assembly-Language Summary

Constants

XPP csCode

```
xCall            EQU      246    ;csCode for XPP extended calls
```

XPP Driver Unit Reference Number

```
xppUnitNum       EQU      9      ;XPP unit number
```

XPP xCall Subcodes for ZIP Commands

```
ZGetMyZone       EQU      7      ;selector for GetMyZone command
ZGetZoneList     EQU      8      ;selector for GetZoneList command
ZGetLocalZones   EQU      9      ;selector for GetLocalZones command
```

Data Structures

XPP Parameter Block Common Fields for ZIP Routines

0	qLink	long	reserved
4	qType	word	reserved
6	ioTrap	word	reserved
8	ioCmdAddr	long	reserved
12	ioCompletion	long	address of completion routine
16	ioResult	word	result code
18	cmdResult	long	reserved
22	ioVRefNum	word	reserved
24	ioRefNum	word	driver reference number

GetMyZone

28	xppSubCode	word	always `zipGetZoneList` for this function
30	xppTimeout	byte	retry interval in seconds
31	xppRetry	byte	retry count
34	zipBuffPtr	long	pointer to data buffer
42	zipInfoField	70 bytes	data buffer for use by ZIP; first word set to 0

GetLocalZones

28	xppSubCode	word	always `zipGetLocalZones` for this function
30	xppTimeout	byte	retry interval in seconds
31	xppRetry	byte	retry count
34	zipBuffPtr	long	pointer to data buffer
38	zipNumZones	word	number of names returned
40	zipLastFlag	byte	nonzero if no more names
42	zipInfoField	70 bytes	data buffer for use by ZIP; first word set to 0

GetZoneList

28	xppSubCode	word	always `zipGetZoneList` for this function
30	xppTimeout	byte	retry interval in seconds
31	xppRetry	byte	retry count
34	zipBuffPtr	long	pointer to data buffer
38	zipNumZones	word	number of names returned
40	zipLastFlag	byte	nonzero if no more names
42	zipInfoField	70 bytes	data buffer for use by ZIP; first word set to 0

Result Codes

noErr	0	No error
noBridgeErr	−93	No router is available
reqFailed	−1096	Request to contact router failed; retry count exceeded
tooManyReqs	−1097	Too many concurrent requests
noDataArea	−1104	Too many outstanding ATP calls

4

Zone Information Protocol (ZIP)

AppleTalk Data Stream Protocol (ADSP)

Contents

This chapter describes the AppleTalk Data Stream Protocol (ADSP) that you use to establish a session to exchange data between two network processes or applications in which both parties have equal control over the communication. You should read this chapter if you want to write an application that supports the exchange of more than a small amount of data between two parties who each can both send and receive streams of data.

This chapter also describes the AppleTalk Secure Data Stream Protocol (ASDSP), a secure version of ADSP, that allows users of your application to communicate over an ADSP session after the users' identities have been authenticated. Users can then exchange encrypted data over the session. For your application to use ASDSP, the system on which it runs must have the AppleTalk Open Collaboration Environment (AOCE) software installed and must have access to an AOCE server. To use ASDSP, you must also use the Authentication Manager, which is a component of the AOCE software. For information on the Authentication Manager, refer to *Inside Macintosh: AOCE Application Programming Interfaces.*

ASDSP enhances ADSP with authentication and encryption features. When this chapter discusses components of ADSP, such as connection ends and connection listeners, you can assume that the information also applies to ASDSP. The sections in this chapter that discuss ASDSP describe any specific differences between it and the standard version of ADSP. To use ASDSP, you should be familiar with ADSP.

For an overview of ADSP and how it fits within the AppleTalk protocol stack, read the chapter "Introduction to AppleTalk" in this book, which also introduces and defines some of the terminology used in this chapter. For a complete explanation of the ADSP specification, see *Inside AppleTalk,* second edition.

About ADSP

ADSP includes both session and transport services, and it is the most commonly used of the AppleTalk transport protocols. The .DSP driver implements ADSP. ADSP allows you to establish and maintain a connection between two AppleTalk network entities and transfer data across this connection as a continuous stream. Because ADSP is a client of DDP, data that you transmit using ADSP is actually sent and received over the AppleTalk internet in packets. However, ADSP builds a session connection on top of the packet transfer services that DDP provides so that applications using ADSP can exchange data as a continuous stream. Figure 5-1 on page 5-4 shows ADSP and the underlying protocols that it uses; ADSP is a client of DDP, just as your application is a client of ADSP.

Figure 5-1   ADSP and its underlying protocols

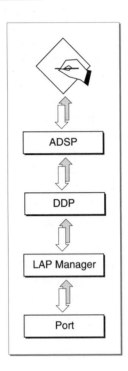

Communication between two applications using ADSP occurs over a connection that is made between the two sockets that these network entities use; ADSP assigns a socket to be used when you initialize each end of the connection, and your application becomes a client of that socket. Because this connection exists for the duration of the exchange, ADSP is called a *connection-oriented* protocol. ADSP manages and controls the data flow between the two sockets throughout the session to ensure that

- the data is delivered and received in the order in which it was sent

- duplicate data is not sent

- the application or process at the receiving end of the connection has the buffer capacity to accept the data

In an ADSP session, both ends of the connection have equal control over the communication in a **peer-to-peer** relationship. For the two ends of an ADSP connection to function properly, each must maintain information to control the connection and determine the connection state. To accommodate these requirements, the socket at either end of the connection has associated with it information that defines the state of the connection and information that the application and ADSP use to control the connection and communicate over it. The combination of a socket and the ADSP information maintained by the socket client is referred to as a **connection end.** To create a connection, two connection ends must be set up and initialized. Each connection end views itself as the local end and the other as the remote end.

AppleTalk Data Stream Protocol (ADSP)

Your application can use ADSP to

■ create a connection end

■ request a connection with a remote connection end

■ create a **connection listener** to wait passively for connection requests from remote connection ends (see "Connection Listeners" on page 5-7 for more information)

■ read data from and write it to an open connection

■ close a connection without removing it

■ remove a connection end

Figure 5-2 shows the order in which applications commonly call the ADSP routines to perform these functions for a connection end. (Figure 5-4 on page 5-8 shows this for a connection listener.)

Figure 5-2   Steps for creating an ADSP connection end

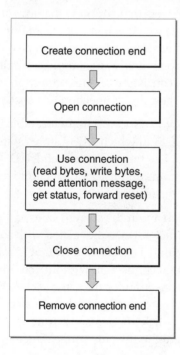

ADSP provides for a full-duplex data stream between the two ends of the connection that allows for a full-duplex dialog; this means that either end of the connection can call routines to send data at any time. (However, full-duplex does not mean that both connection ends actually send electrical signals at the same time; ADSP controls this process.) See the chapter "Introduction to AppleTalk" in this book for more information on full-duplex communication.

In addition to the full-duplex data stream that an ADSP session maintains, ADSP allows either end of a connection to send an attention message to the other end without interrupting the primary flow of data.

Among the features that ADSP provides are

■ an end-of-message feature that lets you break streams of data into logical messages

■ an attention-message feature that lets you and your partner application signal to each other outside the normal exchange of data

■ a forward-reset feature that lets you cancel the delivery of any data that is in your connection end's send queue and any data that you have sent that is in transit and that the remote connection end has not received

■ a built-in flow control feature that ensures that your application sends data only if its remote partner has the buffer capacity to receive it

Connections, Connection Ends, and Connection States

A connection is an association between two sockets that supports the flow of data between the clients of those sockets in a reliable way. Each socket can maintain concurrent ADSP connections with several other sockets, but there can be only one ADSP connection between any two sockets at one time. For example, a single socket on node A can have multiple concurrent sessions consisting of one connection to a socket on node B, one connection to a socket on node C, and one connection to a socket on node D.

When you establish an ADSP connection end, you allocate a nonrelocatable block of memory called a **connection control block (CCB)** in which ADSP stores state information about the connection end. When you initialize the connection end, ADSP uses the CCB to set up control information that it maintains and uses for synchronizing communication with the other socket client and for error checking.

You can read the CCB fields to gain information about the current state of the connection end. In addition to the unique AppleTalk internet address associated with a socket, each instance of a connection end has associated with it a connection ID that identifies it. You can open a connection for a socket and close that connection without actually removing the connection end, and then open another connection for the same socket. When you close a connection, the socket number remains associated with the connection, as do the data structures whose memory you allocated. ADSP uses this to ensure that any data meant for the old connection end is not delivered to the new connection end using the same socket number and data structures.

ADSP cannot deliver packets to a connection end based on the AppleTalk internet socket address alone. The connection ID ensures that a packet is delivered to the specific connection end for which it was intended. You call the new connection ID (dspNewCID) routine to cause ADSP to assign a connection ID to the connection end before you open a connection. ADSP assigns a connection ID number, which it includes in every packet that it delivers from your connection end to a remote connection end.

AppleTalk Data Stream Protocol (ADSP)

Figure 5-3   ADSP connection ends and their components

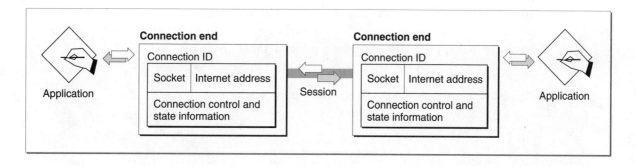

Figure 5-3 shows two connection ends and the client applications that use them to participate in a session with each other over an ADSP connection. This figure shows the components that constitute a connection end.

At any time, either end of a potential ADSP connection can initiate a session. Also, either end of the connection can tear down the connection when it is no longer needed.

- When two connection ends establish communication, the connection is considered an **open connection.**

- When both connection ends terminate the connection and dispose of the connection information each maintains, the connection is considered a **closed connection.**

- If one connection end is established but the other connection end is unreachable or has disposed of its connection information, the connection is considered a **half-open connection.**

No communication can occur over a half-open or closed connection.

To prevent a half-open connection from tying up resources, ADSP automatically closes any half-open connection that cannot reestablish communication within two minutes and informs its client that the connection is closed. Under these circumstances, ADSP will call the application-supplied completion routine for any pending asynchronous ADSP routine, if one was provided. Otherwise, the pending ADSP routine will return to the calling program with an `errState` error message. If you attempt to call an ADSP routine on a half-open connection, ADSP also returns the `errState` error message.

Connection Listeners

A connection listener or a connection-listening socket is a socket that accepts open-connection requests and passes them along to its client, a connection server process, for further processing. The server then selects a socket and requests ADSP to open a connection using that socket. The connection listener can also deny an open-connection request. By specifying filtering values for the network address of the requester, you can control which requests are accepted or denied. The use of a connection listener is typical of a server environment in which a server, such as a file server, is registered with NBP

AppleTalk Data Stream Protocol (ADSP)

using a single name. Various connection ends throughout the network contact the server's connection listener with open-connection requests. The connection server can honor the requests, or it can deny them. It might deny a request, for example, when its resources are exhausted. Figure 5-4 shows the tasks for an ADSP connection listener in the order that applications commonly perform them.

Figure 5-4   Standard tasks for an ADSP connection listener

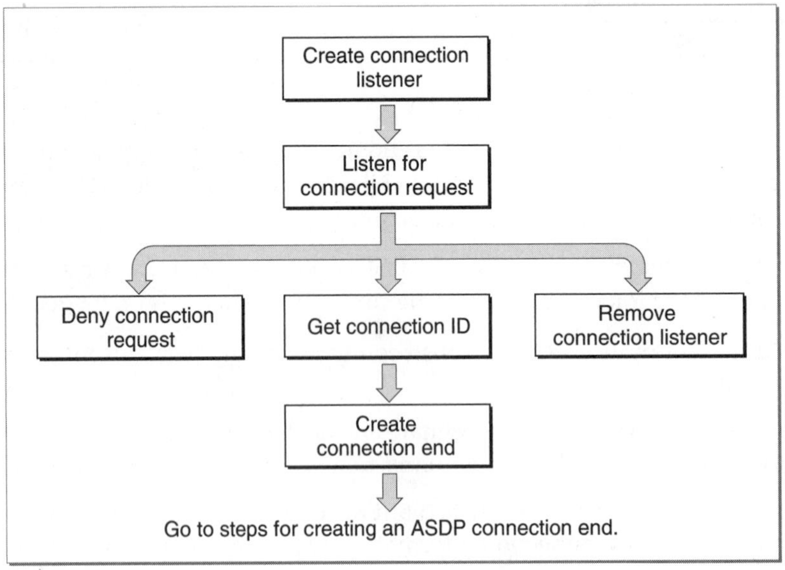

Reliable Delivery of Data

ADSP guarantees that data bytes are delivered in the same order as they were sent and that they are free of duplicates. It ensures that all data sent is delivered to the remote connection end's receive buffer. To accomplish this, ADSP associates a sequence number with each byte that it sends. ADSP discards any out-of-sequence data or any duplicates that are delivered. ADSP uses the sequence numbers to ensure that all of the data that one end sends is received by the other end. If data is lost, ADSP retransmits it. ADSP can send the data again because the data remains in the sending connection end's send queue until the remote end actually receives a copy of it. For more information about how ADSP delivers data, see *Inside AppleTalk*, second edition.

Unsolicited ADSP Events

After you open a connection, you can receive events that are not generated in response to any of the ADSP calls that your application makes. The other connection end or ADSP initiates these events. For example, the remote connection end can send you an attention message or a forward reset.

You receive a **forward reset** event when the remote connection end cancels delivery of all outstanding data to your connection end. A forward reset causes ADSP to discard all data in the send queue, all data in transit to the remote connection end, and all data in the remote connection end's receive queue that the client has not yet read.

The remote connection end can close the connection, and this, too, will generate an event notification for your connection end. You also receive event notification when ADSP tears down a connection because the remote end has become unreachable.

ADSP sets the bits of your connection end's connection control block user flags field to identify the type of event. For more information about this field, see "Creating and Using a Connection Control Block" on page 5-12. You can provide a user routine that ADSP is to call whenever you receive one of these events. This user routine is similar in concept and use to an `ioCompletion` routine that many of the other AppleTalk protocols use. See "Writing a User Routine for Connection Events" on page 5-26 for information on how to write a user routine.

About ASDSP

This section describes the secure version of ADSP referred to as **AppleTalk Secure Data Stream Protocol (ASDSP).** ASDSP is a superset of ADSP that includes authentication and encryption features. To use ASDSP, you should be familiar with both ADSP and ASDSP.

ASDSP features allow you to provide users of your application with the ability to exchange encrypted data across a **secure session** that is established after the users' identities are proven through what is known as the **authentication process.** Before transmitting the data that a user sends, ASDSP encrypts it and then decrypts the data before delivering it to the application at the remote connection end. Users might want to identify one another, for example, to verify that a piece of electronic mail came from the sender who claimed to be its author, and they might want to encrypt data that traverses a network if that data is considered confidential or private and they do not want others to intercept and read the data.

To verify the identities of two ends of a connection, an ASDSP application relies on information that is provided by an Apple Open Collaboration Environment (AOCE) authentication server. Your ASDSP client application at the connection end that initiates the session calls the AOCE Authentication Manager to acquire the information necessary for the authentication process from the authentication server, and then it passes this information on to ASDSP.

Note
Because ASDSP is dependent on information from the authentication server, your ASDSP application can only run on systems that also run AOCE and that have access to an AOCE authentication server. If the AOCE software is installed on the system that runs your application and if the system has access to an AOCE authentication server, your application can use ASDSP. ◆

You perform the first part of the authentication process by requesting information from the authentication server and giving that information to ASDSP to transmit to the other end of the connection. The authentication process culminates in a challenge-and-reply handshake that the ASDSP code performs on behalf of your ASDSP client application at each end of the connection to ensure that the application users are who they claim to be. The ASDSP client application of the connection end that retrieves the information from the authentication server and makes the request to open the session is called the **initiator;** the ASDSP client application of the connection end that receives the request and the information from the server is called the **recipient.**

The Authentication Process

This section describes the general strategy of the authentication process. Understanding what this process entails can be helpful in understanding the meaning and use of the parameters that you get from the authentication server and pass to ASDSP.

The initiator and the recipient each have a **private key.** The private key, also called a *user key* or *client key*, is a number that is derived from a password; the number is used by an encryption algorithm.

The initiator calls the authentication server to request information and **credentials** to be used by ASDSP in establishing an authenticated session. The credentials contain information that is required in order to prove that the users of both ends of the connection are who they claim to be. The user of the initiator ASDSP client application gives the authentication server his own name or identity and that of the user of the recipient ASDSP client application.

The authentication server returns to the initiator a unique session key that the server generates exclusively for use by the authentication process for this session; the session key is valid for a limited time only. The authentication server also returns to the initiator a set of credentials that are encrypted in the recipient's private key. The credentials contain the session key also and the initiator's identity, as well as the identity of an **intermediary** or proxy, if one was used to obtain the credentials from the authentication server.

The initiator passes a block of data containing the credentials to ASDSP, and ASDSP on the initiator's end sends the credentials to ASDSP on the recipient's end. The latter decrypts the entire credentials block, obtaining the session key from the credentials block. ASDSP on the recipient's end then uses the session key in the authentication process that it performs on behalf of the recipient. ASDSP has the recipient's private key, which it uses to decrypt the credentials. If the authentication process succeeds, ASDSP returns all of the credentials to the recipient.

Because the initiator and ASDSP on behalf of the recipient must each decrypt the session key using their own private key, they can each be convinced that the other is who they claim to be if they can conclude that the other knows the session key. The need for this conviction begins the challenge-and-reply authentication process that enables each end to confirm that the other end also knows the unique session key.

ASDSP performs the challenge-and-reply process on behalf of the client applications in a manner that is transparent to the applications. If the authentication process completes successfully, ASDSP opens a secure connection; if the authentication process fails, ASDSP returns an error code to both the initiator and the recipient and tears down the connection that was established to perform the authentication process. To learn more about the challenge-and-reply process, see the chapter "Authentication Manager" in *Inside Macintosh: AOCE Application Programming Interfaces*.

The Data Encryption Feature

After ASDSP successfully completes the authentication process, the two ends of the connection whose identities have been verified can exchange data and they can also encrypt that data. The ASDSP encryption feature allows each party to send data that can be trusted to be securely transmitted in a manner that is unreadable by anyone other than the intended recipient until that data is decrypted by ASDSP and delivered to the recipient at the other end of the ASDSP session connection. ASDSP encrypts only data in the main data stream; it does not encrypt data in attention messages or ASDSP packet headers.

Using ADSP

This section describes how to use ADSP to

- open and maintain an ADSP connection, including how to
  - initialize the connection end (dspInit)
  - set options that control the behavior of the connection end (dspOptions)
  - open the connection (dspOpen)
  - read (dspRead) and write (dspWrite) data over the connection
  - send an attention code and an attention message to the remote connection end (dspAttention)
  - close the connection (dspClose) and remove it (dspRemove)
- create and use a connection listener, including how to
  - initialize a connection listener (dspCLInit)
  - activate the connection listener, causing it to listen for an open-connection request (dspCLListen), filtering requests that you will accept by restricting network addresses
  - initialize (dspInit) and open (dspOpen) a connection end in response to an open request that you want to accept
  - read (dspRead) and write (dspWrite) data over the connection and close the connection (dspClose)
  - remove the connection listener when you are finished with it (dspCLRemove)
- handle unsolicited connection events using your own user routine

You execute ADSP routines by calling the Device Manager's `PBControl` function. When you call the `PBControl` function for an ADSP routine, you provide a pointer to a parameter block of type `DSPParamBlock`.

You use the parameter block fields to specify the input parameters that ADSP requires to execute the command. The parameter block also includes fields whose values ADSP returns. For a complete description of the DSP parameter block and its fields, see "The DSP Parameter Block" beginning on page 5-38.

Allocating Memory for ADSP

To open and maintain an ADSP session, you must allocate memory required for the session. Depending on the ADSP routine that you call, you must allocate the following:

- storage of the state information that ADSP maintains at either end of a connection (see the discussion of the connection control block in "Connections, Connection Ends, and Connection States" on page 5-6)

- a parameter block that you use to pass parameters when you execute an ADSP routine

- a send queue and a receive queue

- an attention message buffer

This memory belongs to ADSP until you explicitly remove the connection end.

Creating and Using a Connection Control Block

When you establish an ADSP connection end, you must allocate a nonrelocatable block of memory for (and provide a pointer to) a connection control block (CCB) data structure, which ADSP uses to store state information about the connection end. This memory belongs to ADSP until you explicitly remove the connection end using the `dspRemove` routine (see "dspRemove" on page 5-62). Only then can you release or reuse the memory that you allocated for the CCB.

Most of the fields of the CCB are for ADSP's internal use. Although you must not alter any of the CCB fields except one, the `userFlags` field, you may poll them to gain information about the current state of the connection end.

When your connection end receives an unsolicited event, such as an attention message or a forward reset, ADSP's interrupt handler sets a bit corresponding to the event type in the `userFlags` field and calls your user routine, if you provided one. If you did not provide a user routine, you can test these bits to determine when an unsolicited event occurs on the connection end.

After you read them, you must clear the bits either through your user routine or directly before you handle the event.

The CCB is a record of type `TRCCB` that must consist of 242 bytes. See "The ADSP Connection Control Block Record" beginning on page 5-35 for a description of the CCB and the fields that comprise it.

Opening and Maintaining an ADSP Connection

To use ADSP to establish and maintain a connection between a socket on your local node and a remote socket, use the following procedure:

1. Use the Device Manager's `OpenDriver` function to open the .MPP driver, and then use it again to open the .DSP driver. The .MPP driver must be open before you open the .DSP driver. The `OpenDriver` function call for the .DSP driver returns the driver reference number. You must supply this reference number each time you call the Device Manager's `PBControl` function to execute an ADSP routine.

2. Allocate nonrelocatable memory for a CCB, send and receive queues, and an attention-message buffer. If you need to allocate the memory dynamically while the program is running, use the `NewPtr` routine. Otherwise, the way in which you allocate the memory depends on the compiler you are using. (Listing 5-1 on page 5-17 shows how to do this in Pascal.) The memory that you allocate becomes the property of ADSP when you call the `dspInit` routine to establish a connection end. You cannot write any data to this memory except by calling ADSP, and you must ensure that the memory remains locked until you call the `dspRemove` routine to eliminate the connection end.

   The CCB is 242 bytes. The attention-message buffer must be 570 bytes. When you send bytes to a remote connection end, ADSP stores the bytes in a buffer called the **send queue.** Until the remote connection end acknowledges their receipt, ADSP keeps the bytes you sent in the send queue so that they are available to be retransmitted if necessary. When the local connection end receives bytes, it stores them in a buffer, called the **receive queue,** until you read them. The sizes you need for the send and receive queues depend on the lengths of the messages being sent.

   ADSP does not transmit data from the remote connection end until there is room for it in your receive queue. If your send or receive queues are too small, they limit the speed with which you can transmit and receive data. A queue size of 600 bytes should work well for most applications. If you are using ADSP to send a continuous flow of data, a larger data buffer improves performance. If your application is sending or receiving the user's keystrokes, a smaller buffer should be adequate. The constant `minDSPQueueSize`, which is defined in the MPW interface file for ADSP, indicates the minimum queue size that you can use.

   If you are using a version of the .DSP driver prior to version 1.5, you must allocate send and receive queues that are 12 percent larger than the actual buffer sizes you need. You must do this in order to provide some extra space for use by the .DSP driver. Version 1.5 and later versions of the .DSP driver use a much smaller, and variable, portion of buffer space for overhead. The .DSP driver version number is stored in the low byte of the `qFlags` field, which is the first field in the `dCtlQHdr` field in the driver's device control entry (DCE) data structure. Version 1.5 of the .DSP driver has a version number of 4 in the DCE. See the chapter "Device Manager" in *Inside Macintosh: Devices* for information on the DCE.

3. Use the `dspInit` routine to establish a connection end. You must provide pointers to the CCB, send queue, receive queue, and attention-message buffer. You may also provide a pointer to a user routine that ADSP calls when your connection end receives an unsolicited connection event. See the section"Writing a User Routine for Connection Events" on page 5-26 for information on providing a user routine.

If there is a specific socket that you want to use for the connection end, you can specify the socket number in the localSocket parameter. If you want ADSP to assign the socket for you, specify 0 for the localSocket parameter; in this case, ADSP returns the socket number when the dspInit routine completes execution.

4. If you wish, you can use the Name-Binding Protocol (NBP) routines to add the name and address of your connection end to the node's names table. See the chapter "Name-Binding Protocol (NBP)" in this book for information on NBP.

5. You can use the dspOptions routine to set several parameters that control the behavior of the connection end. Because every parameter has a default value, the use of the dspOptions routine is optional. You can specify values for the following parameters:

   □ The sendBlocking parameter, which sets the maximum number of bytes that may accumulate in the send queue before ADSP sends a packet to the remote connection end. You can experiment with different values of the sendBlocking parameter to determine which provides the best performance. Under most circumstances, the default value of 16 bytes gives good performance.

   □ The badSeqMax parameter, which sets the maximum number of out-of-sequence data packets that the local connection end can receive before requesting the remote connection end to retransmit the missing data. Under most circumstances, the default value of 3 provides good performance.

   □ The useCheckSum parameter, which determines whether the Datagram Delivery Protocol (DDP) should compute a checksum and include it in each packet that it sends to the remote connection end. Using checksums slows communications slightly. Normally ADSP and DDP perform enough error checking to ensure safe delivery of all data. Set the useCheckSum parameter to 1 only if you feel that the network is highly unreliable.

6. Call the dspOpen routine to open the connection. The dspOpen routine has four possible modes of operation: ocAccept, ocEstablish, ocRequest, and ocPassive. Normally you use either the ocRequest or ocPassive mode. You must specify one of these four modes for the ocMode parameter when you call the dspOpen routine.

   The ocAccept mode is used only by connection servers. The ocEstablish mode is used by routines that determine their connection-opening parameters and establish a connection independently of ADSP, but use ADSP to transmit and receive data.

   Use the ocRequest mode when you want to establish communications with a specific socket on the AppleTalk internet. When you execute the dspOpen routine in the ocRequest mode, ADSP sends an open-connection request to the address you specify.

   If the socket to which you send the open-connection request is a connection listener, the connection server that operates that connection listener can select any socket on the internet to be the connection end that responds to the open-connection request. To restrict the socket from which you will accept a response to your open-connection request, specify a value for the filterAddress parameter to the dspOpen routine. When your connection end receives a response from a socket that meets the restrictions of the filterAddress parameter, it acknowledges the response and ADSP completes the connection.

To use the `ocRequest` mode, you must know the complete internet address of the remote socket, and the ADSP client at that address must either be a connection listener or have executed the `dspOpen` routine in the `ocPassive` mode. You can use the NBP routines to obtain a list of names of objects on the internet and to determine the internet address of a socket when you know its name. See the chapter "Name-Binding Protocol (NBP)" in this book for information on the NBP routines.

Use the `ocPassive` mode when you expect to receive an open-connection request from a remote socket. You can specify a value for the `filterAddress` parameter to restrict the network number, node ID, or socket number from which you will accept an open-connection request. When your connection end receives an open-connection request that meets the restrictions of the `filterAddress` parameter, it acknowledges the request and ADSP completes the connection.

You can poll the state field in the CCB to determine when the connection end is waiting to receive an open-connection request, when the connection end is waiting to receive an acknowledgment of an open-connection request, and when the connection is open. See the section "The ADSP Connection Control Block Record" beginning on page 5-35 for a description of the CCB fields. Alternatively, you can check the result code for the `dspOpen` routine when the routine completes execution. If the routine returns the `noErr` result code, then the connection is open.

7. Use the `dspRead` routine to read data that your connection end has received from the remote connection end. Use the `dspWrite` routine to send data to the remote connection end. Use the `dspAttention` routine to send attention messages to the remote connection end.

The `dspWrite` routine places data in the send queue. ADSP is a full-duplex, symmetric communications protocol: You can send data at any time, and your connection end can receive data at any time, even at the same time as you are sending data. ADSP transmits the data in the send queue when one of the following conditions occurs:

☐ You call the `dspWrite` routine with the flush parameter set to a nonzero number.

☐ The number of bytes in the send queue equals or exceeds the blocking factor that you set with the `dspOptions` routine.

☐ The send timer expires. The send timer sets the maximum amount of time that can pass before ADSP sends all unsent data in the send queue to the remote connection end. ADSP calculates the best value to use for this timer and sets it automatically.

☐ A connection event requires that the local connection end send an acknowledgment packet to the remote connection end.

If you send more data to the send queue than it can hold, the `dspWrite` routine does not complete execution until it has written all the data to the send queue. If you execute the `dspWrite` routine asynchronously, ADSP returns control to your program and writes the data to the send queue as quickly as it can. This technique provides the most efficient use of the send queue by your program and by ADSP. Because ADSP does not remove data from the send queue until that data has been not only sent but also acknowledged by the remote connection end, using the `flush` parameter to the `dspWrite` routine does not guarantee that the send queue is empty. You can use the `dspStatus` routine to determine how much free buffer space is available in the send queue.

The dspRead routine reads data from the receive queue into your application's private data buffer. ADSP does not transmit data until there is space available in the other end's receive queue to accept it. Because a full receive queue slows the communications rate, you should read data from the receive queue as often as necessary to keep sufficient buffer space available for new data. You can use either of two techniques to do this:

☐ Allocate a small receive queue (about 600 bytes) and call the dspRead routine asynchronously. Your completion routine for the dspRead routine should then call the dspRead routine again.

☐ Allocate a large receive queue and call the dspRead routine less frequently.

If there is less data in the receive queue than the amount you specify with the reqCount parameter to the dspRead command, the command does not complete execution until there is enough data available to satisfy the request. There are three exceptions to this rule:

☐ If the end-of-message bit in the ADSP packet header is set, the dspRead command reads the data in the receive queue, returns the actual amount of data read in the actCount parameter, and returns the eom parameter set to 1.

☐ If you have closed the connection end before calling the dspRead routine (that is, the connection is half open), the command reads whatever data is available and returns the actual amount of data read in the actCount parameter.

☐ If ADSP has closed the connection before you call the dspRead routine and there is no data in the receive queue, the routine returns the noErr result code with the actCount parameter set to 0 and the eom parameter set to 0.

In addition to the byte-stream data format implemented by the dspRead and dspWrite routines, ADSP provides a mechanism for sending and receiving control signals or information separate from the byte stream. You use the dspAttention routine to send an attention code and an attention message to the remote connection end. When your connection end receives an attention message, ADSP's interrupt handler sets the eAttention flag in the userFlags field of the CCB and calls your user routine. Your user routine must first clear the userFlags field. Then your routine can read the attention code and attention message and take whatever action you deem appropriate.

Because ADSP is often used by terminal emulation programs and other applications that pass the data they receive on to the user without processing it, attention messages provide a mechanism for the applications that are clients of the connection ends to communicate with each other. For example, you could use attention messages to implement a handshaking and data-checking protocol for a program that transfers disk files between two applications, neither one of which is a file server. Or a database server on a mainframe computer that uses ADSP to communicate with Macintosh computer workstations could use the attention mechanism to inform the workstations when the database is about to be closed down for maintenance.

8. When you are ready to close the ADSP connection, you can use the dspClose or dspRemove routine to close the connection end. Use the dspClose routine if you intend to use that connection end to open another connection and do not want to release the memory you allocated for the connection end. Use the dspRemove routine if you are completely finished with the connection end and want to release the memory.

You can continue to read data from the receive queue after you have called the dspClose routine, but not after you have called the dspRemove routine. You can use the dspStatus routine to determine whether any data is remaining in the receive queue, or you can read data from the receive queue until both the actCount and eom fields of the dspRead parameter block return 0.

If you set the abort parameter for the dspClose or dspRemove routine to 0, then ADSP does not close the connection or the connection end until it has sent—and received acknowledgment for—all data in the send queue and any pending attention messages. If you set the abort parameter to 1, then ADSP discards any data in the send queue and any attention messages that have not already been sent.

After you have executed the dspRemove routine, you can release the memory you allocated for the CCB and data buffers.

Listing 5-1 illustrates the use of ADSP. This routine opens the .MPP and .DSP drivers and allocates memory for its internal data buffers, for the CCB, and for the send, receive, and attention-message buffers. Then the routine uses the dspInit routine to establish a connection end and uses NBP to register the name of the connection end on the internet. (The user routine specified by the userRoutine parameter to the dspInit function is shown in Listing 5-3 on page 5-28.) Next, Listing 5-1 uses the dspOptions routine to set the blocking factor to 24 bytes. This routine then uses NBP to determine the address of a socket whose name was selected by the user and sends an open-connection request (dspOpen) to that socket. When the dspOpen routine completes execution, it sends data and an attention message to the remote connection end and reads data from its receive queue. Finally, the routine closes the connection end with the dspRemove routine and releases the memory it allocated.

Listing 5-1   Using ADSP to establish and use a connection

```
PROCEDURE MyADSP;

CONST
   qSize =  600;                          {queue space}
   myDataSize =   128;                    {size of internal read/write buffers}
   blockFact = 24;                        {blocking factor}


TYPE
{Modify the connection control block to add storage for A5.}
myTRCCB =
   RECORD
      myA5: LongInt;
      u: TRCCB;
   END;

VAR
   dspSendQPtr:       Ptr;
   dspRecvQPtr:       Ptr;
```

```
    dspAttnBufPtr:       Ptr;
    myData2ReadPtr:      Ptr;
    myData2WritePtr:     Ptr;
    myAttnMsgPtr:        Ptr;
    dspCCB:              myTRCCB;
    myDSPPBPtr:          DSPPBPtr;
    myMPPPBPtr:          MPPPBPtr;
    myNTEName:           NamesTableEntry;
    myAddrBlk:           AddrBlock;
    drvrRefNum:          Integer;
    mppRefNum:           Integer;
    connRefNum:          Integer;
    gReceivedAnEvent:    Boolean;
    myAttnCode:          Integer;
    tempFlag:            Byte;
    tempCFlag:           Integer;
    myErr:               OSErr;

BEGIN
    myErr := OpenDriver('.MPP', mppRefNum);      {open .MPP driver}
    IF myErr <> noErr THEN DoErr(myErr);         {check and handle error}
    myErr := OpenDriver('.DSP', drvrRefNum);     {open .DSP driver}
    IF myErr <> noErr THEN DoErr(myErr);         {check and handle error}

    {Allocate memory for data buffers.}
    dspSendQPtr := NewPtr(qSize);                {ADSP use only}
    dspRecvQPtr := NewPtr(qSize);                {ADSP use only}
    dspAttnBufPtr := NewPtr(attnBufSize);        {ADSP use only}
    myData2ReadPtr := NewPtr(myDataSize);
    myData2WritePtr := NewPtr(myDataSize);
    myAttnMsgPtr := NewPtr(myDataSize);
    myDSPPBPtr := DSPPBPtr(NewPtr(SizeOf(DSPParamBlock)));
    myMPPPBPtr := MPPPBPtr(NewPtr(SizeOf(MPPParamBlock)));

    WITH myDSPPBPtr^ DO                          {set up dspInit parameters}
    BEGIN
        ioCRefNum := drvrRefNum;                 {ADSP driver ref num}
        csCode := dspInit;
        ccbPtr := @dspCCB;                       {pointer to CCB}
        userRoutine := @myConnectionEvtUserRoutine;
                                                 {see Listing 5-3}
        sendQSize := qSize;                      {size of send queue}
        sendQueue := dspSendQPtr;                {send-queue buffer}
        recvQSize := qSize;                      {size of receive queue}
```

AppleTalk Data Stream Protocol (ADSP)

```
      recvQueue := dspRecvQPtr;                   {receive-queue buffer}
      attnPtr := dspAttnBufPtr;                   {receive-attention buffer}
      localSocket := 0;                           {let ADSP assign socket}
  END;


  gReceivedAnEvent := FALSE;
  dspCCB.myA5 := SetCurrentA5;                     {save A5 for the user routine}
  {Establish a connection end.}
  myErr := PBControl(ParmBlkPtr(myDSPPBPtr), FALSE);
  IF myErr <> noErr THEN DoErr(myErr);
                                                   {check and handle error}

  connRefNum := myDSPPBPtr^.ccbRefNum;
                                                   {save CCB ref num for later}

  NBPSetNTE(@myNTEName, 'The Object', 'The Type',
           '*', myDSPPBPtr^.localSocket);
                                                   {set up NBP names table entry}
  WITH myMPPPBPtr^ DO                              {set up PRegisterName }
                                                   { parameters}

  BEGIN
      interval := 7;                               {retransmit every 7*8=56 ticks}
      count := 3;                                  {retry 3 times}
      entityPtr := @myNTEName;                     {name to register}
      verifyFlag := 1;                             {verify this name}
  END;
  {Register this socket.}
  myErr := PRegisterName(myMPPPBPtr, FALSE);
                                                   {register this socket}

  IF myErr <> noErr THEN DoErr(myErr);
                                                   {check and handle error}

  WITH myDSPPBPtr^ DO                              {set up dspOptions parameters}
  BEGIN
      ioCRefNum := drvrRefNum;                     {ADSP driver ref num}
      csCode := dspOptions;
      ccbRefNum := connRefNum;                     {connection ref num}
      sendBlocking := blockFact;                   {quantum for data packet}
      badSeqMax := 0;                              {use default}
      useCheckSum := 0;                            {don't calculate checksum}
  END;
  myErr := PBControl(ParmBlkPtr(myDSPPBPtr), FALSE);
                                                   {set options}

  IF myErr <> noErr THEN DoErr(myErr);
                                                   {check and handle error}
```

```
    PickASocket(myAddrBlk);                       {routine using the PLookupName }
                                                  { function to pick a socket }
                                                  { for the connection}
{Open a connection with the selected socket.}
WITH myDSPPBPtr^ DO                               {set up dspOpen parameters}
BEGIN
    ioCRefNum := drvrRefNum;                      {ADSP driver ref num}
    csCode := dspOpen;
    ccbRefNum := connRefNum;                      {connection ref num}
    remoteAddress := myAddrBlk;                   {address of remote socket }
                                                  { from PLookupName function}
    filterAddress := myAddrBlk;                   {address filter,specified }
                                                  { socket address only}
    ocMode := ocRequest;                          {open connection mode}
    ocInterval := 0;                              {use default retry interval}
    ocMaximum := 0;                               {use default retry maximum}
END;
myErr := PBControl(ParmBlkPtr(myDSPPBPtr), FALSE);
                                                  {open a connection}
IF myErr <> noErr THEN DoErr(myErr);              {check and handle error}

{The connection with the selected socket is open, so now send }
{ to the send queue exactly myDataSize number of bytes.}
WITH myDSPPBPtr^ DO                               {set up dspWrite parameters}
BEGIN
    ioCRefNum := drvrRefNum;                      {ADSP driver ref num}
    csCode := dspWrite;
    ccbRefNum := connRefNum;                      {connection ref num}
    reqCount := myDataSize;                       {write this number of bytes}

    dataPtr := myData2WritePtr;                   {pointer to send queue}
    eom := 1;                                     {1 means last byte is }
                                                  { logical end-of-message}
    flush := 1;                                   {1 means send data now}
END;
myErr := PBControl(ParmBlkPtr(myDSPPBPtr), FALSE);
                                                  {send data to the remote }
                                                  { connection}
IF myErr <> noErr THEN DoErr(myErr);

                                                  {check and handle error}
```

```
{Now send an attention message to the remote connection end.}
WITH myDSPPBPtr^ DO                            {set up dspAttention parameters}
BEGIN
    ioCRefNum := drvrRefNum;                   {ADSP driver ref num}
    csCode := dspAttention;
    ccbRefNum := connRefNum;                   {connection ref num}
    attnCode := 0;                             {user-defined attention code}
    attnSize := myDataSize;                    {length of attention message}
    attnData := myAttnMsgPtr;                  {attention message}
END;
myErr := PBControl(ParmBlkPtr(myDSPPBPtr), FALSE);
IF myErr <> noErr THEN DoErr(myErr);
                                               {check and handle error}


{Now read from the receive queue exactly myDataSize number }
{ of bytes.}
WITH myDSPPBPtr^ DO                            {set up dspRead parameters}
BEGIN
    ioCRefNum := drvrRefNum;                   {ADSP driver ref num}
    csCode := dspRead;
    ccbRefNum := connRefNum;                   {connection ref num}
    reqCount := myDataSize;                    {read this number of bytes}
    dataPtr := myData2ReadPtr;                 {pointer to read buffer}
END;
myErr := PBControl(ParmBlkPtr(myDSPPBPtr), FALSE);
                                               {read data from the remote }
                                               { connection}
IF myErr <> noErr THEN DoErr(myErr);           {check and handle error}


{We're finished with the connection, so remove it.}
WITH myDSPPBPtr^ DO                            {set up dspRemove parameters}
BEGIN
    ioCRefNum := drvrRefNum;                   {ADSP driver ref num}
    csCode := dspRemove;

    ccbRefNum := connRefNum;                   {connection ref num}
    abort := 0;                                {don't close until }
                                               { everything is sent and }
                                               { received}
END;
myErr := PBControl(ParmBlkPtr(myDSPPBPtr), FALSE);
                                               {close and remove the }
                                               { connection}
IF myErr <> noErr THEN DOErr(myErr);

                                               {check and handle error}
```

5

AppleTalk Data Stream Protocol (ADSP)

```
{You're finished with this connection, so release the memory.}
DisposPtr(dspSendQPtr);
DisposPtr(dspRecvQPtr);
DisposPtr(dspAttnBufPtr);
DisposPtr(myData2ReadPtr);
DisposPtr(myData2WritePtr);
DisposPtr(myAttnMsgPtr);
DisposPtr(Ptr(myDSPPBPtr));
DisposPtr(Ptr(myMPPPBPtr));

END;        {MyADSP}
```

Creating and Using a Connection Listener

A connection listener is a special sort of ADSP connection end that cannot receive or transmit data streams or attention messages. The sole function of a connection listener is to wait passively to receive an open-connection request and to inform its client, the connection server, when it receives one. The connection server can then accept or deny the open-connection request. If it accepts the request, the connection server selects a socket to use as a connection end, establishes a connection end on that socket, and sends an acknowledgment and connection request back to the requesting connection end. The connection server can use the same socket as it used for the connection listener, or it can select a different socket as the connection end.

Use the following procedure to establish a connection listener and to use that connection listener to open a connection with a remote connection end:

1. Use the Device Manager's `OpenDriver` function to open the .MPP driver and then use the `OpenDriver` function to open the .DSP driver. The `OpenDriver` function returns the reference number for the .DSP driver. You must supply this reference number each time you call the .DSP driver.

2. Allocate nonrelocatable memory for a connection control block, which is described in "Connections, Connection Ends, and Connection States" on page 5-6. The CCB is 242 bytes. A connection listener does not need send and receive queues or an attention-message buffer. The memory that you allocate becomes the property of ADSP when you call the `dspCLInit` routine to establish a connection listener. You cannot write any data to this memory except by calling ADSP, and you must ensure that the memory remains locked until you call the `dspRemove` routine to eliminate the connection end.

3. Call the `dspCLInit` routine to establish a connection listener. You must provide a pointer to the CCB.

   If there is a specific socket that you want to use for the connection listener, you can specify the socket number in the `localSocket` parameter. If you want ADSP to assign the socket for you, specify 0 for the `localSocket` parameter. ADSP returns the socket number when the `dspCLInit` routine completes execution.

4. If you wish, you can use the NBP routines to add the name and address of your connection listener to the node's names table. See the chapter "Name-Binding Protocol (NBP)" in this book for information on NBP.

5. Use the `dspCLListen` routine to cause the connection listener to wait for an open-connection request. Because the `dspCLListen` routine does not complete execution until it receives a connection request, you should call this routine asynchronously. You can specify a value for the `filterAddress` parameter to restrict the network number, node ID, or socket number from which you will accept an open-connection request.

   When the `dspCLListen` routine receives an open-connection request that meets the restrictions of the `filterAddress` parameter, it returns a `noErr` result code (if you executed the routine asynchronously, it places a `noErr` result code in the `ioResult` parameter) and places values in the parameter block for the `remoteCID`, `remoteAddress`, `sendSeq`, `sendWindow`, and `attnSendSeq` parameters.

6. If you want to open the connection, call the `dspInit` routine to establish a connection end. You can use any available socket on the node for the connection end, including the socket that you used for the connection listener. Because a single socket can have more than one CCB connected with it, the socket can function simultaneously as a connection end and a connection listener.

   You can check the address of the remote socket to determine if it meets your criteria for a connection end. Although the `filterAddress` parameter to the `dspCLListen` routine provides some screening of socket addresses, it cannot check for network number ranges, for example, or for a specific set of socket numbers. If for some reason you want to deny the connection request, call the `dspDeny` routine, specifying the CCB of the connection listener in the `ccbRefNum` parameter. Because the `dspCLListen` routine completes execution when it receives an open-connection request, you must return to step 5 to wait for another connection request.

7. Call the `dspOpen` routine to open the connection. Specify the value `ocAccept` for the `ocMode` parameter and specify in the `ccbRefNum` parameter the reference number of the CCB for the connection end that you want to use. When you call the `dspOpen` routine, you must provide the values returned by the `dspCLListen` routine for the `remoteCID`, `remoteAddress`, `sendSeq`, `sendWindow`, and `attnSendSeq` parameters.

   You can poll the state field in the CCB to determine when the connection is open. Alternatively, you can check the result code for the `dspOpen` routine when the routine completes execution. If the routine returns the `noErr` result code, then the connection is open.

8. You can now send and receive data and attention messages over the connection, as described in "Opening and Maintaining an ADSP Connection" beginning on page 5-13. When you are ready to close the connection, you can use the `dspClose` or `dspRemove` routine, both of which are also described in the section "Creating and Using a Connection Control Block."

9. When you are finished using the connection listener, you can use the `dspCLRemove` routine to eliminate it. Once you have called the `dspCLRemove` routine, you can release the memory you allocated for the connection listener's CCB.

AppleTalk Data Stream Protocol (ADSP)

Listing 5-2 illustrates the use of ADSP to establish and use a connection listener. It opens the .MPP and .DSP drivers and allocates memory for the CCB. Then it uses the dspCLInit routine to establish a connection listener, uses NBP to register the name of the connection end on the internet, and uses the dspCLListen routine to wait for a connection request. When the routine receives a connection request, it calls the dspOpen routine to complete the connection.

Listing 5-2   Using ADSP to establish and use a connection listener

```
VAR
    dspCCBPtr:     TPCCB;
    myDSPPBPtr:    DSPPBPtr;
    myMPPPBPtr:    MPPPBPtr;
    myNTEName:     NamesTableEntry;
    drvrRefNum:    Integer;
    mppRefNum:     Integer;
    connRefNum:    Integer;
    myErr:         OSErr;

BEGIN
    myErr := OpenDriver('.MPP', mppRefNum);
                                {open .MPP driver}
    IF myErr <> noErr THEN DoErr(myErr);
                                {check and handle error}
    myErr := OpenDriver('.DSP', drvrRefNum);
                                {open .DSP driver}
    IF myErr <> noErr THEN DoErr(myErr);
                                {check and handle error}
    {Allocate memory for data buffers.}
    dspCCBPtr := TPCCB(NewPtr(SizeOf(TRCCB)));
    myDSPPBPtr := DSPPBPtr(NewPtr(SizeOf(DSPParamBlock)));
    myMPPPBPtr := MPPPBPtr(NewPtr(SizeOf(MPPParamBlock)));
    WITH myDSPPBPtr^ DO         {set up dspCLInit parameters}
    BEGIN
        ioCRefNum := drvrRefNum;   {ADSP driver ref num}
        csCode := dspCLInit;
        ccbPtr := dspCCBPtr;       {pointer to CCB}
        localSocket := 0;          {local socket number}
    END;
    myErr := PBControl(ParmBlkPtr(myDSPPBPtr), FALSE);
                                {establish a connection listener}
    IF myErr <> noErr THEN DoErr(myErr);
                                {check and handle error}
    connRefNum := myDSPPBPtr^.ccbRefNum;
                                {save CCB ref num for later}
```

```
NBPSetNTE(@myNTEName, 'The Object', 'The Type',
         '*', myDSPPBPtr^.localSocket);
                                {set up NBP names table entry}
WITH myMPPPBPtr^ DO             {set up PRegisterName parameters}
BEGIN
   interval := 7;               {retransmit every 7*8=56 ticks }
   count := 3;                  { and retry 3 times}
   entityPtr := @myNTEname;     {name to register}
   verifyFlag := 1;             {verify this name}
END;
myErr := PRegisterName(myMPPPBPtr, FALSE);
                                {register this name}
IF myErr <> noErr THEN DoErr(myErr);
                                {check and handle error}

WITH myDSPPBPtr^ DO             {set up dspCLListen parameters}
BEGIN
   ioCRefNum := drvrRefNum;     {ADSP driver ref num}
   csCode := dspCLListen;
   ccbRefNum := connRefNum;     {connection ref num}
   filterAddress := AddrBlock(0);
                                {connect with anybody}
END;
myErr := PBControl(ParmBlkPtr(myDSPPBPtr), TRUE);
                                {listen for connection requests}
WHILE myDSPPBPtr^.ioResult = 1 DO
BEGIN
{Return control to user while waiting for a connection }
{ request.}
   GoDoSomething;
END;
IF myErr <> noErr THEN DoErr(myErr);
                                {check and handle error}

WITH myDSPPBPtr^ DO             {set up dspInit parameters}
BEGIN
   ioCRefNum := drvrRefNum;     {ADSP driver ref num}
   csCode := dspInit;
   ccbPtr := @dspCCB;           {pointer to CCB}
   userRoutine := @myConnectionEvtUserRoutine;
   sendQSize := qSize;          {size of send queue}
   sendQueue := dspSendQPtr;    {send-queue buffer}
   recvQSize := qSize;          {size of receive queue}
   recvQueue := dspRecvQPtr;    {receive-queue buffer}
```

```
      attnPtr := dspAttnBufPtr;    {receive-attention buffer}
      localSocket := 0;           {let ADSP assign socket}
   END;


   dspCCB.myA5 := SetCurrentA5;   {save A5 for the user routine}


   {Establish a connection end.}
   myErr := PBControl(ParmBlkPtr(myDSPPBPtr), FALSE);
   IF myErr <> noErr THEN DoErr(myErr);
                                 {check and handle error}
   connRefNum := myDSPPBPtr^.ccbRefNum;
                                 {save CCB ref num for later}


   {You received a connection request: now open a connection. }
   { The dspCLListen call has returned values into the }
   { remoteCID, remoteAddress, sendSeq, sendWindow, }
   { and attnSendSeq fields of the parameter block.}


   WITH myDSPPBPtr^ DO            {set up dspOpen parameters}
   BEGIN
      ioCRefNum := drvrRefNum;    {ADSP driver ref num}
      csCode := dspOpen;
      ccbRefNum := connRefNum;    {connection ref num}
      ocMode := ocAccept;         {open connection mode}
      ocInterval := 0;            {use default retry interval}
      ocMaximum := 0;             {use default retry maximum}
   END;
   myErr := PBControl(ParmBlkPtr(myDSPPBPtr), FALSE);
                                 {open a connection}
   IF myErr <> noErr THEN DoErr(myErr)
                                 {check and handle error}
END;      {MyCLADSP}
```

Writing a User Routine for Connection Events

When you execute the dspInit routine, you can specify a pointer to a routine that
you provide (referred to as the *user routine*). Whenever an unsolicited connection event
occurs, ADSP sets a flag in the CCB and calls the user routine. The user routine must
clear the flag to acknowledge that it has read the flag field, and then it can respond to the
event in any manner you deem appropriate. The CCB flags are described in"The ADSP
Connection Control Block Record" beginning on page 5-35. The four following types
of unsolicited connection events set flags in the CCB:

■ ADSP has been informed by the remote connection end that the remote connection
   end is about to close the connection. An appropriate response might be to store a flag

indicating that the connection end is about to close. When your application regains control, it can then display a dialog box informing the user of this event and asking whether the application should attempt to reconnect later.

■ ADSP has determined that the remote connection end is not responding and so has closed the connection. Your user routine can attempt to open a new connection immediately. Alternatively, you can store a flag indicating that the connection has closed, and when your application regains control, it can display a dialog box asking the user whether to attempt to reconnect.

■ ADSP has received an attention message from the remote connection end. Depending on what you are using the attention-message mechanism for, you might want to read the attention code in the `attnCode` field of the CCB and the attention message pointed to by the `attnPtr` field of the CCB.

■ ADSP has received a forward reset command from the remote client end. It has then discarded all ADSP data not yet delivered, including the data in the receive queue of the local client end, and has resynchronized the connection. Your response to this event depends on the purpose for which you are using the forward reset mechanism. You might want to resend the last data you have sent or inform the user of the event.

When ADSP calls your user routine, the CPU is in interrupt-processing mode and register A1 contains a pointer to the CCB of the connection end that generated the event. You can examine the `userFlags` field of the CCB to determine what event caused the interrupt, and you can examine the `state` field of the CCB to determine the current state of the connection.

Because the CPU is set to interrupt-processing mode, your user routine must preserve all registers other than A0, A1, D0, D1, and D2. Your routine must not make any direct or indirect calls to the Memory Manager, and it cannot depend on handles to unlocked blocks being valid. If you want to use any of your application's global variables, you must save the contents of the A5 register before using the variables, and you must restore the A5 register before your routine terminates. Listing 5-1 and Listing 5-3 illustrate the use of the CCB to store the pointer to your application's global variables.

If you want to execute a routine each time an unsolicited connection event occurs but the interrupt environment is too restrictive, you can specify a `NIL` pointer to the user routine and periodically poll the `userFlags` field of the CCB.

▲ **WARNING**
When an unsolicited connection event occurs, you must clear the bit in the `userFlags` field by setting it to 0 or the connection will hang. To ensure that you do not lose any attention messages, you must read any attention messages into an internal buffer before you clear the bit in the `userFlags` field. ▲

Listing 5-3 on page 5-28 shows the user routine called by Listing 5-1 on page 5-17. When this routine is called, it first checks the CCB to determine the source of the interrupt and then clears the bit in the `userFlags` field of the CCB. If the routine has received an attention message, the user routine reads the message into an internal buffer before it clears the `flag` bit. The definitions of procedures `PushA5`, `GetMyTRCCBA5`, and `PopA5` are shown in Listing 5-3 for your convenience. In a complete application these procedures would be defined in the calling routine (see Listing 5-1 for an example).

Listing 5-3   An ADSP user routine

```
PROCEDURE PushA5;                {moves current value of A5 onto stack}
   INLINE $2F0D;                 {MOVE.L A5,-(SP)}


PROCEDURE GetMyTRCCBA5;          {retrieves A5 from the head of the TRCCB }
                                 { (pointed to by A1) and puts it in A5 register}
   INLINE $2A69, $FFFC;          {MOVE.L -4(A1), A5}


PROCEDURE PopA5;                 {restores A5 from stack}
   INLINE $2A5F;                 {MOVE.L (SP)+, A5}


PROCEDURE MyConnectionEvtUserRoutine;

BEGIN
{The connection received an unexpected connection event. Find }
{ out what kind and process accordingly.}

   PushA5;                       {save the current A5}
   GetMyTRCCBA5;                 {set up A5 to point to your }
                                 { application's global variables}

   WITH dspCCB.u DO
   BEGIN
      IF BAND(userFlags, eClosed) <> 0 THEN TellUserItsClosed;
      IF BAND(userFlags, eTearDown) <> 0 THEN TellUserItsBroken;
      IF BAND(userFlags, eFwdReset) <> 0 THEN TellUserItsReset;
      IF BAND(userFlags, eAttention) <> 0 THEN
      BEGIN                      {the event is an attention message}
         myAttnCode := AttnCode;
                                 {get the attention code}
         CopyAttnMsg(AttnPtr, AttnSize, @myAttnData);
                                 {copy the attention message into your buffer}
         tempFlag := userFlags;
         tempCFlag := eAttention;
         BClr(LongInt(tempFlag), tempCFlag);
                                 {clear the flag}
         userFlags := tempFlag;
         {Do something with the message.}
      END;
      gReceivedAnEvent := TRUE
   END;
   PopA5                         {restore the current A5}
END;
```

Using ASDSP

You can write an application that uses the AppleTalk Secure Data Stream Protocol (ASDSP) to

- open a secure ASDSP connection (`sdspOpen`)

- transmit encrypted data across a secure session (`dspWrite` using the encrypt flag)

- read data decrypted by ASDSP that was sent as encrypted across a secure session (`dspRead`)

The initiator end of your ASDSP client application must call the AOCE Authentication Manager to obtain credentials to pass on to ASDSP. ASDSP passes these credentials to the recipient end of the client application and uses them to establish a secure session in which the users of the client applications at both ends of the connection are positively identified. See "About ASDSP" beginning on page 5-9 for more information about this process. ASDSP client applications at either end of a connection can send data to each other that ASDSP encrypts for transmission and then decrypts before delivering it to the client at the receiving end.

An application that currently uses ADSP needs little modification to use ASDSP. To open an ASDSP connection, the client application at each end must issue the secure data stream protocol open routine (`sdspOpen`) instead of the standard open routine (`dspOpen`). The `sdspOpen` routine uses a parameter block that, in addition to the standard ADSP parameters required to open a connection, contains the identity and credentials used in the challenge process; only the initiator end of the connection passes the credentials to ASDSP as input parameter values. The initiator and the recipient ends of a session each open the connection in a different manner:

- The initiator end of a session calls the `sdspOpen` routine using the request mode to direct ASDSP to open a connection with a specific socket.

- The recipient end of a session calls the `sdspOpen` routine in either passive mode or accept mode. A recipient end of a connection can be either of the following:
  - □ a specific socket that waits passively to receive an ASDSP connection request (the connection end associated with the socket calls the `sdspOpen` routine with a value of `ocPassive` for the `ocMode` parameter)
  - □ a connection listener that listens for connection requests and passes them on to a connection server (the connection listener calls the `sdspOpen` routine with a value of `ocAccept` for the `ocMode` parameter, and the connection server accepts and acknowledges receipt of a connection request)

You issue the `sdspOpen` routine by calling the Device Manager's `PBControl` function and passing it a pointer to the DSP parameter block for ASDSP that holds all of the input and output parameters for the call. The parameters that the `sdspOpen` call requires differ for the initiator and recipient ends of a connection. The next section describes how to open an ASDSP connection and how to send encrypted data across it.

Opening a Secure Connection

To open a secure ASDSP connection, both the initiator and the recipient must call the `sdspOpen` routine after calling the `dspInit` routine and, optionally, the `dspOptions` routine. First this section describes how the initiator part of an application opens a secure connection. Then it describes how the recipient end of an application opens a secure connection.

From the Initiator's End

An initiator can send a request to open a secure session to

■ a specific socket whose client application has opened a connection end to wait passively for a connection request

■ a connection listener whose function is to accept requests for secure connections and pass those requests on to a connection server

The initiator makes either an AOCE `AuthTradeProxyForCredentials` call or an AOCE `AuthGetCredentials` call to the authentication server. It passes to the authentication server its own name and the name of the recipient and gets back the session key and the credentials for the session. For an explanation of the calls that the initiator must make to the Authentication Manager, see the chapter "Authentication Manager" in *Inside Macintosh: AOCE Application Programming Interfaces*.

Through the `sdspOpen` call, the initiator passes the credentials to ASDSP to send to the recipient. ASDSP decrypts the credentials and passes the decrypted credential information to the recipient.

To open a secure ASDSP connection, the initiator performs the following procedure:

1. Determine if the Apple Open Collaboration Environment (AOCE) software is installed by calling the `Gestalt` function. See the chapter "Introduction to AOCE" in *Inside Macintosh: AOCE Application Programming Interfaces* for a description of the selector values that you use.

2. Allocate memory for the required data structures identified in this step. The memory belongs to ASDSP until the routine completes execution, after which you can either release or reuse the memory. You must either allocate nonrelocatable memory or lock the memory until the routine completes. See the chapter "Authentication Manager" in *Inside Macintosh: AOCE Application Programming Interfaces* for a description of the memory that you need to allocate for calls that you make to that interface. The data structures that you need to allocate memory for are listed here:

   □ An ASDSP parameter block of type `SDSPParamBlock`. You pass a pointer to this parameter block as the value of the `paramBlock` parameter to the `PBControl` function. (See "The ASDSP Parameter Block" on page 5-41.)

   □ A workspace buffer that the `sdspOpen` routine uses internally whose size is equal to `sdspWorkSize`. The memory for this buffer must be aligned on an even boundary. You pass a pointer to this buffer as the value of the `workspace` parameter.

   □ A buffer for the credentials retrieved from the authentication server and passed to ASDSP.

   □ A buffer for the session key retrieved from the authentication server and passed to ASDSP. This is a data structure of type `AuthKey`.

3. Call the Authentication Manager's `AuthGetUTCTime` function to get the universal coordinated time (UTC). You base the credentials expiration time that you specify as input to the `AuthGetCredentials` function on the UTC. See the chapter "Authentication Manager" for a description of the `AuthGetUTCTime` function.

4. Obtain your (the initiator's) identity and the recipient's record ID. (You can use the local identity or get a specific identity for the initiator.) You need to pass these values to the authentication server to get the session key and credential block from the server. See the chapter "Authentication Manager" for a discussion of identities and complete instruction on how to get these values.

5. Call the Authentication Manager's `AuthGetCredentials` function or `AuthTradeProxyForCredentials` function to get the credentials and the session key. You use these values as input to the `sdspOpen` routine. See the chapter "Authentication Manager" for information on the `AuthGetCredentials` and `AuthTradeProxyForCredentials` functions.

   You pass the `AuthGetCredentials` function or `AuthTradeProxyForCredentials` function the following values returned from the functions that you called in the previous steps:

   □ The initiator's identity.

   □ A pointer to a buffer containing the record ID for the recipient.

   □ The desired expiration time of the credentials. You use the `expiry` parameter to specify for how long you want the credentials to be valid. Credentials are valid for at most eight hours after they are returned to the initiator by the server. You base the expiration time on the UTC time returned by the `AuthGetUTCTime` function.

   □ The expected length of the credentials. A buffer three times the size of a packed record ID is usually sufficient for credentials. The AOCE constant `kPackedRecordIDMaxBytes` specifies the size of a single packed record ID.

6. Call the `sdspOpen` routine to open a secure connection. To call the `sdspOpen` routine, you call the Device Manager's `PBControl` function and specify `sdspOpen` as the value of the `csCode` parameter. The parameter block for the `sdspOpen` routine includes fields also used for the standard `dspOpen` routine. In addition to these parameters, you specify parameters used in the authentication process to establish the secure connection.

   The initiator application calls the `sdspOpen` routine with a value of `ocRequest` for the `ocMode` parameter to direct ASDSP to open a connection with a specific socket on the AppleTalk internet. When you execute the `sdspOpen` routine in the `ocRequest` mode, ASDSP sends an open-connection request to the address you specify.

   If the socket to which you send the open-connection request is a connection listener, the connection server that operates that connection listener can select any socket on the internet to be the connection end that responds to the open-connection request. To restrict the socket from which you will accept a response to your open-connection request, specify a value for the `filterAddress` parameter to the `sdspOpen` routine.

   To use the `ocRequest` mode, you must know the complete internet address of the remote socket, and the ASDSP client at that address must either be a connection listener or have executed the `sdspOpen` routine in the `ocPassive` mode. You can use the NBP routines to obtain a list of the names of objects on the internet and to determine the internet address of a socket when you know its name. See the chapter "Name-Binding Protocol (NBP)" in this book for information on the NBP routines.

In addition to the standard ADSP parameters required for a `dspOpen` call, the initiator supplies the following input values to the `sdspOpen` call:

Parameter	Value
secure	To open a secure authenticated connection, pass a value of TRUE. To open a normal, unauthenticated connection, pass a value of FALSE.
sessionKey	A pointer to the encryption key returned from the `AuthGetCredentials` or `AuthTradeProxyForCredentials` function.
credentialsSize	The value that the `AuthGetCredentials` function or the `AuthTradeProxyForCredentials` function returned that specifies the length of the credentials.
credentials	A pointer to the credentials that the `AuthGetCredentials` function or the `AuthTradeProxyForCredentials` function returned.
workspace	A pointer to the workspace buffer that you allocated, which is for ASDSP's internal use.

From the Recipient End

To open a secure ASDSP connection, the recipient performs the following procedure:

1. Allocate memory for the following data structures. The memory belongs to ASDSP until the routine completes execution, after which you can either release or reuse the memory. You must either allocate nonrelocatable memory or lock the memory until the routine completes.

   □ An ASDSP secure parameter block of type `SDSPParamBlock`. You pass a pointer to this parameter block as the value of the `paramBlock` parameter to the `PBControl` function. (See "The ASDSP Parameter Block" beginning on page 5-41.)

   □ A workspace buffer that the `sdspOpen` routine uses internally whose size is equal to `sdspWorkSize`. The memory for this buffer must be aligned on an even boundary. You must pass a pointer to the buffer as the value of the `workspace` parameter.

   □ A data structure of type `AuthKey` for the session key retrieved from the authentication server and passed to ASDSP. ASDSP breaks out from the credentials block the session key encrypted in the recipient's private key and returns the session key to the recipient in the `sessionKey` buffer.

   □ A buffer for the record ID of the initiator that ASDSP returns to the recipient in response to the recipient's `sdspOpen` routine. You pass a pointer to this buffer as the value of the `initiator` parameter. ASDSP breaks out the initiator's record ID from the credential block that the initiator passes to ASDSP and returns it to the recipient. See the chapter "Authentication Manager" in *Inside Macintosh: AOCE Application Programming Interfaces* for a description of how to create a maximum-size record ID structure that is large enough to hold any record ID.

   □ A buffer for the record ID of the intermediary that ASDSP returns to the recipient if an intermediary is found in the credentials. You pass a pointer to this buffer as the value of the `intermediary` parameter. An intermediary is a proxy that has used the `AuthTradeProxyForCredentials` function to obtain the credentials used in the authentication process. See the chapter "Authentication Manager" in *Inside Macintosh: AOCE Application Programming Interfaces* for a discussion of the use of an intermediary and the `AuthTradeProxyForCredentials` function and for a description of how to create a maximum-size record ID structure that is large enough to hold any record ID.

2. Call the `sdspOpen` routine to open a secure connection. To call the `sdspOpen` routine, you call the Device Manager's `PBControl` function and specify `sdspOpen` as the value of the `csCode` parameter. The parameter block for the `sdspOpen` routine includes fields also used for the standard `dspOpen` routine. In addition to these parameters, you specify parameters used in the authentication process to establish the secure connection.

A recipient end of a connection can be either a connection listener that listens for connection requests and passes them on to a connection server or a socket that waits passively to receive a connection request.

If the recipient is a connection listener, it calls the `sdspOpen` routine with a value of `ocAccept` for the `ocMode` parameter. The connection server accepts and acknowledges receipt of a connection request. When you call the `sdspOpen` routine, you must provide the values returned by the `dspCLListen` routine for the `remoteCID`, `remoteAddress`, `sendSeq`, `sendWindow`, and `attnSendSeq` parameters. You can poll the `state` field in the CCB to determine when the connection is open. Alternatively, you can check the result code for the `sdspOpen` routine when the routine completes execution. If the routine returns the `noErr` result code, then the connection is open.

If the recipient is a connection end associated with a passive socket that calls the `sdspOpen` routine with a value of `ocPassive` for the `ocMode` parameter, use the `ocPassive` mode when you expect to receive an open-connection request from a remote socket. You can specify a value for the `filterAddress` parameter to restrict the network number, node ID, or socket number from which you will accept an open-connection request.

You can poll the state field in the CCB to determine when the connection end is waiting to receive an open-connection request, when the connection end is waiting to receive an acknowledgment of an open-connection request, and when the connection is open. See the section "The ADSP Connection Control Block Record" beginning on page 5-35 for a description of the CCB fields. Alternatively, you can check the result code for the `dspOpen` routine when the routine completes execution. If the routine returns the `noErr` result code, then the connection is open.

In addition to the standard ADSP parameters required for a `dspOpen` call, the recipient supplies the following input values to the `sdspOpen` call:

Parameter	Value
`sessionKey`	A pointer to a data structure of type `AuthKey`, which you allocated. ASDSP copies the session key into this buffer if an authenticated connection was successfully opened.
`workspace`	A pointer to the workspace buffer that you allocated, which is for ASDSP's internal use.
`recipient`	The identity of the recipient.

continued

Parameter	Value
initiator	A pointer to a maximum-size record ID. ASDSP copies the initiator's record ID into this structure if an authenticated connection was successfully opened.
intermediary	A pointer to a maximum-size record ID. ASDSP copies the intermediary's record ID into this structure if an authenticated connection was successfully opened and an intermediary was used to obtain the credentials used to authenticate the call.

If a secure connection was successfully opened, ASDSP returns the following values:

Parameter	Value
issueTime	The time when the credentials were issued. ASDSP copies this value from the credentials.
expiry	The time when the credentials expire. ASDSP copies this value from the credentials.
sessionKey	The encryption key for the session. ASDSP copies this value from the credentials.
initiator	A pointer to a maximum-size record ID structure. If an authenticated connection was successfully opened, this structure holds the initiator's record ID.
hasIntermediary	A flag that is set to TRUE if an intermediary was used to obtain the credentials.
intermediary	A pointer to a maximum-size record ID. If an authentication connection was successfully opened and an intermediary was used to obtain the credentials, this structure holds the intermediary's record ID.

Sending Encrypted Data Across a Secure Connection

After a secure connection is established, both ends can send encrypted data over the session. ASDSP client applications use the dspWrite routine to send data, encrypted or not, over a secure connection. You can turn the encryption feature on or off on a message-by-message basis by setting one flag to direct ASDSP to encrypt the data and setting another flag to terminate the message.

To set these flags, you use the bits of the end-of-message (eom) field; this field is part of the ioParams variant record of the DSP parameter block that you pass to the dspWrite routine. For secure connections, the eom field comprises these two single-bit flags instead of a zero-nonzero byte. You can use the dspEncryptMask and dspEOMMask masks to set these flags, or you can use the dspEncryptBit or dspEOMBit constant.

Note

Apart from the dspWrite routine's eom parameter, the interface to ADSP remains unchanged in regard to encryption. ◆

The encryption process is transparent to the client application that receives the data; ASDSP determines if the received information is encrypted, and, if so, it decrypts the byte stream before copying the data to the read buffer specified by the dspRead routine.

To write data that ASDSP encrypts and then transmits or to terminate data encryption, you call the dspWrite routine using the Device Manager's PBControl function.

■ Set the encrypt bit of the eom field (bit 1) of the DSP parameter block. To set the encrypt bit, you use the dspEncryptMask mask or the dspEncryptBit constant. Note that ASDSP checks this flag on the first write of the connection or the first write following a write for which the end-of-message flag (bit 0 of the eom field) is set.

■ Set the end-of-message bit (bit 0) of the eom field to terminate the encrypted message. To set the end-of-message bit, you use the dspEOMMask mask or the dspEOMBit constant.

If you want to encrypt all messages, you can simply set the encrypt bit on all dspWrite calls.

ADSP Reference

This section describes the data structures and routines that are specific to ADSP and to its secure version, ASDSP. The "Data Structures" section shows the Pascal data structures for

■ the ADSP connection control block

■ the address block record

■ the DSP parameter block

■ the ASDSP version of the DSP parameter block

■ the TRSecureParams record

The "Routines" section describes routines for setting up and tearing down an ADSP or an ASDSP (secure) connection, setting up and tearing down an ADSP connection listener, and maintaining an ADSP connection over which to send and receive data and enable encryption of the data to be sent.

Data Structures

This section describes the connection control block that you allocate for use by ADSP in maintaining the state of a connection end and the DSP parameter block that you use to specify input parameters for and receive output parameters from an ADSP routine. It also describes the address block record that you use to specify the remote connection end's AppleTalk internet address.

The ADSP Connection Control Block Record

The connection control block (CCB) data structure is a record of type TRCCB that consists of 242 bytes. ADSP uses the CCB to store state information about the connection end. You allocate a nonrelocatable block of memory for this data structure when you create a connection end. You may read the fields in the CCB to obtain information about the connection end, but you are not allowed to write to any of the fields except one, the userFlags field.

```
TYPE TRCCB =
PACKED RECORD
    ccbLink:        TPCCB;      {link to next CCB}
    refNum:         Integer;    {reference number}
    state:          Integer;    {state of the connection end}
    userFlags:      Byte;       {user flags for connection}
    localSocket:    Byte;       {local socket number}
    remoteAddress:  AddrBlock;  {remote end internet address}
    attnCode:       Integer;    {attention code received}
    attnSize:       Integer;    {size of attention data}
    attnPtr:        Ptr;        {pointer to attention data}
    reserved:       PACKED ARRAY[1..220] OF Byte;
                                {reserved for use by ADSP}
END;
```

Field descriptions

ccbLink   A pointer to the next CCB. This field is for use by ADSP only.

refNum   The reference number of the CCB. This number is assigned by ADSP when you establish the connection end.

state   The state of the connection end, as follows:

State	Value	Meaning
sListening	1	The socket is a connection listener—that is, a socket that accepts ADSP requests to open connections and passes them on to a socket client. A connection listening socket passes the open-connection request on to a routine that can establish the connection on any socket. The connection listening state is ordinarily used only by connection servers.
sPassive	2	The socket client is inactive but capable of accepting an ADSP request to open a connection. Unlike a connection listening socket, a socket client in the sPassive state can accept an open-connection request only to establish itself as a connection end.
sOpening	3	The socket client has sent an open-connection request and is waiting for acknowledgment.
sOpen	4	The connection is open.

State	Value	Meaning
sClosing	5	The socket client has requested that ADSP close the connection, and ADSP is sending data or waiting for acknowledgment of data it has sent before closing the connection.
sClosed	6	The connection is closed.

userFlags
: Flags that indicate an unsolicited connection event has occurred. An unsolicited connection event is an event initiated by ADSP or the remote connection end that is not in response to any ADSP routine that you executed.

Each time an unsolicited connection event occurs, ADSP sets a flag in the userFlags field of the CCB and calls the routine you specified in the userRoutine parameter to the dspInit routine (if any). The user routine must read the userFlags field and then clear the flag to 0. ADSP cannot notify your routine of future events unless you clear the flag after each event.

ADSP recognizes four types of unsolicited connection events, one corresponding to each of the flags in this field. The events and flags are defined as follows, where bit 7 is the most significant bit:

Event	Flag bit	Meaning
eClosed	7	ADSP has been informed by the remote connection end that the remote connection end has closed the connection.
eTearDown	6	ADSP has determined that the remote connection end is not responding and so has closed the connection.
eAttention	5	ADSP has received an attention message from the remote connection end.
eFwdReset	4	ADSP has received a forward reset command from the remote connection end, has discarded all ADSP data not yet delivered—including the data in the local client end's receive queue— and has resynchronized the connection.
None	3–0	Reserved.

localSocket
: The socket number through which DDP transmits and receives the ADSP packets.

remoteAddress
: The AppleTalk internet address of the socket used by the remote connection end.

attnCode	The attention code received by ADSP when the remote connection end sends an attention message.
attnSize	The size of the attention message received by ADSP when the remote connection end sends an attention message.
attnPtr	A pointer to a buffer containing the attention message received by ADSP from the remote connection end.
reserved	A data buffer reserved for use by ADSP.

The Address Block Record

The address block record defines a data structure of `AddrBlock` type. ADSP routines use this data type to specify the AppleTalk internet socket address of the remote connection end in the CCB. You can use NBP to get the address of an application that is registered with NBP. See the chapter "Name-Binding Protocol (NBP)" in this book for more information. ATP functions also use this data type to specify AppleTalk internet socket addresses.

```
TYPE AddrBlock =
PACKED RECORD
    aNet:        Integer;    {network number}
    aNode:       Byte;       {node ID}
    aSocket:     Byte;       {socket number}
END;
```

Field descriptions

aNet	The network number to which the node belongs that is running the ADSP or ATP client application whose address you are specifying.
aNode	The node ID of the machine running the ADSP or ATP client application whose address you are specifying.
aSocket	The number of the socket used for the ADSP or ATP client application.

The DSP Parameter Block

The ADSP routines, which you execute by calling the Device Manager's `PBControl` function, require a pointer to a DSP parameter block that holds all of the input and output values associated with the routine. The DSP parameter block contains variant records used by particular routines. The `DSPParamBlock` data type defines the DSP parameter block.

This section defines the fields that are common to all ADSP routines that use the DSP parameter block. The fields that are used for specific routines only are defined in the descriptions of the routines to which they apply. The reserved fields, which are used internally by the .DSP driver or not at all, are not defined.

CHAPTER 5

AppleTalk Data Stream Protocol (ADSP)

```
TYPE DSPParamBlock =
PACKED RECORD
    qLink:             QElemPtr;    {reserved}
    qType:             Integer;     {reserved}
    ioTrap:            Integer;     {reserved}
    ioCmdAddr:         Ptr;         {reserved}
    ioCompletion:      ProcPtr;     {completion routine}
    ioResult:          OSErr;       {result code}
    ioNamePtr:         StringPtr;   {reserved}
    ioVRefNum:         Integer;     {reserved}
    ioCRefNum:         Integer;     {driver reference number}
    csCode:            Integer;     {primary command code}
    qStatus:           LongInt;     {reserved}
    ccbRefNum:         Integer;     {CCB reference number}
CASE Integer OF
dspInit, dspCLInit:
    (ccbPtr:           TPCCB;       {pointer to CCB}
    userRoutine:       ProcPtr;     {pointer to user routine}
    sendQSize:         Integer;     {size of send queue}
    sendQueue:         Ptr;         {pointer to send queue}
    recvQSize:         Integer;     {size of receive queue}
    recvQueue:         Ptr;         {pointer to receive queue}
    attnPtr:           Ptr;         {pointer to attention-message }
                                    { buffer}
    localSocket:       Byte;        {local socket number}
    filler1:           Byte);       {filler for proper alignment}
dspOpen, dspCLListen, dspCLDeny:
    (localCID:         Integer;     {local connection ID}
    remoteCID:         Integer;     {remote connection ID}
    remoteAddress:     AddrBlock;   {remote internet address}
    filterAddress:     AddrBlock;   {address filter}
    sendSeq:           LongInt;     {send sequence number}
    sendWindow:        Integer;     {size of remote buffer}
    recvSeq:           LongInt;     {receive sequence number}
    attnSendSeq:       LongInt;     {attention send seq number}
    attnRecvSeq:       LongInt;     {attention receive seq num}
    ocMode:            Byte;        {connection-opening mode}
    ocInterval:        Byte;        {interval bet. open requests}
    ocMaximum:         Byte;        {retries of open-conn req}
    filler2:           Byte);       {filler for proper alignment}
dspClose, dspRemove:
    (abort:            Byte;        {abort send requests}
    filler3:           Byte);       {filler for proper alignment}
```

```
dspStatus:
    (statusCCB:      TPCCB;         {pointer to CCB}
     sendQPending:   Integer;       {bytes waiting in send queue}
     sendQFree:      Integer;       {available send-queue buffer}
     recvQPending:   Integer;       {bytes in receive queue}
     recvQFree:      Integer);      {avail receive-queue buffer}
dspRead, dspWrite:
    (reqCount:       Integer;       {requested number of bytes}
     actCount:       Integer;       {actual number of bytes}
     dataPtr:        Ptr;           {pointer to data buffer}
     eom:            Byte;          {1 if end of message}
     flush:          Byte);         {1 to send data now}
dspAttention:
    (attnCode:       Integer;       {client attention code}
     attnSize:       Integer;       {size of attention data}
     attnData:       Ptr;           {pointer to attention data}
     attnInterval:   Byte;          {reserved}
     filler4:        Byte);         {filler for proper alignment}
dspOptions:
    (sendBlocking:   Integer;       {send-blocking threshold}
     sendTimer:      Byte;          {reserved}
     rtmtTimer:      Byte;          {reserved}
     badSeqMax:      Byte;          {retransmit advice threshold}
     useCheckSum:    Byte);         {DDP checksum for packets}
dspNewCID:
    (newCID:         Integer);      {new connection ID}
END;
```

Field descriptions

ioCompletion   A pointer to a completion routine that you can provide; the Device
                Manager calls your completion routine when it completes execution
                of the PBControl function, if you execute PBControl asynchro-
                nously and you specify a pointer to the routine as the value of this
                field. Specify NIL for this field if you do not wish to provide a
                completion routine. If you execute a function synchronously,
                AppleTalk ignores the ioCompletion field. For information about
                completion routines, see the chapter "Introduction to AppleTalk" in
                this book.

ioResult   The result of the function. If you call the routine asynchronously,
                the Device Manager sets this field to 1 as soon as you call the
                routine and it changes the field to the actual result code when the
                routine completes execution.

ioCRefNum   The driver reference number that is returned by the OpenDriver function. You must specify this number every time you call the .DSP driver.

csCode   The command code for the ADSP routine to be executed. You must fill in this field before calling the PBControl function. You use the following constants as values for this field:

csCode command	Action
dspInit	Create a new connection end
dspRemove	Remove a connection end
dspOpen	Open a connection
dspClose	Close a connection
dspCLInit	Create a connection listener
dspCLRemove	Remove a connection listener
dspCLListen	Post a listener request
dspCLDeny	Deny an open-connection request
dspStatus	Get status of connection end
dspRead	Read data from the connection
dspWrite	Write data on the connection
dspAttention	Send an attention message
dspOptions	Set connection end options
dspReset	Forward reset the connection
dspNewCID	Generate a CID for a connection end

qStatus   This field is reserved for use by ADSP.

ccbRefNum   The reference number of the connection control block (CCB). ADSP returns the CCB reference number in response to the dspInit routine. You must specify this number as a parameter to every .DSP driver routine you call subsequently.

The ASDSP Parameter Block

To open an ASDSP connection, the client application at each end must call the Device Manager's PBControl function with a command code that specifies the ASDSP open routine (sdspOpen). This section describes the ASDSP parameter block whose pointer you pass to PBControl to execute the sdspOpen routine. The ASDSP parameter block contains fields that carry the input and output parameters associated with the function. The SDSPParamBlock data type defines the ASDSP parameter block.

For a description of the fields that are common to both the DSP and ASDSP parameter blocks and that are used in exactly the same way, see "The DSP Parameter Block" beginning on page 5-38. For a description of the fields that are particular to the sdspOpen routine, see "sdspOpen" beginning on page 5-54.

```
SDSPParamBlock =
PACKED RECORD
CASE INTEGER OF
    1: (dspParamBlock: DSPParamBlock);
    2: (qLink:         QElemPtr;             {reserved}
        qType:         Integer;              {reserved}
        ioTrap:        Integer;              {reserved}
        ioCmdAddr:     Ptr;                  {reserved}
        ioCompletion:  ProcPtr;              {pointer to completion routine}
        ioResult:      OSErr;                {routine result}
        ioNamePtr:     StringPtr;            {reserved}
        ioVRefNum:     Integer;              {reserved}
        ioCRefNum:     Integer;              {ASDSP driver refNum}
        csCode:        Integer;              {ASDSP driver control code}
        qStatus:       LongInt;              {reserved}
        ccbRefNum:     Integer;              {connection end refNum}
        secureParams:  TRSecureParams);      {dspOpenSecure}
END;

SDSPPBPtr = ^SDSPParamBlock;
```

Field descriptions

csCode   The command code for the ASDSP routine to be executed. You must fill in this field before calling the PBControl function. To call the sdspOpen routine to open a secure connection, you specify the constant sdspOpen as the value of this parameter.

secureParams   A record of type TRSecureParams that contains the additional parameters required to open a secure ASDSP session.

The TRSecureParams Record

The ASDSP parameter block is a variant parameter block that includes a field that is a record of type TRSecureParams, which defines the additional parameters required for an ASDSP session. This section shows the declaration for the TRSecureParams record. The routine description "sdspOpen" beginning on page 5-54 includes the field definitions for the TRSecureParams record.

The TRSecureParams record is defined as follows:

```
TYPE  TRSecureParams =
PACKED RECORD
    localCID:          Integer;       {local connection ID}
    remoteCID:         Integer;       {remote connection ID}
    remoteAddress:     AddrBlock;     {address of remote end}
    filterAddress:     AddrBlock;     {address filter}
    sendSeq:           Longint;       {local send sequence number}
```

```
    sendWindow:              Integer;          {send window size}
    recvSeq:                 LongInt;          {receive sequence number}
    attnSendSeq:             LongInt;          {attention send sequence number}
    attnRecvSeq:             LongInt;          {attention receive sequence number}
    ocMode:                  Byte;             {open connection mode}
    ocInterval:              Byte;             {open connection request retry }
                                               { interval}
    ocMaximum:               Byte;             {open connection request retry }
                                               { maximum}
    secure:                  Boolean;          {for initiator, TRUE if session is
                                               { authenticated }
                                               {for recipient, TRUE if session was }
                                               { authenticated}
    sessionKey:              AuthKeyPtr;       {encryption key for session}
    credentialsSize:         LongInt;          {length of credentials}
    credentials:             Ptr;              {pointer to credentials}
    workspace:               Ptr;              {pointer to workspace for }
                                               { connection. Align on even boundary }
                                               { and length = sdspWorkSize}
    recipient:               AuthIdentity;     {identity of recipient or initiator }
                                               { if active mode}
    issueTime:               UTCTime;          {time when credentials were issued}
    expiry:                  UTCTime;          {time when credentials expire}
    initiator:               RecordIDPtr;      {RecordID of initiator returned in }
                                               { buffer pointed to by this field}
    hasIntermediary:         Boolean;          {set if credentials has an }
                                               { intermediary}
    intermediary:            RecordIDPtr;      {RecordID of intermediary returned }
                                               { here}
END;
```

Routines

This section describes the ADSP and ASDSP routines that you use to

- establish and terminate an ADSP connection

- establish a secure (ASDSP) connection

- establish and terminate an ADSP connection listener

- maintain an ADSP connection, including sending and receiving data across an ADSP or ASDSP connection and enabling encryption of the data to be sent

You use the Device Manager's `PBControl` function for all of the ADSP and ASDSP routine calls.

```
FUNCTION PBControl (paramBlock: ParmBlkPtr;
                        async: Boolean): OSErr;
```

paramBlock
> A pointer to the DSP parameter block that the `PBControl` function uses for DSP routines.

async
> A Boolean that specifies whether the function is to execute synchronously or asynchronously. Set the `async` parameter to `TRUE` to execute the function asynchronously.

DESCRIPTION

All of the ADSP routines are implemented through a call to the `PBControl` function. The `PBControl` function takes a pointer to a parameter block and a Boolean value that specifies the mode in which the function is to be executed. You use the DSP parameter block for all ADSP calls.

The parameter block includes a field, `csCode`, in which you specify the routine selector for the particular routine to be executed; you must specify a value for this field. Each ADSP routine may use different fields of the DSP parameter block for parameters specific to that routine. The description of a function in this section includes the specific parameters used for that function. See the section "The DSP Parameter Block" beginning on page 5-38 for the complete DSP parameter block data structure.

An arrow preceding a parameter indicates whether the parameter is an input parameter, an output parameter, or both:

Arrow	Meaning
→	Input
←	Output
↔	Both

Establishing and Terminating an ADSP Connection

You can use the routines described in this section to

- establish and initialize a connection end

- set the values for parameters that control the behavior of a connection end

- open an ADSP or ASDSP connection

- assign an identification number to a connection end

- close a connection end

- eliminate a connection end

dspInit

The dspInit routine establishes a connection end, that is, it assigns a specific socket for the ADSP connection end to use and initializes the variables that ADSP uses to maintain the connection. You use the PBControl function to call the dspInit routine. See "Routines" beginning on page 5-43 for a description of the PBControl function.

Parameter block

→	ioCompletion	ProcPtr	A pointer to a completion routine.
←	ioResult	OSErr	The function result.
→	ioCRefNum	Integer	The driver reference number.
→	csCode	Integer	Always dspInit for this function.
←	ccbRefNum	Integer	The CCB reference number.
→	ccbPtr	TPCCB	A pointer to the CCB.
→	userRoutine	ProcPtr	A pointer to a routine to call on connection events.
→	sendQSize	Integer	The size in bytes of the send queue.
→	sendQueue	Ptr	A pointer to the send queue.
→	recvQSize	Ptr	The size in bytes of the receive queue.
→	recvQueue	Ptr	A pointer to the receive queue.
→	attnPtr	Ptr	A pointer to the buffer for incoming attention messages.
↔	localSocket	Byte	The DDP socket number for this connection end.

Field descriptions

csCode   The routine selector, always equal to dspInit for this routine.

ccbRefNum   The connection control block (CCB) reference number. The dspInit routine returns the CCB reference number for this connection end as the value of the ccbRefNum parameter. You must provide this number in all subsequent calls to this connection end.

ccbPtr   A pointer to the CCB that you allocated to be used by this connection end. The CCB is 242 bytes in size and is described in "The ADSP Connection Control Block Record" beginning on page 5-35. See also "Creating and Using a Connection Control Block" on page 5-12.

userRoutine   A pointer to a routine that ADSP is to call each time the connection end receives an unsolicited connection event. Specify NIL for this parameter if you do not want to supply a user routine. Connection events and user routines are discussed in "Writing a User Routine for Connection Events" beginning on page 5-26.

sendQSize   The size in bytes of the send queue. A queue size of 600 bytes should work well for most applications. If you are using ADSP to send a continuous flow of data, a larger data buffer improves performance. If your application is sending the user's keystrokes, a smaller buffer should be adequate. The constant minDSPQueueSize indicates the minimum queue size that you can use.

sendQueue   A pointer to the send queue that you allocated.

recvQSize	The size in bytes of the receive queue. A queue size of 600 bytes should work well for most applications. If you are using ADSP to receive a continuous flow of data, a larger data buffer improves performance. If your application is receiving a user's keystrokes, a smaller buffer should be adequate. The constant minDSPQueueSize indicates the minimum queue size that you can use.
recvQueue	A pointer to the receive queue that you allocated.
attnPtr	A pointer to the attention-message buffer that you allocated. The attention-message buffer must be the size of the constant attnBufSize.
localSocket	The DDP socket number of the socket that you want ADSP to use for this connection end. Specify 0 for this parameter to cause ADSP to assign the socket; in this case, ADSP returns the socket number when the dspInit routine completes execution.

DESCRIPTION

The dspInit routine creates and initializes a connection end. The dspInit routine does not open the connection end or establish a connection with a remote connection end; you must follow the dspInit routine with the dspOpen routine to perform those tasks.

When you send bytes to a remote connection end, ADSP stores the bytes in a buffer called the *send queue*. Until the remote connection end acknowledges their receipt, ADSP keeps the bytes you sent in the send queue so that they are available to be retransmitted if necessary. When the local connection end receives bytes, it stores them in a buffer called the *receive queue* until you read them.

You must allocate memory for the send (sendQueue) and receive (recvQSize) queues and for a buffer (attnPtr) that holds incoming attention messages. You must also allocate a nonrelocatable block of memory (ccbPtr) for the CCB for this connection end.

SPECIAL CONSIDERATIONS

You must allocate nonrelocatable memory for the CCB, the send queue, the receive queue, and the attention-message buffer, and ensure that the memory remains locked until you explicitly remove the connection end by calling the dspRemove routine. Do not write any data to this memory except by calling ADSP routines.

ASSEMBLY-LANGUAGE INFORMATION

To execute the dspInit routine from assembly language, call the _Control trap macro with a value of dspInit in the csCode field of the parameter block.

RESULT CODES

noErr	0	No error
ddpSktErr	–91	Error opening DDP socket
errDSPQueueSize	–1274	Send or receive queue is too small

dspOptions

The `dspOptions` routine allows you to set values for several parameters that affect the behavior of the local connection end. You use the `PBControl` function to call the `dspOptions` routine. See "Routines" on page 5-43 for a description of the `PBControl` function.

Parameter block

→	ioCompletion	ProcPtr	A pointer to a completion routine.
←	ioResult	OSErr	The function result.
→	ioCRefNum	Integer	The driver reference number.
→	csCode	Integer	Always dspOptions for this function.
→	ccbRefNum	Integer	The CCB reference number.
→	sendBlocking	Integer	The send-blocking threshold.
→	badSeqMax	Byte	The threshold to send retransmit advice.
→	useCheckSum	Byte	A DDP checksum flag.

Field descriptions

csCode   The routine selector, always equal to `dspOptions` for this routine.

ccbRefNum   The connection control block (CCB) reference number that the `dspInit` routine returned.

sendBlocking   The maximum number of bytes that may accumulate in the send queue before ADSP sends a packet to the remote connection end. ADSP sends a packet before the maximum number of bytes accumulates if the period specified by the send timer expires, if you execute the `dspWrite` routine with the flush parameter set to 1, or if a connection event requires that the local connection end send an acknowledgment packet to the remote connection end.

You can set the `sendBlocking` parameter to any value from 1 byte to the maximum size of a packet (572 bytes). If you set the `sendBlocking` parameter to 0, the current value for this parameter is not changed. The default value for the `sendBlocking` parameter is 16 bytes.

badSeqMax   The maximum number of out-of-sequence data packets that the local connection end can receive before requesting the remote connection end to retransmit the missing data. Because a connection end does not acknowledge the receipt of a data packet received out of sequence, the retransmit timer of the remote connection end will expire eventually and the connection end will retransmit the data. The `badSeqMax` parameter allows you to cause the data to be retransmitted before the retransmit timer of the remote connection end has expired.

You can set the `badSeqMax` parameter to any value from 1 to 255. If you set the `badSeqMax` parameter to 0, the current value for this parameter is not changed. The default value for the `badSeqMax` parameter is 3.

useCheckSum   A flag specifying whether DDP should compute a checksum and include it in each packet that it sends to the remote connection end. Set this parameter to 1 if you want DDP to use checksums or to 0 if you do not want DDP to use checksums. The default value for useCheckSum is 0.

ADSP cannot include a checksum in a packet that has a short DDP header—that is, a packet being sent over LocalTalk to a remote socket that is on the same cable as the local socket. Note that the useCheckSum parameter affects only whether ADSP includes a checksum in a packet that it is sending. If ADSP receives a packet that includes a checksum, it validates the checksum regardless of the setting of the useCheckSum parameter.

DESCRIPTION

The dspOptions routine lets you set values that determine the behavior of a connection end, such as the blocking factor, which is maximum number of bytes that should accumulate in the connection end's send queue before ADSP sends a packet to the remote connection end, the maximum number of out-of-sequence packets received by the connection end before ADSP sends a request for the missing packets, and whether or not DDP should use checksums for all the packets that it transmits. You can set the options for any established connection end, whether or not the connection end is open.

ASSEMBLY-LANGUAGE INFORMATION

To execute the dspOptions routine from assembly language, call the _Control trap macro with a value of dspOptions in the csCode field of the parameter block.

RESULT CODES

noErr   0   No error
errRefNum   –1280   Bad connection reference number

SEE ALSO

Use the dspInit routine, described on page 5-45, to return the connection control block (CCB) reference number.

dspOpen

The dspOpen routine opens a connection end. You can open a connection end in request mode, passive mode, accept mode, or establish mode. You use the PBControl function to call the dspOpen routine. See "Routines" on page 5-43 for a description of the PBControl function.

Parameter block

→	ioCompletion	ProcPtr	A pointer to completion routine.
←	ioResult	OSErr	The function result.
→	ioCRefNum	Integer	The driver reference number.
→	csCode	Integer	Always dspOpen for this function.
→	ccbRefNum	Integer	The CCB reference number.
←	localCID	Integer	The ID of this connection end.
↔	remoteCID	Integer	The ID of remote connection end.
↔	remoteAddress	AddrBlock	A remote internet address.
→	filterAddress	AddrBlock	A filter for open-connection requests.
↔	sendSeq	LongInt	The initial send sequence number.
↔	sendWindow	Integer	The initial size of remote receive queue.
→	recvSeq	LongInt	The initial receive sequence number.
↔	attnSendSeq	LongInt	The attention send sequence number.
→	attnRecvSeq	LongInt	The attention receive sequence number.
→	ocMode	Byte	The connection-opening mode.
→	ocInterval	Byte	The interval between open requests.
→	ocMaximum	Byte	The number of open-connection request retries.

The use of parameters by the dspOpen routine depends on the mode in which the routine is executed, as follows:

ocRequest		**ocPassive**		**ocAccept**		**ocEstablish**	
→	ioCompletion	→	ioCompletion	→	ioCompletion	→	ioCompletion
←	ioResult	←	ioResult	←	ioResult	←	ioResult
→	ioCRefNum	→	ioCRefNum	→	ioCRefNum	→	ioCRefNum
→	csCode	→	csCode	→	csCode	→	csCode
→	ccbRefNum	→	ccbRefNum	→	ccbRefNum	→	ccbRefNum
←	localCID	←	localCID	←	localCID	—	localCID
←	remoteCID	←	remoteCID	→	remoteCID	→	remoteCID
→	remoteAddress	←	remoteAddress	→	remoteAddress	→	remoteAddress
→	filterAddress	→	filterAddress	—	filterAddress	—	filterAddress
←	sendSeq	←	sendSeq	→	sendSeq	→	sendSeq
←	sendWindow	←	sendWindow	→	sendWindow	→	sendWindow
—	recvSeq	—	recvSeq	—	recvSeq	→	recvSeq
←	attnSendSeq	←	attnSendSeq	→	attnSendSeq	→	attnSendSeq
—	attnRecvSeq	—	attnRecvSeq	—	attnRecvSeq	→	attnRecvSeq
→	ocMode	→	ocMode	→	ocMode	→	ocMode
→	ocInterval	→	ocInterval	→	ocInterval	—	ocInterval
→	ocMaximum	→	ocMaximum	→	ocMaximum	—	ocMaximum

Key: → input   ← output   ↔ input and output   — not used

Field descriptions

csCode   The routine selector, always equal to dspOpen for this routine.

ccbRefNum   The connection control block (CCB) reference number that was
                  returned by the dspInit routine for the connection end that you
                  want to use.

localCID   The identification number of the local connection end. This number
                  is assigned by ADSP when you open the connection. ADSP includes
                  this number in every packet sent to a remote connection end. Before
                  you call the dspOpen routine in ocEstablish mode, you must
                  call the dspNewCID routine to cause ADSP to assign this value.

remoteCID   The identification number of the remote connection end. This
                  parameter is returned by the dspOpen routine in the ocRequest
                  and ocPassive modes. A connection server must provide this
                  number to the dspOpen routine when the server executes the
                  routine in ocAccept mode; in this case, the connection server
                  obtains the remoteCID value from the dspCLListen routine. You
                  must provide the remoteCID value to the dspOpen routine when
                  you use the routine in ocEstablish mode.

remoteAddress   The internet address of the remote socket with which you wish to
                  establish communications. This address consists of a 2-byte network
                  number, a 1-byte node ID, and a 1-byte socket number. You must
                  provide this parameter when you call the dspOpen routine in the
                  ocRequest or ocEstablish mode. This parameter is returned by
                  the dspOpen routine when you call the routine in the ocPassive
                  mode. When you call the dspOpen routine in the ocAccept mode,
                  you must use the value for the remoteAddress parameter that
                  was returned by the dspCLListen routine.

filterAddress   The internet address of the socket from which you will accept a
                  connection request. The address consists of three fields: a 2-byte
                  network number, a 1-byte node ID, and a 1-byte socket number.
                  Specify 0 for any of these fields for which you wish to impose no
                  restrictions. If you specify a filter address of $00082500, for example,
                  the connection end accepts a connection request from any socket at
                  node $25 of network $0008. Set the filterAddress parameter
                  equal to the remoteAddress parameter to accept a connection
                  only with the socket to which you sent a connection request.

                  When you execute the dspOpen routine in the ocPassive mode,
                  you can receive a connection request from any ADSP connection
                  end on the internet. When you execute the dspOpen routine in the
                  ocRequest mode, your connection end can receive a connection
                  request acknowledgment from an address different from the one
                  you specified in the remoteAddress parameter only if the remote
                  address you specified was that of a connection listener. In either
                  case, you can use the filterAddress parameter to avoid acknowl-
                  edging unwanted connection requests.

                  When you execute the dspOpen routine in the ocAccept mode,
                  your connection listener has already received and decided to accept
                  the connection request. You can specify a filter address for a

connection listener with the dspCLListen routine. A connection server can use the dspCLDeny routine to deny a connection request that was accepted by its connection listener.

You cannot use the filter address when you execute the dspOpen routine in ocEstablish mode.

sendSeq   The sequence number of the first byte that the local connection end will send to the remote connection end. ADSP uses this number to coordinate communications and to check for errors. ADSP returns a value for the sendSeq parameter when you execute the dspOpen routine in the ocRequest or ocPassive mode. When you execute the dspOpen routine in the ocAccept mode, you must specify the value for the sendSeq parameter that was returned by the dspCLListen routine. You must provide the value for this parameter when you execute the dspOpen routine in the ocEstablish mode.

sendWindow   The sequence number of the last byte that the remote connection end has buffer space to receive. ADSP uses this number to coordinate communications and to check for errors. ADSP returns a value for the sendWindow parameter when you execute the dspOpen routine in the ocRequest or ocPassive mode. When you execute the dspOpen routine in the ocAccept mode, you must specify the value for the sendWindow parameter that was returned by the dspCLListen routine. You must provide the value for this parameter when you execute the dspOpen routine in the ocEstablish mode.

recvSeq   The sequence number of the next byte that the local connection end expects to receive. ADSP uses this number to coordinate communications and to check for errors. You must provide the value for this parameter when you execute the dspOpen routine in the ocEstablish mode. The dspOpen routine does not use this parameter when you execute it in any other mode.

attnSendSeq   The sequence number of the next attention packet that the local connection end will transmit. ADSP uses this number to coordinate communications and to check for errors. ADSP returns a value for the attnSendSeq parameter when you execute the dspOpen routine in the ocRequest or ocPassive mode. When you execute the dspOpen routine in the ocAccept mode, you must specify the value for the attnSendSeq parameter that was returned by the dspCLListen routine. You must provide the value for this parameter when you execute the dspOpen routine in the ocEstablish mode.

attnRecvSeq   The sequence number of the next attention packet that the local connection end expects to receive. ADSP uses this number to ensure that packets are delivered in the correct order and to check for errors. You must provide a value for this parameter when you execute the dspOpen routine in the ocEstablish mode. The dspOpen routine does not use this parameter when you execute it in any other mode.

ocMode   The mode in which the dspOpen routine is to operate, as follows:

Mode	Value	Meaning
ocRequest	1	ADSP attempts to open a connection with the socket you specify.
ocPassive	2	The connection end waits to receive a connection request.
ocAccept	3	The connection server accepts and acknowledges receipt of a connection request.
ocEstablish	4	ADSP considers the connection established and open; you are responsible for setting up and synchronizing both connection ends.

ocInterval   The period between transmissions of open-connection requests. If the remote connection end does not acknowledge or deny an open-connection request, ADSP retransmits the request after a time period specified by this parameter. The time period used by ADSP is (ocInterval × 10) ticks, or (ocInterval / 6) seconds. For example, if you set the ocInterval parameter to 3, the time period between retransmissions is 30 ticks ($^1/_2$ second). You can set the ocInterval parameter to any value from 1 ($^1/_6$ second) to 180 (30 seconds). If you specify 0 for the ocInterval parameter, ADSP uses the default value of 6 (1 second).

You must provide a value for the ocInterval parameter when you execute the dspOpen routine in the ocRequest, ocPassive, or ocAccept mode. The dspOpen routine does not use this parameter when you execute it in the ocEstablish mode.

ocMaximum   The maximum number of times to retransmit an open-connection request before ADSP terminates execution of the dspOpen routine. If you specify 0 for the ocMaximum parameter, ADSP uses the default value of 3. If you specify 255 for the ocMaximum parameter, ADSP retransmits the open-connection request indefinitely until the remote connection end either acknowledges or denies the request.

You must provide a value for the ocMaximum parameter when you execute the dspOpen routine in the ocRequest, ocPassive, or ocAccept mode. The dspOpen routine does not use this parameter when you execute it in the ocEstablish mode.

DESCRIPTION

The dspOpen routine opens a connection end. You set the ocMode field of the parameter block to specify the opening mode that the dspOpen routine is to use. The dspOpen routine puts a connection end into one of the four following opening modes:

- The ocRequest mode, in which ADSP attempts to open a connection with the socket at the internet address you specify as the remoteAddress parameter. If the socket you specify as a remote address is a connection listener, it is possible that your application will receive a connection acknowledgment and request from a different address than the one to which you sent the open-connection request. You can use the `filterAddress` parameter to restrict the addresses with which you will accept a connection.

The `dspOpen` routine completes execution in the `ocRequest` mode when one of the following occurs: ADSP establishes a connection, your connection end receives a connection denial from the remote connection end, your connection end denies the connection request returned by a connection listener, or ADSP cannot complete the connection within the maximum number of retries that you specified with the `ocMaximum` parameter.

■ The `ocPassive` mode, in which the connection end waits to receive an open-connection request from a remote connection end. You can use the `filterAddress` parameter to restrict the addresses from which you will accept a connection request.

The `dspOpen` routine completes execution in the `ocPassive` mode when ADSP establishes a connection or when either connection end receives a connection denial.

■ The `ocAccept` mode, used by connection servers to complete an open-connection dialog. When a connection server is informed by its connection listener that the connection listener has received an open-connection request, the connection server calls the `dspInit` routine to establish a connection end and then calls the `dspOpen` routine in `ocAccept` mode to complete the connection. You must obtain the following parameters from the `dspCLListen` routine and provide them to the `dspOpen` routine: `remoteAddress`, `remoteCID`, `sendSeq`, `sendWindow`, and `attnSendSeq`. Connection listeners and connection servers are described in "Creating and Using a Connection Listener" beginning on page 5-22 and in "Establishing and Terminating an ADSP Connection" beginning on page 5-44. See "Connection Listeners" on page 5-7 for a brief introduction to connection listeners.

The `dspOpen` routine completes execution in the `ocAccept` mode when ADSP establishes a connection or when either connection end receives a connection denial.

■ The `ocEstablish` mode, in which ADSP considers the connection end established and the connection state open. This mode is for use by clients that determine their connection-opening parameters without using ADSP or the .DSP driver to do so.

You must first use the `dspInit` routine to establish a connection end and then execute the `dspNewCID` routine to obtain an identification number (ID) for the local connection end. You must then communicate with the remote connection end to send it the local connection ID and to determine the values of the following parameters: `remoteAddress`, `remoteCID`, `sendSeq`, `sendWindow`, `recvSeq`, `attnSendSeq`, and `attnRecvSeq`. Only then can you execute the `dspOpen` routine in the `ocEstablish` mode.

The `dspOpen` routine completes execution in the `ocEstablish` mode immediately.

ASSEMBLY-LANGUAGE INFORMATION

To execute the `dspOpen` routine from assembly language, call the `_Control` trap macro with a value of `dspOpen` in the `csCode` field of the parameter block.

RESULT CODES

noErr	0	No error
errOpenDenied	–1273	Open request denied by recipient
errOpening	–1277	Attempt to open connection failed
errState	–1278	Connection end must be closed
errAborted	–1279	Request aborted by dspRemove or dspClose routine
errRefNum	–1280	Bad connection reference number

sdspOpen

The sdspOpen routine opens a secure (ASDSP) connection and causes ASDSP to perform the challenge-and-reply process that authenticates the ASDSP clients at either end of the connection. You use the PBControl function to call the sdspOpen routine. See "Routines" on page 5-43 for a description of the PBControl function.

Parameter block

ioCompletion	ProcPtr	A pointer to completion routine.
ioResult	OSErr	A result code.
ioCRefNum	Integer	The ADSP driver reference number.
csCode	Integer	Always sdspOpen for this function.
ccbRefNum	Integer	The CCB reference number for connection end.
localCID	Integer	The ID of this connection end.
remoteCID	Integer	The ID of remote connection end.
remoteAddress	AddrBlock	A remote internet address.
filterAddress	AddrBlock	A filter for open connection end.
sendSeq	LongInt	The initial send sequence number.
sendWindow	Integer	The initial size of remote receive queue.
recvSeq	LongInt	Not used for ASDSP.
attnSendSeq	LongInt	The attention send sequence number.
attnRecvSeq	LongInt	Not used for ASDSP.
ocMode	Byte	The connection-opening mode.
ocInterval	Byte	The interval between open requests.
ocMaximum	Byte	The maximum number of retries of the open-connection request.
secure	Boolean	A flag that determines if ASDSP authenticates the connection.
sessionKey	AuthKeyPtr	A pointer to the session encryption key.
credentialsSize	LongInt	The length of credentials.
credentials	Ptr	A pointer to credentials.
workspace	Ptr	A pointer to workspace for connection.
recipient	AuthIdentity	The identity of recipient.
issueTime	UTCTime	The time when credentials were issued.
expiry	UTCTime	The time when credentials expire.
initiator	RecordIDPtr	A pointer to record ID of initiator.
hasIntermediary	Boolean	TRUE if credentials has an intermediary.
intermediary	RecordIDPtr	A pointer to record ID of intermediary.

The use of parameters by the sdspOpen routine depends on the mode in which the routine is executed, as follows:

ocRequest		ocPassive		ocAccept	
→	ioCompletion	→	ioCompletion	→	ioCompletion
←	ioResult	←	ioResult	←	ioResult
→	ioCRefNum	→	ioCRefNum	→	ioCRefNum
→	csCode	→	csCode	→	csCode
→	ccbRefNum	→	ccbRefNum	→	ccbRefNum
←	localCID	←	localCID	←	localCID
←	remoteCID	←	remoteCID	→	remoteCID
→	remoteAddress	←	remoteAddress	→	remoteAddress
→	filterAddress	→	filterAddress	—	filterAddress
←	sendSeq	←	sendSeq	→	sendSeq
←	sendWindow	←	sendWindow	→	sendWindow
—	recvSeq	—	recvSeq	—	recvSeq
←	attnSendSeq	←	attnSendSeq	→	attnSendSeq
—	attnRecvSeq	—	attnRecvSeq	—	attnRecvSeq
→	ocMode	→	ocMode	→	ocMode
→	ocInterval	→	ocInterval	→	ocInterval
→	ocMaximum	→	ocMaximum	→	ocMaximum
→	secure	←	secure	←	secure
→	sessionKey	←	sessionKey	←	sessionKey
→	credentialsSize	—	credentialsSize	—	credentialsSize
→	credentials	—	credentials	—	credentials
→	workspace	→	workspace	→	workspace
—	recipient	→	recipient	→	recipient
—	issueTime	←	issueTime	←	issueTime
—	expiry	←	expiry	←	expiry
—	initiator	↔	initiator	↔	initiator
—	hasIntermediary	←	hasIntermediary	←	hasIntermediary
—	intermediary	↔	intermediary	↔	intermediary

Key: → input ← output ↔ input and output — not used

Field descriptions

csCode	The routine selector, always equal to sdspOpen for this routine.
ccbRefNum	This field is used in the same way that it is used for ADSP. See the description of this field under "dspOpen" beginning on page 5-48.
localCID	This field is used in the same way that it is used for ADSP. See the description of this field under "dspOpen" beginning on page 5-48.

`remoteCID`	The identification number of the remote connection end. This parameter is returned by the `sdspOpen` routine in the `ocRequest` and `ocPassive` modes. A connection server must provide this number to the `sdspOpen` routine when the server executes the routine in `ocAccept` mode; in this case, the connection server obtains the `remoteCID` value from the `dspCLListen` routine.
`remoteAddress`	The internet address of the remote socket with which you wish to establish communications. This address consists of a 2-byte network number, a 1-byte node ID, and a 1-byte socket number. You must provide this parameter when you call the `sdspOpen` routine in the `ocRequest` or `ocAccept` mode. When you call the `sdspOpen` routine in the `ocAccept` mode, you must use the value for the `remoteAddress` parameter that was returned by the `dspCLListen` routine. This parameter is returned by the `sdspOpen` routine when you call the routine in the `ocPassive` mode.
`filterAddress`	This field is used in the same way that it is used for ADSP. See the description of this field under "dspOpen" beginning on page 5-48.
`sendSeq`	The sequence number of the first byte that the local connection end will send to the remote connection end. ASDSP uses this number to coordinate communications and to check for errors. ASDSP returns a value for the `sendSeq` parameter when you execute the `sdspOpen` routine in the `ocRequest` or `ocPassive` mode. When you execute the `sdspOpen` routine in the `ocAccept` mode, you must specify the value for the `sendSeq` parameter that was returned by the `dspCLListen` routine.
`sendWindow`	The sequence number of the last byte that the remote connection end has buffer space to receive. ASDSP uses this number to coordinate communications and to check for errors. ASDSP returns a value for the `sendWindow` parameter when you execute the `sdspOpen` routine in the `ocRequest` or `ocPassive` mode. When you execute the `sdspOpen` routine in the `ocAccept` mode, you must specify the value for the `sendWindow` parameter that was returned by the `dspCLListen` routine.
`recvSeq`	This field is not used by ASDSP.
`attnSendSeq`	The sequence number of the next attention packet that the local connection end will transmit. ASDSP uses this number to coordinate communications and to check for errors. ASDSP returns a value for the `attnSendSeq` parameter when you execute the `sdspOpen` routine in the `ocRequest` or `ocPassive` mode. When you execute the `sdspOpen` routine in the `ocAccept` mode, you must specify the value for the `attnSendSeq` parameter that was returned by the `dspCLListen` routine.
`attnRecvSeq`	This field is not used by ASDSP.

ocMode		The mode in which the `sdspOpen` routine is to operate, as follows:

Mode	Value	Meaning
`ocRequest`	1	ADSP attempts to open a connection with the remote socket you specify.
`ocPassive`	2	The connection end waits to receive a connection request.
`ocAccept`	3	The connection server accepts and acknowledges receipt of a connection request.

ocInterval
This field is used in the same way that it is used for ADSP. See the description of this field under "dspOpen" beginning on page 5-48.

ocMaximum
This field is used in the same way that it is used for ADSP. See the description of this field under "dspOpen" beginning on page 5-48.

secure
A flag that determines whether ASDSP authenticates the connection. On input for the initiator end, you must set this value to TRUE if you want ASDSP to authenticate the connection. You must provide a value for the `secure` parameter when you execute the `sdspOpen` routine in the `ocRequest` mode. ASDSP returns a value of TRUE for this parameter to the recipient for all modes if the session was authenticated.

sessionkey
A pointer to a buffer containing the session key returned by the Authentication Manager's `AuthGetCredentials` or `AuthTradeProxyForCredentials` function. The initiator connection end must provide an input value for this parameter. For the recipient connection end, ASDSP breaks out the session key from the credentials block and returns a copy of the session key as the value of this parameter. See the description of the data structures that you need to allocate for ASDSP in the section "Opening a Secure Connection" beginning on page 5-30 for more information about the buffer.

credentialsSize
The size in bytes of credentials returned by the Authentication Manager's `AuthTradeProxyForCredentials` or `AuthGetCredentials` function. You must provide a value for the `credentialsSize` parameter when you execute the `sdspOpen` routine in the `ocRequest` mode. This parameter is not used for the recipient end of the connection when you call the `sdspOpen` routine in `ocAccept` mode or `ocPassive` mode.

credentials
A pointer to the credentials for this session that the Authentication Manager's `AuthTradeProxyForCredentials` or `AuthGetCredentials` function returned when you called it. Specify the size in bytes of the credential block pointed to by this parameter as the value of the `credentialsSize` parameter when you call the `sdspOpen` routine in the `ocRequest` mode. This parameter is not used for the recipient end of the connection when you call the `sdspOpen` routine in `ocAccept` mode or `ocPassive` mode. See the chapter "Authentication Manager" in *Inside Macintosh: AOCE Application Programming Interfaces*.

workspace
A pointer to a buffer that you allocate as workspace for the `sdspOpen` routine's internal use. The memory for the buffer that you allocate must be aligned on an even boundary and must be equal in size to the `sdspWorkSize` constant, which is 2048 bytes.

recipient
When the value of the `ocMode` parameter is `ocAccept`, you specify the identity of the connection server as the value of the `recipient` parameter. When the value of the `ocMode` parameter is `ocPassive`, you specify the identity of the socket that is the recipient of the request call as the value of the `recipient` parameter. This field is not used when the `ocMode` parameter value is `ocRequest`.

issueTime
The time when the authentication credentials were issued. Together with the `expiry` parameter value, the `issueTime` parameter specifies the period of time for which the credentials are valid. ASDSP extracts the value for the `issueTime` parameter from the decrypted credentials. ASDSP returns this value when the mode is `ocPassive` or `ocAccept`. The `issueTime` field is not used when the `ocMode` parameter value is `ocRequest`.

expiry
The time when the authentication credentials expire. Together with the `issueTime` parameter value, the `expiry` parameter specifies the duration for which the credentials are valid. ASDSP extracts the value for the `expiry` parameter from the decrypted credentials. This field is not used when the `ocMode` parameter value is `ocRequest`.

initiator
A pointer to the record ID of the initiator that ASDSP returns when the value of the `ocMode` parameter is `ocAccept` or `ocPassive`. ASDSP extracts this value from the encrypted credentials. This field is not used when the `ocMode` parameter value is `ocRequest`.

hasIntermediary
A flag that ASDSP sets if the credentials have an intermediary. When this flag is set, a proxy was used; an intermediary used the `AuthTradeProxyForCredentials` function to obtain the credentials used in the authentication process. The `sdspOpen` routine returns this value when the `ocMode` parameter value is `ocPassive` or `ocAccept`.

intermediary
A pointer to a buffer that is used to store the record ID of the intermediary, if ASDSP finds an intermediary in the credentials. The `sdspOpen` routine returns this value when the `ocMode` parameter value is `ocPassive` or `ocAccept`.

DESCRIPTION

The `sdspOpen` routine opens a secure connection end if the identities of both the initiator and the recipient connection ends can be proven in the authentication process. You set the `ocMode` field of the parameter block to specify the opening mode that the `sdspOpen` routine is to use. The `sdspOpen` routine puts a connection end into one of the three following opening modes:

■ In the `ocRequest` mode, ASDSP attempts to open a connection with the socket at the internet address you specify as the `remoteAddress` parameter.

- In the ocPassive mode, the connection end waits to receive an open-connection request from a remote connection end. You can use the filterAddress parameter to restrict the addresses from which you will accept a connection request.

- In the ocAccept mode, connection servers complete open-connection dialogs. When a connection server is informed by its connection listener that the connection listener has received an open-connection request, the connection server calls the dspInit routine to establish a connection end and then calls the sdspOpen routine in ocAccept mode to complete the connection. Connection listeners and connection servers are described in "Creating and Using a Connection Listener" beginning on page 5-22 and in "Establishing and Terminating an ADSP Connection" beginning on page 5-44. See "Connection Listeners" on page 5-7 for a brief introduction to connection listeners.

Except for the authentication process, these three modes are used by ASDSP and ADSP in the same way and their behavior is the same. See the description of how these modes are used in "dspOpen" beginning on page 5-48.

If ASDSP cannot successfully complete the authentication process, ASDSP tears down the connection and the sdspOpen calls made by both the initiator and the recipient return a result code reporting the reason why the authentication process failed. For the conditions that can cause the authentication process to fail, see the list of result codes that follows.

ASSEMBLY-LANGUAGE INFORMATION

To execute the sdspOpen routine from assembly language, call the _Control trap macro with a value of sdspOpen in the csCode field of the parameter block.

RESULT CODES

noErr	0	No error
errOpenDenied	−1273	Open request denied by recipient
errFwdReset	−1276	A forward reset caused ASDSP to terminate the request
errOpening	−1277	Attempt to open connection failed
errState	−1278	Connection end is not open
errAborted	−1279	Request aborted by dspRemove or dspClose routine
errRefNum	−1280	Bad connection reference number
kOCEUnsupportedCredentialsVersion	−1543	Credentials version not supported
kOCEBadEncryptionMethod	−1559	During the authentication process, the ASDSP implementations could not agree on an encryption method to be used (ASDSP can support multiple stream encryption methods. In Release 1, only RC4 and "no encryption" are supported.)
kOCENoASDSPWorkSpace	−1570	You passed NIL for the workspace parameter
kOCEAuthenticationTrouble	−1571	Authentication process failed

dspNewCID

The dspNewCID routine creates a connection ID to be used in setting up a connection. You use the PBControl function to call the dspNewCID routine. See "Routines" on page 5-43 for a description of the PBControl function.

Parameter block

→	ioCompletion	ProcPtr	A pointer to a completion routine.
←	ioResult	OSErr	The function result.
→	ioCRefNum	Integer	The driver reference number.
→	csCode	Integer	Always dspNewCID for this function.
→	ccbRefNum	Integer	The CCB reference number.
←	newCID	Integer	The ID of new connection.

Field descriptions

csCode   The routine selector, always equal to dspNewCID for this routine.

ccbRefNum   The connection control block (CCB) reference number that was returned by the dspNewCID routine for the connection end that you want to use.

newCID   The connection-end ID that this routine returns. You must provide this number to the client of the remote connection end so that it can use it for the remoteCID parameter when it calls the dspOpen routine.

DESCRIPTION

The dspNewCID routine causes ADSP to assign an ID to a connection end without opening the connection end or attempting to establish a connection with a remote connection end. Use this routine only if you implement your own protocol to establish communication with a remote connection end. You must first use the dspInit routine to establish a connection end. Next, you must call the dspNewCID routine to obtain a connection-end ID. Then you must establish communication with a remote connection end and pass the ID to the remote connection end. Finally, you must call the dspOpen routine in ocEstablish mode to cause ADSP to open the connection.

ASSEMBLY-LANGUAGE INFORMATION

To execute the dspNewCID routine from assembly language, call the _Control trap macro with a value of dspNewCID in the csCode field of the parameter block.

RESULT CODES

noErr	0	No error
errState	−1278	Connection is not closed
errRefNum	−1280	Bad connection reference number

SEE ALSO

To establish a connection, use the dspInit routine, described on page 5-45.

To obtain a connection-end ID, use the sdspOpen routine, described on page 5-54.

To open a connection in ocEstablish mode, use the dspOpen routine, described on see page 5-48.

dspClose

The dspClose routine closes a connection end. You use the PBControl function to call the dspClose routine. See "Routines" on page 5-43 for a description of the PBControl function.

Parameter block

→	ioCompletion	ProcPtr	A pointer to a completion routine.
←	ioResult	OSErr	The function result.
→	ioCRefNum	Integer	The driver reference number.
→	csCode	Integer	Always dspClose for this function.
→	ccbRefNum	Integer	The CCB reference number.
→	abort	Byte	A value specifying to abort send requests if not 0.

Field descriptions

csCode   The routine selector, always equal to dspClose for this routine.

ccbRefNum   The connection control block (CCB) reference number that was returned by the dspNewCID routine for the connection end that you want to close.

abort   A value that specifies whether or not to send all of the data in the send queue and all outstanding messages before closing the connection end. If the abort parameter is nonzero, ADSP cancels any outstanding requests to send data packets (such as the dspAttention routine) and discards all data in the send queue. If the abort parameter is 0, ADSP does not close the connection end until all of the data in the send queue and all outstanding attention messages have been sent and acknowledged.

DESCRIPTION

The `dspClose` routine closes the connection end. The connection end is still established; that is, ADSP retains ownership of the CCB, send queue, receive queue, and attention-message buffer. You can continue to read bytes from the receive queue after you have called the `dspClose` routine. Use the `dspRemove` routine instead of the `dspClose` routine if you are finished with reading bytes from the receive queue and want to release the memory associated with the connection end.

SPECIAL CONSIDERATIONS

The `dspClose` routine does not return an error if you call it for a connection end that is already closed.

ASSEMBLY-LANGUAGE INFORMATION

To execute the `dspClose` routine from assembly language, call the `_Control` trap macro with a value of `dspClose` in the `csCode` field of the parameter block.

RESULT CODES

noErr	0	No error
errRefNum	−1280	Bad connection reference number

SEE ALSO

For information on how to remove a connection end and release the memory associated with it, see the description of the `dspRemove` routine that follows.

dspRemove

The `dspRemove` routine closes any open connection and eliminates the connection end, releasing all memory associated with it. You use the `PBControl` function to call the `dspRemove` routine. See "Routines" on page 5-43 for a description of the `PBControl` function.

Parameter block

→	ioCompletion	ProcPtr	A pointer to a completion routine.
←	ioResult	OSErr	The function result.
→	ioCRefNum	Integer	The driver reference number.
→	csCode	Integer	Always dspRemove for this function.
→	ccbRefNum	Integer	The CCB reference number.
→	abort	Byte	A value specifying to abort connection if not 0.

Field descriptions

csCode	The routine selector, always equal to `dspRemove` for this routine.
ccbRefNum	The connection control block (CCB) reference number that was returned by the `dspNewCID` routine for the connection end that you want to remove.
abort	A value that specifies whether or not to send all of the data in the send queue and all outstanding messages before closing the connection end. If the abort parameter is nonzero, ADSP cancels any outstanding requests to send data packets (such as the `dspAttention` routine) and discards all data in the send queue. If the abort parameter is 0, ADSP does not close the connection end until all of the data in the send queue and all outstanding attention messages have been sent and acknowledged.

DESCRIPTION

The `dspRemove` routine closes the connection end whose connection control block (CCB) you specify, and it eliminates that connection end; that is, ADSP no longer retains control of the CCB, send queue, receive queue, and attention-message buffer. You cannot continue to read bytes from the receive queue after you have called the `dspRemove` routine. After you call the `dspRemove` routine, you can release all of the memory you allocated for the connection end if you do not intend to reopen the connection end.

ASSEMBLY-LANGUAGE INFORMATION

To execute the `dspRemove` routine from assembly language, call the `_Control` trap macro with a value of `dspRemove` in the `csCode` field of the parameter block.

RESULT CODES

noErr	0	No error
errRefNum	–1280	Bad connection reference number

Establishing and Terminating an ADSP Connection Listener

A connection listener is a special kind of connection end that listens for open-connection requests from remote connection ends. Connection listeners are used by **connection servers**—that is, programs that assign a socket for the local connection end only after they receive a connection request from a remote connection end. A single connection listener can receive connection requests from any number of remote connection ends.

You can use the routines in this section to

- establish a connection listener

- cause the connection listener to listen for a connection request

- deny a connection request

- close and eliminate a connection listener

dspCLInit

The dspCLInit routine establishes and initializes a connection listener. You use the PBControl function to call the dspCLInit routine. See "Routines" on page 5-43 for a description of the PBControl function.

Parameter block

→	ioCompletion	ProcPtr	A pointer to a completion routine.
←	ioResult	OSErr	The function result.
→	ioCRefNum	Integer	The driver reference number.
→	csCode	Integer	Always dspCLInit for this function.
←	ccbRefNum	Integer	The CCB reference number.
→	ccbPtr	TPCCB	A pointer to CCB.
↔	localSocket	Byte	The local DDP socket number.

Field descriptions

csCode
: The routine selector, always equal to dspCLInit for this routine.

ccbRefNum
: The connection control block (CCB) reference number. The dspCLInit routine returns this value. You must provide this number in all subsequent dspCLListen and dspCLRemove calls to this connection listener.

ccbPtr
: A pointer to the CCB that you allocated. The CCB is 242 bytes in size.

localSocket
: The number of the DDP socket that you want ADSP to use for this connection end. Specify 0 for this parameter to cause ADSP to assign the socket; in this case, ADSP returns the socket number when the dspCLInit routine completes execution.

DESCRIPTION

The dspCLInit routine establishes a connection listener; that is, it assigns a specific socket for use by ADSP and initializes the variables that ADSP uses to maintain a connection listener. The dspCLInit routine does not cause the connection listener to listen for connection requests; you must follow the dspCLInit routine with the dspCLListen routine to activate the connection listener.

You must allocate a block of nonrelocatable memory for a CCB before you call the dspCLInit routine and pass a pointer to that CCB as the value of the ccbPtr parameter. See the section "Creating and Using a Connection Control Block" on page 5-12 and the section "The ADSP Connection Control Block Record" on page 5-35 for more information.

SPECIAL CONSIDERATIONS

The connection control block for which you allocate memory belongs to ADSP until you explicitly remove the connection listener. You cannot release the memory for the CCB until after you eliminate the connection listener.

ASSEMBLY-LANGUAGE INFORMATION

To execute the dspCLInit routine from assembly language, call the _Control trap macro with a value of dspCLInit in the csCode field of the parameter block.

RESULT CODES

noErr	0	No error
ddpSktErr	–91	Error opening socket

SEE ALSO

To establish a connection end that is not a connection listener, use the dspInit routine described on page 5-45.

To eliminate a connection listener, use the dspCLRemove routine, described on page 5-68.

dspCLListen

The dspCLListen routine causes a connection listener to listen for connection requests. You use the PBControl function to call the dspCLListen routine. See "Routines" on page 5-43 for a description of the PBControl function.

Parameter block

→	ioCompletion	ProcPtr	A pointer to a completion routine.
←	ioResult	OSErr	The function result.
→	ioCRefNum	Integer	The driver reference number.
→	csCode	Integer	Always dspCLListen for this function.
→	ccbRefNum	Integer	The CCB reference number.
←	remoteCID	Integer	The ID of the remote connection end.
←	remoteAddress	AddrBlock	The remote internet address.
→	filterAddress	AddrBlock	A filter for open-connection requests.
←	sendSeq	LongInt	The initial send sequence number.
←	sendWindow	Integer	The initial size of the remote receive queue.
←	attnSendSeq	LongInt	The attention send sequence number.

Field descriptions

csCode   The routine selector, always dspCLListen for this routine.

ccbRefNum   The CCB reference number that the dspCLInit routine returned.

remoteCID   The identification number of the remote connection end. You must pass this value to the dspOpen routine when you open the connection or to the dspCLDeny routine when you deny the connection request. The dspCLListen routine returns this number.

remoteAddress   The internet address of the remote socket that sent a request to open a connection. This address consists of a 2-byte network number, a 1-byte node ID, and a 1-byte socket number. You must pass this value to the dspOpen routine when you open the connection or to the dspCLDeny routine when you deny the connection request.

filterAddress   The internet address of the socket from which you will accept a connection request. The address consists of three fields: a 2-byte network number, a 1-byte node ID, and a 1-byte socket number. Specify 0 for any of these fields for which you wish to impose no restrictions. If you specify a filter address of $00082500, for example, the connection listener accepts a connection request from any socket at node $25 of network $0008.

sendSeq   The sequence number of the first byte that the local connection end will send to the remote connection end. ADSP uses this number to coordinate communications and to check for errors. You must pass this value to the dspOpen routine when you open the connection.

sendWindow   The sequence number of the last byte that the remote connection end has buffer space to receive. ADSP uses this number to coordinate communications and to check for errors. You must pass this value to the dspOpen routine when you open the connection.

attnSendSeq   The sequence number of the next attention packet that the local connection end will transmit. ADSP uses this number to ensure that attention packets are delivered in the correct order and to check for errors. You must pass this value to the dspOpen routine when you open the connection.

DESCRIPTION

The dspCLListen routine initiates the connection listener. You must have already used the dspCLInit routine to establish a connection listener before using the dspCLListen routine. The dspCLListen routine is used only by connection servers.

When ADSP receives an open-connection request from a socket that satisfies the address requirements of the filterAddress parameter, it returns values for the remoteCID, remoteAddress, sendSeq, sendWindow, and attnSendSeq parameters and completes execution of the dspCLListen routine. You must then either accept the open-connection request by calling the dspOpen routine in the ocAccept mode or deny the request by calling the dspCLDeny routine.

You can call the dspCLListen routine several times, specifying the same connection listener. For example, if you wanted to accept connections from any or all of three different addresses, you could call the dspCLListen routine three times with a different value for the filterAddress parameter each time. Note that you must execute the dspCLListen routine asynchronously to take advantage of this feature.

ASSEMBLY-LANGUAGE INFORMATION

To execute the dspCLListen routine from assembly language, call the _Control trap macro with a value of dspCLListen in the csCode field of the parameter block.

RESULT CODES

noErr	0	No error
errState	−1278	Not a connection listener
errAborted	−1279	Request aborted by the dspRemove routine
errRefNum	−1280	Bad connection reference number

dspCLDeny

The dspCLDeny routine denies a connection request from a remote connection end. You use the PBControl function to call the dspCLDeny routine. See "Routines" on page 5-43 for a description of the PBControl function.

Parameter block.

→	ioCompletion	ProcPtr	A pointer to a completion routine.
←	ioResult	OsErr	The function result.
→	ioCRefNum	Integer	The driver reference number.
→	csCode	Integer	Always dspCLDeny for this function.
→	ccbRefNum	Integer	The CCB reference number.
→	remoteCID	Integer	The ID of the remote connection end.
→	remoteAddress	AddrBlock	The remote internet address.

Field descriptions

csCode   The routine selector, always dspCLDeny for this routine.

ccbRefNum   The CCB reference number for the connection listener that received the request. This is the CBB number that the dspCLInit routine returned for the connection listener when you established a connection listener.

remoteCID   The ID of the remote connection end. The dspCLListen routine returns this value.

remoteAddress   The internet address of the remote connection end. The dspCLListen routine returns this value.

DESCRIPTION

A connection server uses the dspCLDeny routine to inform a remote connection end that its request to open a connection cannot be honored. If you want your connection listener to continue to listen for further connection requests, you must call the dspCLListen request again after you call dspCLDeny.

ASSEMBLY-LANGUAGE INFORMATION

To execute the dspCLDeny routine from assembly language, call the _Control trap macro with a value of dspCLDeny in the csCode field of the parameter block.

RESULT CODES

noErr	0	No error
errState	−1278	Not a connection listener
errAborted	−1279	Request aborted by the dspRemove routine
errRefNum	−1280	Bad connection reference number

dspCLRemove

The dspCLRemove routine closes a connection end used as a connection listener. You use the PBControl function to call the dspCLRemove routine. See "Routines" on page 5-43 for a description of the PBControl function.

Parameter block

→	ioCompletion	ProcPtr	A pointer to a completion routine.
←	ioResult	OSErr	The function result.
→	ioCRefNum	Integer	The driver reference number.
→	csCode	Integer	Always dspCLRemove for this function.
→	ccbRefNum	Integer	The CCB reference number.
→	abort	Byte	A value specifying to abort outstanding requests if not 0.

Field descriptions

csCode   The routine selector, always dspCLRemove for this routine.

ccbRefNum   The connection control block (CCB) reference number that the dspCLInit routine returned.

abort   A value directing ADSP whether or not to cancel any outstanding listen and deny requests. If this value is nonzero, ADSP cancels outstanding dspCLListen and dspCLDeny requests. If this value is 0, ADSP does not cancel these requests.

DESCRIPTION

The dspCLRemove routine closes a connection end used as a connection listener. After you call the dspCLRemove routine, you can release the memory that you allocated for the CCB if you do not intend to reopen the connection end.

ASSEMBLY-LANGUAGE INFORMATION

To execute the dspCLRemove routine from assembly language, call the _Control trap macro with a value of dspCLRemove in the csCode field of the parameter block.

RESULT CODES

noErr	0	No error
errRefNum	−1280	Bad connection reference number

Maintaining an ADSP Connection and Using It to Exchange Data

Once you have established a connection end and opened a connection, you can send and receive data over the connection. You can use the routines in this section to

- determine the status of a connection

- read bytes from the connection end's receive queue

- write bytes to the connection end's send queue and transmit them to the remote connection end

- send an attention message to the remote connection end

- discard all data that has been sent but not yet delivered, and reset the connection

dspStatus

The dspStatus routine returns the number of bytes waiting to be read and sent and the amount of space available in the send and receive queues. You use the PBControl function to call the dspStatus routine. See "Routines" on page 5-43 for a description of the PBControl function.

Parameter block

→	ioCompletion	ProcPtr	A pointer to a completion routine.
←	ioResult	OSErr	The function result.
→	ioCRefNum	Integer	The driver reference number.
→	csCode	Integer	Always dspStatus for this function.
→	ccbRefNum	Integer	The CCB reference number.
←	statusCCB	TPCCB	A pointer to the CCB.
←	sendQPending	Integer	Bytes waiting to be sent or acknowledged.
←	sendQFree	Integer	Available send queue in bytes.
←	recvQPending	Integer	Bytes waiting to be read from queue.
←	recvQFree	Integer	Available receive queue in bytes.

Field descriptions

csCode
The routine selector, always dspStatus for this routine.

ccbRefNum
The connection control block (CCB) reference number that the dspInit routine returned.

statusCCB
A pointer to the CCB of the connection specified by the ccbRefNum parameter value.

sendQPending
The number of bytes of data that are in the send queue waiting to be sent, including 1 byte for each logical end-of-message (EOM) indicator in the send queue. (ADSP counts 1 byte for each EOM, even though no actual data corresponds to the EOM indicator.) The send queue contains all data that has been sent to ADSP for transmission and that has not yet been acknowledged. Some of the data in the send queue might have already been transmitted, but ADSP retains it in the send queue until the remote connection end acknowledges its receipt in case the data has to be retransmitted.

sendQFree	The number of bytes available in the send queue for additional data.
recvQPending	The number of bytes in the receive queue, including 1 byte for each EOM if the EOM bit is set in an ADSP packet header. The receive queue contains all of the data that has been received by the connection end but not yet read by the connection end's client.
recvQFree	The number of bytes available in the receive queue for additional data.

DESCRIPTION

The dspStatus routine provides information about an open connection. In addition to returning the number of bytes waiting to be read and sent and the space available in the send and receive queues, this routine also returns a pointer to the CCB, which contains information about the state of the connection end and about connection events received by the connection end. For more information about the CCB, see "Creating and Using a Connection Control Block" on page 5-12 and "The ADSP Connection Control Block Record" beginning on page 5-35.

ASSEMBLY-LANGUAGE INFORMATION

To execute the dspStatus routine from assembly language, call the _Control trap macro with a value of dspStatus in the csCode field of the parameter block.

RESULT CODES

noErr	0	No error
errRefNum	–1280	Bad connection reference number

dspRead

The dspRead routine reads data from a connection end's receive queue and writes the data to a buffer that you specify. You use the PBControl function to call the dspRead routine. See "Routines" on page 5-43 for a description of the PBControl function.

Parameter block

→	ioCompletion	ProcPtr	A pointer to a completion routine.
←	ioResult	OSErr	The function result.
→	ioCRefNum	Integer	The driver reference number.
→	csCode	Integer	Always dspRead for this function.
→	ccbRefNum	Integer	The CCB reference number.
→	reqCount	Integer	The requested number of bytes.
←	actCount	Integer	The actual number of bytes read.
→	dataPtr	Ptr	A pointer to the data buffer.
←	eom	Byte	A flag indicating the end of message.

Field descriptions

csCode	The routine selector, always dspRead for this routine.
ccbRefNum	The connection control block (CCB) reference number that the dspInit routine returned.
reqCount	The number of bytes that ADSP is to read.
actCount	The actual number of bytes that ADSP read.
dataPtr	A pointer to the buffer into which ADSP is to place the data.
eom	A flag indicating if the last byte that ADSP read was a logical end-of-message indicator. If the last byte constitutes an EOM, ADSP sets this parameter to 1. If not, it sets this parameter to 0.

DESCRIPTION

The dspRead routine reads data from an ADSP connection. You can continue to read bytes as long as data is in the receive queue, even after you have called the dspClose routine or after the remote connection end has called the dspClose or dspRemove routine. The dspRead routine completes execution when it has read the number of bytes you specify or when it encounters an end of message (that is, the last byte of data in an ADSP packet that has the EOM bit set in the packet header).

You can call the dspStatus routine to determine the number of bytes remaining to be read from the read queue, or you can continue to call the dspRead routine until the actCount and eom parameters both return 0.

If either end closes the connection before you call the dspRead routine, the command reads whatever data is available and returns the actual amount of data read in the actCount parameter. If the connection is closed and there is no data in the receive queue, the dspRead routine returns the noErr result code with the actCount parameter set to 0 and the eom parameter set to 0.

ASSEMBLY-LANGUAGE INFORMATION

To execute the dspRead routine from assembly language, call the _Control trap macro with a value of dspRead in the csCode field of the parameter block.

RESULT CODES

noErr	0	No error
errFwdReset	–1275	Read terminated by forward reset
errState	–1278	State isn't open, closing, or closed
errAborted	–1279	Request aborted by dspRemove or dspClose routine
errRefNum	–1280	Bad connection reference number

dspWrite

The dspWrite routine writes bytes into a connection end's send queue for ADSP or ASDSP to transmit across a connection. When ASDSP is used and the encrypt bit is set, ASDSP encrypts the data before sending it. You use the PBControl function to call the dspWrite routine. See "Routines" on page 5-43 for a description of the PBControl function.

Parameter block

→	ioCompletion	ProcPtr	A pointer to a completion routine.
←	ioResult	OSErr	The function result.
→	ioCRefNum	Integer	The driver reference number.
→	csCode	Integer	Always dspWrite for this function.
→	ccbRefNum	Integer	The CCB reference number.
→	reqCount	Integer	The requested number of bytes.
←	actCount	Integer	The actual number of bytes written.
→	dataPtr	Ptr	A pointer to the data buffer.
→	eom	Byte	For ADSP: a flag indicating end of message. For ASDSP: a flag indicating end of message or encryption.
→	flush	Byte	A flag indicating whether to send buffered data.

Field descriptions

csCode   The routine selector, always dspWrite for this routine.

ccbRefNum   The connection control block (CCB) reference number that the dspInit routine returned.

reqCount   The number of bytes to write.

actCount   The actual number of bytes written to the send queue.

dataPtr   A pointer to the buffer from which ADSP or ASDSP should read the data that is to be sent.

eom   For ADSP, a flag indicating if the last byte written to the send queue was a logical end-of-message indicator. If the last byte constitutes an EOM, you set this parameter to 1. If not, you set this parameter to 0. The high-order bits of the eom parameter are reserved for use by ADSP; you must leave these bits equal to 0.

              For ASDSP, if this is a secure connection, this field constitutes two single-bit flags instead of a zero/nonzero byte. If set to 1, bit 0 indicates the end of message; if set to 1, bit 1 turns on encryption. Note that ASDSP checks this flag on the first write of the connection and the first write following a write for which the end-of-message flag (bit 0 of the eom field) is set.

flush   A flag indicting whether or not ADSP or ASDSP should immediately send the data in the send queue to the remote connection. Set flush to 1 to cause ADSP or ASDSP to immediately transmit any data in the send queue that has not already been transmitted. Set flush to 0 to allow data to accumulate in the send queue until another condition occurs that causes data to be transmitted. The high-order bits of the `flush` parameter are reserved for use by ADSP or ASDSP; you must leave these bits equal to 0.

DESCRIPTION

The `dspWrite` routine sends data across an ADSP or ASDSP connection. The send queue contains all data that has been sent to ADSP or ASDSP for transmission and that has not yet been acknowledged. Some of the data in the send queue might have already been transmitted, but ADSP or ASDSP retains it in the send queue until the remote connection end acknowledges its receipt in case the data has to be retransmitted. The `dspWrite` routine completes execution when it has copied all of the data from the data buffer into the send queue.

ADSP or ASDSP transmits the data in the send queue when the remote connection end has room to accept the data and one of the following conditions occurs:

■ You call the `dspWrite` routine with the flush parameter set to a nonzero number.

■ The number of bytes in the send queue equals or exceeds the blocking factor. (You use the `sendBlocking` parameter to the `dspOptions` routine to set the blocking factor.)

■ The send timer expires.

■ A connection event requires that the local connection end send an acknowledgment packet to the remote connection end.

For an ADSP `dspWrite` call, you can set the `reqCount` parameter to 0 and the `eom` parameter to 1 to indicate that the last byte you sent the previous time you called the `dspWrite` routine was the end of the message. You can set the `reqCount` parameter to a value larger than the size of the send queue. If you do so, the `dspWrite` routine writes as much data as it can into the send queue, sends the data and waits for acknowledgment, and then writes more data into the send queue until it has written the amount of data you requested. In this case, the routine does not complete execution until it has finished writing all of the data into the send queue.

For an ASDSP `dspWrite` call, you can set the encrypt bit of the `eom` field (bit 1) of the DSP parameter block. Note that ASDSP checks this flag on the first write of the connection or the first write following a write for which the end-of-message flag (bit 0 of the `eom` field) is set. You can set the end-of-message bit (bit 0) of the `eom` field to indicate the end of the message.

■ To set the encrypt bit, you use the `dspEncryptMask` mask or the `dspEncryptBit` constant.

■ To set the end-of-message bit, you use the `dspEOMMask` mask or the `dspEOMBit` constant.

Set the `flush` parameter to 1 to cause ADSP to immediately transmit any data in the send queue that has not already been transmitted. Set the `flush` parameter to 0 to allow data to accumulate in the send queue until another condition occurs that causes data to be transmitted.

If you want to encrypt all messages, you can simply set the encrypt bit on all calls to the dspWrite function.

ASSEMBLY-LANGUAGE INFORMATION

To execute the dspWrite routine from assembly language, call the _Control trap macro with a value of dspWrite in the csCode field of the parameter block.

RESULT CODES

noErr	0	No error
errState	–1278	Connection is not open
errAborted	–1279	Request aborted by dspRemove or dspClose routine
errRefNum	–1280	Bad connection reference number

dspAttention

The dspAttention routine sends an attention code and an attention message to the remote connection end. You use the PBControl function to call the dspAttention routine. See "Routines" on page 5-43 for a description of the PBControl function.

Parameter block

→	ioCompletion	ProcPtr	A pointer to a completion routine.
←	ioResult	OSErr	The function result.
→	ioCRefNum	Integer	The driver reference number.
→	csCode	Integer	Always dspAttention for this function.
→	ccbRefNum	Integer	The CCB reference number.
→	attnCode	Integer	The client attention code.
→	attnSize	Integer	The size of attention data in bytes.
→	attnData	Ptr	A pointer to attention data.

Field descriptions

csCode   The routine selector, always dspAttention for this routine.

ccbRefNum   The connection control block (CCB) reference number that the dspInit routine returned.

attnCode   The 2-byte attention code that you wish to send to the remote connection end. You can use any value from $0000 through $EFFF for the attention code. The values $F000 through $FFFF are reserved for use by ADSP.

attnSize   The size in bytes of the attention message you wish to send.

attnData   A pointer to the attention message. The attention message can be any size from 0 through 570 bytes. There are no restrictions on the content of the attention message.

DESCRIPTION

The dspAttention routine sends an attention code and message. Attention codes and attention messages can have any meaning that your application and the application at the remote connection end both recognize. The purpose of attention codes and messages is to allow clients of ADSP to send messages outside the normal data stream.

For example, if a connection end on a mainframe computer is connected to several connection ends in Macintosh computers being used as remote terminals, the mainframe computer might wish to inform the remote terminals that all connections will be terminated in ten minutes. The mainframe application could send an attention message to each of the remote terminals informing them of this fact, and the terminal emulation programs in the Macintosh computers could then display an alert message on the screen so that the users could prepare to shut down.

ASSEMBLY-LANGUAGE INFORMATION

To execute the dspAttention routine from assembly language, call the _Control trap macro with a value of dspAttention in the csCode field of the parameter block.

RESULT CODES

noErr	0	No error
errAttention	−1276	Attention message too long
errState	−1278	Connection is not open
errAborted	−1279	Request aborted by dspRemove or dspClose routine
errRefNum	−1280	Bad connection reference number

dspReset

The dspReset routine clears all the data associated with the connection that the remote connection client has not already read and resynchronizes the connection. You use the PBControl function to call the dspReset routine. See "Routines" on page 5-43 for a description of the PBControl function.

Parameter block

→	ioCompletion	ProcPtr	A pointer to a completion routine.
←	ioResult	OSErr	The function result.
→	ioCRefNum	Integer	The driver reference number.
→	csCode	Integer	Always dspReset for this routine.
→	ccbRefNum	Integer	The CCB reference number.

Field descriptions

csCode	The routine selector, always dspReset for this routine.
ccbRefNum	The connection control block (CCB) reference number that the dspInit routine returned.

AppleTalk Data Stream Protocol (ADSP)

DESCRIPTION

The dspReset routine causes ADSP to discard all data in the send queue, all data in transit to the remote connection end, and all data in the remote connection end's receive queue that the client has not yet read. This process is known as a *forward reset*. ADSP then resynchronizes the connection. You can determine that your connection end has received a forward reset and has discarded all data in the receive queue by checking the eFwdReset flag in the userFlags field of the CCB. For information on the CCB, see "Connections, Connection Ends, and Connection States" beginning on page 5-6.

ASSEMBLY-LANGUAGE INFORMATION

To execute the dspReset routine from assembly language, call the _Control trap macro with a value of dspReset in the csCode field of the parameter block.

RESULT CODES

noErr	0	No error
errState	−1278	Connection is not open
errAborted	−1279	Request aborted by dspRemove or dspClose routine
errRefNum	−1280	Bad connection reference number

Summary of ADSP

Pascal Summary

Constants

```
CONST
   {ADSP routine selectors}
   dspInit              = 255;        {create a new connection end}
   dspRemove            = 254;        {remove a connection end}
   dspOpen              = 253;        {open a connection}
   dspClose             = 252;        {close a connection}
   dspCLInit            = 251;        {create a connection listener}
   dspCLRemove          = 250;        {remove a connection listener}
   dspCLListen          = 249;        {post a listener request}
   dspCLDeny            = 248;        {deny an open-connection request}
   dspStatus            = 247;        {get status of connection end}
   dspRead              = 246;        {read data from the connection}
   dspWrite             = 245;        {write data on the connection}
   dspAttention         = 244;        {send an attention message}
   dspOptions           = 243;        {set connection end options}
   dspReset             = 242;        {forward reset the connection}
   dspNewCID            = 241;        {generate a CID for a }
                                      { connection end}

   sdspOpen             = 229;        {open a secure connection}

   {ADSP connection-opening modes}
   ocRequest            = 1;          {request a connection with a }
                                      { remote connection end}

   ocPassive            = 2;          {wait for a connection request }
                                      { from remote connection end}

   ocAccept             = 3;          {accept request as delivered by }
                                      { listener}

   ocEstablish          = 4;          {consider connection to be open}

   {ADSP connection end states}
   sListening           = 1;          {for connection listeners}
   sPassive             = 2;          {waiting for a connection }
                                      { request from remote }
                                      { connection end}
```

```
sOpening                = 3;            {requesting a connection }
                                        { with remote connection end}
sOpen                   = 4;            {connection is open}
sClosing                = 5;            {connection is being torn down}
sClosed                 = 6;            {connection end state is closed}


{ASDSP end-of-message and encrypt flags and masks}
dspEncryptBit           = 1;            {set to encrypt message}
dspEOMBit               = 0;            {set if EOM at end of write}
dspEOMMask              = $1;           {mask for setting the EOM bit}
dspEncryptMask          = $2;           {mask for setting the encrypt bit}


{ADSP client event flags}
eClosed                 = $80;          {received connection-closed event}
eTearDown               = $40;          {closed due to broken connection}
eAttention              = $20;          {received attention message}
eFwdReset               = $10;          {received forward reset event}


{miscellaneous ADSP constants}
attnBufSize             = 570;          {size of client attention buffer}
minDSPQueueSize         = 100;          {minimum size of receive or }
                                        { send queue}


{driver control ioResults}
errRefNum               = -1280;        {bad connection refNum}
errAborted              = -1279;        {control call was aborted}
errState                = -1278;        {bad connection state for this }
                                        { operation}
errOpening              = -1277;        {open connection request failed}
errAttention            = -1276;        {attention message too long}
errFwdReset             = -1275;        {read terminated by forward reset}
errDSPQueueSize         = -1274;        {DSP read/write queue too small}
errOpenDenied           = -1273;        {open connection request denied}
```

Data Types

The ADSP Connection Control Block Record

```
TYPE TRCCB =
  PACKED RECORD
    ccbLink:          TPCCB;       {link to next CCB}
    refNum:           Integer;     {reference number}
    state:            Integer;     {state of the connection end}
```

```
    userFlags:         Byte;        {user flags for connection}
    localSocket:       Byte;        {local socket number}
    remoteAddress:     AddrBlock;   {remote end internet address}
    attnCode:          Integer;     {attention code received}
    attnSize:          Integer;     {size of attention data}
    attnPtr:           Ptr;         {pointer to attention data}
    reserved:          PACKED ARRAY[1..220] OF Byte;
                                    {reserved for use by ADSP}
    END;
```

The Address Block Record

```
TYPE AddrBlock =
    PACKED RECORD
        aNet:          Integer;     {network number}
        aNode:         Byte;        {node ID}
        aSocket:       Byte;        {socket number}
    END;
```

The DSP Parameter Block

```
TYPE DSPParamBlock =
    PACKED RECORD
        qLink:         QElemPtr;    {reserved}
        qType:         Integer;     {reserved}
        ioTrap:        Integer;     {reserved}
        ioCmdAddr:     Ptr;         {reserved}
        ioCompletion:  ProcPtr;     {completion routine}
        ioResult:      OSErr;       {result code}
        ioNamePtr:     StringPtr;   {reserved}
        ioVRefNum:     Integer;     {reserved}
        ioCRefNum:     Integer;     {driver reference number}
        csCode:        Integer;     {primary command code}
        qStatus:       LongInt;     {reserved}
        ccbRefNum:     Integer;     {CCB reference number}
    CASE Integer OF
    dspInit, dspCLInit:
        (ccbPtr:       TPCCB;       {pointer to CCB}
        userRoutine:   ProcPtr;     {pointer to user routine}
        sendQSize:     Integer;     {size of send queue}
        sendQueue:     Ptr;         {pointer to send queue}
        recvQSize:     Integer;     {size of receive queue}
        recvQueue:     Ptr;         {pointer to receive queue}
        attnPtr:       Ptr;         {pointer to attention-message buffer}
```

AppleTalk Data Stream Protocol (ADSP)

```
        localSocket:      Byte;             {local socket number}
        filler1:          Byte);            {filler for proper alignment}
dspOpen, dspCLListen, dspCLDeny:
        (localCID:        Integer;          {local connection ID}
        remoteCID:        Integer;          {remote connection ID}
        remoteAddress:    AddrBlock;        {remote internet address}
        filterAddress:    AddrBlock;        {address filter}
        sendSeq:          LongInt;          {send sequence number}
        sendWindow:       Integer;          {size of remote buffer}
        recvSeq:          LongInt;          {receive sequence number}
        attnSendSeq:      LongInt;          {attention send seq number}
        attnRecvSeq:      LongInt;          {attention receive seq num}
        ocMode:           Byte;             {connection-opening mode}
        ocInterval:       Byte;             {interval bet. open requests}
        ocMaximum:        Byte;             {retries of open-conn req}
        filler2:          Byte);            {filler for proper alignment}
dspClose, dspRemove:
        (abort:           Byte;             {abort send requests}
        filler3:          Byte);            {filler for proper alignment}
dspStatus:
        (statusCCB:       TPCCB;            {pointer to CCB}
        sendQPending:     Integer;          {bytes waiting in send queue}
        sendQFree:        Integer;          {available send-queue buffer}
        recvQPending:     Integer;          {bytes in receive queue}
        recvQFree:        Integer);         {avail receive-queue buffer}
dspRead, dspWrite:
        (reqCount:        Integer;          {requested number of bytes}
        actCount:         Integer;          {actual number of bytes}
        dataPtr:          Ptr;              {pointer to data buffer}
        eom:              Byte;             {1 if end of message}
        flush:            Byte);            {1 to send data now}
dspAttention:
        (attnCode:        Integer;          {client attention code}
        attnSize:         Integer;          {size of attention data}
        attnData:         Ptr;              {pointer to attention data}
        attnInterval:     Byte;             {reserved}
        filler4:          Byte);            {filler for proper alignment}
dspOptions:
        (sendBlocking:    Integer;          {send-blocking threshold}
        sendTimer:        Byte;             {reserved}
        rtmtTimer:        Byte;             {reserved}
        badSeqMax:        Byte;             {retransmit advice threshold}
        useCheckSum:      Byte);            {DDP checksum for packets}
```

```
    dspNewCID:
        (newCID:              Integer);     {new connection ID}
    END;


DSPPBPtr = ^DSPParamBlock;
```

The ASDSP Parameter Block

```
TYPE SDSPParamBlock =
    PACKED RECORD
    CASE INTEGER OF
        1: (dspParamBlock: DSPParamBlock);
        2: (qLink:        QElemPtr;        {reserved}
            qType:        Integer;         {reserved}
            ioTrap:       Integer;         {reserved}
            ioCmdAddr:    Ptr;             {reserved}
            ioCompletion: ProcPtr;         {completion routine}
            ioResult:     OSErr;           {result code}
            ioNamePtr:    StringPtr;       {reserved}
            ioVRefNum:    Integer;         {reserved}
            ioCRefNum:    Integer;         {adsp driver refNum}
            csCode:       Integer;         {asdsp driver control code}
            qStatus:      Longint;         {reserved}
            ccbRefNum:    Integer;         {connection end refNum}
            secureParams: TRSecureParams); {parameters for dspOpenSecure}
    END;


SDSPPBPtr = ^SDSPParamBlock;
```

The TRSecureParams Record

```
TYPE  TRSecureParams =
    PACKED RECORD
        localCID:        Integer;      {local connection ID}
        remoteCID:       Integer;      {remote connection ID}
        remoteAddress:   AddrBlock;    {address of remote end}
        filterAddress:   AddrBlock;    {address filter}
        sendSeq:         Longint;      {local send sequence number}
        sendWindow:      Integer;      {send window size}
        recvSeq:         Longint;      {receive sequence number}
        attnSendSeq:     Longint;      {attention send sequence number}
        attnRecvSeq:     Longint;      {attention receive sequence number}
        ocMode:          Byte;         {open connection mode}
```

```
    ocInterval:        Byte;          {open connection request }
                                      { retry interval}
    ocMaximum:         Byte;          {open connection request }
                                      { retry maximum}
    secure:            Boolean;       {for initiator, TRUE if session is }
                                      { authenticated}
                                      {for recipient, TRUE if session was }
                                      { authenticated}
    sessionKey:        AuthKeyPtr;    {encryption key for session}
    credentialsSize:   Longint;       {length of credentials}
    credentials:       Ptr;           {pointer to credentials}
    workspace:         Ptr;           {pointer to workspace for }
                                      { connection. Align on }
                                      { even boundary and }
                                      { length = sdspWorkSize}
    recipient:         AuthIdentity;  {identity of recipient }
                                      { or initiator if active mode}
    issueTime:         UTCTime;       {time when credentials were issued}
    expiry:            UTCTime;       {time when credentials expire}
    initiator:         RecordIDPtr;   {RecordID of initiator returned in }
                                      { the buffer pointed to by this field}
    hasIntermediary:   Boolean;       {set if credentials has an }
                                      { intermediary}
    intermediary:      RecordIDPtr;   {Record ID of intermediary returned}
END;
```

C Summary

Constants

```
/*workspace used internally by ASDSP for the sdspOpen call*/
#define sdspWorkSize        2048            /*size of ASDSP workspace*/

enum{                                       /*ADSP routine selectors*/
    dspInit            = 255,               /*create a new connection end*/
    dspRemove          = 254,               /*remove a connection end*/
    dspOpen            = 253,               /*open a connection*/
    dspClose           = 252,               /*close a connection*/
    dspCLInit          = 251,               /*create a connection listener*/
    dspCLRemove        = 250,               /*remove a connection listener*/
    dspCLListen        = 249,               /*post a listener request*/
```

```
    dspCLDeny           = 248,       /*an open-connection request*/
    dspStatus           = 247,       /*get status of connection end*/
    dspRead             = 246,       /*read data from the connection*/
    dspWrite            = 245,       /*write data on the connection*/
    dspAttention        = 244,       /*send an attention message*/
    dspOptions          = 243,       /*set connection end options*/
    dspReset            = 242,       /*forward reset the connection*/
    dspNewCID           = 241,       /*generate a CID for a */
                                     /* connection end*/

    sdspOpen            = 229;       /*open a secure connection*/

enum {                               /*ADSP connection-opening modes*/
    ocRequest           = 1,         /*request a connection with a */
                                     /* remote connection end*/

    ocPassive           = 2,         /*wait for a connection request */
                                     /* from remote connection end*/

    ocAccept            = 3,         /*accept request as delivered by */
                                     /* listener*/

    ocEstablish         = 4};        /*consider connection to be */
                                     /* open*/


enum {                               /*ADSP connection end states*/
    sListening          = 1,         /*for connection listeners*/
    sPassive            = 2,         /*waiting for a connection */
                                     /* request from remote */
                                     /* connection end*/

    sOpening            = 3,         /*requesting a connection */
                                     /* with remote connection end*/

    sOpen               = 4,         /*connection is open*/
    sClosing            = 5,         /*connection is being torn down*/
    sClosed             = 6};        /*connection end state */
                                     /* is closed*/


/*ASDSP end-of-message and encrypt flags and masks*/
enum {
    dspEOMBit           = 0,         /*set if EOM at end of write*/
    dspEncryptBit       = 1};        /*set to encrypt message*/

enum {
    dspEOMMask          = 1<<dspEOMBit,
    dspEncryptMask      = 1<<dspEncryptBit
};
```

```
enum {                                  /*ADSP client event flags*/
    eClosed            = $80,           /*received connection-closed */
                                        /* event*/
    eTearDown          = $40,           /*closed due to broken */
                                        /* connection*/
    eAttention         = $20,           /*received attention message*/
    eFwdReset          = $10};          /*received forward reset event*/


enum {                                  /*miscellaneous ADSP constants*/
    attnBufSize        = 570,           /*size of client attention */
                                        /* buffer*/
    minDSPQueueSize    = 100};          /*minimum size of receive or */
                                        /* send queue*/


enum {                                  /*driver control ioResults*/
    errRefNum          = -1280,         /*bad connection refNum*/
    errAborted         = -1279,         /*control call was aborted*/
    errState           = -1278,         /*bad connection state for this */
                                        /* operation*/
    errOpening         = -1277,         /*open connection request */
                                        /* failed*/
    errAttention       = -1276,         /*attention message too long*/
    errFwdReset        = -1275,         /*read terminated */
                                        /* by forward reset*/
    errDSPQueueSize    = -1274,         /*DSP read/write queue */
                                        /* too small*/
    errOpenDenied      = -1273};        /*open connection request */
                                        /* denied*/
```

Data Types

The ADSP Connection Control Block Record

```
struct TRCCB {
    unsigned char      *ccbLink;        /*link to next CCB*/
    unsigned short     refNum;          /*reference number*/
    unsigned short     state;           /*state of the connection end*/
    unsigned char      userFlags;       /*user flags for connection*/
    unsigned char      localSocket;     /*local socket number*/
    AddrBlock          remoteAddress;   /*remote end internet address*/
    unsigned short     attnCode;        /*attention code received*/
    unsigned short     attnSize;        /*size of attention data*/
```

```
    unsigned char      *attnPtr;           /*pointer to attention data*/
    unsigned char      reserved[220];      /*reserved*/
};

typedef struct TRCCB TRCCB;
typedef TRCCB *TPCCB;
```

The Address Block Record

```
struct AddrBlock {
    short              aNet;               /*network number*/
    unsigned char      aNode;              /*node ID*/
    unsigned char      aSocket;            /*socket number*/
};

typedef struct AddrBlock AddrBlock;
```

Parameter Block for dspInit and dspCLInit

```
struct TRinitParams {
    TPCCB              ccbPtr;             /*pointer to connection control block*/
    ProcPtr            userRoutine;        /*client routine to call on event*/
    unsigned short     sendQSize;          /*size of send queue (0..64K bytes)*/
    unsigned char      *sendQueue;         /*client passed send queue buffer*/
    unsigned short     recvQSize;          /*size of receive queue */
                                           /* (0..64K bytes)*/
    unsigned char      *recvQueue;         /*client passed receive queue buffer*/
    unsigned char      *attnPtr;           /*client passed receive attention */
                                           /* buffer*/
    unsigned char      localSocket;        /*local socket number*/
};

typedef struct TRinitParams TRinitParams;
```

Parameter Block for dspOpen, dspCLListen, and dspCLDeny

```
struct TRopenParams {
    unsigned short     localCID;           /*local connection ID*/
    unsigned short     remoteCID;          /*remote connection ID*/
    AddrBlock          remoteAddress;      /*address of remote end*/
    AddrBlock          filterAddress;      /*address filter*/
    unsigned long      sendSeq;            /*local send sequence number*/
    unsigned short     sendWindow;         /*send window size*/
    unsigned long      recvSeq;            /*receive sequence number*/
```

```
    unsigned long       attnSendSeq;        /*attention send sequence number*/
    unsigned long       attnRecvSeq;        /*attention receive sequence */
                                            /* number*/
    unsigned char       ocMode;             /*open connection mode*/
    unsigned char       ocInterval;         /*open connection request retry */
                                            /* interval*/
    unsigned char       ocMaximum;          /*open connection request retry */
};                                          /* maximum*/

typedef struct TRopenParams TRopenParams;
```

Parameter Block for dspClose and dspRemove

```
struct TRcloseParams {
    unsigned char       abort; /*abort connection immediately if nonzero*/
};

typedef struct TRcloseParams TRcloseParams;
```

Parameter Block for dspStatus

```
struct TRstatusParams {
    TPCCB               ccbPtr;         /*pointer to ccb*/
    unsigned short      sendQPending;   /*pending bytes in send queue*/
    unsigned short      sendQFree;      /*available buffer space in send */
                                        /* queue*/
    unsigned short      recvQPending;   /*pending bytes in receive queue*/
    unsigned short      recvQFree;      /*available buffer space in */
};                                      /* receive queue*/

typedef struct TRstatusParams TRstatusParams;
```

Parameter Block for dspRead and dspWrite

```
struct TRioParams {
    unsigned short      reqCount;       /*requested number of bytes*/
    unsigned short      actCount;       /*actual number of bytes*/
    unsigned char       *dataPtr;       /*pointer to data buffer*/
    unsigned char       eom;            /*indicates logical end of message*/
    unsigned char       flush;          /*send data now*/
};

typedef struct TRioParams TRioParams;
```

Parameter Block for dspAttention

```
struct TRattnParams {
    unsigned short         attnCode;      /*client attention code*/
    unsigned short         attnSize;      /*size of attention data*/
    unsigned char          *attnData;     /*pointer to attention data*/
    unsigned char          attnInterval;  /*retransmit timer in 10-tick */
                                          /* intervals*/
};

typedef struct TRattnParams TRattnParams;
```

Parameter Block for dspOptions

```
struct TRoptionParams {
    unsigned short         sendBlocking;  /*quantum for data packets*/
    unsigned char          sendTimer;     /*send timer in 10-tick intervals*/
    unsigned char          rtmtTimer;     /*retransmit timer in 10-tick */
                                          /* intervals*/
    unsigned char          badSeqMax;     /*threshold for sending retransmit */
                                          /* advice*/
    unsigned char          useCheckSum;   /*use ddp packet checksum*/
};

typedef struct TRoptionParams TRoptionParams;
```

Parameter Block for dspNewCID

```
struct TRnewcidParams {
    unsigned short         newcid;        /*new connection ID returned*/
};

typedef struct TRnewcidParams TRnewcidParams;
```

The DSP Parameter Block

```
struct DSPParamBlock {
    struct QElem    *qLink;         /*reserved*/
    short           qType;          /*reserved*/
    short           ioTrap;         /*reserved*/
    Ptr             ioCmdAddr;      /*reserved*/
    ProcPtr         ioCompletion;   /*pointer to completion routine*/
    OSErr           ioResult;       /*routine result*/
    char            *ioNamePtr;     /*reserved*/
    short           ioVRefNum;      /*reserved*/
```

```
    short            ioCRefNum;          /*ADSP driver refNum*/
    short            csCode;             /*ADSP driver control code*/
    long             qStatus;            /*reserved*/
    short            ccbRefNum;
union{
    TRinitParams     initParams;         /*dspInit, dspCLInit*/
    TRopenParams     openParams;         /*dspOpen, dspCLListen, dspCLDeny*/
    TRcloseParams    closeParams;        /*dspClose, dspRemove*/
    TRioParams       ioParams;           /*dspRead, dspWrite*/
    TRattnParams     attnParams;         /*dspAttention*/
    TRstatusParams   statusParams;       /*dspStatus*/
    TRoptionParams   optionParams;       /*dspOptions*/
    TRnewcidParams   newCIDParams;       /*dspNewCID*/
    } u;
};

typedef struct DSPParamBlock DSPParamBlock;
typedef DSPParamBlock *DSPPBPtr;
```

The ASDSP Parameter Block

```
struct TRSecureParams {
    unsigned short   localCID;           /*local connection ID*/
    unsigned short   remoteCID;          /*remote connection ID*/
    AddrBlock        remoteAddress;      /*address of remote end*/
    AddrBlock        filterAddress;      /*address filter*/
    unsigned long    sendSeq;            /*local send sequence number*/
    unsigned short   sendWindow;         /*send window size*/
    unsigned long    recvSeq;            /*receive sequence number*/
    unsigned long    attnSendSeq;        /*attention send sequence number*/
    unsigned long    attnRecvSeq;        /*attention receive sequence */
                                         /* number*/
    unsigned char    ocMode;             /*open connection mode*/
    unsigned char    ocInterval;         /*open connection request retry */
                                         /* interval*/
    unsigned char    ocMaximum;          /*open connection request retry */
                                         /* maximum*/
    Boolean          secure;             /*TRUE if session was */
                                         /* authenticated*/
    AuthKeyPtr       sessionKey;         /*encryption key for session*/
    unsigned         longcredentialsSize;
                                         /*length of credentials*/
    Ptr              credentials;        /*pointer to credentials*/
```

```
    Ptr                 workspace;          /*pointer to workspace for */
                                            /* connection. align on even */
                                            /* boundary and length equals */
                                            /* sdspWorkSize*/

    AuthIdentity        recipient;          /*identity of recipient */
                                            /* (or initiator if active mode)*/
    UTCTime             issueTime;          /*when credentials were issued*/
    UTCTime             expiry;             /*when credentials expire*/
    RecordIDPtr         initiator;          /*pointer to RecordID of */
                                            /* initiator returned*/

    Boolean             hasIntermediary;    /*is set if credentials */
                                            /* have an intermediary*/

    RecordIDPtr         intermediary;       /*pointer to RecordID of */
                                            /* intermediary returned*/

    };
```

The TRSecureParams Record

```
typedef struct TRSecureParams TRSecureParams;

struct SDSPParamBlock {
    struct QElem    *qLink;             /*reserved*/
    short           qType;              /*reserved*/
    short           ioTrap;             /*reserved*/
    Ptr             ioCmdAddr;          /*reserved*/
    ProcPtr         ioCompletion;
                                        /*pointer to completion routine*/
    OSErr           ioResult;           /*routine result*/
    char            *ioNamePtr;         /*reserved*/
    short           ioVRefNum;          /*reserved*/
    short           ioCRefNum;          /*ADSP driver refNum*/
    short           csCode;             /*ADSP driver control code*/
    long            qStatus;            /*ADSP internal use*/
    short           ccbRefNum;          /*connection end refNum*/

    union {
      TRinitParams      initParams;     /*dspInit, dspCLInit*/
      TRopenParams      openParams;     /*dspOpen, dspCLListen, dspCLDeny*/
      TRcloseParams     closeParams;    /*dspClose, dspRemove*/
      TRioParams        ioParams;       /*dspRead, dspWrite*/
      TRattnParams      attnParams;     /*dspAttention*/
      TRstatusParams    statusParams;   /*dspStatus*/
      TRoptionParams    optionParams;   /*dspOptions*/
```

```
     TRnewcidParams     newCIDParams;   /*dspNewCID*/
     TRSecureParams     secureParams;   /*dspOpenSecure*/
  } u;
};

typedef struct SDSPParamBlock SDSPParamBlock;
typedef SDSPParamBlock *SDSPPBPtr;
```

Assembly-Language Summary

Constants

ADSP Queue Element Equates and Sizes

```
csQStatus       EQU       CSParam         ;ADSP internal use
csCCBRef        EQU       csQStatus+4     ;refnum of ccb
```

Command Codes

```
dspInit         EQU       255             ;create a new connection end
dspRemove       EQU       254             ;remove a connection end
dspOpen         EQU       253             ;open a connection
dspClose        EQU       252             ;close a connection
dspCLInit       EQU       251             ;create a connection listener
dspCLRemove     EQU       250             ;remove a connection listener
dspCLListen     EQU       249             ;post a listener request
dspCLDeny       EQU       248             ;deny an open connection request
dspStatus       EQU       247             ;get status of connection end
dspRead         EQU       246             ;read data from the connection
dspWrite        EQU       245             ;write data on the connection
dspAttention    EQU       244             ;send an attention message
dspOptions      EQU       243             ;set connection end options
dspReset        EQU       242             ;forward reset the connection
dspNewCID       EQU       241             ;generate a cid for a connection end
sdspOpen        EQU       229             ;open a secure connection
```

Open Connection Modes

ocRequest	EQU	1	;request a connection with remote
ocPassive	EQU	2	;wait for a connection request from
			; remote
ocAccept	EQU	3	;accept request as delivered by
			; listener
ocEstablish	EQU	4	;consider connection to be open

Connection States

sListening	EQU	1	;for connection listeners
sPassive	EQU	2	;waiting for a connection request
			; from remote
sOpening	EQU	3	;requesting a connection with remote
sOpen	EQU	4	;connection is open
sClosing	EQU	5	;connection is being torn down
sClosed	EQU	6	;connection end state is closed

Client Event Flags (Bit-Mask)

eClosed	EQU	$80	;received connection closed advice
eTearDown	EQU	$40	;closed due to broken connection
eAttention	EQU	$20	;received attention message
eFwdReset	EQU	$10	;received forward reset advice

Miscellaneous Equates

attnBufSize	EQU	570	;size of client attention message
minDSPQueueSize			
	EQU	100	;minimum size for both receive and
			; send queues
sdspWorkSize	EQU	2048	;size of ASDSP workspace

ASDSP Encrypt and End-of-Message Flags and Masks

dspEOMBit	EQU	0	;set if EOM at end of write
dspEncryptBit	EQU	1	;set to encrypt message
dspEncryptMask	EQU	$1	;mask for setting the encrypt bit
dspEOMMask	EQU	$2	;mask for setting the EOM bit

Data Structures

ADSP Connection Control Block Data Structure

0	ccbLink	long	link to next CCB
4	refNum	word	reference number
6	state	word	state of the connection end
8	userFlags	byte	user flags for connection
9	localSocket	byte	local socket number
10	remoteAddress	long	internet address of remote end
14	attnCode	word	attention code received
16	attnSize	word	size of received attention data
18	attnPtr	long	pointer to received attention data
22	reserved	220 bytes	reserved

DPS Parameter Block Common Fields for ADSP and ASDSP

0	qLink	long	reserved
4	qType	word	reserved
6	ioTrap	word	reserved
8	ioCmdAddr	long	reserved
12	ioCompletion	long	address of completion routine
16	ioResult	word	result code
18	ioNamePtr	long	reserved
22	ioVRefNum	word	reserved
24	ioCRefNum	word	driver reference number
28	qStatus	long	reserved
32	ccbRefNum	word	reference number of CCB

dspInit and dspCLInit Parameter Variant

26	csCode	word	dspInit or dspCLInit
34	ccbPtr	long	pointer to CCB
38	userRoutine	long	pointer to routine to call on connection events
42	sendQSize	word	size in bytes of the send queue
44	sendQueue	long	pointer to send queue
48	recvQSize	word	size in bytes of the receive queue
50	recvQueue	long	pointer to receive queue
54	attnPtr	long	pointer to buffer for incoming attention messages
58	localSocket	byte	DDP socket number for this connection end

dspOptions Parameter Variant

16	ioResult	word	result code
24	ioCRefNum	word	driver reference number
26	csCode	word	always dspOptions
34	sendBlocking	word	send-blocking threshold
38	badSeqMax	byte	threshold to send retransmit advice
39	useCheckSum	byte	DDP checksum flag

dspOpen, dspCLListen, and dspCLDeny Parameter Variant

26	csCode	word	dspOpen, dspCLListen, or dspCLDeny
34	localCID	word	ID of this connection end
36	remoteCID	word	ID of remote connection end
38	remoteAddress	long	remote internet address
42	filterAddress	long	filter for open-connection requests
46	sendSeq	long	initial send sequence number
50	sendWindow	word	initial size of remote receive queue
52	recvSeq	long	initial receive sequence number
56	attnSendSeq	long	attention send sequence number
60	attnRecvSeq	long	attention receive sequence number
64	ocMode	byte	connection-opening mode
65	ocInterval	byte	interval between open requests
66	ocMaximum	byte	retries of open-connection request

sdspOpen Parameter Variant

26	csCode	word	sdspOpen
34	localCID	word	ID of this connection end
36	remoteCID	word	ID of remote connection end
38	remoteAddress	long	remote internet address
42	filterAddress	long	filter for open-connection requests
46	sendSeq	long	initial send sequence number
50	sendWindow	word	initial size of remote receive queue
52	recvSeq	long	not used for ASDSP
56	attnSendSeq	long	attention send sequence number
60	attnRecvSeq	long	not used for ASDSP
64	ocMode	byte	connection-opening mode
65	ocInterval	byte	interval between open requests
66	ocMaximum	byte	retries of open-connection request
68	secure	word	flag that determines if ASDSP authenticates the connection
70	sessionKey	long	pointer to the encryption key for the session
74	credentialsSize	long	length of credentials
78	credentials	long	pointer to credentials
82	workspace	long	pointer to workspace for connection
86	recipient	long	identity of recipient
90	issueTime	long	time when credentials were issued
94	expiry	long	time when credentials expire
98	initiator	long	pointer to record ID of initiator
102	hasIntermediary	word	TRUE if credentials have an intermediary
104	intermediary	long	pointer to record ID of intermediary

dspNewCID Parameter Variant

26	csCode	word	always dspNewCID
34	newCID	word	ID of new connection

dspClose, dspRemove, and dspCLRemove Parameter Variant

26	csCode	word	dspClose, dspRemove, or dspCLRemove
34	abort	byte	abort send requests or connection listener if not 0

dspStatus Parameter Variant

26	csCode	word	always dspStatus
34	statusCCB	pointer	pointer to CCB
38	sendQPending	word	bytes waiting to be sent or acknowledged
40	sendQFree	word	available send queue in bytes
42	recvQPending	word	bytes waiting to be read from queue
44	recvQFree	word	available receive queue in bytes

dspRead and dspWrite Parameter Variant

26	csCode	word	dspRead or dspWrite
34	reqCount	word	requested number of bytes
36	actCount	word	actual number of bytes read or written
38	dataPtr	pointer	pointer to data buffer
42	eom	byte	for ADSP: 1 if end of message; 0 otherwise for ASDSP: bit 0 = end of message; bit 1 turns on encryption, if set
43	flush	byte	1 to send data now; 0 otherwise

dspAttention and dspReset Parameter Variant

26	csCode	word	dspAttention or dspReset
34	attnCode	word	client attention code
36	attnSize	word	size of attention data in bytes
38	attnData	pointer	pointer to attention data

Result Codes

noErr	0	No error or unrecognized event code
ddpSktErr	−91	Error opening socket
errOpenDenied	−1273	Open request denied by recipient
errDSPQueueSize	−1274	Send or receive queue is too small
errFwdReset	−1275	Read terminated by forward reset
errAttention	−1276	Attention message too long
errOpening	−1277	Attempt to open connection failed
errState	−1278	Bad connection state for this operation
errAborted	−1279	Request aborted by dspRemove or dspClose routine
errRefNum	−1280	Bad connection reference number
kOCEUnsupportedCredentialsVersion	−1543	Credentials version not supported
kOCEBadEncryptionMethod	−1559	During the authentication process, the ASDSP implementations could not agree on an encryption method to be used (ASDSP can support multiple stream encryption methods. In Release 1, only RC4 and "no encryption" are supported.)
kOCENoASDSPWorkSpace	−1570	You passed NIL for the workspace parameter
kOCEAuthenticationTrouble	−1571	Authentication process failed

AppleTalk Transaction Protocol (ATP)

Contents

Contents

This chapter describes the AppleTalk Transaction Protocol (ATP) that you use to send a request from one application or process to another that can satisfy the request and respond to it. Because ATP is transaction-based—that is, the response data is bound to the request data and the exchange of information is limited to the transaction—you do not incur the overhead entailed in establishing, maintaining, and breaking a connection that is associated with connection-oriented protocols, such as ADSP. However, you can transfer only a limited amount of data using ATP.

You should read this chapter if you want to write an application that requires reliable delivery of data while allowing one side of the communication to ask the other side to perform a service and return a small amount of data.

For an overview of ATP and how it fits within the AppleTalk protocol stack, read the chapter "Introduction to AppleTalk" in this book, which also introduces and defines some of the terminology used in this chapter. For complete explanation of the ATP specification, see *Inside AppleTalk,* second edition.

About ATP

The AppleTalk Transaction Protocol offers a simple, efficient means of transferring *small* amounts of data across a network; it lets one network entity request information of another entity that possesses only the ability to respond to the request. ATP ensures that data is delivered without error or packet loss.

ATP communication is based on the concept of a **transaction:** one party, the **requester,** makes a request of another party, the **responder,** to perform a service and return a response. This discussion uses the term *requester* to refer to an application that uses ATP to make a request and *responder* to refer to an application that uses ATP to respond to a request.

When it receives a request, the responder application performs the necessary processing to service it and sends a response message back to the requester, completing the transaction. The response message can be data that reports the result of the trans-action or information produced as a result of the processing. Here is how a basic transaction occurs:

- The requester application calls the .ATP interface, and the .ATP driver on the requester side sends the request to the .ATP driver on the responder side.

- The .ATP driver on the responder side passes the request to the responder application, which is listening for incoming .ATP requests.

- The responder application satisfies the request and prepares a response, then calls the ATP interface to transmit the response via the .ATP driver back to the requester application.

Figure 6-1 shows this interaction.

Figure 6-1   An ATP transaction

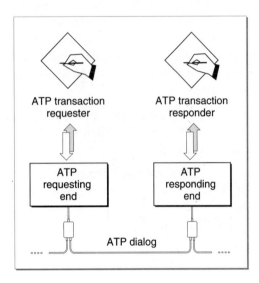

The amount of data that a requester application can send is limited to 578 bytes; the amount of data that a responder application can return is limited to 4624 bytes. The ATP programming interface includes a function that lets you add one or more single packets to follow the initial response, up to a total of eight packets including the initial number of packets sent, if you do not send eight packets in the initial response.

Note
Although you can use the ATP add-response function to extend the amount of response data, if you intend for your application to transfer large amounts of data, you should choose a transport protocol other than ATP. For example, you can use ADSP, which allows you to send and receive continuous streams of data. ◆

You can implement applications that use ATP to perform network-based transactions in the following two ways:

■ You can write a single application that handles both the responder and requester actions of an ATP transaction and run that application on two networked nodes. This method allows each application to act as either the requester or the responder. The interaction remains asymmetric; only one side can control the communication during a single transaction. However, each side has the capacity to initiate a transaction by sending a request to the other side.

■ You can write two distinct applications, one application that implements only the requester part of a transaction and another application that implements only the responder side. This scenario lends itself to a client-server model in which many nodes on a network run the requester application (client), while one or more nodes run the responder application (server); one server can respond to transaction requests from various clients.

AppleTalk Transaction Protocol (ATP)

ATP is a direct client of DDP, and it adds reliable delivery of data to the transport delivery services that DDP provides. Figure 6-2 shows ATP and the underlying protocol stack.

Figure 6-2   ATP and its underlying protocols

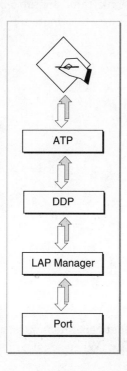

The ATP Packet Format

An ATP packet includes an 8-byte header followed by up to 578 bytes of data. An ATP packet is preceded by the DDP header that, in turn, is preceded by the data-link header, referred to as the *frame* header.

The ATP header contains the following information:

■ The first byte consists of control information. Bits within this byte are set to identify aspects of a request or a response function.

■ The second byte contains a **bitmap/sequence number.** This field is 8 bits wide, and its use and significance depend on whether the ATP packet is a request packet or a response packet. For request packets, this field is referred to as the **transaction bitmap,** and it identifies the number of buffers that a requester application has reserved for the response data. For response packets, this field is referred to as the **ATP sequence number,** and it is used to identify the sequential position of the response packet in the complete response message; ATP uses the sequence number to manage and handle lost or out-of-sequence response packets.

■ The third and fourth bytes carry the transaction ID assigned to a request and used by the response to that request.

■ The fifth through eighth bytes carry user data; an application can use these bytes for its own purposes, for example, to transfer command information.

The ATP data follows the header. It can consist of from 0 to 578 bytes. An ATP packet is enclosed in a DDP datagram that is enclosed in a data-link frame. Figure 6-3 shows a close-up view of the first byte of the ATP header, the control information byte.

Figure 6-3   The ATP packet header control information byte

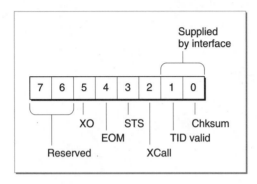

The Control Information Byte

ATP applications call response and request functions that generate request and response packets. (ATP uses the release packet internally.) When set, the bits have the following meanings:

Bit	Meaning
0	Use the DDP checksum feature for this packet.
1	ATP has assigned the request transaction ID; the TID field value is now valid.
2	This request uses an extended parameter block.
3	To the requester: retransmit the request immediately (send-transmission status).
4	This is the last packet of the response message (end of message).
5	This request is an exactly-once transaction.

The Bitmap/Sequence Number

ATP ensures reliable delivery of data. This means that ATP retransmits all lost or dropped packets, and if it is unable to complete a transaction properly, ATP returns an error as the function result. To receive all the packets that make up a response message, a requester application must provide enough buffer space to hold the data. A request message consists of a single packet, while each **response message** can contain up to eight response packets.

Response packets are numbered from 0 to 7. ATP uses the sequence number to manage the transmission and receipt of response packets; the packet header ATP sequence number field contains 8 bits, 1 for each response packet.

ATP sets the sequence number in the request header to tell the .ATP driver code on the responder side which response packets the requester has not received. When a requester does not receive a complete response message, the .ATP driver code on the responder side can then send again only the packets that the requester side has not received, based on the bit settings of the transaction sequence number. ATP handles the retransmission of data internally without requiring any action on the part of your application. For information about the buffer records, see "The Buffer Data Structure" on page 6-20.

The Transaction ID

The third and fourth bytes of the ATP header carry a 16-bit transaction ID. The .ATP driver code on the requester side of a transaction assigns a unique transaction ID to each request that a requester application makes. The responder application that services the request includes this number as a parameter to the response call that it issues to send its response back to the requester. The transaction ID ties together the request and its response, ensuring that ATP delivers the correct data in response to each request. An application can issue and have pending multiple concurrent asynchronous requests; ATP uses the transaction ID to keep track of them.

User Bytes

ATP does not concern itself with the last 4 bytes of the ATP header. They are reserved for your use. You can use these bytes for any purpose prearranged by the requester and responder applications. The ATP functions include a parameter that you use to specify this data.

At-Least-Once and Exactly-Once Transactions

ATP supports two types of transactions: at-least-once transactions and exactly-once transactions. An **at-least-once transaction** ensures that the responder application receives every request directed to it at least once. However, this mode allows for the possibility of a responder application receiving duplicate requests.

For example, when you send a request that the .ATP driver code on the responder side receives, it passes the request on to the responder application. Your responder application then processes the request and creates a response to it. The ATP responder driver sends that response to your requester application. If the response is lost during the transmission, ATP retransmits the request after a period of time passes; you can set a value to control this timeout period. The ATP responder driver code receives the duplicate request and repeats the cycle of passing it on to your responder application for processing. At-least-once transactions ensure that the data is delivered at least once, and possibly more than once. You can use this transaction mode if it does not have adverse affects on the responder application.

An **exactly-once transaction** ensures that the responder application receives a specific request only once. These are also referred to as *XO*, as in *exactly-once* transactions. To create this result, the ATP responder code saves the response packets until the transaction is complete. This means that ATP itself can retransmit packets without requiring that your responder application reprocess the request.

The ATP responder code saves the response packets until the ATP code on the requester side indicates that it has received all of the packets. The ATP code on the requester side sends a transaction release packet to the ATP code on the responder side to signal that the requester application has received all of the response packets, so that ATP can now release them.

Because the transaction release packet could also be lost during transmission, ATP backs up this process with a transaction release timer. ATP marks packets saved for retransmission with a timestamp. When a packet ages beyond the amount of time that you set for the responder's release timer, ATP discards the packet.

You can set the release timer value that the ATP code on the responder end uses from your requester application; the send request functions include a release timer parameter for this purpose. For more information about this parameter, see "PSendRequest" on page 6-24 or "PNSendRequest" on page 6-27.

The Buffer Data Structure

The responder application needs to provide space to store the data to be sent to the requester until the requester application has received all of the data. The requester application needs to provide space to receive the data that it expects to receive as a result of the transaction. Each response can include up to eight packets. To handle the storage of these packets, the ATP client application at each end of the transaction provides a buffer data structure. The buffer data structure is designed to allow ATP to easily manage reliable transfer of multiple packets belonging to a single response message. A buffer data structure consists of an array of eight elements, each of which contains a pointer to a record of type `BDSElement`.

Each record contains a field for the size of the buffer created to hold the data and a pointer to that buffer. It also contains fields for the size of the data in the response packet and the user bytes that were passed in the packet header, if these bytes were used to communicate additional information. You can create your own buffer data structures, or you can use the ATP utility provided for this purpose. For a description of the BDS data type, see "The Buffer Data Structure" on page 6-20. For a description of the utility that you can use to build the buffer data structure, see "BuildBDS" on page 6-44.

ATP Flags

Many of the functions that you use for an ATP transaction pass control information in an ATP parameter block field called `atpFlags`. This field comprises a single byte whose bits you can set to signal control information, if appropriate. In some cases, ATP sets these flag bits for its own use. The discussion of each function that uses these flags includes the control information about the bits specific to that function. Table 6-1 shows the Pascal and assembly constants defined for these bits.

Table 6-1   Constants for ATP flag bits

Bit	Pascal constant	Assembly constant	Meaning
0	`atpSendChkvalue`	`sendChk`	Use DDP's checksum feature when sending a packet.
1	`atpTIDValidvalue`	`tidValid`	The transaction ID value that ATP assigns is set; you can check the `reqTID` field now.
2	None	`atpXcall`	This exactly-once transaction request uses an extended parameter block, the last field of which (`TRelTime`) is set to the release timer value for the ATP responder side.
3	`atpSTSvalue`	`atpSTSBit`	The ATP requester must retransmit a request immediately. (ATP sets the send-transmission-status bit, which it uses internally.)
4	`atpEOMvalue`	`atpEOMBit`	The last packet in this response is the end of the message.
5	`atpXOvalue`	`atpXOBit`	This request is an exactly-once transaction.

Using ATP

This section describes how to use ATP to

- send a transaction request to a responder application that is an ATP socket client
- receive a request from an ATP requester application and respond to it
- cancel pending ATP requests and responses

You can write a single ATP application that includes both the responder and requester code or two ATP applications that separately provide the responder and the requester services. This section describes how to write a requester application, and then it describes how to write a responder application.

Writing a Requester ATP Application

You use the `PSendRequest` function or the `PNSendRequest` function to send an ATP request to another socket.

Before you can use ATP, you must first open the .MPP driver, which in turn opens the .ATP driver. Use the Device Manager's `OpenDriver` function to open the .MPP driver. Even if you suspect that the .MPP and the .ATP drivers are open, you should call the `OpenDriver` function for the .MPP driver to ensure that this is the case. Calling `OpenDriver` for a driver that is already open will not produce harmful repercussions. See the chapter "Device Manager" in *Inside Macintosh: Devices* for information on the `OpenDriver` function. Do not close the .MPP driver when you are finished using

ATP because other applications dependent on it or on the .ATP driver require that it remain open.

To send an ATP request, follow these steps:

1. Create a buffer data structure (BDS) to hold the data that you expect to receive in response to your request. For information on how to do this, see "Creating a Buffer Data Structure" on page 6-12.

2. To allow ATP to assign the socket to be used to send the request, use the `PSendRequest` function. To specify a particular socket to be used to send the request, use the `PNSendRequest` function; in this case, you must call `POpenATPSocket` to first open the socket (see "POpenATPSkt" on page 6-30 for information about this function). For information on the parameters required for these functions, see "Specifying the Parameters for the Send Request Function" on page 6-12.

3. You can get the transaction ID that ATP assigns to a request from the `reqTID` parameter; you need this ID to cancel a request. However, before you check this field, make sure that the valid transaction ID (`atpTIDValidvalue`) bit (bit 1) of the `atpFlags` parameter is set. ATP sets this bit to inform you that it has assigned a transaction ID and that the `reqTID` field is now valid.

4. If you opened a socket to be used for the `PNSendRequest` call, close the socket using `PCloseATPSkt`. See"PCloseATPSkt" on page 6-31 for information on how to use this function. If you use the `PSendRequest` function, ATP allocates a socket and opens and closes it for you.

The code in Listing 6-1 shows how to open a socket and issue a call to the `PSendRequest` function. The code uses the `BuildBDS` function to create a buffer data structure to hold the response data it expects in response. This segment of code assumes that the application has already called the `OpenDriver` function to open the .MPP and .ATP drivers.

Listing 6-1   Opening a socket and sending an ATP request

```
CONST
    kMaxPacketSize = 578;              {maximum packet size we can receive}
    kNRespBuffs = 8;                   {you allow eight response buffers}
    kOurRespBufSize = kMaxPacketSize * kNRespBuffs;
                                       {response buffer size}
VAR
    err:            OSErr;
    reqLength:      Integer;
    nBufs:          Integer;
    ref:            Integer;
    targetAddr:     AddrBlock;
    gAtpPBPtr:      ATPPBPtr;
    gReqBufPtr:     Ptr;
    gRespBufPtr:    Ptr;
    gSRespBdsPtr:   BDSPtr;
```

```
BEGIN
    gAtpPBPtr := ATPPBPtr(NewPtr(SizeOf(ATPParamBlock)));
    gReqBufPtr := NewPtr(kMaxPacketSize);
    gRespBufPtr := NewPtr(kOurRespBufSize);
    gSRespBdsPtr := BDSPtr(NewPtr(SizeOf (BDSType)));
    err := OpenDriver('MPP',ref);
    if err <> noErr THEN DoErr(err);
    WITH gAtpPBPtr^ DO

    BEGIN
        atpSocket := 0;                    {dynamically allocate a socket}
        addrBlock.aNet := 0;               {accept requests from anyone}
        addrBlock.aNode := 0;
        addrBlock.aSocket := 0;
    END;
    err := POpenATPSkt(gAtpPBPtr,false);{socket is returned in }
                                         { gAtpPBPtr^.atpSocket}


    IF err <> noErr THEN DoErr(err);
    IF gAtpPBPtr^.ioResult <> noErr THEN DoErr(err);


    MyPrepareRequestData(gReqBufPtr,@reqLength);
                                         {user routine that prepares the }
                                         { request data to be sent}
    MyLocateTargetAddress(@targetAddr);
                                         {user routine that locates the }
                                         { target machine}


    {Set up your BDS structure.}
    nBufs := BuildBDS(gRespBufPtr,Ptr(gSRespBdsPtr),kOurRespBufSize);


    WITH gAtpPBPtr^ DO
    BEGIN
        atpFlags := atpXOvalue;            {issue an exactly-once transaction}
        addrBlock.aNet := targetAddr.aNet;
                                           {set up the target machine}
        addrBlock.aNode := targetAddr.aNode;
        addrBlock.aSocket := targetAddr.aSocket;

        reqLength := reqLength;            {size of your request data}
        reqPointer := gReqBufPtr;          {pointer to actual request data}
        numOfBuffs := nBufs;              {number of responses expected}
        bdsPointer := Ptr(gSRespBdsPtr);  {your BDS pointer}
        timeOutVal := 3;                   {timeout interval}
        retryCount := 5;                   {number of retries}
    END;
    err := PSendRequest(gAtpPBPtr,false);
```

```
    IF err <> noErr THEN DoErr(err);

    MyProcessResponses(gAtpPBPtr^.bdsPointer,gAtpPBPtr^.numOfResps);
                                    {user routine to process the }
                                    { response data returned}

    {Clean up after you are done.}
    DisposePtr(Ptr(gAtpPBPtr));
    DisposePtr(gReqBufPtr);
    DisposePtr(gRespBufPtr);
    DisposePtr(Ptr(gSRespBdsPtr));
END.
```

Creating a Buffer Data Structure

Response data can comprise up to eight packets. ATP uses the organization of the buffer data structure (BDS) to manage these packets and ensure their complete delivery. The BDS must be an array of up to eight elements. You can create the buffer data structure yourself, or you can use the BuildBDS function for this purpose. You pass BuildBDS a pointer to a buffer and the length of the buffer, and it creates up to eight elements, one for each packet, depending on the size of the buffer that you supply. BuildBDS returns as its function result the number of elements that it creates; you pass this number and a pointer to the buffer data structure to the PSendRequest or PNSendRequest function that you call to issue the request. The memory that you allocate for the buffer must be nonrelocatable until the PSendResponse call completes execution. After PSendResponse returns, you should release this memory if you do not intend to reuse it.

Specifying the Parameters for the Send Request Function

When you call either the PSendRequest function or the PNSendRequest function to send an ATP request, you must do these tasks:

- Specify as the value of the addrBlock parameter the AppleTalk internet address of the socket whose client responder application you are sending the request to.

- Specify in the reqLength field the size in bytes of the request and in the reqPointer field a pointer to the request data. The buffer that you use to store the request belongs to ATP until the PSendRequest (or PNSendRequest) function completes execution, after which you can either reuse the memory or release it.

- Set the timeOutVal and retryCount parameters appropriately for your network. See the following section, "Setting the Timeout and Retry Count Parameters." If this is an exactly-once request, set bit 5 (atpXOvalue) of the atpFlags parameter to ensure that the responder application receives a specific request only once. For additional information about exactly-once transactions, see "At-Least-Once and Exactly-Once Transactions" on page 6-7.

You can send up to 4 bytes of additional information in the userData parameter, and ATP will pass this to the responder application in the userData parameter of its PGetRequest call. To make this parameter meaningful, both the requester and the responder applications should agree on the use of these additional data bytes that are separate from the request or response data sent in an ATP transaction.

Setting the Timeout and Retry Count Parameters

When a transaction does not complete on the first transmission, ATP retries it a number of times. You can control ATP's retry behavior by setting these two parameters: the timeOutVal field and the retryCount field. The timeOutVal value determines in seconds how long ATP waits before resending the original request packet; the retryCount value determines how many times ATP retries to send the request.

ATP optimizes how it performs retries based on the response bitmap; ATP on the requester side resends the request with the header bitmap indicating to the ATP driver on the responder side which packets it should resend. (See the "The Bitmap/Sequence Number" on page 6-6 for more information.) ATP makes this request to resend until it receives all of the packets or it exhausts the number of retry attempts that you specify. If ATP exhausts all of the retry attempts before the requester side receives all of the packets, ATP returns an error.

To choose the correct timeout value and retry count combination, you should consider the speed and complexity of your network—for example, take into account the degree of traffic congestion and whether your network contains multiple routers. You can use the AppleTalk Echo Protocol (AEP) echo socket to test the network performance and adjust the values accordingly. For more information about using the AEP echo socket to test network performance, see the chapter "Datagram Delivery Protocol (DDP)" in this book. You can store various pairs of values in a preferences resource file so that you can easily change them to adapt to the speed of the network.

If you want ATP to retry indefinitely to send the request, you can set the retryCount parameter to 255. In this case, ATP will send the request repeatedly until either the ATP responder end satisfies the request and sends back a response or you cancel the request. To cancel a PSendRequest call, you can use either the PKillSendReq function or the PRelTCB function. To cancel a PNSendRequest call, you can use the PKillSendReq function only.

Setting the Release Timer Value

For exactly-once transactions, the ATP responder code saves the response packets until the ATP code on the requester side indicates that it has received all of them. When this is the case, the ATP code on the requester side sends a transaction release packet to tell the ATP code on the responder side to release the response packets. Because this packet could be dropped or lost during transmission, ATP uses a release timer to discard the retained packets after a specified amount of time and to release the memory used to store them.

If the nodes at both ends of the ATP connection are running AppleTalk Phase 2 drivers, you can control the release timer value that determines when ATP releases the response packets by setting the 3 lower bits of the `TRelTime` parameter to one of the following values:

TRelTime	Setting of release timer
000	30 seconds
001	1 minute
010	4 minutes
100	8 minutes

Writing a Responder ATP Application

A responder application receives incoming ATP requests, processes them, and sends a response to the requester application. To write a responder application, you open a socket that you set up to listen for requests. When you receive a request, you process it and send a response back to the requester application. The response can consist of a message reporting the outcome of the processing you performed or data resulting from the processing.

Before you can use ATP, you must first open the .MPP driver, which in turn opens the .ATP driver. Use the Device Manager's `OpenDriver` function to open the .MPP driver. Even if you suspect that the .MPP and the .ATP drivers are open, you should call the `OpenDriver` function for the .MPP driver to ensure that this is the case. Calling `OpenDriver` for a driver that is already open will not produce harmful repercussions. See the chapter "Device Manager" in *Inside Macintosh: Devices* for information on the `OpenDriver` function. Do not close the .MPP driver when you are finished using ATP because other applications dependent on it or the .ATP driver require that it remain open.

Opening and Setting Up a Socket to Receive Requests

To open a socket to receive incoming requests, you use the following procedure:

1. To open the socket, call the `POpenATPSkt` function, providing it with values as follows:
   □ To direct ATP to open a specific socket, provide the number of that socket as the value of the `atpSocket` parameter; to allow ATP to dynamically assign a socket, specify 0 as the value of this field.
   □ To filter the sockets from which you will accept requests, set the internet socket address fields of the `addrBlock` parameter; to accept requests from any socket, set all three fields to 0. You can filter requests based on network, socket, or node numbers. For example, to accept requests from all sockets on the node whose ID is 112, you set the network and socket number fields of the address block record to 0 and the node ID field to 112.

2. To set up the socket to receive requests, call the `PGetRequest` function, which listens for an incoming request on the socket you specify. You provide it with the parameter values as follows:

☐ Allocate a buffer to store the incoming request; you pass `PGetRequest` a pointer to this buffer and the length of the buffer. Unless you know the exact size of the incoming request, allocate at least 578 bytes of nonrelocatable memory for this buffer to accommodate the maximum request packet size. Set the `reqPointer` parameter to point to the buffer, and set the `reqLength` parameter to the size in bytes of the buffer.

☐ Set the `atpSocket` parameter to the number of the socket to be used to listen for the request; this is the socket you opened through the `POpenATPSkt` call.

☐ Set the `ioCompletion` parameter. In most cases, you should issue the `PGetRequest` call asynchronously so that your application can continue execution while `PGetRequest` listens for an incoming call; the `PGetRequest` function returns after it receives an incoming request or encounters an error condition. If you issue this call asynchronously, you must either specify a completion routine or set the `ioCompletion` parameter to `NIL`. If you use a completion routine, before it exits, your completion routine can call the `PGetRequest` function again to listen for the next incoming request. If you do not use a completion routine, you must poll the `ioResult` field for indication of an incoming request to determine when the function completes execution and whether an error condition or an incoming request caused the function to complete. For more information on calling a routine asynchronously, see the chapter "Introduction to AppleTalk" in this book.

3. Process the values that `PGetRequest` returns. The `PGetRequest` function returns the following values that may be of use to your application:

☐ The request transaction ID `reqTID` that ATP assigns to this request. If you intend to respond to the request, save this value because you will need to pass it to the `PSendResponse` function and the `PAddResponse` function to identify the request for which the response message is intended. For more information on the transaction ID, see the discussion in the section "The ATP Packet Format" beginning on page 6-5.

☐ The `userData` parameter, which contains any additional information that the requester application has sent. To make this parameter meaningful, both the requester and the responder applications should agree on the use of these additional data bytes that are separate from the request or response data sent in an ATP transaction.

☐ The exactly-once bit (bit 5) of the `atpFlags` parameter, which is set if the request received is part of an exactly-once transaction. ATP uses this information internally to ensure that your responder application receives this request only once.

Listing 6-2 on page 6-17 shows how to open a socket and issue a call to the `PGetRequest` function to receive requests.

Responding to Requests

After you process a request and create a response message, you call the PSendResponse function to send the response. ATP assembles the response packets into a message and returns them to the requester application. You can send the request through the same socket that you use to receive incoming requests, or you can specify a different socket to be used for this purpose. To use a different socket, you must first open the socket by calling POpenATPSocket. The code in Listing 6-2 opens a new socket that it uses to send the response.

1. Create a buffer data structure to hold the response data that you want to send.

   The buffer data structure (BDS) must be an array of up to eight elements. You can use the BuildBDS function to create the BDS. You pass BuildBDS a pointer to a buffer and the length of the buffer, and it creates up to eight elements depending on the size of the buffer that you supply. BuildBDS returns as its function result the number of elements that it creates; you pass this number and a pointer to the buffer data structure to the PSendResponse call. The memory that you allocate for the buffer must be nonrelocatable until the PSendResponse call completes execution. After PSendResponse returns, you should release this memory.

2. To send the response, call the PSendResponse function. The response data cannot exceed 4624 bytes. If you need to send more information, you can follow the PSendResponse function with one or more calls to the PAddResponse function until you have sent a total of eight packets, including the packets that you sent when you called the PSendResponse function; each time you call the PAddResponse function, you can send one additional packet consisting of 578 bytes of data.

   □ For the input address block (addrBlock) and transaction ID (transID) parameters to PSendResponse, use the address block (addrBlock) and request transaction ID (reqTID) parameter values that the PGetRequest function returned.

   □ Set the numOfBuffs field to the number of response packets that you are sending. If you are sending fewer packets than the requester expects to receive, you must set the end-of-message (atpEOMvalue) bit (bit 4) in the atpFlags field to indicate that the last packet is the final one in the response message. The bitmap returned by the PGetRequest function indicates the number of packets that the requester expects in response.

   □ Set the atpSocket field to the number of the socket that you are using to send the response.

3. Call the CloseATPSkt function to close the socket that you opened to receive requests and respond to them after you are finished with this socket. You can use the socket to continue to listen for requests until your application completes execution, but you should explicitly close the socket before exiting the program.

The code in Listing 6-2 first shows how to open a socket and issue a call to the PGetRequest function to receive requests. Then it shows how to prepare the response data and send it.

Listing 6-2 Opening a socket to receive a request and sending response data

```
CONST
    kMaxPacketSize = 578;              {maximum packet size you can receive}
    kMaxResponses = 8;                 {maximum number of responses to expect}
    kRespBufSize = kMaxPacketSize * kMaxResponses;
                                       {your response buffer}
VAR
    err:               OSErr;
    NumOfBufs:         Integer;
    ref:               Integer;
    nBufs:             Integer;
    ReqBitMap:         BitMapType;
    thisBit:           LongInt;
    gAtpPBPtr:         ATPPBPtr;
    gSendRespPBPtr:    ATPPBPtr;
    gGetReqBufPtr:     Ptr;
    gSRespBuf:         Ptr;
    gSRespBdsPtr:      BDSPtr;
BEGIN
    gAtpPBPtr := ATPPBPtr(NewPtr(SizeOf(ATPParamBlock)));
    gSendRespPBPtr := ATPPBPtr(NewPtr(SizeOf(ATPParamBlock)));
    gGetReqBufPtr := NewPtr(kMaxPacketSize);
    gSRespBdsPtr := BDSPtr(NewPtr(SizeOf(BDSType)));
    gSRespBuf := NewPtr(kRespBufSize);

    err := OpenDriver('MPP',ref);
    if err <> noErr THEN DoErr(err);

WITH gAtpPBPtr^ DO
BEGIN
    atpSocket := 0;                    {dynamically allocate a socket}
    addrBlock.aNet := 0;               {accept requests from anyone}
    addrBlock.aNode := 0;
    addrBlock.aSocket := 0;
END;
err := POpenATPSkt(gAtpPBPtr,false);{socket is returned in }
                                    { gAtpPBPtr^.atpSocket}

IF err <> noErr THEN DoErr(err);
IF gAtpPBPtr^.ioResult <> noErr THEN DoErr(err);
```

```
WITH gAtpPBPtr^ DO
BEGIN
    reqLength := 0;                        {request data length will be returned }
                                           { to you here}
    reqPointer := gGetReqBufPtr;           {pointer to buffer for incoming request }
                                           { data}
END;
    err := PGetRequest(gAtpPBPtr,TRUE);{asynchronous PGetRequest}

    IF err <> noErr THEN DoErr(err);

    {Poll ioResult until the call completes.}
    WHILE gAtpPBPtr^.ioResult > noErr DO
    BEGIN
        GoDoSomething;                     {return control to user while you wait }
                                           { for PGetRequest to complete}
    END;

    IF gAtpPBPtr^.ioResult <> noErr THEN DoErr(err);

    MyProcessRequestReceived(gAtpPBPtr^.reqPointer,gAtpPBPtr^.reqLength)
                                           {user routine that looks at the request }
                                           { data received}

    {Walk through the bitmap and see how many response buffers you need.}
    NumOfBufs := 0;
    FOR thisBit := 0 to 7 DO
    BEGIN
        {Each bit that is set corresponds to a buffer.}
        if BitTst(@gAtpPBPtr^.bitMap,thisBit) = TRUE THEN
    BEGIN
        {Your routine to fill in the appropriate response data.}
        SetUpResponseData(gSRespBuf,thisBit);
        NumOfBufs := NumOfBufs + 1;
    END
END;

{Put your response data into the BDS structure.}
nBufs := BuildBDS(gSRespBuf,Ptr(gSRespBdsPtr),(NumOfBufs * kMaxPacketSize));
```

```
WITH gSendRespPBPtr^ DO
BEGIN
   atpSocket := gAtpPBPtr^.atpSocket;
   atpFlags := atpEOMvalue;            {indicate end of message}

{Send response to the machine that sent you the request.}
   addrBlock.aNet := gAtpPBPtr^.addrBlock.aNet;
   addrBlock.aNode := gAtpPBPtr^.addrBlock.aNode;
   addrBlock.aSocket := gAtpPBPtr^.addrBlock.aSocket;
   bdsPointer := Ptr(gSRespBdsPtr);
   numOfBuffs := NumOfBufs;            {send all of the responses back now}
   bdsSize := nBufs;                   {indicate how many responses you are }
                                       { sending}
   transID := gAtpPBPtr^.transID;      {use transID returned from the }
                                       { PGetRequest function}
END;
err := PSendResponse(gSendRespPBPtr,FALSE);

IF err <> noErr THEN DoErr(err);

{Clean up after you are done.}
DisposePtr(Ptr(gAtpPBPtr));
DisposePtr(Ptr(gSendRespPBPtr));
DisposePtr(gGetReqBufPtr);
DisposePtr(Ptr(gSRespBdsPtr));
DisposePtr(gSRespBuf);
END.
```

Canceling an ATP Function

You can cancel all pending ATP function calls made on a specific socket by closing the socket. However, ATP provides functions that allow you to cancel individual function calls or all function calls of a particular kind. If you want to close a socket for which there are still pending requests that you don't want executed, you should first explicitly cancel those requests by using the ATP function provided for this purpose, instead of simply closing the socket.

You can use the following functions to cancel specific requests:

■ To cancel a PGetRequest function, use the PKillGetReq function, which is described on page 6-41. You identify the request to be canceled by specifying the pointer to the parameter block that you passed to the PGetRequest function when you called it.

6

AppleTalk Transaction Protocol (ATP)

AppleTalk Transaction Protocol (ATP)

- To cancel all pending `PGetRequest` functions on a certain socket, use the `ATPKillAllGetReq` function described on page 6-42; you specify the socket number, whose pending get requests you want to cancel, as the value of the `atpSocket` parameter.

- To cancel a `PSendRequest` or a `PNSendRequest` function, use the `PKillSendReq` function described beginning on page 6-38. You identify the request to be canceled by specifying the pointer to the parameter block that you passed to the function when you issued it. To cancel a `PSendRequest` function, use the `PRelTCB` function described beginning on page 6-40. You identify the request to be canceled by specifying the request transaction ID as the `transID` parameter and the destination socket of the request as the `addrBlock` parameter.

- To cancel an exactly-once `PSendResponse` function, use the `PRelRspCB` function, described beginning on page 6-43. You identify the request to be canceled by specifying the transaction ID of the associated request as the `transID` parameter and the `PSendResponse` destination socket number as the `atpSocket` parameter.

ATP Reference

This section describes the data structures and routines that are specific to ATP.

- The "Data Structures" section shows the Pascal data structures for the buffer data structure (BDS) array, the ATP parameter block, and the address block record.

- The "Routines" section describes the ATP routines for making a transaction request, receiving and responding to a transaction request, canceling a call to an ATP function, and building a buffer data structure to be used to hold response data to be sent and received.

Data Structures

This section describes the data structures that are specific to ATP. These data structures include the buffer data structure that is used to hold the response data packets to be sent from one application and received by another, the ATP parameter block that is used to hold input and output values for ATP functions, and the address block record data structure that ATP functions use to specify an AppleTalk internet socket address.

The Buffer Data Structure

The buffer data structure (BDS) is an array of type `BDSElement` containing up to eight records, each of which is used to hold a response packet. You create a BDS to hold the response data that you send using the `PSendResponse` function. You also create a BDS to receive the response packets that you request through a `PSendRequest` or `PNSendRequest` function. You can use the `BuildBDS` function to create this data structure, or you can create the data structure in Pascal.

CHAPTER 6

```
TYPE  BDSElement =
RECORD
    buffSize: Integer;
    buffPtr: Ptr;
    dataSize: Integer;
    userBytes: Longint;
END;
BDSType = ARRAY[0..7] OF BDSElement;
BDSPtr = ^BDSType;
BitMapType = PACKED ARRAY[0..7] OF Boolean;
```

Field descriptions

buffSize   The size in bytes of the buffer.

buffPtr   A pointer to the buffer.

dataSize   The size of the data received.

userBytes   Up to 4 bytes of additional data separate from the response data.

The ATP Parameter Block

The ATP functions require a pointer to an ATP parameter block that is used to pass the input and output parameters associated with the function. The ATPParamBlock data type defines the ATP parameter block. The ATP parameter block includes variant records for the fields that are particular to an ATP routine.

This section defines the fields that are common to all ATP functions that use the ATP parameter block. (The BuildBDS function does not use the ATP parameter block.) These common fields are either filled in by the MPW interface or returned by the function; your application does not need to provide values for these fields. This section does not define reserved fields, which are used internally by the .ATP driver or not at all. The fields that are used for specific functions only are defined in the descriptions of the functions to which they apply.

```
TYPE ATPParamBlock =
PACKED RECORD
    qLink:          QElemPtr;          {reserved}
    qType:          Integer;           {reserved}
    ioTrap:         Integer;           {reserved}
    ioCmdAddr:      Ptr;               {reserved}
    ioCompletion:   ProcPtr;           {completion routine}
    ioResult:       OSErr;             {result code}
    userData:       Longint;           {ATP user bytes}
    reqTID:         Integer;           {request transaction ID}
    ioRefNum:       Integer;           {driver reference number}
    csCode:         Integer;           {call command code}
    atpSocket:      Byte;              {currBitMap or socket number}
```

```
CASE MPPParmType OF
   SendRequestParm,
   SendResponseParm,
   GetRequestParm,
   AddResponseParm,
   KillSendReqParm:
      (atpFlags:        Byte;     {control information}
       addrBlock:       AddrBlock;
                                  {source/dest. socket address}
       reqLength:       Integer;  {request/response length}
       reqPointer:      Ptr;      {ptr to request/response data}
       bdsPointer:      Ptr;      {ptr to response BDS}
   CASE MPPParmType OF
      SendRequestParm:
         (numOfBuffs:   Byte;     {number of responses expected}
          timeOutVal:   Byte;     {timeout interval}
          numOfResps:   Byte;     {number of responses }
                                  { actually received}
          retryCount:   Byte;     {number of retries}
          intBuff:      Integer;  {used internally for }
                                  { PNSendRequest}
          TRelTime:     Byte);    {TRelease time for extended }
                                  { send request}
      SendResponseParm:
         (filler0:      Byte;     {bitmap}
          bdsSize:      Byte;     {number of BDS elements}
          transID:      Integer); {transaction ID}
      GetRequestParm:
         (bitmap:       Byte;     {bitmap}
          filler1:      Byte);    {reserved}
      AddResponseParm:
         (rspNum:       Byte;     {sequence number}
          filler2:      Byte);    {reserved}
      KillSendReqParm
         (aKillQEl:     Ptr));    {ptr to (queue element) function to }
                                  { cancel}
END;


ATPPBPtr  =  ^ATPParamBlock;
```

Field descriptions

ioCompletion   A pointer to a completion routine that you can provide. When you
                 execute a function asynchronously, the .ATP driver calls your
                 completion routine when it completes execution of the function if

you specify a pointer to the routine as the value of this field. Specify NIL for this field if you do not wish to provide a completion routine. If you execute a function synchronously, the .ATP driver ignores the ioCompletion field. For information about completion routines, see the chapter "Introduction to AppleTalk" in this book.

ioResult   The result of the function. If you call the function asynchronously, the .ATP driver sets this field to 1 as soon as you call the function, and it changes the field to the actual result code when the function completes execution.

ioRefNum   The .ATP driver reference number. The MPW interface fills in this field.

csCode   The command code for the ATP function to be executed. The MPW interface fills in this value for you.

The Address Block Record

The address block record defines a data structure of AddrBlock type. The following ATP functions use this data type to specify AppleTalk internet socket addresses: PSendRequest, PSendResponse, PNSendResponse, POpenATPSkt, PGetRequest, PSendResponse, PAddResponse, PRelTCB, PRelRspCB.

```
TYPE AddrBlock =
PACKED RECORD
    aNet:          Integer;      {network number}
    aNode:         Byte;         {node ID}
    aSocket:       Byte;         {socket number}
END;
```

Field descriptions

aNet   The network number to which the node belongs that is running the ATP client application whose address you are specifying.

aNode   The node ID of the machine running the ATP client application whose address you are specifying.

aSocket   The number of the socket used for the ATP client application.

Routines

This section describes the ATP routines that you use to

■ send a request to a responder socket client

■ open and close an ATP socket

■ set up a socket to listen for a request

■ send a response to a requester socket client

■ cancel a response or a request function

■ build a buffer data structure to store the response data

All of the ATP functions except the `BuildBDS` function use the ATP parameter block to pass input and output parameters. Each function description shows the parameter block for that function. An arrow preceding a parameter indicates whether the parameter is an input parameter, an output parameter, or both:

Arrow	Meaning
→	Input
←	Output
↔	Both

Sending an ATP Request

This section describes the `PSendRequest` function that you use to send a request to another socket's client application, allowing ATP to dynamically allocate the socket to be used to send the request; in this case, ATP opens the socket when you issue the function and closes it after the call completes execution. It also describes the `PNSendRequest` function that you can use to send a request to another socket while specifying the socket to be used to send the request; you must open the socket to be used and close it when you're finished with it.

PSendRequest

The `PSendRequest` function sends a request to another socket whose client application is to respond to the request. `PSendRequest` then waits for a response before completing execution.

```
FUNCTION PSendRequest (thePBPtr: ATPPBPt; async: Boolean): OSErr;
```

thePBPtr   A pointer to an ATP parameter block.

async   A Boolean that indicates whether the function should be executed
                asynchronously or synchronously. Specify TRUE for asynchronous
                execution.

Parameter block

→	iocompletion	ProcPtr	A pointer to a completion routine.
←	ioResult	OSErr	The function result.
→	userData	LongInt	Four bytes of user data.
←	reqTID	Integer	The transaction ID for this request.
→	csCode	Integer	Always sendRequest for this function.
←	currBitMap	Byte	A bitmap.
↔	atpFlags	Byte	The control information.
→	addrBlock	AddrBlock	The destination socket address.
→	reqLength	Integer	The size in bytes of the request.

→	`reqPointer`	Ptr	A pointer to request data.
→	`bdsPointer`	Ptr	A pointer to response data.
→	`numOfBuffs`	Byte	The number of responses expected.
→	`timeOutVal`	Byte	The timeout interval.
←	`numOfResps`	Byte	The number of responses received.
↔	`retryCount`	Byte	The number of retries.
→	`TRelTime`	Byte	The release timer setting.

Field descriptions

`userData`
Four bytes of user data that are sent in the header of the message. You can use these bytes for any purpose that you wish.

`reqTID`
A number that identifies this transaction request. If you want to use the `PRelTCB` function to cancel the transaction, you must pass it this number.

`currBitMap`
A bitmap showing which packets of the transaction were received.

`atpFlags`
A control information field whose bits, numbered 0–7, are used as flags.

You set bit 5 (`atpXOvalue`) to specify an exactly-once transaction. To specify an at-least-once transaction, you clear the bit.

To set the other connection end's release timer, set bit 2 of this flag, and use the `TRelTime` field to indicate the amount of time. Bit 2 (`atpXcallvalue`) indicates that the parameter block is extended to include the release timer field.

ATP sets the `atpTIDValidvalue` bit (bit 1) of this field to indicate that the transaction ID field (`reqTID`) now contains valid data; you should determine if this bit is set before you check the request transaction ID.

To direct ATP to use DDP's checksum feature, set the send checksum (`atpSendChkvalue`) bit (bit 0) of this flag.

`addrBlock`
The AppleTalk internet address of the socket to which the request is to be sent.

`reqLength`
The size of the request to be sent.

`reqPointer`
A pointer to the request data to be sent.

`bdsPointer`
A pointer to a buffer data structure (BDS) that is to be used to hold the responses.

`numOfBuffs`
On input, the number of response packets that you expect from the responder application. If this field contains a nonzero number on return, you can examine the `currBitMap` field to determine which packets of the transaction were actually received.

`timeOutVal`
The number of seconds that ATP should wait for a response before resending the request.

`numOfResps`
The number of responses actually received.

`retryCount`
The maximum number of times ATP should retry to send the request. This field is used to monitor the number of retries; for each retry, ATP decrements it by 1.

TRelTime   The release timer setting. Set the 3 lower bits of this field value to
                  indicate the time to which the release timer should be set for the
                  other end of the connection:

TRelTime	Setting of release timer
000	30 seconds
001	1 minute
010	4 minutes
100	8 minutes

DESCRIPTION

The PSendRequest function sends your request data to the destination ATP socket that you specify, and then it waits for that socket's client to return a response message. ATP dynamically assigns and opens the socket to be used to send the request, and it closes the socket when the function completes execution. Before you call the PSendRequest function, you must build a buffer data structure to hold the response data. You can use the BuildBDS function to do this. See "The Buffer Data Structure" on page 6-8 and "BuildBDS" on page 6-44 for a discussion of this function.

If you want to include additional information along with the request message, you can use the user bytes to include it; for example, you can use these bytes for command information.

The PSendRequest function completes execution when it receives an entire response or when the retry count is exceeded. The timeout value (timeOutVal) determines how many seconds PSendRequest waits before resending the original request packet. The retry count (retryCount) value determines the maximum number of times that ATP is to resend the request. Together the timeout value and the retry count determine the total retry time in seconds (timeOutVal x retryCount = total retry time). ATP modifies the retry count field value during execution of the PSendRequest function if it resends the request; ATP decrements the field by 1 for each retry. See "Writing a Requester ATP Application" beginning on page 6-9 for information on how to select these values.

The .ATP driver maintains a timer, called the *release timer,* for each call to the PSendResponse function that is part of an exactly-once (XO) transaction. If the timer expires before the transaction is complete (that is, before the socket receives the transaction release packet), the driver completes the PSendResponse function. Before AppleTalk Phase 2, the release timer was always set to 30 seconds. You can set the responding socket's release timer to a value other than 30 seconds. To do this, set the extended call bit (bit 2) of the atpFlags field in the parameter block for the PSendRequest function and specify the release timer parameter as the value of the

`TRelTime` field. The nodes at both ends of the ATP connection must be running AppleTalk Phase 2 drivers for this feature to work. For a discussion of exactly-once transactions and use of the release timer, see "At-Least-Once and Exactly-Once Transactions" on page 6-7. You should set the exactly-once flag (bit 5) if you want the request to be part of an exactly-once transaction.

You can use the `PKillSendReq` function or the `PRelTCB` function to cancel a `PSendRequest` call. For the `PRelTCB` function, you need the request transaction ID that ATP returns in the request transaction ID (`reqTID`) field of the `PSendRequest` call's parameter block. You can examine the request transaction ID field before the completion of the call, but its contents are valid only after the `tidValid` bit (bit 1) of the `atpFlags` field has been set. You should determine if this bit is set before you check the request transaction ID.

ASSEMBLY-LANGUAGE INFORMATION

To execute the `PSendRequest` function from assembly language, call the `_Control` trap macro with a value of `sendRequest` in the `csCode` field of the parameter block. To execute this function from assembly language, you must also specify the .ATP driver reference number.

RESULT CODES

noErr	0	No error
reqFailed	–1096	Retry count exceeded
tooManyReqs	–1097	Too many concurrent requests
noDataArea	–1104	Too many outstanding ATP calls
reqAborted	–1105	Request canceled

PNSendRequest

The `PNSendRequest` function sends a request to another socket's client. It uses the socket that you specify to send the request.

```
FUNCTION PNSendRequest (thePBPtr: ATPPBPtr; async: Boolean): OSErr;
```

thePBPtr   A pointer to an ATP parameter block.

async   A Boolean that indicates whether the function should be executed asynchronously or synchronously. Specify TRUE for asynchronous execution.

AppleTalk Transaction Protocol (ATP)

Parameter block

→	iocompletion	ProcPtr	A pointer to a completion routine.
←	ioResult	OSErr	The function result.
→	userData	LongInt	Four bytes of user data.
←	reqTID	Integer	The transaction ID for this request.
→	csCode	Integer	Always nSendRequest for this function.
→	atpSocket	Byte	The socket number to send the request.
↔	atpFlags	Byte	The control information.
→	addrBlock	AddrBlock	The destination socket address.
→	reqLength	Integer	The size in bytes of the request.
→	reqPointer	Ptr	A pointer to the request data.
→	bdsPointer	Pointer	A pointer to the BDS.
→	numOfBuffs	Byte	The number of responses expected.
→	timeOutVal	Byte	The timeout interval.
←	numOfResps	Byte	The number of responses received.
↔	retryCount	Byte	The number of retries.
←	intBuff	Integer	A buffer that ATP uses internally.
→	TRelTime	Byte	The release timer setting.

Field descriptions

userData	Four bytes of user data that are sent in the header of the message. You can use these bytes for any purpose that you wish.
reqTID	A number that identifies this transaction request.
atpSocket	The socket to be used to send the request. You must have previously opened this socket by calling the POpenATPSkt function.
atpFlags	A control information field whose bits, numbered 0–7, are used as flags.
	You set bit 5 (atpXOvalue) to specify an exactly-once transaction. To specify an at-least-once transaction, you clear the bit.
	To set the other connection end's release timer, set bit 2 of this flag (atpXcallvalue) to signal that this is an extended call and that the parameter block includes an additional field. Then you use the TRelTime field to indicate the amount of time.
	ATP sets the atpTIDidValidvalue bit (bit 1) of this field to indicate that the transaction ID field (reqTID) now contains valid data; you should determine if this bit is set before you check the request transaction ID.
	To direct ATP to use DDP's checksum feature, set the atpSendChkvalue bit (bit 0) of this flag.
addrBlock	The AppleTalk internet socket address of the application to which the request is being sent.
reqLength	The size in bytes of the request data to be sent.
reqPointer	A pointer to the request data to be sent.
bdsPointer	A pointer to the buffer data structure (BDS) that is to hold the data returned in response to the request.
numOfBuffs	The number of response packets requested and expected from the responder application.

timeOutVal	The number of seconds that ATP should wait for a response before resending the request.
numOfResps	The number of response packets actually received.
retryCount	The maximum number of times ATP should retry to send the request. This field value is used to monitor the number of retries; for each retry, ATP decrements the value by 1.
intBuff	Two bytes that are used internally by ATP.
TRelTime	The release timer setting. The 3 lower bits of this field value indicate the time to which the release timer is to be set, as follows:

TRelTime	Setting of release timer
000	30 seconds
001	1 minute
010	4 minutes
100	8 minutes

DESCRIPTION

The PNSendRequest function is similar to the PSendRequest function except that rather than relying on ATP to dynamically allocate a socket to use for the transaction, PNSendRequest lets you specify the socket to be used to send the request. You set the atpSocket field of the parameter block to the number of the socket to be used for the request; you must have previously opened the socket by calling the POpenATPSkt function. POpenATPSkt lets you send more than one asynchronous request using the same socket. The number of concurrent requests that you send using PNSendRequest is machine dependent. If you exceed this limit, ATP returns an error message (tooManyReqs) indicating this. Note that if you call the PNSendRequest function without having previously opened the socket that you specify for the send request, ATP returns a bad ATP socket (badATPSkt) error.

The .ATP driver maintains a timer, called the *release timer,* for each call to the PSendResponse function that is part of an exactly-once (XO) transaction. If the timer expires before the transaction is complete (that is, before the socket receives the transaction release packet), the driver completes the PSendResponse function. Before AppleTalk Phase 2, the release timer was always set to 30 seconds. To set the other connection end's release timer to another value, set bit 2 of the atpFlags field in the parameter block for the PNSendRequest function to indicate that this is an extended call, then set the TRelTime field to the new value. The nodes at both ends of the ATP connection must be running AppleTalk Phase 2 drivers for this feature to work. For a discussion of exactly-once transactions and use of the release timer, see "At-Least-Once and Exactly-Once Transactions" on page 6-7. You should set the exactly-once flag if you want the request to be part of an exactly-once transaction.

You can use the PKillSendReq function to cancel a pending PNSendRequest call. Unlike PSendRequest, you cannot use the PRelTCB function to kill this request call.

SPECIAL CONSIDERATIONS

The parameter block for the `PNSendRequest` function requires 2 additional bytes, `intBuff`, for ATP's internal use. You must not modify these bytes.

ASSEMBLY-LANGUAGE INFORMATION

To execute the `PNSendRequest` function from assembly language, call the `_Control` trap macro with a value of `nSendRequest` in the `csCode` field of the parameter block. To execute this function from assembly language, you must also specify the .ATP driver reference number.

RESULT CODES

noErr	0	No error
reqFailed	–1096	Retry count exceeded
tooManyReqs	–1097	Too many concurrent requests
badATPSkt	–1099	Specified socket is not opened
noDataArea	–1104	Too many outstanding ATP calls
reqAborted	–1105	Request canceled

Opening and Closing an ATP Socket

This section describes the `POpenATPSkt` function that you use to open a socket for receiving ATP requests from another socket's client application. It also describes the `PCloseATPSkt` function that you use to close a socket used for receiving requests after you are finished with that socket. You also use the `POpenATPSkt` and `PCloseATPSkt` functions to open and close a socket that you want to use to send requests through a specific socket by calling the `PNSendRequest` function.

POpenATPSkt

The `POpenATPSkt` function opens a socket to be used to receive ATP requests or to be used to send ATP requests through the `PNSendRequest` function.

```
FUNCTION POpenATPSkt (thePBptr: ATPPBPtr; async: Boolean): OSErr;
```

thePBptr   A pointer to an ATP parameter block.

async   A Boolean that indicates whether the function should be executed asynchronously or synchronously. Specify TRUE for asynchronous execution.

Parameter block

→	ioCompletion	ProcPtr	A pointer to a completion routine.
←	ioResult	OSErr	The function result.
→	csCode	Integer	Always openATPSkt for this function.
↔	atpSocket	Byte	The socket number to be used.
→	addrBlock	AddrBlock	The socket request specification.

Field descriptions

atpSocket   The number of the socket that ATP is to open. To direct ATP to
                   dynamically assign a socket number, which it returns as the value
                   of this field, specify 0.

addrBlock   A value that specifies the AppleTalk internet socket addresses
                   that the atpSocket field will receive requests from; specify 0 for
                   the network number, the node ID, or the socket number to accept
                   all requests based on the value of that part of the AppleTalk internet
                   socket address.

DESCRIPTION

The POpenATPSkt routine serves two purposes: you use it to open a socket to be used
for incoming requests, and you use it to open a socket to send requests using a specific
socket. (The PNSendRequest function lets you send a request using a specific socket,
but you must first open that socket using POpenATPSkt.) You can use the addrBlock
field to filter requests that you will accept by restricting network addresses.

ASSEMBLY-LANGUAGE INFORMATION

To execute the POpenATPSkt function from assembly language, call the _Control trap
macro with a value of openATPSkt in the csCode field of the parameter block. To
execute this function from assembly language, you must also specify the .ATP driver
reference number.

RESULT CODES

noErr	0	No error
tooManySkts	−1098	Too many responding sockets
noDataArea	−1104	Too many outstanding ATP calls

SEE ALSO

The PNSendRequest function is described on page 6-27.

PCloseATPSkt

The PCloseATPSkt function closes a socket that was opened to receive ATP requests or
to send requests over a specific socket.

```
FUNCTION PCloseATPSkt (thePBPtr: ATPPBPtr; async: Boolean): OSErr;
```

thePBPtr   A pointer to an ATP parameter block.

async   A Boolean that indicates whether the function should be executed
                   asynchronously or synchronously. Specify TRUE for asynchronous
                   execution.

Parameter block

→	ioCompletion	ProcPtr	A pointer to a completion routine.
←	ioResult	OSErr	The function result.
→	csCode	Integer	Always `closeATPSkt` for this function.
→	atpSocket	Byte	The socket number.

Field descriptions

atpSocket   The number of the socket to be closed.

DESCRIPTION

The `PCloseATPSkt` function closes the socket that you opened to receive ATP requests or to send them over a specific socket.

ASSEMBLY-LANGUAGE INFORMATION

To execute the `PCloseATPSkt` function from assembly language, call the `_Control` trap macro with a value of `closeATPSkt` in the `csCode` field of the parameter block. To execute this function from assembly language, you must also specify the .ATP driver reference number.

RESULT CODES

noErr	0	No error
noDataArea	−1104	Too many outstanding ATP calls

Setting Up a Socket to Listen for Requests

After you open a socket to be used to response to requests, you need to set up that socket to receive requests. You use the `PGetRequest` function for this purpose.

PGetRequest

The `PGetRequest` function sets up a socket to listen for a request from another socket.

```
FUNCTION PGetRequest (thePBPtr: ATPPBPtr; async: Boolean): OSErr;
```

thePBPtr   A pointer to an ATP parameter block.

async   A Boolean that indicates whether the function should be executed asynchronously or synchronously. Specify TRUE for asynchronous execution.

AppleTalk Transaction Protocol (ATP)

Parameter block

→	ioCompletion	ProcPtr	A pointer to a completion routine.
←	ioResult	OSErr	The function result.
←	userData	LongInt	Four bytes of user data.
←	reqTID	Word	The transaction ID.
→	csCode	Integer	Always getRequest for this function.
→	atpSocket	Byte	The socket number.
←	atpFlags	Byte	The control information.
←	addrBlock	LongInt	The destination socket address.
↔	reqLength	Word	On input, the request buffer size. On return, the actual of the request received.
→	reqPointer	Ptr	A pointer to the request buffer.
←	bitMap	Byte	A bitmap.

Field descriptions

userData   The 4 user bytes from the request.

reqTID   The transaction ID of the request that PGetRequest has received. ATP supplies this value.

atpSocket   The number of the socket that is to be used to listen for requests. This is the number of a socket you opened using the POpenATPSkt function call.

atpFlags   A control information field whose bits, numbered 0–7, are used as flags.

                  ATP sets bit 5, the exactly-once flag (atpXOvalue), if the request received is part of an exactly-once transaction.

addrBlock   The AppleTalk internet address of the socket from which the request was sent. ATP returns this value.

reqLength   On input, the size in bytes of the buffer to be used to store the incoming request. On return, the actual number of bytes of the request received.

reqPointer   A pointer to the location of the buffer to be used to store the incoming request.

bitMap   A bitmap of the transaction that ATP returns.

DESCRIPTION

To receive an ATP request, you must set up a socket to listen for incoming requests; you use the PGetRequest function to do this. In almost all cases, you should call the PGetRequest function asynchronously to avoid delaying execution of your program until after an ATP request comes in. The PGetRequest function completes execution after it receives an ATP request.

The PGetRequest function returns the transaction ID of the request that it receives in the reqTID field. You should save this value if you intend to respond to the request; this transaction ID is used as an input parameter to the PSendResponse and PAddResponse functions. To determine that the request transaction ID specified in the reqTID field is valid, first check the atpTIDValidvalue bit (bit 1) of the atpFlags field. If this bit is set, the reqTID field value is valid.

You must allocate nonrelocatable memory to be used as the buffer to hold an incoming request. Make sure that you allocate enough memory to hold the entire request; ATP will not deliver more data than will fit in the amount of buffer space that you specified as the value of the reqLength field. The buffer should be 578 bytes long, which is the maximum size of a request packet, unless you know the exact size of the request.

SPECIAL CONSIDERATIONS

Memory used for the incoming request buffer belongs to ATP for the life of the call.

ASSEMBLY-LANGUAGE INFORMATION

To execute the PGetRequest function from assembly language, call the _Control trap macro with a value of getRequest in the csCode field of the parameter block. To execute this function from assembly language, you must also specify the .ATP driver reference number.

RESULT CODES

noErr	0	No error
badATPSkt	–1099	Bad responding socket

SEE ALSO

For information on opening a socket that you can set up to receive requests, use the POpenATPSkt function, described on page 6-30.

Responding to Requests

After you receive and process a request, you can call the PSendResponse function to send the response data to the requesting socket. If you need to send additional data, you can call the PAddResponse function after you call PSendResponse. This section discusses the PSendResponse and PAddResponse functions.

PSendResponse

The PSendResponse function sends the response message to the requester.

```
FUNCTION PSendResponse (thePBPtr: ATPPBPtr; async: Boolean): OSErr;
```

thePBPtr   A pointer to an ATP parameter block.

async   A Boolean that indicates whether the function should be executed asynchronously or synchronously. Specify TRUE for asynchronous execution.

Parameter block

→	ioCompletion	ProcPtr	A pointer to a completion routine.
←	ioResult	OSErr	The function result.
→	userData	LongInt	Four bytes of user data.
→	csCode	Integer	Always sendResponse for this function.
→	atpSocket	Byte	The socket number.
→	atpFlags	Byte	The control information.
→	addrBlock	AddrBlock	The destination socket address.
→	bdsPointer	Ptr	A pointer to the response BDS.
→	numOfBuffs	Byte	The number of response packets to be sent.
→	bdsSize	Byte	The BDS size in elements.
→	transID	Integer	The transaction ID.

Field descriptions

userData   Four bytes of user data that are sent in the header of the message. If the response was part of an exactly-once transaction, this field contains the user bytes from the TRel packet.

atpSocket   The number of the socket that is sending the response.

atpFlags   A control information field whose bits, numbered 0–7, are used as flags.

To signal that this packet is the last packet in the transaction's response message when the number of responses is less than expected, set the end-of-message (atpEOMvalue) bit (bit 4).

ATP sets the send-transmission-status (atpSTSvalue) bit (bit 3) to force the requester to retransmit a request immediately, when this is necessary.

To direct ATP to use DDP's checksum feature, set the send checksum (atpSendChkvalue) bit (bit 0) of this flag.

addrBlock   The AppleTalk internet socket address of the socket to which the response is to be sent.

bdsPointer   A pointer to the response buffer data structure (BDS) that contains the response data.

numOfBuffs   The number of response packets to be sent.

bdsSize   The number of elements in the buffer data structure (BDS).

transID   The transaction ID of the request for which this response is meant.

DESCRIPTION

You call PSendResponse when you receive a request, and after you have created a response message. The PSendResponse function sends the data to the socket whose address you specify; this is the address of the requester socket. If you cannot or do not want to send the entire response at one time, you can call PSendResponse to send the first part of it, then call PAddResponse later to send the remainder of the response.

To signal the requester socket that you are sending fewer response packets than it expects to receive, you must set the end-of-message flag (bit 4) of the atpFlags parameter.

For each call to the PSendResponse function that is part of an exactly-once (XO) transaction, ATP maintains a timer, called the *release timer*. If the timer expires before the transaction is completed, that is, before the socket receives the transaction release packet, ATP completes the PSendResponse function. Before AppleTalk Phase 2, the release timer was always set to 30 seconds. The PSendRequest or the PNSendRequest function can set the release timer for the responder to a different value. For more information about sending a response, see "Responding to Requests" beginning on page 6-16.

SPECIAL CONSIDERATIONS

During exactly-once transactions, PSendResponse doesn't complete until either a TRel packet is received from the socket that made the request or the retry count is exceeded.

ASSEMBLY-LANGUAGE INFORMATION

To execute the PSendResponse function from assembly language, call the _Control trap macro with a value of sendResponse in the csCode field of the parameter block. To execute this function from assembly language, you must also specify the .ATP driver reference number.

RESULT CODES

noErr	0	No error
badATPSkt	–1099	Bad responding socket
badBuffNum	–1100	Sequence number out of range
noRelErr	–1101	No release received
noDataArea	–1104	Too many outstanding ATP calls

SEE ALSO

See the chapter "Introduction to AppleTalk" in this book for a description of the AppleTalk internet socket address structure.

For a description of the possible release timer values that PSendRequest or PNSendRequest can set, see either the PSendRequest function on page 6-24 or the PNSendRequest function on page 6-27.

PAddResponse

The PAddResponse function sends an additional response packet to a socket that has already been sent the first part of the response message through the PSendResponse function.

```
FUNCTION PAddResponse (thePBPtr: ATPPBPtr; async: Boolean): OSErr;
```

thePBPtr   A pointer to an ATP parameter block.

async   A Boolean that indicates whether the function should be executed
            asynchronously or synchronously. Specify TRUE for asynchronous
            execution.

Parameter block

→	ioCompletion	ProcPtr	A pointer to a completion routine.
←	ioResult	OSErr	The function result.
→	userData	LongInt	Four bytes of user data.
→	csCode	Integer	Always addResponse for this function.
→	atpSocket	Byte	The source socket number.
→	atpFlags	Byte	The control information.
→	addrBlock	AddrBlock	The destination socket address.
→	reqLength	Integer	The size in bytes of the response data.
→	reqPointer	Ptr	A pointer to the response data.
→	rspNum	Byte	The sequence number.
→	transID	Integer	The transaction ID.

Field descriptions

userData   Four bytes of user data that are sent in the header of the message.
            You can use these bytes for any purpose that you wish.

atpSocket   The number of the socket that is used to send the additional
            response.

atpFlags   A control information field whose bits, numbered 0–7, are used
            as flags.

            To signal that this packet is the last packet in the transaction's
            response message when the number of responses is less than
            expected, set the end-of-message (atpEOMvalue) bit (bit 4).

            ATP sets the send-transmission-status (atpSTSvalue) bit (bit 3) to
            force the requester to retransmit a request immediately, when this
            is necessary.

            To direct ATP to use DDP's checksum feature, set the send
            checksum (atpSendChkvalue) bit (bit 0) of this flag.

addrBlock   The number of the socket to which the additional response packet is
            to be sent.

reqLength   The size in bytes of the response data to be sent.

reqPointer A pointer to the response data to be sent.

rspNum   The sequence number of the response, in the range of 0 to 7.

reqTID   The transaction ID of the request for which this response is meant.

DESCRIPTION

The PAddResponse function sends an additional response packet, following the initial
response sent in return to a PSendResponse request message. You can send multiple
additional response packets, one at a time, up to a total of eight packets including the
initial response packets sent in the PSendResponse function.

You cannot issue a PAddResponse call without having first called PSendResponse. You must provide a pointer to the buffer containing the data to be sent and specify the amount of data. Each packet can contain up to 578 bytes of data. You also must specify the sequence number of the response.

SPECIAL CONSIDERATIONS

If the transaction is part of an exactly-once transaction, you must allocate nonrelocatable memory for the buffer that you use for the response data, and you must not alter the contents of this buffer until the corresponding PSendRequest function has completed execution.

ASSEMBLY-LANGUAGE INFORMATION

To execute the PAddResponse function from assembly language, call the _Control trap macro with a value of addResponse in the csCode field of the parameter block. To execute this function from assembly language, you must also specify the .ATP driver reference number.

RESULT CODES

noErr	0	No error
badATPSkt	–1099	Bad responding socket
badBuffNum	–1100	Sequence number out of range
noSendResp	–1103	PAddResponse issued before PSendResponse
noDataArea	–1104	Too many outstanding ATP calls

Canceling Pending ATP Functions

This section describes the functions that you use to cancel pending ATP functions. It describes the PKillSendReq function that you use to cancel a PSendRequest or PNSendRequest function, the PRelTCB function that you use to cancel a PSendRequest function, the PKillGetReq function that you use to cancel a PGetRequest function, the ATPKillAllGetReq function that you use to cancel all pending PGetRequest functions, and the PRelRspCB function that you use to cancel a PSendResponse call that specifies an exactly-once transaction.

PKillSendReq

The PKillSendReq function cancels the pending PSendRequest or PNSendRequest functions whose queue element pointer you specify.

```
FUNCTION PKillSendReq (thePBPtr: ATPPBPtr; async: Boolean): OSErr;
```

thePBPtr   A pointer to an ATP parameter block.

async   A Boolean that indicates whether the function should be executed
                asynchronously or synchronously. Specify TRUE for asynchronous
                execution.

Parameter block

→	ioCompletion	ProcPtr	A pointer to the completion routine.
←	ioResult	OSErr	The function result.
→	csCode	Integer	Always killSendReq for this function.
→	aKillQEl	Ptr	A pointer to queue element of function to be removed.

Field descriptions

aKillQEl   A pointer to the queue element of the pending function that is to be
                canceled. This is the pointer to the parameter block that you passed
                to the send request function when you issued the function.

DESCRIPTION

To cancel a specific pending PSendRequest or PNSendRequest function, you specify
the pointer to the queue element for the function in the aKillQEl field of the parameter
block for the PKillSendReq function, then call the function. If the function has
already completed execution or if it is not in the ATP queue for any other reason,
PKillSendReq returns a message (cbNotFound) indicating that it could not find the
parameter block.

ASSEMBLY-LANGUAGE INFORMATION

To execute the PKillSendReq function from assembly language, call the _Control
trap macro with a value of killSendReq in the csCode field of the parameter block. To
execute this function from assembly language, you must also specify the .ATP driver
reference number.

RESULT CODES

noErr	0	No error
cbNotFound	−1102	The aKillQEl parameter does not point to a PSendRequest or PNSendRequest queue element

SEE ALSO

To send requests, use the PSendRequest function, described on page 6-24, and the
PNSendRequest function, described on page 6-27.

PRelTCB

The PRelTCB function cancels the pending PSendRequest function that you specify.

```
FUNCTION PRelTCB (thePBPtr: ATPPBPtr; async: Boolean): OSErr;
```

thePBPtr   A pointer to an ATP parameter block.

async   A Boolean that indicates whether the function should be executed asynchronously or synchronously. Specify TRUE for asynchronous execution.

Parameter block

→	ioCompletion	ProcPtr	A pointer to a completion routine.
←	ioResult	OSErr	The function result.
→	csCode	Integer	Always relTCB for this function.
→	addrBlock	AddrBlock	The destination socket address.
→	transID	Integer	The transaction ID of the request to be canceled.

Field descriptions

addrBlock   The AppleTalk internet address of the destination socket for which the PSendRequest function that is to be canceled was meant.

transID   The transaction ID of the PSendRequest function to be canceled. You can get the transaction ID from the reqTID field of the PSendRequest parameter block queue entry.

DESCRIPTION

The PRelTCB function releases the queued parameter block for the PSendRequest function whose transaction ID you specify. The PRelTCB function returns a function result of reqAborted for the canceled PSendRequest function.

SPECIAL CONSIDERATIONS

You cannot use this function to cancel a send request that you made using the PNSendRequest function.

ASSEMBLY-LANGUAGE INFORMATION

To execute the PRelTCB function from assembly language, call the _Control trap macro with a value of relTCB in the csCode field of the parameter block. To execute this function from assembly language, you must also specify the .ATP driver reference number.

RESULT CODES

noErr	0	No error
cbNotFound	–1102	The ATP control block was not found
noDataArea	–1104	Too many outstanding ATP functions

PKillGetReq

The `PKillGetReq` function cancels the pending `PGetRequest` function that you specify.

```
FUNCTION PKillGetReq (thePBPtr: ATPPBPtr; async: Boolean): OSErr;
```

thePBPtr   A pointer to an ATP parameter block.

async   A Boolean that indicates whether the function should be executed asynchronously or synchronously. Specify TRUE for asynchronous execution.

Parameter block

→	ioCompletion	ProcPtr	A pointer to a completion routine.
←	ioResult	OSErr	The function result.
→	csCode	Integer	Always killGetReq for this function.
→	aKillQEl	Pointer	A pointer to the queue element

Field descriptions

aKillQEl   A pointer to the queue element of the pending call that is to be canceled.

DESCRIPTION

The `PKillGetReq` function lets you cancel a specific outstanding `PGetRequest` function without having to cancel all pending get requests or having to close the socket to do this; closing the socket cancels all outstanding functions on that socket.

To cancel a specific pending `PGetRequest` function, you specify the pointer to the queue element for the function in the `aKillQEl` field of the parameter block for the `PKillGetReq` function. The queue element pointer is the pointer to the parameter block of the `PGetRequest` function to be canceled. If the function has already completed execution or if it is not in the ATP queue for any other reason, `PKillGetReq` returns a message (`cbNotFound`) indicating that it could not find the parameter block.

ASSEMBLY-LANGUAGE INFORMATION

To execute the `PKillGetReq` function from assembly language, call the `_Control` trap macro with a value of `killGetReq` in the `csCode` field of the parameter block. To execute this function from assembly language, you must also specify the .ATP driver reference number.

RESULT CODES

noErr	0	No error
cbNotFound	−1102	The aKillQEl parameter does not point to a PGetRequest queue element

ATPKillAllGetReq

The ATPKillAllGetReq function cancels all pending calls to the PGetRequest function for a specific socket.

```
FUNCTION ATPKillAllGetReq (thePBPtr: ATPPBPtr;
                           async: Boolean): OSErr;
```

thePBPtr   A pointer to an ATP parameter block.

async   A Boolean that indicates whether the function should be executed asynchronously or synchronously. Specify TRUE for asynchronous execution.

Parameter block

→	ioCompletion	ProcPtr	A pointer to the completion routine.
←	ioResult	OSErr	The function result.
→	csCode	Integer	Always killAllGetReq for this function.
→	atpSocket	Byte	The socket number whose pending PGetRequest functions are to be canceled.

Field descriptions

atpSocket   The socket whose pending PGetRequest functions are to be canceled.

DESCRIPTION

The ATPKillAllGetReq function cancels all pending PGetRequest functions issued on a specific socket without closing the socket. For each function executed asynchronously, ATPKillAllGetReq also calls the completion routine with the value reqAborted (–1105) in the D0 register. You should call the ATPKillAllGetReq function before closing a socket.

ASSEMBLY-LANGUAGE INFORMATION

To execute the ATPKillAllGetReq function from assembly language, call the _Control trap macro with a value of killAllGetReq in the csCode field of the parameter block. To execute this function from assembly language, you must also specify the .ATP driver reference number.

RESULT CODES

noErr	0	No error
cbNotFound	–1102	Control block not found; no pending asynchronous calls

PRelRspCB

The `PRelRspCB` function cancels a `PSendResponse` function that is an exactly-once transaction.

```
FUNCTION PRelRspCB (thePBPtr: ATPPBPtr; async: Boolean): OSErr;
```

thePBPtr   A pointer to an ATP parameter block.

async   A Boolean that indicates whether the function should be executed asynchronously or synchronously. Specify TRUE for asynchronous execution.

Parameter block

→	ioCompletion	ProcPtr	A pointer to the completion routine.
←	ioResult	OSErr	The function result.
→	csCode	Integer	Always relRspCB for this function.
→	atpSocket	Byte	The number of the socket on which the request was received.
→	addrBlock	AddrBlock	The internet socket address of the source of the request.
→	transID	Byte	The transaction ID of the request with which the PSendResponse function to be canceled is associated.

Field descriptions

atpSocket   The number of the socket on which the request was received and from which the `PSendResponse` function that is to be canceled was sent.

addrBlock   The internet socket address of the application that issued the request.

transID   The transaction ID of the `PSendResponse` call to be canceled. You can get the transaction ID from the `reqTID` field of the `PSendResponse` parameter block queue entry.

DESCRIPTION

The `PRelRspCB` function releases the queued parameter block for the exactly-once transaction `PSendResponse` function without waiting for the release timer to expire or for a `TRel` packet to be received; `PRelRspCB` returns a function result of `noErr` for the canceled `PSendResponse` call.

If you call `PRelRspCB` to cancel a transaction that is not an exactly-once service, `RelRspCB` returns a function result of `cbNotFound` for the `PSendResponse` call.

To execute the `PRelRspCB` function from assembly language, call the `_Control` trap macro with a value of `relRspCB` in the `csCode` field of the parameter block. To execute this function from assembly language, you must also specify the .ATP driver reference number.

RESULT CODES

noErr	0	No error
cbNotFound	–1102	Control block not found; no pending asynchronous calls

Building a Buffer Data Structure

You need to provide a buffer data structure (BDS) to hold data that comprises multiple response packets whether you are sending the response data or receiving it. This section describes a utility, `BuildBDS`, that ATP provides that allows you to create a BDS to be used for this purpose.

BuildBDS

From the buffer that you supply, the `BuildBDS` function creates a buffer data structure (BDS) to be used to hold data for ATP functions that send and receive response data.

```
FUNCTION BuildBDS (buffPtr: Ptr; bdsPtr: Ptr;
                   buffSize: Integer): Integer;
```

buffPtr   A pointer to a data buffer.

buffSize   The length in bytes of the buffer data structure.

DESCRIPTION

The `PSendResponse`, `PSendRequest`, and `PNSendRequest` functions require a buffer data structure of a specific format to be used to hold the response data. You can use the `BuildBDS` function to create this data structure, or you can build it yourself from Pascal.

The `BuildBDS` function creates a buffer data structure consisting of an array of elements—one for each response packet—to be used to hold response data. You pass this function a pointer to the memory to be used for this buffer and the size in bytes of the memory. You should allocate enough memory to hold the response data that you are either sending or receiving. Because an entire response message cannot exceed 4624 bytes, the amount of memory that you allocate for this data structure should not exceed this size.

BuildBDS creates up to eight elements for a buffer data structure. If you provide the maximum space of 4624 bytes, BuildBDS returns eight elements; if the response message is shorter and you specify fewer bytes, BuildBDS returns the equivalent number of elements. BuildBDS returns as a function result the number of buffer data structure elements that it creates. For more information about the BDS data structure, see "The Buffer Data Structure" on page 6-20.

RESULT CODES

noErr	0	No error
paramErr	−50	Version number is too high

SEE ALSO

See "PSendResponse" on page 6-34, "PSendRequest" on page 6-24, and "PNSendRequest" on page 6-27 for more information about the functions that require a buffer data structure.

Summary of ATP

Pascal Summary

Constants

```
CONST
   {csCodes}
   nSendRequest         = 248;        {send request using a specific socket}
   relRspCB             = 249;        {release RspCB}
   closeATPSkt          = 250;        {close ATP socket}
   addResponse          = 251;        {add response}
   sendResponse         = 252;        {send response}
   getRequest           = 253;        {get request}
   openATPSkt           = 254;        {open ATP socket}
   sendRequest          = 255;        {send request}
   relTCB               = 256;        {release TCB}
   killGetReq           = 257;        {kill getRequest}
   killSendReq          = 258;        {kill sendRequest}
   killAllGetReq        = 259;        {kill all getRequests for a socket}

   {ATP flags}
   atpXOvalue           = 32;         {ATP exactly-once bit}
   atpEOMvalue          = 16;         {ATP end-of-message bit}
   atpSTSvalue          = 8;          {ATP send-transmission-status bit}
   atpTIDValidvalue     = 2;          {ATP trans. ID valid bit}
   atpSendChkvalue      = 1;          {ATP send checksum bit}
```

Data Types

The Buffer Data Structure

```
TYPE  BDSElement =
   RECORD
      buffSize:   Integer;
      buffPtr:    Ptr;
      dataSize:   Integer;
      userBytes:  LongInt;
   END;
```

```
BDSType = ARRAY[0..7] OF BDSElement;
BDSPtr = ^BDSType;
BitMapType = PACKED ARRAY[0..7] OF Boolean;
```

The Address Block Record

```
TYPE AddrBlock =
   PACKED RECORD
      aNet:          Integer;              {network number}
      aNode:         Byte;                 {node ID}
      aSocket:       Byte;                 {socket number}
   END;
```

The ATP Parameter Block

```
TYPE ATPParamBlock =
   PACKED RECORD
      qLink:         QElemPtr;             {next queue entry}
      qType:         Integer;              {queue type}
      ioTrap:        Integer;              {routine trap}
      ioCmdAddr:     Ptr;                  {routine address}
      ioCompletion:  ProcPtr;              {completion routine}
      ioResult:      OSErr;                {result code}
      userData:      Longint;              {ATP user bytes}
      reqTID:        Integer;              {request transaction ID}
      ioRefNum:      Integer;              {driver reference number}
      csCode:        Integer;              {call command code }
                                           { automatically set}
      atpSocket:     Byte;                 {currBitMap or socket number}
      CASE MPPParmType OF
         SendRequestParm,
         SendResponseParm,
         GetRequestParm,
         AddResponseParm,
         KillSendReqParm:
            (atpFlags:     Byte;      {control information}
             addrBlock:    AddrBlock;
                                      {source/dest. socket address}
             reqLength:    Integer;   {request/response length}
             reqPointer:   Ptr;       {ptr to request/response data}
             bdsPointer:   Ptr;       {ptr to response BDS}
         CASE MPPParmType OF
            SendRequestParm:
               (numOfBuffs: Byte;     {number of responses expected}
```

```
                    timeOutVal:    Byte;      {timeout interval}
                    numOfResps:    Byte;      {number of responses }
                                              { actually received}
                    retryCount:    Byte;      {number of retries}
                    intBuff:       Integer;   {used internally for PNSendRequest}
                    TRelTime:      Byte);     {TRelease time for extended }
                                              { send request}
                SendResponseParm:
                    (filler0:      Byte;      {numOfBuffs}
                    bdsSize:       Byte;      {number of BDS elements}
                    transID:       Integer);  {transaction ID}
                GetRequestParm:
                    (bitMap:       Byte;      {bitmap}
                    filler1:       Byte);
                AddResponseParm:
                    (rspNum:       Byte;      {sequence number}
                    filler2:       Byte);
                KillSendReqParm:
                    (aKillQEl:     Ptr));     {pointer to queue element to cancel}
        END;


ATPPBPtr = ^ATPParamBlock;
```

Routines

Sending an ATP Request

```
FUNCTION PSendRequest        (thePBPtr: ATPPBPt; async: Boolean): OSErr;
FUNCTION PNSendRequest       (thePBPtr: ATPPBPtr; async: Boolean): OSErr;
```

Opening and Closing an ATP Socket

```
FUNCTION POpenATPSkt         (thePBptr: ATPPBPtr; async: Boolean): OSErr;
FUNCTION PCloseATPSkt        (thePBPtr: ATPPBPtr; async: Boolean): OSErr;
```

Setting Up a Socket to Listen for Requests

```
FUNCTION PGetRequest         (thePBPtr: ATPPBPtr; async: Boolean): OSErr;
```

Responding to Requests

```
FUNCTION PSendResponse       (thePBPtr: ATPPBPtr; async: Boolean): OSErr;
FUNCTION PAddResponse        (thePBPtr: ATPPBPtr; async: Boolean): OSErr;
```

Canceling Pending ATP Functions

```
FUNCTION PKillSendReq        (thePBPtr: ATPPBPtr; async: Boolean): OSErr;

FUNCTION PRelTCB             (thePBPtr: ATPPBPtr; async: Boolean): OSErr;

FUNCTION PKillGetReq         (thePBPtr: ATPPBPtr; async: Boolean): OSErr;

FUNCTION ATPKillAllGetReq    (thePBPtr: ATPPBPtr; async: Boolean): OSErr;

FUNCTION PRelRspCB           (thePBPtr: ATPPBPtr; async: Boolean): OSErr;
```

Building a Buffer Data Structure

```
FUNCTION BuildBDS            (buffPtr: Ptr; bdsPtr: Ptr; buffSize: Integer):
                              Integer;
```

C Summary

Constants

```
/*ATP parameter constants*/
#define ATPioCompletion ATP.ioCompletion
#define ATPioResult ATP.ioResult
#define ATPuserData ATP.userData
#define ATPreqTID ATP.reqTID
#define ATPioRefNum ATP.ioRefNum
#define ATPcsCode ATP.csCode
#define ATPatpSocket ATP.atpSocket
#define ATPatpFlags ATP.atpFlags
#define ATPaddrBlock ATP.addrBlock
#define ATPreqLength ATP.reqLength
#define ATPreqPointer ATP.reqPointer
#define ATPbdsPointer ATP.bdsPointer
#define ATPtimeOutVal SREQ.timeOutVal
#define ATPnumOfResps SREQ.numOfResps
#define ATPretryCount SREQ.retryCount
#define ATPnumOfBuffs OTH1.u0.numOfBuffs
#define ATPbitMap OTH1.u0.bitMap
#define ATPrspNum OTH1.u0.rspNum
#define ATPbdsSize OTH2.bdsSize
#define ATPtransID OTH2.transID
#define ATPaKillQEl KILL.aKillQEl
```

```
/*csCodes*/
enum {                                          /*csCodes*/
   nSendRequest          = 248,                 /*send request using a specific */
                                                /* socket*/

   relRspCB              = 249,                 /*release RspCB*/
   closeATPSkt           = 250,                 /*close ATP socket*/
   addResponse           = 251,                 /*add response*/
   sendResponse          = 252,                 /*send response*/
   getRequest            = 253,                 /*get request*/
   openATPSkt            = 254,                 /*open ATP socket*/
   sendRequest           = 255,                 /*send request*/
   relTCB                = 256,                 /*release TCB*/
   killGetReq            = 257,                 /*kill getRequest*/
   killSendReq           = 258,                 /*kill sendRequest*/
   killAllGetReq         = 259};                /*kill all getRequests for */
                                                /* a socket*/


/*ATP flags*/
enum {
   atpXOvalue            = 32,                  /*ATP exactly-once bit*/
   atpEOMvalue           = 16,                  /*ATP end-of-message bit*/
   atpSTSvalue           = 8,                   /*ATP send-transmission-status */
                                                /* bit*/
   atpTIDValidvalue      = 2,                   /*ATP trans. ID valid bit*/
   atpSendChkvalue       = 1};                  /*ATP send checksum bit*/
```

Data Types

The Buffer Data Structure

```
struct    BDSElement {
   short        buffSize;
   Ptr          buffPtr;
   short        dataSize;
   long         userBytes;
};


typedef struct BDSElement BDSElement;

typedef BDSElement BDSType[8];
typedef BDSElement *BDSPtr;
typedef char BitMapType;
```

The Address Block Record

```
struct AddrBlock {
    short            aNet;
    unsigned char    aNode;
    unsigned char    aSocket;
};


typedef struct AddrBlock AddrBlock;
```

The ATP Parameter Block

```
#define MPPATPHeader \
    QElem        *qLink;            /*next queue entry*/\
    short        qType;             /*queue type*/\
    short        ioTrap;            /*routine trap*/\
    Ptr          ioCmdAddr;         /*routine address*/\
    ProcPtr      ioCompletion;      /*completion routine*/\
    OSErr        ioResult;          /*result code*/\
    long         userData;          /*command result (ATP user bytes)*/\
    short        reqTID;            /*request transaction ID*/\
    short        ioRefNum;          /*driver reference number*/\
    short        csCode;            /*call command code*/


typedef struct {
    MPPATPHeader
}MPPparms;


#define MOREATPHeader \
    char         atpSocket;         /*currbitmap for requests or ATP */\
                                    /* socket number*/\

    char         atpFlags;          /*control information*/\
    AddrBlock    addrBlock;         /*source/dest. socket address*/\
    short        reqLength;         /*request/response length*/\
    Ptr          reqPointer;        /*pointer to request/response data*/\
    Ptr          bdsPointer;        /*pointer to response BDS*/


typedef struct {
    MPPATPHeader
    MOREATPHeader
}ATPparms;
```

```
typedef struct {
   MPPATPHeader
   MOREATPHeader
   char          filler;                /*numOfBuffs*/
   char          timeOutVal;            /*timeout interval*/
   char          numOfResps;            /*number of responses actually */
                                        /* received*/
   char          retryCount;            /*number of retries*/
   short         intBuff;               /*used internally for NSendRequest*/
   char          TRelTime;              /*TRelease time for extended send */
                                        /* request*/

}SendReqparms;

typedef struct {
   MPPATPHeader
   MOREATPHeader
   union {
      char       bitMap;                /*bitmap received*/
      char       numOfBuffs;            /*number of responses being sent*/
      char       rspNum;                /*sequence number*/
   } u0;
}ATPmisc1;

typedef struct {
   MPPATPHeader
   MOREATPHeader
   char          filler;
   char          bdsSize;               /*number of BDS elements*/
   short         transID;               /*transaction ID*/
}ATPmisc2;

typedef struct {
   MPPATPHeader
   MOREATPHeader
   Ptr           aKillQEl;              /*pointer to i/o queue element to */
                                        /* cancel*/

}Killparms;

union ATPParamBlock {
   ATPparms      ATP;                    /*general ATP parms*/
   SendReqparms  SREQ;                   /*send request parms*/
   ATPmisc1      OTH1;                   /*miscellaneous parms*/
   ATPmisc2      OTH2;                   /*miscellaneous parms*/
   Killparms     KILL;                   /*kill request parms*/
};
```

```
typedef union ATPParamBlock ATPParamBlock;
typedef ATPParamBlock *ATPPBPtr;
```

Routines

Sending an ATP Request

```
pascal OSErr PSendRequest    (ATPPBPtr thePBPtr,Boolean async);
pascal OSErr PNSendRequest   (ATPPBPtr thePBPtr,Boolean async);
```

Opening and Closing an ATP Socket

```
pascal OSErr POpenATPSkt     (ATPPBPtr thePBptr,Boolean async);
pascal OSErr PCloseATPSkt    (ATPPBPtr thePBPtr,Boolean async);
```

Setting Up a Socket to Listen for Requests

```
pascal OSErr PGetRequest     (ATPPBPtr thePBPtr,Boolean async);
```

Responding to Requests

```
pascal OSErr PSendResponse   (ATPPBPtr thePBPtr,Boolean async);
pascal OSErr PAddResponse    (ATPPBPtr thePBPtr,Boolean async);
```

Canceling Pending ATP Functions

```
pascal OSErr PKillSendReq    (ATPPBPtr thePBPtr,Boolean async);
pascal OSErr PRelTCB         (ATPPBPtr thePBPtr,Boolean async);
pascal OSErr PKillGetReq     (ATPPBPtr thePBPtr,Boolean async);
pascal OSErr ATPKillAllGetReq
                             (ATPPBPtr thePBPtr,Boolean async);
pascal OSErr PRelRspCB       (ATPPBPtr thePBPtr,Boolean async);
```

Building a Buffer Data Structure

```
pascal short BuildBDS        (Ptr buffPtr,Ptr bdsPtr,short buffSize);
```

Assembly-Language Summary

Constants

ATP Header

atpControl	EQU	0	;control field (byte)
atpBitmap	EQU	1	;bitmap (requests only) (byte)
atpRespNo	EQU	1	;response number (responses only) (byte)
atpTransID	EQU	2	;transaction ID (word)
atpUserData	EQU	4	;start of user data (long)
atpHdSz	EQU	8	;size of ATP header

ATP Control Field

atpReqCode	EQU	$40	;request code after masking
atpRspCode	EQU	$80	;response code after masking
atpRelCode	EQU	$C0	;release code after masking
atpXOBit	EQU	5	;bit number of exactly-once bit
atpEOMBit	EQU	4	;bit number of end-of-message bit
atpSTSBit	EQU	3	;send transmission status bit number
flagMask	EQU	$3F	;mask for just flags
controlMask	EQU	$F8	;mask for good control bits

ATP Type Code

atp	EQU	$3	;ATP type code (in DDP header)

ATP Limits

atpMaxNum	EQU	8	;maximum number of responses per request
atpMaxData	EQU	$242	;maximum data size in ATP packet

ATP Command Codes

nSendRequest	EQU	248	;PNSendRequest code
relRspCB	EQU	249	;release RspCB
closeATPSkt	EQU	250	;close ATP socket
addResponse	EQU	251	;add response code
sendResponse	EQU	252	;send response code
getRequest	EQU	253	;get request code

```
openATPSkt      EQU     254        ;open ATP socket
sendRequest     EQU     255        ;send request code
relTCB          EQU     256        ;release TCB
killGetReq      EQU     257        ;kill GetRequest
killSendReq     EQU     258        ;kill SendRequest
killAllGetReq   EQU     259        ;kill all getRequests for a socket
```

ATPQueue Element Standard Structure

```
;arguments passed in the CSParam area

atpSocket       EQU     $1C        ;socket number is first parameter [byte]
atpFlags        EQU     $1D        ;flag [byte]
addrBlock       EQU     $1E        ;start of address block
reqLength       EQU     $22        ;size of request buffer [word]
reqPointer      EQU     $24        ;pointer to request buffer or data
bdsPointer      EQU     $28        ;pointer to buffer data structure (BDS)
guArea          EQU     $2C        ;start of general-use area
userData        EQU     $12        ;user bytes
```

ATP Bits

```
sendCHK         EQU     0          ;bit number of send-checksum bit in flags
tidValid        EQU     1          ;bit set when TID valid in SendRequest
```

Data Structures

Buffer Data Structure (BDS)

```
bdsBuffSz       EQU     0          ;send: data length
                                   ; receive: buffer length
bdsBuffAdr      EQU     2          ;send: data address
                                   ; receive: buffer address
bdsDataSz       EQU     6          ;send: used internally
                                   ; receive: data length
bdsUserData     EQU     8          ;send: 4 user bytes
                                   ; receive: 4 user bytes
bdsEntrySz      EQU     12         ;size of a BDS entry
```

ATP Parameter Block Common Fields

0	qLink	long	reserved
4	qType	word	reserved
6	ioTrap	word	reserved
8	ioCmdAddr	long	reserved
12	ioCompletion	long	address of completion routine
16	ioResult	word	result code
18	userData	long	user bytes
22	reqTID	word	request transaction ID
24	ioRefNum	word	driver reference number
26	csCode	word	command code
28	atpSocket	byte	current bitmap or socket number

SendRequest Parameter Variant

26	csCode	word	command code; always sendRequest
28	currBitMap	byte	current bitmap
29	atpFlags	byte	control information
30	addrBlock	long	destination socket address
34	reqLength	word	request size in bytes
36	reqPointer	long	pointer to request data
40	bdsPointer	long	pointer to response BDS
44	numOfBuffs	byte	number of responses expected
45	timeOutVal	byte	timeout interval
46	numOfResps	byte	number of responses received
47	retryCount	byte	number of retries
50	TRelTime	byte	release time for extended send request

NSendRequest Parameter Variant

22	reqTID	word	request transaction ID
26	csCode	word	command code; always nSendRequest
29	atpFlags	byte	control information
30	addrBlock	long	destination socket address
34	reqLength	word	request size in bytes
36	reqPointer	long	pointer to request data
40	bdsPointer	long	pointer to response BDS
44	numOfBuffs	byte	number of responses expected
45	timeOutVal	byte	timeout interval
46	numOfResps	byte	number of responses received
47	retryCount	byte	number of retries
50	TRelTime	byte	release time for extended send request

OpenATPSkt Parameter Variant

26	csCode	word	command code; always openATPSkt
30	addrBlock	long	socket request specification

CloseATPSkt Parameter Variant

26	csCode	word	command code; always closeATPSkt

GetRequest Parameter Variant

22	reqTID	word	request transaction ID
26	csCode	word	command code; always getRequest
29	atpFlags	byte	control information
30	addrBlock	long	destination socket address
34	reqLength	word	request size in bytes
36	reqPointer	long	pointer to request data
44	bitMap	byte	current bitmap

SendResponse Parameter Variant

26	csCode	word	command code; always sendResponse
29	atpFlags	byte	control information
30	addrBlock	long	destination socket address
40	bdsPointer	long	pointer to response BDS
44	numOfBuffs	byte	number of responses expected
45	bdsSize	byte	BDS size in elements
46	transID	word	transaction ID

AddResponse Parameter Variant

26	csCode	word	command code; always addResponse
29	atpFlags	byte	control information
30	addrBlock	long	destination socket address
34	reqLength	word	response size in bytes
36	reqPointer	long	pointer to response data
44	rspNum	byte	sequence number
46	transID	word	transaction ID

KillSendReq Parameter Variant

26	csCode	word	command code; always killSendReq
44	aKillQEl	long	pointer to queue element of function to be removed

RelTCB Parameter Variant

26	csCode	word	command code; always relTCB
30	addrBlock	long	destination socket address of request
46	transID	word	transaction ID of request to be canceled

KillGetReq Parameter Variant

26	csCode	word	command code; always killGetReq
44	aKillQEl	long	pointer to queue element of function to be removed

KillAllGetReq Parameter Variant

| 26 | csCode | word | command code; always `killAllGetReq` |

RelRspCB Parameter Variant

26	csCode	word	command code; always `relRspCB`
30	addrBlock	long	internet socket address of the source of the request
46	transID	word	transaction ID of request with which the `PSendResponse` function to be canceled is associated

Result Codes

noErr	0	No error
paramErr	–50	Version number is too high
reqFailed	–1096	Retry count exceeded
tooManyReqs	–1097	Too many concurrent requests
tooManySkts	–1098	Too many responding sockets
badATPSkt	–1099	Bad responding socket
badBuffNum	–1100	Sequence number out of range
noRelErr	–1101	No release received
cbNotFound	–1102	The `aKillQEl` parameter does not point to a `PSendRequest` or `PNSendRequest` queue element
noSendResp	–1103	`PAddResponse` issued before `PSendResponse`
noDataArea	–1104	Too many outstanding ATP calls
reqAborted	–1105	Request canceled

Datagram Delivery Protocol (DDP)

Contents

This chapter describes how you can use the Datagram Delivery Protocol (DDP) to send data to and receive it from another socket across an AppleTalk internet. To use DDP, you send and receive data as discrete packets, each packet carrying its own addressing information. DDP does not allow you to set up a connection between two sockets, nor does DDP ensure that data is delivered error free as do some of the AppleTalk protocols that are built on top of it.

You should use DDP if your application does not require reliable delivery of data and you do not want to incur the additional processing associated with the use of a protocol that entails setting up and breaking down a connection. Because it is connectionless and does not include reliability services, DDP offers faster performance than do the higher-level protocols that add these services. Applications such as diagnostic tools that retransmit packets at regular intervals to estimate averages or games that can tolerate packet loss are good candidates for the use of DDP.

A series of DDP packets transmitted over an AppleTalk internet from one node to another may traverse a single high-speed EtherTalk network or they may wind across multiple intermediate data links such as LocalTalk or TokenTalk, which are connected by routers. During the course of this process, some packet loss can occur, for example, as a result of collisions. If you do not plan on implementing recovery from packet loss in your application, but your application requires it, you should consider using an AppleTalk transport protocol, such as the AppleTalk Data Stream Protocol (ADSP) or the AppleTalk Transaction Protocol (ATP); these protocols protect against packet loss and ensure reliability by using positive acknowledgment with packet retransmission mechanisms.

This chapter describes how to

- open and close sockets for sending and receiving DDP packets
- prepare the data and addressing information for each packet that you want to send
- write a socket listener that receives packets addressed to the DDP socket associated with your application
- measure packet-delivery performance

This chapter includes a sample socket listener that you can use as a model for your own socket listener or modify to fit your application's requirements.

For an overview of DDP and how it fits within the AppleTalk protocol stack, read the chapter "Introduction to AppleTalk" in this book, which also introduces and defines some of the terminology used in this chapter.

For an explanation of the DDP specification, see *Inside AppleTalk,* second edition.

About DDP

The protocol implementations at the physical and data-link layers of the AppleTalk protocol stack provide node-to-node delivery of data on the internet. DDP is a client of the link-access protocol—whether LLAP, ELAP, TLAP, or FDDILAP—and it uses the node-to-node delivery services provided by the data link to send and receive data. DDP is responsible for delivering data from socket to socket over an AppleTalk internet.

DDP is central to the process of sending and receiving data across an AppleTalk internet. Regardless of which data link is being used and which (if any) higher-level protocols are processing data, all AppleTalk data is carried in the form of DDP packets known as **datagrams.** (This chapter uses the terms *datagram* and *DDP packet* interchangeably.) A datagram consists of a header followed by data.

DDP lets you send and receive data a packet at a time. If you use DDP, you must address each data packet to the **socket** for which it is intended. A socket is a piece of software that serves as an addressable entity in a networked node. Sockets are numbered, and each application that uses DDP to transfer data is associated with a unique socket. You cannot open and maintain a session between two sockets using DDP, and for this reason, DDP is called a *connectionless protocol.*

To use DDP, you must provide a **socket listener** and a routine that reads packets from the socket listener code after it receives them. A socket listener is a process that receives packets addressed to the DDP socket associated with your application. Because the driver that implements DDP, the .MPP driver, uses registers not accessible from higher-level languages such as Pascal to pass information to your socket listener, you must write the socket listener code in assembly language.

DDP is said to provide a best-effort socket-to-socket delivery of datagrams over the internet.

- *Socket-to-socket delivery* means that when the data link delivers a packet to a node, the DDP implementation in that node determines the socket for which the packet is intended and calls the socket listener for that socket.

- *Best-effort delivery* means that DDP attempts to deliver any datagram that has a valid address to an open socket, as long as the length of the datagram received is the same as the length indicated by the header, the data is not longer than 586 bytes, and the datagram does not include an invalid checksum. DDP has no provision for requesting the sender to retransmit a lost or damaged datagram.

Note

You can send DDP packets to another socket in your own node if you have enabled the intranode delivery feature of AppleTalk. By default, intranode delivery is disabled; to turn it on, you use the `PSetSelfSend` function, which is described in the chapter "AppleTalk Utilities" in this book. ◆

About Sockets and Socket Listeners

Every application that uses DDP to transfer data must send or receive that data through a socket. The use of sockets allows DDP to determine for which application a packet is intended. Each node supports up to 254 sockets, and each socket is identified by an 8-bit number that combines with the network number and the node ID to form the internet socket address of the application. When an application or process calls DDP to open a socket, DDP associates the number of that socket with the application, making the application distinct from other applications on the same node. An application that is associated with a specific socket through DDP is the client of that socket, or a **socket client.**

The use of sockets allows multiple processes or applications that run on a single node connected to AppleTalk to be open at the same time. In Figure 7-1, a printer server client application and a file server client application are open on the same node at the same time. Each application is associated with a unique socket, and packets for that application are addressed to that socket number.

Figure 7-1 Two applications running on the same node, each with its own socket

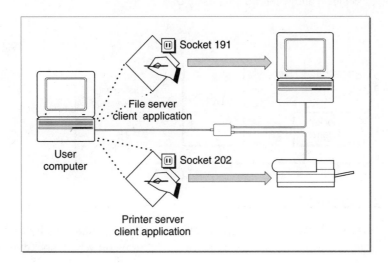

Applications exchange data with each other through their sockets. A socket client can send and receive datagrams only through its associated socket. Moreover, every socket-client application that uses DDP directly to transfer data must have associated with it a socket listener that receives datagrams addressed to the socket on behalf of that socket's client application.

A socket listener is a process that you provide as part of your client application. You must write your socket listener in assembly language and adhere to specific requirements in regard to the use of registers and the routines that you call to receive packets. Beyond meeting these AppleTalk requirements, your socket listener can perform any other functions that your socket-client application requires. See "A Sample Socket Listener" beginning on page 7-20 for more details.

When you call DDP to open a socket, you provide a pointer to your socket listener for that socket. DDP maintains a **socket table** that includes an entry for every open socket and its socket listener. When the .MPP driver receives a packet, it does not read and process the packet. Instead, it reads the socket number portion of the internet socket address and then checks the socket table to determine if that socket is open. If so, the .MPP driver calls the socket listener associated with the socket to handle reception of the packet for the client application. The use of socket listeners helps to maximize throughput between DDP and the link-access protocol layer by eliminating unnecessary buffer copying.

Datagram Delivery Protocol (DDP)

Figure 7-2 shows a socket-client application that calls DDP to send data to another socket. The socket-client application includes code that comprises its socket listener. When DDP receives a packet addressed to this socket, it checks the socket table for the entry that contains the socket number and the address of the socket listener belonging to the application that owns the socket; then DDP calls the socket listener to receive the packet for the application.

Figure 7-2   Sending and receiving data using DDP

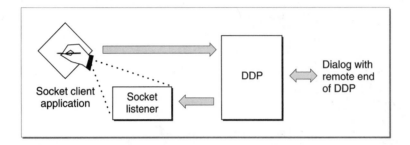

Assigning Socket Numbers

DDP maintains two classes of sockets: sockets that are assigned statically and sockets that are assigned dynamically. There are some restrictions on which socket numbers they use:

- Statically assigned sockets have numbers in the range of 1–127.
  - □ Socket numbers 1–63 are reserved for use by Apple Computer, Inc.
  - □ Socket numbers 64–127 are available for program development.
- Dynamically assigned sockets have numbers within the range of 128–254.

To use a statically assigned socket, an application must request a specific socket number. In most cases, you should not use statically assigned sockets.

IMPORTANT

Although you can use statically assigned sockets whose numbers fall within the range of 64–127 for program development, you must *not* use a statically assigned socket number for a released product. To do so creates the possibility of conflicts arising, for example, when two applications that both use the same statically assigned socket are open on the same node at the same time. Data intended for one application could be delivered to the other application, and vice versa. ▲

DDP maintains a pool of available sockets from which it selects a socket number to assign dynamically for your use when you call DDP to open a socket and you do not specify a number within the range of statically assigned sockets.

Figure 7-3 illustrates conceptually what happens when an application calls DDP to open and assign a socket dynamically. In this example, DDP assigns socket number 130 to the application that requests a socket. (Socket number 129 is already assigned to an application.)

Figure 7-3   Assigning sockets

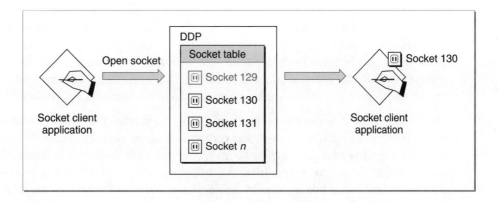

To let DDP choose a socket number from the pool of available sockets within the range of dynamically assigned sockets, you specify 0 for the socket number. However, you can choose a specific socket within that range and pass the number of that socket to DDP to open. If that socket is available, DDP opens it, assigns it to your application, and associates your socket listener with it. If the socket number you specify is not available, DDP returns an error result.

DDP Client Protocol Types

AppleTalk allows for the implementation of up to 254 parallel protocols that are clients of DDP. The DDP protocol type field, which is the last field of the DDP packet header, specifies the type of protocol that the packet is intended for. Figure 7-6 on page 7-15 shows the 1-byte DDP protocol type field of the DDP packet header.

The socket listener for a single socket can receive packets whose protocol type fields contain different values. It is the responsibility of your socket-client application to define its own protocol types. Your socket-client application can define more than one DDP protocol type and receive packets for any of the protocol types it handles, sorting them by reading the value of the DDP protocol type field.

For example, if you are implementing a server, you might define one protocol type for data and another for attention messages, and have separate routines to handle the different packet types. You fill in the DDP protocol type field when you build the contents of a DDP packet to be sent to another socket.

For more information on how to specify a protocol type for a DDP client application and the range of valid values for the DDP protocol type field, see Appendix C in *Inside AppleTalk*, second edition.

Obtaining Data From the Network

DDP supports a number of client protocols that are built on top of it, and DDP itself is a client protocol of the underlying data-link protocol. DDP has its own protocol handler that the link-access protocol calls when it receives a DDP packet. A **protocol handler** is a process that receives packets for a specific protocol type much like a socket listener receives packets for a specific socket. A DDP packet or datagram is sent from its source socket through one or more AppleTalk networks to its destination network.

A datagram is sent across the network enclosed in a **frame.** The frame contains additional information that the link-access protocol requires, such as addressing information that identifies the node and the socket number for which the frame is meant. The frame addressing information is contained in the frame's header, which is followed by the datagram. The frame header also identifies the protocol type of the enclosed packet. In addition to a header, a frame also contains a trailer that follows the datagram. The frame trailer contains a frame check sequence number that the AppleTalk hardware generates and uses to detect transmission errors.

The link-access protocol in the destination network delivers the frame to the node containing the destination socket. When a frame addressed to a particular node arrives at that node, the node's CPU is interrupted and the .MPP driver's interrupt handler gets control to service the interrupt. As the frame's first 3 bytes are read into the first-in first-out (FIFO) buffer, the .MPP driver's interrupt handler moves these bytes into its own internal buffer.

If the frame is a data frame containing a packet intended for a higher-level protocol, the .MPP driver's interrupt handler passes control to the protocol handler for the protocol type specified in the frame's header. For example, when a frame whose header specifies the DDP protocol type is delivered to a node, the link-access protocol passes control to the .MPP driver. The .MPP driver then calls the DDP protocol handler. DDP, which is implemented by the .MPP driver, determines for which socket the packet is meant and calls the socket listener that is associated with the socket. The socket listener, in turn, actually reads in the packet.

Using DDP

This section describes how to send data packets to a socket and how to receive them from another socket over an AppleTalk network or internet using DDP. It also describes how to use the AEP Echoer to measure packet-delivery performance and to determine if a node is on the network.

Note
You do not need to use the AEP Echoer to send and receive data using DDP. This chapter describes the AEP Echoer because you must use the programming interface to DDP in order to use the AEP Echoer. Applications that use higher-level AppleTalk protocols, such as ATP or ADSP, can also use the AEP Echoer to measure packet-delivery performance. ◆

Sending and Receiving Data: An Overview

To send data, you must address each packet to the socket for which it is intended because you cannot open and maintain a connection between two sockets using DDP. To receive a data packet using DDP, you must provide a socket listener process that DDP associates with the socket that your application uses. When you open the socket for your application to use, you must provide a pointer to the socket listener. DDP associates the address of the socket listener with your application's socket so that the .MPP driver can call your socket listener when it receives a packet that is addressed to your socket-client application. DDP maintains a separate entry in its socket table for each socket and socket listener pair.

Applications developers commonly write a single socket-client application that both sends and receives data and that includes a socket listener process to receive data. To clarify the steps involved in sending and receiving data, this section gives you an overview of these tasks as separate sequences after it explains how to open a socket. The steps for sending and receiving data refer to sections that are provided later in this chapter that describe how to

- create a write-data structure, which you need to send data

- use the registers that the .MPP driver uses to pass parameters to your socket listener

- write a socket listener, with sample code illustrating this

If you want to provide features in addition to the DDP checksum feature to check data and correct errors, you can include them in your application, you can define your own AppleTalk protocol, or you can use a higher-level AppleTalk protocol such as ATP or ADSP instead of calling DDP directly. (For information about DDP checksums, see "Using Checksums" beginning on page 7-19.)

To make your application available to other users of AppleTalk, you must use the NBP `PRegisterName` function to register the name that represents your socket-client application. When you are finished using the socket, you must use the NBP `PRemoveName` function to remove this name from the NBP names table. See the chapter "Name-Binding Protocol (NBP)" in this book for more information about these functions.

Opening a Socket

To send and receive data using DDP, your application must first open a socket. Opening a socket makes your application a client of that socket. You open a socket with the `POpenSkt` function. When you open a socket, you must provide a pointer to your socket listener and you must specify 0 for the socket number if you want DDP to dynamically assign a socket.

The `POpenSkt` function assigns a socket number to your application and enters the number in the socket table along with the pointer to the socket listener that you provide. The `POpenSkt` function returns the socket number to you in the `socket` field of the parameter block.

Associating a single socket listener with more than one socket

If your application includes processes that each have their own sockets, you can assign a single socket listener to more than one socket, but each socket should have its own buffer or set of buffers for receiving data. ◆

If you do not want DDP to randomly assign a socket number to your application, you can specify the number of a particular socket for DDP to open. For information on the range of socket numbers from which you can select, see "Assigning Socket Numbers" on page 7-6.

IMPORTANT

You cannot specify a `NIL` pointer to the socket listener. If you do, the system on which your application is running will crash. ▲

When your application is finished using a socket, you must use the `PCloseSkt` function to close the socket.

Sending Data

To send data, you must create a write-data structure that contains the data in a specific format and then call a DDP function to send the data. After you have opened a socket using the `POpenSkt` function, here are the steps that you follow to send data using DDP:

1. Create a write-data structure.

2. Use the DDP function `PWriteDDP` to send the data.

See "Creating a DDP Write-Data Structure" beginning on page 7-12 for information about how to create a write-data structure using the DDP procedure `BuildDDPwds` or your own code.

Packets with long headers can include a checksum that can be used to verify the integrity of the packet data. For information on how to direct DDP to calculate a checksum for data that you want to send, see "Using Checksums" beginning on page 7-19. For details of the contents of a long header, see "The DDP Packet and Frame Headers" beginning on page 7-14.

Receiving Data

To receive data using DDP, you must provide a socket listener that is part of your socket-client application. The socket listener code must

■ be written in assembly language because it must read from and write to the CPU's registers

■ include buffers to hold the data that it reads

■ use the register values that the .MPP driver passes to your socket listener

■ determine the type of packet, if you have defined more than one protocol type that your application handles

■ if the packet includes a long header, calculate the checksum value, if one is used

There are many ways to design and write a socket-client application and socket listener. This chapter offers one possibility. For details of this sample socket listener and for its code, see "A Sample Socket Listener" beginning on page 7-20.

Note

Your socket-client application should test to find out when the socket listener finishes processing a packet so that the socket-client application can begin its own packet reading and processing. ◆

To receive data, your application must have already opened a socket using the POpenSkt function and have passed the POpenSkt function a pointer to your socket listener.

Here are the tasks involved in receiving data using DDP:

1. The .MPP driver calls your socket listener when it receives a packet addressed to your socket-client application. The .MPP driver passes values to you in the CPU's registers. You need to know how the .MPP driver uses these registers and how you can use them. For information about these registers, see "How the .MPP Driver Calls Your Socket Listener" beginning on page 7-13. One of the values that the .MPP driver passes to you is a pointer to the buffer that holds the DDP packet header. You need to know how the DDP packet header and the frame header are structured. For information about these headers, see "The DDP Packet and Frame Headers" beginning on page 7-14.

2. To hold the data that it reads, your socket listener must allocate memory for buffers. In addition to allocating data buffers, either your socket-client application or the socket listener (if you write the socket listener code to carry out this function) must perform some initialization tasks. For information about these tasks and how the sample socket listener handles them, see "Socket Listener Queues and Buffers" beginning on page 7-20, "Setting Up the Socket Listener" beginning on page 7-22, and "Initializing the Socket Listener" beginning on page 7-24.

3. When the .MPP driver calls your socket listener, the socket listener must read the incoming packet into one or more data buffers. To do this, the socket listener uses two processes, ReadPacket and ReadRest, which are implemented as a single routine in the hardware driver. The .MPP driver passes you the address of this routine in one of the CPU's registers. For more information, see "Reading an Incoming Packet" beginning on page 7-17.

4. If you have defined more than one DDP protocol type that your application handles, check the DDP protocol type field of the datagram header (see Figure 7-6 on page 7-15) to determine the protocol type of the packet you have just received.

   The AppleTalk internet address (network number, node ID, and socket number) is insufficient to distinguish between packets intended for different processes that are using the same socket. Your socket listener must use some other information (such as the DDP protocol type or a higher-level protocol header imbedded in the DDP packet data) to make this distinction.

5. If the packet contains a long header, the socket listener needs to find out if the header contains a checksum. If it does, the socket listener needs to calculate the checksum to determine if the packet's data has been corrupted. For more information, see "Using Checksums" beginning on page 7-19.

6. The socket listener can now process the packet or pass it to the client application for processing. The sample socket listener provided here writes the packet buffer to a queue that it uses for successfully processed packets and removes the packet from the queue for incoming packets. For a description of how the sample socket listener does this, see "Processing a Packet" beginning on page 7-25.

7. The client application can now read in the packet for its own purposes. The client application should include code that periodically checks to determine whether the socket listener has finished processing an incoming packet. For a description of how the sample socket listener's client application performs this task and some sample code, see "Testing for Available Packets" beginning on page 7-31.

Creating a DDP Write-Data Structure

When you use the PWriteDDP function to send a DDP packet to another socket, you provide a pointer to a write-data structure that you have already created. A write-data structure contains a series of pairs of length words and pointers and ends with a 0 word. Each pair indicates the length and location of a portion of the data that constitutes the packet to be sent over the network. The first entry in the write-data structure consists of only a pointer. It does not include a length word, because the length is always the same.

The first pointer indicates a 16-byte header block, which must start at an odd address. You fill in the destination network number, destination node ID, destination socket number, and DDP protocol type, and the .MPP driver fills in the other fields of the packet header. DDP protocol types 1 through 15 are reserved for use by Apple. A DDP packet may have a maximum of 586 bytes of data. Figure 7-4 shows the write-data structure and the header block.

Because the first pointer in the write-data structure must point to an odd address, it is difficult to use Pascal to create a write-data structure. If you are programming in Pascal, you can use the BuildDDPwds procedure to create a write-data structure. You must provide a 17-byte buffer for the header block, a 14-byte buffer to hold the write-data structure, and a pointer to the data you want to send. The header block is only 16 bytes, but because it begins on an odd address, the first byte is not used. The write-data structure created by the BuildDDPwds procedure is 14 bytes long, consisting of only a pointer to the header, a length-pointer pair for the data block, and the terminating 0 word. Although a write-data structure allows you to divide the data into as many blocks as you wish, the BuildDDPwds procedure assumes that the data is in a single block.

In most cases, if you are using DDP directly to send data across a network, a single block of data should be adequate. However, if you are implementing a protocol on top of DDP and you want to send blocks of data that are stored separately as parts of the same datagram, you will have to build your own write-data structure that includes multiple pairs of pointers and lengths. For a description of the write-data structure that you need to build in this case, see "The Write-Data Structure" on page 7-35. Notice that the pointer to the first entry indicates an odd address and that there is no length word for the first entry.

Datagram Delivery Protocol (DDP)

Figure 7-4   DDP write-data structure

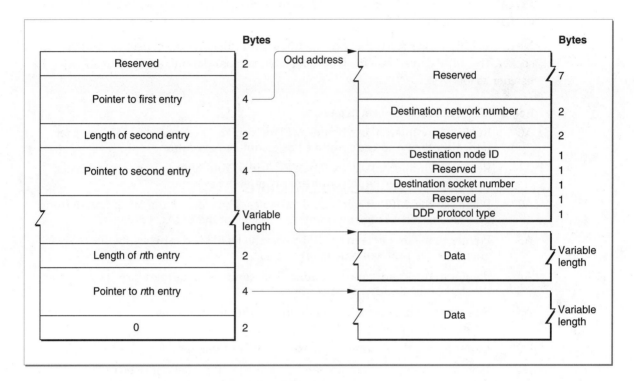

Using Registers and Packet Headers

To receive data at the DDP level, you need to include as part of your socket-client application a socket listener that reads packets addressed to your application and passes them to the application for further processing. DDP maintains a table with an entry for each socket and socket listener pair.

When the .MPP driver receives a packet addressed to your socket-client application, it calls your socket listener, using the CPU's registers to pass pointers to the internal buffer where it has stored the packet's headers and to some data values that your socket listener uses during its processing.

The CPU's registers that the .MPP driver uses to pass parameters to your socket listener are not directly accessible from Pascal. Because a DDP socket listener must read from and write to the CPU's registers, you must write a socket listener in assembly language; you cannot use Pascal. However, you can write the remainder of the client application that includes the socket listener in a high-level language such as Pascal. The client application sample code that this chapter shows is written in the Pascal language.

How the .MPP Driver Calls Your Socket Listener

When a frame addressed to a particular node arrives at that node and the frame contains a DDP packet, the node's CPU is interrupted and the link-access protocol calls the .MPP driver to receive the packet. When the .MPP driver receives a DDP packet, it reads the first 3 bytes of the frame header into an internal buffer called the **read-header area (RHA).** After the frame header is read into the RHA, 8 bytes of the RHA are still available for your use.

Next, the .MPP driver reads the socket address and calls the socket listener for that socket. The .MPP driver uses the CPU's registers to pass parameters to your socket listener as follows:

Registers on call to DDP socket listener

A0   Reserved for internal use by the .MPP driver. You must preserve this register until after the `ReadRest` routine has completed execution.

A1   Reserved for internal use by the .MPP driver. You must preserve this register until after the `ReadRest` routine has completed execution.

A2   Pointer to the .MPP driver's local variables. The value at the offset `toRHA` from the value in the A2 register points to the start of the RHA.

A3   Pointer to the first byte in the RHA past the DDP header bytes (the first byte after the DDP protocol type field).

A4   Pointer to the `ReadPacket` routine. The `ReadRest` routine starts 2 bytes after the start of the `ReadPacket` routine.

A5   Free for your use before and until your socket listener calls the `ReadRest` routine.

D0   Lower byte is the destination socket number of the packet.

D1   Word indicating the number of bytes in the DDP packet left to be read (that is, the number of bytes following the DDP header).

D2   Free for your use.

D3   Free for your use.

When the .MPP driver calls your socket listener, you can read the destination socket number that is in the D0 register and the frame header that is in the RHA. You should assume that only 8 bytes are still available in the RHA for your use. Figure 7-5 shows the beginning of the RHA where the frame header begins; the frame header is followed by either a short or a long DDP header.

The DDP Packet and Frame Headers

A DDP packet includes a packet header followed by data. The DDP packet header is preceded by the frame header. Figure 7-6 shows both headers; they do not include the data portion. The DDP packet header can be long or short; if the destination and source network numbers are different, DDP uses a long header, which includes some additional fields.

The frame header includes

■ the source and destination node IDs

■ the DDP header type (1 = short, 2 = long)

Figure 7-5   The RHA for both long and short DDP headers

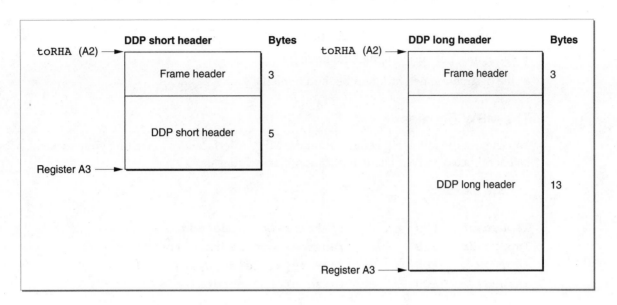

Figure 7-6   Data-link frame header and DDP packet header

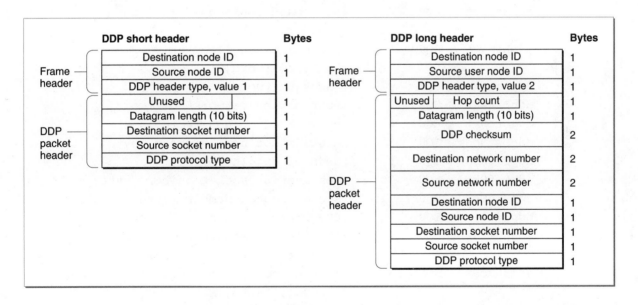

The DDP long and short packet headers have these fields in common:

- the datagram length (10 bits)
- the destination socket number
- the source socket number
- the DDP protocol type

Datagram Delivery Protocol (DDP)

A long DDP packet header also includes

- a hop count
- a checksum value, if one was calculated
- the source network number and node ID
- the destination network number and node ID

The MPW Equates

You can use the following equates from the MPW interface files in writing your socket listener process and the client application that includes it:

```
;frame header
;
lapDstAdr    EQU    0      ;destination node address [byte]
lapSrcAdr    EQU    1      ;source node address [byte]
lapType      EQU    2      ;LAP type field [byte]
lapHdSz      EQU    3      ;size of LAP header

;DDP packet header
;
ddpHopCnt    EQU    0      ;hop count (only used in long
                          ; header) [byte]
ddpLength    EQU    0      ;packet length (from this word
                          ; onward) [word]
ddpChecksum  EQU    2      ;checksum [word]
ddpDstNet    EQU    4      ;destination network no. [word]
ddpSrcNet    EQU    6      ;network of origin [word]
ddpDstNode   EQU    8      ;destination node address [byte]
ddpSrcNode   EQU    9      ;node of origin [byte]
ddpDstSkt    EQU    10     ;destination socket number [byte]
ddpSrcSkt    EQU    11     ;source socket number [byte]
ddpType      EQU    12     ;DDP protocol type field [byte]
sddpDstSkt   EQU    2      ;destination socket number (short
                          ; header) [byte]
sddpSrcSkt   EQU    3      ;source socket number (short
                          ; header) [byte]
sddpType     EQU    4      ;DDP protocol type field (short header)
                          ; [byte]
;
ddphSzLong   EQU    13     ;size of extended DDP header
ddphSzShort  EQU    5      ;size of short DDP header
;
shortDDP     EQU    $01    ;LAP type code for DDP (short header)
longDDP      EQU    $02    ;LAP type code for DDP (long header)
```

Reading an Incoming Packet

Your socket listener calls the ReadPacket and ReadRest processes to read the incoming data packet. You can call ReadPacket as many times as you like to read the data piece by piece into one or more data buffers, but you must always use ReadRest to read the final piece of the data packet. Alternatively, you can read all of the data using only ReadRest. The ReadRest routine restores the machine state (the stack pointers, status register, and so forth) and checks for error conditions.

Note
You can ignore any remaining data instead of reading it by setting the D3 register to 0 and calling ReadRest. ◆

Before you call the ReadPacket routine, you must allocate memory for a data buffer and place a pointer to the buffer in the A3 register. You must also place the number of bytes you want to read in the D3 register. You must not request more bytes than remain in the data packet.

The buffer that you allocate must be large enough to hold all of the data and—if your socket listener places the packet header in the buffer—the header as well. The maximum amount of data in a DDP data packet is 586 bytes. A long DDP packet header is 13 bytes long; a short header is 5 bytes. The frame header is 3 bytes. Therefore, the maximum amount of data from the packet that the socket listener can return is 602 bytes. You can use the buffer as a data structure to hold other information as well, such as the number of bytes of data actually read by the socket listener, a flag that indicates when the data has been returned, and result codes.

After you have called the ReadRest routine, you can use registers A0 through A3 and D0 through D3 for your own use, but you must preserve all other registers. You cannot depend on having access to your application's global variables.

To call the ReadPacket routine, execute a JSR instruction to the address in the A4 register. The ReadPacket routine uses the registers as follows:

Registers on entry to the ReadPacket routine

A3   Pointer to a buffer to hold the data you want to read

D3   Number of bytes to read; must be nonzero

Registers on exit from the ReadPacket routine

A0   Unchanged

A1   Unchanged

A2   Unchanged

A3   Address of the first byte after the last byte read into buffer

A4   Unchanged

D0   Changed

D1   Number of bytes left to be read

D2   Unchanged

D3   Equals 0 if requested number of bytes were read, nonzero if error

After every time you call `ReadPacket` or `ReadRest`, you must check the zero (`z`) flag in the status register for errors because the `ReadPacket` routine indicates an error by clearing it to 0. If the `ReadPacket` routine returns an error, you must terminate execution of your socket listener with an RTS instruction without calling `ReadPacket` again or calling `ReadRest` at all.

Call the `ReadRest` routine to read the last portion of the data packet, or call it after you have read all the data with `ReadPacket` routines and before you do any other processing or terminate execution. After you call the `ReadRest` routine, you must terminate execution of your socket listener with an RTS instruction whether or not the `ReadRest` routine returns an error.

When you call the `ReadRest` routine, you must provide in the A3 register a pointer to a data buffer and must indicate in the D3 register the size of the data buffer. If you have already read all of the data with calls to the `ReadPacket` routine, specify a buffer of size 0.

▲ **WARNING**
If you do not call the `ReadRest` routine after the last time you call the `ReadPacket` routine successfully, the system will crash. You do not need to call the `ReadPacket` routine; you can call only the `ReadRest` routine to read in the entire packet. However, you must call the `ReadRest` routine. ▲

To call the `ReadRest` routine, execute a JSR instruction to an address 2 bytes past the address in the A4 register. The `ReadRest` routine uses the registers as follows:

Registers on entry to the `ReadRest` routine

A3 Pointer to a buffer to hold the data you want to read

D3 Size of the buffer (word length); may be 0

Registers on exit from the `ReadRest` routine

A0 Unchanged

A1 Unchanged

A2 Unchanged

A3 Pointer to first byte after the last byte read into buffer

D0 Changed

D1 Changed

D2 Unchanged

D3 Equals 0 if requested number of bytes exactly equaled the size of the buffer; less than 0 if more data was left than would fit in buffer (extra data equals –D3 bytes); greater than 0 if less data was left than the size of the buffer (extra buffer space equals D3 bytes)

Calling `ReadPacket` and `ReadRest` when LocalTalk is the data link

If LocalTalk is the data link that is being used, your socket listener has less than 95 microseconds (best case) to read more data with a `ReadPacket` or `ReadRest` call. If you need more time, you can read another 3 bytes into the RHA, which will allow you an additional 95 microseconds. ◆

In implementing your socket listener, you can use the registers as follows:

- You can use registers D0, D2, and D3 freely throughout the socket listener code.

- You must preserve the contents of registers A6 and D4 to D7.

- From entry to your socket listener until you call `ReadRest`
  - □ you can use A5 register
  - □ you must preserve registers A0 to A2, A4, and D1

- From `ReadRest` until your application exits from the socket listener
  - □ you must preserve register A5
  - □ you can use registers A0 to A3 and D0 to D3

Using Checksums

For packets that include a long header, DDP includes a checksum feature that you can use to verify that the packet data has not been corrupted by memory or data bus errors within routers on the internet.

When you use the `PWriteDDP` function to send a DDP packet across an AppleTalk internet, you can set a flag (`checksumFlag`) to direct DDP to calculate a checksum for the packet.

If the checksum flag is set and the socket to which you are sending the packet (the destination socket) has a network number that is different from that of the socket from which you are sending the packet (the source socket), then the `PWriteDDP` function calculates a checksum for the datagram and includes it in the datagram packet header. In this case, DDP uses a long header for the packet; Figure 7-6 on page 7-15 shows both the long and short DDP headers.

When your socket listener receives a packet that has a long header, the socket listener must determine whether DDP calculated a checksum for the packet, and if so, use the checksum to verify that the data was delivered intact. You can use the equates from the MPW interface files in calculating checksums: see "The MPW Equates" on page 7-16.

To determine this, your socket listener code should take the following steps:

1. Check the DDP header type field. This is set to 2 for a packet with a long header and 1 for a packet with a short header.

2. Check the checksum field (`checksumFlag`). This is set to a nonzero value if the sender specified that DDP should calculate a checksum for the packet; a short header does not include a checksum field.

3. Calculate the checksum using the following algorithm to calculate the checksum, starting with the byte immediately following the checksum field in the header and ending with the last data byte:

checksum := checksum + next byte; {unsigned addition}
Rotate the most significant bit to the least significant bit
Repeat

4. Compare the calculated checksum against the value set in the checksum field of the DDP packet header.

You can use the equates from the MPW interface files in calculating checksums: see "The MPW Equates" on page 7-16.

A Sample Socket Listener

There are many ways to implement a socket listener that follow the requirements described previously for using and preserving registers and reading packets. This section uses a sample socket listener that shows one way to implement the process within a DDP socket-client application that reads in the packet contents. The sample code also shows those segments of the sample client application that set up the socket listener and check to determine when a packet that the socket listener has read is available for processing by the client application.

Some of the tasks that your socket listener can do that this sample socket listener does not illustrate are how to

■ route packets to different sockets based on the socket number in register D0 when more than one socket uses your socket listener

■ check the DDP protocol type field and ignore any packets that do not match the desired packet types that your socket listener is set up to receive

■ check the source node ID and ignore any packets that don't come from a desired node

■ implement a completion routine to be executed after a packet is processed

The sample socket listener does, however, show you how to

■ buffer multiple packets

■ retrieve the frame and DDP packet header information that DDP has already read into the RHA

■ calculate and compare the packet checksum when a packet uses a long DDP header that includes the checksum value

Socket Listener Queues and Buffers

The sample socket listener uses two standard operating-system queues to manage the contents of the packets that it receives and makes available to the socket-client application. It calls these linked lists a *free queue* and a *used queue*. The use of two queues allows the socket listener to receive and process packets while the client application is reading the data from those packets that the socket listener has already processed.

The free queue is used to manage available buffers that consist of data structures declared as `PacketBuffer` records. The sample socket listener uses the buffers in the free queue one at a time to hold the contents of an incoming packet as it processes the packet header and data fields. The socket listener's initialization module, `SL_InitSktListener`, shown in Listing 7-5 on page 7-24, releases the first element or buffer of the free queue and points to it from the current queue element (`current_qelem`) variable; it is this buffer that the socket listener uses when the .MPP driver calls the socket listener with a packet for it to process.

After the socket listener fills in the fields of the record pointed to by `current_qelem` with the processed contents of the packet, it moves the buffer into the used queue, pointed to by `used_queue`, for the client application to read. Then the socket listener releases the next record buffer from the free queue and points to it using the `current_qelem` variable. The sample code in Listing 7-7 on page 7-31 shows that when the client application has finished reading the contents of a used queue buffer element, it returns the buffer to the free queue pointed to by `free_queue` to make the buffer available again to the socket listener.

The socket listener uses the variables declared in Listing 7-1 to point to

- the free queue's queue header
- the used queue's queue header
- the current buffer queue element

Listing 7-1   Declarations for pointers to the sample socket listener's queues and packet buffer

```
SL_Locals     PROC
          ENTRY free_queue,used_queue,current_qelem
free_queue        DC.L     0        ;pointer to freeQ QHdr ;
                                    ; initialized by InitSktListener
used_queue        DC.L     0        ;pointer to usedQ QHdr ;
                                    ; initialized by InitSktListener
current_qelem     DC.L     0        ;pointer to current
                                    ; PacketBuffer record
ENDP;
```

Listing 7-4 on page 7-23 shows the Pascal-language client application `SetUpSocketListener` procedure. This procedure calls the `SL_InitSktListener` function to pass to the socket listener pointers to these two operating-system queues.

When the .MPP driver calls the socket listener, if there is an available buffer, the socket listener processes the packet and returns in the fields of the packet buffer record the DDP type, the destination node ID, the source address in `AddrBlock` format, the hop count, the size of the packet, a flag to indicate whether a checksum error occurred, and the data delivered in the packet. If you use the sample record data structure as a model, you can extend it to include fields to hold additional values, such as the tick count at the time when the .MPP driver called your socket listener. Listing 7-2 shows the assembly-language declaration for the `PacketBuffer` record.

Listing 7-2   Declaration for the sample socket listener's packet buffer record

```
PacketBuffer        RECORD      0
qLink               DS.L        1
qType               DS.W        1
buffer_Type         DS.W        1       ;DDP protocol type
buffer_NodeID       DS.W        1       ;destination node
buffer_Address      DS.L        1       ;source address in AddrBlock format
buffer_Hops         DS.W        1       ;hop count
buffer_ActCount     DS.W        1       ;length of DDP datagram
buffer_CheckSum     DS.W        1       ;chksum error returned here
                                        ; (cksumErr or noErr)
buffer_Data         DS.B        ddpMaxData
                                        ;the DDP datagram
                    ENDR
```

Listing 7-3 shows the socket listener's declaration for the queue header record, which is defined and used to make the code easier to read.

Listing 7-3   Declaration for the sample socket listener's queue header record

```
QHdr      RECORD      0
qFlags    DS.W        1
qHead     DS.L        1
qTail     DS.L        1
          ENDR
```

Setting Up the Socket Listener

The client application that includes the sample socket listener uses a Pascal procedure, SetUpSocketListener, to set up the socket listener's initialization routine. The SetUpSocketListener procedure defines

- the free and used queue variables of type QHdr

- a packet buffer record of type PacketBuffer to match the data structure defined in the socket listener code (The sample Pascal code declares an array of 10 packet buffer records.)

If you base your own code on the sample code, you can add new fields to the record declaration, if you need them. If you do this, you must modify the packet buffer data structure defined in the socket listener code to match the high-level language record declaration.

Listing 7-4 shows the client-application's Pascal code that initializes the packet buffer records and then adds them to the free queue using the _Enqueue trap. The code calls the SL_InitSktListener routine and passes to it pointers to the queue header for the free queue and the queue header for the used queue.

Listing 7-4   Setting up the socket listener from the client application

```
CONST
    ddpMaxData = 586;
TYPE
    PacketBuffer = RECORD
        qLink: QElemPtr;
        qType: Integer;
        buffer_Type: Integer;
        buffer_NodeID: Integer;
        buffer_Address: AddrBlock;
        buffer_Hops: Integer;
        buffer_ActCount: Integer;
        buffer_CheckSum: OSErr;
        buffer_Data: ARRAY[1..ddpMaxData] OF SignedByte;
END;

VAR
    freeQ, usedQ: QHdr;
    Buffers: ARRAY[1..10] OF PacketBuffer;

PROCEDURE SL_TheListener;
External;

FUNCTION SL_InitSktListener (freeQ, usedQ: QHdrPtr): OSErr;
External;

PROCEDURE SetUpSocketListener;
    VAR
        err: OSErr;
        i: Integer;
    BEGIN
        freeQ.QHead := NIL;       {initialize to nil to indicate empty queue}
        freeQ.QTail := NIL;       {initialize to nil to indicate end of queue}
        usedQ.QHead := NIL;       {initialize to nil to indicate empty queue}
        usedQ.QTail := NIL;       {initialize to nil to indicate end of queue}

        FOR i := 1 TO 10 DO       {add all buffers to the free queue}
            Enqueue(@Buffers[i], @freeQ);

        err := SL_InitSktListener(@freeQ, @usedQ);
                                  {initialize the socket listener code}
```

```
IF err <> noErr THEN
    BEGIN
        {Perform error processing here}
    END;
{You can now call POpenSkt because the socket listener is ready to }
{ process packets.}
END;
```

Initializing the Socket Listener

The sample socket-client application procedure SetUpSocketListener (shown in the preceding listing) calls the socket listener SL_InitSktListener initialization routine provided in Listing 7-5 to pass it pointers to the two operating-system queues (used and free) that the socket listener uses after the SetUpSocketListener procedure initializes these queues.

The SL_InitSktListener routine sets up its local variables used_queue and free_queue to point to the queue headers for the two queues. Then the routine releases from the free queue the first buffer and sets the current_qelem variable to point to it. This is the buffer that the socket listener uses when it next reads a packet.

Listing 7-5   Initializing the socket listener

```
;Function SL_InitSktListener(freeQ, usedQ: QHdrPtr): OSErr;
;
SL_InitSktListener PROC EXPORT

StackFrame      RECORD      {A6Link},DECR ;build a stack frame record
Result1         DS.W        1             ;function's result returned to caller
ParamBegin      EQU         *             ;start parameters after this point
freeQ           DS.L        1             ;freeQ parameter
usedQ           DS.L        1             ;usedQ parameter
ParamSize       EQU         ParamBegin-*  ;size of all the passed parameters
RetAddr         DS.L        1             ;placeholder for return address
A6Link          DS.L        1             ;placeholder for A6 link
LocalSize       EQU         *             ;size of all the local variables
                ENDR

    WITH        StackFrame,QHdr;          ;use these record types
    LINK        A6,#LocalSize             ;allocate your local stack frame

;Copy the queue header pointers into our local storage for use in the
; listener
```

Datagram Delivery Protocol (DDP)

```
          LEA          used_queue,A0              ;copy usedQ into used_queue
          MOVE.L       usedQ(A6),(A0)


          LEA          free_queue,A0              ;copy freeQ into free_queue
          MOVE.L       freeQ(A6),(A0)


;Release the first buffer record from freeQ and set current_qelem to it


          MOVEA.L      freeQ(A6),A1               ; A1 = ^freeQ
          LEA          current_qelem,A0           ;copy freeQ.qHead into current_qelem
          MOVE.L       qHead(A1),(A0)
          MOVEA.L      qHead(A1),A0               ;A0 = freeQ.qHead
          _Dequeue
          MOVE.W       D0,Result1(A6)             ;return status


@1  UNLK          A6                              ;destroy the link
          MOVEA.L      (SP)+,A0                   ;pull off the return address
          ADDA.L       #ParamSize,SP              ;strip all of the caller's parameters
          JMP          (A0)                       ;return to the caller
          ENDP
          END
```

Processing a Packet

When the .MPP driver calls the sample socket listener, the socket listener's main module, the SL_TheListener procedure, reads and processes a packet addressed to the socket-client application. However, the socket listener can only process a packet if there is a packet buffer record available to hold the processed packet.

The code shown in Listing 7-6 determines if the current_qelem variable is NIL or not. If it is not NIL, the code gets a buffer, if one is available.

- If there is no buffer available, the code ignores the packet and calls the ReadRest routine with a buffer size value of 0. Before returning to the calling program, the code calls its GetNextBuffer routine to set up the current_qelem variable to point to the next available buffer, if there is one.

- If there is a buffer available, the code reads in the packet data and processes it.

If the socket listener reads the packet successfully, it processes the header information that the hardware driver has stored in the .MPP driver's local variable space pointed to by the value in register A2. To do this, the socket listener

- fills in a value for the hop count field of the packet buffer record and determines the packet length

- determines whether the DDP header is short or long and fills in the remaining fields of the packet buffer

Using DDP

■ tests the checksum field of long DDP headers to determine if they are nonzero, indicating that the packet contains a checksum, and, if so, calculates the checksum

■ adds the packet buffer to the used queue and then gets the next free buffer from the free queue and points to it with `current_qelem`

The socket listener then returns control to the calling program and waits until the .MPP driver calls it again when the .MPP driver next receives a packet addressed to a socket that is associated with the socket listener. Listing 7-6 shows the `SL_TheListener` procedure.

Listing 7-6   Receiving and processing a DDP packet

```
;SL_TheListener
;Input:
;      D0 (byte) = packet's destination socket number
;      D1 (word) = number of bytes left to read in packet
;      A0 points to the bytes to checksum
;      A1 points to the bytes to checksum
;      A2 points to MPP's local variables
;      A3 points to next free byte in read-header area
;      A4 points to ReadPacket and ReadRest jump table
;
;Return:
;      D0 is modified
;      D3 (word) = accumulated checksum

SL_TheListener  PROC      EXPORT
   WITH    PacketBuffer

;Get pointer to current PacketBuffer.
GetBuffer:
   LEA          current_qelem,A3    ;get the pointer to PacketBuffer
   MOVE.L       (A3),A3
   MOVE.L       A3,D0               ;if no PacketBuffer
   BEQ.S        NoBuffer            ; then ignore packet

;Read rest of packet into PacketBuffer.datagramData.
   MOVE.L       D1,D3               ;read rest of packet
   LEA          buffer_data(A3),A3  ;A3 = ^bufferData
   JSR          2(A4)               ;call ReadRest
   BEQ.S        ProcessPacket       ;if no error, continue
   BRA          RcvRTS              ;if error, ignore the packet
;No buffer; ignore the packet.
NoBuffer         CLR D3             ;set to ignore packet (buffer size = 0)
```

```
        JSR         2(A4)                   ;call ReadRest
        BRA         GetNextBuffer           ;no buffer available, so read next packet;
                                            ; maybe there will be a buffer
                                            ; for the next packet
```

```
;Process the packet you just read in.
; ReadRest has been called so registers A0-A3 and D0-D3 are free
; to use. Use registers this way:
PktBuff         EQU     A0      ;current PacketBuffer
MPPLocals       EQU     A2      ;pointer to MPP's local variables
                                ; (still set up from entry to
                                ; socket listener)
HopCount        EQU     D0      ;gets the hop count
DatagramLength  EQU     D1      ;determines the datagram length
SourceNetAddr   EQU     D2      ;builds the source network address
ProcessPacket:
    LEA         current_qelem,PktBuff
                                ;PktBuff =  current_qelem
    MOVE.L      (PktBuff),PktBuff
```

```
;Do everything that's common to both long and short DDP headers
; first, clear buffer_Type and buffer_NodeID to ensure their high
; bytes are 0.
    CLR.W       buffer_Type(PktBuff)
                                ;clear buffer_Type
    CLR.W       buffer_NodeID(PktBuff)
                                ;clear buffer_NodeID
```

```
;Clear SourceNetAddr to prepare to build network address.
    MOVEQ       #0,SourceNetAddr    ;build the network address in
                                    ; SourceNetAddr
;Get the hop count
    MOVE.W      toRHA+lapHdSz+ddpLength(MPPLocals),HopCount
                                    ;get hop/length field
    ANDI.W      #DDPHopsMask,HopCount
                                    ;mask off the hop count bits
    LSR.W       #2,HopCount         ;shift hop count into low bits
                                    ; of high byte
    LSR.W       #8,HopCount         ;shift hop count into low byte
    MOVE.W      HopCount,buffer_Hops(PktBuff)
                                    ; and move it into the
                                    ; PacketBuffer
```

Datagram Delivery Protocol (DDP)

```
;Get the packet length (including the DDP header).
    MOVE.W        toRHA+lapHdSz+ddpLength(MPPLocals),DatagramLength
                                    ;get length field
    ANDI.W        #ddpLenMask,DatagramLength
                                    ;mask off the hop count bits

;Now, find out if the DDP header is long or short.
    MOVE.B        toRHA+lapType(MPPLocals),D3
                                    ;get LAP type
    CMPI.B        #shortDDP,D3       ;is this a long or short DDP
                                    ; header?
    BEQ.S         IsShortHdr         ;skip if short DDP header

;It's a long DDP header.
    MOVE.B toRHA+lapHdSz+ddpType(MPPLocals),buffer_Type+1(PktBuff)
                                    ;get DDP type
    MOVE.B
        toRHA+lapHdSz+ddpDstNode(MPPLocals),buffer_NodeID+1(PktBuff)
                                    ;get destination node from frame header
    MOVE.L        toRHA+lapHdSz+ddpSrcNet(MPPLocals),SourceNetAddr
                                    ;source network in high word,
                                    ; source node in low byte
    LSL.W         #8,SourceNetAddr   ;shift source node up to high byte
                                    ; of low word; get source socket
                                    ; from DDP header
    MOVE.B        toRHA+lapHdSz+ddpSrcSkt(MPPLocals),SourceNetAddr
    SUB.W         #ddpType+1,DatagramLength
                                    ;DatagramLength = number of
                                    ; bytes in datagram
    BRA.S         MoveToBuffer

;Determine if there is a checksum.
    TST.W         toRHA+lapHdSz+ddpChecksum(MPPLocals)
                                    ;does packet have checksum?
    BEQ.S         noChecksum

;Calculate checksum for the DDP header.
    MOVE.L        DatagramLength,-(SP);save DatagramLength (D1)
    CLR           D3                 ;set checksum to 0
    MOVEQ         #ddphSzLong-ddpDstNet,D1
                                    ;D1 = length of header part to
                                    ; checksum pointer to destination
                                    ; network number in DDP header
```

```
    LEA         toRHA+lapHdSz+ddpDstNet(MPPLocals),A1
    JSR         SL_DoChksum             ;checksum of DDP header part
                                        ; (D3 holds accumulated
                                        ; checksum)


;Calculate checksum for the data portion of the packet (if any).
    MOVE.L      buffer_Data(PktBuff),A1
                                        ;pointer to datagram
    MOVE.L      (SP)+,DatagramLength
                                        ;restore DatagramLength (D1)
    MOVE.L      DatagramLength,-(SP)
                                        ;save DatagramLength (D1)
                                        ; before calling SL_DoChksum
    BEQ.S       TestChecksum            ;don't checksum datagram if
                                        ; its length = 0
    JSR         SL_DoChksum             ;checksum of DDP datagram part
                                        ; (D3 holds accumulated checksum)


TestChecksum:
    MOVE.L      (SP)+,DatagramLength
                                        ;restore DatagramLength (D1)


;Now make sure the checksum is OK.
    TST.W       D3                      ;is the calculated value 0?
    BNE.S       NotZero                 ;if nonzero, go and use it
    SUBQ.W      #1,D3                   ;if 0, make it -1


NotZero:
    CMP.W       toRHA+lapHdSz+ddpChecksum(MPPLocals),D3
    BNE.S       ChecksumErr             ;bad checksum
    MOVE.W      #0,buffer_CheckSum(A0)
                                        ;no errors
    BRA.S       noChecksum


ChecksumErr:
    MOVE.W      #ckSumErr,buffer_CheckSum(PktBuff)
                                        ;checksum error


noChecksum:
    BRA.S       MoveToBuffer
```

```
;It's a short DDP header.
IsShortHdr:
    MOVE.B      toRHA+lapHdSz+sddpType(MPPLocals),buffer_Type+1(PktBuff)
                                ;get DDP type
    MOVE.B      toRHA+lapDstAdr(MPPLocals),buffer_NodeID+1(PktBuff)
                                ;get destination node from LAP header
    MOVE.B      toRHA+lapSrcAdr(MPPLocals),SourceNetAddr
                                ;get source node from LAP header
    LSL.W       #8,SourceNetAddr    ;shift src node up to high byte of low word
    MOVE.B      toRHA+lapHdSz+sddpSrcSkt(MPPLocals),SourceNetAddr
                                ;get source socket from short DDP header
    SUB.W       #sddpType+1,DatagramLength
                                ;DatagramLength = number of bytes in
                                ; datagram
MoveToBuffer:
    MOVE.L      SourceNetAddr,buffer_Address(PktBuff)
                                ;move source network address into
                                ; PacketBufffer
    MOVE.W      DatagramLength,buffer_ActCount(PktBuff)
                                ;move datagram length into PacketBuffer

;Write the packet into the used queue and
; get another buffer from the free queue for the next packet.
    LEA         used_queue,A1       ;A1 = ^used_queue
    MOVE.L      (A1),A1             ;A1 = used_queue (pointer to usedQ)
    _Enqueue                        ;put the PacketBuffer in the used queue

GetNextBuffer:
    LEA         free_queue,A1       ;A1 = ^free_queue
    MOVE.L      (A1),A1             ;A1 = free_queue (pointer to freeQ)
    LEA         current_qelem,A0    ;copy freeQ.qHead into current_qelem
    MOVE.L      qHead(A1),(A0)
    MOVEA.L     qHead(A1),A0        ;A0 = freeQ.qHead
    _Dequeue

RcvRTS:
    RTS                             ;return to caller
    ENDP
```

Testing for Available Packets

Your client application must include a routine that determines if the socket listener has processed a packet for a socket associated with your client application. If it has, your client application routine must itself read and process the packet's contents, which are made available by the socket listener.

If your client application includes several processes each with its own socket that use the same socket listener, your client application routine must include a mechanism to scan for packets addressed to specific sockets.

If you expect to receive multiple packets for a specific socket, you should anticipate the possibility that the client application might handle the first packet for a socket before the socket listener processes the second packet for that socket. For example, to prepare for reception of multiple related packets addressed to the same socket, the sample client application's routine could check the socket listener's used queue QHead field for additional packets periodically after it read the first packet.

If you design your socket listener based on the sample one, your client's application should define a sufficient number of packet buffers so that as the client application releases a buffer from the used queue, processes its contents, and then moves that buffer back into the free queue for the socket listener to use, there are always buffers available in the free queue.

Listing 7-7 shows the code that the sample client application uses for this purpose. It periodically checks the QHead element of the socket listener's used queue. When QHead is not NIL, the client application knows that a packet is available for processing.

Listing 7-7   Determining if the socket listener has processed a packet

```
TYPE
    PacketBuffer = RECORD
        qLink: QElemPtr;
        qType: Integer;
        buffer_Type: Integer;
        buffer_NodeID: Integer;
        buffer_Address: AddrBlock;
        buffer_Hops: Integer;
        buffer_ActCount: Integer;
        buffer_CheckSum: OSErr;
        buffer_Data: ARRAY[1..ddpMaxData] OF SignedByte;
END;
PacketPtr = ^PacketBuffer;


VAR
    freeQ, usedQ: QHdr;
    bufPtr : PacketPtr;
```

```
            •
            •
            •
    WHILE (usedQ.QHead <> nil) DO
        BEGIN
            bufPtr := PacketPtr(usedQ.QHead); {get the packet ptr}
            IF (Dequeue(QElemPtr(bufPtr), @usedQ) <> noErr) THEN
                BEGIN
                                              {process the packet information}
                Enqueue(QElemPtr(bufPtr), @freeQ);
                                              {requeue the packet buffer for use}
        END
            ELSE
                BEGIN
                    {Error occurred dequeueing packet - perform error }
                    { processing here. However, because this is the only }
                    { place in the code where buffers are dequeued, your error }
                    { code should never be called. You can include a debugging }
                    { statement here.}
        END;
END;
```

Measuring Packet-Delivery Performance

You use the AppleTalk Echo Protocol (AEP) to measure the performance of an AppleTalk network. Knowing the approximate speed at which an AppleTalk internet delivers packets is helpful in tuning the behavior of an application that uses one of the higher-level AppleTalk protocols, such as ATP and ADSP. You can also use AEP to test whether a node is on the network.

To tune an application, you need to know the round-trip time of a packet between two nodes on an AppleTalk internet. This is dependent on such factors as the network configuration, the number of routers and bridges that a packet must traverse, and the amount of traffic on the network; as these change, so does the packet transmission time. Routines belonging to the interfaces of both ATP and ADSP let you specify retry count and interval numbers whose optimum values you can better assess if you know the average round-trip time of a packet on your application's network.

AEP is implemented in each node as a DDP client process referred to as the **AEP Echoer.** The AEP Echoer uses a statically assigned socket, socket number 4, known as the **echoer socket.** The AEP Echoer listens for packets received through this socket.

Whenever it receives a packet, the AEP Echoer examines the packet's protocol type field to determine if the packet is an AEP packet, indicated by a value of 4. If it is, the first byte of the data portion of the packet serves as a function field. AEP uses two function codes:

- A value of 1 identifies the packet as an Echo Request packet.

- A value of 2 identifies the packet as an Echo Reply packet.

The AEP Echoer sets this field to a value of 2 to indicate that the packet is now a reply packet, then it calls DDP to send a copy of the packet back to the socket from which it originated. The AEP packet that you send is referred to as an **Echo Request packet;** the modified AEP packet that the AEP Echoer sends back to you is referred to as an **Echo Reply packet.**

Here are some general guidelines that you should follow in using the AEP Echoer:

- Use the maximum packet size that you plan on using in your application.

- To test if a node is on the network, send several packets to that node because DDP can sometimes drop a packet.

- To test packet-delivery performance, send more than one packet and calculate the average round-trip time.

  Typically, you should receive an Echo Reply packet within a few milliseconds. If you do not get a response after about 10 seconds, you can assume that DDP dropped or lost your Echo Request packet, and you should resend the packet.

  The Echo Reply packet contains the same data that you sent in the Echo Request packet. If you send multiple packets to determine an average turnaround time and to compensate for the possibility of lost or dropped packets, you should include different data in the data portion of each packet; this will allow you to distinguish between replies to different request packets in the event that some replies are not delivered in the same order that you sent them or that some packets are dropped.

- To test packet-delivery performance time, your socket listener can include a field in its packet buffer record that saves the time in ticks when you sent the packet to compare against the response time.

- Accept only packets from the target node. Use your socket listener to filter out packets from nodes other than the target node to which you sent the Echo Request packet.

Follow these steps to send a packet to a target node and have AEP echo that packet back to your socket listener:

1. Write a socket listener to be used to receive an Echo Reply packet back from the target node to which you are sending the Echo Request packet.

   The AEP Echoer will send the Echo Reply packet to the socket from which you send the Echo Request packet. Follow the general instructions described earlier in this chapter that explain how to write a socket listener.

2. Call the POpenSkt function to open a socket from which to send an Echo Request packet, and assign your socket listener to that socket.

3. Determine the internet address of the target node to which you want to send an Echo Request packet.

You can use the Name-Binding Protocol (NBP) to get the address of the destination application for which you want to measure round-trip packet delivery, and substitute the socket ID of the AEP Echoer; the socket number of the AEP Echoer is always 4 on every node. NBP routines are described in the chapter "Name-Binding Protocol (NBP)" in this book.

4. Prepare the datagram to be sent to the AEP Echoer on the target node by building a write-data structure with specific values for certain fields. You can use the `BuildDDPwds` procedure for this purpose.

Set the destination socket number equal to 4 to indicate that it's the Echoer socket; set the DDP protocol type field also equal to 4 to indicate that the packet belongs to the AEP implementation on the target node; set the first byte of the data portion equal to 1 to indicate that this is an Echo Request packet. Fill in the destination network number and node ID for the target system; these are the numbers that NBP returned to you (see the preceding step).

5. Call the `PWriteDDP` function to send the Echo Request to the target node. As the value of the `wdsPointer parameter`, specify the pointer to the write data structure that you created.

DDP Reference

This section describes the data structures and routines that are specific to DDP. The "Data Structures" section shows the Pascal data structures for the records and parameter block that functions use for the protocol interface. The "Routines" section describes the DDP routines.

Data Structures

This section describes the data structures that you use to provide information to and receive it from DDP. It includes

- the write-data structure
- the address block record
- the MPP parameter block

The Write-Data Structure

A write-data structure is of type `WDSElement` and contains a series of pairs of length words and pointers. Each pair indicates the length and location of a portion of the data, including the header information, that constitutes the packet to be sent over the network.

You pass the `PWriteDDP` function a pointer to a write-data structure to send a DDP packet to another socket. You can use the `BuildDDPwds` procedure described on page 7-42 to create a write-data structure.

```
TYPE  WDSElement =
RECORD
    entryLength:   Integer;
    entryPtr:      Ptr;
END;
```

Field descriptions

entryLength   The length of the data pointed to by `entryPtr`.

entryPtr   A pointer to the DDP packet data to be sent using the `PWriteDDP` function.

The Address Block Record

The address block record defines a data structure of `AddrBlock` type. The `destAddress` parameter of the `BuildDDPwds` procedure takes an AppleTalk internet address value specified in this format.

You use NBP routines to get the address of an application that is registered with NBP. For more information about these routines, see the chapter "Name-Binding Protocol (NBP)" in this book.

```
TYPE AddrBlock =
PACKED RECORD
    aNet:      Integer;     {network number}
    aNode:     Byte;        {node ID}
    aSocket:   Byte;        {socket number}
END;
```

Field descriptions

aNet   The number of the network to which the node belongs that is running the DDP client application whose address you are specifying.

aNode   The node ID of the machine running the DDP client application whose address you are specifying.

aSocket   The number of the socket used for the DDP client application.

MPP Parameter Block

The DDP POpenSkt, PCloseSkt, and PWriteDDP functions use the following variant record of the MPP parameter block, defined by the MPPParamBlock data type, to pass information to and receive it from the .MPP driver.

This section defines the fields that are common to all of the DDP functions that use the MPP parameter block. (The BuildDDPwds procedure does not use the MPP parameter block.) The fields that are used for specific functions only are defined in the descriptions of the functions to which they apply. This section does not define reserved fields, which are used either internally by the .MPP driver or not at all.

```
TYPE MPPParamBlock =
PACKED RECORD
    qLink:              QElemPtr;      {reserved}
    qType:              Integer;       {reserved}
    ioTrap:             Integer;       {reserved}
    ioCmdAddr:          Ptr;           {reserved}
    ioCompletion:       ProcPtr;       {completion routine}
    ioResult:           OSErr;         {result code}
    ioNamePtr:          StringPtr;     {reserved}
    ioVRefNum:          Integer;       {reserved}
    ioRefNum:           Integer;       {driver reference number}
    csCode:             Integer;       {primary command code}
    CASE MPPParmType OF
        OpenSktParm,
        CloseSktParm,
        WriteDDPParm:
        (
            socket:         Byte;      {socket number}
            checksumFlag:   Byte;      {checksum flag}
            listener:       Ptr;       {For POpenSkt, pointer to socket }
                                       { listener routine. For PWriteDDP, }
                                       { pointer to write-data structure.}
```

Field descriptions

ioCompletion   A pointer to a completion routine that you can provide. When you execute the POpenSkt function asynchronously, DDP calls your completion routine when it completes execution of the function. Specify NIL for this field if you do not wish to provide a completion routine. If you execute the POpenSkt function synchronously, it ignores the ioCompletion field.

ioResult   The result of the function. When you execute the function asynchronously, the function sets this field to 1 and returns a function result of noErr as soon as the function begins execution. When the function completes execution, it sets the ioResult field to the actual result code.

ioRefNum	The .MPP driver reference number. The MPW interface fills in this field.
csCode	The command code of the MPP command to be executed. The MPW interface fills in this field.
socket	The number of the socket to be opened, closed, or from which to send data.

Routines

This section describes these DDP interface routines:

- the POpenSkt function that you use to open a DDP socket

- the PCloseSkt function that you use to close a socket that you opened with the POpenSkt function

- the PWriteDDP function that you use to send a datagram to another socket

- the BuildDDPwds procedure that you use to create a data structure to hold the header and data information that you want DDP to send

You pass parameters to and receive them from DDP in the fields of the parameter block whose pointer you pass directly to the routine that you call. An arrow preceding each parameter indicates whether it is an input parameter, an output parameter, or both:

Arrow	Meaning
→	Input
←	Output
↔	Both

Opening and Closing DDP Sockets

DDP delivers datagrams from socket to socket. You must open a socket before you use DDP to send or receive a DDP datagram.

- You use the POpenSkt function to open a DDP socket and associate your socket listener with it.

- You use the PCloseSkt function to close a socket that you opened with the POpenSkt function.

To receive a DDP datagram from another socket, you must provide a socket listener to receive packets and your own routine to read the data. When you open a socket, you specify a pointer to the socket listener for that socket.

Datagram Delivery Protocol (DDP)

POpenSkt

The POpenSkt function opens a socket for your application to use, and it adds that socket to the socket table along with a pointer to the socket listener that you provide.

```
FUNCTION POpenSkt (thePBptr: MPPPBPtr; async: Boolean): OSErr;
```

thePBptr   A pointer to an MPP parameter block.

async   A Boolean that specifies whether or not the function should be executed asynchronously. Specify TRUE for asynchronous execution.

Parameter block

→	ioCompletion	ProcPtr	A pointer to completion routine.
←	ioResult	OSErr	The result code.
→	csCode	Integer	Always openSkt for this function.
↔	socket	Byte	The socket number.
→	listener	Ptr	A pointer to socket listener.

Field descriptions

socket   The number of the socket you wish to open. Specify 0 for this field to have DDP assign a socket number in the range 128 through 254 and return it in this field. Socket numbers 1 through 63 are reserved for use by Apple Computer, Inc. You can use socket numbers 64 through 127 for this field during program development; however, it is recommended that you not use these numbers in a commercial product as there is no mechanism for resolving conflicts in the case that someone else uses the same socket number.

listener   Pointer to a socket listener that you provide. You cannot specify NIL for this field. See "A Sample Socket Listener" beginning on page 7-20 for information on writing a socket listener.

DESCRIPTION

The POpenSkt function opens a DDP socket and associates that socket with the socket listener whose pointer you specify. If you specify 0 for the socket field, DDP dynamically assigns a socket, which it opens, and DDP returns the number of that socket to you.

Alternatively, you can specify a socket number as the value of the socket field. The POpenSkt function returns a result code of ddpSktErr if any of the following conditions is true:

■ You specify the number of an already open socket.

■ You pass a socket number greater than 127.

■ The socket table is full.

The POpenSkt function is equivalent to calling the PBControl function with a value of openSkt in the csCode field of the parameter block.

7-38   DDP Reference

You must provide a socket listener when you call the POpenSkt function. If you do not intend to listen for DDP datagrams through the socket you open with this function, you can provide a socket listener that does nothing but immediately return control to DDP.

DDP reads the destination socket address and delivers datagrams to the socket listener associated with the socket. The socket listener can be part of a DDP client application or a higher-level AppleTalk protocol that is also a client of DDP.

If you want a process using a socket to be visible to other processes using the AppleTalk network, use the NBP PRegisterName function to register the name that is associated with the socket and address of the process. See the chapter "Name-Binding Protocol (NBP)" in this book for more information about NBP.

SPECIAL CONSIDERATIONS

You cannot specify NIL for the listener parameter; if you do so, your application will crash and the computer on which it is running will hang.

ASSEMBLY-LANGUAGE INFORMATION

To execute the POpenSkt function from assembly language, call the _Control trap macro with a value of openSkt in the csCode field of the parameter block. You must also specify the .MPP driver reference number. To execute the _Control trap asynchronously, include the value ,ASYNC in the operand field.

RESULT CODES

noErr	0	No error
ddpSktErr	–91	Bad socket number or socket table is full

SEE ALSO

For information about how to use the POpenSkt function in sequence with other routines to send and receive data over an AppleTalk network, see "Sending and Receiving Data: An Overview" beginning on page 7-9.

PCloseSkt

The PCloseSkt function removes the entry for a specific socket from the socket table.

```
FUNCTION PCloseSkt (thePBptr: MPPPBPtr; async: Boolean): OSErr;
```

thePBptr   A pointer to an MPP parameter block.

async   A Boolean that specifies whether or not the function should be executed asynchronously. Specify TRUE for asynchronous execution.

Parameter block

→	ioCompletion	ProcPtr	A completion routine.
←	ioResult	OSErr	The result code.
→	csCode	Integer	Always closeSkt for this function.
→	socket	Byte	The number of the socket to close.

Field descriptions

socket   The number of the socket you wish to close. You cannot use 0 for this field.

DESCRIPTION

Use the PCloseSkt function to close a socket that you opened with the POpenSkt function. The PCloseSkt function returns a result code of ddpSktErr if you specify a socket number of 0 or if there is no open socket with the socket number you specify.

The PCloseSkt function is equivalent to calling the PBControl function with a value of closeSkt in the csCode field of the parameter block.

ASSEMBLY-LANGUAGE INFORMATION

To execute the PCloseSkt function from assembly language, call the _Control trap macro with a value of closeSkt in the csCode field of the parameter block. You must also specify the .MPP driver reference number. To execute the _Control trap asynchronously, include the value ,ASYNC in the operand field.

RESULT CODES

noErr	0	No error
ddpSktErr	–91	Bad socket number

SEE ALSO

For information on the assignment of socket numbers, see "POpenSkt" beginning on page 7-38.

Sending DDP Datagrams

To send a DDP datagram to another socket, you must first open a socket with the POpenSkt function, prepare a write-data structure, and finally send the packet using the PWriteDDP function described in this section. You can use the BuildDDPwds procedure described in this section to create the write-data structure.

PWriteDDP

The PWriteDDP function sends a DDP datagram to another socket.

```
FUNCTION PWriteDDP (thePBptr: MPPPBPtr; async: Boolean): OSErr;
```

thePBptr   A pointer to an MPP parameter block.

async   A Boolean that specifies whether the function should be executed
             asynchronously. Specify TRUE for asynchronous execution.

Parameter block

→	ioCompletion	ProcPtr	A completion routine.
←	ioResult	OSErr	The result code.
→	csCode	Integer	Always writeDDP for this function.
→	socket	Byte	The number of socket to send data from.
→	checksumFlag	Byte	The checksum flag; nonzero to compute checksum.
→	wdsPointer	Ptr	A pointer to write-data structure.

Field descriptions

socket   The number of the socket from which you want to send data. See
               the description of the POpenSkt function for information on the
               assignment of socket numbers.

checksumFlag   The checksum flag. If you set this field to a nonzero value and if
               DDP uses a long header for the datagram (that is, if the destination
               socket has a network number different from that of the source
               socket), then the PWriteDDP function calculates a checksum for the
               datagram and includes it in the datagram header. Set this field to 0
               if you do not want the PWriteDDP function to calculate a checksum.

wdsPointer   A pointer to a write-data structure. The write-data structure
               provides the destination address and the data for the datagram.
               The DDP write-data structure is described in "Creating a DDP
               Write-Data Structure" on page 7-12.

DESCRIPTION

Before you call the PWriteDDP function, you must prepare a write-data structure.
The write-data structure, shown in Figure 7-4 on page 7-13, includes a pointer to the
destination address and pointers to buffers containing the data you wish to send.
You can use the BuildDDPwds procedure to build a write-data structure.

Set the checksum flag field when you call the PWriteDDP function to have the function
calculate the checksum and include it in the packet header. Note, however, that only
long packet headers include a checksum field, and that whether the checksum is used
for error checking depends on how the socket listener code at the destination socket is
implemented.

The PWriteDDP function is equivalent to calling the PBControl function with a value
of writeDDP in the csCode field of the parameter block.

SPECIAL CONSIDERATIONS

Memory used for the write-data structure belongs to DDP and must be nonrelocatable until the `PWriteDDP` function completes execution, after which you can either reuse the memory or release it.

ASSEMBLY-LANGUAGE INFORMATION

To execute the `PWriteDDP` function from assembly language, call the `_Control` trap macro with a value of `writeDDP` in the `csCode` field of the parameter block. You must also specify the .MPP driver reference number. To execute the `_Control` trap asynchronously, include the value `,ASYNC` in the operand field.

RESULT CODES

noErr	0	No error
ddpSktErr	–91	Bad socket number
ddpLenErr	–92	Datagram data exceeds 586 bytes
noBridgeErr	–93	Could not find router to forward packet

SEE ALSO

For a description of the DDP write-data structure, see "Creating a DDP Write-Data Structure" on page 7-12.

If you are programming in Pascal or C, see the description of the `BuildDDPwds` procedure that follows for help in creating a write-data structure.

BuildDDPwds

The `BuildDDPwds` procedure creates a write-data structure that you can use to send a DDP packet to a remote socket.

```
PROCEDURE BuildDDPwds (wdsPtr,headerPtr,dataPtr: Ptr;
                       destAddress: AddrBlock; DDPType: Integer;
                       dataLen: Integer);
```

wdsPtr   A pointer to a buffer that you provide that will contain the write-data structure. The write-data structure created by `BuildDDPwds` is 14 bytes long.

headerPtr   A pointer to a buffer that you provide that will contain the packet header. This buffer must be at least 17 bytes long.

dataPtr   A pointer to the data that you want to send. The maximum amount of data that you can include in a DDP data packet is 586 bytes.

destAddress

The address of the socket to which you want to send the data. The address consists of the network number, the node ID, and the socket number in `AddrBlock` format; see "The Address Block Record" on page 7-35.

A node ID of 255 is the broadcast address; that is, the datagram is broadcast to all nodes in the network. Note, however, that broadcast datagrams are not forwarded by routers and so are not sent to nodes on other networks in the internet.

DDPType   The DDP protocol type of the packet you are sending. DDP protocol types 1 through 15 are reserved for use by Apple Computer, Inc. You can use other protocol types as you see fit.

dataLen   The length of the data pointed to by the `dataPtr` parameter.

DESCRIPTION

The `BuildDDPwds` procedure creates a write-data structure that consists of a pointer for the header, a length word and pointer for the data, and a terminating 0 word. Because the first pointer in the write-data structure must point to an odd address, it is difficult to use Pascal to create a write-data structure. In this case, using the `BuildDDPwds` procedure simplifies the process. However, the `BuildDDPwds` procedure assumes that the data that you are sending is in a single block. In most cases, if you are using DDP directly to send data across a network, a single block of data should be adequate.

You must provide a 17-byte buffer for the header block, a 14-byte buffer to hold the write-data structure, and a pointer to the data you want to send. (The header block is only 16 bytes, but because it begins on an odd address, the first byte is not used.)

SPECIAL CONSIDERATIONS

Memory that you allocate for the write-data structure buffers belongs to DDP and must be nonrelocatable until the `PWriteDDP` function completes execution, after which you can either reuse the memory or release it.

ASSEMBLY-LANGUAGE INFORMATION

The `BuildDDPwds` procedure is implemented entirely in the MPW interface files. There is no assembly-language equivalent to this procedure.

SEE ALSO

The write-data structure is defined in "Creating a DDP Write-Data Structure" on page 7-12.

To send the data pointed to by your write-data structure, use the `PWriteDDP` function described on page 7-41.

Summary of DDP

Pascal Summary

Constants

```
CONST
   {.MPP driver unit and reference numbers}
   mppUnitNum      =      9;          {MPP unit number}
   mppRefNum       =    -10;          {MPP reference number}

   {csCodes}
   writeDDP        =    246;          {write out DDP packet, csCode}
   closeSkt        =    247;          {close DDP socket, csCode}
   openSkt         =    248;          {open DDP socket, csCode}
```

Data Types

The Write-Data Structure

```
TYPE  WDSElement =
   RECORD
      entryLength:    Integer;
      entryPtr:       Ptr;
   END;
```

The Address Block Record

```
TYPE AddrBlock =
   PACKED RECORD
      aNet:        Integer;     {network number}
      aNode:       Byte;        {node ID}
      aSocket:     Byte;        {socket number}
   END;
```

MPP Parameter Block

```
MPPParmType = (...OpenSktParm,CloseSktParm,WriteDDPParm ...)

TYPE MPPParamBlock =
    PACKED RECORD
        qLink:              QElemPtr;       {reserved}
        qType:              Integer;        {reserved}
        ioTrap:             Integer;        {reserved}
        ioCmdAddr:          Ptr;            {reserved}
        ioCompletion:       ProcPtr;        {completion routine}
        ioResult:           OSErr;          {result code}
        ioNamePtr:          StringPtr;      {reserved}
        ioVRefNum:          Integer;        {reserved}
        ioRefNum:           Integer;        {driver reference number}
        csCode:             Integer;        {command code}
        CASE MPPParmType OF
            OpenSktParm,
            CloseSktParm,
            WriteDDPParm:
            (
                socket:         Byte;       {socket number}
                checksumFlag:   Byte;       {checksum flag}
                listener:       Ptr;        {For POpenSkt, pointer to socket }
                                            { listener routine. For PWriteDDP, }
                                            { pointer to write-data structure.}

            )
    END;

MPPPBPtr = ^MPPParamBlock;
```

Routines

Opening and Closing DDP Sockets

```
FUNCTION POpenSkt          (thePBptr: MPPPBPtr; async: Boolean): OSErr;
FUNCTION PCloseSkt         (thePBptr: MPPPBPtr; async: Boolean): OSErr;
```

Sending DDP Datagrams

```
FUNCTION PWriteDDP         (thePBptr: MPPPBPtr; async: Boolean): OSErr;
PROCEDURE BuildDDPwds      (wdsPtr,headerPtr,dataPtr: Ptr;
                            destAddress: AddrBlock; DDPType: Integer;
                            dataLen: Integer);
```

C Summary

Constants

```
/*DDP parameter constants*/
#define MPPioCompletion MPP.ioCompletion
#define MPPioResult MPP.ioResult
#define MPPioRefNum MPP.ioRefNum
#define MPPcsCode MPP.csCode
#define DDPsocket DDP.socket
#define DDPchecksumFlag DDP.checksumFlag
#define DDPwdsPointer DDP.DDPptrs.wdsPointer
#define DDPlistener DDP.DDPptrs.listener

/*.MPP driver unit and reference number*/
enum {
    mppUnitNum     =        9,           /*MPP unit number*/
    mppRefNum      =      -10            /*MPP reference number*/
};

/*DDP csCodes*/
enum {
    writeDDP       =      246,           /*send DDP packet*/
    closeSkt       =      247,           /*close DDP socket*/
    openSkt        =      248            /*open DDP socket*/
};
```

Data Types

The Write-Data Structure

```
struct    WDSElement {
    short     entryLength;
    Ptr       entryPtr;
} WDSElement;
```

The Address Block Record

```
struct AddrBlock {
    short                 aNet;                   /*network number*/
    unsigned char         aNode;                  /*node ID*/
    unsigned char         aSocket;                /*socket number*/
};

typedef struct AddrBlock AddrBlock;
```

MPP Parameter Block

```
#define MPPATPHeader\
    QElem           *qLink;          /*reserved*/\
    short           qType;           /*reserved*/\
    short           ioTrap;          /*reserved */\
    Ptr             ioCmdAddr;       /*reserved*/\
    ProcPtr         ioCompletion;    /*completion routine*/\
    OSErr           ioResult;        /*result code*/\
    long            ioNameptr;       /*command result (ATP user bytes)*/\
    short           ioVRefNum;       /*request transaction ID*/\
    short           ioRefNum;        /*driver reference number*/\
    short           csCode;          /*command code*/

typedef struct {
   MPPATPHeader
}MPPparms;

union ParamBlockRec {
   MPPparms     MPP;                 /*general MPP parms*/
   DDPparms     DDP;                 /*DDP calls*/
};
typedef MPPParamBlock    *MPPPBtr;

typedef struct {
MPPATPHeader
    char socket;                     /*socket number*/
    char checksumFlag;               /*checksum flag*/
    union {
    Ptr wdsPointer;                  /*pointer to write-data structure*/
    Ptr listener;                    /*pointer to write-data structure or */
                                     /* pointer to socket listener*/
} DDPptrs;
}DDPparms;
```

Routines

Opening and Closing DDP Sockets

```
pascal OSErr POpenSkt       (MPPPBPtr the PBptr, Boolean async);
pascal OSErr PCloseSkt      (MPPPBPtr thePBptr, Boolean async);
```

Sending DDP Datagrams

```
pascal OSErr PWriteDDP        (MPPPBPtr the PBptr, Boolean async);
pascal void BuildDDPwds       (Ptr wdsPtr, header Ptr, Ptr dataPtr,
                               const AddrBlock netAddr, short ddpType,
                               short dataLen);
```

Assembly-Language Summary

Constants

```
mppUnitNum      EQU     9           ;MPP unit number

;csCodes for DDP
writeDDP        EQU     246         ;write out DDP packet
closeSkt        EQU     247         ;close DDP socket
openSkt         EQU     248         ;open DDP socket

;long DDP packet header
ddpHopCnt       EQU     0           ;hop count (byte)
ddpLength       EQU     0           ;packet length (word)
ddpChecksum     EQU     2           ;checksum (word)
ddpDstNet       EQU     4           ;destination network number (word)
ddpSrcNet       EQU     6           ;source network number (word)
ddpDstNode      EQU     8           ;destination node address (byte)
ddpSrcNode      EQU     9           ;source node address (byte)
ddpDstSkt       EQU     10          ;destination socket number (byte)
ddpSrcSkt       EQU     11          ;source socket number (byte)
ddpType         EQU     12          ;DDP protocol type field (byte)

;short DDP packet header
sddpDstSkt      EQU     2           ;destination socket number (byte)
sddpSrcSkt      EQU     3           ;source socket number (byte)
sddpType        EQU     4           ;DDP protocol type field (byte)

;DDP long header size
ddphSzLong      EQU     13          ;size of extended DDP header

DDP short header size
ddphSzShort     EQU     5           ;size of short DDP header

shortDDP        EQU     $01         ;LAP type code for DDP (short header)
longDDP         EQU     $02         ;LAP type code for DDP (long header)
```

```
;DDP miscellaneous
ddpMaxWKS       EQU      $7F       ;highest valid well-known socket
ddpMaxData      EQU      586       ;maximum DDP data size
ddpLenMask      EQU      $03FF     ;mask for DDP length
rhaSize         EQU      $18       ;size of read-header area
toRHA           EQU      1         ;top of the read-header area

wdsEntrySz      EQU      6         ;size of a write-data structure entry
DDPHopsMask     EQU      $3C00     ;mask hop count bits from field in DDP
                                   ; header

;command codes (csCodes)
writeDDP        EQU      246       ;write out DDP packet
closeSkt        EQU      247       ;close DDP socket
openSkt         EQU      248       ;open DDP socket
```

Data Structures

MPP Parameter Block Common Fields for DDP Routines

0	qLink	long	reserved
4	qType	word	reserved
6	ioTrap	word	reserved
8	ioCmdAddr	long	reserved
12	ioCompletion	long	address of completion routine
16	ioResult	word	result code
18	ioNamePtr	long	reserved
22	ioVRefNum	word	reserved
24	ioRefNum	word	driver reference number

OpenSkt Parameter Variant

26	csCode	word	command code; always openSkt
28	socket	byte	socket number
30	listener	long	pointer to socket listener

CloseSkt Parameter Variant

26	csCode	word	command code; always closeSkt
28	socket	byte	number of socket to be closed

WriteDDP Parameter Variant

26	csCode	word	command code; always writeDDP
28	socket	byte	number of socket to write from
30	listener	long	pointer to write-data structure

Result Codes

`noErr`	0	No error
`ddpSktErr`	–91	Bad socket number or socket table is full
`ddpLenErr`	–92	Datagram data exceeds 586 bytes
`noBridgeErr`	–93	Could not find router to forward packet

AppleTalk Session Protocol (ASP)

Contents

This chapter describes the AppleTalk Session Protocol (ASP) that you can use to establish a session between an ASP workstation application or process and an ASP server application. An ASP session is asymmetrical: all communication is initiated by the ASP workstation and responded to by the ASP server.

ASP provides an application programming interface for the workstation side only. ASP is not commonly used by application program developers. The primary use of ASP is to provide services for the AppleTalk Filing Protocol (AFP) that, in turn, provides all of the services necessary to access an AppleTalk AppleShare server. Most developers who want to write an AppleTalk application that establishes a session use the AppleTalk Data Stream Protocol (ADSP) because it provides peer-to-peer services. For these reasons, this chapter includes "About" and "Reference" sections only; it does not include a "Using" section, as do most of the other chapters in this book. This chapter is included to complete the coverage of the AppleTalk protocol stack in this book.

However, if you want to use ASP to write an application that runs on a workstation and initiates a session with an ASP server, you should read this chapter and the chapter in *Inside AppleTalk,* second edition, that describes the AppleTalk Session Protocol specification.

You can use ASP to open and close a session with an ASP server; you can also send commands and data across the session to the server and receive replies in response. The commands that you send to the ASP server must adhere to the syntax of a higher-level protocol that is built on top of the ASP server. ASP transfers the commands; it does not interpret or execute them.

This chapter does not describe how to implement an ASP server. If you want to implement an ASP server, you must use the programming interface to the AppleTalk Transaction Protocol (ATP) and follow the AppleTalk Session Protocol specification as defined in *Inside AppleTalk,* second edition.

If you want to write an application that supports a peer-to-peer session in which each end of the session can send and receive data at any time, you should use the AppleTalk Data Stream Protocol (ADSP) instead of ASP. The chapter "AppleTalk Data Stream Protocol (ADSP)" in this book describes ADSP.

For an overview of ASP and how it fits within the AppleTalk protocol stack, read the chapter "Introduction to AppleTalk" in this book. "Introduction to AppleTalk" also introduces and defines some of the terminology used in this chapter. Because ASP is built on top of ATP, possessing an understanding of ATP will help you to understand ASP. The chapter "AppleTalk Transaction Protocol (ATP)" in this book describes ATP.

About ASP

The AppleTalk Session Protocol (ASP) allows one or more ASP workstation applications or processes to establish a session with the same server at the same time. To track communication from various sessions, ASP assigns a unique session identifier that is referred to as a **session reference number** to each session. ASP is an *asymmetrical protocol* that provides one set of services to the workstation and a different set of services to the server. The ASP workstation application always initiates the process of setting up a session and the communication across a session, and the ASP server replies to commands that it receives. (ASP is built on top of ATP, and it follows the transaction model of ATP while adding session-connection services.) The only case in which an ASP server can initiate communication is through the ASP attention mechanism. Figure 8-1 shows ASP and its underlying protocols.

Figure 8-1   ASP and its underlying protocols

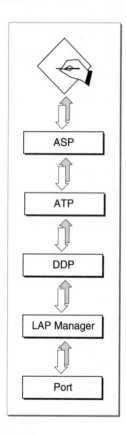

Note

To open a session with an ASP server, you must know the server's internet socket address; you can use the Name-Binding Protocol (NBP) to obtain the internet socket address of any ASP server that advertises its services on the network. ◆

You can open an ASP session and send commands to the ASP server for a higher-level protocol, such as AFP, to interpret and execute. The commands that you send to an ASP server must follow the syntax prescribed by the higher-level protocol that is a client of the ASP server. ASP simply transfers the commands, and the ASP server returns a response.

For example, the AppleShare server is AppleTalk's ASP server implementation. AFP uses the services of ASP to allow a user to manipulate files on an AppleShare server. (AFP is an example of an ASP workstation application.) As long as the ASP session is open, the workstation can send AFP commands to request directory information, change filenames, and so forth.

ASP ensures that commands from a workstation are delivered to the ASP server without duplication in the same order in which they were sent. This feature is useful for implementing applications that are *state dependent*, that is, applications in which the response to a request is dependent on a previous request. A workstation application connecting to a file server to read a file is an example of a state-dependent application: before the application can read the file, it must have first issued a request to open the file.

ASP also provides an attention mechanism that allows the server to send a message to the workstation. For example, a file server can use this messaging system to notify all of the workstations that are using the file server that it is shutting down. ASP is responsible for closing down the session if one end fails or becomes unreachable, and it will inform the workstation applications of its action. The .XPP driver implements ASP.

Once again, if your application requires a session-oriented protocol, you should consider whether to use ADSP instead of ASP. ASP and ADSP have in common the salient feature that they are both session-oriented protocols. However, they each provide a different type of session-oriented service. Although the differences between them are not parallel, in contrasting the two protocols it is helpful to recognize that ASP is limited by the structure of a transaction because it is built on top of ATP and that ADSP entails more flexibility because it is built directly on top of DDP. Figure 8-2 illustrates the different behavior and functions of the two protocols.

Figure 8-2   Differences between ASP and ADSP

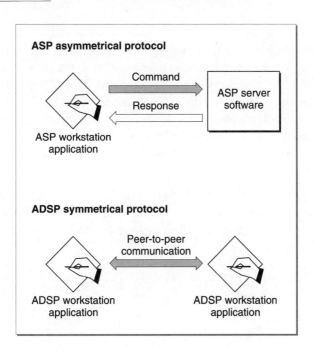

Please read this note before you continue
ASP provides an application programming interface for the workstation side only. The primary use of ASP is to provide services for the AppleTalk Filing Protocol (AFP). In most cases, you will not need to use ASP. Because very few application program developers use ASP, this chapter does not include a "Using" section. It includes only an overview of ASP and an ASP reference section. ◆

ASP Reference

This section describes the data structures and routines that are specific to the AppleTalk Session Protocol (ASP).

The "Data Structures" section shows the Pascal data structure for the XPP parameter block for ASP. The "Routines" section describes the routines for opening an ASP session, closing a specific ASP session or all ASP sessions on your node, sending commands and data across a session to a server, obtaining information about ASP sessions on your node or about a server, and canceling a request to open a session.

Data Structures

This section describes the XPP parameter block that ASP functions use to pass information to and receive it from the .XPP driver.

XPP Parameter Block for ASP

The ASP functions use the XPP parameter block defined by the `XPPParamBlock` data type to pass input and receive output parameters. In addition to the standard XPP parameter block fields, the ASP functions use variant records. The `ASPOpenSession` function uses the `ASPOpenPrm` variant record. The `ASPAbortOS` function uses the `ASPAbortPrm` variant record. The `ASPGetParms` function uses the `ASPSizeBlk` variant record. The `ASPUserCommand` and `ASPUserWrite` functions uses the `ASPSubPrm` variant record. The `ASPUserWrite`, `ASPUserCommand`, and `ASPGetStatus` functions use the `ASPEndPrm` variant record.

This section defines the parameter block fields that are common to all ASP functions. It does not define reserved fields, which are used either internally by the .XPP driver or not at all. The fields that are used by a particular function are defined in the section that describes the function.

```
XPPPrmBlkType = (...XPPPrmBlk,ASPAbortPrm,ASPSizeBlk...);
XPPSubPrmType = (ASPOpenPrm,ASPSubPrm);
XPPEndPrmType = (...ASPEndPrm);
```

```
XPPParamBlock = PACKED RECORD
    qLink:              QElemPtr;           {reserved}
    qType:              Integer;            {reserved}
    ioTrap:             Integer;            {reserved}
    ioCmdAddr:          Ptr;                {reserved}
    ioCompletion:       ProcPtr;            {completion routine}
    ioResult:           OSErr;              {result code}
    cmdResult:          LongInt;            {command result (ATP user bytes)}
    ioVRefNum:          Integer;            {reserved}
    ioRefNum:           Integer;            {driver reference number}
    csCode:             Integer;            {call command code}
    CASE XPPPrmBlkType OF
    ASPAbortPrm:
        (abortSCBPtr: Ptr);                 {SCB pointer for AbortOS}
    ASPSizeBlk:
        (aspMaxCmdSize: Integer;            {for ASPGetParms}
         aspQuantumSize: Integer;           {for ASPGetParms}
         numSesss: Integer);                {for SPGetParms}
    XPPPrmBlk:
        (sessRefnum: Integer;               {offset to session refnum}
         aspTimeout: Byte;                  {timeout for ATP}
         aspRetry: Byte;                    {retry count for ATP}
    CASE XPPSubPrmType OF
    ASPOpenPrm:
        (serverAddr: AddrBlock;             {server address block}
         scbPointer: Ptr;                   {SCB pointer}
         attnRoutine: Ptr);                 {attention routine pointer}
    ASPSubPrm:
        (cbSize: Integer;                   {command block size}
         cbPtr: Ptr;                        {command block pointer}
         rbSize: Integer;                   {reply buffer size}
         rbPtr: Ptr;                        {reply buffer pointer}
    CASE XPPEndPrmType OF
    ASPEndPrm:
        (wdSize: Integer;                   {write data size}
         wdPtr: Ptr;                        {write data pointer}
         ccbStart: ARRAY[0..295] OF Byte))); {beginning of command control }
                                             { block}
    END;
XPPParmBlkPtr = ^XPPParamBlock;
```

Field descriptions

`ioCompletion`	A pointer to a completion routine that you can provide. When you execute a function asynchronously, AppleTalk calls your completion routine when it completes execution of the function if you specify a pointer to the routine as the value of this field. Specify `NIL` for this field if you do not wish to provide a completion routine. If you execute a function synchronously, AppleTalk ignores the `ioCompletion` field. For information about completion routines, see the chapter "Introduction to AppleTalk" in this book.
`ioResult`	The result of the function. When you execute the function asynchronously, the function sets this field to 1 and returns a function result of `noErr` as soon as the function begins execution. When the function completes execution, it sets the `ioResult` field to the actual result code.
`ioRefNum`	The driver reference number for the .XPP driver. The Device Manager's `OpenDriver` function that you use to open the .XPP driver returns the driver reference number in the `refnum` field. You must supply this value. You can call this function to obtain the .XPP driver's reference number even if the .XPP driver is already open. The MPW interface does not fill in this value. For information on opening the .XPP driver, see the chapter "AppleTalk Utilities" in this book. For information on the `OpenDriver` function, see the chapter "Device Manager" in *Inside Macintosh: Devices*.
`csCode`	The command code of the XPP command to be executed. The MPW interface fills in this field.

Routines

This section describes the ASP functions that you use to

- open an ASP session from an ASP workstation application or process

- close one or all ASP sessions for a workstation from your ASP workstation application or process

- send commands and data across the session from the workstation to the server

- obtain information about the maximum capacities of the ASP implementation on your node, such as the number of concurrent ASP sessions and the amount of data that you can send

- obtain status information about a server without establishing a session with that server

Before you can open an ASP session or call any of the ASP functions, you must open the .XPP driver. You use the Device Manager's `OpenDriver` function to open the .XPP driver. The .MPP and .ATP drivers must be open before you open the .XPP driver. For information on opening the .XPP driver, see the chapter "AppleTalk Utilities" in this book. For information on the `OpenDriver` function, see the chapter "Device Manager" in *Inside Macintosh: Devices*.

The chapter "AppleTalk Utilities" also describes how to close the .XPP driver. However, in most circumstances, you should not close the .XPP driver because other applications and processes could be using the protocols implemented by the .XPP driver.

You must pass the .XPP driver reference number as a parameter to each of the ASP functions; the MPW interface does not fill in this value. The OpenDriver function that you use to open the .XPP driver returns the driver reference number in the refnum field. You can call this function to obtain the .XPP driver's reference number even if the .XPP driver is already open.

An arrow preceding a parameter indicates whether the parameter is an input parameter, an output parameter, or both:

Arrow	Meaning
→	Input
←	Output
↔	Both

Opening and Closing ASP Sessions

This section describes how to open and close an ASP session from your workstation application or process. It includes

■ the ASPOpenSession function that you use to open a session with a server

■ the ASPCloseSession function that you use to close a single session when you are finished using the connection

■ the ASPCloseAll function that you use to close all of the ASP sessions running on your node

ASPOpenSession

The ASPOpenSession function opens an ASP session between an ASP workstation application and an ASP server application.

```
FUNCTION ASPOpenSession (thePBptr: XPPParmBlkPtr;
                         async: Boolean): OSErr;
```

thePBptr   A pointer to an XPP parameter block.

async   A Boolean that specifies whether the function should be executed asynchronously or synchronously. Specify TRUE for asynchronous execution.

Parameter block

→	`ioCompletion`	`ProcPtr`	A pointer to a completion routine.
←	`ioResult`	`OSErr`	The function result.
→	`ioRefNum`	`Integer`	The .XPP driver reference number.
→	`csCode`	`Integer`	Always `openSess` for this function.
←	`sessRefnum`	`Integer`	The session reference number.
→	`aspTimeout`	`Byte`	The retry interval in seconds.
→	`aspRetry`	`Byte`	The number of retries.
→	`serverAddr`	`AddrBlock`	The server socket address.
→	`scbPointer`	`Ptr`	A pointer to the session control block.
→	`attnRoutine`	`Ptr`	A pointer to an attention routine.

Field descriptions

`sessRefnum`
A unique number that the .XPP driver assigns to the session that it opens if the function completes successfully.

`aspTimeout`
The interval in seconds between retries of the open session request.

`aspRetry`
The number of times that ASP will retry to open a session.

`serverAddr`
The internet socket address of the socket that the server is using to listen for requests to open a session.

`scbPointer`
A pointer to a session control block (SCB) that the .XPP driver requires to maintain an open session. The `scbMemSize` constant defines the size of the session control block. The memory that you allocate for the SCB must be nonrelocatable or locked because it belongs to the .XPP driver for the life of the session.

`attnRoutine`
A pointer to a routine that ASP calls if the workstation component of ASP receives an attention request from the server or if the session is closed. If you do not want to specify an attention routine to be called, set this pointer to NIL.

DESCRIPTION

To gain access to an ASP server, you must call the `ASPOpenSession` function to open a session. Before calling the `ASPOpenSession` function, you must obtain the internet socket address of the socket that the ASP server uses to listen for incoming session requests. The server uses a session listening socket (SLS) for this purpose. You can use the Name-Binding Protocol (NBP) to get the internet socket address of an SLS. You pass the internet socket address of the SLS as the value of the `serverAddr` parameter.

You also pass the `ASPOpenSession` function a pointer to a session control block (SCB) in the `scbPointer` parameter. The .XPP driver uses the SCB internally to manage the session. Each session requires its own SCB. You must either allocate nonrelocatable memory for the session control block or lock the memory and not modify it for the duration of the session. The SCB size is defined by the constant `scbMemSize`. The memory belongs to the .XPP driver for the life of the session. You can reuse an SCB after either of the following events occurs:

■ You have called the `ASPCloseSession` function to close the session and it has completed successfully.

■ The server end of the ASP session has closed the session or the .XPP driver has closed the session. In both cases, the .XPP driver returns an `aspParamErr` result code as the result of a call for that session.

You can also pass the `ASPOpenSession` function a pointer to an attention routine that the .XPP driver calls when it receives an attention request from the server and when the session is closing. ASP provides an attention mechanism that allows the ASP server to notify the ASP workstation application of some event or critical piece of information. As the value of the `attnRoutine` parameter, you can specify a pointer to your attention routine, and the .XPP driver will call this routine when it receives an attention request from the server or when the server, the workstation, or ASP closes the session; ASP, as implemented in the .XPP driver, will close a session if it cannot successfully open the session before it exhausts the number of retries.

Because the .XPP driver calls your attention routine at interrupt level, you must observe the following interrupt conventions in writing the attention routine:

■ An attention routine can change registers A0 through A3 and D0 through D3.

■ The routine must not call any Memory Manager routines.

The .XPP driver calls your attention routine with

■ D0 (word) equal to the session reference number (`sessRefnum`) for that session. This is the number that ASP returns on completion of the `ASPOpenSession` function.

■ D1 (word) equal to the attention bytes passed by the server or 0 if the session is closing.

To resume normal execution, your attention routine must return with an RTS (return from subroutine) instruction.

If you code your program in a high-level language such as Pascal, you might not want to provide an attention routine written in assembly language. If you do not want to provide an attention routine, you can poll the attention bytes to determine if your ASP workstation application has received an attention request from the server. The attention bytes are the first 2 bytes of the session control block. When the .XPP driver receives an `ASPOpenSession` function call, it sets these 2 bytes to 0. When the server sends an attention request to the workstation, the .XPP driver receives the request and sets the first 2 bytes of the SCB to the attention bytes from the packet. (A higher-level protocol that uses the services of ASP defines the attention code that the 2 attention bytes in the packet carry.) If the first 2 bytes of the SCB are nonzero when your Pascal program polls them, the program will know that it has received an attention request from the server. Your program can handle the request, based on the conventions defined by the higher-level protocol, and reset the SCB's attention bytes to 0. However, using this method to determine if the workstation has received an attention request from the server has limitations: two or more attention requests could be received between successive polls and only the last one would be preserved.

When the .XPP driver receives an `ASPOpenSession` function, it sends a special open session (`OpenSession`) packet as an ATP request to the SLS; this packet carries the address of the socket that the ASP workstation application or process is using for the session. The open session packet also carries a version number so that both ends can verify that they are using the same version of ASP.

AppleTalk Session Protocol (ASP)

Once you open a session, you can send commands and data to the server and receive command replies from the server. However, before you open an ASP session, you should call the `ASPGetParms` function to determine the maximum sizes of commands and replies that ASP supports on your node.

SPECIAL CONSIDERATIONS

Note that you must provide the .XPP driver reference number as an input parameter to this function. You can obtain the driver reference number by calling the Device Manager's `OpenDriver` function.

ASSEMBLY-LANGUAGE INFORMATION

To execute the `ASPOpenSession` function from assembly language, call the `_Control` trap macro with a value of `openSess` in the `csCode` field of the parameter block. You must also specify the .XPP driver reference number. To execute the `_Control` trap asynchronously, include the value `,ASYNC` in the operand field.

RESULT CODES

aspBadVersNum	−1066	The server cannot support the ASP version number
aspNoMoreSess	−1068	The .XPP driver cannot support another ASP session (the number of sessions that the driver is capable of supporting is dependent on the machine type)
aspNoServers	−1069	There is no server at the specified `serverAddr` address, or the server did not respond to the request
aspParamErr	−1070	You specified an invalid session reference number, or the session has been closed
aspServerBusy	−1071	The server cannot open another session
reqAborted	−1105	The `ASPOpenSession` function call was aborted by an `ASPAbortOS` function call

SEE ALSO

For information on how to use NBP, see the chapter "Name-Binding Protocol (NBP)" in this book.

You can use the `ASPAbortOS` function described on page 8-25 to cancel an outstanding `ASPOpenSession` function request before it completes execution.

For the maximum sizes of commands and replies that ASP supports on your node, use the `ASPGetParms` function, described on page 8-22.

ASPCloseSession

The `ASPCloseSession` function closes the session that you identify.

```
FUNCTION ASPCloseSession (thePBptr: XPPParmBlkPtr;
                          async: Boolean): OSErr;
```

thePBptr   A pointer to an XPP parameter block.

async   A Boolean that specifies whether the function should be executed
            asynchronously or synchronously. Specify TRUE for asynchronous
            execution.

Parameter block

→	ioCompletion	ProcPtr	A pointer to a completion routine.
←	ioResult	OSErr	The function result.
→	ioRefNum	Integer	The .XPP driver reference number.
→	csCode	Integer	Always closeSess for this function.
→	sessRefnum	Integer	The session reference number.

Field descriptions

sessRefnum   A unique number that the .XPP driver assigned to this session when
              you called the `ASPOpenSession` function to open the session.

DESCRIPTION

To close a single session, you pass the session's reference number to the
`ASPCloseSession` function in the `sessRefnum` field. The session reference number
is the number that the .XPP driver assigns to the session and returns to you in the
`sessRefnum` field when you open a session using the `ASPOpenSession` function. The
`ASPCloseSession` function cancels any function calls that are pending for the session,
closes the session, and calls the attention routine for the session, if there is one, with
an attention code of 0 to indicate that the session is closed.

Note that there are other ways in which a session can be closed: for example, ASP closes
a session when one end of the session fails. A session remains open until it is explicitly
terminated by either the ASP workstation application or the ASP server or until one of
the session's ends fails or becomes unreachable.

SPECIAL CONSIDERATIONS

Note that you must provide the .XPP driver reference number as an input parameter
to this function. You can obtain the driver reference number by calling the Device
Manager's `OpenDriver` function.

ASSEMBLY-LANGUAGE INFORMATION

To execute the `ASPCloseSession` function from assembly language, call the `_Control` trap macro with a value of `closeSess` in the `csCode` field of the parameter block. You must also specify the .XPP driver reference number. To execute the `_Control` trap asynchronously, include the value `,ASYNC` in the operand field.

RESULT CODES

`aspParamErr`	–1070	You specified an invalid session reference number, or the session has been closed
`aspSessClosed`	–1072	The .XPP driver is in the process of closing down the session

SEE ALSO

You can call the `ASPCloseAll` function, described next, to cancel all active ASP sessions on your node. Note that you should use the `ASPCloseAll` function cautiously as applications and processes other than your own that are running on the same node could be using ASP sessions.

ASPCloseAll

The `ASPCloseAll` function closes all of the active ASP sessions on the node.

```
FUNCTION ASPCloseAll (thePBptr: XPPParmBlkPtr;
                      async: Boolean): OSErr;
```

thePBptr   A pointer to an XPP parameter block.

async   A Boolean that specifies whether the function should be executed asynchronously or synchronously. Specify `TRUE` for asynchronous execution.

Parameter block

→	ioCompletion	ProcPtr	A pointer to a completion routine.
←	ioResult	OSErr	The function result.
→	ioRefNum	Integer	The .XPP driver reference number.
→	csCode	Integer	Always `closeAll` for this function.

DESCRIPTION

To close all of the ASP sessions that are active and maintained by the .XPP driver on the node, you call the `ASPCloseAll` function. This function cancels all active requests, and it invokes the attention routines for any active sessions, if attention routines were provided. A good use of this function is as a system-level function call to ensure that all ASP sessions are closed before you close the .XPP driver.

SPECIAL CONSIDERATIONS

Note that you must provide the .XPP driver reference number as an input parameter to this function. You can obtain the driver reference number by calling the Device Manager's `OpenDriver` function.

ASSEMBLY-LANGUAGE INFORMATION

To execute the `ASPCloseAll` function from assembly language, call the `_Control` trap macro with a value of `closeAll` in the `csCode` field of the parameter block. You must also specify the .XPP driver reference number. To execute the `_Control` trap asynchronously, include the value `,ASYNC` in the operand field.

RESULT CODES

`aspParamErr`	–1070	You specified an invalid session reference number, or the session has been closed
`aspSessClosed`	–1072	The .XPP driver is in the process of closing down the session

Sending Commands and Writing Data From the Workstation to the Server

After you open a session, you can send a sequence of commands or a variable-size block of data across the session to the server. ASP returns to your ASP workstation application replies to the commands from the server end of the session. This section describes the `ASPUserCommand` function that you use to send commands to the server and the `ASPUserWrite` function that you use to send data.

ASPUserCommand

The `ASPUserCommand` function sends a command that you define from the workstation to the server across a session between them. ASP does not interpret the command syntax or execute the command; it simply transfers the command to the ASP server.

```
FUNCTION ASPUserCommand (thePBptr: XPPParmBlkPtr;
                         async: Boolean): OSErr;
```

`thePBptr`   A pointer to an XPP parameter block.

`async`   A Boolean that specifies whether the function should be executed asynchronously or synchronously. Specify TRUE for asynchronous execution.

Parameter block

→	ioCompletion	ProcPtr	A pointer to a completion routine.
←	ioResult	OSErr	The function result.
←	cmdResult	LongInt	The ASP command result.
→	ioRefNum	Integer	The .XPP driver reference number.
→	csCode	Integer	Always userCommand for this function.
→	sessRefnum	Integer	The session reference number.
→	aspTimeout	Byte	The retry interval in seconds.
→	cbSize	Integer	The command block size.
→	cbPtr	Ptr	A pointer to the command block.
↔	rbSize	Integer	The reply buffer and reply size.
→	rbPointer	Ptr	A pointer to the reply buffer.
←	ccbStart	Array	The beginning of memory for the CCB.

Field descriptions

cmdResult
: The ASP command result, consisting of 4 bytes of data returned by the server. The ASP client application defines the contents of the command result field. For example, AFP defines this field to specify the result of the AFP command. This field is valid if no system-level error is returned in the ioResult field.

sessRefnum
: The reference number assigned to this session that the ASPOpenSession function returned when you called it to open the session.

aspTimeout
: The time in seconds after which ASP is to retry to send the command across the session. You cannot specify the number of retries, just the time between them. ASP will retry to transmit the command until either it succeeds or the session is closed.

cbSize
: The size in bytes of the buffer that contains the command that ASP is to send to the sever. The command buffer size must not exceed the value of aspMaxCmdSize, which the ASPGetParms function returns.

cbPtr
: A pointer to a buffer containing the command that ASP is to send to the server.

rbSize
: On input, the size in bytes of the buffer that you allocated to contain the command reply that you expect to receive from the server. On return, the size in bytes of the reply data that was actually returned.

rbPointer
: A pointer to the buffer for the command reply.

ccbStart
: The beginning of the memory for the command control block (CCB) that the .XPP driver is to use. The memory allocated for the CCB must not exceed the maximum of 150 bytes for this function. The CCB is an array that is part of the .XPP parameter block.

DESCRIPTION

You use the ASPUserCommand function to send a user command across an ASP session. You pass to the ASPUserCommand function a pointer to a variable-size command block that contains the command data to be sent to the ASP server. The command data must adhere to a format defined by a higher-level protocol that is built on top of the ASP server, such as the AppleTalk Filing Protocol (AFP). The command data requests the server to perform a particular function and return a reply consisting of a variable-size block of data and a command result. Some examples of the types of commands that you can send are

■ a request to open a particular file on a file server (The server would return a small amount of data for this request.)

■ a request to read a range of bytes from a device (The server might send a multiple-packet reply to this request.)

ASP delivers the commands in the same sequence that you send them. ASP does not interpret the command data or in any way participate in executing the command's function. It simply conveys the command data, included in a higher-level format, to the server end of the session and returns the command reply to your ASP workstation application. The command reply consists of a 4-byte command result returned in the cmdResult field and a variable-size command reply returned in the reply buffer that you supply. The higher-level protocol that is the client of ASP defines the content and use of the command result. A command result error is returned in the cmdResult field. All other types of errors are returned in the function's parameter block ioResult field. These error codes report the following error conditions:

■ system-level errors returned by the .XPP driver indicating, for example, that the driver is not open or that a particular system call is not supported

■ .XPP driver errors indicating, for example, that the session is not open

■ AppleTalk errors returned from the underlying AppleTalk protocols

■ an ASP-specific error returned from an ASP server, for example, in response to a failed ASPOpenSession function

Figure 8-3 on page 8-18 shows how these errors are reported.

The .XPP driver uses the memory at the end of the XPP parameter block defined as a CCBStart array as an internal command control block (CCB). To ensure that the function executes successfully, you can specify the maximum size for this array as indicated in particular for the function that uses it.

You can minimize the amount of memory that is used for the CCB in the queue element. To do this, you should understand how ASP uses this memory. ASP uses the CCB to build data structures, including parameter blocks and buffer data structures (BDS), that it needs in order to make function calls to the .ATP driver. (See the chapter "AppleTalk Transaction Protocol [ATP]" in this book for information on ATP and buffer data structures.) The exact size of the memory that ASP needs for the CCB depends on the size of the replies that you expect from the server, and in the case of the ASPUserWrite function, the size of the data to be written. For the ASPUserCommand, ASPUserWrite, and ASPGetStatus functions, ASP must set up a BDS to hold the reply information. The number of entries in the BDS that ASP creates is equal to the size of the reply buffer divided by 578 (the maximum number of data bytes per ATP response packet), rounded up. A BDS cannot exceed eight elements. In addition to a BDS, ASP uses the CCB memory for the queue element to call the .ATP driver.

AppleTalk Session Protocol (ASP)

Figure 8-3   Error reporting in ASP

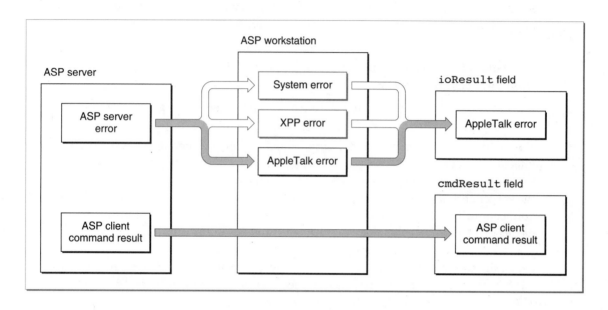

You can use the following equations to determine the minimum size of a CCB for a function that includes a reply buffer (rbSize):

```
bdsSize = MIN (((rbSize DIV 578) + 1),8) * bdsEntrySz
ccbSize = ioQElSize + 4 + bdsSize
```

For functions, such as ASPUserWrite, ASP must create an additional BDS and queue element to use in sending the write data to the server. You can use the following equations to determine the minimum size of a CCB for an ASPUserWrite function; these equations take into account the reply buffer (rbSize) and write data size (wdSize):

```
wrBDSSize = MIN (((wdSize DIV 578) + 1),8) * bdsEntrySz
wrCCBSz = (2 * ioQElSize) + 4 + bdsSize + wrBDSSize
```

Note that bdsEntrySz is equal to 12 and ioQelSize is equal to 50.

SPECIAL CONSIDERATIONS

Note that you must provide the .XPP driver reference number as an input parameter to this function. You can obtain the driver reference number by calling the Device Manager's OpenDriver function.

ASSEMBLY-LANGUAGE INFORMATION

To execute the ASPUserCommand function from assembly language, call the _Control trap macro with a value of userCommand in the csCode field of the parameter block. You must also specify the .XPP driver reference number. To execute the _Control trap asynchronously, include the value ,ASYNC in the operand field.

RESULT CODES

aspBufTooSmall	–1067	The reply data exceeds the size of the reply buffer; the .XPP driver will fill the buffer and truncate the data
aspParamErr	–1070	You specified an invalid session reference number, or the session has been closed
aspSessClosed	–1072	The .XPP driver is in the process of closing down the session
aspSizeErr	–1073	The size of the command block exceeds the maximum size of aspMaxCmdSize

ASPUserWrite

The ASPUserWrite function transfers data from the workstation to the server across a specific session.

```
FUNCTION ASPUserWrite (thePBptr: XPPParmBlkPtr;
                       async: Boolean): OSErr;
```

thePBptr   A pointer to an XPP parameter block.

async   A Boolean that specifies whether the function should be executed asynchronously or synchronously. Specify TRUE for asynchronous execution.

Parameter block

→	ioCompletion	ProcPtr	A pointer to a completion routine.
←	ioResult	OSErr	The function result.
←	cmdResult	LongInt	The ASP command result.
→	ioRefNum	Integer	The .XPP driver reference number.
→	csCode	Integer	Always userWrite for this function.
→	sessRefnum	Integer	The session reference number.
→	aspTimeout	Byte	The retry interval in seconds.
→	cbSize	Integer	The command block size.
→	cbPtr	Ptr	A pointer to command blocks.
↔	rbSize	Integer	The reply buffer size and reply size.
→	rbPointer	Ptr	A pointer to the reply buffer.
↔	wdSize	Integer	The write data size.
→	wdPtr	Ptr	The write data pointer.
←	ccbStart	Array	The beginning of memory for the CCB.

Field descriptions

cmdResult   The ASP command result consisting of 4 bytes of data returned by the server. The ASP client application defines the contents of the command result field. For example, AFP defines this field to specify the result of the AFP command. This field is valid if no system-level error is returned in the ioResult field.

sessRefnum   The reference number of the session that you want to use to transfer data. The session reference number is the unique number that the .XPP driver assigned to this session when you opened the session by calling the ASPOpenSession function.

aspTimeout   The time in seconds after which ASP is to retry to send data across the session.

cbSize   The size in bytes of the command data that ASP is to transfer across the session.

cbPtr   A pointer to the buffer containing the command data to be transferred.

rbSize   On input, the size in bytes of the buffer that you allocated to contain the command reply that you expect to receive from the server. On return, the size in bytes of the reply data that was actually returned.

rbPointer   A pointer to the buffer for the reply data.

wdSize   On input, the size in bytes of the of the write data that the command is to send. On return, the size in bytes of the write data that was actually sent.

wdPtr   A pointer to the buffer containing the data to be written.

ccbStart   The beginning of the memory for the command control block (CCB) that the .XPP driver is to use. The maximum size of this block is 296 bytes. The CCB is an array that is part of the .XPP parameter block.

DESCRIPTION

The ASPUserWrite function allows you to transfer a variable-size block of data to the server end of the ASP session and receive a reply. If you have previously called the ASPUserCommand function to send a command that directs the ASP server to open a file, you can call the ASPUserWrite function to write data to the file.

The .XPP driver uses the memory at the end of the XPP parameter block defined as a CCBStart array as an internal command control block (CCB). To ensure that the function executes successfully, you can specify the maximum size for this array as indicated in particular for the function that uses it. If you want to limit the amount of memory used for the CCB, you can specify the minimum amount of memory required for this array.

A command result error is returned in the cmdResult field. All other types of errors are returned in the function's parameter block ioResult field. Error reporting for the ASPUserWrite function is the same as for the ASPUserCommand.

SPECIAL CONSIDERATIONS

Note that you must provide the .XPP driver reference number as an input parameter to this function. You can obtain the driver reference number by calling the Device Manager's OpenDriver function.

ASSEMBLY-LANGUAGE INFORMATION

To execute the ASPUserWrite function from assembly language, call the _Control trap macro with a value of userWrite in the csCode field of the parameter block. You must also specify the .XPP driver reference number. To execute the _Control trap asynchronously, include the value ,ASYNC in the operand field.

RESULT CODES

aspBufTooSmall	–1067	The reply data exceeds the size of the reply buffer; the .XPP driver will fill the buffer and truncate the data
aspParamErr	–1070	You specified an invalid session reference number, or the session has been closed
aspSessClosed	–1072	The .XPP driver is in the process of closing the session
aspSizeErr	–1073	The size of the command block exceeds the maximum size of 296 bytes

SEE ALSO

To send a command to the server to direct it to perform a prerequisite action before you use the ASPUserWrite command to write data, use the ASPUserCommand function, described on page 8-15. To determine the minimum amount of memory required for the CCB or to find out more about the possible types of error conditions for which errors are returned and how these error results are reported, see the description of the ASPUserCommand function.

Obtaining Information About ASP's Maximum Capacities and the Status of the Server

This section describes the ASPGetParms function that you can use to determine how many concurrent ASP sessions can run on your node and the maximum amount of data that you can send and receive across a session. Before you open an ASP session, you should call the ASPGetParms function to determine the maximum sizes of commands and replies that ASP supports on your node.

This section also describes the ASPGetStatus function that you can use to obtain server status information without opening a session with the server.

ASPGetParms

The `ASPGetParms` function returns the maximum size of the data that you can send and receive across an ASP session and the maximum number of concurrent ASP sessions that the .XPP driver running on your node supports.

```
FUNCTION ASPGetParms (thePBptr: XPPParmBlkPtr;
                      async: Boolean): OSErr;
```

thePBptr   A pointer to an XPP parameter block.

async   A Boolean that specifies whether the function should be executed
           asynchronously or synchronously. Specify TRUE for asynchronous
           execution.

Parameter block

→	ioCompletion	ProcPtr	A pointer to a completion routine.
←	ioResult	OSErr	The function result.
→	ioRefNum	Integer	The .XPP driver reference number.
→	csCode	Integer	Always getParms for this function.
←	aspMaxCmdSize	Integer	The maximum size of command data.
←	aspQuantumSize	Integer	The maximum data size.
←	numSesss	Integer	The number of sessions.

Field descriptions

aspMaxCmdSize   The maximum size in bytes of a command that you can send to
                 the server.

aspQuantumSize   The maximum size in bytes of the data that you can either request
                 ASP to transfer to the server in an `ASPUserWrite` function call or
                 receive from the server in a command reply.

numSesss   The number of concurrent ASP sessions that the .XPP driver
                 supports on your node.

DESCRIPTION

The `ASPGetParms` function returns information about the data capacity of an ASP session that you need to know to send commands using the `ASPUserCommand` and `ASPUserWrite` functions and write data using the `ASPUserWrite` function. It also tells you how many concurrent ASP sessions your node supports. You do not need to establish a session before you call the `ASPGetParms` function.

SPECIAL CONSIDERATIONS

Note that you must provide the .XPP driver reference number as an input parameter to this function. You can obtain the driver reference number by calling the Device Manager's `OpenDriver` function.

ASSEMBLY-LANGUAGE INFORMATION

To execute the `ASPGetParms` function from assembly language, call the `_Control` trap macro with a value of `getParms` in the `csCode` field of the parameter block. You must also specify the .XPP driver reference number. To execute the `_Control` trap asynchronously, include the value `,ASYNC` in the operand field.

RESULT CODES

noErr   0   No error

ASPGetStatus

The `ASPGetStatus` function returns status information about the server whose internet socket address you provide.

```
FUNCTION ASPGetStatus (thePBptr: XPPParmBlkPtr;
                       async: Boolean): OSErr;
```

thePBptr   A pointer to an XPP parameter block.

async   A Boolean that specifies whether the function should be executed asynchronously or synchronously. Specify TRUE for asynchronous execution.

Parameter block

→	ioCompletion	ProcPtr	A pointer to a completion routine.
←	ioResult	OSErr	The function result.
→	ioRefNum	Integer	The .XPP driver reference number.
→	csCode	Integer	Always getStatus for this function.
→	aspTimeout	Byte	The retry interval in seconds.
→	aspRetry	Byte	The number of retries.
→	serverAddr	AddrBlock	The server socket address.
↔	rbSize	Integer	The reply buffer and reply size.
→	rbPtr	Ptr	A pointer to the reply buffer.
←	ccbStart	Array	The beginning of memory for the CCB.

Field descriptions

aspTimeout   The time in seconds after which ASP is to retry to obtain information about the status of the server whose address you provide.

aspRetry   The number of times ASP is to retry to obtain the server status information.

serverAddr   The internet socket address of the server about which you want status information.

rbSize   On input, the size in bytes of the buffer that you allocated to contain the reply that you expect to receive from the server. On return, the size in bytes of the reply (status) data that was actually returned.

rbPtr   A pointer to the buffer for the reply data.

ccbStart   The beginning of the memory for the command control block (CCB)
                    that the .XPP driver is to use. The memory allocated for the CCB
                    must not exceed the maximum of 150 bytes.

DESCRIPTION

You can use the ASPGetStatus function to obtain service status information about a
server without opening a session between your application and that server. ASP does not
impose any structure on the status block. The protocol above ASP defines the structure.
The .XPP driver uses the memory at the end of the XPP parameter block defined as
a CCBStart array as an internal command control block (CCB). To ensure that the
function executes successfully, you can specify the maximum size for this array as
indicated in particular for the function that uses it. If you want to limit the amount of
memory used for the CCB, you can specify the minimum amount of memory required
for this array.

SPECIAL CONSIDERATIONS

Note that you must provide the .XPP driver reference number as an input parameter
to this function. You can obtain the driver reference number by calling the Device
Manager's OpenDriver function.

ASSEMBLY-LANGUAGE INFORMATION

To execute the ASPGetStatus function from assembly language, call the _Control
trap macro with a value of getStatus in the csCode field of the parameter block.
You must also specify the .XPP driver reference number. To execute the _Control
trap asynchronously, include the value ,ASYNC in the operand field.

RESULT CODES

aspBufTooSmall	−1067	The reply data exceeds the size of the reply buffer; the .XPP driver will fill the buffer and truncate the data
aspNoServer	−1069	There was no response from the server whose address you specified as the value of serverAddr

SEE ALSO

To determine the minimum amount of memory required for the CCB, refer to the
description of the ASPUserCommand function on page 8-15.

Canceling an ASP Request to Open a Session

This section describes the `ASPAbortOS` function that you can use to cancel a pending request to open a session.

ASPAbortOS

The `ASPAbortOS` function cancels a specific pending request to open an ASP session function.

```
FUNCTION ASPAbortOS (thePBptr: XPPParmBlkPtr;
                     async: Boolean): OSErr;
```

thePBptr   A pointer to an XPP parameter block.

async   A Boolean that specifies whether the function should be executed asynchronously or synchronously. Specify `TRUE` for asynchronous execution.

Parameter block

→	ioCompletion	ProcPtr	A pointer to a completion routine.
←	ioResult	OSErr	The function result.
→	ioRefNum	Integer	The .XPP driver reference number.
→	csCode	Integer	Always `abortOS` for this function.
→	abortSCBPointer	Ptr	A pointer to the session control block.

Field descriptions

abortSCBPointer

A pointer to the session control block (SCB) that you passed to the `ASPOpenSession` function that you want to cancel.

DESCRIPTION

The `ASPAbortOS` function cancels a single call to the `ASPOpenSession` function if that function has not yet completed execution. You identify the request to be canceled by passing the `ASPAbortOS` function the pointer to the original session control block that you specified to open the session.

SPECIAL CONSIDERATIONS

Note that you must provide the .XPP driver reference number as an input parameter to this function. You can obtain the driver reference number by calling the Device Manager's `OpenDriver` function.

AppleTalk Session Protocol (ASP)

8

ASSEMBLY-LANGUAGE INFORMATION

To execute the ASPAbortOS function from assembly language, call the _Control trap macro with a value of abortOS in the csCode field of the parameter block. You must also specify the .XPP driver reference number. To execute the _Control trap asynchronously, include the value ,ASYNC in the operand field.

RESULT CODES

cbNotFound   –1102   Specified SCB was not found (there is no outstanding open session function call with this SCB)

SEE ALSO

For information on the session control block, see the description of the ASPOpenSession function on page 8-9.

Summary of ASP

Pascal Summary

Constants

```
CONST
   {.XPP driver unit and reference number}
   xppUnitNum      =      40;              {XPP unit number}
   xppRefNum       =     -41;              {XPP reference number}

   {command codes for ASP}
   openSess        =     255;              {open session}
   closeSess       =     254;              {close session}
   userCommand     =     253;              {user command}
   userWrite       =     252;              {user write}
   getStatus       =     251;              {get server status}
   getParms        =     249;              {get parameters for session}
   abortOS         =     248;              {cancel open session request}
   closeAll        =     247;              {close all open sessions}

   {miscellaneous}
   xppLoadedBit    =       5;              {XPP bit in PortBUse}
   scbMemSize      =     192;              {size of memory for SCB}
```

Data Types

Address Block Record

```
TYPE AddrBlock =
   PACKED RECORD
      aNet:        Integer;           {network number}
      aNode:       Byte;              {node ID}
      aSocket:     Byte;              {socket number}
   END;
```

XPP Parameter Block for ASP

```
XPPPrmBlkType = (...XPPPrmBlk,ASPAbortPrm,ASPSizeBlk...);
XPPSubPrmType = (ASPOpenPrm,ASPSubPrm);
XPPEndPrmType = (...ASPEndPrm);

TYPE XPPParamBlock =
   PACKED RECORD
        qLink:            QElemPtr;          {reserved}
        qType:            Integer;           {reserved}
        ioTrap:           Integer;           {reserved}
        ioCmdAddr:        Ptr;               {reserved}
        ioCompletion:     ProcPtr;           {completion routine}
        ioResult:         OSErr;             {result code}
        cmdResult:        LongInt;           {command result (ATP user bytes)}
        ioVRefNum:        Integer;           {reserved}
        ioRefNum:         Integer;           {driver reference number}
        csCode:           Integer;           {call command code}
        CASE XPPPrmBlkType OF
        ASPAbortPrm:
           (abortSCBPtr: Ptr);              {SCB pointer for AbortOS}
        ASPSizeBlk:
           (aspMaxCmdSize: Integer;          {maximum size of data for commands}
            aspQuantumSize:Integer;          {maximum size of data for request }
                                             { commands and receive replies}
            numSesss: Integer);              {number of concurrent sessions }
                                             { for your node}
   }
        XPPPrmBlk:
        (sessRefnum: Integer;                {offset to session refnum}
        aspTimeout: Byte;                    {timeout for ATP}
        aspRetry: Byte;                      {retry count for ATP}
        CASE XPPSubPrmType OF
        ASPOpenPrm:
        (serverAddr: AddrBlock;              {server address block}
        scbPointer: Ptr;                     {SCB pointer}
        attnRoutine: Ptr);                   {attention routine pointer}
        ASPSubPrm:
        (cbSize: Integer;                    {command block size}
        cbPtr: Ptr;                          {command block pointer}
        rbSize: Integer;                     {reply buffer size}
        rbPtr: Ptr;                          {reply buffer pointer}
```

CHAPTER 8

AppleTalk Session Protocol (ASP)

```
     CASE XPPEndPrmType OF
     ASPEndPrm:
     (wdSize: Integer;                    {write data size}
     wdPtr: Ptr;                          {write data pointer}
     ccbStart: ARRAY[0..295] OF Byte)));  {beginning of command control }
                                          { block}

   END;

XPPParmBlkPtr = ^XPPParamBlock;
```

Routines

Opening and Closing ASP Sessions

```
FUNCTION ASPOpenSession     (thePBptr: XPPParmBlkPtr; async: Boolean): OSErr;
FUNCTION ASPCloseSession    (thePBptr: XPPParmBlkPtr; async: Boolean): OSErr;
FUNCTION ASPCloseAll        (thePBptr: XPPParmBlkPtr; async: Boolean): OSErr;
```

Sending Commands and Writing Data From the Workstation to the Server

```
FUNCTION ASPUserCommand     (thePBptr: XPPParmBlkPtr; async: Boolean): OSErr;
FUNCTION ASPUserWrite       (thePBptr: XPPParmBlkPtr; async: Boolean): OSErr;
```

Obtaining Information About ASP's Maximum Capacities and the Status of the Server

```
FUNCTION ASPGetParms        (thePBptr: XPPParmBlkPtr; async: Boolean): OSErr;
FUNCTION ASPGetStatus       (thePBptr: XPPParmBlkPtr; async: Boolean): OSErr;
```

Canceling an ASP Request to Open a Session

```
FUNCTION ASPAbortOS         (thePBptr: XPPParmBlkPtr; async: Boolean): OSErr;
```

C Summary

Constants

```
enum {                              /*.XPP driver unit and reference */
                                    /* number*/
   xppUnitNum    =     40,          /*XPP unit number*/
   xppRefNum     =     -41};        /*XPP reference number*/
```

Summary of ASP

8-29

```
enum {                                         /*command codes for ASP*/
   openSess     =      255,                    /*open session*/
   closeSess    =      254,                    /*close session*/
   userCommand  =      253,                    /*user command*/
   userWrite    =      252,                    /*user write*/
   getStatus    =      251,                    /*get status*/
   getParms     =      249,                    /*get parameters*/
   abortOS      =      248,                    /*cancel open session request*/
   closeAll     =      247};                   /*close all open sessions*/

enum {                                         /*miscellaneous*/
xppLoadedBit    =      5,                       /*XPP bit in PortBUse*/
scbMemSize      =      192};                    /*size of memory for SCB*/
```

Data Types

Address Block Record

```
struct AddrBlock {
   short             aNet;                      /*network name*/
   unsigned char     aNode;                     /*node name*/
   unsigned char     aSocket;                   /*socket number*/
};
```

XPP Parameter Block for ASP

```
#define XPPPBHeader\
   QElem        *qLink;                         /*reserved*/\
   short        qType;                          /*reserved*/\
   short        ioTrap;                         /*reserved*/\
   Ptr          ioCmdAddr;                      /*reserved*/\
   ProcPtr      ioCompletion;                   /*completion routine*/\
   OSErr        ioResult;                       /*result code*/\
   long         cmdResult;                      /*command result (ATP user bytes)*/\
   short        ioVRefNum;                      /*reserved*/\
   short        ioRefNum;                       /*driver reference number*/\
   short        csCode;                         /*command code*/

typedef struct {
   XPPPBHeader
      short        sessRefnum;                  /*offset to session refnum*/
      char         aspTimeout;                  /*timeout for ATP*/
      char         aspRetry;                    /*retry count for ATP*/
```

```
        short          cbSize;                 /*command block size*/
        Ptr            cbPtr;                  /*command block pointer*/
        short          rbSize;                 /*reply buffer size*/
        Ptr            rbPtr;                  /*reply buffer pointer*/
        short          wdSize;                 /*write data size*/
        Ptr            wdPtr;                  /*write data pointer*/
        char           ccbStart[296];          /*CCB memory allocated for */
                                               /* beginning of command control */
                                               /* block*/
}XPPPrmBlk;

typedef struct {
    XPPPBHeader
        short          sessRefnum;             /*offset to session refnum*/
        char           aspTimeout;             /*timeout for ATP*/
        char           aspRetry;               /*retry count for ATP*/
        AddrBlock      serverAddr;             /*server address block*/
        Ptr            scbPointer;             /*SCB pointer*/
        Ptr            attnRoutine;            /*attention routine pointer*/
}ASPOpenPrm;
typedef ASPOpenPrm *ASPOpenPrmPtr;

typedef struct {
    XPPPBHeader
        Ptr            abortSCBPtr;            /*SCB pointer for ASPAbortOS*/
}ASPAbortPrm;

typedef struct {
    XPPPBHeader
        short          aspMaxCmdSize;          /*maximum size of data for commands*/
        short          aspQuantumSize;         /*maximum size of data for request */
                                               /* commands and receive replies*/
        short          numSesss;               /*number of concurrent sessions */
                                               /* for your node*/
}ASPGetparmsBlk;
```

Routines

Opening and Closing ASP Sessions

```
pascal OSErr ASPOpenSession  (ASPOpenPrmPtr thePBptr, Boolean async);
pascal OSErr ASPCloseSession (XPPParmBlkPtr thePBptr, Boolean async);
pascal OSErr ASPCloseAll     (XPPParmBlkPtr thePBptr, Boolean async);
```

Sending Commands and Writing Data From the Workstation to the Server

```
pascal OSErr ASPUserCommand (XPPParmBlkPtr thePBptr, Boolean async);
pascal OSErr ASPUserWrite   (XPPParmBlkPtr thePBptr, Boolean async);
```

Obtaining Information About ASP's Maximum Capacities and the Status of the Server

```
pascal OSErr ASPGetParms    (XPPParmBlkPtr thePBptr, Boolean async);
pascal OSErr ASPGetStatus   (XPPParmBlkPtr thePBptr, Boolean async);
```

Canceling an ASP Request to Open a Session

```
pascal OSErr ASPAbortOS     (XPPParmBlkPtr thePBptr, Boolean async);
```

Assembly-Language Summary

Constants

Offsets in User Bytes

```
aspCmdCode      EQU   0          ;offset to command field
aspWSSNum       EQU   1          ;WSS number in OpenSessions
aspVersNum      EQU   2          ;ASP version number in OpenSessions

aspSSSNum       EQU   0          ;SSS number in OpenSessReplies
aspSessID       EQU   1          ;session ID (requests & OpenSessReply)
aspOpenErr      EQU   2          ;OpenSessReply error code

aspSeqNum       EQU   2          ;sequence number in requests
aspAttnCode     EQU   2          ;attention bytes in attentions
```

Offsets in ATP Data Part

```
aspWrBSize      EQU   0          ;offset to write buffer size
                                 ; (WriteData)
aspWrHdrSz      EQU   2          ;size of data part
```

Command Codes (csCodes)

```
openSess        EQU   255        ;open session
closeSess       EQU   254        ;close session
userCommand     EQU   253        ;user command
userWrite       EQU   252        ;user write
```

getStatus	EQU	251	;get status
afpCall	EQU	250	;AFP command
getParms	EQU	249	;get parameters
abortOS	EQU	248	;abort open session request
closeAll	EQU	247	;close all open sessions

ASP Commands

aspCloseSess	EQU	1	;close session
aspCommand	EQU	2	;user command
aspGetStat	EQU	3	;get status
aspOpenSess	EQU	4	;open session
aspTickle	EQU	5	;tickle
aspWrite	EQU	6	;write
aspDataWrite	EQU	7	;writeData (from server)
aspAttention	EQU	8	;attention (from server)

Miscellaneous

aspVersion	EQU	$0100	;ASP version number
maxCmdSize	EQU	atpMaxData	;maximum command block size
quantumSize	EQU	atpMaxData*atpMaxNum	;maximum reply size
tickleInt	EQU	30	;tickle interval (secs)
tickleTime	EQU	tickleInt*60*4	;tickle timeout (ticks)
xppLoadedBit	EQU	atpLoadedBit+1	;XPP loaded bit number in ; PortBUse

Data Structures

XPP Parameter Block Common Fields for ASP Routines

0	qLink	long	reserved
4	qType	word	reserved
6	ioTrap	word	reserved
8	ioCmdAddr	long	reserved
12	ioCompletion	long	address of completion routine
16	ioResult	word	result code
18	cmdResult	long	pointer to attention routine
22	ioVRefNum	word	reserved
24	ioRefNum	word	driver reference number

ASPOpenSession Parameter Block

26	csCode	word	command code; always openSess
28	sessRefnum	word	session reference number
30	aspTimeout	byte	retry interval in seconds
31	aspRetry	byte	number of retries
32	serverAddr	long	server internet socket address
36	scbPointer	pointer	pointer to session control block
40	attnRoutine	long	pointer to attention routine

ASPCloseSession Parameter Block

26	csCode	word	command code; always closeSess
28	sessRefnum	word	session reference number

ASPCloseAll Parameter Block

26	csCode	word	command code; always closeAll

ASPUserCommand Parameter Block

18	cmdResult	long	ASP command result
26	csCode	word	command code; always userCommand
28	sessRefnum	word	session reference number
30	aspTimeout	byte	retry interval in seconds
32	cbSize	word	command block size
34	cbPtr	pointer	command block pointer
38	rbSize	word	reply buffer and reply size
40	rbPtr	pointer	pointer to reply buffer
50	ccbStart	record	start of memory for CCB

ASPUserWrite Parameter Block

18	cmdResult	long	ASP command result
26	csCode	word	command code; always userWrite
28	sessRefnum	word	session reference number
30	aspTimeout	byte	retry interval in seconds
32	cbSize	word	size of command block
34	cbPtr	pointer	pointer to command block
38	rbSize	word	reply buffer size and reply size
40	rbPtr	pointer	pointer to reply buffer
44	wdSize	word	size of write data
46	wdPtr	pointer	pointer to write data
50	ccbStart	record	start of memory for CCB

ASPGetParms Parameter Block

26	csCode	word	command code; always getParms
28	aspMaxCmdSize	word	maximum size of command block
30	aspQuantumSize	word	maximum data size
32	numSesss	word	maximum number of sessions

ASPGetStatus Parameter Block

26	csCode	word	command code; always `getStatus`
30	aspTimeout	byte	retry interval in seconds
31	aspRetry	byte	number of retries
32	serverAddr	long	server internet socket address
38	rbSize	word	reply buffer and reply size
40	rbPtr	pointer	pointer to reply buffer
50	ccbStart	record	start of memory for CCB

ASPAbortOS Parameter Block

26	csCode	word	command code; always `abortOS`
28	abortSCBPtr	pointer	pointer to session control block

Result Codes

noErr	0	No error
aspBadVersNum	−1066	The server cannot support the ASP version number
aspBufTooSmall	−1067	The reply data exceeds the size of the reply buffer; the .XPP driver will fill the buffer and truncate the data
aspNoMoreSess	−1068	The .XPP driver cannot support another ASP session (the number of sessions that the driver is capable of supporting is dependent on the machine type)
aspNoServers	−1069	There is no server at the specified `serverAddr` address, or the server did not respond to the request
aspParamErr	−1070	You specified an invalid session reference number, or the session has been closed
aspServerBusy	−1071	The server cannot open another session
aspSessClosed	−1072	The .XPP driver is in the process of closing down the session
aspSizeErr	−1073	The size of the command block exceeds the maximum size of `aspMaxCmdSize`
cbNotFound	−1102	Specified SCB was not found (there is no outstanding open session function call with this SCB)
reqAborted	−1105	The `ASPOpenSession` function call was aborted by an `ASPAbortOS` function call

AppleTalk Filing Protocol (AFP)

Contents

This chapter describes the AppleTalk Filing Protocol (AFP) that allows a workstation on an AppleTalk network to access and manipulate files on an AFP file server, such as an AppleShare server.

Because you can use the native file system to access an AFP server from a workstation, in most cases you should not need to use AFP directly. For example, few application developers use AFP to access an AppleShare file server because the existing File Manager commands perform most of the functions needed to access and manipulate files on an AppleShare server.

However, if you want to provide functions that are not implemented by the native file system commands or you want to manipulate files on an AFP server other than an AppleShare server, your application can use the AFP programming interface to directly access AFP to send commands to the server. For example, you can use AFP to list the contents of a directory when you need to obtain ProDOS information. You can also use AFP to retrieve or set parameters for a specific file when ProDOS is used.

This chapter describes the programming interface to the workstation portion of AFP only. It does not describe how to implement an AFP server. For information on how to implement an AFP server, see *Inside AppleTalk,* second edition.

Because AFP is not widely used by application program developers, this chapter provides only the AFP basics. This chapter includes "About" and "Reference" sections. It does not include a "Using" section, as do most of the other chapters in this book. This chapter is included in this book to complete the coverage of the AppleTalk protocol stack.

If you decide to use AFP, it is important to note that to implement an AFP command, you need information in addition to the information that this chapter provides. *Inside AppleTalk*, second edition, and the *AppleShare 3.0 Developer's Kit* version 3.0, provide information describing the AFP commands and the command block data structure required for each command. The *AppleShare 3.0 Developer's Kit* includes extensions to AFP not described in *Inside AppleTalk.*

AFP is built on top of the AppleTalk Session Protocol (ASP) and uses the services of ASP. To use AFP, you should also be familiar with ASP, which is described in the chapter "AppleTalk Session Protocol (ASP)" in this book. For an overview of AFP and how it fits within the AppleTalk protocol stack, read the chapter "Introduction to AppleTalk," which is also in this book.

About AFP

AFP is a remote filing system protocol that provides a workstation on an AppleTalk network with access to a server that is implemented according to the AFP file system structure. AFP also includes user authentication support and an access control mechanism that supports volume-level and folder-level access rights. AppleShare is the AFP file server that is implemented on Macintosh computers.

AppleTalk Filing Protocol (AFP)

Through the native file system and AFP, your application running on one node can manipulate files on another node using the same file system commands on the remote node that it uses to manipulate files on its own node. You can use AFP commands to

■ obtain and modify information about the file server and other parts of the file system structure

■ create and delete files and directories

■ read files or write to them

■ retrieve and store information within individual files

AFP is implemented by the .XPP driver. The .XPP driver maps an AFP function call from the client workstation into one or more ASP function calls. Figure 9-1 shows AFP and its underlying protocols.

Figure 9-1   AFP and its underlying protocols

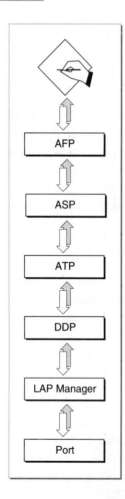

The Pascal programming interface to AFP on the workstation consists of a single function. You use this function to pass to the .XPP driver the command code and parameters for an AFP command. There are four categories of AFP commands: general, login, read, and write. Each of these categories requires a specific format of the XPP parameter block that is used for the AFP function. The next section describes these categories, the commands they include, and the XPP parameter block formats for each category.

Please read this note before you continue

Because the native file system commands implement most of the functions that you need to access an AFP server, in most cases you will not need to use AFP directly. For this reason, this chapter does not include a "Using" section, as do most of the other chapters in this book. If the native file system implements the function that you need, you should use the file system command. If you want to implement a function that is not part of the native file system, you can use AFP directly. In this case, you should continue to read this chapter. ◆

AFP Reference

This section describes the data structures and the function that are specific to the AppleTalk Filing Protocol (AFP).

The "Data Structures" section shows the Pascal data structures for the AFP command block record and the XPP parameter block.

The AFP programming interface consists of a single function, `AFPCommand`, which allows you to call AFP and specify from within a command block a particular command and its parameters to send across the session to the server.

Data Structures

This section describes the data structures that you use to provide information to the AppleTalk Filing Protocol (AFP).

You use an AFP command block record for the AFP read or AFP write format of the `AFPCommand` function.

You use the XPP parameter block as a parameter to the `AFPCommand` function.

AFP Command Block Record

An AFP command block record of type `AFPCommandBlock` defines the structure of the command block that you use to send either a read (`afpRead`) or write (`afpWrite`) command to the server. A **command block** is a data structure that is used to specify an AFP command and its parameters, which the .XPP driver sends to an AFP server to be executed. The XPP parameter block for the `AFPCommand` function contains a pointer to the command block. The read and write commands use different fields of this record. You pass a pointer to the AFP command block record as a field value of the XPP parameter block. The command block record fields are defined in the section describing the command that uses them.

```
AFPCommandBlock =
PACKED RECORD
    cmdByte:            Byte;     {AFP command code}
    startEndFlag:       Byte;     {start/end flag; for the read }
                                  { command, identifies offset }
                                  { relative to fork}
    forkRefNum:         Integer;  {fork reference number}
    rwOffset:           LongInt;  {offset within fork to begin }
                                  { reading or writing}
    reqCount:           LongInt;  {on input, requested size of }
                                  { data; on return, size of data }
                                  { actually read or written}
    newLineFlag:        Byte;     {new line flag}
    newLineChar:        Char;     {new line character}
END;
```

XPP Parameter Block

The `AFPCommand` function, which has four formats, requires a pointer to an XPP parameter block of type `XPPParamBlock`. Because the .XPP driver maps the AFP commands that you specify to ASP commands, the various `AFPCommand` function formats use some of the XPP parameter block fields defined within variant records for ASP functions.

The first four fields of the XPP parameter block, `qLink`, `qType`, `ioTrap`, and `ioCmdAddr`, which are the same for all four formats of the `AFPCommand`, are used internally by the Device Manager.

You must specify the .XPP driver reference number as the input value of the `ioRefNum` field; AFP does not fill in this value. You can use the Device Manager's `OpenDriver` function to obtain the .XPP driver reference number.

The XPP parameter block that follows is defined as the maximum size required for any format of the `AFPCommand` function. Various formats use different size parameter blocks. You can abbreviate the parameter block appropriately for any `AFPCommand` format.

This section defines the parameter block fields that are common to all AFP functions. It does not define reserved fields, which are used either internally by the .XPP driver or not at all. The fields that are used by a particular format are defined in the section that describes that format.

```
XPPPrmBlkType = (XPPPrmBlk...);

XPPSubPrmType = (ASPOpenPrm,ASPSubPrm);

XPPEndPrmType = (AFPLoginPrm,ASPEndPrm);

XPPParmBlkPtr = ^XPPParamBlock;

XPPParamBlock =
PACKED RECORD
    qLink:              QElemPtr;              {reserved}
    qType:              Integer;               {reserved}
    ioTrap:             Integer;               {reserved}
    ioCmdAddr:          Ptr;                   {reserved}
    ioCompletion:       ProcPtr;               {completion routine}
    ioResult:           OSErr;                 {result code}
    cmdResult:          LongInt;               {command result (ATP user bytes)}
    ioVRefNum:          Integer;               {reserved}
    ioRefNum:           Integer;               {driver reference number}
    csCode:             Integer;               {call command code}
CASE XPPPrmBlkType OF
    XPPPrmBlk:
        (sessRefnum:    Integer;               {offset to session refnum}
        aspTimeout:     Byte;                  {timeout for ATP}
        aspRetry:       Byte;                  {retry count for ATP}
CASE XPPSubPrmType OF
    ASPOpenPrm:
        (serverAddr:    AddrBlock;             {server address block}
        scbPointer:     Ptr;                   {SCB pointer}
        attnRoutine:    Ptr);                  {attention routine pointer}
    ASPSubPrm:
        (cbSize:        Integer;               {command block size}
        cbPtr:          Ptr;                   {command block pointer}
        rbSize:         Integer;               {reply buffer size}
        rbPtr:          Ptr;                   {reply buffer pointer}
CASE XPPEndPrmType OF
    AFPLoginPrm:
        (afpAddrBlock:  AddrBlock;             {address block in AFP login}
        afPSCBPtr:      Ptr;                   {SCB pointer in AFP login}
        afpAttnRoutine:Ptr);                   {attn routine pointer in AFP login}
    ASPEndPrm:
        (wdSize:        Integer;               {write data size}
        wdPtr:          Ptr;                   {write data pointer}
        ccbStart:       ARRAY[0..295] OF Byte)));
                                               {beginning of command control }
                                               { block}

END;
XPPParmBlkPtr = ^XPPParamBlock;
```

Field descriptions

ioCompletion   A pointer to a completion routine that you can provide. When you execute a function asynchronously, the .XPP driver calls your completion routine when it completes execution of the function if you specify a pointer to the routine as the value of this field. Specify NIL for this field if you do not wish to provide a completion routine. If you execute a function synchronously, the .XPP driver ignores the ioCompletion field. For information about completion routines, see the chapter "Introduction to AppleTalk" in this book.

ioResult   The result of the function. When you execute the function asynchronously, the function sets this field to 1 and returns a function result of noErr as soon as the function begins execution. When the function completes execution, it sets the ioResult field to the actual result code.

ioRefNum   The driver reference number for the .XPP driver. The Device Manager's OpenDriver function that you use to open the .XPP driver returns the driver reference number in the refnum field. You must supply this value. You can call this function to obtain the .XPP driver's reference number even if the .XPP driver is already open. The MPW interface does not fill in this value. For information on opening the .XPP driver, see the chapter "AppleTalk Utilities" in this book. For information on the OpenDriver function, see the chapter "Device Manager" in *Inside Macintosh: Devices*.

csCode   The .XPP driver command code for the function. For the AFPCommand function, the value of this field is always afpCall. The MPW interface fills in this field.

Routines

The programming interface to AFP is different in form from the programming interfaces to the other AppleTalk protocols described in this book. For AFP, the programming interface consists of a single function, the AFPCommand function, which allows you to call AFP and pass it the command code for a particular AFP command. There are four categories or types of commands that you can send to a server: general, login, write, and read. To use the commands that form these categories, in addition to this chapter, you must also refer to the books *Inside AppleTalk*, second edition, and *AppleShare 3.0 Developer's Kit* version 3.0.

The AFPCommand function requires as a parameter a pointer to an XPP parameter block. This function uses a different parameter block format for each category. You do not specify the command code as a parameter block field value, as you might expect. Instead, as the value of a parameter block field you specify a pointer to a command buffer. You use the command buffer to specify the command code of the AFP command to be sent to the server.

Although the `AFPCommand` function syntax is the same for all four formats, the fields of the XPP parameter block that are used for each format differ. The `AFPCommand` function is defined as follows:

```
FUNCTION AFPCommand (thePBptr: XPPParmBlkPtr;
                     async: Boolean): OSErr;
```

thePBptr   A pointer to the XPP parameter block format for a particular group of AFP commands.

async   A Boolean that specifies whether the function is to execute synchronously or asynchronously. Set the `async` parameter to `TRUE` to execute the function asynchronously.

This section describes the XPP parameter block format for each category of commands. An arrow preceding a parameter block field indicates whether the field's value is an input parameter, an output parameter, or both:

Arrow	Meaning
→	Input
←	Output
↔	Both

Within the parameter block, you specify a pointer to a command block, the first byte of which contains the command code of the command to be sent to the server. The range of command codes is 0 through 255, inclusive, although AppleTalk does not currently implement all command codes and some command codes are invalid. Table 9-1 shows the AFP command codes that are implemented in AppleTalk. This table shows the AFP command code constant, the numeric value, and a description of the command.

Note

The following six constants may not be defined in the header files: `afpGetSrvrMsg`, `afpCreateID`, `afpDeleteID`, `afpResolveID`, `afpExchangeFiles`, and `afpCatSearch`. If you use the commands that these constants identify, you must either specify the numeric values for the commands or declare the constants in your application. ◆

Table 9-1   AFP command codes

AFP command constant	Command code	Action
afpByteRangeLock	1	Locks or unlocks a specified range of bytes within an open fork.
afpVolClose	2	Informs the server that the workstation no longer needs the volume.
afpDirClose	3	Closes a directory and invalidates its directory identifier.

continued

AppleTalk Filing Protocol (AFP)

Table 9-1   AFP command codes (continued)

AFP command constant	Command code	Action
afpForkClose	4	Closes a fork that was opened by afpOpenFork.
afpCopyFile	5	Copies a file from one location to another on the same file server.
afpDirCreate	6	Creates a new directory.
afpFileCreate	7	Creates a new file.
afpDelete	8	Deletes a file or directory.
afpEnumerate	9	Lists the contents of a directory.
afpFlush	10	Writes to a disk any volume data that has been modified.
afpForkFlush	11	Writes to a disk any data buffered from previous afpWrite calls.
afpGetForkParms	14	Retrieves parameters for a file associated with a particular open fork.
afpGetSInfo	15	Obtains a block of descriptive information from the server, without requiring an open session. Use the ASPGetStatus function instead of this command code. See the chapter "AppleTalk Session Protocol (ASP)" in this book for information on ASPGetStatus. Making an afpGetSInfo call using the AFPCommand results in an error.
afpGetSParms	16	Retrieves server parameters.
afpGetVolParms	17	Retrieves parameters for a particular volume.
afpLogin	18	Establishes an AFP session with a server.
afpContLogin	19	Continues the login and user authentication process started by the afpLogin command.
afpLogout	20	Terminates a session with a server.
afpMapID	21	Maps a user ID to a user name, or a group ID to a group name.
afpMapName	22	Maps a user name to a user ID, or a group name to a group ID.
afpMove	23	Moves a directory or file to another location on the same volume.
afpOpenVol	24	Makes a volume available to the workstation.
afpOpenDir	25	Opens a directory on a variable directory ID volume and returns its directory ID.

continued

Table 9-1   AFP command codes (continued)

AFP command constant	Command code	Action
afpOpenFork	26	Opens the data or resource fork of an existing file to read from it or write to it.
afpRead	27	Reads a block of data from an open fork.
afpRename	28	Renames a directory or file.
afpSetDirParms	29	Sets parameters for a specified directory.
afpSetFileParms	30	Sets parameters for a specified file.
afpSetForkParms	31	Sets the fork length for a specified open fork.
afpSetVolParms	32	Sets the backup date for a specified volume.
afpWrite	33	Writes a block of data to an open fork.
afpGetFlDrParms	34	Retrieves parameters for either a file or a directory.
afpSetFlDrParms	35	Sets parameters for a file or directory.
afpGetSrvrMsg*	38	Gets a string message from the server, such as shutdown, user, and login messages.
afpCreateID*	39	Creates a unique file ID for a specified file.
afpDeleteID*	40	Invalidates all instances of a specified file ID.
afpResolveID*	41	Returns parameters for the file referred to by the specified file ID.
afpExchangeFiles*	42	Preserves an existing file ID when an application performs a "Save" or "Save As" operation.
afpCatSearch*	43	Allows an application to efficiently search an entire volume for files that match specified criteria.
afpDTOpen	48	Opens the Desktop database on a particular volume.
afpDTClose	49	Informs the server that the workstation no longer needs the volume's Desktop database.
afpGetIcon	51	Retrieves an icon from the volume's Desktop database.
afpGtIcnInfo	52	Retrieves icon information from the volume's Desktop database.
afpAddAPPL	53	Adds an APPL mapping to the Desktop database.
afpRmvAPPL	54	Removes an APPL mapping from the volume's Desktop database.

continued

9

AppleTalk Filing Protocol (AFP)

Table 9-1   AFP command codes (continued)

AFP command constant	Command code	Action
afpGetAPPL	55	Retrieves an APPL mapping from the volume's Desktop database.
afpAddCmt	56	Adds a comment for a file or directory to the volume's Desktop database.
afpRmvCmt	57	Removes a comment from the volume's Desktop database.
afpGetCmt	58	Retrieves a comment associated with a specified file or directory from the volume's Desktop database.
afpAddIcon	192	Adds an icon bitmap to the volume's Desktop database.

* An asterisk (*) marks the constants that may not be defined in the header files. If you use them, you must first declare the constants in your application.

The command block buffer that you provide for each `AFPCommand` function contains the command code and the command parameters. The format for the command block differs for each command.

For a description of the commands and their required command block formats and parameters, see *Inside AppleTalk*, second edition, and the *AppleShare 3.0 Developer's Kit* version 3.0 as follows:

■ For command codes 38 through 43, inclusive, see the *AppleShare 3.0 Developer's Kit* version 3.0.

■ For all other AFP command codes, see *Inside AppleTalk*, second edition.

The .XPP driver implements most AFP commands by mapping the AFP command to an ASP function, without interpreting or verifying the data. The .XPP driver maps AFP commands to ASP functions according to the following conventions:

AFP commands are mapped to ASP functions, which use the services of ATP to transport data. The following two AFP command codes can send or receive more data than a single eight-packet ATP transaction will support.

■ The `afpRead` command (27) can cause the server to return more data than fits in eight ATP response packets. (The `aspQuantumSize` parameter of the `ASPGetParms` function returns the maximum amount of data that you can receive from the server.) The `afpRead` command can return up to the number of bytes indicated in the command block's requested count (`reqCount`) field. The .XPP driver may issue multiple calls to ASP for this command mapping.

■ The `afpWrite` command (33) can pass more data than fits in eight ATP response packets. The `afpWrite` command can pass up to the number of bytes indicated in the command block's requested count (`reqCount`) field. The .XPP driver may issue multiple calls to ASP for this command mapping.

Table 9-2 summarizes the mapping of AFP commands to ASP functions.

Table 9-2 Mapping of AFP commands to ASP functions

AFP command code	ASP function mapping
0	Invalid AFP command.
1–14, 16, 17, 21–32, 34–190	Mapped to `ASPUserCommand`.
15	Mapped to `ASPGetStatus`. Use `ASPGetStatus` instead of this command code. Making an `afpGetSInfo` call using the `AFPCommand` function results in an error.
18	Mapped to appropriate login dialog including `ASPOpenSession`.
19	Mapped to appropriate login dialog.
20	Mapped to `ASPCloseSession`.
33	Mapped to `ASPUserWrite`.
191	Mapped to `ASPUserCommand`. Reserved for developers; Apple Computer, Inc., will not use this command code.
192–253	Mapped to `ASPUserWrite`.
254	Mapped to `ASPUserWrite`. Reserved for developers; Apple Computer, Inc., will not use this command code.
255	Invalid AFP command.

Before you can call the `AFPCommand` function, you must open the .XPP driver. You can use the Device Manager's `OpenDriver` function to open the .XPP driver. You should not close the .XPP driver because other applications and processes may be using it. For more information on opening the .XPP driver, see the chapter "AppleTalk Utilities" in this book. The .MPP and .ATP drivers must be open before you open the .XPP driver.

The chapter "AppleTalk Utilities" also describes how to close the .XPP driver. However, in most circumstances, you should not close the .XPP driver because other applications and processes could be using the protocols implemented by the .XPP driver.

You must pass the .XPP driver reference number as a parameter to the `AFPCommand` function; the MPW interface does not fill in this value. The `OpenXPP` function that you use to open the .XPP driver returns the driver reference number in the `refnum` field. You can call this function to obtain the .XPP driver's reference number even if the .XPP driver is already open.

For all `AFPCommand` formats, the XPP parameter block includes a `CCBStart` field. The .XPP driver uses the memory at the end of the XPP parameter block defined as a `CCBStart` array as an internal command control block (CCB). To ensure that the function executes successfully, you can specify the maximum size for this array as indicated for the particular function that uses it.

AFP General Command Format

You use the general command format for the `AFPCommand` function to pass any of the AFP commands to the .XPP driver to be sent to the server except `afpLogin`, `afpRead`, and `afpWrite`.

```
FUNCTION AFPCommand (thePBptr: XPPParmBlkPtr;
                     async: Boolean): OSErr;
```

thePBptr   A pointer to the XPP parameter block format for the AFP commands that use the AFP general command format.

async   A Boolean that specifies whether the function is to be executed synchronously or asynchronously. Set the `async` parameter to `TRUE` to execute the function asynchronously.

Parameter block

→	ioCompletion	ProcPtr	A pointer to a completion routine.
←	ioResult	OSErr	The function result.
←	cmdResult	LongInt	The AFP command result.
→	ioRefNum	Integer	The .XPP driver reference number.
→	csCode	Integer	Always `afpCall` for this function.
→	sessRefnum	Integer	The session reference number.
→	aspTimeout	Byte	The retry interval in seconds.
→	cbSize	Integer	The command buffer size.
→	cbPtr	Ptr	The command buffer.
↔	rbSize	Integer	The reply buffer size and reply size.
→	rbPtr	Ptr	A pointer to the reply buffer.
↔	wdSize	Integer	The write data size.
→	wdPtr	Ptr	A pointer to the write data.

Field descriptions

cmdResult   Four bytes of data returned from the server indicating the result of the AFP command.

sessRefnum   The session reference number, which is a unique number that the .XPP driver assigns to the session and returns in response to an `afpLogin` command.

aspTimeout   The interval in seconds that the .XPP driver waits between retries of the AFP command.

cbSize   The size in bytes of the block of data that contains the command and its parameters to be sent to the server across the session. The size of the command block must not exceed the value of `aspMaxCmdSize` that the `ASPGetParms` function returns. For information on the `ASPGetParms` function, see the chapter "AppleTalk Session Protocol (ASP)" in this book.

cbPtr   A pointer to the beginning of the command block that contains the AFP command to be sent across the session to the server. (The `cbSize` field value specifies the command block size.) The first byte of the command block must contain the AFP command. The

<table>
<tr><td></td><td>following bytes contain the parameters for the command. See Inside AppleTalk, second edition, and the AppleShare 3.0 Developer's Kit version 3.0 for the definitions of the AFP commands and their command codes and parameters.</td></tr>
<tr><td>rbSize</td><td>On input, the size in bytes of the reply buffer that is to hold the expected response to the AFP command. On return, the actual size of the reply to the AFP command that the .XPP driver returned in the buffer.</td></tr>
<tr><td>rbPtr</td><td>A pointer to the reply buffer.</td></tr>
<tr><td>wdSize</td><td>The size of the write data buffer that contains the data to be written to the server. This field's value is used only if the AFP command is one that the .XPP driver maps to the ASPUserWrite function.</td></tr>
<tr><td>wdPtr</td><td>A pointer to the write-data buffer. This field's value is used only if the AFP command is one that the .XPP driver maps to the ASPUserWrite function.</td></tr>
</table>

DESCRIPTION

The general format of the AFPCommand function provides a way to pass an AFP command to the server end of an open session and receive a reply. After you open a session with an AFP file server using the login format of the AFPCommand function, you can send a sequence of AFP commands across the session to the server. You use the general format for the AFPCommand function to send all of the AFP commands to the server, except for afpLogin, afpRead, and afpWrite, which have their own AFPCommand formats. AFP delivers the commands in the same order in which you send them and returns replies to the commands in the reply buffer that you provide. The cmdResult field indicates the result of the command that was delivered to the server, not the function result.

SPECIAL CONSIDERATIONS

Note that you must provide the .XPP driver reference number as an input parameter to this function. You can obtain the driver reference number by calling the Device Manager's OpenDriver function. For information on the OpenDriver function, see *Inside Macintosh: Devices*.

Any memory that you allocate for the parameter block, buffers, and command block belongs to the .XPP driver until the function completes execution, after which you can reuse or release the memory.

ASSEMBLY-LANGUAGE INFORMATION

To execute the AFPCommand function from assembly language, call the _Control trap macro with a value of afpCall in the csCode field of the parameter block.

RESULT CODES

aspBufTooSmall	–1067	The command reply from the server is larger than the response buffer; ASP will fill the buffer and truncate the reply data
aspParamErr	–1070	You specified an invalid session reference number, or the session has been closed
aspSessClosed	–1072	The .XPP driver is in the process of closing the session
aspSizeErr	–1073	The size of the command block exceeds the maximum size of aspMaxCmdSize
afpParmError	–5019	The AFP command block size is equal to 0 (this error is also returned when the command block is equal to 0 or $FF [255] or GetSrvrStatus [15])

SEE ALSO

For a list of the AFP commands and their command code numeric values and constants, see Table 9-1 on page 9-9. To determine which AFP commands take the general AFPCommand format, see Table 9-2 on page 9-13. For a description of the AFP commands that you can send to a server and their required command block formats, see *Inside AppleTalk*, second edition, and the *AppleShare 3.0 Developer's Kit* version 3.0.

AFP Login Command Format

You use the login command format for the AFPCommand function to pass the afpLogin command to the .XPP driver to open a session with an AFP file server.

```
FUNCTION AFPCommand (thePBptr: XPPParmBlkPtr;
                     async: Boolean): OSErr;
```

thePBptr   A pointer to the XPP parameter block format for the afpLogin command.

async   A Boolean that specifies whether the function is to execute synchronously or asynchronously. Set the async parameter to TRUE to execute the function asynchronously.

Parameter block

→	ioCompletion	ProcPtr	A pointer to a completion routine.
←	ioResult	OSErr	The function result.
→	ioRefNum	Integer	The .XPP driver reference number.
←	cmdResult	LongInt	The AFP command result.
→	csCode	Integer	Always afpCall for this function.
←	sessRefnum	Integer	The session reference number.
→	aspTimeout	Byte	The retry interval in seconds.
→	aspRetry	Byte	The number of retries.
→	cbSize	Integer	The command buffer size.
→	cbPtr	Integer	A pointer to the command buffer.

↔	rbSize	Integer	On input, the reply buffer size. On return, the actual reply size.
→	rbPtr	Ptr	A pointer to the reply buffer.
→	afpAddrBlock	AddrBlock	The internet socket address of the server.
↔	afpSCBPtr	Ptr	A pointer to the SCB.
↔	afpAttnRoutine	Ptr	A pointer to an attention routine.

Field descriptions

cmdResult   Four bytes of data returned from the server indicating the result of the AFP command.

sessRefnum   The session reference number, which is a unique number that the .XPP driver assigns to the session and returns.

aspTimeout   The interval in seconds that the .XPP driver waits between retries of the AFP command call.

aspRetry   The number of times that the .XPP driver is to retry to execute the AFP command.

cbSize   The size in bytes of the block of data that contains the command and its parameters to be sent to the server across the session. The size of the command block must not exceed the value of aspMaxCmdSize that the ASPGetParms function returns. For information on the ASPGetParms function, see the chapter "AppleTalk Session Protocol (ASP)."

cbPtr   A pointer to the beginning of the command block that contains the AFP login command to be sent across the session to the server. The cbSize field value specifies the command block size. The first byte of the command block must contain the AFP login command. The following command block bytes contain the parameters for the command. For the definitions of the AFP commands and their command codes and parameters, see *Inside AppleTalk*, second edition, and the *AppleShare 3.0 Developer's Kit* version 3.0.

rbSize   On input, the size in bytes of the reply buffer that is to hold the expected response to the AFP login command. On return, the actual size of the reply to the AFP command that the .XPP driver returned in the buffer.

rbPtr   A pointer to the reply buffer.

afpAddrBlock   The internet socket address of the server to which the command is to be sent.

afpSCBPtr   A pointer to a session control block (SCB) that the .XPP driver requires to maintain an open session. The scbMemSize constant defines the size of the session control block. The memory that you allocate for the SCB must be nonrelocatable or locked because it belongs to the .XPP driver for the life of the session. Each session requires its own SCB.

afpAttnRoutine   A pointer to a routine that the .XPP driver calls when it receives an attention request from the server. If you do not want the .XPP driver to call an attention routine, set this field to 0.

AppleTalk Filing Protocol (AFP)

DESCRIPTION

To open a session with an AFP file server, you call the `AFPCommand` function and pass it the `afpLogin` command in the command block that you provide. You point to the command block from the XPP parameter block's `cbPtr` field. You specify the internet socket address of the server that you want to access as the value of the `afpAddrBlock` field.

In addition to allocating memory for the parameter block and the command block, you must provide a session control block (SCB) and pass the `AFPCommand` function a pointer to the SCB in the `afpSCBPtr` field. The .XPP driver uses the SCB internally to manage the session. Each session requires its own SCB. You must either allocate nonrelocatable memory for the session control block or lock the memory and not modify it for the duration of the session. The SCB size is defined by the constant `scbMemSize`. The memory belongs to the .XPP driver for the life of the session. You can reuse an SCB after either of the following events occurs:

- You have called an `AFPCommand` function using the general command format to specify an `afpLogout` command to close the session and the `AFPCommand` function has successfully completed execution.

- The server end of the session has closed the session or the .XPP driver has closed the session.

AFP includes an attention mechanism that allows the server to send an attention request to the workstation. For example, a file server can use this messaging system to notify all of the workstations that are using the file server that it is shutting down. The XPP parameter block for the login format includes a pointer to an attention routine.

When the .XPP driver receives an attention request, it sets the first 2 bytes of the SCB to the attention bytes from the packet. If you have provided an attention routine, the .XPP driver calls it. The .XPP driver also calls the attention routine when the session is closed by either the workstation or the server or AFP itself, for example, because the .XPP driver could not open a session before it exhausted the number of retries.

You code the attention routine in assembly language. Because the .XPP driver calls your attention routine at interrupt level, you must observe the following interrupt conventions in writing the attention routine:

- An attention routine can change registers A0 through A3 and D0 through D3.

- The routine must not call any Memory Manager routines.

The .XPP driver calls your attention routine with

- D0 (word) equal to the session reference number (`sessRefnum`) for that session. This is the number that AFP returns on completion of the `AFPCommand` function for the `afpLogin` command.

- D1 (word) equal to the attention bytes passed by the server or 0 if the session is closing.

To resume normal execution, your attention routine must return with an RTS (return from subroutine) instruction.

If you code your program in a high-level language, such as Pascal, you might not want to provide an attention routine written in assembly language. If you do not want to provide an attention routine, you can poll the attention bytes to determine if your application has received an attention request from the server. The attention bytes are the first 2 bytes of the session control block. When the server sends an attention request to the workstation, the .XPP driver receives the request and it sets the first 2 bytes of the SCB to the attention bytes from the packet. (When the session was opened, the .XPP driver set these bytes to 0.) If the first 2 bytes of the SCB are nonzero when your Pascal program polls them, the program will know that it has received an attention request from the server. Your program can handle the request and reset the SCB's attention bytes to 0. However, using this method to determine if the workstation has received an attention request from the server has limitations; two or more attention requests could be received between successive polls and only the last one would be preserved.

SPECIAL CONSIDERATIONS

Note that you must provide the .XPP driver reference number as an input parameter to this function. You can obtain the driver reference number by calling the Device Manager's OpenDriver function. For more information on the OpenDriver function, see *Inside Macintosh: Devices.*

In the XPP parameter block for the AFPCommand function login format, the afpSCBPointer and afpAttnRoutine fields overlap with the beginning of the CCB and are modified by AFPCommand function.

The memory that you allocate for the XPP parameter block, command block, and reply buffer belongs to AFP until the function completes execution, after which you can reuse the memory or release it. However, the memory that you allocate for the SCB belongs to AFP for the life of the session. You must either allocate nonrelocatable memory for the SCB or lock the memory and not modify it for the duration of the session.

ASSEMBLY-LANGUAGE INFORMATION

To execute the AFPCommand function from assembly language, call the _Control trap macro with a value of afpCall in the csCode field of the parameter block.

RESULT CODES

aspBadVersNum	−1066	The server cannot support the ASP version number
aspBufTooSmall	−1067	The command reply from the server is larger than the response buffer; ASP will fill the buffer and truncate the reply data
aspNoMoreSess	−1068	The .XPP driver cannot support another ASP session
aspNoServers	−1069	There is no server at the specified server address, or the server did not respond to the request
aspParamErr	−1070	You specified an invalid session reference number, or the session has been closed
aspServerBusy	−1071	The server cannot open another session
aspSizeErr	−1073	The size of the command block exceeds the maximum size of aspMaxCmdSize

SEE ALSO

For information on how to obtain the internet socket address of a server, see the chapter "Name-Binding Protocol (NBP)" in this book.

AFP Write Command Format

You use the write command format for the AFPCommand function to pass the afpWrite command to the .XPP driver to send a data block to the server.

```
FUNCTION AFPCommand (thePBptr: XPPParmBlkPtr;
                     async: Boolean): OSErr;
```

thePBptr   A pointer to the XPP parameter block format for the afpWrite command.

async   A Boolean that specifies whether the function is to execute synchronously or asynchronously. Set the async parameter to TRUE to execute the function asynchronously.

Parameter block

→	ioCompletion	ProcPtr	A pointer to a completion routine.
←	ioResult	OSErr	The function result.
←	cmdResult	LongInt	The AFP command result.
→	ioRefNum	Integer	The .XPP driver reference number.
→	csCode	Integer	Always afpCall for this function.
→	sessRefnum	Integer	The session reference number.
→	aspTimeout	Byte	The retry interval in seconds.
→	cbSize	Integer	The command buffer size.
→	cbPtr	Ptr	The command buffer.
↔	rbSize	Integer	On input, the reply buffer size. On return, the actual reply size.
→	rbPtr	Ptr	A pointer to the reply buffer.
↔	wdPtr	Ptr	A pointer to the write data.

Field descriptions

cmdResult   Four bytes of data returned from the server indicating the result of the AFP command.

sessRefnum   The session reference number, which is a unique number that the .XPP driver assigns to the session and returns in response to an afpLogin command.

aspTimeout   The interval in seconds that the .XPP driver waits between retries of the AFP command call.

cbSize   The size in bytes of the block of data that contains the command and its parameters to be sent to the server across the session. The size of the command block must not exceed the value of aspMaxCmdSize that the ASPGetParms function returns. For information on the ASPGetParms function, see the chapter "AppleTalk Session Protocol (ASP)."

cbPtr   A pointer to the beginning of the command block buffer that contains the `afpWrite` command to be sent across the session to the server. The `cbSize` field value specifies the command block buffer size. The first byte of the command block must contain the AFP command. The following command block bytes contain the parameters for the command. The "Description" section that follows explains the command block structure that you use for the `afpWrite` command to be sent to the server.

rbSize   On input, the size in bytes of the reply buffer that is to hold the expected response to the AFP command. On return, the actual size of the reply that the .XPP driver returned in the buffer.

rbPtr   A pointer to the reply buffer.

wdPtr   A pointer to the write data buffer. The .XPP driver updates this field as it proceeds so that the field always points to the section of data that the .XPP driver is currently writing.

DESCRIPTION

After you open a session, you can use the `afpWrite` command to send a block of data to the server. The `AFPCommand` function format for the write command allows you to send more data than a single call to an `ASPUserWrite` function can send. Instead of using a write-data structure to specify the data to be sent, you specify the beginning of the data to be written and the size in bytes of the data as values within the command block. (You do not specify the size of the write data in the parameter block.)

The command block for the `afpWrite` command consists of the following fields. The byte offsets for these fields are relative to the location indicated by the command block pointer (`cbPtr`).

Command block

→	cmdByte	Byte	The AFP command code.
→	startEndFlag	Byte	A flag identifying offset relative to fork.
↔	rwOffset	LongInt	The offset within fork to begin writing.
↔	reqCount	LongInt	On input, requested size of data; on return, size of data actually written.

Field descriptions

cmdByte   The AFP command code, which is always `afpWrite` for this command.

startEndFlag   A 1-bit flag (the high bit of the byte) indicating whether the offset specified in the `rwOffset` field is relative to the beginning or the end of the fork: set the high bit to 0 to specify that the offset is relative to the beginning of the fork; set the high bit to 1 to specify that the offset is relative to the end of the fork. Set all other bits of this byte to 0.

rwOffset   The byte offset within the fork at which the write is to begin. The .XPP driver modifies the value of this field as it proceeds; the field always reflects the current value.

reqCount   On input, the size in bytes of the data to be written. On return, the actual size of the data that was written. The .XPP driver modifies the value of this field as it proceeds; the field always reflects the current value.

SPECIAL CONSIDERATIONS

Note that you must provide the .XPP driver reference number as an input parameter to this function. You can obtain the driver reference number by calling the Device Manager's OpenDriver function. For more information on the OpenDriver function, see *Inside Macintosh: Devices*.

The memory that you allocate for the XPP parameter block, command block, and reply buffer belongs to AFP until the function completes execution, after which you can reuse the memory or release it.

ASSEMBLY-LANGUAGE INFORMATION

To execute the AFPCommand function from assembly language, call the _Control trap macro with a value of afpCall in the csCode field of the parameter block.

RESULT CODES

aspBufTooSmall	–1067	The command reply from the server is larger than the response buffer (ASP will fill the buffer and truncate the reply data)
aspParamErr	–1070	You specified an invalid session reference number, or the session has been closed
aspSessClosed	–1072	The session reference number is valid, but the .XPP driver is in the process of closing the session
aspSizeErr	–1073	The size of the command block exceeds the maximum size of aspMaxCmdSize

SEE ALSO

See "AFP Command Block Record" on page 9-5 for the Pascal structure of the command block for an afpWrite command.

AFP Read Command Format

To read a block of data on an AFP file server, you use the read command format for the AFPCommand function, which passes the afpRead command to the .XPP driver.

```
FUNCTION AFPCommand (thePBptr: XPPParmBlkPtr;
                     async: Boolean): OSErr;
```

thePBptr   A pointer to the XPP parameter block format for a particular group of AFP commands.

async   A Boolean that specifies whether the function is to execute synchronously or asynchronously. Set the async parameter to TRUE to execute the function asynchronously.

Parameter block

→	ioCompletion	ProcPtr	A pointer to a completion routine.
←	ioResult	OSErr	The function result.
←	cmdResult	LongInt	The AFP command result.
→	ioRefNum	Integer	The .XPP driver reference number.
→	csCode	Integer	Always afpCall for this function.
→	sessRefnum	Integer	The session reference number.
→	aspTimeout	Byte	The retry interval in seconds.
→	cbSize	Integer	The command buffer size.
→	cbPtr	Ptr	A pointer to the command buffer.
↔	rbPtr	Ptr	A pointer to the reply buffer.

Field descriptions

cmdResult   Four bytes of data returned from the server indicating the result of the AFP command.

sessRefnum The session reference number, which is a unique number that the .XPP driver assigns to the session and returns in response to an afpLogin command.

aspTimeout The interval in seconds that the .XPP driver waits between retries of the AFP command call.

cbSize   The size in bytes of the block of data that contains the command and its parameters to be sent to the server across the session. The size of the command block must not exceed the value of aspMaxCmdSize that the ASPGetParms function returns. The "Description" section that follows explains the command block structure that you use for the afpRead command. See the chapter "AppleTalk Session Protocol (ASP)" for information on the ASPGetParms function.

cbPtr   A pointer to the beginning of the command block that contains the afpRead command. The cbSize field value specifies the command block size. The first byte of the command block must contain the AFP command. The following command block bytes contain the parameters for the command.

rbPtr   A pointer to the reply buffer. The .XPP driver updates this field as it proceeds; the value of this field points to the section of the buffer into which the . XPP driver is currently reading data.

DESCRIPTION

After you open a session, you can use the afpRead command to read a block of data from the server. The AFPCommand function format for the read command allows you to read more data than you can through a single call to an ASPUserCommand function.

You use the command block buffer to pass the read command and its parameters to the .XPP driver. (You pass the size of the read data buffer in the command block, not in the parameter block.) The command block for the afpRead command consists of the following fields. The byte offsets for these fields are relative to the location indicated by the command block pointer (cbPtr).

Command block

→	cmdByte	Byte	The AFP command code.
↔	rwOffset	LongInt	The offset within fork to begin reading
↔	reqCount	LongInt	On input, size of the read data buffer; on return, size of data actually read into the buffer.
→	newLineFlag	Byte	A flag indicating whether the read is to be terminated at a specified character.
→	newLineChar	Byte	The character used to determine where the read should be terminated.

Field descriptions

cmdByte
: The AFP command code, which is always afpRead for this command.

rwOffset
: The byte offset within the fork at which the read is to begin. The .XPP driver modifies the value of this field as it proceeds; the field always reflects the current value.

reqCount
: On input, the requested size of the read data buffer. On return, the actual size of the data that was read. The .XPP driver modifies the value of this field as it proceeds; the field always reflects the current value.

newLineFlag
: A 1-bit flag (the high bit of the byte) indicating whether the read is to be terminated at a specified character: set the high bit to 0 to indicate that you are *not* specifying a new-line character in the newLineChar field; set the high bit to 1 to indicate that you *are* specifying a new-line character in the newLineChar field. Set all other bits to 0.

newLineChar
: A character from $00 to $FF inclusive that, when encountered in reading the fork, causes the read operation to terminate.

SPECIAL CONSIDERATIONS

Note that you must provide the .XPP driver reference number as an input parameter to this function. You can obtain the driver reference number by calling the Device Manager's OpenDriver function. For more information on the OpenDriver function, see *Inside Macintosh: Devices*.

The memory that you allocate for the XPP parameter block, command block, and reply buffer belongs to AFP until the function completes execution, after which you can reuse the memory or release it.

ASSEMBLY-LANGUAGE INFORMATION

To execute the `AFPCommand` function from assembly language, call the `_Control` trap macro with a value of `afpCall` in the `csCode` field of the parameter block.

RESULT CODES

`aspBufTooSmall`	−1067	The command reply from the server is larger than the response buffer (ASP will fill the buffer and truncate the reply data)
`aspParamErr`	−1070	You specified an invalid session reference number, or the session has been closed
`aspSessClosed`	−1072	The .XPP driver is in the process of closing the session
`aspSizeErr`	−1073	The size of the command block exceeds the maximum size of `aspMaxCmdSize`

SEE ALSO

See "AFP Command Block Record" on page 9-5 for the Pascal structure of the command block for an `afpRead` command.

Summary of AFP

Pascal Summary

Constants

```
CONST
    {.XPP Driver unit and reference numbers}
    xppUnitNum        =    40;         {XPP unit number}
    xppRefNum         =   -41;         {XPP reference number}
    afpCall           =   250;         {AFP call command. Command buffer }
                                       { contains code for the command to be }
                                       { executed}

    {AFP command codes}
    afpByteRangeLock  =    1;
    afpVolClose       =    2;
    afpDirClose       =    3;
    afpForkClose      =    4;
    afpCopyFile       =    5;
    afpDirCreate      =    6;
    afpFileCreate     =    7;
    afpDelete         =    8;
    afpEnumerate      =    9;
    afpFlush          =   10;
    afpForkFlush      =   11;
    afpGetDirParms    =   12;
    afpGetFileParms   =   13;
    afpGetForkParms   =   14;
    afpGetSInfo       =   15;
    afpGetSParms      =   16;
    afpGetVolParms    =   17;
    afpLogin          =   18;
    afpContLogin      =   19;
    afpLogout         =   20;
    afpMapID          =   21;
    afpMapName        =   22;
    afpMove           =   23;
    afpOpenVol        =   24;
```

```
afpOpenDir          =  25;
afpOpenFork         =  26;
afpRead             =  27;
afpRename           =  28;
afpSetDirParms      =  29;
afpSetFileParms     =  30;
afpSetForkParms     =  31;
afpSetVolParms      =  32;
afpWrite            =  33;
afpGetFlDrParms     =  34;
afpSetFlDrParms     =  35;
afpDTOpen           =  48;
afpDTClose          =  49;
afpGetIcon          =  51;
afpGtIcnInfo        =  52;
afpAddAPPL          =  53;
afpRmvAPPL          =  54;
afpGetAPPL          =  55;
afpAddCmt           =  56;
afpRmvCmt           =  57;
afpGetCmt           =  58;
afpAddIcon          =  192;       {special code for ASP write commands}


{miscellaneous}
xppLoadedBit        =  5;         {XPP bit in PortBUse}
scbMemSize          =  192;       {size of memory for SCB}


{constants for AFP command block startEndFlag & newLineFlag fields}
xppFlagClr          =  0;
xppFlagSet          =  128;
```

Data Types

Command Block for AFP Read and AFP Write Commands

```
TYPE AFPCommandBlock =
   PACKED RECORD
      cmdByte:          Byte;        {AFP command}
      startEndFlag:     Byte;        {flag identifying offset relative }
                                     { to fork}
      forkRefNum:       Integer;     {reserved}
      rwOffset:         LongInt;     {offset within fork to begin }
                                     { reading or writing}
```

```
reqCount:               LongInt;      {on input, size of the data buffer; }
                                      { on return, size of the data actually }
                                      { written or read}
newLineFlag:            Byte;         {for read, a flag indicating whether }
                                      { the read is to be terminated at }
                                      { a specific character; not used by }
                                      { write}
newLineChar:            Char;         {character used to determine where }
                                      { the read is to be terminated; not }
                                      { used by write}
        END;
```

XPP Parameter Block for AFP

```
XPPPrmBlkType = (XPPPrmBlk...);
XPPSubPrmType = (ASPOpenPrm,ASPSubPrm);
XPPEndPrmType = (AFPLoginPrm,ASPEndPrm);

TYPE XPPParamBlock =
   PACKED RECORD
      qLink:               QElemPtr;       {reserved}
      qType:               Integer;        {reserved}
      ioTrap:              Integer;        {reserved}
      ioCmdAddr:           Ptr;            {reserved}
      ioCompletion:        ProcPtr;        {completion routine}
      ioResult:            OSErr;          {result code}
      cmdResult:           LongInt;        {command result (ATP user bytes)}
      ioVRefNum:           Integer;        {reserved}
      ioRefNum:            Integer;        {driver reference number}
      csCode:              Integer;        {command code}
   CASE XPPPrmBlkType OF
      XPPPrmBlk:
         (sessRefnum:      Integer;        {offset to session refnum}
         aspTimeout:       Byte;           {timeout for ATP}
         aspRetry:         Byte;           {retry count for ATP}
   CASE XPPSubPrmType OF
      ASPOpenPrm:
         (serverAddr:      AddrBlock;      {server address block}
         scbPointer:       Ptr;            {SCB pointer}
         attnRoutine:      Ptr);           {attention routine pointer}
      ASPSubPrm:
         (cbSize:          Integer;        {command block size}
         cbPtr:            Ptr;            {command block pointer}
         rbSize:           Integer;        {reply buffer size}
         rbPtr:            Ptr;            {reply buffer pointer}
```

```
CASE XPPEndPrmType OF
   AFPLoginPrm:
      (afpAddrBlock:     AddrBlock;        {address block in AFP login}
       afPSCBPtr:        Ptr;              {SCB pointer in AFP login}
       afpAttnRoutine:   Ptr);            {attn routine pointer in AFP login}
   ASPEndPrm:
      (wdSize:           Integer;          {write data size}
       wdPtr:            Ptr;              {write data pointer}
       ccbStart:         ARRAY[0..295] OF Byte)));
                                           {command control block}

   END;


XPPParmBlkPtr = ^XPPParamBlock;


XPPPrmBlkType = (XPPPrmBlk...);
XPPSubPrmType = (ASPOpenPrm,ASPSubPrm);
XPPEndPrmType = (AFPLoginPrm,ASPEndPrm);
```

Routines

```
FUNCTION AFPCommand              (thePBptr: XPPParmBlkPtr; async: Boolean): OSErr;
```

C Summary

Constants

```
enum {
   afpCall      = 250            /*AFP command (buffer has command code)*/
};

enum {                           /*AFPCall command codes*/
   afpFlush        = 10,
   afpForkFlush    = 11,
   afpGetDirParms  = 12,
   afpGetFileParms = 13,
   afpGetForkParms = 14,
   afpGetSInfo     = 15,
   afpGetSParms    = 16,
   afpGetVolParms  = 17,
   afpLogin        = 18,
   afpContLogin    = 19,
```

```
    afpLogout          = 20,
    afpMapID           = 21,
    afpMapName         = 22,
    afpMove            = 23,
    afpOpenVol         = 24,
    afpOpenDir         = 25,
    afpOpenFork        = 26,
    afpRead            = 27,
    afpRename          = 28,
    afpSetDirParms     = 29
};

enum {                              /*AFPCall command codes*/
    afpSetFileParms    = 30,
    afpSetForkParms    = 31,
    afpSetVolParms     = 32,
    afpWrite           = 33,
    afpGetFlDrParms    = 34,
    afpSetFlDrParms    = 35,
    afpDTOpen          = 48,
    afpDTClose         = 49,
    afpGetIcon         = 51,
    afpGtIcnInfo       = 52,
    afpAddAPPL         = 53,
    afpRmvAPPL         = 54,
    afpGetAPPL         = 55,
    afpAddCmt          = 56,
    afpRmvCmt          = 57,
    afpGetCmt          = 58,
    afpAddIcon         = 192        /*special code for ASP write commands*/
};

enum {
    xppLoadedBit       = 5,         /*XPP bit in PortBUse*/
    scbMemSize         = 192,       /*size of memory for SCB*/
    xppFlagClr         = 0          /*cs for AFPCommandBlock*/
};

enum {
xppFlagSet             = 128}       /*startEndFlag & NewLineFlag fields*/
};
```

Data Types

Command Block for AFP Read and AFP Write Commands

```
typedef struct {
    char   cmdByte;              /*AFP command*/
    char   startEndFlag;         /*flag identifying offset relative to fork*/
    short  forkRefNum;           /*reserved*/
    long   rwOffset;             /*offset within fork to begin reading */
                                 /* or writing*/
    long   reqCount;             /*on input, size of the data buffer; */
                                 /* on return, size of the data actually */
                                 /* written or read*/
    char   newLineFlag;          /*for read, a flag indicating whether the */
                                 /* read is to be terminated at a specific */
                                 /* character; not used by write*/
    char   newLineChar;          /*character used to determine where the read */
                                 /* is to be terminated; not used by write*/
} AFPCommandBlock;
```

XPP Parameter Block for AFP

```
#define  XPPPBHeader\
    QElem    *qLink;           /*reserved*/\
    short    qType;            /*reserved*/\
    short    ioTrap;           /*reserved*/\
    Ptr      ioCmdAddr;        /*reserved*/\
    ProcPtr  ioCompletion;     /*completion routine*/\
    OSErr    ioResult;         /*result code*/\
    long     cmdResult;        /*command result*/\
    short    ioVRefNum;        /*reserved*/\
    short    ioRefNum;         /*.XPP driver reference number*/\
    short    csCode;           /*function code*/

typedef struct {
    XPPPBHeader
    short     sessRefnum;      /*offset to session refnum*/
    char      aspTimeout;      /*timeout for ATP*/
    char      aspRetry;        /*retry count for ATP*/
    short     cbSize;          /*command block size*/
    Ptr       cbPtr;           /*command block pointer*/
    short     rbSize;          /*reply buffer size*/
    Ptr       rbPtr;           /*reply buffer pointer*/
```

```
   short      wdSize;           /*write data size*/
   Ptr        wdPtr;            /*write data pointer*/
   char       ccbStart[296];    /*beginning of command control block */
                                /* (CCB)*/
}XPPPrmBlk;

typedef struct {
   XPPPBHeader
   short        sessRefnum;      /*offset to session refnum*/
   char         aspTimeout;      /*timeout for ATP*/
   char         aspRetry;        /*retry count for ATP*/
   short        cbSize;          /*command block size*/
   Ptr          cbPtr;           /*command block pointer*/
   short        rbSize;          /*reply buffer size*/
   Ptr          rbPtr;           /*reply buffer pointer*/
   AddrBlock    afpAddrBlock;    /*block in AFP login*/
   Ptr          afpSCBPtr;       /*SCB pointer in AFP login*/
   Ptr          afpAttnRoutine;  /*attn routine pointer in AFP login*/
   char         ccbFill[144];    /*beginning of command control block*/
}AFPLoginPrm;

typedef struct {
   XPPPBHeader
   short        sessRefnum;      /*offset to session refnum*/
   char         aspTimeout;      /*timeout for ATP*/
   char         aspRetry;        /*retry count for ATP*/
   AddrBlock    serverAddr;      /*server address block*/
   Ptr          scbPointer;      /*SCB pointer*/
   Ptr          attnRoutine;     /*attention routine pointer*/
} ASPOpenPrm;

typedef ASPOpenPrm *ASPOpenPrmPtr;
```

Routines

```
pascal OSErr AFPCommand      (XPPParmBlkPtr thePBptr, Boolean async);
```

Assembly-Language Summary

Constants

XPP Driver Unit Number

xppUnitNum	EQU	40	;XPP unit number
xppLoadedBit	EQU	atpLoadedBit+1	;XPP loaded bit number in ; PortBUse

AFP Control Code

afpCall	EQU	250	;AFP csCode

AFP Command Codes

afpByteRangeLock	EQU	1
afpVolClose	EQU	2
afpDirClose	EQU	3
afpForkClose	EQU	4
afpCopyFile	EQU	5
afpDirCreate	EQU	6
afpFileCreate	EQU	7
afpDelete	EQU	8
afpEnumerate	EQU	9
afpFlush	EQU	10
afpForkFlush	EQU	11
afpGetDirParms	EQU	12
afpGetFileParms	EQU	13
afpGetForkParms	EQU	14
afpGetSInfo	EQU	15
afpGetSParms	EQU	16
afpGetVolParms	EQU	17
afpLogin	EQU	18
afpContLogin	EQU	19
afpLogout	EQU	20
afpMapID	EQU	21
afpMapName	EQU	22
afpMove	EQU	23
afpOpenVol	EQU	24
afpOpenDir	EQU	25
afpOpenFork	EQU	26

AppleTalk Filing Protocol (AFP)

```
afpRead              EQU      27
afpRename            EQU      28
afpSetDirParms       EQU      29
afpSetFileParms      EQU      30
afpSetForkParms      EQU      31
afpSetVolParms       EQU      32
afpWrite             EQU      33
afpGetFlDrParms      EQU      34
afpSetFlDrParms      EQU      35


afpDTOpen            EQU      48
afpDTClose           EQU      49
afpGetIcon           EQU      51
afpGtIcnInfo         EQU      52
afpAddAPPL           EQU      53
afpRmvAPPL           EQU      54
afpGetAPPL           EQU      55
afpAddCmt            EQU      56
afpRmvCmt            EQU      57
afpGetCmt            EQU      58


afpAddIcon           EQU      192     ;special code for ASP write commands
```

Miscellaneous

```
afpUseWrite    EQU    $C0              ;first call in range that maps to an
                                       ; ASPWrite
```

Data Structures

Parameter Block for General Command Format

18	cmdResult	long	AFP command result
26	csCode	word	command code; always afpCall
28	sessRefnum	word	session reference number
30	aspTimeout	byte	retry interval in seconds
32	cbSize	word	command buffer size
34	cbPtr	pointer	command buffer
38	rbSize	word	reply buffer size and actual reply size
40	rbPtr	pointer	reply buffer pointer
44	wdSize	word	write data size
46	wdPtr	pointer	write data pointer
50	ccbStart	record	beginning of memory for CCB

Parameter Block for Login Command Format

18	cmdResult	long	AFP command result
26	csCode	word	command code; alwaysafpCall
28	sessRefnum	word	session reference number
30	aspTimeout	byte	retry interval in seconds
31	aspRetry	byte	number of retries
32	cbSize	word	command buffer size
34	cbPtr	pointer	command buffer
38	rbSize	word	reply buffer size and actual reply size
40	rbPtr	pointer	reply buffer pointer
44	afpAddrBlock	long	server address block
48	afpSCBPtr	pointer	SCB pointer
52	afpAttnRoutine	pointer	attention routine pointer
50	ccbStart	record	beginning of memory for CCB

Parameter Block for AFP Write Command Format

18	cmdResult	long	AFP command result
26	csCode	word	command code; always afpCall
28	sessRefnum	word	session reference number
30	aspTimeout	byte	retry interval in seconds
32	cbSize	word	command buffer size
34	cbPtr	pointer	command buffer
38	rbSize	word	reply buffer size and actual reply size
40	rbPtr	pointer	reply buffer pointer
44	wdSize	word	used internally
46	wdPtr	pointer	write data pointer, updated
50	ccbStart	record	beginning of memory for CCB

Command Block for the AFP Write Command

0	cmdByte	byte	AFP command code
1	startEndFlag	byte	start/end flag
4	rwOffset	long	offset within fork to begin writing
8	reqCount	long	on input, requested size of data; on return, size of data actually written
12	newLineFlag	byte	new line flag
13	newLineChar	byte	new line character

Parameter Block for AFP Read Command Format

18	cmdResult	long	AFP command result
26	csCode	word	command code; always afpCall
28	sessRefnum	word	session reference number
30	aspTimeout	byte	retry interval in seconds
32	cbSize	word	command buffer size
34	cbPtr	pointer	command buffer
38	rbSize	word	used internally
40	rbPtr	pointer	reply buffer pointer (updated)
50	ccbStart	record	beginning of memory for CCB

Command Block for the AFP Read Command

0	cmdByte	byte	AFP command code
1	startEndFlag	byte	flag identifying offset relative to fork
4	rwOffset	long	offset within fork to begin reading
8	reqCount	long	on input, requested size of data; on return, size of data actually read into the buffer

Result Codes

aspBadVersNum	−1066	The server cannot support the ASP version number
aspBufTooSmall	−1067	The command reply from the server is larger than the response buffer (ASP will fill the buffer and truncate the reply data)
aspNoMoreSess	−1068	The .XPP driver cannot support another ASP session
aspNoServers	−1069	There is not a server at the specified server address, or the server did not respond to the request
aspParamErr	−1070	You specified an invalid session reference number, or the session has been closed
aspServerBusy	−1071	The server cannot open another session
aspSessClosed	−1072	The .XPP driver is in the process of closing the session
aspSizeErr	−1073	The size of the command block exceeds the maximum size of aspMaxCmdSize
afpParmError	−5019	The AFP command block size is equal to 0 (this error is also returned when the command block is equal to 0 or $FF [255] or GetSrvrStatus [15])

Link-Access Protocol (LAP) Manager

Contents

The Link-Access Protocol (LAP) Manager is a set of operating-system utilities that provide a standard interface between the higher-level AppleTalk protocols and the various link-access protocols, such as LocalTalk (LLAP), EtherTalk (ELAP), TokenTalk (TLAP), and FDDITalk (FLAP). This chapter describes the LAP Manager programming interfaces to the AppleTalk Transition Queue and the 802.2 packet protocol handlers only. This chapter does not discuss the LAP Manager interface to AppleTalk connection files of type 'adev' that comprise the data links. Apple Computer, Inc. recommends that you not write your own 'adev' files. However, for a description of the LAP Manager that includes the interface to AppleTalk connection files for EtherTalk and other AppleTalk connections, see the *Macintosh AppleTalk Connections Programmer's Guide*.

You should read this chapter if you want the LAP Manager to notify you when a transition occurs or is about to occur. An AppleTalk transition is an event, such as an AppleTalk driver being opened or closed, that can affect your AppleTalk application. This chapter also describes how you can define a transition to notify other applications of a transition event that your application effects.

You should also read this chapter if your application processes 802.2 Type 1 packets. In this case, you must write a protocol handler that reads 802.2 Type 1 data packets and install your protocol handler as a client of the LAP Manager.

For an overview of the LAP Manager and how it fits within the AppleTalk protocol stack, read the chapter "Introduction to AppleTalk" in this book, which also introduces and defines some of the terminology used in this chapter. For additional information on the IEEE 802.2 standard, see *Inside AppleTalk*, second edition.

About the LAP Manager

A Macintosh computer on an AppleTalk network can include one or more AppleTalk connection files. An **AppleTalk connection file** is a file of type 'adev' that contains a link-access protocol implementation for a data link (ELAP for EtherTalk, for example). One important function of an AppleTalk connection file is to implement the AppleTalk Address Resolution Protocol (AARP) that maps hardware layer addresses to AppleTalk node addresses. The LAP Manager makes it possible for the user to select among AppleTalk connection files by using the Network control panel to specify which network is to be used for the node's AppleTalk connection. When the user selects a connection from the Network control panel, the LAP Manager routes AppleTalk communications through the selected link-access protocol and hence through the selected hardware. The LAP Manager acts as a switching mechanism, interceding between the higher-level AppleTalk protocols and the data links so that when a user selects or changes the type of data link to be used, the process is transparent to the higher-level AppleTalk protocols and has no effect on applications that are clients of these protocols. Figure 10-1 shows this service that the LAP Manager provides. This figure does not show an AppleTalk connection file for LLAP because AARP is not used for LLAP and address mapping is not necessary.

CHAPTER 10

Figure 10-1   LAP Manager connecting the higher-level AppleTalk protocols with the selected data link

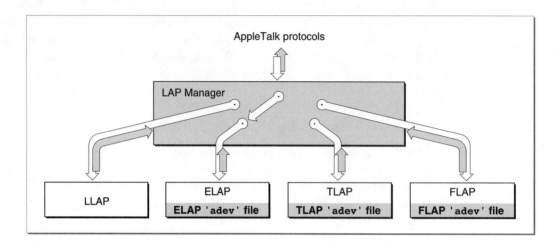

In addition to providing an interface to AppleTalk connection files, the LAP Manager also maintains the **AppleTalk Transition Queue,** which is an operating-system queue that can notify your application each time an AppleTalk transition occurs. An **AppleTalk transition** is an event, such as an AppleTalk driver being opened or closed or a network connection being broken, that can affect your AppleTalk application.

At any given time there might be two or more applications running that use AppleTalk. If one of these applications opens the .MPP driver, the other AppleTalk applications that use the driver are affected. If the operating system closes the AppleTalk .MPP driver, all AppleTalk applications using the driver are affected. To ensure that your application is not adversely affected by such an event, your application can place an entry in the AppleTalk Transition Queue. The LAP Manager sends a message to each entry each time the operating system or any routine performs any of these operations:

- opens the .MPP driver
- closes the .MPP driver
- indicates that it intends to close the .MPP driver
- cancels its intention to close the .MPP driver
- reports that it is changing the flagship name (This is a personalized name that a user can enter to identify the system when it is connected to an AppleTalk network.)
- indicates that it intends to change the flagship name
- cancels its intention to change the flagship name
- reports that the network connectivity has changed (for example, that a previously interconnected network is no longer available)
- reports that the cable range for the current network has been changed
- changes the speed of the CPU
- defines its own AppleTalk event and calls the AppleTalk Transition Queue to inform it that such an event occurred

Each of these events is referred to as an *AppleTalk transition.*

The LAP Manager also includes a protocol handler that reads 802.2 packets and provides an interface that allows you to attach your own **protocol handler** to receive 802.2 Type 1 packets. An 802.2 protocol handler is an application or process that receives, reads, and processes these 802.2 data packets. An 802.2 packet conforms to the 802.2 data-link standard called **Logical Link Control (LLC)** defined by the Institute of Electrical and Electronics Engineers (IEEE) for use on Ethernet, token ring, FDDI, and certain other data links. The 802.2 Type 1 protocol specifies a *connectionless* or *datagram* service. (The AppleTalk ELAP, TLAP, and FLAP implementations process 802.2 Type 1 packets.)

Using the LAP Manager

This section describes how you can use the LAP Manager's AppleTalk Transition Queue. Then it describes how to attach and detach protocol handlers for 802.2 Type 1 data packets using the `L802Attach` and `L802Detach` routines.

To use the AppleTalk Transition Queue, you add an entry for your application that contains a pointer to a transition event handler routine that you must provide to receive notification of transitions and to perform any additional processing that you want to perform in reaction to the transition.

After you add your entry, the LAP Manager will call your transition event handler routine to notify you that an AppleTalk transition either is about to occur or has occurred. The description of how to use the AppleTalk Transition Queue includes

- how to determine if the LAP Manager is installed on the node running your application

- how to add an entry to the AppleTalk Transition Queue

- how to write the routine that you must provide that the LAP Manager calls to notify you of the transition

- how to handle each of the standard AppleTalk transitions that can occur and about which your routine will be notified

- how to handle developer-defined transitions

- how to define your own transition events

Determining if the LAP Manager Is Installed

Before you issue any calls to the LAP Manager, you should check to determine if the LAP Manager is installed on the node that is running your application. The LAP Manager is implemented beginning with AppleTalk version 53. To determine if the LAP Manager is installed, you can check the low-memory global variable `LAPMgrPtr`. However, Apple Computer, Inc. recommends that you use a higher-level method to perform this check, such as the one that the code in Listing 10-1 shows.

Listing 10-1   Checking to determine if the LAP Manager is installed

```
FUNCTION GestaltAvailable: Boolean;
CONST
   _Gestalt = $A1AD;
BEGIN
   GestaltAvailable := TrapAvailable(_Gestalt);
END;

FUNCTION AppleTalkVersion: Integer;
CONST
   versionRequested = 1;    {version of SysEnvRec}
VAR
   refNum: Integer;
   world: SysEnvRec;
   attrib: LongInt;
BEGIN
   AppleTalkVersion := 0;    {default to no AppleTalk}
   IF OpenDriver('.MPP', refNum) = noErr THEN
                          {open the AppleTalk driver}
      IF GestaltAvailable THEN
      BEGIN
         IF (Gestalt(gestaltAppleTalkVersion, attrib) = noErr)
            THEN
            AppleTalkVersion := BAND(attrib, $000000FF);
      END
      ELSE {Gestalt or gestaltAppleTalkVersion selector isn't }
           { available.}
         IF SysEnvirons(versionRequested, world) = noErr THEN
            AppleTalkVersion := world.atDrvrVersNum;
END;

FUNCTION LAPMgrExists: Boolean;
BEGIN
   {AppleTalk Phase 2 is AppleTalk version 53 and later}
   LAPMgrExists := (AppleTalkVersion >= 53);
END;
```

Here is the declaration for the `TrapAvailable` function that the code in
Listing 10-1 calls:

```
FUNCTION TrapAvailable (theTrap: Integer): Boolean;
VAR
   tType: TrapType;
BEGIN
   tType := GetTrapType(theTrap);
   IF tType = ToolTrap THEN
   BEGIN
      theTrap := BAND(theTrap, $07FF);
      IF theTrap >= NumToolboxTraps THEN
         theTrap := _Unimplemented, ToolTrap;
END;
```

Adding an Entry to the AppleTalk Transition Queue

To ensure that your application is not adversely affected by a transition event, your
application places an entry in the AppleTalk Transition Queue.

To do this, you must create an AppleTalk Transition Queue entry record of type
`ATQentry` and give the LAP Manager a pointer to it. See "The AppleTalk Transition
Queue Entry" on page 10-33 for a description of the AppleTalk Transition Queue entry
record. This record includes a `CallAddr` field that holds a pointer to a **transition event
handler routine** that you provide, which is described in the following section "How the
LAP Manager Calls Your Transition Event Handler Routine."

Because you provide the memory for the queue entry, you can add as many fields to the
end of the entry as you wish for your own purposes. Whenever the LAP Manager calls
your transition event handler routine, it provides you with a pointer to the queue entry
so that you can have access to the information you stored at the end of your queue entry.

After you have created the AppleTalk Transition Queue entry record, you use the
`LAPAddATQ` function to add the entry to the AppleTalk Transition Queue. You pass a
pointer to the entry record as the value of the function's `theATQEntry` parameter.
Listing 10-2 shows how to do this using assembly language: you place a routine selector
in the D0 register, place a pointer to your AppleTalk Transition Queue entry in the A0
register, and execute a JSR instruction to an offset past the start of the LAP Manager. The
start of the LAP Manager is contained in the global variable `LAPMgrPtr` ($B18). The
offset to the LAP Manager routines is given by the constant `LAPMgrCall` (2).

Link-Access Protocol (LAP) Manager

Listing 10-2   Adding an AppleTalk Transition Queue entry

```
LAPMgrPtr    EQU      $B18           ;entry point for LAP Manager
LAPMgrCall   EQU      2              ;offset to LAP Manager
                                     ; routines
ATQEntry     EQU      *              ;pointer to ATQ entry


             MOVEQ    #23,D0         ;place routine selector
                                     ; in D0
             MOVE.L   LAPMgrPtr,An   ;put pointer to LAP Mgr in An
             MOVE.L   ATQEntry,A0    ;put ATQ entry in A0
             JSR      LAPMgrCall(An) ;jump to start of LAP Mgr
                                     ; routines
```

When you no longer want to be notified of transition events or before your program exits, you use the LAPRmvATQ function to remove your AppleTalk Transition Queue entry from the queue. Listing 10-3 shows how to do this from assembly language; you place the routine selector in the D0 register, place a pointer to your AppleTalk Transition Queue entry in the A0 register, and execute a JSR instruction to an offset past the start of the LAP Manager. The start of the LAP Manager is contained in the global variable LAPMgrPtr ($B18). The offset to the LAP Manager routines is given by the constant LAPMgrCall (2).

Listing 10-3   Removing an AppleTalk Transition Queue entry

```
LAPMgrPtr    EQU      $B18           ;entry point for LAP Manager
LAPMgrCall   EQU      2              ;offset to LAP Manager
                                     ; routines
ATQEntry     EQU      *              ;pointer to ATQ entry


             MOVEQ    #24,D0         ;place routine selector
                                     ; in D0 (24 to remove an
                                     ; entry)
             MOVE.L   LAPMgrPtr,An   ;put pointer to LAP Mgr in An
             MOVE.L   ATQEntry,A0    ;put ATQ entry in A0
             JSR      LAPMgrCall(An) ;jump to start of LAP Mgr
                                     ; routines
```

How the LAP Manager Calls Your Transition Event Handler Routine

This section describes how to write a transition event handler routine that responds to notification of AppleTalk transitions. Because the LAP Manager calls your transition event routine using C conventions, a transition event handler routine written in Pascal requires glue code to function correctly. To help solve this problem, this section includes a discussion of how to write a transition event routine using Pascal, and it also includes glue code that you will need. This section also describes the standard AppleTalk transitions and how your routine can respond to a particular transition.

When you have used the LAPAddATQ function to add an entry to the AppleTalk Transition Queue, the LAP Manager calls the transition event handler routine, whose pointer you pass to the LAP Manager in the AppleTalk Transition Queue entry record, whenever an AppleTalk transition occurs.

Table 10-1 shows the standard AppleTalk transitions (each of which is discussed later in this section) and their constants and routine selectors.

Table 10-1   AppleTalk transitions and their constants and routine selectors

AppleTalk transition	Constant	Routine selector
Open	ATTransOpen	0
Prepare-to-close	ATTransClose	2
Permission-to-close	ATTransClosePrep	3
Cancel-close	ATTransCancelCATTransCancelClose	4
Network-connection-change	ATTransNetworkTransition*	5
Flagship-name-change	ATTransNameChangeTellTask*	6
Permission-to-change-flagship-name	ATTransNameChangeAskTask*	7
Cancel-flagship-name-change	ATTransCancelNameChange*	8
Cable-range-change	ATTransCableChange*	'rnge'
CPU-speed-change	ATTransSpeedChange*	'sped'

* The constants marked with an asterisk are not included in the header files; you can use the routine selectors for these transitions, or you can define the constants in your application.

Link-Access Protocol (LAP) Manager

From assembly language, when the LAP Manager calls your routine, the stack looks like this:

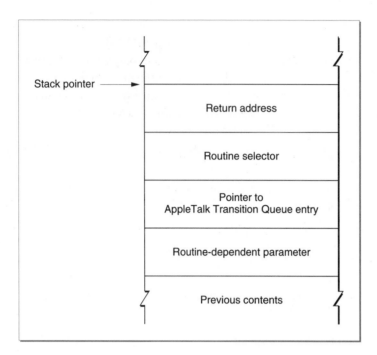

The first item on the stack (after the 4-byte-long return address) is a routine selector. There is one routine selector for each type of transition. Some transition events have a single-digit routine selector. Other transition events are four-character codes. Codes starting with an uppercase letter (A through Z) are reserved for use by developers. All other codes are reserved for use by Apple Computer, Inc.

The second item passed to your routine on the stack is a pointer to your routine's entry in the AppleTalk Transition Queue. You can use this pointer to gain access to any fields at the end of the queue entry that you allocated for your own use. The last item passed to your routine on the stack is a 4-byte-long parameter whose meaning depends on the type of transition.

With the exception of the open transition, the prepare-to-close transition, the flagship-name-change transition, the permission-to-change-flagship-name transition, and the cancel-flagship-name transition, the interface between the AppleTalk Transition Queue and your routine must follow these conventions:

- Your routine must preserve all registers except D0, D1, D2, A0, and A1.

- All parameters are passed on the stack as long words.

- Because your routine might be called at interrupt time, your routine must not make any direct or indirect calls to the Memory Manager, and it cannot depend on handles to unlocked blocks being valid, unless otherwise noted in the description of the transition event.

■ If you want to use any of your application's global variables, you must save the contents of the A5 register before using the variables and you must restore the A5 register before your routine terminates.

Again, these restrictions do not apply to the open transition, the prepare-to-close transition, and the three flagship-name transitions.

IMPORTANT

It is important that you return a 0 in the D0 register whenever you receive a transition event routine selector that you do not recognize or do not choose to handle. Returning a nonzero value in the D0 register might cause the system to cancel an attempt to close AppleTalk, for example, or it might be misinterpreted in some other way. You should only return a nonzero result to known transition events. ▲

Writing a Transition Event Handler Routine Using Pascal

The LAP Manager assumes that you will use the `CallAddr` field of your event record to pass it a pointer to a transition event handler routine that is written in the C programming language. The LAP Manager use C calling conventions when it calls your routine.

If you write your transition event handler routine in Pascal, you must include a glue code wrapper routine. You can use either the sample glue code provided in this section or your own method. To use this glue code, you must modify the AppleTalk Transition Queue entry record to include a field to hold a pointer to your Pascal transition event handler routine. You must add this field directly after the `CallAddr` field. You use the `CallAddr` field to pass the address of the assembly-language glue code routine. Here is the type declaration for an AppleTalk Transition Queue entry record that includes the additional field that is required if you use the glue code:

```
TYPE myATQEntry =
RECORD
    qlink:          Ptr;            {ptr to next queue entry}
    qType:          Integer;        {reserved}
    CallAddr:       ProcPtr;        {ptr to the glue code}
    PATQProcPtr:    ProcPtr;        {ptr to Pascal ATQ }
                                    { routine; this field must }
                                    { follow the CallAddr field. }
                                    { Do not change the order of }
                                    { these fields.}
    globs:          TransEventPtr;  {ptr to user defined globals}
END;

myATQEntryPtr = ^myATQEntry;
myATQEntryHdl = ^myATQEntryPtr;
```

The following segment of code shows how to add an AppleTalk Transition Queue entry to the queue. In this example, the actual transition event handler routine is called `ATQueueProc`. The glue code routine is called `CallTransQueue`. The `LAPAddATQ` function passes the glue code routine to the LAP Manager in the `CallAddr` field of the AppleTalk Transition Queue entry `myATQEntry`.

```
VAR
    gATQEntry: myATQEntry;
    OSErr: err;

BEGIN
    gATQEntry.CallAddr := ProcPtr(@CallTransQueue);
    gATQEntry.PATQProcPtr := ProcPtr(@ATQueueProc);
    err := LAPAddATQ(ATQEntryPtr(@gATQEntry));
```

Listing 10-4 shows the sample assembly-language glue code routine `CallTransQueue` that you can use if you write your transition event handler routine in Pascal. The glue routine takes the parameters from the stack and sets up a Pascal stack, then calls the function pointed to by the `PATQProcPtr` field of the AppleTalk Transition Queue entry record. On return, the glue code pulls the result from the stack and puts it into the D0 register, where the LAP Manager expects to find it.

Listing 10-4   Glue code for a Pascal transition event handler routine

```
;FUNCTION CallTransQueue (selector: LongInt; q: ATQEntryPtr;
;                         p: Ptr): LongInt;
;EXTERNAL;

CallTransQueue PROCEXPORT
    LINK       A6,#$0000         ;set up a local stack frame
    CLR.L      -(A7)             ;set space for return result
    MOVE.L     $0008(A6),-(A7)   ;move selector to stack
    MOVE.L     $000C(A6),-(A7)   ;move ATQPtr to stack
    MOVEA.L    (A7),A0           ;put copy ATQPtr in A0
    MOVEA.L    $000A(A0),A0      ;put pointer to real ATQ in A0
    MOVE.L     $0010(A6),-(A7)   ;move last parameter:
                                 ; pointer to stack
    JSR        (A0)              ;call the Pascal ATQ function
    MOVE.L     (A7)+,D0          ;move result into D0
    UNLK       A6                ;tear down local stack frame
    RTS                          ;return
    ENDP
    END
```

Open Transition

When an application calls the MPPOpen function or the Device Manager's OpenDriver function, AppleTalk attempts to open the .MPP driver. If the .MPP driver is already open, the LAP Manager does not call the AppleTalk Transition Queue transition event handler routines. If AppleTalk successfully opens the .MPP driver, the LAP Manager then calls every routine listed in the AppleTalk Transition Queue with an open transition (ATTransOpen).

When the LAP Manager calls your transition event handler routine, the stack looks like this:

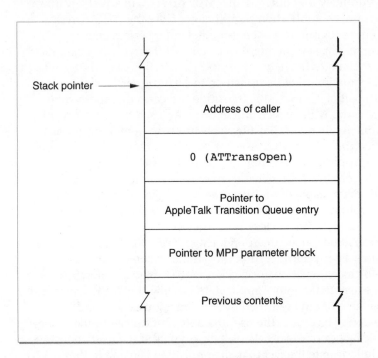

Stack pointer

Address of caller

0 (ATTransOpen)

Pointer to
AppleTalk Transition Queue entry

Pointer to MPP parameter block

Previous contents

The last item on the stack for an open transition is a pointer to the start of the Device Manager extended parameter block used by the routine that opened the .MPP driver. This pointer is provided for your information only; you must not change any of the fields in this parameter block.

Your transition event handler routine can perform any tasks you wish in response to the notification that the .MPP driver has been opened, such as using the Name-Binding Protocol (NBP) to register a name on the internet. Return 0 in the D0 register to indicate that your routine executed with no error.

Note
The open transition event occurs at system task time, during which you can allocate memory. ◆

Prepare-to-Close Transition

When any routine calls the `MPPClose` function or the Device Manager's `CloseDriver` function to close the .MPP driver, the LAP Manager calls every routine listed in the AppleTalk Transition Queue before the .MPP driver closes with an `ATTransClose` transition; if the .MPP driver is already closed when a routine calls either `MPPClose` or `CloseDriver`, the LAP Manager does not call the transition event handler routines in the AppleTalk Transition Queue.

When the system closes the .MPP driver

Whereas it is unlikely that opening the .MPP driver will adversely affect another program, an application should never close the .MPP driver because another program might be using it. Under certain circumstances, however, the system might close the .MPP driver, for example, when the user changes the network connection. In this case, the system will send a permission-to-close transition to each routine in the AppleTalk Transition Queue. This transition indicates that the system intends to close the .MPP driver, and in this way, each transition event handler routine in the queue has the opportunity to deny it permission to do so. When the system sends the permission-to-close transition, any routine in the AppleTalk Transition Queue that wishes to deny permission to close the .MPP driver can return a pointer to a Pascal string that gives the name of the application that placed the entry in the queue. If any routine denies permission to close the .MPP driver, the LAP Manager sends a cancel-close transition to every routine in the AppleTalk Transition Queue that previously received the permission-to-close transition. The application that caused the system to send a permission-to-close transition application may display a dialog box informing the user that another application is using the .MPP driver and showing the name (if any) returned by the transition event handler routine. The dialog box gives the user the option of canceling the request to close AppleTalk or of closing AppleTalk anyway. If the user chooses to close AppleTalk despite the fact that an application is using it, the system calls the `MPPClose` function. The LAP Manager then sends a prepare-to-close transition to each application in the AppleTalk Transition Queue, informing each one that AppleTalk is about to close. In this case, your transition event handler routine must prepare for the imminent closing of AppleTalk; it cannot deny permission to the `MPPClose` function. ◆

When the LAP Manager calls your transition event handler routine, the stack looks like this:

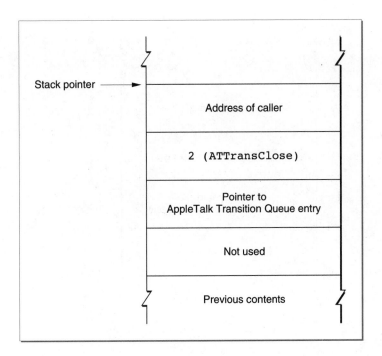

Your routine can perform any tasks you wish to prepare for the imminent closing of AppleTalk, such as ending a session with a remote terminal and informing the user that the connection is being closed. You must return control to the LAP Manager as quickly as possible. Return 0 in the D0 register to indicate that your routine executed with no error.

Note
When the LAP Manager calls your routine with a prepare-to-close transition (that is, a routine selector of ATTransClose), you cannot prevent the .MPP driver from closing. ◆

Permission-to-Close Transition

When a routine calls AppleTalk to inform AppleTalk that it wants to close the .MPP driver, the LAP Manager calls every transition event handler routine to request permission to close the .MPP driver with an ATTransClosePrep transition.

When the LAP Manager calls your transition event handler routine, the stack looks like this:

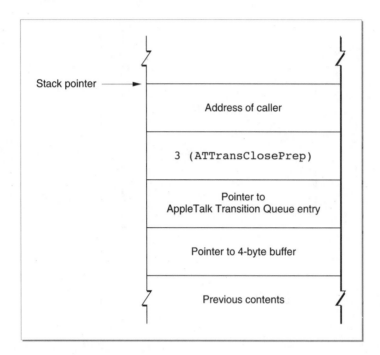

The last parameter on the stack is a pointer to a 4-byte buffer. If you intend to deny the request to close the .MPP driver, you place in the buffer a pointer to a Pascal string containing the name of your application. This string belongs to the LAP Manager until the LAP Manager finishes processing the cancel-close transition. The routine that issued the request to close the .MPP driver can then display a dialog box telling the user the name of the application that is currently using AppleTalk.

Your routine can return either a function result of 0 in the D0 register, indicating that it accepts the request to close, or a 1 in the D0 register, indicating that it denies the request to close. Note that the operating system might elect to close the .MPP driver anyway; for example, if the user grants permission to close in response to a dialog box.

Because the LAP Manager calls your routine again (with the routine selector set to ATTransClose) before the .MPP driver actually closes, it is not necessary for your routine to do anything other than grant or deny permission in response to being called for a permission-to-close transition. However, you might want to prohibit users from opening new sessions or establishing new connections while you are waiting for the .MPP driver to close.

Note
Earlier versions of *Inside Macintosh* referred to the PATalkClosePrep function as a means of requesting permission to close the .MPP driver. The PATalkClosePrep function is now only used internally by the .MPP driver. ◆

Cancel-Close Transition

When any routine in the AppleTalk Transition Queue denies permission for the .MPP driver to close, the LAP Manager calls each routine that has already received the permission-to-close transition with an `ATTransCancelClose` transition to inform it that the request to close the .MPP driver has been canceled.

When the LAP Manager calls your transition event handler routine, the stack looks like this:

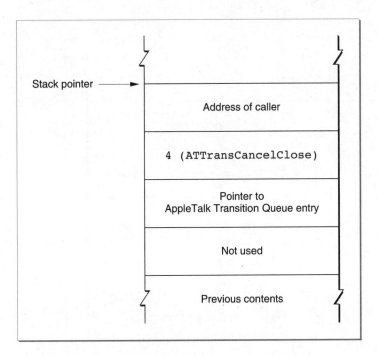

If your routine performed any tasks to prepare for the closing of AppleTalk, it should reverse their effects when it is called with the routine selector set to `ATTransCancelClose`. Return 0 in the D0 register to indicate that your routine executed with no errors.

Network-Connection-Change Transition

To receive notification of network connection changes or transitions, your application should process `ATTransNetworkTransition` transitions. All applications running on an AppleTalk network should handle this event, but especially those applications that use multinode IDs.

For example, Apple Remote Access (ARA), which uses multinode architecture, allows a user to establish a connection between two Macintosh computers over standard telephone lines. If the Macintosh that the user dials into is on an AppleTalk network, such as LocalTalk or EtherTalk, the Macintosh effectively becomes a node on that network, and all of the services on that network become available to the user. Because of this relationship, any application that establishes an ARA connection needs to be notified when new AppleTalk connections are established or broken.

Link-Access Protocol (LAP) Manager

Note

Both the AppleTalk Session Protocol (ASP) and the AppleTalk Data Stream Protocol (ADSP) have been modified to respond to network-connection-change transitions. When the AppleTalk drivers that implement these protocols receive notification of a network disconnect transition, they close down sessions on the remote side of the connection. ◆

When the LAP Manager calls your transition event handler routine, the stack looks like this:

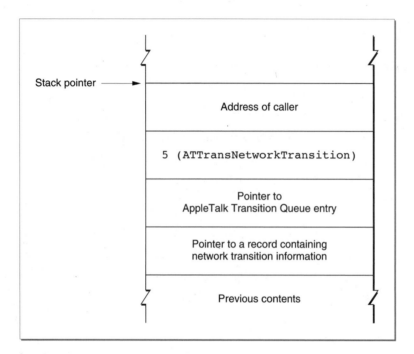

Note

If you want to use the constant `ATTransNetworkTransition` for this transition event, you must first declare it in your application because it is not defined in the MPW interface files. ◆

When the LAP Manager calls your routine, the last parameter on the stack contains a pointer to a record that contains a pointer to a network validation procedure. The process that sends notification of the network connection change uses this record to pass to the transition event handler routines a pointer to the network validation procedure; the transition event handler routines can then use this procedure to determine which networks are no longer connected, which networks remain connected, and which new networks have been added. To read the data in the record that this field points to, you must declare the following record type in your application:

```
TNetworkTransition =
    RECORD
        private:            Ptr;        {pointer used internally by ARA}
        netValidProc:       ProcPtr;    {pointer to the network }
                                        { validation procedure}
        newConnectivity:    Boolean;    {TRUE = new connectivity, }
                                        { FALSE = loss of connectivity}
    END;
```

You cannot access a ProcPtr directly from Pascal. Therefore, if you write your application in Pascal and you want to handle the ATTransNetworkTransition event, you need to include the following glue code so that you can access the network validation procedure pointed to by the netValidProc field. Listing 10-5 shows the CallNetValidProc function glue code that you can use to call the netValidProc validation procedure passed in the TNetworkTransition record.

Listing 10-5   Glue code to handle the network-connection-change transition from Pascal

```
FUNCTION CallNetValidProc (netTrans: TNetworkTransitionPtr;
                           theNet: LongInt; p: ProcPtr): LongInt;

INLINE
$205F, { MOVEA.L  (SP)+,A0 ;get ProcPtr into A0, and make stack
                           ; right for call }
$4E90; { JSR      (A0)     ;call ProcPtr, and return to caller}
```

The code in Listing 10-6 demonstrates the calling sequence of events for the CallNetValidProc glue code.

Listing 10-6   Using the glue code for the network validation procedure

```
CASE selector OF
ATTransNetworkTransition:
BEGIN
    myTNetworkTransitionPtr := TNetworkTransitionPtr(p);
    if (myTNetworkTransitionPtr^.newConnectivity) THEN
    BEGIN
    {
        /*Determine if there is a new connection.*/
    }
    END
```

```
      ELSE
  BEGIN
  {
      /*If there is a new connection, determine which network */
      /* address needs to be validated and assign the value to */
      /* checkThisNet.*/
  }

      checkThisNet = $1234FD00;
                        /*network $1234, node $FD, socket not used*/
      if (CallNetValidProc(myTNetworkTransitionPtr, checkThisNet
      myTNetworkTransitionPtr^.netValidProc) <> 0) THEN

      /*Take the appropriate action depending on result.*/
```

Apple Remote Access (ARA) is an example of a process that generates network-connection-change transitions to inform transition event handler routines and resident processes that network connectivity has changed. ARA uses the `TNetworkTransition` record to inform the routines about the changes. The `newConnectivity` field of the `TNetworkTransition` record identifies the type of change that has occurred:

- If this flag is `TRUE`, the network that your node is connected to through ARA has connected to a new internet. In this case, the LAP Manager will return all network addresses identifying them as reachable.

- If this flag is `FALSE`, specific networks are no longer reachable.

Because ARA is connection oriented, it can identify the location of a specific network and inform transition event handler routines that a network is no longer reachable. You can use this information to identify the loss of connections immediately instead of waiting to discover that the other end of the connection is no longer responding.

The `netValidProc` field of the `TNetWorkTransition` record contains a network validation hook for a function that you can use to query ARA about a specific network to determine if that network is still reachable. If the network is reachable, the validation function returns `TRUE`. You can call this function repeatedly to determine the status of each network that you are interested in. If you use the Pascal language to write your transition event handler routine, you must implement glue code to use the network validation procedure.

The information that the validation function returns is valid only for those routines that use the function in response to a network-connection-change transition.

Note
A network-connection-change transition can be sent at interrupt time. Because of this, you should follow the conventions that apply when a routine is called during an interrupt. For example, your routine should not call routines that move memory and you should not call AppleTalk functions synchronously. ◆

Flagship-Name-Change Transition

System 7 allows a user to enter a personalized name that identifies the system when it is connected to an AppleTalk network. This is called the **flagship name.** An application that provides network services for a workstation should use the flagship name so that the user can personalize the name that identifies the workstation to the network while reserving the use of the Chooser name for server connection identification. If your application utilizes flagship names, your routine should process `ATTransNameChangeTellTask` transitions. When the LAP Manager calls your routine with an `ATTransNameChangeTellTask` transition, you cannot prevent the flagship name from being changed.

When a routine calls the `ATEvent` procedure to change the flagship name, the LAP Manager calls every routine listed in the AppleTalk Transition Queue with an `ATTransNameChangeTellTask` transition. When the LAP Manager calls your transition event handler routine, the stack looks like this:

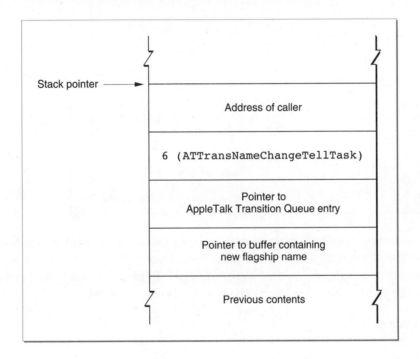

The last item on the stack is a pointer to a Pascal string that is the new flagship name to be registered. Your routine should remove the NBP registrations of entities under the old flagship name. You can make synchronous calls to NBP to remove a registered entity. Return a result of 0 in the D0 register to indicate that your routine executed with no error.

Note
Your application should only respond to flagship name changes about which it receives notification. Do not attempt to change the flagship name. ◆

Permission-to-Change-Flagship-Name Transition

If your application utilizes flagship names, your transition event handler routine should process `ATTransChangeNameAskTask` transitions. When a process makes a request to change the flagship name, the LAP Manager calls every routine listed in the AppleTalk Transition Queue with an `ATTransChangeNameAsk` transition to request permission to change the name. When the LAP Manager calls your transition event handler routine, the stack looks like this:

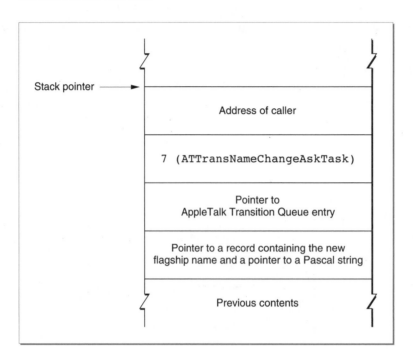

The last item on the stack contains a pointer to a record that holds the new flagship name. The `NameChangeInfo` record also includes a field that you use to identify your application if you deny the name-change request. To read from and write to the record, you must declare the following record type in your application:

```
NameChangeInfo =
   RECORD
      newObjStr:   Str32;       {new flagship name}
      name:        StringPtr;   {pointer to }
   END;                         { application's name}
```

The `newObjStr` field contains the proposed flagship name change. Your routine can inspect the `newObjStr` field. If your routine denies the name-change request, you must provide as the value of the `name` field a pointer to a buffer containing a Pascal string that names your application. The LAP Manager returns this pointer to the process that requested the flagship name change so that the process can then display a dialog box telling the user the name of the application that refused the name change.

If your application does not deny the request, you can make synchronous calls to NBP to attempt to register your application under the new flagship name while your transaction event handler routine is processing the request. Apple Computer, Inc. recommends that you register your application with NBP under the new flagship name while you handle the `ATTransChangeNameAskTask` transition. However, you should not remove the old NBP registration until you are certain that other applications have not denied the request to change the flagship name. If another application denies the name-change request, the LAP Manager will send an `ATTransCancelNameChange` transition to cancel the name-change request.

Return 0 in the D0 register to indicate that you accept the request to change the flagship name. To deny the request, return a nonzero number in the D0 register.

Cancel-Flagship-Name-Change Transition

When any routine in the AppleTalk Transition Queue refuses a request to change the flagship name, the LAP Manager will send an `ATTransCancelNameChange` transition to any transition event handler routines that acknowledged the `ATTransNameChangeAskTask` transition.

When the LAP Manager calls your transition event handler routine, the stack looks like this:

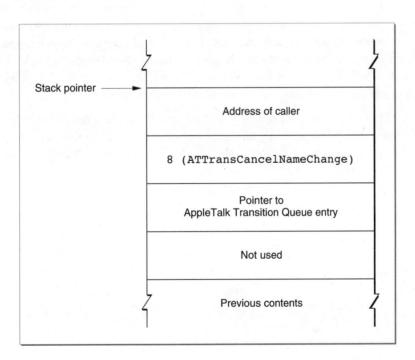

If your routine registered any entities with NBP under the new flagship name while it processed the ATTransNameChangeAskTask, it should remove those entries now. You can make synchronous calls to NBP to remove registration of the entities.

Return a result of 0 in the D0 register to indicate that your routine executed with no errors.

Cable-Range-Change Transition

A cable range is a range of network numbers beginning with the lowest network number and ending with the highest network number defined by a seed router for a network. All node addresses, including multinode addresses, that a system on a network acquires must have a network number within the defined cable range. (For information on multinodes, see the chapter "Multinode Architecture" in this book.)

Note
For nonextended networks, the lowest and the highest numbers are the same. ◆

When the cable range of a network changes because, for example, a router on the network shuts down, the LAP Manager will call your transition event handler routine with an ATTransCableChange transition. This transition notifies you that the cable range has changed for the network to which your node is connected.

Applications that use multinodes are examples of processes that should handle this transition. For multinode applications, after receiving notification of the cable range change, you should check the new cable range and determine if all the multinode IDs that the application acquired before the transition event occurred are still valid. If you discover multinode IDs that are no longer valid, you should call the RemoveNode function to remove them. Then you can call the AddNode function to obtain new multinode IDs that are within the valid cable range. See the chapter "Multinode Architecture" for information on RemoveNode and AddNode.

The LAP Manager sends you notice of a change in the cable range when the following events occur: AppleTalk first identifies the network router, the last router ages out, or AppleTalk first receives a Routing Table Maintenance Protocol (RTMP) broadcast packet that is different from the current range. The ATTransCableChange transition is implemented beginning with AppleTalk version 57. This transition event is issued at system task time only.

When the LAP Manager calls your transition event handler routine, the stack looks like this:

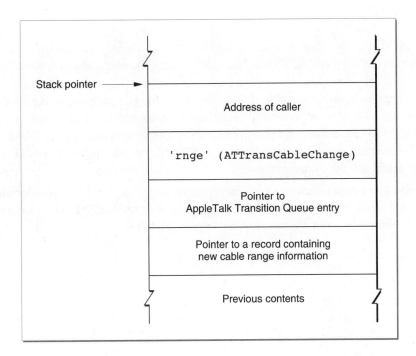

The last item on the stack contains a pointer to a record that holds the new high and low cable numbers that identify the cable range. To access this information, you must declare a record of type TNewCRTrans. Here is the TNewCRTrans record type declaration:

```
TNewCRTrans =
   RECORD
      newCableLo:     Integer; {new low cable in the range, }
                              { received from RTMP}
      newCableHigh:   Integer; {new high cable in the range, }
                              { received from RTMP}
   END;
```

CPU-Speed-Change Transition

Some applications change the CPU speed without rebooting the system. For example, an application may alter the cache states on the 68030 or 68040 CPUs or a third-party accelerator card may support dynamic speed changes made through a control panel 'cdev' file. Time-dependent processes need to be notified of changes to the CPU speed when these changes occur. If your application changes the CPU speed, you should use the ATEvent procedure to send notification of an ATTransSpeedChange transition to time-dependent processes. You must issue this transition event at system task time only. When you call the ATEvent procedure, pass ATTransSpeedChange as the value of the event parameter.

You must always notify LocalTalk when a CPU speed change occurs. LocalTalk includes a module that is time-dependent; the low-level timer values used in this code must be recalculated when the CPU speed changes. Altering the cache state on the 68030 does not affect LocalTalk, whereas altering the cache state on the 68040 does affect the LocalTalk timers. Therefore, an application that dynamically toggles caching on the 68040 should send notification of an ATTransSpeedChange transition. If the application does not do this and LocalTalk is the current network connection, the connection will be broken. LocalTalk implemented in AppleTalk version 57 or later recognizes the CPU-speed-change transition event notification.

The transition event handler routine of any time-dependent process should handle the ATTransSpeedChange transition notification. When the LAP Manager calls your transition event handler routine, the stack looks like this:

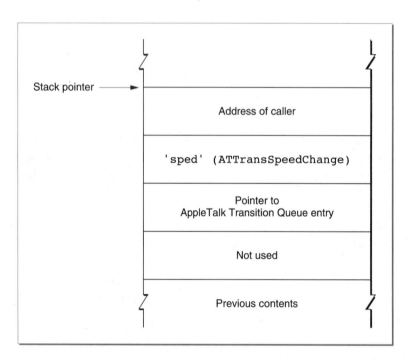

Developer-Defined Transitions

Any AppleTalk transition event code that begins with an uppercase letter (that is, any value in the range $41 00 00 00 through $5A FF FF FF) indicates a developer-defined event. Because you cannot tell how the originator of such an event might interpret a nonzero function result, you must always return 0 in the D0 register for any AppleTalk transition event code that you do not recognize.

When you return a nonzero result code for certain developer-defined transitions, the LAP Manager may call your transition event handler routine a second time with a cancel transition analogous to the cancel-close transition.

Defining Your Own AppleTalk Transition

You can define AppleTalk transitions and use such events to send messages to your own entries in the AppleTalk Transition Queue, or you can define events and make them public for others to use.

You can define your own AppleTalk transition to have any meaning you choose. For example, you might want to call every routine in the AppleTalk Transition Queue each time you open or close a custom protocol stack.

You can use either the `ATEvent` procedure or the `ATPreFlightEvent` function to notify all of the routines in the AppleTalk Transition Queue that your AppleTalk transition has occurred. Whereas the `ATEvent` procedure only calls the routines in the queue with a transition event, the `ATPreFlightEvent` function also allows each routine in the AppleTalk Transition Queue to return a result code and other information to your calling routine.

A developer-defined event, as with any event, always begins with an uppercase letter (that is, any value in the range $41 00 00 00 through $5A FF FF FF).

Note

You can call the `ATEvent` and `ATPreFlightEvent` routines only at virtual-memory safe time. See *Inside Macintosh: Memory* for information on virtual memory. ◆

The LAP Manager and 802.2 Protocol Packets

The Institute of Electrical and Electronics Engineers (IEEE) has defined a series of communications protocols for use on a variety of networks. At the physical level, these protocols include the 802.3 CSMA/CD protocol, the 802.4 token bus protocol, and the 802.5 token ring protocol. At the data-link level, you access these protocols through the IEEE 802.2 Logical Link Control (LLC) protocol. If you write an application that handles 802.2 Type 1 data packets, you must include a protocol handler to read the data. You can install your application as a client of the LAP Manager to receive 802.2 packets from an Ethernet, token ring, or FDDI driver.

The LAP Manager includes two routines that allow you to attach and detach protocol handlers for 802.2 Type 1 data packets: the `L802Attach` and `L802Detach` routines. The LAP Manager contains a generic protocol handler that receives data from the hardware device drivers and determines for which application the 802.2 packet is meant based on the protocol type. The LAP Manager's protocol handler then calls the destination application's protocol handler to read in the data. This section uses Ethernet to illustrate how this process works; however, the same process applies to token ring and FDDI packets.

The ANSI/IEEE standards for the 802 protocols are published by the IEEE. The first 14 bytes of a packet sent or received by the .ENET driver constitute the header. The first 12 bytes consist of the destination and source data-link addresses, such as the Ethernet hardware addresses. If the value of the last 2 bytes in the header is greater than 1500, then the .ENET driver treats that field as an Ethernet protocol type discriminator; this indicates that the packet is an Ethernet Phase 1 packet. If the value of the last 2 bytes in the header is less than or equal to 1500, then the field contains the length of the 802.2 packet, not including the 14-byte header, and this indicates that the packet is an Ethernet Phase 2 packet. The .ENET driver passes all Phase 2 packets to the LAP Manager.

The IEEE LLC standard defines the concept of a Service Access Point (SAP). A SAP is a 1-byte value that is used to distinguish the different protocols using 802.2 in a single node. Most SAPs are reserved for use by IEEE standard protocols. IEEE has reserved one SAP, whose value is $AA, for use by protocols other than the standard IEEE protocols. AppleTalk and many other protocol families use SAP $AA. Because other protocol families can also use this SAP, the value of another field that contains the **subnetwork access protocol (SNAP)** type is used to discriminate for which protocol family a packet with a destination subnetwork access protocol value of $AA is intended.

At the physical level, a packet contains the 802.3 header, the data field of which contains either an Ethernet protocol type discriminator (for Phase 1 packets) or the 802.2 packet length (for Phase 2 packets). For all Phase 2 packets, the LAP Manager receives the entire 802.3 packet from the .ENET driver. The first 14 bytes of the 802.3 data constitute the frame header, and they are followed by the 802.2 protocol header.

The first byte of the 802.2 header is the **destination service access point (DSAP).** If the DSAP value is equal to $AA, then the first 5 bytes of the 802.2 data constitute a SNAP protocol type discriminator. If the SNAP type value is $00000080F3, indicating the AppleTalk Address Resolution Protocol (AARP), then the next 4 bytes of the 802.2 data constitute the AARP packet type field. AARP is not discussed at length in this book; for complete information about AARP, see *Inside AppleTalk,* second edition.

Figure 10-2 shows an Ethernet packet containing AppleTalk Phase 1 data. Phase 1 packets are the original version of Ethernet packets. The last 2 bytes in the header contain a value greater than 1500, indicating that this field is to be treated as a protocol type discriminator.

Figure 10-2   Ethernet Phase 1 packet formats

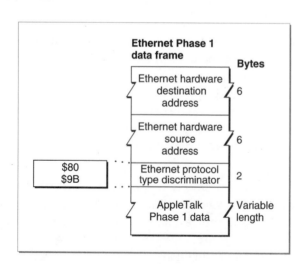

Figure 10-3 shows two Phase 2 packets. For Phase 2 packets, the last 2 bytes of the 802.3 header contain the 802.2 packet length, not including the 14-byte header; the 802.2 packet length is a value from 0 through 1500.

The data frame on the left shows an Ethernet 802.3 packet containing an 802.2 packet that holds AppleTalk Phase 2 data. The Ethernet driver would deliver this entire packet to the LAP Manager; the 802.2 packet is enclosed in the 802.3 packet, which is also referred to as a frame. The data frame on the right shows an Ethernet 802.3 packet containing an 802.2 packet to be delivered to the Phase 2 Ethernet AARP handler; the SNAP type value is $00000080F3, indicating the AppleTalk Address Resolution Protocol (AARP).

Figure 10-3   Ethernet Phase 2 packet formats

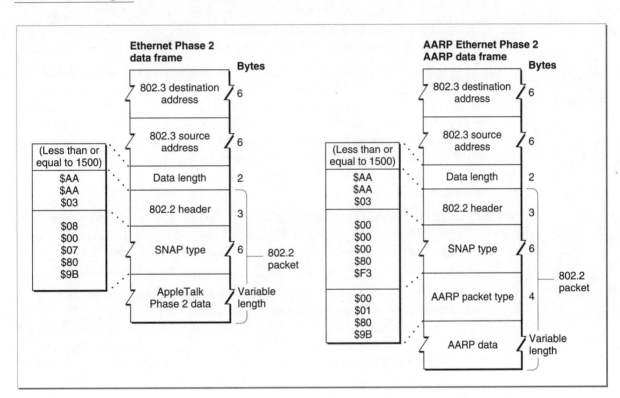

When you call the L802Attach routine, you provide a pointer to your protocol handler, the reference number of the .ENET driver, and a pointer to a string containing one or more type fields. The type fields indicate the DSAP value and any other protocol type fields (such as the SNAP type and the AARP type). The LAP Manager delivers to your protocol handler any 802.2 data packets that have the protocol type you specify.

Attaching and Detaching 802.2 Protocol Handlers

You must use the LAP Manager to attach your protocol handler for 802.2 protocols to receive Ethernet Phase 2 packets and all token ring and FDDI packets.

The LAP Manager is designed to install a generic protocol handler that receives packets from the hardware device drivers for 802.2 protocols and that also serves as a dispatcher. The LAP Manager's protocol handler maintains an index of registered protocol types and pointers to their protocol handlers. When an application calls the LAP Manager to attach a protocol handler, the LAP Manager adds an entry for the application's protocol type and protocol handler to its protocol handler index.

The LAP Manager's protocol handler determines for which application data is meant. When processing a packet, the LAP Manager reads the destination SAP; if the SAP value is $AA, the LAP Manager then checks the SNAP header for the protocol type, and then it searches for a protocol type match in its protocol handler index. If the LAP Manager finds a protocol type match, it calls the destination application's protocol handler to read in the data. You cannot replace or override the permanent LAP Manager protocol handler.

The first time that a process or application calls the LAP Manager to attach a protocol handler for 802.2 packets, the LAP Manager calls the specified hardware device driver directly to install its own generic protocol handler. The LAP Manager then registers in its index the protocol handler and the protocol type for the process that initially called it. When a process or application subsequently calls the LAP Manager to attach a protocol handler to receive 802.2 packets from the same type of hardware device driver, the LAP Manager simply adds the protocol handler and protocol type information for that process to its index.

The LAP Manager allows for the concurrent use of hardware device drivers by more than one application. For example, Figure 10-4 shows three scenarios. In the first instance at the top of the figure, only AppleTalk is using the Ethernet driver to receive data; AppleTalk always uses the LAP Manager, which provides for its link independence.

In the second instance in the middle of the figure, both AppleTalk and a developer-written application have attached their protocol handlers to the LAP Manager. AppleTalk is configured to use the Ethernet driver; when the LAP Manager's protocol handler reads a packet, it determines if the data is meant for AppleTalk, and if so, the LAP Manager calls the DDP protocol handler to receive the data. If the data is meant for the other application, the LAP Manager calls that application's protocol handler.

In the third instance at the bottom of the figure, both AppleTalk and the developer-written application have attached their protocol handlers to the LAP Manager to receive data from the token ring driver. The LAP Manager receives the data, determines the destination, then calls the appropriate protocol handler, either the DDP protocol handler or the developer-written application's protocol handler to receive the data.

Figure 10-4   Using the LAP Manager to receive data for 802.2 protocols

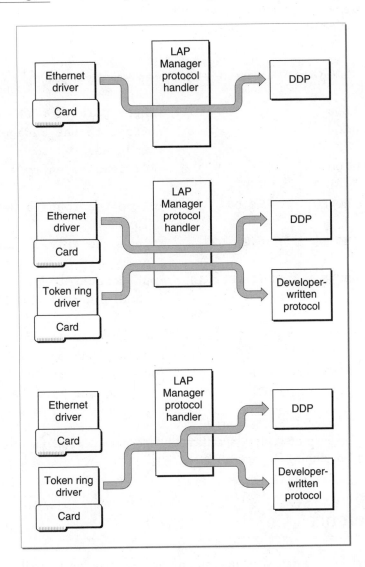

There are no high-level interfaces for the LAP Manager 802.2 protocol routines. You call these routines from assembly language by placing a routine selector in the D0 register and executing a JSR instruction to an offset 2 bytes past the start of the LAP Manager. The start of the LAP Manager is contained in the global variable `LAPMgrPtr` ($B18).

Before you call these routines, you must place the reference number of the .ENET driver in the D2 register and a pointer to the protocol type specification in the A1 register. Before you call the `L802Attach` routine, you must also place a pointer to your protocol handler in the A0 register. Both routines return a nonzero value in the D0 register if there is an error.

Listing 10-7 shows how to call either the LAP Manager's `L802Attach` or `L802Detach` routine from assembly language. To specify either of these routines, you place the routine selector in register D0, as indicated in the sample code.

Listing 10-7   Calling a LAP Manager 802.2 routine from assembly language

```
LAPMgrPtr     EQU    $B18           ;entry point for LAP Manager
LAPMgrCall    EQU    2              ;offset to LAP Manager
                                    ; routines
L802Entry     EQU    *              ;802 routine entry

              MOVEQ  #RSel,D0        ;place the routine selector
                                    ; in D0
              MOVEQ  #refNum,D2      ;place the driver reference
                                    ; number in D2
              MOVE.L PHndlrPtr,A0    ;put pointer to protocol
                                    ; handler in A0 (L802Attach
                                    ; only)
              MOVE.L PSpecPtr,A1     ;put pointer to protocol
                                    ; specification in A1
              MOVE.L LAPMgrPtr,An    ;put pointer to LAP Mgr in An
              JSR    LAPMgrCall(An)  ;jump to start of LAP Mgr
                                    ; routines
```

For information on the protocol type specification whose pointer you place in register A1, see "L802Attach" beginning on page 10-40.

LAP Manager Reference

This section describes the data structures and routines that are specific to the LAP Manager.

The "Data Structures" section shows the Pascal data structure for the AppleTalk Transition Queue entry record.

The "Routines" section describes routines for adding and removing an AppleTalk Transition Queue entry, requesting permission to close the .MPP driver, notifying the routines specified by AppleTalk Transition Queue entries when a transition occurs that your application has defined, and attaching and detaching your own 802.2 protocol handler for Type 1 packets.

Data Structures

This section describes the `ATQEntry` record that you use to specify your AppleTalk Transition Queue entry routine to be called when a transition event occurs. You pass a pointer to this record as a parameter to the `LAPAddATQ` function, which you call to place your entry in the AppleTalk Transition Queue.

The AppleTalk Transition Queue Entry

You use the AppleTalk Transition Queue entry record to specify an entry to be added to the transition queue. The `ATQEntry` data type defines an AppleTalk Transition Queue entry.

```
TYPE ATQEntry =
RECORD
    qLink:      ATQEntryPtr;        {next queue entry}
    qType:      Integer;            {reserved}
    CallAddr:   ProcPtr;            {pointer to your routine}
END;
```

Field descriptions

qLink   A pointer to the next queue entry. Set this field to `NIL`; the LAP Manager fills it in when an application adds another entry to the queue.

qType   Reserved.

CallAddr   A pointer to a transition event handler routine that you provide. The LAP Manager calls your routine when an AppleTalk transition event occurs.

Because you provide the memory for the AppleTalk Transition Queue entry, you can add as many fields to the end of the entry as you wish for your own purposes. Whenever your routine is called, the caller provides you with a pointer to the queue entry so that you can have access to the information you stored at the end of your queue entry.

Routines

This section describes the LAP Manager's Pascal interface to the AppleTalk Transition Queue that allows you to place an entry for your application in the queue so that you will be notified when an AppleTalk transition occurs.

The Pascal interface to the AppleTalk Transition Queue consists of four routines:

■ The `LAPAddATQ` function adds an entry to the AppleTalk Transition Queue.

■ The `LAPRmvATQ` function removes an entry from the AppleTalk Transition Queue.

■ The `ATEvent` procedure calls all the entries in the AppleTalk Transition Queue with an AppleTalk transition event code that you specify.

■ The ATPreFlightEvent function calls all the entries in the AppleTalk Transition Queue with an AppleTalk transition event code that you specify in the event parameter. If any routine returns a nonzero function result, the LAP Manager calls all of the entries with the transition event code that you specify in ATPreFlightEvent function's cancel parameter.

This section also describes the LAP Manager's assembly-language interface that allows you to install and remove your own protocol handler for a specific IEEE 802.2 protocol type. You can write a protocol handler application that reads 802.2 Type 1 data packets, and you can install your application as a client of the LAP Manager.

The assembly-language routines that allow you to attach and detach protocol handlers for 802.2 Type 1 data packets are

■ the L802Attach routine, which installs your protocol handler for a specific IEEE 802.2 protocol type

■ the L802Detach routine, which detaches from the LAP Manager your protocol handler for a specific IEEE 802.2 protocol type

Note
The ANSI/IEEE standards for the 802 protocols are published by the IEEE. ◆

Adding and Removing AppleTalk Transition Queue Entries

This section describes the LAPAddATQ function that you use to add an entry to the AppleTalk Transition Queue and the LAPRmvATQ function that you use to remove an entry from the queue.

LAPAddATQ

The LAPAddATQ function adds an entry to the AppleTalk Transition Queue.

FUNCTION LAPAddATQ (theATQEntry: ATQEntryPtr): OSErr;

theATQEntry
    A pointer to a record of type ATQEntry to be added to the AppleTalk Transition Queue.

DESCRIPTION

You use the LAPAddATQ function to add an entry for your application to the AppleTalk Transition Queue. Before you call the LAPAddATQ function, you must create an AppleTalk Transition Queue entry record of type ATQEntry that defines your entry. "The AppleTalk Transition Queue Entry" on page 10-33 describes the ATQEntry record. You provide a pointer to this record as the value of the theATQEntry parameter when you call the LAPAddATQ function.

In the `CallAddr` field of the AppleTalk Transition Queue entry record, you provide a pointer to a routine that the LAP Manager is to call when an AppleTalk transition event occurs. The LAP Manager calls your routine to notify you when any of the following events occurs:

- A process opens the .MPP driver.

- A process requests permission to close AppleTalk.

- A process closes the .MPP driver.

- A request to close AppleTalk is canceled. One of the routines pointed to by an entry in the AppleTalk Transition Queue denies permission to close AppleTalk, and so the request to do so is canceled.

- A process calls the `ATEvent` procedure or the `ATPreFlightEvent` function to send its own AppleTalk transition event to the entries in the AppleTalk Transition Queue.

- A process reports that it is changing the flagship name.

- A process makes a request to change the flagship name.

- A request to change the flagship name is canceled. One process denies another's request to change the flagship name, and so the request is canceled.

- The network connectivity has changed. This transition event is sent if a node is connected to an AppleTalk network and, for some reason, a particular interconnected AppleTalk network is longer be reachable.

- The cable range for the current network has been changed.

- The speed of the CPU has been changed.

SPECIAL CONSIDERATIONS

You must allocate nonrelocatable memory for the `ATQEntry` record and not alter or manipulate this memory until you remove the AppleTalk Transition Queue entry from the transition queue using the `LAPRmvATQ` function.

When LAP Manager calls your transition event handler routine, the LAP Manager passes parameters to your routine using the C stack calling conventions, and expects your routine to return a result in register D0. If you write your transition event handler routine in Pascal, you must use an assembly glue code routine. For a sample glue code routine, see "Writing a Transition Event Handler Routine Using Pascal" beginning on page 10-11.

ASSEMBLY-LANGUAGE INFORMATION

From assembly language, you add an AppleTalk Transition Queue entry by placing a routine selector in the D0 register, placing a pointer to your AppleTalk Transition Queue entry in the A0 register, and executing a JSR instruction to an offset past the start of the LAP Manager. The start of the LAP Manager is contained in the global variable `LAPMgrPtr` ($B18). The offset to the LAP Manager routines is given by the constant `LAPMgrCall` (2).

Registers on entry

D0   23

A0   Pointer to AppleTalk Transition Queue entry

Registers on exit

D0   Result code

RESULT CODES

noErr   0   No error

SEE ALSO

"Adding an Entry to the AppleTalk Transition Queue" on page 10-7 describes the process of creating an AppleTalk Transition Queue entry and adding it to the queue.

For the details of each transition, see "How the LAP Manager Calls Your Transition Event Handler Routine" beginning on page 10-9.

LAPRmvATQ

The LAPRmvATQ function removes an entry from the AppleTalk Transition Queue.

```
FUNCTION LAPRmvATQ (theATQEntry: ATQEntryPtr): OSErr;
```

theATQEntry
     A pointer to the ATQEntry record to be removed from the AppleTalk Transition Queue.

DESCRIPTION

You use the LAPRmvATQ function to remove your application's entry from the AppleTalk Transition Queue. To identify the entry to be removed, you pass the LAPRmvATQ function the same pointer to the AppleTalk Transition Queue entry record that you provided as the value of the theATQEntry parameter when you called the LAPAddATQ function to place the entry in the queue.

SPECIAL CONSIDERATIONS

You must not call the LAPRmvATQ function at interrupt time or through a callback routine. This restriction is to prevent any routine from removing an entry from the AppleTalk Transition Queue while another routine is in the process of adding or removing an entry.

ASSEMBLY-LANGUAGE INFORMATION

From assembly language, you remove an AppleTalk Transition Queue entry by placing a routine selector in the D0 register, placing a pointer to your AppleTalk Transition Queue entry in the A0 register, and executing a JSR instruction to an offset past the start of the LAP Manager. The start of the LAP Manager is contained in the global variable `LAPMgrPtr` ($B18). The offset to the LAP Manager routines is given by the constant `LAPMgrCall` (2).

Registers on entry

D0   24

A0   Pointer to AppleTalk Transition Queue entry

Registers on exit

D0   Result code

RESULT CODES

noErr	0	No error
qErr	−1	Queue element not found

Notifying Routines When Your Application-Defined Transition Occurs

This section describes the `ATEvent` and `ATPreFlightEvent` routines that you can use to notify all of the entries in the AppleTalk Transition Queue that an AppleTalk transition that you have defined has occurred.

You can define your own AppleTalk transition to have any meaning you choose. For example, you might want to call every routine in the AppleTalk Transition Queue each time you open an AppleTalk Data Stream Protocol (ADSP) connection.

ATEvent

The `ATEvent` procedure calls the routines specified by each of the entries in the AppleTalk Transition Queue with notification of a transition event that you have defined.

```
PROCEDURE ATEvent (event: LongInt; infoPtr: Ptr);
```

event   The AppleTalk transition event code for your application-defined transition. This can be any four-character string that starts with an uppercase letter—that is, any value in the range $41 00 00 00 through $5A FF FF FF.

infoPtr   A pointer to information that you make available to the AppleTalk Transition Queue entry routines. If you do not want to pass any information to these routines, set the `infoPtr` parameter to NIL.

DESCRIPTION

The `ATEvent` procedure calls the routines in the queue with the AppleTalk transition event code you specify in the `event` parameter. You can use the `infoPtr` parameter to point to any information that you want to make available to the transition event handler routines; for an ADSP-open transition, for example, you might pass a pointer to the parameter block used by the `dspOpen` routine.

You use the `ATEvent` procedure to send notification of an `ATTransSpeedChange` transition to time-dependent processes. You must send this transition event notification if your application changes the CPU speed. Note that you must issue this transition event at system task time only.

For transition events that you define, you can issue the `ATEvent` procedure at interrupt time provided that the transition event handler routines follow the standard rules for interrupt operation.

SPECIAL CONSIDERATIONS

You can call the `ATEvent` procedure only at virtual-memory safe time.

AppleTalk transitions defined by developers might return other result codes.

RESULT CODES

noErr   0   No error, or unrecognized event code

SEE ALSO

For more information about the `ATTransSpeedChange` event, see "CPU-Speed-Change Transition" on page 10-25.

For more information about developer-defined transition events, see "Developer-Defined Transitions" on page 10-26 and "Defining Your Own AppleTalk Transition" on page 10-27.

For information on virtual memory, see *Inside Macintosh: Memory*.

ATPreFlightEvent

The `ATPreFlightEvent` function calls the routines specified by each of the entries in the AppleTalk Transition Queue with notification of a transition event that you have defined and allows each routine in the AppleTalk Transition Queue to return a result code and other information to your calling routine.

```
FUNCTION ATPreFlightEvent (event,cancel: LongInt;
                           infoPtr: Ptr): OSErr;
```

event   The AppleTalk transition event code for the initial transition about which you want to notify the AppleTalk Transition Queue event routines. This code can be any four-character string that starts with an uppercase letter—that is, any value in the range $41 00 00 00 through $5A FF FF FF.

cancel   The AppleTalk transition event code for the transition that notifies the AppleTalk Transition Queue event routines that your original transition notification is canceled. This code can be any four-character string that starts with an uppercase letter—that is, any value in the range $41 00 00 00 through $5A FF FF FF.

infoPtr   A pointer to information that you make available to the AppleTalk Transition Queue entry routines. If you do not want to pass any information to these routines, set the infoPtr parameter to NIL.

DESCRIPTION

The ATPreFlightEvent function calls all of the routines in the AppleTalk Transition Queue with the AppleTalk transition event code you specify in the event parameter. If any routine in the AppleTalk Transition Queue returns a nonzero function result, the ATPreFlightEvent function calls each of the routines that it has already called, this time with the AppleTalk transition event code you specify in the cancel parameter.

SPECIAL CONSIDERATIONS

You can call the ATPreFlightEvent function only at virtual-memory safe time.

AppleTalk transitions defined by developers might return other result codes.

RESULT CODES

noErr   0   No error, or unrecognized event code

SEE ALSO

See *Inside Macintosh: Memory* for information on virtual memory.

For information about developer-defined transition events, see "Developer-Defined Transitions" on page 10-26 and "Defining Your Own AppleTalk Transition" on page 10-27.

Attaching and Detaching 802.2 Protocol Handlers

You can attach to the LAP Manager your own protocol handler for 802.2 protocols. The LAP Manager has a generic protocol handler that it attaches at the hardware device driver level for all 802.2 packets; you must not replace or override this protocol handler. You can also detach from the LAP Manager any 802.2 protocol handler that you have provided and attached.

You use the `L802Attach` routine to attach your protocol handler and the `L802Detach` routine to detach your protocol handler. There are no high-level interfaces for the LAP Manager 802.2 protocol routines. You must call these routines from assembly language.

L802Attach

The `L802Attach` routine attaches to the LAP Manager a protocol handler for a specific IEEE 802.2 protocol type.

DESCRIPTION

You call the `L802Attach` routine from assembly language by placing the routine selector of 21 in the D0 register and the reference number of the Ethernet, token ring, or FDDI driver in the D2 register that the `OpenSlot` or `OpenDriver` function returns. Then, you execute a JSR instruction to an offset 2 bytes past the start of the LAP Manager. The start of the LAP Manager is contained in the global variable `LAPMgrPtr` ($B18).

Here are the register contents that you supply on entry and the value that is returned to you.

Registers on entry

D0   21
D2   Reference number of hardware device driver
A0   Pointer to your protocol handler
A1   Pointer to protocol-type specification

Registers on exit

D0   Nonzero if error

You must put a pointer to your protocol handler in the A0 register and a pointer to the protocol-type specification for this protocol handler in the A1 register. The protocol-type specification consists of one or more protocol-type fields, each preceded by a length byte. The LAP Manager reads the fields in the 802.2 data packet header to determine to which protocol handler (if any) to deliver the packet. The first type field in your protocol specification is the 1-byte DSAP. If the DSAP type field is equal to $AA, then the packet is a SNAP packet. In this case, the protocol-type specification must contain a second type field, the 5-byte SNAP type. If the SNAP type field is $00000080F3, indicating the AppleTalk Address Resolution Protocol (AARP), then the protocol-type specification must contain a third type field, the 4-byte AARP protocol type. Terminate the list of protocol-type fields with a byte of zeros.

The following protocol-type specification, for example, is for the permanent LAP Manager protocol handler for an 802.3 packet containing AppleTalk data. The .ENET driver would deliver this packet to the LAP Manager. The first byte, $01, is the length byte for the first protocol-type field (the DSAP type field), $AA, contained in the second byte. The DSAP value of $AA is reserved for use with protocol-type specifications that include a SNAP field. The third byte, $05, is the length byte for the next protocol-type field, the SNAP type field, $0800078098. The SNAP value of $08 00 07 80 9B is reserved for AppleTalk data. The final byte ($00) terminates the type specification.

```
01 AA 05 08 00 07 80 9B 00
```

The following protocol-type specification is for the permanent LAP Manager protocol handler for an 802.3 packet to be delivered to the EtherTalk AARP handler. Notice that the SNAP field is followed by an additional type field, the AARP protocol type.

```
01 AA 05 00 00 00 80 F3 04 00 01 80 9B 00
```

The SNAP value of $00 00 00 80 F3 is reserved for AARP data. The AARP protocol type value of $00 01 80 9B is reserved for Ethernet AARP packets.

SPECIAL CONSIDERATIONS

For token ring, the Apple Computer, Inc. specification for the device driver that the hardware vendor must implement requires that the driver process only SNAP packets, that is, packets with a SAP value of $AA. For Ethernet and FDDI, your protocol can receive packets with a SAP value of $AA or any other SAP value.

You can only use the L802Attach routine if the hardware device driver interface conforms to the Apple specification for that driver type.

RESULT CODES

The L802Attach routine returns a nonzero value in the D0 register if there is an error.

SEE ALSO

See the "The LAP Manager and 802.2 Protocol Packets" on page 10-27 and the ANSI/IEEE standard 802.2 for more information about 802.2 protocols, and see *Inside AppleTalk,* second edition, for more information about AARP.

See *Inside Macintosh: Devices* for information on the OpenSlot function.

L802Detach

The L802Detach routine detaches from the LAP Manager a protocol handler for a specific IEEE 802.2 protocol type.

DESCRIPTION

You use the L802Detach routine to remove a protocol handler that you have written and attached using the L802Attach routine. You call the L802Detach routine from assembly language by placing the routine selector of 22 in the D0 register and the reference number of the Ethernet, token ring, or FDDI driver in the D2 register that the OpenSlot or OpenDriver function returns. Then, you execute a JSR instruction to an offset 2 bytes past the start of the LAP Manager. The start of the LAP Manager is contained in the global variable LAPMgrPtr ($B18).

Here are the register contents that you supply on entry and the value that is returned to you.

Registers on entry

D0   22

D2   Reference number of the hardware device driver

A1   Pointer to protocol specification

Registers on exit

D0   Nonzero if error

You must put a pointer to the protocol-type specification for this protocol handler in the A1 register. You must specify exactly the same protocol type as you specified for the L802Attach routine when you attached the protocol handler.

RESULT CODES

L802Detach routine returns a nonzero value in the D0 register if there is an error.

SEE ALSO

See *Inside Macintosh: Devices* for information on the OpenSlot and OpenDriver functions.

Summary of the LAP Manager

Pascal Summary

Constants

```
CONST
   {Transition Queue transition types}
   ATTransOpen            =         0;       {AppleTalk has been opened}
   ATTransClose           =         2;       {AppleTalk is about to close}
   ATTransClosePrep       =         3;       {permission to close AppleTalk}
   ATTransCancelClose     =         4;       {cancel the ClosePrep transition}

{To use the following six constants, you must first declare them in your }
{ application. They are not included in the MPW interface files.}
   ATTransNetworkTransition  =  5;           {change in network connection for }
                                             { Apple Remote Access (ARA)}

   ATTransNameChangeTellTask =  6;           {flagship name change}
   ATTransNameChangeAskTask  =  7;           {permission to change flagship }
                                             { name}

   ATTransCancelNameChange   =  8;           {cancel flagship name change}
   ATTransCableChange     =  'rnge';         {change in cable range}
   ATTransSpeedChange     =  'sped';         {change in CPU speed}
```

Data Types

AppleTalk Transition Queue Entry

```
TYPE ATQEntry =
RECORD
   qLink:      ATQEntryPtr;      {next queue entry}
   qType:      Integer;          {reserved}
   CallAddr:   ProcPtr;          {pointer to your routine}
END;


ATQEntryPtr = ^ATQEntry;
```

Routines

Adding and Removing AppleTalk Transition Queue Entries

```
FUNCTION LAPAddATQ          (theATQEntry: ATQEntryPtr): OSErr;
FUNCTION LAPRmvATQ          (theATQEntry: ATQEntryPtr): OSErr;
```

Notifying Routines When Your Application-Defined Transition Occurs

```
PROCEDURE ATEvent           (event: LongInt; infoPtr: Ptr);
FUNCTION ATPreFlightEvent   (event: LongInt; cancel: LongInt; infoPtr: Ptr):
                             OSErr;
```

C Summary

Constants

```
/*LAP Manager parameter constants*/
#define LAPprotType LAP.protType
#define LAPwdsPointer LAP.LAPptrs.wdsPointer
#define LAPhandler LAP.LAPptrs.handler

enum {                                      /*AppleTalk Transition Queue */
                                            /* transition types*/
ATTransOpen             =       0,          /*AppleTalk has opened*/
ATTransClose            =       2,          /*AppleTalk is about to close*/
ATTransClosePrep        =       3,          /*permission to close AppleTalk*/
ATTransCancelClose      =       4,          /*cancel ClosePrep transition*/

/*To use the following six constants, you must first define them in */
/* your application. They are not defined in the MPW interface files.*/
ATTransNetworkTransition =      5,          /*change in network connection */
                                            /* for ARA*/
ATTransNameChangeTellTask =     6,          /*flagship name change*/
ATTransNameChangeAskTask =      7,          /*permission to change */
                                            /* flagship name*/
ATTransCancelNameChange =       8,          /*cancel flagship name change*/
ATTransCableChange      =       'rnge',     /*change in cable range*/
ATTransSpeedChange      =       'sped',     /*change in CPU speed*/
};
```

Data Types

AppleTalk Transition Queue Entry

```
struct ATQEntry {
    struct ATQEntry    *qLink;        /*reserved*/
    short              qType;         /*reserved*/
    ProcPtr            CallAddr;      /*pointer to your routine*/
};


typedef struct ATQEntry ATQEntry;
typedef ATQEntry *ATQEntryPtr;
```

Routines

Adding and Removing AppleTalk Transition Queue Entries

```
pascal OSErr           LAPAddATQ(ATQEntryPtr theATQEntry);
pascal OSErr           LAPRmvATQ(ATQEntryPtr theATQEntry);
```

Notifying Routines When Your Application-Defined Transition Occurs

```
pascal void            ATEvent(long event, Ptr infoPtr);
pascal OSErr           ATPreFlightEvent(long event, long cancel, Ptr
                         infoPtr);
```

Assembly-Language Summary

Constants

```
;routine selectors to attach and detach an 802.2 protocol handler
L802Attach             EQU    21        ;attach an 802.2 protocol handler
L802Detach             EQU    22        ;detach an 802.2 protocol handler

;miscellaneous LAP Manager values
LAPMgrPtr              EQU    $B18      ;entry point for LAP Manager
LAPMgrCall             EQU    2         ;offset to LAP routines
LAddAEQ                EQU    23        ;LAPAddATQ routine selector
LRmvAEQ                EQU    24        ;LAPRmvATQ routine selector
```

Data Structures

AppleTalk Transition Queue Entry Data Structure

0	AeQQLink	long	next queue entry
4	AeQQType	word	reserved
6	AeQCallAddr	long	pointer to your transition event handler routine

Result Codes

noErr	0	No error, or unrecognized event code
qErr	−1	Queue element not found

Ethernet, Token Ring, and Fiber Distributed Data Interface

Contents

This chapter describes how to write data directly to an Ethernet, token ring, or Fiber Distributed Data Interface (FDDI) driver. For Ethernet Phase 1 packets, that is, the original version of Ethernet packets, this chapter also describes how to read data directly from an Ethernet driver using either the default protocol handler that Apple provides or your own protocol handler.

For Phase 2 packets, that is, IEEE 802.2 packets, you must use the interface to the Link-Access Protocol (LAP) Manager to attach your protocol handler to read data from an Ethernet, token ring, or FDDI driver.

For a description of how to attach a protocol handler to read 802.2 packets, see the chapter "Link-Access Protocol (LAP) Manager" in this book, which also explains Ethernet Phase 1 packets and Phase 2 packets for Ethernet, token ring, and FDDI.

For an introduction to the hardware and software of an entire AppleTalk network, see *Understanding Computer Networks* and the *AppleTalk Network System Overview.* For information on designing circuit cards and device drivers for Macintosh computers, see *Designing Cards and Drivers for the Macintosh Family,* second edition.

To use this chapter, you should be familiar with the information on Ethernet and token ring provided in *Inside AppleTalk,* second edition. (*Inside AppleTalk* does not address FDDI.) To gain an understanding of the relationship between the AppleTalk data links and the physical device drivers, see the chapter "Introduction to AppleTalk" in this book, which also introduces some of the terminology used in this chapter.

About Ethernet, Token Ring, and FDDI Support

You can write an application that processes packets for a protocol other than AppleTalk and run your application on Macintosh computers that also run the AppleTalk protocol stack. To send data from your application, you need to communicate directly with a network hardware device driver. To read data, you either use the LAP Manager or directly communicate with the hardware device driver, depending on the type of packet that your application processes. To read data from the network hardware device driver, you must use a protocol handler, which is code that the driver calls, in this case, to process an incoming packet for a specific protocol type.

Ethernet Phase 1 packets are IEEE 802.3 protocol packets. If your application processes Ethernet Phase 1 packets, you can use the default protocol handler that Apple Computer, Inc. provides to read data addressed to the protocol type that your application handles, or you can create and attach your own protocol handler to read that data. The chapter "Link-Access Protocol (LAP) Manager" in this book provides more information about Phase 1 and Phase 2 packets, including figures that show the two packet formats.

For Ethernet Phase 1 packets, the Apple Ethernet implementation supports multiple protocol types, and more than one protocol handler can be attached to the Ethernet driver at the same time. For example, you can write an application implementing a protocol stack that uses the default Apple Ethernet protocol handler. Another developer can write an application implementing a different protocol stack, and it, too, can use the default Apple Ethernet protocol handler. A third developer can write an application implementing yet another protocol stack that supplies and attaches its own protocol handler to the Ethernet driver. All of these applications can run concurrently on the same machine. Figure 11-1 shows three developer-provided applications that implement protocol stacks, all using the Ethernet driver at the same time.

Figure 11-1 Using protocol handlers to read data directly from the Ethernet driver

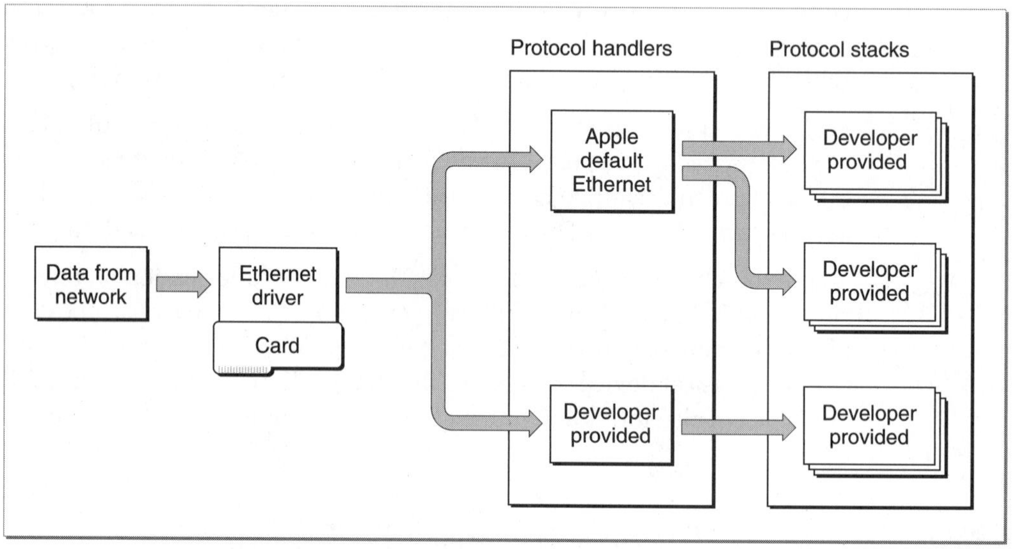

The Ethernet driver maintains a list that identifies the protocol handler for each protocol type. When you attach your protocol handler to the Ethernet driver, it adds an entry to its list for the type of protocol that your application supports along with the pointer to your protocol handler. When a packet arrives for your application, the driver reads the protocol type, locates the pointer to the protocol handler, and calls the protocol handler to read the data.

For all 802.2 packets, which includes Ethernet Phase 2 packets and all token ring and FDDI packets, Apple Computer, Inc. recommends that you attach your protocol handler using the LAP Manager interface. All AppleTalk packets are 802.2 packets. (For more information about using the LAP Manager to attach protocol handlers, see the chapter "Link-Access Protocol [LAP] Manager" in this book.)

At the hardware device driver level, only one protocol handler can be attached to receive 802.2 packets. Although you can attach more than one protocol handler at this level, if you do so, you will cause problems for AppleTalk. The AppleTalk protocol stack uses the LAP Manager's protocol handler for 802.2 packets to connect to a hardware device driver. (All AppleTalk packets are 802.2 packets.) If you attach your own protocol handler for 802.2 packets, the LAP Manager will be unable to attach its protocol handler, and you will have excluded AppleTalk from using the hardware device driver simultaneously.

For example, suppose a user is running your application with its own protocol handler over token ring and AppleTalk over Ethernet. If the user decides to change the AppleTalk network type to token ring, the attempted connection switch will fail because the LAP Manager will not be able to attach its protocol handler to the token ring device driver. To avoid problems such as these, Apple recommends that you attach your protocol handler to read Ethernet Phase 2, token ring, or FDDI 802.2 packets through the LAP Manager.

The LAP Manager installs a protocol handler at the hardware device driver level that receives 802.2 packets and that also serves as a dispatcher. This protocol handler maintains an index of registered protocol types and pointers to their protocol handlers, which allows the LAP Manager to act as a dispatcher, thereby permitting the concurrent use of a token ring or FDDI hardware device driver by more than one application, including AppleTalk.

Notes for applications that handle token ring and FDDI 802.2 packets

Apple provides specifications for both token ring and FDDI drivers that result in these implications for network applications:

- Only one protocol handler can be attached at the hardware device driver level.
- Only one protocol type is supported: the IEEE 802.2 Type 1 protocol that provides for a connectionless, or datagram, service.
- Apple does not provide a default protocol handler for token ring or FDDI.

These limitations do not restrict you from attaching your own protocol handler directly to a token ring or an FDDI hardware device driver, but doing so results in the consequences stated previously. ◆

About Multivendor Network Interface Controller (NIC) Support

Before AppleTalk version 56, a networked Macintosh computer could support only one Ethernet or token ring connection at a time. This posed a limitation for many developers who wanted multiple concurrent Ethernet or token ring connections. The original architecture also lacked support for the concurrent use of a NuBus slot device and a non-NuBus device, such as a SCSI Ethernet connection or the processor-direct slot (PDS) device.

To solve this problem, Apple implemented **multivendor architecture** to provide support that allows you to use different brands of Ethernet, token ring, or FDDI NuBus hardware in the same machine at the same time. For example, multivendor architecture allows a single machine to run AppleTalk over one Ethernet card (or through an Ethernet network connector that uses the SCSI port) and to run another application that implements a different protocol, such as TCP/IP, over another Ethernet card at the same time.

The user can select the network type to be used depending on the NuBus cards and slotless devices that are installed in the Macintosh computer. In addition to supporting various types of network hardware, multivendor architecture allows AppleTalk users to also select which brand of card to use. Your application can also provide support that allows a user to select a particular brand of card for a particular type of network connection.

Figure 11-2 shows three different brands of Ethernet cards installed in a single machine and indicates the path that data follows from the LAP Manager through the driver of the selected Ethernet card and out to the network when AppleTalk is used. The user can choose which Ethernet card is used as the network connector.

Figure 11-2   How AppleTalk uses multivendor support

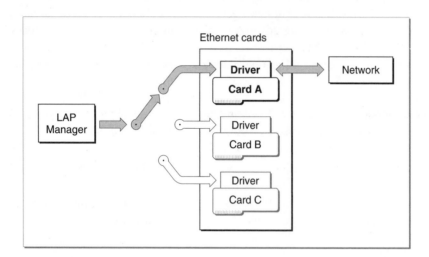

To make possible the use of multiple brands of network cards, Apple provides a driver shell for each of the following types of networks:

- For Ethernet, the name of the driver shell is .ENET.
- For token ring, the name of the driver shell is .TOKN.
- For FDDI, the name of the driver shell is .FDDI.

These driver shells consist of commands that locate and load the driver software for a particular card of that network type.

Note
For configurations that are not NuBus based, such as PDS-based and SCSI-based hardware solutions, you must open and use the following drivers, not the driver shells: .ENET0 for Ethernet, .TOKN0 for token ring, .FDDI0 for FDDI. ◆

The EGetInfo function returns information about the .ENET driver. If the Ethernet card that you are using has a SONIC chip, you can use the EGetInfo function to obtain information pertaining to the SONIC-based network interface controller (NIC). Beginning with version 58 of AppleTalk, the EGetInfo function returns this additional information. For the details regarding Ethernet cards with SONIC chips, see "EGetInfo" beginning on page 11-36.

About Multicast Addressing

At the hardware device driver level, Apple supports multicast addressing. A **multicast address** is a hardware address that is shared by a subset of nodes on a particular data link. This is similar in concept to a broadcast hardware address, but a multicast address is used to send directed broadcasts to the subset group of nodes only, and not to all nodes on the data link. A broadcast address is shared by all nodes on a particular type of network. Packets sent to the Ethernet broadcast address are sent to all nodes on the Ethernet data link. Ethernet and FDDI networks use multicast addresses; the token ring equivalent of a multicast address is a **functional address.**

A network type, such as an Ethernet data link, can also have associated with it one or more multicast addresses. Each data link is identified by a unique hardware address to which packets for that network hardware are sent. In addition to this unique hardware address, a data link can receive packets that contain the broadcast address for its own network type—Ethernet, for example.

When a node on a data link transmits a packet that has a multicast hardware address as its destination hardware address, then only a specific subset of the nodes on the link will receive the packet. Each node can have any number of multicast addresses, and any number of nodes can have the same multicast address. Some nodes on the link may not have a multicast address; other nodes may have more than one multicast addresses. (For more information on multicast and functional addresses, see *Inside AppleTalk*, second edition. See also "EAddMulti" on page 11-40.)

Using Ethernet, Token Ring, and FDDI Drivers

This section describes how to write an application that implements a protocol other than AppleTalk and that reads data from and writes it to the hardware device driver for a particular network interface controller.

For Ethernet, this section describes how to locate the installed Ethernet cards and open the Ethernet driver for a particular card or a slotless device. Then it describes how to write data to the driver. Next it describes how to attach either the Apple default protocol handler or your own protocol handler to the Ethernet driver to read data for Ethernet Phase 1 packets.

For token ring and FDDI, this section describes the differences between using the Ethernet driver and the token ring or FDDI driver, including the steps to follow to read data from and write it to this driver.

Using the Ethernet Driver

You can write your own protocol stack or application that uses the Ethernet driver directly rather than going through the LAP Manager. Apple provides an .ENET driver shell that locates and loads the driver for the selected Ethernet NuBus card. The driver shell searches the following locations for existing Ethernet driver resources, and it uses the most current one:

- the system resource file

- the card's declaration ROM

- the motherboard's ROM

See *Designing Cards and Drivers for the Macintosh Family,* second edition, for discussions of NuBus board IDs and slot resources.

Opening the Ethernet Driver

Before you use the Device Manager's `OpenSlot` function to open the .ENET driver, you use the `SGetTypeSRsrc` function described in the Slot Manager chapter of *Inside Macintosh: Devices* to determine which NuBus slots contain Ethernet cards. To find Ethernet NuBus cards, use the value `catNetwork` in the field `spCategory` of the `GetTypeSRsrc` function parameter block, and use the value `typeEthernet` in the field `spCType`. If you cannot find any Ethernet NuBus cards, you should also attempt to open the .ENET0 driver in case non-NuBus Ethernet hardware is attached to the system. You should provide a user interface that allows the user to select a specific Ethernet card in the case that more than one is present. (The chapter "Device Manager" in *Inside Macintosh: Devices* describes the `OpenSlot` function.)

Note

This section refers to the .ENET driver shell, which facilitates multivendor support, as the .ENET driver. When you open the .ENET driver shell, it loads and opens the particular card's driver. ◆

Listing 11-1 illustrates how to identify and open an Ethernet driver.

Listing 11-1   Finding an Ethernet card and opening the .ENET driver

```
FUNCTION Get_And_Open_ENET_Driver: Integer;
   VAR
       mySBlk:     SpBlock;
       myPBRec:    ParamBlockRec;
       myErr:      OSErr;
       Found:      Integer;
       ENETRefNum: Integer;
       EnetStr:    Str15;
       Enet0Str:   Str15;


BEGIN
   Found := 0;                  {assume no sResource found}
   ENETRefNum := 0;             {indicate no driver found}
```

```
    WITH mySBlk DO                     {set up the SpBlock}
        BEGIN
            spParamData := 1;          {include search of disabled resources }
                                       { starting searching from spSlot and }
                                       { the slots above it}

            spCategory := catNetwork;
            spCType := typeEthernet;
            spDrvrSW := 0;
            spDrvrHW := 0;
            spTBMask := 3;             {match only Category and }
                                       { CType fields}
            spSlot := 0;               {start search from here}
            spID := 0;                 {start search from here}
            spExtDev := 0;             {ID of the external device}
        END;
            .
            .
            .

        {REPEAT}
            .

        {At this point you could implement a repeat loop to check }
        { for multiple Ethernet cards. This sample uses the first card.}
            .

myErr := SGetTypeSRsrc(@mySBlk);
IF myErr = noErr THEN                  {found an sResource match; }
                                       { save it for later}

    BEGIN
        Found := Found + 1;
        (SaveSInfo(@mySBlk);           {save slot info for later use}
    END;
        {until myErr = smNoMoresRsrcs;}

  IF Found > 1 THEN
    BEGIN
        {If you find more than one sResource, put up a dialog box }
        { to let the user select one. If any of the sResources }
        { that you found were disabled, let the user know that they }
        { are not available.}
        {This code sample assumes that the selected slot is }
        { returned in mySBlk.spSlot, that the corresponding }
        { sResource ID is returned in mySBlk.spID, and that Found }
        { remains > 1 to indicate that it is okay to open the }
        { driver.}
    END;
```

11

Ethernet, Token Ring, and Fiber Distributed Data Interface

```
IF found <> 0 THEN
    BEGIN
        EnetStr := '.ENET';
        WITH myPBRec DO
            BEGIN
                ioCompletion := NIL;              {call made synchronously}
                ioNamePtr := @EnetStr;
                ioPermssn := fsCurPerm;
                ioFlags := 0;                     {reserved for driver use}
                ioSlot := mySBlk.spSlot;          {slot of Ethernet card to open}
                ioID := mySBlk.spID;              {sResource ID for slot}
            END;
        myErr := OpenSlot(@myPBRec, FALSE);
        IF myErr = noErr THEN
        ENETRefNum := myPBRec.ioRefNum;
    END
ELSE
    BEGIN
        Enet0Str := '.ENET0';
        myErr := OpenDriver(Enet0Str, ENETRefNum);
    END;
IF myErr <> noErr THEN
    DoError(myErr); {handle the error}
Get_And_Open_ENET_Driver := ENETRefNum;    {return the refNum or }
                                           { 0 if unsuccessful}
END;
```

Using a Write-Data Structure to Transmit Ethernet Data

You use the EWrite function to send data to the .ENET driver for transmission over the Ethernet network. When you do this, you provide a pointer to a write-data structure containing one or more pairs of length words and pointers. (Figure 11-3 shows multiple pairs.) Each pair indicates the length and location of a portion of the data packet to be sent over the network. The first length-pointer pair points to a header block that is at least 14 bytes long and that starts with the destination node hardware address. Note that this is not the AppleTalk address, but is the *hardware* address of the destination node. (Note that this address can also be a multicast address or the broadcast address for the link type.)

The next 6 bytes of the header block are reserved for use by the .ENET driver. These bytes are followed by the 2-byte Ethernet protocol type field (Ethernet Phase 2 packets use this field to indicate the amount of data in the packet). Data may follow the header block; all other length-pointer pairs point to data. The write-data structure terminates with a 0 word.

Note

Instead of using multiple buffers and length-pointer pairs, you can create a write-data structure that consists of a single buffer that specifies the header block followed directly by the data. For more information about write-data structures, see the chapter "Datagram Delivery Protocol (DDP)" in this book. ◆

When you first open the .ENET driver, it allocates a 768-byte buffer that it uses for transmitting data packets. This buffer is large enough to hold the largest EtherTalk packet, which is 621 bytes in size. If you want to transmit data packets larger than 768 bytes, call the `ESetGeneral` function; the .ENET driver can then allocate a data buffer large enough to send packets up to 1514 bytes in size. Figure 11-3 shows the write-data structure that you use to send data to the .ENET driver.

Figure 11-3   An Ethernet write-data structure

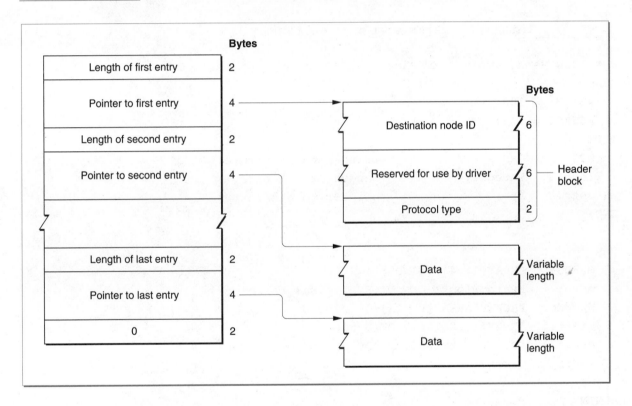

The sample code in Listing 11-2 uses a multicast address instead of a local hardware address. The multicast address is a packet array that is defined as follows:

```
VAR
    gMultiCastAddr: PACKED ARRAY[0..5] OF Byte;
```

The following procedure initializes the gMultiCastAddr global variable:

```
PROCEDURE Init_Multicast_Address;
BEGIN
    gMultiCastAddr[1] := $09;
    gMultiCastAddr[2] := $00;
    gMultiCastAddr[3] := $2B;
    gMultiCastAddr[4] := $00;
    gMultiCastAddr[5] := $00;
    gMultiCastAddr[6] := $04;
END;
```

The code in Listing 11-2 defines an Ethernet write-data structure, and then it calls the EWrite function to send a data packet over Ethernet.

Listing 11-2   Sending a data packet over Ethernet

```
FUNCTION Send_Sample_ENET_Packet (ENETRefNum: Integer): OSErr;
CONST
    kSIZE1 = 100;
    kSIZE2 = 333;
TYPE
    WDS = RECORD                {write-data structure}
    length:  Integer;          {length of nth entry}
    aptr:    Ptr;              {pointer to nth entry}
END;

VAR
    myWDS:   ARRAY[1..4] OF WDS;
    myPB:    EParamBlock;       {.ENET parameter block}
    wheader: PACKED ARRAY[0..13] OF Byte;
    stuff1:  ARRAY[1..kSIZE1] OF Byte;
    stuff2:  ARRAY[1..kSIZE2] OF Byte;
    myErr:   OSErr;

BEGIN
    BlockMove(@gMultiCastAddr, @wheader, 6);   {multicast address}
    wheader[12] := $90;                         {protocol type}
    wheader[13] := $90;                         {must match kProtocol value}
    myWDS[1].length := 14;
    myWDS[1].aptr := @wheader;
    myWDS[2].length := kSIZE1;
    myWDS[2].aptr := @stuff1;
    myWDS[3].length := kSIZE2;
```

```
    myWDS[3].aptr := @stuff2;
    myWDS[4].length := 0;
    myPB.ePointer := @myWDS;
    myPB.ioRefNum := ENETRefNum;

{Send something.}
    myErr := EWrite(@myPB, FALSE);
    IF myErr <> noErr THEN
        DoError(myErr);
    Send_Sample_ENET_Packet := myErr;
END;
```

Using the Default Ethernet Protocol Handler to Read Data

This section describes how to write an application that uses the Apple default protocol handler for Ethernet Phase 1 packets. For Ethernet Phase 2 packets, the process is largely the same, except that you must code and provide your own protocol handler and use the LAP Manager to attach it.

When the Ethernet NuBus card or other Ethernet hardware receives a data packet, it generates an interrupt to the CPU. The interrupt handler in ROM determines the source of the interrupt and calls the .ENET driver. The .ENET driver reads the packet header to determine the protocol type of the data packet and checks to see if any client has specified that protocol type in a call to the EAttachPH function. If so, the client either specified a NIL pointer to a protocol handler or provided its own protocol handler. If the client specified a NIL pointer, the .ENET driver uses its default protocol handler to read the data. If no one has specified the protocol type that the packet header contains in a call to the EAttachPH function, the .ENET driver discards the data. (For more information about the EAttachPH function, see "EAttachPH" on page 11-28.)

The Ethernet driver looks for a pending ERead function with a protocol type that matches the packet protocol type. (When you call the ERead function, you pass it a protocol type.) The Ethernet driver places the entire packet—including the packet header—into the buffer specified by that function. The function returns the number of bytes actually read. If the packet is larger than the data buffer, the ERead function places as much of the packet as will fit into the buffer and returns the buf2SmallErr result code.

You must call the ERead function asynchronously to await the next data packet. When the .ENET driver receives the data packet, it completes execution of the ERead function and calls your completion routine. Your completion routine should call the ERead function again so that an ERead function is always pending execution. If the .ENET driver receives a data packet with a protocol type for which you specified the default protocol handler while no ERead function is pending, the .ENET driver discards the packet.

You can have several asynchronous calls to the ERead function pending execution simultaneously as long as you use different buffers and a different parameter block for each call.

Alternatively, after the ERead function completes execution, you can call the function again from your completion routine, and reuse the same parameter block. This is the approach the code in Listing 11-3 takes.

The code in Listing 11-3 calls the EAttachPH function to specify that the .ENET driver should use the default protocol handler to process packets for the protocol type defined by the following constant:

```
CONST
    kMyProtocol = $9090;                    {must be > $5DC}
```

In practice, you should call the EAttachPH function very early, during your program initialization sequence, if possible. As soon as the connection is established and you are expecting data, you should call the ERead function asynchronously. The code in Listing 11-3 shows how to attach a protocol handler and read a packet for an Ethernet Phase 1 packet.

Listing 11-3   Attaching a protocol handler and reading a packet

```
FUNCTION Sample_AttachPH_And_Read_Packet (ENETRefNum: Integer): OSErr;
CONST
    kBigBytes = 8888;

VAR
    myPB:        MyEParamBlock;
    myEPBPtr:    MyEParamBlkPtr;
    aptr:        Ptr;
    myErr:       OSErr;

BEGIN
    myEPBPtr := @myPB;                          {set up EAttachPH parameters}
    WITH myPB.pb DO
        BEGIN
            eProtType := kMyProtocol;           {protocol type}
            ePointer := NIL;                    {use default protocol handler}
            ioRefNum := ENETRefNum;             {.ENET driver reference number}
        END;
    myErr := EAttachPH(EParamBlkPtr(myEPBPtr), FALSE);

    IF myErr <> noErr THEN                       {check if error occurred while }
        DoError(myErr)                           { attaching protocol handler}
    ELSE
        BEGIN
            aptr := NewPtr(kBigBytes);
            myPB.myA5 := SetCurrentA5;           {store the current A5 world}
```

```
WITH myPB.pb DO
    BEGIN
        ioCompletion := @MyCompRoutine;
                                        {ptr to completion routine}

        eProtType := kMyProtocol;       {protocol type to respond to}
        ePointer := aptr;               {pointer to read-data buffer}
        eBuffSize := kBigBytes;         {size of read-data buffer}
        ioRefNum := ENETRefNum;         {.ENET driver refNum}
    END;
    myErr := ERead(EParamBlkPtr(myEPBPtr), TRUE);

    IF myErr <> noErr THEN
        {check if error occurred queueing read request}
        BEGIN
            DoError(myErr);                 {process error result}
            Detach_SamplePH(ENETRefNum);    {detach protocol handler}
        END;
END;
Sample_AttachPH_And_Read_Packet := myErr;
END;
```

When the .ENET driver receives a packet, it then calls your completion routine if you called the ERead function asynchronously and the ioCompletion routine field is not NIL. Your completion routine should process the packet, after which it can then queue another asynchronous call to the ERead function to await the next packet.

The sample completion routine that Listing 11-4 shows uses the following inline function that gets the pointer to the parameter block from register A0.

```
FUNCTION GetParamBlockPtr: Ptr;
INLINE
    $2E88;              {MOVE.L A0,(SP)}
```

Because register A0 is a utility register that compilers often use for their own purposes, the sample code uses the following stub completion routine technique to minimize the possibility that a compiler will overwrite the value in register A0. The stub completion routine calls GetParamBlockPtr and then calls the actual completion routine.

```
PROCEDURE MyStubCompRoutine;

VAR
    myEPBPtr: MyEParamBlkPtr;

BEGIN
    myEPBPtr := MyEParamBlkPtr(GetParamBlockPtr);
                {get parameter block pointer from register A0}
    myCompRoutine(myEPBPtr);
                {now call the actual completion routine}
END;
```

Listing 11-4 shows the actual completion routine that the stub completion routine calls. This completion routine reuses the original parameter block when it calls the ERead function again. The code also shows how to access global variables from within the completion routine. Note that if you call the ERead function from within the completion routine, you must call the function asynchronously. You must not call the ERead function synchronously at interrupt time.

Listing 11-4   Completion routine to process received packet and await the next packet

```
PROCEDURE MyCompRoutine (myEPBPtr: MyEParamBlkPtr);
VAR
    myErr:   OSErr;
    saveA5: LongInt;
    aptr: Ptr;

BEGIN
    saveA5 := SetA5(myEPBPtr^.myA5);      {set A5 to our world}
    IF (myEPBPtr^.pb.ioResult < noErr) THEN
                                          {was ERead successful?}
    BEGIN
       IF (myEPBPtr^.pb.ioResult <> reqAborted) THEN
                                          {was request aborted?}
          DoError(myEPBPtr^.pb.ioResult)
       END
    ELSE
    BEGIN                                 {process the packet}
       aptr := myEPBPtr^.pb.EPointer;
       ProcessData(aptr);                 {use the data}
    END;

  IF NOT gDone THEN                       {check if we have been called}
    BEGIN                                 {if not, call ERead again}
       myErr := ERead(EParamBlkPtr(myEPBPtr), TRUE);
       IF myErr <> noErr THEN
          DoError(myErr);                 {check if error occurred while }
                                          { queueing call to ERead}
    END;
    saveA5 := SetA5(saveA5);              {restore the A5 world}
END; {of MyCompletion routine}
```

Using Your Own Ethernet Protocol Handler to Read Data

If a client of the .ENET driver has used the `EAttachPH` function to provide a pointer to its own protocol handler, the .ENET driver calls that protocol handler, which must in turn call the .ENET driver's `ReadPacket` and `ReadRest` routines to read the data. Your protocol handler calls these routines in essentially the same way as you called these routines to implement a DDP socket listener. (The chapter "Datagram Delivery Protocol [DDP]" describes how you use these routines to implement a DDP socket listener.)

The following sections describe how the .ENET driver calls a custom protocol handler and the `ReadPacket` and `ReadRest` routines.

Note
Because an Ethernet protocol handler must read from and write to the CPU's registers, you must write the protocol handler in assembly language; you cannot write a protocol handler in Pascal. ◆

How the .ENET Driver Calls Your Protocol Handler

You can provide an Ethernet protocol handler for a particular protocol type and use the `EAttachPH` function to attach it to the .ENET driver. When the driver receives an Ethernet packet, it reads the packet header into an internal buffer, reads the protocol type, and calls the protocol handler for that protocol type. The CPU is in interrupt mode, and the registers are used as follows:

Registers on call to Ethernet protocol handler

A0	Reserved for internal use by the .ENET driver (You must preserve this register until after the `ReadRest` routine has completed execution.)
A1	Reserved for internal use by the .ENET driver (You must preserve this register until after the `ReadRest` routine has completed execution.)
A2	Free for your use
A3	Pointer to first byte past data-link header bytes (the first byte after the 2-byte protocol-type field)
A4	Pointer to the `ReadPacket` routine (The `ReadRest` routine starts 2 bytes after the start of the `ReadPacket` routine.)
A5	Free for your use until after the `ReadRest` routine has completed execution
D0	Free for your use
D1	Number of bytes in the Ethernet packet left to be read (that is, the number of bytes following the Ethernet header)
D2	Free for your use
D3	Free for your use

If your protocol handler processes more than one protocol type, you can read the protocol type field in the frame header to determine the protocol type of the packet. The protocol-type field starts 2 bytes before the address pointed to by the A3 register.

Note

The source address starts 8 bytes before the address pointed to by the A3 register, and the destination address starts 14 bytes before the address pointed to by the A3 register. ◆

After you have called the ReadRest routine, you can use registers A0 through A3 and D0 through D3 for your own use, but you must preserve all other registers. You cannot depend on having access to your application global variables.

How Your Protocol Handler Calls the .ENET Driver Routines

Your protocol handler must call the .ENET driver routines ReadPacket and ReadRest to read the incoming data packet.

Note

Before the Ethernet driver calls your protocol handler at interrupt time, you must have already allocated memory for one or more data buffers to hold the incoming data. ◆

You may call the ReadPacket routine as many times as you like to read the data piece by piece into one or more data buffers, but you must always use the ReadRest routine to read the final piece of the data packet. The ReadRest routine restores the machine state (the stack pointers, status register, and so forth) and checks for error conditions.

Before you call the ReadPacket routine, you must place a pointer to the data buffer in the A3 register. You place the number of bytes you want to read in the D3 register. You must not request more bytes than remain in the data packet.

To call the ReadPacket routine, execute a JSR instruction to the address in the A4 register. The ReadPacket routine uses the registers as follows:

Registers on entry to the ReadPacket routine

A3 Pointer to a buffer to hold the data you want to read

D3 Number of bytes to read; must be nonzero

Registers on exit from the ReadPacket routine

A0 Unchanged

A1 Unchanged

A2 Unchanged

A3 First byte after the last byte read into buffer

D0 Changed

D1 Number of bytes left to be read

D2 Unchanged

D3 Equals 0 if requested number of bytes were read, nonzero if error

The ReadPacket routine indicates an error by clearing to 0 the zero (z) flag in the status register. If the ReadPacket routine returns an error, you must terminate execution of your protocol handler with an RTS instruction without calling ReadPacket again or calling ReadRest at all.

Call the ReadRest routine to read the last portion of the data packet, or call it after you have read all the data with ReadPacket routines and before you do any other processing or terminate execution. You must provide in the A3 register a pointer to a data buffer and must indicate in the D3 register the size of the data buffer. If you have already read all of the data with calls to the ReadPacket routine, you can specify a buffer of size 0.

▲ **WARNING**
If you do not call the ReadRest routine after your last call to the ReadPacket routine, the system will crash. ▲

To call the ReadRest routine, execute a JSR instruction to an address 2 bytes past the address in the A4 register. The ReadRest routine uses the registers as follows:

Registers on entry to the ReadRest routine

A3   Pointer to a buffer to hold the data you want to read

D3   Size of the buffer (word length); may be 0

Registers on exit from the ReadRest routine

A0   Unchanged

A1   Unchanged

A2   Unchanged

A3   Pointer to first byte after the last byte read into buffer

D0   Changed

D1   Changed

D2   Unchanged

D3   Equals 0 if requested number of bytes were read; less than 0 if more data was left than would fit in buffer (extra data equals –D3 bytes); greater than 0 if less data was left than the size of the buffer (extra buffer space equals D3 bytes)

The ReadRest routine indicates an error by clearing to 0 the zero (z) flag in the status register. You must terminate execution of your protocol handler with an RTS instruction whether or not the ReadRest routine returns an error.

Changing the Ethernet Hardware Address

Each Ethernet NuBus card or other Ethernet hardware interface device contains a unique 6-byte hardware address assigned by the manufacturer of the device. The .ENET driver normally uses this address to determine whether to receive a packet. To change the hardware address for your node, place in the System file a resource of type 'eadr' with a resource ID equal to the slot number of the Ethernet NuBus card.

The 'eadr' resource consists only of a 6-byte number. Do not use the broadcast address or a multicast address for this number. (Refer to *Inside AppleTalk,* second edition, for the broadcast and multicast address formats.)

When you open the .ENET driver, it looks for an 'eadr' resource with the resource ID that matches the slot number of the card. If it finds one, the driver substitutes the number in this resource for the Ethernet hardware address and uses it until the driver is closed or reset.

Note

To avoid address collisions, you should never arbitrarily change the Ethernet hardware address. This feature should be used only by a system administrator who can keep track of all the Ethernet addresses in the system. ◆

Using the Token Ring Driver

You can write an application implementing a protocol other than AppleTalk that reads data from and writes it to the token ring driver defined by Apple.

To write data to the token ring driver and to perform other functions such as adding a functional address for the token ring hardware, you use the Ethernet functions described earlier, with the modifications noted later in this section. To read 802.2 packets from the token ring driver, you need to attach your protocol handler to the LAP Manager.

The Apple token ring driver implementation supports only the IEEE 802.2 Type 1 protocol and allows for the attachment of only one protocol handler that reads 802.2 packets that contain an SAP value of $AA.

Although it is possible to attach your own protocol handler at the hardware device driver level, Apple recommends that you not do this because it excludes AppleTalk from using the token ring driver. So that more than one protocol can receive packets from the token ring driver concurrently, Apple recommends that you attach your protocol handler to the LAP Manager. The LAP Manager attaches its own protocol handler to the token ring driver, and when it receives a packet for your protocol, the LAP Manager calls your protocol handler. When it receives a packet for another protocol, such as AppleTalk, the LAP Manager calls that application's protocol handler.

For a description of how to attach and detach your protocol handler for token ring, see the chapter "Link-Access Protocol (LAP) Manager" included in this book and the discussion of token ring and FDDI in "About Ethernet, Token Ring, and FDDI Support" beginning on page 11-3 in this chapter. The chapter "Link-Access Protocol (LAP) Manager" also gives more information on the SAP field value for 802.2 Type 1 packets.

Applying Ethernet Functions

The Apple token ring driver implements many but not all of the functions that the Apple Ethernet driver implements.

For those Ethernet functions that do apply to token ring, you use the function for token ring in the same way that you do for Ethernet: you pass parameters in a parameter block and you use the Ethernet control code in the `csCode` field to call the function. The only difference is that instead of specifying the Ethernet driver reference number in the parameter block's `ioRefNum` field, you specify the token ring driver reference number. Here are the Ethernet functions that apply to token ring:

■ You use the `EAddMulti` function to add a functional address for token ring and the `EDelMulti` function to remove one. Be careful not to specify the broadcast address as a functional address. See *Inside AppleTalk*, second edition, for a description and the format of functional and broadcast addresses for token ring.

■ You use the `EWrite` function to send data to the token ring driver for transmission over the network.

Here are the Ethernet functions that do not apply to token ring:

■ The `ERead` and `ERdCancel` functions are not valid for token ring because Apple does not specify a default protocol handler for the token ring driver. These two functions are used exclusively by applications that use the default Ethernet protocol handler. If an application calls these functions for token ring, the driver will return an error.

■ The `ESetGeneral` function switches to a mode that allows the .ENET driver to transmit a larger Ethernet data packet than the standard size. Because token ring is not normally restricted to the limited packet size, this function does not apply. However, the token ring driver will return a result of `noErr` if you call this function.

There are some other differences between Ethernet and token ring:

■ The token ring packet size is determined by the token ring hardware developer. However, for Logical Link Control (LLC) type packets, the packet length cannot exceed 1500 bytes.

■ The token ring interface uses functional addresses instead of multicast addresses. Be careful not to use the broadcast address for a functional address. For information about both kinds of token ring addresses, see *Inside AppleTalk*, second edition.

■ For token ring, the vendor who supplies the hardware device driver provides a control panel that allows you to specify an alternative hardware address. (For general information about alternative hardware addresses, see "Changing the Ethernet Hardware Address" on page 11-19.)

Note

Although you can use the `EAttachPH` function to attach a protocol handler to the token ring driver and the `EDetachPH` function to remove one, Apple recommends that you not use these functions. Instead, you should use the LAP Manager's `L802Attach` and `L802Detach` routines. ◆

Sending and Receiving Data

The tasks involved in sending data to and receiving it from a token ring driver are similar to those that you use for Ethernet. The primary difference is that you use the LAP Manager to attach your protocol handler. Any vendor implementing a token ring driver to run on a Macintosh computer must follow rules that direct them to return packet information in the same manner as does the Ethernet driver for 802.2 packets. From the

Ethernet, Token Ring, and Fiber Distributed Data Interface

perspective of an application that uses the token ring driver, this means that when the LAP Manager calls your protocol handler, you can expect the token ring hardware addresses that you reference from register A3 to follow the same format that is used for Ethernet addresses, regardless of how the token ring address might appear at the hardware level.

Here are the steps that you follow to send data to and receive it from a token ring driver:

1. Locate the token ring cards that are installed in the system. Use the Slot Manager to identify installed token ring cards. Use the SGetTypeSRsrc function described in the Slot Manager chapter of *Inside Macintosh: Devices* to determine which NuBus slots contain token ring cards. To find token ring cards, use the value catNetwork (0x4) in the spCategory field and the value typeTokenRing (0x2) in the spCType field. You should provide a user interface that allows the user to select a specific token ring card in the case that more than one is present.

2. Use the OpenSlot function to open the token ring driver. Set the ioNamePtr field to .TOKN. If you did not locate any NuBus token ring cards in step 1, you should also attempt to open the .TOKN0 driver in case non-NuBus token ring hardware is attached to the system. Use the Device Manager's OpenDriver function to open the .TOKN0 driver. (For information on the OpenSlot and OpenDriver functions, see the chapter "Device Manager" in *Inside Macintosh: Devices*.)

   Note that this section refers to the .TOKN driver shell, which facilitates multi-vendor support, as the .TOKN driver. Opening the .TOKN driver shell, which loads and opens the card's driver, is effectively the same as directly opening the token ring driver.

3. If your application requires a functional address, use the EAddMulti function to register one. Functional addresses are the token ring equivalent of Ethernet and FDDI multicast addresses. (For information on functional addresses, see *Inside AppleTalk*, second edition. For a description of multicast addresses, see "About Multicast Addressing" on page 11-7.)

4. Use the LAP Manager's L802Attach routine to install your protocol handler. (See the chapter "Link-Access Protocol [LAP] Manager" in this book for more information.)

5. Use the EWrite function to send packets to the token ring driver for transmission across the network. To use the EWrite function, you provide a pointer to a write-data structure. The first buffer in the write-data structure must be at least 14 bytes long: the first 6 bytes of that buffer must contain the destination address. Bytes 13 and 14 must contain the packet length, which must not exceed 1500 bytes. The token ring driver fills in bytes 7–12 with the source address. (For more information on the write-data structure, see "Using a Write-Data Structure to Transmit Ethernet Data" on page 11-10.)

6. When you are finished using the token ring driver, use the LAP Manager's L802Detach routine to remove your protocol handler.

7. When you are finished using a functional address, use the EDelMulti function to remove it.

11-22   Using Ethernet, Token Ring, and FDDI Drivers

Using the FDDI Driver

You can write an application implementing a protocol other than AppleTalk that processes 802.2 packets and that sends and receives data over a Fiber Distributed Data Interface (FDDI) network. To do this, you read data from and write it to the FDDI driver defined by Apple. Your application can run on a node that is also running AppleTalk.

To write data to the FDDI driver and to perform other functions such as adding a multicast address for the FDDI hardware, you use the Ethernet functions described earlier in this chapter. To receive 802.2 packets from the FDDI driver, you attach your protocol handler to the LAP Manager using the interface to the LAP Manager.

The Apple FDDI driver implementation support allows for the attachment of only one protocol handler. The Apple FDDI driver specification requires that an FDDI driver handle 802.2 packets to service access points (SAP) other than SAP $AA.

Although it is possible to attach your own protocol handler at the hardware device driver level, Apple Computer, Inc. recommends that you not do this because it excludes AppleTalk from using the FDDI driver. So that more than one protocol can receive packets from the FDDI driver concurrently, Apple recommends that you attach your protocol handler to the LAP Manager. The LAP Manager attaches its own protocol handler to the FDDI driver, and when it receives a packet for your protocol, the LAP Manager calls your protocol handler. When it receives a packet for another protocol, such as AppleTalk, the LAP Manager calls that application's protocol handler.

For a description of how to attach and detach your protocol handler for FDDI, see the chapter "Link-Access Protocol (LAP) Manager" included in this book and the discussion of token ring and FDDI in "About Ethernet, Token Ring, and FDDI Support" beginning on page 11-3 in this chapter. The chapter "Link-Access Protocol (LAP) Manager" also explains the concept and use of the SAP field value for 802.2 Type 1 packets.

Applying Ethernet Functions

The Apple FDDI driver implements many but not all of the functions that the Apple Ethernet driver implements.

For those Ethernet functions that do apply to FDDI, you use the function for FDDI in the same way that you do for Ethernet: you pass parameters in a parameter block and you use the Ethernet control code in the csCode field to call the function. The only difference is that instead of specifying the Ethernet driver reference number in the parameter block's ioRefNum field, you specify the FDDI driver reference number. Here are the Ethernet functions that apply to FDDI:

- You use the EAddMulti function to add a multicast address for FDDI and the EDelMulti function to remove one. Be careful not to use the broadcast address as a multicast address. The broadcast and multicast addresses are the same for FDDI and Ethernet. For information about these addresses and their formats, see the discussion of them for Ethernet in *Inside AppleTalk*, second edition.

- You use the EWrite function to send data to the FDDI driver for transmission over the network.

Here are the Ethernet functions that do not apply to FDDI:

- The `ERead` and `ERdCancel` functions are not valid for FDDI because Apple does not specify a default protocol handler for the FDDI driver. These two functions are used exclusively by applications that use the default Ethernet protocol handler. If an application calls these functions for FDDI, the driver will return an error.

- The `ESetGeneral` function switches to a mode that allows the .ENET driver to transmit a larger Ethernet data packet than the standard size. Because FDDI is not normally restricted to the limited packet size, this function does not apply. However, the FDDI driver will return a result of `noErr` if you call this function.

There are some other differences between Ethernet and FDDI:

- The FDDI packet size is determined by the FDDI hardware developer. However, for Logical Link Control (LLC) type packets, the packet length cannot exceed 1500 bytes.

- The FDDI driver searches for a resource of type `'fadr'` instead of `'eadr'` in the System file for an alternative hardware address. (For general information about alternative hardware addresses, see "Changing the Ethernet Hardware Address" on page 11-19.)

Note

Although you can use the `EAttachPH` function to attach a protocol handler to the FDDI driver and the `EDetachPH` function to remove one, Apple recommends that you not use these functions. Instead, you should use the LAP Manager's `L802Attach` and `L802Detach` routines. ◆

Sending and Receiving Data

The tasks involved in sending data to and receiving it from an FDDI driver are similar to those that you use for Ethernet. The primary difference is that you use the LAP Manager to attach your protocol handler. Any vendor implementing an FDDI driver to run on a Macintosh computer must follow rules that direct them to return packet information in the same manner as does the Ethernet driver for 802.2 packets. From the perspective of an application that uses the FDDI driver, this means that when the LAP Manager calls your protocol handler, you can expect the FDDI hardware addresses that you reference from register A3 to follow the same format that is used for Ethernet addresses, regardless of how the FDDI address might appear in the packet. The chapter "Link-Access Protocol (LAP) Manager" in this book explains this in detail.

Here are the steps that you follow to send data to and receive it from an FDDI driver:

1. Locate the FDDI cards that are installed in the system. Use the Slot Manager to identify installed FDDI cards. Use the `SGetTypeSRsrc` function described in the Slot Manager chapter of *Inside Macintosh: Devices* to determine which NuBus slots contain FDDI cards. To find FDDI cards, use the value `catNetwork (0x4)` in the `spCategory` field and the value `typeFDDI (0x11)` in the `spCType` field. You should provide a user interface that allows the user to select a specific FDDI card in the case that more than one is present.

2. Use the `OpenSlot` function to open the FDDI driver. Set the `ioNamePtr` field to .FDDI. If you did not locate any NuBus FDDI cards in step 1, you should also attempt to open the .FDDI0 driver in case non-NuBus FDDI hardware is attached to the

system. Use the Device Manager's `OpenDriver` function to open the .FDDI0 driver. (For information on the `OpenSlot` and `OpenDriver` functions, see the chapter "Device Manager" in *Inside Macintosh: Devices*.)

Note that this section refers to the .FDDI driver shell, which facilitates multivendor support, as the .FDDI driver. Opening the .FDDI driver shell, which loads and opens the card's driver, is effectively the same as directly opening the FDDI driver.

3. If your application requires a multicast address, use the `EAddMulti` function to register a multicast address. (For information on multicast addresses, see *Inside AppleTalk*, second edition. For a description of multicast addresses, see "About Multicast Addressing" on page 11-7.)

4. Use the LAP Manager's `L802Attach` routine to install your protocol handler. (See the chapter "Link-Access Protocol [LAP] Manager" in this book for more information.)

5. Use the `EWrite` function to send packets to the FDDI driver for transmission across the network. To use the `EWrite` function, you provide a pointer to a write-data structure. The first buffer in the write-data structure must be at least 14 bytes long: the first 6 bytes of that buffer must contain the destination address. Bytes 13 and 14 must contain the packet length, which must not exceed 1500 bytes. The FDDI driver fills in bytes 7–12 with the source address. (For more information on the write-data structure, see "Using a Write-Data Structure to Transmit Ethernet Data" on page 11-10.)

6. When you are finished using the FDDI driver, use the LAP Manager's `L802Detach` routine to remove your protocol handler.

7. When you are finished using a multicast address, use the `EDelMulti` function to remove it.

Ethernet, Token Ring, and FDDI Reference

This section describes the Ethernet data structures and functions. You use these data structures and functions to communicate directly with the Ethernet, token ring, and FDDI drivers. The functions were originally designed to read data from and write it to the Ethernet driver. However, by specifying the appropriate driver reference number, you can also use many of these functions for the token ring and FDDI drivers.

Some of the Ethernet functions do not apply to token ring and FDDI. Each of the functions includes a section called *Token Ring and FDDI Considerations* that identifies whether the function is valid for these drivers.

The "Data Structures" section shows the Pascal data structures for the write-data structure and the ENET parameter block of type `EParamBlock`.

The "Routines" section describes how to

■ attach and detach a protocol handler to receive data from an Ethernet driver

■ write data to the Ethernet, token ring, or FDDI driver

■ read data from the Ethernet driver and cancel a function request to read data from the driver when you use the default Ethernet protocol handler

- obtain information about the Ethernet driver and switch its mode to handle larger packets
- add and remove a multicast address for an application that uses the Ethernet or FDDI driver and a functional address for an application that uses the token ring driver

Data Structures

This section describes the data structures that you use to provide information to the Ethernet, token ring, and FDDI drivers. You use the write-data structure to provide the addressing information and data to send to another node over the network. You use the ENET parameter block of type `EParamBlock` to pass information to and receive it from the functions for Ethernet, token ring, and FDDI drivers.

The Write-Data Structure

To send data directly from the Ethernet, token ring, or FDDI driver, you must provide a write-data structure and pass the `EWrite` function a pointer to it. A write-data structure contains a series of pairs of length words and pointers. Each pair indicates the length and location of a portion of the data that constitutes the packet to be sent over the network. The interface files for the driver do not include a type declaration for the write-data structure. Here is an example type declaration that you can include in your application.

```
TYPE  WDSElement =
RECORD
    entryLength:   Integer;
    entryPtr:      Ptr;
END;
```

Field descriptions

entryLength   The length of the data pointer to by `entryPtr`.

entryPtr   A pointer to the data that is part of the packet to be sent using the `EWrite` function.

For more information about the write-data structure, see "Using a Write-Data Structure to Transmit Ethernet Data" beginning on page 11-10.

The Parameter Block for Ethernet, Token Ring, and FDDI Driver Functions

All of the driver functions—`EAttachPH`, `EDetachPH`, `EWrite`, `ERead`, `ERdCancel`, `EGetInfo`, `ESetGeneral`, `EAddMulti`, `EDelMulti`—require a pointer to an ENET parameter block of type `EParamBlock`.

This section defines the fields that are common to all of the driver functions that use the ENET parameter block. The ENET parameter block contains reserved fields that are used internally by the .ENET driver; these fields are not described. The fields that are used for specific functions only are defined in the descriptions of the functions to which they apply.

```
TYPE EParamBlock =
  PACKED RECORD
        qLink:          QElemPtr;         {reserved}
        qType:          Integer;          {reserved}
        ioTrap:         Integer;          {reserved}
        ioCmdAddr:      Ptr;              {reserved}
        ioCompletion:   ProcPtr;          {completion routine}
        ioResult:       OSErr;            {result code}
        ioNamePtr:      StringPtr;        {reserved}
        ioVRefNum:      Integer;          {reserved}
        ioRefNum:       Integer;          {driver reference number}
        csCode:         Integer;          {primary command code}
     CASE Integer OF
        ENetWrite, ENetAttachPH, ENetDetachPH, ENetRead,
        ENetRdCancel,ENetGetInfo,ENetSetGeneral:
           (eProtType:  Integer;          {Ethernet protocol type}
            ePointer:   Ptr;              {pointer; use depends on function}
            eBuffSize:  Integer;          {buffer size}
            eDataSize:  Integer);         {number of bytes read}
        ENetAddMulti,ENetDelMulti:
           (eMultiAddr: ARRAY[0..5] OF Char;)    {multicast address}
  END;
```

Field descriptions

ioCompletion	A pointer to a completion routine that you can provide. When you execute a function asynchronously, the system calls your completion routine when it completes execution of the function. Specify NIL for this field if you do not wish to provide a completion routine.
ioResult	The result of the function. If you call the function asynchronously, the function sets this field to 1 as soon as it begins execution, and it changes the field to the actual result code when it completes execution.
ioRefNum	The driver reference number that the OpenDriver function or the OpenSlot function returns.
csCode	A routine selector for the function to be executed. Each function has a unique routine selector. The MPW interface automatically sets this value for you.

Routines

An application that uses AppleTalk Manager routines for network communication can communicate with whatever AppleTalk network the user has selected through the Network control panel. However, you can choose to write an application that talks only to the hardware device driver for a particular type of network, such as Ethernet; in this case, your application has to address the hardware driver directly. This section describes the functions that you use to

■ attach a protocol handler to the .ENET driver

■ detach a protocol handler that you previously attached

■ send data directly to a hardware device driver

■ read data from the .ENET driver

■ cancel a pending call to read data from the .ENET driver

■ obtain information about the .ENET driver

■ switch the .ENET driver mode

■ add a multicast or functional address

■ remove a multicast or functional address

Attaching and Detaching an Ethernet Protocol Handler

You can use the functions that this section describes to attach a protocol handler to the .ENET driver, to specify which protocol handler the .ENET driver is to use for each protocol type, and to detach a protocol handler that you previously attached.

Note
Apple Computer, Inc. recommends that you attach a protocol handler for a token ring or an FDDI driver using the interface to the LAP Manager. ◆

EAttachPH

The EAttachPH function attaches a protocol handler to the .ENET driver to receive packets of a particular protocol type. You can provide and attach your own protocol handler or use the default protocol handler provided by Apple.

```
FUNCTION EAttachPH (thePBptr: EParamBlkPtr;
                    async: Boolean): OSErr;
```

thePBptr   A pointer to a parameter block of type EParamBlock.

async   A Boolean value that specifies whether the function is to be executed asynchronously or synchronously. Specify TRUE for asynchronous execution.

Ethernet, Token Ring, and Fiber Distributed Data Interface

Parameter block

→	ioCompletion	ProcPtr	A pointer to completion routine.
←	ioResult	OSErr	The result code.
→	ioRefNum	Integer	The driver reference number.
→	csCode	Integer	Always ENetAttachPH for this function.
→	eProtType	Integer	The Ethernet protocol type.
→	ePointer	Ptr	A pointer to protocol handler.

Field descriptions

eProtType — The protocol type for which you are attaching a protocol handler. To attach a protocol handler for Ethernet Phase 1 packets, specify 0 as the value of this field. (Ethernet Phase 1 packets are IEEE 802.3 protocol packets.)

ePointer — A pointer to your protocol handler application. To use the default protocol handler that Apple provides, set this field value to NIL.

DESCRIPTION

The EAttachPH function serves two purposes: you can use it to attach to the .ENET driver your own protocol handler for a specific protocol type, or you can use it to specify that the .ENET driver should call the default protocol handler for your protocol type. If you attach your own protocol handler, the .ENET driver calls that protocol handler each time it receives a packet with the protocol type you specified. If you specify that the .ENET driver should use the default protocol handler, then you use the ERead command to read packets with that protocol type. In practice, you should call the EAttachPH function very early, during your program initialization sequence, if possible.

You specify the protocol type in the eProtType parameter and provide a pointer to the protocol handler in the ePointer parameter. If you specify NIL for the ePointer parameter, then the .ENET driver uses the default protocol handler for that protocol type.

SPECIAL CONSIDERATIONS

Instead of using the EAttachPH function to install a protocol handler for an Ethernet Phase 2 packet, you should use the LAP Manager's L802Attach routine. In the case of an 802.3 protocol packet, the .ENET driver passes the packet to the LAP Manager 802.2 protocol handler. If the packet has the protocol type you specified with the L802Attach routine, the LAP Manager passes the packet on to your protocol handler. For information about the L802Attach routine, see the chapter "Link-Access Protocol (LAP) Manager" in this book.

TOKEN RING AND FDDI CONSIDERATIONS

This function is available for token ring and FDDI also. However, Apple Computer, Inc. recommends that you use the LAP Manager's L802Attach routine instead to attach your protocol handlers for token ring and FDDI. For information about the L802Attach routine, see the chapter "Link-Access Protocol (LAP) Manager" in this book.

Note that if you use this function for token ring or FDDI, you exclude other processes, such as AppleTalk, from attaching their protocol handlers to the driver at the same time. If you use the LAP Manager interface, other applications can also attach their protocol handlers and use the driver concurrently.

If you use this function for token ring, you can only install a protocol handler for protocol type 0. To use this function for either token ring or FDDI, you must set the ioRefNum field to the driver reference number that the OpenSlot or the OpenDriver function returns.

Apple does not provide a default protocol handler for token ring or FDDI.

ASSEMBLY-LANGUAGE INFORMATION

To execute the EAttachPH function from assembly language, call the _Control trap macro with a value of ENetAttachPH in the csCode field of the parameter block. To execute the _Control trap asynchronously, include the value ,ASYNC in the operand field.

RESULT CODES

noErr	0	No error
LAPProtErr	–94	Protocol handler is already attached or node's protocol table is full

SEE ALSO

For more information on how to use the EAttachPH function, see "Using the Default Ethernet Protocol Handler to Read Data" beginning on page 11-13.

For information on the IEEE 802.2 and 802.3 protocols, see the chapter "Link-Access Protocol (LAP) Manager" in this book.

EDetachPH

The EDetachPH function detaches a protocol handler from the .ENET driver.

```
FUNCTION EDetachPH (thePBptr: EParamBlkPtr;
                      async: Boolean): OSErr;
```

thePBptr   A pointer to a parameter block of type EParamBlock.

async   A Boolean value that specifies whether the function should be executed asynchronously or synchronously. Specify TRUE for asynchronous execution.

Parameter block

→	`ioCompletion`	`ProcPtr`	A pointer to completion routine.
←	`ioResult`	`OSErr`	The result code.
→	`ioRefNum`	`Integer`	The driver reference number.
→	`csCode`	`Integer`	Always `ENetDetachPH` for this function.
→	`eProtType`	`Integer`	The Ethernet protocol typ.

Field descriptions

`eProtType`   The protocol type whose protocol handler you want to remove.

DESCRIPTION

You use the `EDetachPH` function to remove from the .ENET driver a protocol handler that you attached using the `EAttachPH` function. When you call the `EDetachPH` function to remove the protocol handler, `EDetachPH` removes the protocol type from the node's protocol table. Once the protocol type is removed from the node's table, the .ENET driver no longer delivers packets with that protocol type. You specify the protocol type in the `eProtType` parameter.

If you specified your protocol type and attached the default protocol handler, `EDetachPH` removes the entry from the node's protocol table. When you call the `EDetachPH` function, any pending calls to the `ERead` function terminate with the `reqAborted` result code.

TOKEN RING AND FDDI CONSIDERATIONS

This function is available for token ring and FDDI also. However, Apple Computer, Inc. recommends that you use the LAP Manager interface to attach and detach a protocol handler for token ring and FDDI. To detach a protocol handler, you use the LAP Manager's `L802Detach` routine. For information about the `L802Detach` routine, see the chapter "Link-Access Protocol (LAP) Manager" in this book.

Note that if you use this function for token ring or FDDI, you must set the `ioRefNum` field to the driver reference number that the `OpenSlot` or `OpenDriver` function returns. For token ring, you can only detach a protocol handler for protocol type 0.

ASSEMBLY-LANGUAGE INFORMATION

To execute the `EDetachPH` function from assembly language, call the `_Control` trap macro with a value of `ENetDetachPH` in the `csCode` field of the parameter block. To execute the `_Control` trap asynchronously, include the value `,ASYNC` in the operand field.

RESULT CODES

`noErr`	0	No error
`LAPProtErr`	−94	No protocol handler is attached

Writing and Reading Ethernet Packets

You can use the functions in this section to send data to an Ethernet, token ring, or FDDI driver to be transmitted over the network. When you use the default Ethernet protocol handler, you can use the ERead and ERdCancel functions to read Ethernet packets and cancel execution of a read operation.

EWrite

The EWrite function allows you to send data directly to a hardware device driver for a particular network type for transmission across the network.

```
FUNCTION EWrite (thePBptr: EParamBlkPtr; async: Boolean): OSErr;
```

thePBptr   A pointer to a parameter block of type EParamBlock.

async   A Boolean value that specifies whether the function should be executed asynchronously or synchronously. Specify TRUE for asynchronous execution.

Parameter block

→	ioCompletion	ProcPtr	A pointer to completion routine.
←	ioResult	OSErr	The result code.
→	ioRefNum	Integer	The driver reference number.
→	csCode	Integer	Always ENetWrite for this function.
→	ePointer	Ptr	A pointer to write-data structure.

Field descriptions

ePointer   A pointer to the write-data structure that contains the data that you want to send.

DESCRIPTION

You use the EWrite function to send a data packet over an Ethernet, a token ring, or an FDDI network by communicating directly with the hardware device driver for that network type. You must first prepare a write-data structure that specifies the destination address and the protocol type and contains the data that you want to send. You place a pointer to the write-data structure in the ePointer parameter.

For Ethernet, if you want to send a packet larger than 768 bytes, you must first call the ESetGeneral function to put the .ENET driver in general-transmission mode. If the size of the packet you provide is less than 60 bytes, the driver adds pad bytes to the packet.

TOKEN RING AND FDDI CONSIDERATIONS

You can use this function to send data to a token ring or FDDI driver. Note that the packet size for token ring and FDDI is hardware dependent. However, for Logical Link Control (LLC) type packets, the packet length cannot exceed 1500 bytes.

To use this function for token ring or FDDI, you must set the `ioRefNum` field to the driver reference number that the `OpenSlot` or `OpenDriver` function returns.

You must also provide a pointer to a write-data structure. The first buffer in the write-data structure must be at least 14 bytes long: the first 6 bytes of that buffer must contain the destination address. Bytes 13 and 14 must contain the packet length, which must not exceed 1500 bytes. The token ring driver fills in bytes 7–12 with the source address.

ASSEMBLY-LANGUAGE INFORMATION

To execute the `EWrite` function from assembly language, call the `_Control` trap macro with a value of `ENetWrite` in the `csCode` field of the parameter block. To execute the `_Control` trap asynchronously, include the value `,ASYNC` in the operand field.

RESULT CODES

`noErr`	0	No error
`eLenErr`	–92	Packet too large or first entry of the write-data structure did not contain the full 14-byte header
`excessCollsns`	–95	Hardware error

SEE ALSO

For information on how to use the `EWrite` function and how to create a write-data structure, see "Using a Write-Data Structure to Transmit Ethernet Data" beginning on page 11-10.

ERead

When you use the default protocol handler for Ethernet that Apple provides, you must use the `ERead` function to read a data packet and place it in a data buffer.

```
FUNCTION ERead (thePBptr: EParamBlkPtr; async: Boolean): OSErr;
```

`thePBptr` A pointer to a parameter block of type `EParamBlock`.

`async` A Boolean value that specifies whether the function should be executed asynchronously or synchronously. Specify `TRUE` for asynchronous execution.

Parameter block

→	ioCompletion	ProcPtr	A pointer to completion routine.
←	ioResult	OSErr	The result code.
→	ioRefNum	Integer	The driver reference number.
→	csCode	Integer	Always ENetRead for this function.
→	eProtType	Integer	The Ethernet protocol type.
→	ePointer	Ptr	A pointer to a data buffer.
→	eBuffSize	Integer	The size of the data buffer.
←	eDataSize	Integer	The number of bytes read.

Field descriptions

eProtType   The protocol type of the packet you want to read.

ePointer   A pointer to the data buffer into which you want to read data.

eBuffSize   The size of the data buffer. If you are expecting Ethernet data packets, the buffer should be at least 621 bytes in size; if you are expecting general Ethernet data packets, the buffer should be at least 1514 bytes in size.

eDataSize   The number of bytes of data actually read.

DESCRIPTION

You can use the ERead function to read packets of a particular protocol type only after you have used the EAttachPH function to specify a NIL pointer to the protocol handler to indicate that you want to use the default protocol handler. In practice, you should call the EAttachPH function very early, during your program initialization sequence, if possible. As soon as the connection is established and you are expecting data, you should call the ERead function asynchronously.

The ERead function places the entire packet, including the packet header, into your buffer. The function returns in the eDataSize parameter the number of bytes actually read. If the packet is larger than the data buffer, the ERead function places as much of the packet as will fit into the buffer and returns the buf2SmallErr result code.

Call the ERead function asynchronously to await the next data packet. When the .ENET driver receives the data packet, it completes execution of the ERead function and calls your completion routine. If the .ENET driver receives a data packet with a protocol type for which you specified the default protocol handler while no ERead command is pending, the driver discards the data packet.

You can have several asynchronous calls to the ERead function pending execution simultaneously as long as you use a different parameter block for each call.

SPECIAL CONSIDERATIONS

You must not use the ERead function to read packets if you supply and attach your own protocol handler. In this case, you use the driver's ReadPacket and ReadRest routines from within your protocol handler.

TOKEN RING AND FDDI CONSIDERATIONS

This function does not apply to token ring and FDDI.

ASSEMBLY-LANGUAGE INFORMATION

To execute the `ERead` function from assembly language, call the `_Control` trap macro with a value of `ENetRead` in the `csCode` field of the parameter block. To execute the `_Control` trap asynchronously, include the value `,ASYNC` in the operand field.

RESULT CODES

noErr	0	No error
LAPProtErr	–94	No protocol is attached or protocol handler pointer was not 0
reqAborted	–1105	ERdCancel or EDetachPH function called
buf2SmallErr	–3101	Packet too large for buffer; partial data returned

SEE ALSO

See "Using the Default Ethernet Protocol Handler to Read Data" beginning on page 11-13 for more information on using the `ERead` function.

ERdCancel

The `ERdCancel` function cancels execution of a specific call to the `ERead` function.

```
FUNCTION ERdCancel (thePBptr: EParamBlkPtr;
                    async: Boolean): OSErr;
```

thePBptr   A pointer to a parameter block of type `EParamBlock`.

async   A Boolean value that specifies whether the function should be executed asynchronously or synchronously. Specify `TRUE` for asynchronous execution.

Parameter block

→	ioCompletion	ProcPtr	A pointer to completion routine.
←	ioResult	OSErr	The result code.
→	ioRefNum	Integer	The driver reference number.
→	csCode	Integer	Always `ENetRdCancel` for this function.
→	ePointer	Ptr	A pointer to `ERead` parameter block.

Field descriptions

ePointer   A pointer to the .ENET parameter block that you specified when you called the `ERead` function that you want to cancel.

DESCRIPTION

To cancel an ERead function request using the ERdCancel function, you must have called the ERead function asynchronously. You specify in the ePointer parameter a pointer to the parameter block that you used when you called the ERead function.

When you call the ERdCancel function, the pending ERead function that you cancel receives the reqAborted result code.

TOKEN RING AND FDDI CONSIDERATIONS

This function is not valid for token ring and FDDI.

ASSEMBLY-LANGUAGE INFORMATION

To execute the ERdCancel function from assembly language, call the _Control trap macro with a value of ENetRdCancel in the csCode field of the parameter block. To execute the _Control trap asynchronously, include the value ,ASYNC in the operand field.

RESULT CODES

noErr	0	No error
cbNotFound	–1102	ERead not active

Obtaining Information About the Ethernet Driver and Switching Its Mode

The functions in this section return information about the .ENET driver and switch the .ENET driver from limited-transmission mode to general-transmission mode.

EGetInfo

The EGetInfo function returns information about the .ENET driver.

```
FUNCTION EGetInfo (thePBptr: EParamBlkPtr;
                   async: Boolean): OSErr;
```

thePBptr   A pointer to a parameter block of type EParamBlock.

async   A Boolean value that specifies whether the function should be executed asynchronously or synchronously. Specify TRUE for asynchronous execution.

Parameter block

→	ioCompletion	ProcPtr	A pointer to completion routine.
←	ioResult	OSErr	The result code.
→	ioRefNum	Integer	The driver reference number.
→	csCode	Integer	Always ENetGetInfo for this function.
→	ePointer	Ptr	A pointer to a buffer.
→	eBuffSize	Integer	The size of the buffer.
←	eDataSize	Integer	The number of bytes returned.

Field descriptions

ePointer	A pointer to a buffer that is at least 18 bytes in size. The EGetInfo function returns the information about the .ENET driver in this buffer.
eBuffSize	The size of the buffer pointed to by ePointer.
eDataSize	The number of bytes of information that EGetInfo returns in the buffer pointed to by ePointer.

DESCRIPTION

The EGetInfo function returns information about the .ENET driver. Beginning with version 58 of AppleTalk, the EGetInfo function returns additional information for SONIC-based network interface controllers (NICs). For these cards, EGetInfo can return up to 78 bytes of information. The eDataSize field returns the number of bytes of information that EGetInfo has placed in the data buffer that you provide. You can use the value returned in this field to determine whether or not the Ethernet card uses a SONIC chip. For all cards that are not SONIC based, this field will contain a value of 18.

If you do not know whether the Ethernet card that you are using has a SONIC chip, you should provide a data buffer that is at least 78 bytes in length. If you are certain that the Ethernet card that you are using is not SONIC based, you must provide a data buffer that is at least 18 bytes. Put a pointer to the buffer in the ePointer parameter and the size of the buffer in the eBuffSize parameter.

For Ethernet cards that are not SONIC based, the EGetInfo function places the following information in the data buffer:

Bytes	Information
1–6	Ethernet address of the node on which the driver is installed
7–10	Number of times the receive queue has overflowed
11–14	Number of data transmission operations that have timed out
15–18	Number of packets received that contain an incorrect address

An incorrect Ethernet address is one that is neither the broadcast address, a multicast address for which this node is registered, nor the node's data-link address. A node could receive an incorrect Ethernet address due to a hardware or software error.

For SONIC-based Ethernet cards, the last 60 bytes in the buffer return information from the SONIC chip network statistic counters. The EGetInfo function places the following information in the data buffer:

Bytes	Information
1–6	Ethernet address of the node on which the driver is installed
7–10	No information returned (zero-filled)
11–14	No information returned (zero-filled)
15–18	No information returned (zero-filled)
19–22	Frames transmitted without error
23–26	Single collision frames
27–30	Multiple collision frames
31–34	Collision frames
35–38	Frames with deferred transmission
39–42	Late collision
43–46	Excessive collisions
47–50	Excessive deferrals
51–54	Internal MAC transmit error
55–58	Frames received without error
59–62	Multicast frames received without error
63–66	Broadcast frames received without error
67–70	Frame check sequence errors
71–74	Alignment errors
75–78	Frames lost due to internal MAC receive errors

TOKEN RING AND FDDI CONSIDERATIONS

This function does not apply to token ring and FDDI.

ASSEMBLY-LANGUAGE INFORMATION

To execute the EGetInfo function from assembly language, call the _Control trap macro with a value of ENetGetInfo in the csCode field of the parameter block. To execute the _Control trap asynchronously, include the value ,ASYNC in the operand field.

RESULT CODES

noErr   0   No error

ESetGeneral

The ESetGeneral function switches the .ENET driver from limited-transmission mode to general-transmission mode, allowing it to transmit a larger data packet.

```
FUNCTION ESetGeneral (thePBptr: EParamBlkPtr;
                      async: Boolean): OSErr;
```

thePBptr   A pointer to a parameter block of type EParamBlock.

async   A Boolean value that specifies whether the function should be executed asynchronously or synchronously. Specify TRUE for asynchronous execution.

Parameter block

→	ioCompletion	ProcPtr	A pointer to completion routine.
←	ioResult	OSErr	The result code.
→	ioRefNum	Integer	The driver reference number.
→	csCode	Integer	Always ENetSetGeneral for this function.

DESCRIPTION

The ESetGeneral function switches the .ENET driver from limited-transmission mode to general-transmission mode, which enables the .ENET driver to transmit an Ethernet data packet of up to 1514 bytes. In limited-transmission mode, the .ENET driver allocates a write-data buffer of 768 bytes. This buffer size is more than sufficient to hold an Ethernet data packet, which can be no larger than 621 bytes. However, if you want to send a packet that is larger than the Ethernet data packet, you must use the general-transmission mode.

SPECIAL CONSIDERATIONS

There is no command to switch the .ENET driver from general-transmission mode to limited-transmission mode. To switch back to limited-transmission mode, you have to reset the driver by restarting the computer.

TOKEN RING AND FDDI CONSIDERATIONS

This function does not apply to token ring and FDDI. However, if an application calls this function for token ring or FDDI, the driver will return a value of noErr in register D0.

ASSEMBLY-LANGUAGE INFORMATION

To execute the ESetGeneral function from assembly language, call the _Control trap macro with a value of ENetSetGeneral in the csCode field of the parameter block. To execute the _Control trap asynchronously, include the value ,ASYNC in the operand field.

RESULT CODES

noErr	0	No error
memFullErr	−108	Insufficient memory in heap

Adding and Removing Ethernet Multicast Addresses

The functions in this section add or delete multicast addresses for Ethernet or FDDI for a particular node and functional addresses for token ring for a particular node.

EAddMulti

The `EAddMulti` function adds a multicast address or a functional address to the node that is running your application.

```
FUNCTION EAddMulti (thePBptr: EParamBlkPtr;
                    async: Boolean): OSErr;
```

thePBptr   A pointer to a parameter block of type `EParamBlock`.

async   A Boolean value that specifies whether the function should be executed asynchronously or synchronously. Specify `TRUE` for asynchronous execution.

Parameter block

→	ioCompletion	ProcPtr	A pointer to completion routine.
←	ioResult	OSErr	Result code.
→	ioRefNum	Integer	Driver reference number.
→	csCode	Integer	Always `ENetAddMulti` for this function.
→	eMultiAddr	6-byte array	Multicast address.

Field descriptions

eMultiAddr   The multicast address that you want to add and use.

DESCRIPTION

You use the `EAddMulti` function to add a multicast address for Ethernet or FDDI to the node that is running your application so that the hardware device driver for that network type will accept packets delivered to that address. You can also use this function to add a functional address that serves the same purpose for token ring.

Each time a client of a hardware device driver calls the `EAddMulti` function for a particular multicast address, the driver increments a counter for that multicast address. Each time a client of the hardware device driver calls the `EDelMulti` function, the driver decrements the counter for that address. As long as the count for a multicast address is equal to or greater than 1, the hardware device driver accepts packets directed to that multicast address. Therefore, if any client of the hardware device driver in the node has called the `EAddMulti` function for a particular multicast address, the driver receives packets delivered to that address. This process also applies to token ring for functional addresses. For information on how to specify multicast and functional addresses, see *Inside AppleTalk,* second edition. Be careful not to use the broadcast address, which is also described in *Inside AppleTalk,* as a functional address.

TOKEN RING AND FDDI CONSIDERATIONS

If your token ring application requires a functional address, use the `EAddMulti` function to register a functional address. Functional addresses are the token ring equivalent of Ethernet and FDDI multicast addresses. If your FDDI application requires a multicast address, use the `EAddMulti` function to register a multicast address.

ASSEMBLY-LANGUAGE INFORMATION

To execute the `EAddMulti` function from assembly language, call the `_Control` trap macro with a value of `ENetAddMulti` in the `csCode` field of the parameter block. To execute the `_Control` trap asynchronously, include the value `,ASYNC` in the operand field.

RESULT CODES

noErr	0	No error
eMultiErr	−91	Invalid address or table is full

EDelMulti

The `EDelMulti` function decrements the counter kept by the hardware device driver for a particular multicast address for Ethernet or FDDI or a particular functional address for token ring.

```
FUNCTION EDelMulti (thePBptr: EParamBlkPtr;
                    async: Boolean): OSErr;
```

thePBptr   A pointer to a parameter block of type `EParamBlock`.

async   A Boolean value that specifies whether the function should be executed asynchronously or synchronously. Specify `TRUE` for asynchronous execution.

Parameter block

→	ioCompletion	ProcPtr	A pointer to completion routine.
←	ioResult	OSErr	The result code.
→	ioRefNum	Integer	The driver reference number.
→	csCode	Integer	Always `ENetDelMulti` for this function.
→	eMultiAddr	6-byte array	A multicast address.

Field descriptions

eMultiAddr   The multicast address that you no longer want to use.

DESCRIPTION

Each time a client of either the Ethernet or FDDI hardware device driver calls the `EAddMulti` function, the driver increments a counter for the multicast address specified by the `eMultiAddr` parameter. Each time a client of either the Ethernet or FDDI hardware device driver calls the `EDelMulti` function, the driver decrements the counter for the address specified by the `eMultiAddr` parameter.

As long as the count for a multicast address is equal to or greater than 1, the hardware device driver accepts packets directed to that multicast address. When the count for an address equals 0, the driver removes that address from the list of multicast addresses that it accepts. For token ring, the same process applies to functional addresses.

SPECIAL CONSIDERATIONS

Because more than one client of the .ENET driver might be using a particular multicast address, you should call the `EDelMulti` function only once for each time you called the `EAddMulti` function.

TOKEN RING AND FDDI CONSIDERATIONS

If your application added a multicast address for FDDI, you use this function to delete the address when you no longer need it. If your application added a functional address for token ring, use this function to delete the address when you no longer need it. Functional addresses are the token ring equivalent of Ethernet and FDDI multicast addresses. Be careful not to use the broadcast address as either a multicast or a functional address. (For information on all three types of addresses, see *Inside AppleTalk,* second edition.)

ASSEMBLY-LANGUAGE INFORMATION

To execute the `EDelMulti` function from assembly language, call the `_Control` trap macro with a value of `ENetDelMulti` in the `csCode` field of the parameter block. To execute the `_Control` trap asynchronously, include the value `,ASYNC` in the operand field.

RESULT CODES

noErr	0	No error
eMultiErr	−91	Address not found

Summary of Ethernet, Token Ring, and FDDI

Pascal Summary

Constants

```
CONST
{.ENET, .TOKN, and .FDDI driver values}
    catNetwork              = 4;         {spCategory for Ethernet NB card}
    typeEtherNet            = 1;         {spCType for Ethernet NB card}
    typeTokenRing           = 2;         {spCType for token ring NB card}
    typeFDDI                = 11;        {spCType for FDDI NB card}

{.ENET driver routine selectors}
    ENetSetGeneral          = 253;       {set to general transmission mode}
    ENetGetInfo             = 252;       {get info}
    ENetRdCancel            = 251;       {cancel read}
    ENetRead                = 250;       {read}
    ENetWrite               = 249;       {write}
    ENetDetachPH            = 248;       {detach protocol handler}
    ENetAttachPH            = 247;       {attach protocol handler}
    ENetAddMulti            = 246;       {add a multicast address}
    ENetDelMulti            = 245;       {delete a multicast address}
```

Data Structures

```
TYPE EParamBlock =
    PACKED RECORD
        qLink:          QElemPtr;        {reserved}
        qType:          Integer;         {reserved}
        ioTrap:         Integer;         {reserved}
        ioCmdAddr:      Ptr;             {reserved}
        ioCompletion:   ProcPtr;         {completion routine}
        ioResult:       OSErr;           {result code}
        ioNamePtr:      StringPtr;       {reserved}
        ioVRefNum:      Integer;         {reserved}
        ioRefNum:       Integer;         {driver reference number}
        csCode:         Integer;         {primary command code}
```

```
    CASE Integer OF
        ENetWrite, ENetAttachPH, ENetDetachPH, ENetRead, ENetRdCancel,
            ENetGetInfo, ENetSetGeneral:
            (
            eProtType:      Integer;         {Ethernet protocol type}
            ePointer:       Ptr;             {pointer; use depends on }
                                             { function}
            eBuffSize:      Integer;         {buffer size}
            eDataSize:      Integer;         {number of bytes read}
            );

        ENetAddMulti,ENetDelMulti:
            (
            eMultiAddr:     ARRAY[0..5] OF Char; {multicast address}
            )
        END;

EParamBlkPtr = ^EParamBlock;
```

Routines

Attaching and Detaching an Ethernet Protocol Handler

```
FUNCTION EAttachPH          (thePBptr: EParamBlkPtr; async: Boolean): OSErr;
FUNCTION EDetachPH          (thePBptr: EParamBlkPtr; async: Boolean): OSErr;
```

Writing and Reading Ethernet Packets

```
FUNCTION EWrite             (thePBptr: EParamBlkPtr; async: Boolean): OSErr;
FUNCTION ERead              (thePBptr: EParamBlkPtr; async: Boolean):OSErr;
FUNCTION ERdCancel          (thePBptr: EParamBlkPtr; async: Boolean): OSErr;
```

Obtaining Information About the Ethernet Driver and Switching Its Mode

```
FUNCTION EGetInfo           (thePBptr: EParamBlkPtr; async: Boolean): OSErr;
FUNCTION ESetGeneral        (thePBptr: EParamBlkPtr; async: Boolean): OSErr;
```

Adding and Removing Ethernet Multicast Addresses

```
FUNCTION EAddMulti          (thePBptr: EParamBlkPtr; async: Boolean): OSErr;
FUNCTION EDelMulti          (thePBptr: EParamBlkPtr; async: Boolean): OSErr;
```

C Summary

Constants

```
enum {
    ENetSetGeneral    = 253,        /*set "general" mode*/
    ENetGetInfo       = 252,        /*get info*/
    ENetRdCancel      = 251,        /*cancel read*/
    ENetRead          = 250,        /*read*/
    ENetWrite         = 249,        /*write*/
    ENetDetachPH      = 248,        /*detach protocol handler*/
    ENetAttachPH      = 247,        /*attach protocol handler*/
    ENetAddMulti      = 246,        /*add a multicast address*/
    ENetDelMulti      = 245,        /*delete a multicast address*/
};
```

Data Types

```
#define EParamHeader \
    QElem       *qLink;             /*reserved*/\
    short       qType;              /*reserved*/\
    short       ioTrap;             /*reserved*/\
    Ptr         ioCmdAddr;          /*reserved*/\
    ProcPtr     ioCompletion;       /*completion routine*/\
    OSErr       ioResult;           /*result code*/\
    StringPtr   ioNamePtr;          /*reserved*/\
    short       ioVRefNum;          /*reserved*/\
    short       ioRefNum;           /*driver reference number*/\
    short       csCode;             /*call command code*/

struct EParamMisc1 {
    EParamHeader                    /*general EParams*/
    short       eProtType;          /*Ethernet protocol type*/
    Ptr         ePointer;
    short       eBuffSize;          /*buffer size*/
    short       eDataSize;          /*number of bytes read*/
};
```

Ethernet, Token Ring, and Fiber Distributed Data Interface

Note

The C interface file contains the following structure type definition, which is incorrect. A corrected version follows it. ◆

```
typedef struct EParamMisc1 EParamMisc1;

struct EParamMisc2 {
    EParamMisc1 EParms1;
    char  eMultiAddr[6];               /*multicast address*/
};
```

Note

The following structure type definition is a correction to the preceding structure that may exist in the interface file. You should declare the following struct in your application instead of relying on the interface file. ◆

```
typedef struct {
    EParamHeader
    char eMultiAddr[5];               /*multicast address*/
}EParamMisc2;

typedef struct EParamMisc2 EParamMisc2;

union EParamBlock {
    EParamMisc1 EParms1;
    EParamMisc2 EParms2;
};

typedef union EParamBlock EParamBlock;

typedef EParamBlock *EParamBlkPtr;
```

Routines

Attaching and Detaching an Ethernet Protocol Handler

```
pascal OSErr EAttachPH        (EParamBlkPtr thePBptr, Boolean async);
pascal OSErr EDetachPH        (EParamBlkPtr thePBptr, Boolean async);
```

Writing and Reading Ethernet Packets

```
pascal OSErr EWrite           (EParamBlkPtr thePBptr, Boolean async);
pascal OSErr ERead            (EParamBlkPtr thePBptr, Boolean async);
pascal OSErr ERdCancel        (EParamBlkPtr thePBptr, Boolean async);
```

Obtaining Information About the Ethernet Driver and Switching Its Mode

```
pascal OSErr EGetInfo      (EParamBlkPtr thePBptr, Boolean async);
pascal OSErr ESetGeneral   (EParamBlkPtr thePBptr, Boolean async);
```

Adding and Removing Ethernet Multicast Addresses

```
pascal OSErr EAddMulti     (EParamBlkPtr thePBptr, Boolean async);
pascal OSErr EDelMulti     (EParamBlkPtr thePBptr, Boolean async);
```

Assembly-Language Summary

Constants

```
ENetSetGeneral    EQU    253    ;set to general transmission mode
ENetGetInfo       EQU    252    ;get info
ENetRdCancel      EQU    251    ;cancel read
ENetRead          EQU    250    ;read
ENetWrite         EQU    249    ;write
ENetDetachPH      EQU    248    ;detach protocol handler
ENetAttachPH      EQU    247    ;attach protocol handler
ENetAddMulti      EQU    246    ;add a multicast address
ENetDelMulti      EQU    245    ;delete a multicast address
```

Data Structures

EParamBlock Parameter Block

16	ioResult	word	result code
26	csCode	word	routine selected
28	eMultiAddr	6 bytes	multicast address
28	eProtType	word	Ethernet protocol type
30	ePointer	long	pointer
34	eBuffSize	word	size of buffer
36	eDataSize	word	number of bytes read

Result Codes

noErr	0	No error
eMultiErr	–91	Address not found
eLenErr	–92	Packet too large or first entry of the write-data structure did not contain the full 14-byte header
LAPProtErr	–94	No protocol handler is attached
excessCollsns	–95	Hardware error
memFullErr	–108	Insufficient memory in heap
cbNotFound	–1102	ERead not active
reqAborted	–1105	ERdCancel or EDetachPH function called
buf2SmallErr	–3101	Packet too large for buffer; partial data returned

Multinode Architecture

Contents

Multinode Architecture

This chapter describes how you can use AppleTalk's multinode architecture to acquire one or more node IDs, called **multinodes,** in addition to the standard user node ID. **Multinode architecture** is an AppleTalk feature that is provided to meet the needs of special-purpose applications that receive and process AppleTalk packets in a custom manner instead of passing them directly on to a higher-level AppleTalk protocol for processing. A multinode ID allows the system that is running your application to appear as multiple nodes on the network. The prime example of a multinode application is Apple Remote Access (ARA).

A multinode ID is distinct from the user node ID. AppleTalk separates packets addressed to a multinode from those addressed to the user node sockets on the same machine, and it passes the multinode packets on to a receive routine that you must supply for the multinode.

Multinode architecture is implemented in the .MPP driver and exists at the same level of the AppleTalk protocol stack as does the Datagram Delivery Protocol (DDP), but unlike DDP, multinode does not use DDP sockets, nor is it connected to the AppleTalk protocol stack above the data-link level.

This chapter describes the fundamental tasks that you perform to

- add a multinode for your application's use

- write a required routine that receives packets addressed to the multinode

- prepare and send data from the multinode

- remove a multinode when you are finished with it

Because multinode is not connected to the AppleTalk protocol stack above the data-link level, if you want your multinode application to be compatible with AppleTalk, you must implement the higher-level AppleTalk protocols. Multinode also requires that you code a receive routine in assembly language. For these reasons, you should consider using multinode only if your application requires that you process AppleTalk packets in a custom manner. You do not need to use the multinode architecture for other application requirements.

The receive routine that you must provide to handle packets addressed to your multinode ID is similar to the DDP socket-listener code that an application must include to receive packets addressed to its DDP socket. The chapter "Datagram Delivery Protocol (DDP)" in this book describes how to write a socket listener, which provides useful background information on how to write a multinode receive routine.

At the data-link level, multinode architecture relies on the AppleTalk connection file of type `'adev'` that is implemented for a particular link type. For more information about AppleTalk connection files, see the *Macintosh AppleTalk Connections Programmer's Guide.*

For information describing how to implement the higher-level AppleTalk protocols, see *Inside AppleTalk,* second edition.

About Multinode Architecture

AppleTalk multinode architecture lets you acquire multiple node addresses for a single machine, allowing that machine to act and appear as several nodes on a network. You can think of a multinode as a virtual node and the user node as the physical node. A single machine or physical node can have associated with it one or more multinodes. You can obtain a multinode ID after a node that is running your application connects to the AppleTalk network and AppleTalk assigns the standard user node ID to that system. The use of multinode addresses does not affect the functions of the standard user node address, which uniquely identifies the physical node on the network and forms part of the internet socket address of a DDP socket-client application.

Multinode architecture communicates similarly to DDP in that you send data from a multinode as discrete packets, with each packet carrying the full addressing information required to deliver the data to its destination.

Multinode architecture is a client of the data-link layer and all of the supported data-link types. It is connected to the AppleTalk protocol stack from the data-link layer down through the hardware. It is not connected to the AppleTalk protocols above it, and there are no hooks that a multinode application can use to pass a packet up through the AppleTalk protocol stack for processing by a higher-level protocol.

Therefore, a multinode application that receives DDP packets for higher-level AppleTalk protocols must process these packets itself, in its own way. For example, if a multinode application receives an AppleTalk AEP Echoer request packet, it must determine how to handle the request packet, that is, whether or not to respond to the packet as the AppleTalk Echo Protocol (AEP) implementation does. (For more information on AEP, see the discussion in the chapter "Datagram Delivery Protocol [DDP]" in this book and the AEP protocol specification in *Inside AppleTalk,* second edition.)

After a packet is delivered to the node, the .MPP driver checks the DDP packet header and passes packets addressed to a user node socket on to the appropriate socket listener, while passing packets addressed to a multinode on to the receive routine that you provide as part of your multinode application. Your receive routine must receive both packets addressed to the multinode and broadcast packets. A receive routine is similar to a socket listener. You must code the receive routine in assembly language because the .MPP driver passes values to your routine in registers when it calls the routine.

Multinode architecture does not provide for the establishing of sessions—that is, the ability to set up a connection and send streams of data over it, nor does it include support for error recovery. If you want these features, you need to provide them in your multinode application.

AppleTalk delivers all packets to the physical node based on the user node ID assigned to the node, which is carried in the frame header as the destination node ID. Multinode architecture always uses a long DDP packet header; Figure 12-1 shows the structure of the long DDP packet header. It also shows the frame header.

Multinode Architecture

Figure 12-1   The long DDP packet header used for multinode

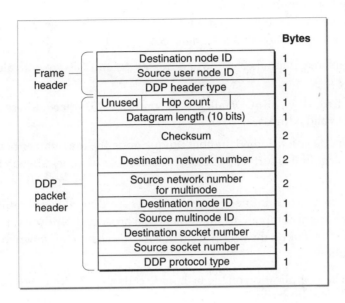

When you send a packet from a multinode:

- The frame header always contains the source user node ID, which identifies the physical node on the network from which the packet was transmitted.

- The DDP packet header always contains the source multinode ID, which identifies the virtual multinode from which you are sending the packet.

A packet is always transmitted from the physical node's network hardware, and the frame header contains the user node ID of the physical node that transmitted the packet. Your multinode application uses a multinode ID, which you can think of as a virtual node from which you are sending data. The DDP header identifies this multinode. Your application sends data, but the networking hardware and its device driver actually transmit the packet containing the data across the network to its destination.

A single networked machine may have associated with it one or more multinode IDs. Packets sent from several multinode applications running on the same machine include different source multinode IDs, but because they are all transmitted from the same physical node, the packets all have the same source user node ID.

Because the source multinode ID is associated with the application that sent the packet and the source user node ID is associated with the machine that transmitted the packet, the source user node ID in the frame header and the source multinode ID in the DDP packet header are always different values.

Note
Even if the destination node of a packet is on the same LocalTalk network as the source user node, a packet sent from a multinode always contains a long DDP header to allow for the inclusion of the two separate source node IDs: the user node ID and the multinode ID. ◆

About Multinode Architecture

To acquire a multinode, you call the `AddNode` routine. You can obtain only one multinode at a time. The number of multinodes that a single machine can support is limited by the maximum number of multinodes supported by the underlying AppleTalk connection file of type `'adev'` for the data link that is being used:

- For LocalTalk, the maximum is 254 node addresses ($0 and $FF are not valid addresses).

- For EtherTalk, TokenTalk, or FDDITalk, the maximum is 253 node addresses ($0, $FF, and $FE are not valid addresses).

Because the multinode is considered another unique node ID, the number of multinodes that can be acquired is further limited by the number of nodes already active on the network.

As an example of one use of multinodes, consider how a multinode application that includes server and client components might handle a broadcast NBP lookup packet. The following events occur on the user node that runs the client component of the multinode application:

1. A DDP socket-client application on the user node calls an NBP function that generates a broadcast NBP lookup packet.

2. The .MPP driver sends the packet out to the network. Because it is a broadcast packet, the .MPP driver also sends the NBP lookup packet to the multinode on the same machine.

3. The multinode client application's receive routine receives the packet.

4. The multinode client application processes the packet's contents and repackages them in its own multinode packet, which it sends out through the serial port over the modem and telephone line to the multinode application on the server node.

The following events occur on the node that is running the server component of the multinode application.

1. The server multinode application receives the multinode packet through the system's serial port.

2. This application uses the `NetWrite` routine to decode the multinode packet and uses the packet contents as the data for a DDP packet. It builds the required data structure to contain the data for a standard DDP packet.

3. The server multinode application then sends the broadcast packet down through the AppleTalk protocol stack from the link-access layer, through the hardware, and out to the network for a response. It also sends the packet to the user node on the same machine.

Figure 12-2 illustrates this process.

Figure 12-2   How a server-client multinode application might send a broadcast NBP
lookup packet

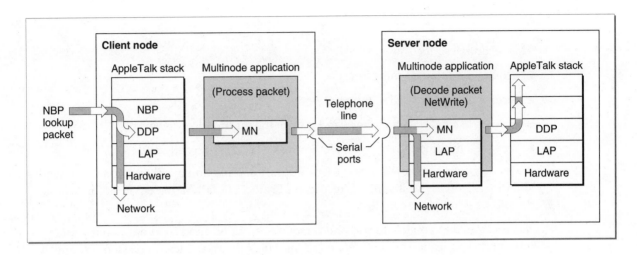

The primary use of the multinode architecture for an application is to provide router-like
services as part of the application. One of the advantages of multinode is that your
application receives all Name-Binding Protocol (NBP) request packets because they are
broadcast packets. In fact, the first packets that your application is likely to receive are
NBP lookup packets. These include NBP register requests that generate an NBP lookup
request if the sender specified that NBP should verify the uniqueness of the entity name
to be registered. (For an explanation of NBP and its components, see the chapter "Name-
Binding Protocol [NBP]" in this book.)

How you handle the NBP lookup packets is application-specific. However, if you want
your application to be visible throughout the network, you need to meet certain
AppleTalk compatibility requirements. In this case, your application needs to implement
the NBP protocol. You can implement your own NBP names table for the multinode to
determine if your application handles the services requested in the lookup packet. For
example, your application can check to determine if an NBP lookup packet's entity name
object and type fields match the object and type fields of any of the entity name entries in
your NBP names table. Any response that you return to the requester must conform to
the AppleTalk packet format. You may also want to implement the AppleTalk Echo
Protocol (AEP), and in this case, too, any responses that you return to the sender must
meet the specifications for an AEP AppleTalk packet. (For a description of AEP, see the
chapter "Datagram Delivery Protocol [DDP]" in this book.) *Inside AppleTalk*, second
edition, describes how to implement NBP and AEP.

Using Multinode Architecture

This section describes how to

- acquire a multinode (`AddNode`)

- receive data addressed to the multinode

- prepare to send data and then send it from the multinode (`NetWrite`)

- remove a multinode when you are finished with it (`RemoveNode`)

It also mentions the cable-range-change AppleTalk transition event that you must handle and directs you to the chapter "Link-Access Protocol (LAP) Manager" for information describing what you must do.

The routines that you use to add and remove a multinode and send data from your multinode application are not defined in the MPW interface files. To use these routines from a high-level language, you must call the Device Manager directly and specify the routine's `csCode` in the parameter block. For the `AddNode` routine, you must issue the function as an immediate control call and define a function for this purpose. (For an example of how to do this, see Listing 12-1 on page 12-9.) For the `NetWrite` and `RemoveNode` routines, you call the Device Manager's `PBControl` function. (For information about how to do this, see "Routines" beginning on page 12-20.)

Note

AppleTalk version 57 or later must be installed on the system that is running your application if you use the multinode feature. AppleTalk version 57 is compatible with system software version 6.0.5 and later. You should include AppleTalk version 57 with any product that uses multinodes. Contact Apple's Software Licensing department for information on licensing AppleTalk. ◆

Acquiring and Removing Multinodes

You can add an AppleTalk multinode once the physical node that runs your application has connected to the AppleTalk network and AppleTalk has assigned to it a user node ID. After you are finished using the multinode, your application must remove it. This section describes how to do these tasks.

To acquire a multinode address, perform the following steps:

1. Use the Device Manager's `OpenDriver` function to open the .MPP driver.

   □ The .MPP driver must be opened before you call the multinode routines. The `OpenDriver` function call returns the .MPP driver's reference number.

   □ Save the returned value because you must supply this reference number as an input parameter in the `ioRefNum` field of the multinode parameter block when you call the multinode routines.

2. Create a receive routine to receive broadcast messages and packets addressed to your multinode. See "Receiving Packets Addressed to Your Multinode" beginning on page 12-10 for details.

   ☐ You pass the address of the receive routine to the .MPP driver when you call the AddNode routine to acquire a multinode.

   ☐ When the .MPP driver receives a packet addressed to your multinode or a broadcast message, it calls your receive routine for that multinode to handle the packet reception.

3. Allocate storage and set parameter block fields as needed.

   ☐ Define a multinode parameter block of type MNParamBlock. Allocate storage for a multinode parameter block that includes the fields required for the AddNode routine. See "The Multinode Parameter Block" on page 12-19.

   ☐ You must set the csCode parameter block field to the numeric value of 262 for the AddNode routine. For the other required parameter block fields, see "AddNode" beginning on page 12-22.

4. Call the AddNode routine once for each multinode that you need.

   ☐ You can acquire only one multinode through each request. You can request a specific multinode address, and if that multinode is available, the .MPP driver will assign it to you. Otherwise, the .MPP driver will return a multinode address that it selects randomly.

   ☐ Because the AddNode routine is not defined in the MPW interface files, you must call the Device Manager directly and execute the AddNode routine as an immediate synchronous control call.

From assembly language, you can directly make an immed _Control trap macro call. To issue the AddNode routine as an immediate synchronous control call from a high-level language such as Pascal or C, you must define a function as part of your application. Listing 12-1 shows how to do this in the Pascal language.

Listing 12-1   Defining a Pascal function that makes an immediate AddNode call

```
FUNCTION PBControlImmedSync(paramBlock: ParmBlkPtr): OSErr;
    INLINE $205F,$A204,$3E80;


FUNCTION AddNode(thePBptr: MNParmBlkPtr): OSErr;
CONST
    tryAddNodeAgainErr   = -1021;
VAR
    err: OSErr;


BEGIN
    thePBptr^.csCode   := 262; {addNode}
    thePBptr^.ioRefNum := mppUnitNum;
{If the call returns tryAddNodeAgainErr, make the call repeatedly
until it no longer returns this error.}
```

```
    REPEAT
        err    := PBControlImmedSync(ParmBlkPtr(thePBptr));
        UNTIL (err <> tryAddNodeAgainErr);
        AddNode := err;
END;
```

You must issue the `AddNode` call synchronously because you need to call `AddNode` repeatedly if the call returns an error of –1021, which indicates that the .MPP driver could not satisfy the `AddNode` request and that you should try the request again immediately.

The .MPP driver internally associates the address of your receive routine with the multinode address that it returns to you. See "AddNode" beginning on page 12-22 for a complete description of this routine and the parameters that you must pass it.

When you are finished using the multinode, you call the `RemoveNode` routine to remove the multinode.

1. Allocate nonrelocatable memory for a multinode parameter block that includes the fields required for the `RemoveNode` routine. See "The Multinode Parameter Block" beginning on page 12-19. The multinode parameter block belongs to the .MPP driver for the life of the `RemoveNode` call.

2. You issue the `RemoveNode` routine as a Device Manager's `PBControl` call. See "RemoveNode" beginning on page 12-24 for details on this routine and the parameters it requires. You must specify the `csCode` numeric value 263 for the `RemoveNode` routine.

Handling an AppleTalk Cable-Range-Change Transition Event

A cable range is a range of network numbers beginning with the lowest network number and ending with the highest network number defined by a seed router for a network. All node addresses, including multinode addresses, that a system on a network acquires must have a network number within the defined cable range.

An AppleTalk cable-range-change transition event occurs when the current cable range for a network changes. Your multinode application needs to be able to receive notification of a cable-range-change transition and respond to that event by checking the new cable range to determine if all the multinode IDs that the application acquired before the transition event occurred are still valid. If you discover multinode IDs that are no longer valid, you must remove them with the `RemoveNode` function. You can obtain new multinodes to replace them with the `AddNode` function.

Receiving Packets Addressed to Your Multinode

Your application must provide a routine that receives packets addressed to the multinode and broadcast packets. Because the .MPP driver passes values to your multinode receive routine in registers when it calls the routine, you must code the receive routine in assembly language.

You pass the address of your receive routine to the .MPP driver when you call the `AddNode` routine to open a multinode. The .MPP driver internally associates your receive routine with the multinode address that it assigns, and it calls your receive routine to handle a packet addressed to the multinode or a broadcast packet.

If your application acquires more than one multinode, you can use the same receive routine for each of these multinodes. If you use the same receive routine to receive and process packets for more than one multinode, the .MPP driver will call that receive routine only once for each broadcast packet that it receives.

A multinode receive routine is similar in concept to a socket listener that receives packets addressed to a specific socket. The chapter "Datagram Delivery Protocol (DDP)" in this book includes a sample socket listener. To create a receive routine, perform the following steps:

1. Allocate a buffer to hold the data that you expect to receive.

   □ The maximum amount of data in a DDP packet is 586 bytes. All packets addressed to multinodes use a long header, which is 13 bytes long. If your receive routine places the packet header as well as the data portion in the buffer, make the buffer large enough to hold both parts of the packet contents.

   □ If you use the same receive routine to receive and process packets for more than one multinode, you should provide a separate buffer to store the data for each multinode. You can define a single buffer for each multinode to hold the contents of both the header and data portions of a packet, or you can define a pair of buffers for each multinode to separate the packet's contents.

2. Determine the number of bytes that have already been read into the .MPP driver's internal buffer, called the RHA.

   □ To do this, subtract the beginning address of the *read-header area (RHA)* from the value in register A3, which points past the last byte read into the RHA. To locate the offset at the beginning of the RHA, you can use the `toRHA` equate.

   When a frame that contains either a DDP packet that is addressed to your multinode or a broadcast packet is delivered to the node that is running your multinode application, the node's CPU is interrupted and the .MPP driver's interrupt handler gets control to service the interrupt. As the frame's first 3 bytes are read into a FIFO buffer, the .MPP driver's interrupt handler moves these bytes into the RHA.

3. Use the `ReadPacket` and `ReadRest` routines to read the rest of the incoming data that constitutes the packet.

   How you handle a packet after you read it is particular to your application. For example, if your application implements NBP, you can check the packet's entity name object and type fields against entries in your names table to determine whether to process the packet and respond to the sender. If you respond, the packet you send must adhere to the structure of a standard AppleTalk packet. (See *Inside AppleTalk*, second edition, for the AppleTalk packet structure.) For a brief description of how ARA uses multinode, see the discussion on page 12-6.

   □ You can call the `ReadPacket` routine as many times as you like to read the data piece by piece into one or more data buffers that you have defined, but you must always use the `ReadRest` routine to read the final piece of the data packet. The `ReadRest` routine restores the machine state (the stack pointers, status register, and so forth) and checks for error conditions.

□ Before you call the `ReadPacket` routine, you must place a pointer to the data buffer for which you allocated memory in the A3 register. You must also place the number of bytes you want to read in the D3 register. You must not request more bytes than remain in the data packet.

□ After you have called the `ReadRest` routine, you can use registers A0 through A3 and D0 through D3 for your own use, but you must preserve all other registers. You cannot depend on having access to your application's global variables.

Calling `ReadPacket` and `ReadRest` when LocalTalk is the data link

If LocalTalk is the data link that is being used, your receive routine has less than 95 microseconds (best case) to read more data with a `ReadPacket` or `ReadRest` routine. If you need more time, you can read another 3 bytes into the RHA, which will allow you an additional 95 microseconds. Note that the RHA may only have 8 bytes still available. ◆

4. If the packet header contains a checksum, you can calculate a checksum for both the header and data portions of the packet and then verify the sum of these two values against the value in the `checksum` field of the packet header. If the checksum you calculate does not match the one in the header, the data has been corrupted in some way. (Figure 12-1 on page 12-5 shows the DDP packet header, including the checksum field.)

The chapter "Datagram Delivery Protocol (DDP)" in this book contains a sample checksum routine to be used for a socket listener; this routine is equally applicable to a multinode receive routine.

Calling ReadPacket to Read in the Packet Contents

To call the `ReadPacket` routine, execute a JSR instruction to the address in the A4 register. The `ReadPacket` routine uses the registers as follows:

Registers on entry to the `ReadPacket` routine

A3   Pointer to a buffer to hold the data you want to read

D3   Size in of bytes to be read; must be nonzero

Registers on exit from the `ReadPacket` routine

A0   Unchanged

A1   Unchanged

A2   Unchanged

A3   Pointer to the first byte after the last byte read into buffer

A4   Unchanged

D0   Changed

D1   Number of bytes left to be read

D2   Unchanged

D3   Equals 0 if the requested number of bytes were read, nonzero if error

After every time that you call ReadPacket, you must check the zero (z) flag in the status register for errors because the ReadPacket routine indicates an error by clearing it to 0. If the ReadPacket routine returns an error, you must terminate execution of your receive routine with an RTS instruction without calling ReadPacket again or calling ReadRest at all.

Calling ReadRest to Complete Reading in the Packet Contents

Call the ReadRest routine to read the last portion of the data packet, or call it after you have read all the data with ReadPacket routines and before you do any other processing or terminate execution. After you call ReadRest, you must check the zero (z) flag in the status register for errors.

After you call the ReadRest routine, you must terminate execution of your receive routine with an RTS instruction whether or not the ReadRest routine returns an error.

When you call the ReadRest routine, you must provide in the A3 register a pointer to a data buffer and you must indicate in the D3 register the size of the data buffer. If you have already read all of the data using the ReadPacket routine, specify a buffer of size 0.

▲ **WARNING**
If you do not call the ReadRest routine after the last time you call the ReadPacket routine successfully, the system will crash. ▲

To call the ReadRest routine, execute a JSR instruction to an address 2 bytes past the address in the A4 register:

```
JSR 2(A4)
```

The ReadRest routine uses the registers as follows:

Registers on entry to the ReadRest routine

A3	Pointer to a buffer to hold the data you want to read
D3	Size of the buffer (word length); may be 0

Registers on exit from the ReadRest routine

A0	Unchanged
A1	Unchanged
A2	Unchanged
A3	Pointer to first byte after the last byte read into buffer
D0	Changed
D1	Changed: number of bytes left to be read
D2	Unchanged
D3	Equals 0 if the requested number of bytes were read, is less than 0 if the packet data was too large to fit in the buffer and the data was truncated, and is greater than 0 to indicate the number of bytes that were not read

For more information on how your receive routine can use the registers, see the discussion of the socket listener routine in the chapter "Datagram Delivery Protocol (DDP)" in this book.

Sending Packets Using a Multinode

You can use a multinode to send packets that contain data that you have already received; in this case you forward the data from the multinode using the NetWrite call. You can also use the multinode to send original data using the NetWrite call. In both cases, you must use a structure called the **write-data structure** to indicate to the .MPP driver where the DDP packet header portion and the data portion to be sent are stored. Why you send data is particular to your application. For example, if your application implements AEP, it would send an Echo Reply packet in response to the Echo Request packet that the application receives. For a brief description of using multinode, see the discussion on page 12-6.

To send data from the multinode, you perform the following steps:

1. Create a write-data structure, as described in the next section, "Preparing a Write-Data Structure."

2. Allocate nonrelocatable memory for a multinode parameter block that includes the fields required for the NetWrite routine. See "The Multinode Parameter Block" beginning on page 12-19. The multinode parameter block belongs to the .MPP driver for the life of the NetWrite call.

3. Call the NetWrite routine to send the data. You issue the NetWrite routine as a Device Manager's PBControl call. See "NetWrite" beginning on page 12-25 for details on this routine and the parameters it requires.

   □ Set the parameter block field values belonging to the NetWrite call, including the checksum flag (checkSumFlag) parameter. See "Using a Checksum" on page 12-16.

   □ You must set the csCode parameter block field to the numeric value of 261 for the NetWrite routine.

Preparing a Write-Data Structure

The .MPP driver uses a write-data structure that you create to locate the header and data portions of the packet to be transmitted. When you call the NetWrite routine to send data from a multinode, you pass it a pointer to the write-data structure that you have already prepared. A write-data structure contains a series of pairs of length words and pointers, and each pair indicates the length and location of a portion of the data. The first pair must indicate the DDP header of the packet to be transmitted. It ends with a 0 word.

The .MPP driver constructs the packet to be transmitted, building the packet contents from the header and data information that you provide.

The write-data structure that you use for a multinode is similar to the write-data structure that you use to send a packet from a DDP socket except that for a multinode write-data structure, you must also include the source network number and the source multinode ID. This is because the source user node ID of the physical node, which is carried in the frame header, is different from the source multinode ID, which is carried in the DDP packet header. The source address information that you provide identifies the multinode from which you are sending the data. The multinode write-data structure also contains a checksum field that you can set to 0 if you do not want a checksum calculated for this packet. Figure 12-3 shows the write-data structure; it also shows how you must define the header information in the storage that you allocate for it.

You create a write-data structure in one of three different forms:

- You can provide a single length-pointer pair that identifies one storage block that contains both the header and data information. In this case, the header information must come first, and it must begin at an odd address.

- You can use two length-pointer pairs, one for the header portion and one for the data portion.

- You could also use more than two length-pointer pairs, one for the header, and one for each separate block of data.

In many cases, the header and data components of a packet are not stored contiguously, which requires that the write-data structure contain at least two length-pointer pairs. Typically, the data portion is stored as a single block. However, some implementations send blocks of data that are stored separately as parts of the same datagram; if the complete data portion is stored as several separate blocks, then the write-data structure needs to contain a length-pointer pair for each block of data.

Figure 12-3   The write-data structure for a multinode

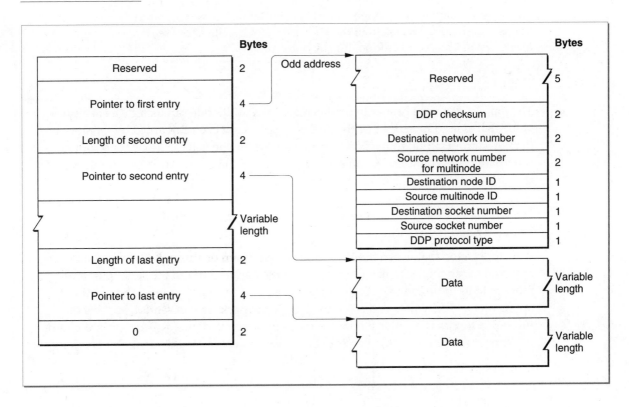

12

Multinode Architecture

Note

The header block that the write-data structure points to consists of 16 bytes. The first pointer in the write-data structure must point to an odd address, so if you create the write-data structure in Pascal, the first byte is not used. ◆

For the header, you must fill in the following:

- the destination network number

- the source network number of the multinode

- the destination node ID

- the source multinode ID

- the destination socket number

- the source socket number (if you are forwarding from the multinode a DDP packet that contains an existing value for the source socket number, you can pass that value on in this field)

- DDP protocol type (DDP protocol types 1 through 15 are reserved for use by Apple)

Note

A multinode is not associated with a DDP socket. If the source socket field contains a value, it must adhere to the conventions that the AppleTalk DDP protocol specification describes for the use of sockets. For example, this field must not specify socket number 0 ($00); rather the value should be constrained to socket number values belonging to the user-defined range stated in the DDP protocol specification; see *Inside AppleTalk*, second edition, for this information. ◆

Using a Checksum

The long DDP packet header that you create for a multinode can include a checksum value that is used to verify that the packet data has not been corrupted by memory or data bus errors within routers on the internet. When you call the `NetWrite` routine to send data from a multinode, you specify a value for the `checkSumFlag` parameter of the multinode parameter block. You use the `checkSumFlag` parameter differently to send data from a multinode than how you would use it to send data from a DDP socket, even though in both cases the flag's value controls the use of the long DDP packet header's `checksum` field.

Any application that uses a multinode can receive packets through that multinode. The application can then repackage and forward the packet through the serial port and modem to its multinode-application counterpart on a remote system. The multinode application at the remote end can then decode the package and send the packet on through a `NetWrite` call to a node on the network or a user-node process on the same machine. An existing packet that is to be forwarded could already contain a checksum value. When you issue the `NetWrite` call, you can preserve that checksum value and pass it on as part of the header in the packet. You use the `checkSumFlag` parameter of the `NetWrite` routine for this purpose.

■ If you do not want the current value in the packet header's checksum field to be altered, you set `checkSumFlag` to 0, and the existing checksum value in the DDP header will not be changed. (If a checksum has already been calculated, it will be passed along unmodified.)

■ If you want the checksum for the datagram to be calculated and placed in the DDP packet header's checksum field before the .MPP driver transmits the packet, set `checkSumFlag` to a nonzero number.

Note that if you want to send a packet that does not include a checksum, you must hardcode the value by setting to 0 the checksum field of the data structure that contains the packet header that you point to from the write-data structure.

How the Apple Remote Access program uses the checksum flag

The Apple Remote Access (ARA) program is an example of an application that sets the `checkSumFlag` flag to 0 in order to preserve a packet's original checksum value. The ARA client multinode can receive a DDP packet addressed to that multinode or a broadcast packet, such as an NBP lookup packet. In either case, the packet is a standard DDP packet that could contain a checksum value. The client ARA software passes the packet on to the ARA software on the server through the serial port and modem. The ARA software on the server node sets `checkSumFlag` to 0 when it calls the `NetWrite` routine to send the packet down from the multinode through the AppleTalk stack and out to a node on the network. ◆

Multinode Architecture Reference

This section describes the data structures and routines that are specific to the multinode architecture.

The "Data Structures" section shows the Pascal data structures for the write-data structure, the address block record, and the multinode parameter block to the .MPP driver.

The "Routines" section describes the routines that you use to add a multinode address, remove a multinode address, and send data from the multinode to be transmitted over the network. Unlike most of the routines comprising the protocol implementations described in this book, the multinode routines are not defined in the MPW interface files. To call these routines from a high-level language, you must use the Device Manager's interface. The "Routines" section describes how to do this.

Data Structures

This section describes the data structures that you use to provide information to the multinode architecture implementation in the .MPP driver.

- You use the write-data structure to pass information to the NetWrite routine that identifies the length and location of the header and data portions of a packet to be sent from the multinode.

- You use the address block record to pass to the AddNode routine the address of the multinode that you wish to acquire and to receive from the routine the actual multinode address that the .MPP driver assigns.

- You use the multinode parameter block to pass and receive the input and output parameters for each multinode call.

The Write-Data Structure

A write-data structure contains a series of pairs of length words and pointers. Each pair indicates the length and location of a portion of the data, including the header information, that constitutes the packet to be sent over the network.

You create a write-data structure, then pass its pointer to the NetWrite routine to send a packet from a multinode.

```
TYPE   WDSElement =
RECORD
    entryLength:    Integer;
    entryPtr:       Ptr;
END;
```

Field descriptions

entryLength   The length of the data pointed to by entryPtr.

entryPtr   A pointer to the data that is part of the packet to be sent using the NetWrite routine. The data storage area pointed to can contain the header information, the data to be transmitted, or both.

The Address Block Record

The address block record defines a data structure of AddrBlock type. You use this record type for

- the reqNodeAddr field value of the multinode parameter block to specify the preferred network number and multinode ID of the multinode that you wish to acquire when you execute the AddNode routine

- the actNodeAddr parameter block field for the AddNode routine for the .MPP driver to return the multinode address that it assigns to you

- the nodeAddr parameter block field for the RemoveNode routine to specify the address of the multinode to be removed

```
TYPE AddrBlock =
PACKED RECORD
    aNet:           Integer;        {network number}
    aNode:          Byte;           {node ID}
    aSocket:        Byte;           {socket number}
END;
```

Field descriptions

aNet   The number of the desired network to which the multinode node that you are requesting or assigned belongs.

aNode   The node ID of the multinode that you request or that MPP assigns.

aSocket   The value of this field should always be 0.

The Multinode Parameter Block

The multinode routines that you use to add and remove a node and send a packet from a multinode require a pointer to a multinode parameter block. The multinode parameter block holds all of the input and output values associated with the routine. The multinode parameter block is a variant record parameter block, defined by the `MNParamBlock` data type.

IMPORTANT

For the multinode parameter block, you must define the `MNParamBlock` type in your application because it is not included in the MPW interface files. ▲

This section defines the fields that are common to the three multinode routines that use the multinode parameter block. It does not define reserved fields, which are used either internally by the .MPP driver or not at all. The fields that are used for specific routines only are defined in the description of the routines to which they apply.

```
TYPE
MNParmType =    (AddNodeParm,RemoveNodeParm);
MNParamBlock    =
PACKED RECORD
        qLink:          QElemPtr;           {reserved}
        qType:          Integer;            {reserved}
        ioTrap:         Integer;            {reserved}
        ioCmdAddr:      Ptr;                {reserved}
        ioCompletion:   ProcPtr;            {completion routine}
        ioResult:       OSErr;              {result code}
        ioNamePtr:      StringPtr;          {reserved}
        ioVRefNum:      Integer;            {reserved}
        ioRefNum:       Integer;            {driver reference number}
        csCode:         Integer;            {command code}
        filler1:        Byte;
```

```
checkSumFlag:       Byte;                    {perform checksum on datagram}
    wdsPointer:     Ptr;                     {pointer to write-data structure}
    filler2:        Integer;
    CASE MNParmType of
       AddNodeParm:
          (reqNodeAddr:   AddrBlock;   {preferred address requested}
           actNodeAddr:   AddrBlock;   {actual node address acquired}
           recvRoutine:   ProcPtr;     {address of packet receive routine}
           reqCableLo:    Integer;     {preferred network range for the }
           reqCableHi:    Integer;     { node being acquired}
           reserved: PACKED ARRAY[1..70] OF Byte);
       RemoveNodeParm:
          (nodeAddr: AddrBlock);       {node address to be deleted}
    END;
```

Field descriptions

ioResult	The result of the function. When you execute the function asynchronously, the function sets this field to 1 and returns a function result of noErr as soon as the function begins execution. When the function completes execution, it sets the ioResult field to the actual result code.
ioRefNum	The .MPP driver reference number. You must fill in this value.
csCode	The command code of the multinode command to be executed. You must fill in a numeric value for this field.

Routines

This section describes the multinode routines that you use to

- acquire a multinode address

- remove a multinode address once you are finished with it

- send packets from a specific multinode

The multinode architecture is implemented in the .MPP driver. To pass parameters required for a multinode routine, you use the multinode parameter block of type MNParamBlock. You must define this parameter block type in your application. (See "The Multinode Parameter Block" on page 12-19.) An arrow preceding a parameter indicates whether the parameter is an input or an output parameter:

Arrow	Meaning
→	Input
←	Output

The AddNode, RemoveNode, and NetWrite routines use different fields of the multinode parameter block for parameters specific to the routine. The description of each routine identifies the parameter block values that the routine requires.

Assembly-language note

You call the multinode commands from assembly language by putting a routine selector in the `csCode` field of the parameter block and calling the `_Control` trap. To execute the `_Control` trap asynchronously, include the value `,ASYNC` in the operand field. Note, however, that you must execute the `AddNode` routine as an immediate (`immed`) synchronous routine. ◆

Because the MPW interface files do not define an interface for the multinode architecture, you must use the Device Manager's interface to call the multinode routines from a high-level language.

To acquire a multinode address, you execute the `AddNode` routine specifying a routine selector of 262 in the `csCode` field. You must issue the `AddNode` routine as an immediate control call to the Device Manager. See Listing 12-1 on page 12-9 for an example of how to make an immediate control call from the Pascal language.

To issue the `RemoveNode` (`csCode` equals 263) and `NetWrite` (`csCode` equals 261) routines, you use the Device Manager's `PBControl` function. The `PBControl` function is defined as follows:

```
FUNCTION PBControl (paramBlock: ParmBlkPtr; async: Boolean): OSErr;
```

`paramBlock`   A pointer to the multinode parameter block of type `MNParamBlock` that contains the parameters required by the multinode routine to be executed.

`async`   A Boolean value that specifies whether the function is to be executed synchronously or asynchronously. Set the `async` parameter to `TRUE` to execute the function asynchronously.

DESCRIPTION

You can execute the `PBControl` function synchronously or asynchronously by setting the `async` flag. The `PBControl` function takes a pointer to a multinode parameter block that contains a `csCode` field in which you specify the routine selector for the particular routine to be executed; you must specify a numeric value for this field. You must also specify the .MPP driver reference number as the value of the multinode parameter block's `ioRefNum` field. The Device Manager's `OpenDriver` function returns the .MPP driver reference number when you call it to open the .MPP driver.

Adding and Removing Multinode Addresses

This section describes the multinode routines that you call to add or remove a multinode address for your application or process to use. You use the `AddNode` routine to add a multinode ID after you open the .MPP driver. You use the `RemoveNode` routine to remove the multinode ID when you no longer require the additional node address.

AddNode

You use the `AddNode` routine to acquire a multinode ID that is separate from and in addition to the standard user node ID assigned to the system. You call the `AddNode` routine once for each additional multinode that you require. You use the `PBControl` function to call the `AddNode` routine. See "Routines" on page 12-20 for a description of the `PBControl` function. You use a synchronous immediate control call to issue the `AddNode` routine.

Parameter block

←	`ioResult`	OSErr	The result code.
→	`ioRefNum`	Integer	The .MPP driver reference number. You must fill in this value.
→	`csCode`	Integer	The routine selector. Always equal to 262 for this routine. You must fill in this value.
→	`reqNodeAddr`	AddrBlock	The requested multinode address.
←	`actNodeAddr`	AddrBlock	The actual multinode address assigned and returned by the .MPP driver.
→	`recvRoutine`	LongInt	The address of the application's receive routine.
→	`reqCableLo`	Integer	The start of requested network number range for the multinode.
→	`reqCableHi`	Integer	The end of the requested network number range for the multinode.
→	`reserved`	char	70 reserved bytes required by the .MPP driver.

Field descriptions

`reqNodeAddr`   The desired network address of the multinode to be acquired. You specify a value for this field in `AddrBlock` format. (See "The Address Block Record" on page 12-18.) The value of the `aSocket` field of the `AddrBlock` record must always be 0. Set the `aNet` and `aNode` fields to the desired network number and multinode ID. If the address that you specify is in use or is invalid, the .MPP driver will assign a different multinode address. To allow the .MPP driver to randomly generate the multinode address to be assigned, specify 0 for all three fields of the `AddrBlock` record. The .MPP driver returns in the `actNodeAddr` field of the parameter block either the multinode address that you request or the one that it selects.

`actNodeAddr`   The actual network address of the multinode that the .MPP driver assigned and returned to you.

`recvRoutine`   The address of the routine that you provide as part of your application to receive packets addressed to this multinode. The .MPP driver calls this routine when it receives either a packet addressed to the multinode or a broadcast packet.

`reqCableLo`   The network number that defines the low end of the range of network numbers from which you would like the .MPP driver to select a multinode ID for your use. The `reqCableHi` field contains the network number that defines the high end of this range. The

.MPP driver uses the values that you specify for the cable range if all of the following conditions are true: the .MPP driver could not assign the multinode number that you specified in the `reqNodeAddr` field (if you specified one), there is no router on the network, and all the multinode addresses belonging to the network whose number is specified in the `NetHint` field are being used. The `NetHint` field contains the last used network number stored in RAM.

The network range for the system on which your application is running is defined by the seed router on a network.

If your application does not require that the multinode ID that the .MPP driver assigns to it belong to a specific network cable range, you can set the `reqCableLo` and `reqCableHi` fields to 0.

reqCableHi   The network number that defines the high end of the range of network numbers from which you would like the .MPP driver to select a multinode ID for your use. The `reqCableLo` field value delimits the low end of the range.

reserved   70 bytes that are reserved for internal use by the .MPP driver.

DESCRIPTION

The `AddNode` routine acquires the multinode address that you specify as the value of the `reqNodeAddr` parameter if that multinode ID is available and the .MPP driver is able to service the call.

If the requested node is already in use or is invalid, or if you do not request a specific multinode ID, the .MPP driver will randomly select a multinode ID and return it as the value of the `actNodeAddr` parameter.

If the .MPP driver is unable to service the call, it will return a result code of −1021, which indicates that you should try the `AddNode` routine again. If you receive this result code, you can retry the `AddNode` routine call repeatedly until either the .MPP driver assigns and returns a multinode ID to you or you receive a different error message. Because of this need to be able to retry this call repeatedly, you cannot issue the `AddNode` call asynchronously.

Your application must provide the address of a receive routine that it uses to receive both packets addressed to the multinode and broadcast packets. You pass the address of this routine to the .MPP driver in the `recvRoutine` parameter. For more information about the receive routine, see "Receiving Packets Addressed to Your Multinode" beginning on page 12-10.

SPECIAL CONSIDERATIONS

You must issue the `AddNode` routine as a synchronous immediate control call at system task time.

ASSEMBLY-LANGUAGE INFORMATION

To execute the `AddNode` routine from assembly language, call the `_Control` trap macro with a value of 262 in the `csCode` field of the parameter block. You must issue the routine request as an immediate call.

RESULT CODES

noErr	0	No error
tryAddNodeAgainErr	–1021	The .MPP driver was not able to add the multinode; try again
mnNotSupported	–1022	Multinode is not supported by the current AppleTalk connection file of type 'adev'
noMoreMultiNodes	–1023	No multinode addresses are available on the network

SEE ALSO

For an example of how to issue the AddNode routine as a synchronous immediate control call from the Pascal language, see Listing 12-1 on page 12-9.

RemoveNode

You use the RemoveNode routine to remove a multinode address that you acquired through the AddNode routine. You use the PBControl function to call the RemoveNode routine. See "Routines" on page 12-20 for a description of the PBControl function.

Parameter block

→	ioCompletion	ProcPtr	A pointer to a completion routine.
←	ioResult	OSErr	The result code.
→	ioRefNum	Integer	The .MPP driver reference number. You must fill in this value.
→	csCode	Integer	A routine selector. Always equal to 263 for this routine. You must fill in this value.
→	nodeAddr	AddrBlock	An address of the multinode to be removed.

Field descriptions

ioCompletion   A pointer to a completion routine that you can provide. When you execute a function asynchronously, AppleTalk calls your completion routine when it completes execution of the function if you specify a pointer to the routine as the value of this field. Specify NIL for this field if you do not wish to provide a completion routine. If you execute a function synchronously, AppleTalk ignores the ioCompletion field. For information about completion routines, see the chapter "Introduction to AppleTalk" in this book.

nodeAddr   The address of the multinode to be removed. You specify a value for this field in AddrBlock format. (See "The Address Block Record" on page 12-18.) The value of the aSocket field of the AddrBlock record must always be 0. Set the aNet and aNode fields to the network number and multinode ID values of the multinode to be deleted.

DESCRIPTION

The RemoveNode routine removes the multinode address that you specify. You should remove only a multinode address using this routine; you must not attempt to remove the user node address.

ASSEMBLY-LANGUAGE INFORMATION

To execute the RemoveNode routine from assembly language, call the _Control trap macro with a value of 263 in the csCode field of the parameter block.

RESULT CODES

noErr	0	No error
paramErr	–50	Bad parameter value

Sending Datagrams Through Multinodes

This section describes the NetWrite routine that you use to send a packet from a multinode. You can use a multinode to send a packet down through the AppleTalk protocol stack and across the AppleTalk network to another multinode or to a socket client application or process, or you can send the packet from the multinode to a socket-client application of the user node on the same system.

NetWrite

You use the NetWrite routine to send a packet from a multinode to another multinode or socket-client application. You use the PBControl function to call the NetWrite routine. See "Routines" on page 12-20 for a description of the PBControl call.

Parameter block

→	ioCompletion	ProcPtr	A pointer to a completion routine.
←	ioResult	OSErr	The result code.
→	ioRefNum	Integer	The .MPP driver reference number. You must fill in this value.
→	csCode	Integer	A routine selector. Always equal to 261 for this routine. You must fill in this value.
→	checkSumFlag	Byte	A flag indicating whether the checksum should be calculated or the existing checksum left unmodified.
→	wdsPointer	Ptr	A pointer to the write-data structure for the function.

Field descriptions

ioCompletion
A pointer to a completion routine that you can provide. When you execute a function asynchronously, AppleTalk calls your completion routine when it completes execution of the function if you specify a pointer to the routine as the value of this field. Specify NIL for this field if you do not wish to provide a completion routine. If you execute a function synchronously, AppleTalk ignores the ioCompletion field. For information about completion routines, see the chapter "Introduction to AppleTalk" in this book.

checkSumFlag
A flag whose value you set to a nonzero number if you want the checksum for the datagram to be calculated and placed in the DDP header of the packet. If you do not want the current value in the packet header's checksum field to be altered, you set this field to 0.

wdsPointer
A pointer to the write-data structure that contains a series of length words and pointers that indicate the length and location of a portion of the data, including the header information, that constitutes the packet to be sent over the network.

DESCRIPTION

To send a packet over an AppleTalk network from a multinode, you must first prepare a write-data structure, and then call the NetWrite routine, passing it a pointer to the write-data structure.

The write-data structure that you create for multinodes differs slightly from the standard write-data structure that you create to send a DDP packet using the PWriteDDP function. For a multinode, you must specify both the source multinode address and the destination address in the packet header information data areas that you point to from the write-data structure. You can also set the checksum field of the write-data structure to 0 to direct AppleTalk to not calculate a checksum for this packet.

You specify the source network number and the source multinode ID of the multinode; the .MPP driver does not set these values for you in the header area of a packet sent from a multinode as it does for a standard DDP packet, although both packets are transmitted as DDP datagrams.

If you are sending the contents of an existing DDP packet through the NetWrite call, you can leave the value of the source socket field unchanged. The value in the source socket field should adhere to the conventions that the AppleTalk DDP protocol specification describes for the use of sockets. The socket number value must fall within the defined user range as stated in the DDP protocol specification. (See *Inside AppleTalk*, second edition, for this information.)

The checkSumFlag parameter block field of the NetWrite routine relates to the standard DDP header checksum field. However, the multinode architecture uses this flag differently than the DDP interface uses it.

■ If you want the checksum for the datagram to be calculated and placed in the DDP header before the .MPP driver transmits the packet, you set this field to a nonzero number.

■ If you want the checksum field of the DDP packet header not to be modified, you set this field to 0, and the existing checksum value in the DDP header will not be changed.

Note that if you want to send a packet that does not include a checksum, you must hardcode the value by setting to 0 the checksum field of the data structure that contains the packet header that you point to from the write-data structure.

All packets that you send using the NetWrite routine are built with the long DDP packet header to allow for inclusion of the source multinode address. The DDP packet header includes the source multinode address even when the destination and source nodes are on the same LocalTalk network.

Because the source multinode ID is associated with the application that sent the packet and the source user node ID is associated with the machine that transmitted the packet, the source user node ID in the frame header and the source multinode ID in the DDP packet header are always different values.

IMPORTANT

Do not set the socket number to 0 ($00) for the source socket number that you specify in the data area pointed to by the write-data structure. You do this in the address block record socket field for the AddNode routine because the socket number does not apply when you are acquiring a multinode, but you must not do it for the NetWrite call because NetWrite causes the .MPP driver to build a DDP packet, and socket number 0 has special meaning to DDP that is outside the valid user socket range. ▲

SPECIAL CONSIDERATIONS

Memory used for the write-data structure belongs to the multinode implementation in the .MPP driver for the life of the NetWrite call and must be nonrelocatable. After the NetWrite call completes execution, you must release the memory that you used for the write-data structure.

ASSEMBLY-LANGUAGE INFORMATION

To execute the NetWrite routine from assembly language, call the _Control trap macro with a value of 261 in the csCode field of the parameter block.

RESULT CODES

noErr	0	No error
ddpLenErr	–92	Datagram is too long
noBridgeErr	–93	No router found
excessCollsns	–95	Excessive collisions on write

SEE ALSO

See the section "Preparing a Write-Data Structure" on page 12-14 for information on how to create the write-data structure.

Summary of Multinode Architecture

The multinode architecture MPP parameter block data structure and symbolic constants for routines and result codes are not defined in the MPW interface files. (The write-data structure and the address block record are defined in the MPW interface files for use with other protocols, but you can use them for multinode also.)

You must declare the MPP parameter block for multinode in your application. If you want to use the symbolic constants for the routines and result codes, you need to declare them also.

You use the Device Manager's `PBControl` function to call the `RemoveNode` and `NetWrite` routines from the Pascal and C languages. You must issue the `AddNode` routine as an immediate synchronous control call from the Pascal and C languages. You must define a function as part of your application. (See Listing 12-1 on page 12-9 for an example of how to do this in Pascal.) From assembly language, you can directly make an `immed _Control` trap macro call.

Pascal Summary

Constants

(Declare the following constants in your application.)

```
CONST
    {csCodes}
    netWrite   = 261;          {send packet through multinode}
    addNode    = 262;          {request a multinode}
    removeNode = 263;          {remove multinode}
```

Data Types

The Write-Data Structure

```
TYPE  WDSElement =
   RECORD
      entryLength:   Integer;
      entryPtr:      Ptr;
   END;
```

The Address Block Record

```
TYPE AddrBlock =
    PACKED RECORD
        aNet:          Integer;      {network number for multinode}
        aNode:         Byte;         {multinode ID}
        aSocket:       Byte;         {socket number; always 0}
    END;
```

The Multinode Parameter Block

(Declare this data type in your application.)

```
TYPEMNParmType = (AddNodeParm,RemoveNodeParm);
TYPE MNParamBlock =
    PACKED RECORD
        qLink:         QElemPtr;            {reserved}
        qType:         Integer;             {reserved}
        ioTrap:        Integer;             {reserved}
        ioCmdAddr:     Ptr;                 {reserved}
        ioCompletion:  ProcPtr;             {completion routine}
        ioResult:      OSErr;               {result code}
        ioNamePtr:     StringPtr;           {reserved}
        ioVRefNum:     Integer;             {reserved}
        ioRefNum:      Integer;             {driver reference number}
        csCode:        Integer;             {call command code}
            filler1:       Byte;            {reserved}
            checkSumFlag:  Byte;            {perform checksum on datagram}
            wdsPointer:    Ptr;             {pointer to write-data structure}
            filler2:       Integer;         {reserved}
            CASE MNParmType OF
                AddNodeParm:
                (reqNodeAddr:  AddrBlock;       {preferred address requested}
                 actNodeAddr:  AddrBlock;       {actual node address returned}
                 recvRoutine:  ProcPtr;         {pointer to packet receive routine}
                 reqCableLo:   Integer;         {preferred network range for the }
                 reqCableHi:   Integer;         { node being acquired}
                 reserved:     PACKED ARRAY[1..70] OF Byte);
                RemoveNodeParm:
                (nodeAddr:     AddrBlock);      {node address to be deleted}
    END;

MNParmBlkPtr = ^MNParamBlock;
```

C Summary

Constants

(Declare the following constants in your application.)

```
/*csCodes*/
enum {
    netWrite      = 261,              /*send packet through multinode*/
    addNode       = 262,              /*request a multinode*/
    removeNode    = 263               /*remove multinode*/
};
```

Data Types

The Write-Data Structure

```
struct    WDSElement {
    short      entryLength;
    Ptr        entryPtr;
} WDSElement;
```

The Address Block Record

```
struct AddrBlock {
    short              aNet;          /*network number for multinode*/
    unsigned char      aNode;         /*multinode ID*/
    unsigned char      aSocket;       /*socket number; always 0*/
};

typedef struct AddrBlock AddrBlock;
```

The MPP Parameter Block for Multinode

(Declare this data type in your application.)

```
typedef struct {
    MPPATPHeader
        char              filler1;        /*reserved*/
        unsigned char     checkSumFlag;   /*perform checksum on datagram*/
        Ptr               wdsPointer;     /*pointer to write-data structure*/
        char              filler2[2];     /*reserved*/
        union {
```

```
            AddrBlock        reqNodeAddr;     /*preferred address requested*/
            AddrBlock        nodeAddr;        /*node address to be deleted*/
                  } MNaddrs;
        AddrBlock        actNodeAddr;         /*actual node address acquired*/
        Ptr              recvRoutine;         /*address of packet receive routine*/
        short            reqCableLo;          /*preferred network range for the */
        short            reqCableHi;          /* node being acquired*/
        char             reserved[70];
} MNParamBlock;

typedef MNParamBlock*MNParmBlkPtr;
```

Assembly-Language Summary

MPP Parameter Block Common Fields for Multinode Routines

0	qLink	long	reserved
4	qType	word	reserved
6	ioTrap	word	reserved
8	ioCmdAddr	long	reserved
12	ioCompletion	long	address of completion routine
16	ioResult	word	result code
18	ioNamePtr	long	reserved
22	ioVRefNum	word	reserved
24	ioRefNum	word	driver reference number

AddNode Parameter Variant

26	csCode	word	routine selector; always 262 for this routine
36	reqNodeAddr	long	requested multinode address
40	actNodeAddr	long	actual multinode address assigned
44	recvRoutine	long	address of the application's receive routine
48	reqCableLo	word	beginning of requested network number range for the multinode
50	reqCableHi	word	end of the requested network number range for the multinode
52	reserved	array	70 reserved bytes required by the .MPP driver

(Note that to execute the AddNode routine from assembly language, you call the _Control trap macro and issue the routine request as an immediate call.)

RemoveNode Parameter Variant

26	csCode	word	routine selector; always 263 for this routine
36	nodeAddr	long	actual multinode address assigned

NetWrite Parameter Variant

26	csCode	word	routine selector; always 261 for this routine
29	checkSumFlag	byte	a flag indicating whether the checksum should be calculated or the existing checksum left unmodified
30	wdsPointer	long	a pointer to the write-data structure for this routine

Result Codes

noErr	0	No error
paramErr	–50	Bad parameter value
ddpLenErr	–92	Datagram is too long
noBridgeErr	–93	No router found
excessColl sns	–95	Excessive collisions on write
tryAddNodeAgainErr	–1021	The .MPP driver was not able to add node; try again
mnNotSupported	–1022	Multinode is not supported by the current AppleTalk connection file of type 'adev'
noMoreMultiNodes	–1023	No node address is available on the network

Glossary

'adev' file   See **AppleTalk connection file.**

ADSP   See **AppleTalk Data Stream Protocol.**

AEP   See **AppleTalk Echo Protocol.**

AEP Echoer   The implementation of the AppleTalk Echo Protocol (AEP) on each node that uses the AEP Echoer or echoer socket; the AEP Echoer listens for packets received through this socket and sends a copy of them back to the sender. Applications use the AEP Echoer to measure the round-trip packet delivery time in analyzing network performance.

AFP   See **AppleTalk Filing Protocol.**

alternate interface   The first version of the AppleTalk Pascal interfaces. The alternate interface was replaced with the current version of AppleTalk Pascal interfaces, which was originally referred to as the *preferred interface.*

AppleTalk connection file   A file of type 'adev' that contains a link-access protocol implementation for a data link (ELAP for EtherTalk, for example).

AppleTalk Data Stream Protocol (ADSP)   A connection-oriented protocol that provides a reliable, full-duplex, byte-stream service between any two sockets in an AppleTalk internet. This protocol appears to its clients to maintain an open pipeline between two entities on an AppleTalk internet. Either entity can write a stream of bytes to the pipeline or read data bytes from the pipeline. ADSP is a symmetrical protocol.

AppleTalk Echo Protocol (AEP)   A simple protocol that allows a node to send a packet to the echoer socket of any other node in an AppleTalk internet and receive an echoed copy of that packet in return. AEP is implemented in each node as a DDP client process that is referred to in this book as the *AEP Echoer.*

AppleTalk Filing Protocol (AFP)   A protocol that allows users to share data files and application programs that reside in a shared file server.

AppleTalk internet   A type of network in which more than one AppleTalk network are interconnected through routers. An AppleTalk internet can consist of a mix of LocalTalk, TokenTalk, EtherTalk, and FDDITalk networks, or it can consist of more than one network of a single type, such as several LocalTalk networks.

AppleTalk Manager   A collection of the application programming interfaces to the AppleTalk protocols.

AppleTalk multivendor architecture   See **multivendor architecture.**

AppleTalk protocol stack   The AppleTalk networking system, which consists of a number of protocols arranged in layers.

AppleTalk Secure Data Stream Protocol (ASDSP)   A superset of ADSP that includes authentication and encryption features.

AppleTalk Session Protocol (ASP)   A protocol that provides asymmetric session support. It uses the services of ATP to establish, maintain, and break down the session.

AppleTalk Transaction Protocol (ATP)   A transport protocol that provides a loss-free transaction service between sockets. ATP allows for the exchange of a limited amount of data in which a client requester application sends a request to a client responder application that can satisfy the request and respond to it. Because it is transaction-based, ATP does not incur the overhead entailed in establishing, maintaining, and breaking a connection that is associated with connection-oriented protocols, such as ADSP. ATP provides reliable delivery of data.

AppleTalk transition   A change in AppleTalk's current state or function, such as an AppleTalk driver being opened or closed or a network connection or link being dropped, that can affect active AppleTalk applications.

AppleTalk Transition Queue (ATQ)   An operating-system queue that the LAP Manager maintains that can notify an application each time an AppleTalk driver is opened or closed or each time certain other network-related transitions occur.

ASDSP   See **AppleTalk Secure Data Stream Protocol.**

ASP   See **AppleTalk Session Protocol.**

asymmetrical session   A session in which only one end of the connection can control the communication. One end of the connection makes a request to which the other end can only respond.

asynchronous execution   A mode of executing a routine in which the system returns control to the calling program directly after the program calls the routine so that the calling program can continue with other processing while the routine is either queued for execution or completes execution.

at-least-once transaction   A type of ATP transaction that ensures that the responder application receives every request directed to it at least once. This type of ATP transaction allows for the possibility of a responder application receiving duplicate requests. Compare with **exactly-once (XO) transaction.**

ATP   See **AppleTalk Transaction Protocol.**

ATP sequence number   The bitmap/sequence number field of the header, when the ATP packet is a response packet. The ATP sequence number is used to identify the sequential position of the response packet in the complete response message; ATP uses the sequence number to manage and handle lost or out-of-sequence response packets.

authentication process   A process that ASDSP performs to positively identify two parties who want to communicate over a secure ADSP connection. The process, which is a kind of handshake, involves the use of a session key.

best-effort delivery   The level of reliability for the data delivery services that a connectionless protocol offers. The network attempts to deliver packets that meet certain requirements, such as containing a valid destination address, but it does not inform the sender when it is unable to deliver the packet; nor does it attempt to recover from error conditions and packet loss.

bitmap/sequence number   An ATP header field that is 8 bits long, the use and significance of which depend on whether the ATP packet is a request packet or a response packet. For request packets, this is the transaction bitmap; for response packets, this is the ATP sequence number.

CCB   See **connection control block, command control block.**

checksum   A calculated value based on the contents of a packet's header and data information. A checksum is used to verify that the packet contents have not been corrupted by memory or data bus errors within routers on the internet.

client   In AppleTalk, a protocol that uses the services of another protocol in order to carry out some functions. An application or process that uses the services of a protocol is also considered a client of the protocol.

closed connection   A connection state in which both connection ends have terminated the connection and disposed of the connection information that each maintains. Compare **half-open connection, open connection.**

command block   A data structure specifying an AFP command and its parameters that the .XPP driver sends to an AFP server to be executed. The XPP parameter block for the `AFPCommand` function contains a pointer to the command block.

command control block (CCB)   An array at the end of the XPP parameter block that the .XPP driver uses internally to build the data structures, parameter blocks, and buffer data structures (BDS) that it needs to make function calls to the .ATP driver.

connection control block (CCB)   A data structure that is used by ADSP to store state information about the connection end.

connection end The combination of a socket and the ADSP information maintained by a socket client for establishing and maintaining a session. The client applications associated with either end of a connection can communicate with each other over the session connection.

connectionless network A network over which an application or process can directly send and receive data one packet at a time without having to first set up a session or connection. A connectionless network is also referred to as a *packet-oriented network* or *datagram network*. A protocol can also be connectionless.

connection listener A socket that accepts open-connection requests and passes them along to its client, a connection server process, for further processing. A connection listener can also deny an open request.

connection-oriented protocol A protocol that requires that a path or session be established over which the two communicating parties at either end of the connection can send and receive data. The process of establishing a session often requires that the two parties identify themselves in a handshake.

connection server A routine that accepts an open-connection request passed to it by a connection listener and selects a socket to respond to the request.

connection state One of three conditions that define the association between two connection ends: open connection, closed connection, and half-open connection.

connectivity The ability to connect to one or another type of data link or network. The connectivity infrastructure includes the communication hardware and the associated link-access protocols for controlling access to the hardware links.

credentials Information that is required to prove that the potential users of both ends of an ASDSP connection are who they claim to be before ASDSP can establish an authenticated session between the two ends. This information includes the session key, the initiator's identity, and an intermediary, if one is used.

datagram See **packet.**

Datagram Delivery Protocol (DDP) A connectionless AppleTalk protocol that provides best-effort delivery. DDP, which is implemented at the network level, transfers datagrams between sockets over an AppleTalk internet with each packet carrying its destination internet socket address. See also **packet.**

datagram network See **connectionless network.**

DDP See **Datagram Delivery Protocol.**

destination service access point (DSAP) An 802.2 packet header field that is used to differentiate between different protocols using the 802.2 interface in a single node. One service access point, $AA, is reserved for use by protocols that are not standard IEEE protocols.

DSAP See **destination service access point.**

dynamically assigned socket One of two classes of sockets that DDP maintains. When an application opens a socket without specifying a number within the range of statically assigned sockets, DDP dynamically assigns the application a socket from a pool of available sockets. See also **statically assigned socket.**

echoer socket On every node, the statically assigned DDP socket, socket number 4, that AEP uses to receive packets sent from other nodes over DDP and echo those packets back to the sending node. See also **AEP Echoer, AppleTalk Echo Protocol.**

Echo Reply packet A packet sent from the AEP Echoer to the originator of the Echo Request packet. Whenever the AEP Echoer receives an Echo Request packet, it modifies the function field, which is the first byte in the packet's data portion, setting it to a value of 2 to indicate that the packet is now a reply packet, then it calls DDP to send a copy of the packet back to the socket from which it originated. See also **Echo Request Packet.**

Echo Request packet A packet send to the AEP Echoer from a DDP client. The first byte of the data portion of the packet serves as a function field. When this byte is set to 1, the packet is an Echo Request packet. When the AEP Echoer receives an Echo Request packet, it modifies the function field to now identify the packet as an Echo Reply packet. Then the AEP Echoer calls

DDP to send a copy of the packet back to the socket from which it originated. See also **Echo Reply packet.**

ELAP   See **EtherTalk Link-Access Protocol.**

encryption   The process of encoding data based on an algorithm that makes the data unreadable by anyone other than the intended recipient.

entity name   A name that is associated with a network entity to register that entity with NBP. An entity name consists of three fields: object, type, and zone.

Ethernet Phase 1 packets   The original style of Ethernet packet as defined by the IEEE 802.3 protocol. If the value of the last 2 bytes in the packet header is greater than 1500, the packet is an Ethernet Phase 1 packet.

Ethernet Phase 2 packets   The style of Ethernet packet defined by the IEEE 802.2 protocol. If the value of the last 2 bytes in the header is less than or equal to 1500, the packet is an Ethernet Phase 2 packet.

EtherTalk   The data link that allows an AppleTalk network to be connected by Ethernet cables.

EtherTalk Link-Access Protocol (ELAP)   The AppleTalk link-access protocol used in an EtherTalk network. ELAP is built on top of the standard Ethernet data-link layer.

exactly-once (XO) transaction   A type of ATP transaction that ensures that the responder application receives a specific request only once.

extended addressing   A method of addressing that allows an extended network to use a range of network numbers. In principle, extended addressing allows an extended network to have over 16 million (2^{24}) nodes. In any specific implementation, the hardware or software might limit the network to fewer nodes.

extended DDP header   See **long DDP header.**

extended network   An AppleTalk network that allows addressing of more than 254 nodes. An extended network can support multiple zones.

FDDITalk   The data link that allows an AppleTalk network to be connected by FDDI fiber-optic cables.

FDDITalk Link-Access Protocol (FLAP)   The AppleTalk link-access protocol used in an FDDITalk network. FLAP is built on top of the standard FDDI data-link layer.

fiber optics   The thin transparent fibers of glass or plastic in which data is transmitted through light pulses.

flagship name   A personalized name that users can enter to identify their nodes when they are connected to an AppleTalk network. The flagship name is different from the Chooser name that a node uses for server-connection identification.

Flagship Naming Service   A feature that allows users to specify a flagship name to identify their nodes when the node is connected to an AppleTalk network.

FLAP   See **FDDITalk Link-Access Protocol.**

forward reset   The event that occurs when one connection end cancels delivery of all outstanding data to the other connection end, causing ADSP to discard all data in the send queue, all data in transit to the remote connection end, and all data in the other connection end's receive queue that the client has not yet read.

frame   A group of bits that form a discrete transmission unit that is sent between data-link protocol implementations across an AppleTalk internet. Each frame includes its own addressing and control information in the header. The first several bits in a frame form the header, followed by the message data, and ending with a check sequence for error detection. A DDP datagram or packet is enclosed within a frame to transmit the packet at the data-link layer. Whether the data-link type is LocalTalk, TokenTalk, EtherTalk, or FDDITalk, all data-link frames are constructed as LLAP (LocalTalk Link-Access Protocol) frames because that is the frame format that AppleTalk recognizes and expects to receive.

full-duplex dialog   A transmission method that permits simultaneous two-way communication.

functional address   A token ring hardware address that is shared by a subset of nodes on a particular data link.

function field   The first byte of the data portion of a packet sent to or from the AEP Echoer that indicates whether the packet is an Echo Request packet (1) or an Echo Reply packet (2).

half-duplex dialog   A transmission method that permits communication in either direction, but in only one direction at a time.

half-open connection   A connection state in which one connection end is established but the other connection end is unreachable or has disposed of its connection information. Compare **closed connection, open connection.**

handshake   The exchange of predetermined signals between two processes engaged in establishing a connection.

header   The information that comes at the beginning of a frame or a packet before the message text. It often includes control and addressing information.

hop count   The number of internet routers that a datagram passes through in transit to its destination; each internet router counts as one hop.

initiator   The ASDSP client application of a connection end that retrieves information from an authentication server and makes a request to open a session.

intermediary   A proxy that has used the `AuthTradeProxyForCredentials` function to obtain from the AOCE server the credentials used in the authentication process that is required to establish an ASDSP session.

internet address   See **internet socket address.**

internet socket address   The combination of the socket number, the node ID, and the network number associated with an application or process. An internet socket address provides a unique identifier for any socket in the AppleTalk internet.

intranode delivery   An AppleTalk feature that allows two programs running on the same node to communicate with each other through AppleTalk protocols. The AppleTalk `PSetSelfSend` function enables or disables intranode delivery.

LAP Manager   See **Link-Access Protocol Manager.**

link   A data transmission medium shared by nodes and used for communication among these nodes. A link forms the basis for networking these nodes.

Link-Access Protocol (LAP) Manager   A set of operating-system utilities that makes it possible for the user to select among AppleTalk connection files by using the Network control panel to specify which network is to be used for the node's AppleTalk connection. The LAP Manager provides for AppleTalk's data-link independence.

link independence   The ability to connect to various types of data links that are installed on a node and to switch among those data links.

Logical Link Control (LLC)   A data-link standard defined by the Institute of Electrical and Electronics Engineers (IEEE) for use on Ethernet, token ring, FDDI, and certain other data links. At the physical level, these protocols include the 802.3 CSMA/CD protocol, the 802.4 token bus protocol, and the 802.5 token ring protocol. At the data-link level, you access these protocols through the IEEE 802.2 Logical Link Control (LLC) protocol.

long DDP header   A DDP packet header that includes the source node ID as well as the destination node ID.

multicast address   A hardware address that is shared by a subset of nodes on a particular data link—an Ethernet network, a token ring network, or an FDDI network. A multicast address is used to send directed broadcasts to this group of nodes rather than to all nodes on the data link.

multinode   A node ID that an application or process can acquire that is in addition to the standard user-node ID that is assigned to a system when it connects to an AppleTalk network. Multinodes are used by special-purpose applications that receive and process AppleTalk packets in a custom manner instead of passing them directly on to a higher-level AppleTalk protocol for processing.

multinode application   An application that uses a multinode to receive DDP packets from and send them to another multinode or socket on an AppleTalk network. A multinode application typically implements custom processing of an

AppleTalk packet. A multinode application cannot pass a packet on to a higher-level AppleTalk protocol for processing because a multinode is not connected to the AppleTalk protocol stack above the data-link layer. Multinode applications must include a receive routine to read in a packet's contents.

multinode architecture   A part of the AppleTalk protocol stack that implements a feature that allows an application or process to acquire multinode IDs. Multinodes allow a single system to appear and act as multiple nodes on an AppleTalk network. The multinode architecture is not connected to the AppleTalk protocol stack above the data-link level, and applications that use it cannot access the higher-level AppleTalk protocols, such as ADSP, from a multinode.

multivendor architecture   An AppleTalk feature that allows for multiple brands of Ethernet, token ring, and FDDI network interface controllers to be installed and used on a single node at the same time.

Name-Binding Protocol (NBP)   An AppleTalk protocol that provides a way to map user-friendly names associated with applications and processes to their machine-readable addresses. Users can choose an application based on its NBP name, and applications and processes can contact another application or process based on its address.

names table   A table that NBP builds on each node; the table contains the name and internet address of each entity in that node that is registered with NBP.

NBP   See **Name-Binding Protocol.**

NBP names directory   The collection of NBP names tables on all the nodes in an internet.

network architecture   The design or assemblage of the various components of a network into a unified structure.

network number   A 16-bit number used to indicate the AppleTalk network that a node is connected to.

network number range   For an extended network, the range of network numbers that are valid for use by nodes on a particular AppleTalk network.

network-visible entity   A network entity that is registered with NBP. After the entity is registered, it is made visible and is available to other entities throughout the network.

node   A data-link addressable entity on an AppleTalk network. All physical devices on an AppleTalk network, such as personal computer workstations, printers, and Macintosh computers acting as file servers, print servers, and routers, are nodes.

node ID   An 8-bit number assigned to a node on an AppleTalk network that is used to identify that node in conjunction with the network number. A node ID is part of the addressing information used to deliver packets across a network or internet.

nonextended network   An AppleTalk network that is assigned only one network number and supports only one zone. LocalTalk is an example of a nonextended network.

object   The field of an NBP entity name that identifies the user of the system or the system itself, in the case of a server.

open connection   An association or connection set up between two sockets in which both ends have been established so that data can flow between them.

packet   A unit of data that is sent as a unit within a frame from one node to another across a network or internet. A packet includes a header portion that contains addressing and control information and a data portion that contains the message text. The terms *packet* and *datagram* are synonymous.

packet-oriented network   See **connectionless network.**

peer-to-peer communication   A connection in which both ends have equal control over the exchange of data and either end can begin or end the session.

peer-to-peer session   See **symmetrical session.**

preferred interface   The AppleTalk interface standard designed to be similar to that of the Device Manager and the File Manager. Its routines use parameter blocks to pass input and output values. The interface glue code converts the parameter block values into a Device Manager control call to the appropriate AppleTalk device driver.

private key   A number that is derived from a password and used by an encryption algorithm. The ASDSP initiator and recipient each have a private key, which is used in the authentication process. The private key is also called a *user key* or *client key.*

protocol   A formalized set of rules that networked computers use to communicate. Network software developers implement these rules in programs that carry out the functions specified by the protocol. AppleTalk consists of a number of protocols, many of which are implemented in drivers.

protocol discriminators   A series of hierarchical type fields in a packet header that incrementally distinguish for which protocol handler a packet is intended. The value of a higher field can affect the possible values of a field that follows it.

protocol handler   A piece of assembly-language code that controls the reception of packets of a given protocol type that are delivered to a node. A protocol handler receives packets for a specific protocol type much like a socket listener receives packets for a specific socket. The data link determines the type of the packet and passes it on to the appropriate protocol handler.

read-header area (RHA)   A buffer that is internal to the .MPP driver. When the .MPP driver receives a frame containing a DDP packet, the .MPP driver's interrupt handler moves the frame's first 3 bytes (the frame header) into the read-header area (RHA). Eight bytes of the RHA are then available for the application's use.

receive queue   An ADSP buffer in which the local connection end receives and stores bytes of data from the remote connection end until the local connection end's client application reads them.

receive routine   A software process that a multinode application must include in order to read in the contents of packets delivered to that multinode. Because the .MPP driver passes values in registers to a multinode application's receive routine when the .MPP driver calls the routine, receive routines must be written in assembly language.

recipient   The ASDSP client application of the connection end that receives the request and the information from the server.

reliable delivery of data   The services a protocol provides that include error checking and recovery from error or packet loss.

requester   An ATP application that transmits a request for some action to be performed to an ATP responder application that carries out the action and transmits a response reporting the outcome.

responder   An ATP application that carries out a request sent to it from an ATP requester application, and then transmits a response to the requester returning the resulting data or reporting the outcome.

response message   A message comprising up to eight packets that the responder client application can send to the requester client application. ATP maintains and manages the correct sequence of these packets.

router   Software that interconnects AppleTalk networks to create a single, large, dispersed AppleTalk internet.

Routing Table Maintenance Protocol (RTMP)   An AppleTalk protocol that provides routers with a means of managing routing tables used to determine how to forward a packet from one socket to another across an internet based on the packet's destination network number.

RTMP   See **Routing Table Maintenance Protocol.**

secure session   An ADSP session that uses ASDSP to perform an authentication process in which the identities of the users at both ends of the connection are verified. Users can exchange data over a secure session, and direct ASDSP to encrypt the data before transmitting it and decrypt the data before delivering to the recipient.

send queue   A buffer in which ADSP stores the bytes of data being sent until the remote connection end acknowledges their receipt.

server node ID   A node ID that falls within the numeric range of 128–254 ($80–$FE). An application or process must explicitly request a node ID within the server range by making an extended `Open` call and setting to 1 the high bit (bit 31) of the extension `ioMix` field.

session   A logical (as opposed to physical) connection between two entities on an internet.

session control block (SCB)   A block of memory that an ASP workstation client application must allocate for the .XPP driver to use internally to manage a session.

session establishment   The process of setting up a connection over which a dialog between two applications or processes can occur. Session-oriented protocols provide this service.

session key   A unique key that the AOCE authentication server generates and returns to the ASDSP initiator in a secure manner. The authentication server generates the session key exclusively for use by the authentication process for the session that the initiator attempts to open. The session key is valid for a limited time only.

session listening socket (SLS)   A socket that the ASP server uses to listen for incoming session requests.

session reference number   A unique session identifier that ASP assigns to a session that it opens successfully. The ASP server uses this number to distinguish between communication from various concurrent sessions.

SNAP   See **subnetwork access protocol.**

socket   A piece of software that serves as an addressable entity on a node. Applications and processes send and receive data through sockets. See also **statically assigned socket, dynamically assigned socket.**

socket client   An application or process that is associated with a socket and that sends and receives data through the socket.

socket listener   A piece of assembly-language code that a socket client application provides that receives datagrams that are addressed to that socket.

socket number   An 8-bit number that identifies a socket. A socket number is one of the three parts that together constitute an AppleTalk internet address.

socket table   A table that DDP builds and maintains that contains entries for open sockets; each entry identifies the socket number and the socket listener that are associated with it.

state dependence   A condition in which a response to a request is dependent on a previous request.

statically assigned socket   One of the two classes of sockets that DDP maintains. To use a statically assigned socket, an application must request a specific socket number. Statically assigned sockets have numbers in the range of 1–127. See also **dynamically assigned socket.**

subnetwork access protocol (SNAP)   An 802.2 packet header field that is used to discriminate for which protocol family a packet with a DSAP of $AA is intended.

symmetrical session   A session in which both ends of the connection have equal control over the communication. Both ends can send and receive data at the same time and initiate or terminate the session. A symmetrical session is also referred to as a *peer-to-peer session.*

synchronous execution   A mode of executing a routine in which the routine is executed as soon as possible and the calling program is prevented from doing any other processing until the routine completes execution.

TLAP   See **TokenTalk Link-Access Protocol.**

TokenTalk   The data link that allows an AppleTalk network to be connected by token ring cables.

TokenTalk Link-Access Protocol (TLAP)   The AppleTalk link-access protocol used in a TokenTalk network. TLAP is built on top of the standard token ring data-link layer.

transaction   The exchange of data between two ATP client applications in which the requester application sends a request to the responder application to perform. The exchange of data is limited to the request-response interaction, and the response data is bound to the request data by a transaction ID.

transaction-based protocol   A communications protocol in which one socket client transmits a request for some action and the other socket client carries out the action and transmits a response.

transaction bitmap   The bitmap/sequence number field of the header, when the ATP packet is a request packet. The transaction bitmap identifies the number of buffers that a requester application has reserved for the response data.

transition   An AppleTalk event, such as an AppleTalk driver being opened or closed, that can affect an AppleTalk application.

transition event handler routine   A developer-supplied routine that the LAP Manager calls to handle a transition event. Entries in the AppleTalk Transition Queue contain a field that holds a pointer to the transition event handler routine.

transport protocol   A protocol that includes services that determine how data is to be transferred across an AppleTalk internet.

tuple   The NBP name and internet socket address pair that an entity provides to register itself with NBP. NBP adds the tuple as a names table entry to its names table.

type   The field of an NBP entity name that is used to identify the type of service that the entity provides. Entities of the same type can find potential partners by looking up addresses of other entities that are registered with NBP based on the type portion of the name.

user node ID   A node ID that falls within the numeric range of 1–127 ($01–$7F). Unless a program explicitly requests assignment of a node ID within the server range, AppleTalk dynamically assigns a user node ID to a system when an application or process on that system opens AppleTalk.

write-data structure   A data structure that contains a series of pairs of length words and pointers. Each pair indicates the length and location of a portion of the data that constitutes the packet to be sent over the network.

ZIP table   A zone information table that contains a complete mapping of network numbers to zone names for an AppleTalk internet. Each AppleTalk internet router maintains a ZIP table.

zone   A logical grouping of nodes in an AppleTalk internet. A zone is typically used to identify an affiliation between a group of nodes, such as a group of nodes belonging to a particular department within an organization.

Zone Information Protocol (ZIP)   An AppleTalk protocol that maintains the mapping between zone names and network numbers and provides applications and processes with access to zone names.

zone name hint   The name of the parameter stored in RAM that is the last zone to which the node belonged.

Index

W

wildcards, with NBP entity names 3-14, 3-31
write-data structures 11-22, 11-25
    for DDP 7-12 to 7-13, 7-35, 7-41 to 7-42
    for Ethernet 11-10 to 11-13, 11-26, 11-33
    for FDDI 11-25, 11-26, 11-33
    for token ring 11-22, 11-25, 11-33
    for multinodes 12-14 to 12-15, 12-18, 12-26

X, Y

`xCallParam` variant record 4-5
.XPP driver
    implementing protocols 1-17, 4-3, 8-5
    opening 2-22, 9-13
`XPPParamBlock` data type 4-10 to 4-11, 8-6 to 8-8, 9-6 to 9-8
XPP parameter blocks
    for AFP 9-6 to 9-8
    for ASP 8-6 to 8-8
    for ZIP 4-10 to 4-11

Z

ZIP. *See* Zone Information Protocol
ZIP tables 4-3
Zone Information Protocol (ZIP) 4-3 to 4-23
    and ATP 4-5
    buffers for 4-5, 4-13, 4-15, 4-17
    data structures for 4-10, 4-11
    driver for 1-17, 4-4
    introduced 1-12, 1-21
    routines for 4-11 to 4-18
    uses of 1-23, 4-3
    and the .XPP driver 4-4
    XPP parameter block for 4-10 to 4-11
zone information tables. *See* ZIP tables
zone name hint 2-13
zone names 2-5, 2-14
zones 1-10, 3-3
    defined 1-7, 4-3
    getting lists of 4-7 to 4-9, 4-14 to 4-18
    getting names of 2-14, 4-6, 4-12, 4-13
    identifying 1-23
    in NBP entity names 3-8

This Apple manual was written, edited, and composed on a desktop publishing system using Apple Macintosh computers and FrameMaker software. Proof pages were created on an Apple LaserWriter Pro printer. Final page negatives were output directly from text files on an Optrotech SPrint 220 imagesetter. Line art was created using Adobe™ Illustrator and Adobe Photoshop. PostScript™, the page-description language for the LaserWriter, was developed by Adobe Systems Incorporated.

Text type is Palatino® and display type is Helvetica®. Bullets are ITC Zapf Dingbats®. Some elements, such as program listings, are set in Apple Courier.

LEAD WRITER
Paul Black

WRITER
Judy Melanson

DEVELOPMENTAL EDITOR
Sanborn Hodgkins

ILLUSTRATORS
Barbara Carey, Peggy Kunz, Bruce Lee, Shawn Morningstar

PRODUCTION EDITOR
Rex Wolf

PROJECT MANAGER
Trish Eastman

TECHNICAL ADVISORS
Rich Kubota, Scott Kuechle, Jim Luther

Special thanks to Rick Andrews, Tim Monroe, David Schlesinger, and Beverly Zegarski

About Inside Macintosh

Inside Macintosh is a collection of books, organized by topic, that describe the system software of Macintosh computers. Together, these books provide the essential reference for programmers, designers, and engineers creating applications for the Macintosh family of computers.

Inside Macintosh: Overview

This book provides a general introduction to the Macintosh Operating System, the Macintosh Toolbox, and other system software services. It illustrates how to write a Macintosh application by gradually dissecting the source code of a sample application. The book also provides guidelines for writing software that is compatible with all supported Macintosh computers.

272 pages, ISBN 0-201-63247-0

Inside Macintosh: Macintosh Toolbox Essentials

This book describes how to implement essential user interface components in a Macintosh application. The Macintosh Toolbox is at the heart of the Macintosh, and every programmer creating a Macintosh application needs to be familiar with the material in this book. This book explains how to create menus; create windows, dialog boxes, and alerts boxes; create controls such as buttons and scroll bars; and create icons for an application and its documents. This book provides a complete technical reference for the Event Manager, Menu Manager, Window Manager, Control Manager, and Dialog Manager.

928 pages, ISBN 0-201-63243-8

Inside Macintosh: More Macintosh Toolbox

A companion to *Inside Macintosh: Macintosh Toolbox Essentials*, this book describes important features such as how to support copy and paste, provide Balloon Help, and create control panels. This book provides a complete technical reference to the Resource Manager, Scrap Manager, Help Manager, List Manager, Component Manager, Translation Manager, and Desktop Manager.

928 pages, ISBN 0-201-63299-3

Inside Macintosh: Imaging With QuickDraw

This book describes QuickDraw, the part of the Macintosh Toolbox that performs graphics operations, and the Printing Manager, which allows applications to print the images created with QuickDraw. This book explains how to create images, display them in black and white or color, and print them.

832 pages (tentative), ISBN 0-201-63242-X

Inside Macintosh: Text

This book describes how to create applications that can perform all kinds of text handling—from simple character display to complex, multi-language text processing. It provides a brief introduction to the unique Macintosh approach to text handling and shows how to draw characters, strings, and lines of text; how to work with fonts in any size, style, and language; how to use utility routines to format numbers, dates, and times; and how to use the WorldScript technology to design an application that handles text in any language.

1120 pages, ISBN 0-201-63298-5

Inside Macintosh: Files

This book describes the parts of the Macintosh Operating System that allow you to manage files and other objects in the file system. It describes how to create an application that can handle the commands typically found in the File menu. This books also provides a complete technical reference for the File Manager, the Standard File Package, the Alias Manager, the Disk Initialization Manager, and other file-related services provided by the system software.

544 pages, ISBN 0-201-63244-6

Inside Macintosh: Memory

This book describes the parts of the Macintosh Operating System that allow you to directly allocate, release, or otherwise manipulate memory. It shows how an application can manage the memory partition that it is allocated and perform other memory-related operations. This book also provides a complete technical reference for the Memory Manager, the Virtual Memory Manager, and other memory-related utilities provided by the system software.

312 pages, ISBN 0-201-63240-3

Inside Macintosh: Processes

This book describes the parts of the Macintosh Operating System that allow you to manage processes and tasks. It shows in detail how an application can manage processes and tasks and provides a complete technical reference for the Process Manager, the Notification Manager, the Time Manager, the Deferred Task Manager, and other task-related services provided by the system software.

208 pages, ISBN 0-201-63241-1

Inside Macintosh: Operating System Utilities

This book describes the parts of the Macintosh Operating System that allow you to manage low-level aspects of the Operating System. It describes how you can get information about the available software features, how to manage operating-system queues, get information about parameter RAM settings, and manipulate the trap dispatch tables. It also describes other utilities, such as mathematical and logical utilities; date, time, and measurement utilities; and the System Error Handler. This book provides a complete technical reference to the Gestalt Manager, Trap Manager, Start Manager, and Package Manager.

400 pages (tentative), ISBN 0-201-62270-X

Inside Macintosh: Devices

This book is a companion volume to both *Guide to Macintosh Family Hardware* and *Designing Cards and Drivers for the Macintosh Family*. It is written for anyone writing software that interacts with built-in and peripheral hardware devices and covers critical hardware and device programming topics including the Device Manager, SCSI Manager, Power Manager, ADB Manager, Serial Driver, and Slot Manager.

560 pages (tentative), ISBN 0-201-62271-8

Inside Macintosh: Interapplication Communication

This book explains how to create applications that work with other applications to give users even greater power and flexibility in accomplishing their tasks. It provides an introduction to how applications work together in a cooperative environment and discusses how they can share data with other applications, request information or services from other applications, and respond to scripts written in a scripting language. This book provides a complete technical reference to the Apple Event Manager, the AppleScript component, the Program-to-Program Communications Toolbox, and the Data Access Manager.

1008 pages, ISBN 0-201-62200-9

Inside Macintosh: Networking

This book describes key concepts of networking the Macintosh with other computers. It describes in detail the components and organization of AppleTalk, how to select an AppleTalk protocol, and how to write software that uses AppleTalk networking protocols.

592 pages, ISBN 0-201-62269-6

Inside Macintosh: QuickTime

This book describes how to create applications that can use QuickTime, Apple's system software extension that supports time-based data in the Macintosh desktop environment. Time-based data is any information that changes over time, such as sound, video, or animation. *Inside Macintosh: QuickTime* discusses how to manipulate time-based data in the same way that you work with text and graphic elements, and it describes how to use the Movie Toolbox to load, play, create, edit, and store objects that contain time-based data. It also explains how to use image compression and decompression to enhance the performance of QuickTime movies in an application.

736 pages, ISBN 0-201-62201-7

Inside Macintosh: QuickTime Components

This book is a companion to *Inside Macintosh: QuickTime*. It describes how you can use or develop QuickTime components such as clock components, image compressors, movie controllers, sequence grabbers, and video digitizers.

848 pages, ISBN 0-201-62202-5

Inside Macintosh: Sound

This book describes the parts of the Macintosh Toolbox that allow you to manipulate sound and speech. It shows how to use the Sound Manager, the Sound Input Manager, and the Speech Manager to create and record sounds, and to convert written text to speech.

432 pages (tentative), ISBN 0-201-62272-6

Inside Macintosh: AOCE Application Interfaces

This book describes the application interfaces to the Apple Open Collaboration Environment (AOCE), the technology behind the PowerTalk system software. This book is intended for anyone who wants to add mail services, messaging services, catalog services, digital signatures, or authentication services to their application. It also shows how to write templates that extend the Finder ability of display information in PowerTalk catalogs.

Inside Macintosh: AOCE Service Access Modules

A companion book to *Inside Macintosh: AOCE Application Interfaces*, this book is required reading for anyone developing software modules that give users and PowerTalk-enabled applications access to a new or existing mail and messaging service or catalog service. It also describes how to provide an interface that lets a user install and set up the service.

Inside Macintosh: PowerPC System Software

This book describes the new process execution environment and system software services provided with the first release of PowerPC processor-based Macintosh computers. It describes the 68LC040 Emulator, which allows existing 680x0 applications to execute unchanged on PowerPC processor-based Macintosh computers, as well as the Mixed Mode Manager, which handles switching between the PowerPC and 680x0 environments. It also documents the Code Fragment Manager and the Exception Manager.

224 pages (tentative), ISBN 0-201-40727-2

Inside Macintosh: PowerPC Numerics

This book describes the floating-point numerics provided with the first release of PowerPC processor-based Macintosh computers. It provides a description of the IEEE Standard 754 for floating-point arithmetic and shows how PowerPC Numerics complies with it. This book also shows how to create floating-point values and how to perform operations on floating-point values in high-level languages such as C and in PowerPC assembly language.

336 pages (tentative), ISBN 0-201-40728-0

Inside Macintosh QuickDraw GX Library

QuickDraw GX is the powerful new graphics architecture for the Macintosh that provides a unified approach to graphics and typography, and that gives programmers unprecedented flexibility and power in drawing and printing all kinds of shapes, images, and text. This extension to Macintosh system software is documented in a suite of books that are themselves an extension to the Inside Macintosh series. The Inside Macintosh QuickDraw GX Library contains volumes that are clear, concise, and organized by topic. They contain detailed explanations and abundant programming examples.

Inside Macintosh: Getting Started With QuickDraw GX

This book provides an introduction to the QuickDraw GX development environment. It begins with an overview of QuickDraw GX and the key elements of QuickDraw GX programs and then moves on to illustrate these features using practical programming examples.

Inside Macintosh: QuickDraw GX Objects

This book gets you started in understanding how to work with QuickDraw GX and how to create the objects that underlie all of its capabilities. It focuses on the object architecture as a whole, and how to use the objects that make up a QuickDraw GX shape: the shape object, the style object, the ink object, and the transform object.

640 pages (tentative), ISBN 0-201-40675-6

Inside Macintosh: QuickDraw GX Graphics

This book shows you how to create and manipulate the fundamental geometric shapes of QuickDraw GX to generate a vast range of graphic entities. It also shows you how to work with bitmaps and pictures, specialized QuickDraw GX graphic shapes.

655 pages (tentative), ISBN 0-201-40673-X

Inside Macintosh: QuickDraw GX Typography

This books shows you how to create and manipulate the three different types of text shapes supported by QuickDraw GX, and how to support sophisticated text layout, including text with mixed directions and multiple language text.

672 pages (tentative), ISBN 0-201-40679-9

Inside Macintosh: QuickDraw GX Printing

This book shows you how to support basic printing features including desktop printers, and how to use QuickDraw GX printing objects to customize printing and perform advanced printing-related tasks.

480 pages (tentative), ISBN 0-201-40677-2

Inside Macintosh: QuickDraw GX Printing Extensions and Drivers

This book shows you how to extend the printing capabilities of QuickDraw GX by creating a printing extension that can work with any application and any kind of printer. It also shows how to create a QuickDraw GX printer driver.

512 pages (tentative), ISBN 0-201-40678-0

Inside Macintosh: QuickDraw GX Environment and Utilities

This book shows you how to set up your program to use QuickDraw GX, how QuickDraw GX relates to the rest of the Macintosh environment, and how to handle errors and debug your code. It also describes a public data format for objects, and documents several managers that extend the object architecture and provide utility functions.

640 pages (tentative), ISBN 0-201-40676-4

Inside Macintosh

Book title	Information on
Inside Macintosh: Macintosh Toolbox Essentials	Control Manager; Dialog Manager; Event Manager; Finder Interface; Menu Manager; Window Manager
Inside Macintosh: More Macintosh Toolbox	Component Manager; Control Panels; Desktop Manager; Help Manager; Icon Utilities; List Manager; Resource Manager; Scrap Manager; Translation Manager
Inside Macintosh: Imaging With QuickDraw	Color QuickDraw; Cursor Utilities; Graphics Devices; Offscreen Graphics Worlds; Printing Manager; QuickDraw
Inside Macintosh: Text	Dictionary Manager; Font Manager; International Resources; Keyboard Resources; QuickDraw Text; Script Manager; TextEdit; Text Services Manager; Text Utilities; WorldScript Extensions
Inside Macintosh: Files	Alias Manager; Disk Initialization Manager; File Manager; Standard File Package
Inside Macintosh: Memory	Memory Management Utilities; Memory Manager; Virtual Memory Manager
Inside Macintosh: Processes	Deferred Task Manager; Notification Manager; Process Manager; Segment Manager; Shutdown Manager; Time Manager; Vertical Retrace Manager
Inside Macintosh: Operating System Utilities	Control Panel Extensions; Date, Time, and Measurement Utilities; Gestalt Manager; Mathematical and Logical Utilities; Package Manager; PRAM Utilities; Queue Utilities; Start Manager; System Error Handler; Trap Manager
Inside Macintosh: Devices	Apple Desktop Bus Manager; Device Manager; Disk Driver; Power Manager; SCSI Manager; Serial Driver; Slot Manager
Inside Macintosh: Interapplication Communication	Apple Event Manager; AppleScript Component; Data Access Manager; Edition Manager; Program-to-Program Communications Toolbox
Inside Macintosh: Networking	AppleTalk Data Stream Protocol (ADSP); AppleTalk Filing Protocol (AFP); AppleTalk Session Protocol (ASP); AppleTalk Transaction Protocol (ATP); AppleTalk Utilities; Datagram Delivery Protocol (DDP); Ethernet, Token Ring, and FDDI Drivers; Link-Access Protocol (LAP) Manager; Name-Binding Protocol (NBP); Zone Information Protocol (ZIP)

Inside Macintosh (continued)

Book title	Information on
Inside Macintosh: QuickTime	Image Compression Manager; Movie Toolbox
Inside Macintosh: QuickTime Components	Clock Components; Derived Media Handler Components; Image Compressor Components; Movie Controller Components; Movie Data Exchange Components; Preview Components; Sequence Grabber Components; Standard Image-Compressor Dialog Components; Video Digitizer Components
Inside Macintosh: Sound	Sound Input Manager; Sound Manager; Speech Manager
Inside Macintosh: AOCE Application Interfaces	AOCE Utilities; Authentication Manager; Catalog Manager; Digital Signature Manager; Interprogram Messaging Manager; Standard Catalog Package; Standard Mail Package
Inside Macintosh: AOCE Service Access Modules	Catalog Service Access Modules; Messaging Service Access Modules
Inside Macintosh: QuickDraw GX Objects	Color Objects; Ink Objects; Shape Objects; Style Objects; Tag Objects; Transform Objects; View Objects
Inside Macintosh: QuickDraw GX Graphics	Bitmap Shapes; Geometric Operations; Geometric Shapes; Geometric Styles; Picture Shapes
Inside Macintosh: QuickDraw GX Typography	Fonts; Glyph Shapes; Layout Shapes; Text Shapes; Typographic Shapes; Typographic Styles
Inside Macintosh: QuickDraw GX Printing	Dialog Box Customization; Page Formatting; Printing
Inside Macintosh: QuickDraw GX Printing Extensions and Drivers	Printer Drivers; Printing Extensions; Printing Functions; Printing Messages; Printing Resources
Inside Macintosh: QuickDraw GX Environment and Utilities	Collection Manager; Debugging; Mathematical Functions; Memory Management; Message Manager; Stream Format
Inside Macintosh: PowerPC System Software	Code Fragment Manager; Exception Manager; Mixed Mode Manager
Inside Macintosh: PowerPC Numerics	Conversions; Environmental Controls; Numeric Operations and Functions

Please keep me informed about future volumes in
New Inside Macintosh.

Name _____

Company _____

Address _____

_____

City _____

State _____

Zip _____

Please tear out card, put in an envelope, and mail to:
Chris Platt
Addison-Wesley Publishing Company
One Jacob Way
Reading, MA 01867

APDA

Your main source for Apple development products

Get easy access to *New Inside Macintosh* and over 300 other programming products through APDA, Apple's worldwide source for Apple and third-party development products. Ordering is easy. APDA offers convenient payment and shipping options.

Call today for your FREE APDA Tools Catalog

1-800-282-2732   U.S.

1-800-637-0029   Canada

(716) 871-6555   International

Site licensing is available for many of the development tools. For information, contact Apple Software Licensing at (408) 974-4667.

© 1992 Apple Computer, Inc. Apple, the Apple logo, APDA, and Macintosh are registered trademarks of Apple Computer, Inc.